ne is

PLASTERING

PLAIN AND DECORATIVE
FOURTH EDITION

By William Millar and George P. Bankart

With an introduction by Jeff Orton and Tim Ratcliffe

DONHEAD

First Edition published in 1897 by B.T. Batsford, High Holborn, London.
Fourth revised and updated edition published in 1927 by B.T. Batsford,
with an introduction by George P. Bankart

This reprinted edition © Donhead Publishing 2009

Simultaneously published in the United Kingdom and Michigan, USA by
Donhead Publishing Ltd

Donhead Publishing Ltd
Lower Coombe
Donhead St Mary
Shaftesbury
Dorset SP7 9LY
Tel. 01747 828422
www.donhead.com

New introduction to this edition © Jeff Orton and Tim Ratcliffe 2009

ISBN 978 1 873394 87 8

A CIP catalogue for this book is available from the British Library

Printed in Great Britain by Cromwell Press Group, Trowbridge, Wiltshire

Introduction to the 2009 edition

William Millar's classic book *Plastering Plain and Decorative* is universally referred to as the 'Plasterer's Bible'. It was first published in 1897 and was clearly a great success, with a second edition following two years later in 1899 and a third edition in 1905 (a reprint of the first edition is also available from Donhead). In 1927 the publishers, B. T. Batsford Ltd, decided that it was time to republish Millar's *magnum opus*, and that the fourth edition should be revised and updated. William Millar had died more than twenty years before, so they asked George P. Bankart, an architect/craftsman and author, who had already written another book on plasterwork for them, to take on this task.

George Percy Bankart was an architect highly influenced by the Arts and Crafts movement, who had chosen to work as a decorative craftsman. Arts and Crafts was, at least initially, an English movement dedicated to the idea that architecture could be inspired by a revival of traditional building crafts and materials. It started with the writings of John Ruskin and was driven by the ideas of William Morris. Although most people associate the movement with the late nineteenth and very early twentieth centuries, there were still many active Arts and Crafts architects and thinkers around in the 1920s.

Bankart was born in Leicester on 20 January 1866, and was a great friend of Ernest W. Gimson, another Leicester born architect, just over a year his elder. Both men studied and became architects, and shared a creative passion for the handicrafts. While Gimson's career included embroidery design, traditional chair-making and furniture design, as well as decorative modelled plasterwork, Bankart concentrated primarily on plasterwork. Their different activities were true to the ideas of the Arts and Crafts movement, and their designs reflect the movement's interest in a return to nature.

Bankart's career as an author started in 1909, with the publication of *The Art of The Plasterer* (B. T. Batsford Ltd). He seems to have taken a break from writing until the mid-1920s, when, together with his son G. Edward Bankart, he produced two books, *Modern Plasterwork Construction* (1926) and *Modern Plasterwork Design* (1927), both published by the Architectural Press. These were in drawing portfolio form, with large loose-leaf plates. It was also in 1927 that B. T. Batsford Ltd published the revised fourth edition of Millar's *Plastering Plain and Decorative*.

One only has to look at the title page of the fourth edition to get an idea of Bankart's confidence and belief in the post-Victorian view of craft and design. He refers to this edition being revised and enlarged, even though it is actually shorter (347 pages compared to 604 pages in the first edition). He and the publishers clearly believed that bringing it up to date with added knowledge and information, along with the removal of (in his view) immaterial parts, had actually increased the scope of the book. The fourth edition has nineteen chapters, as opposed to twenty-one in the first, but more significantly one can sense the change in attitudes and understanding as George Bankart picks out and patches in paragraphs and chapters around William Millar's original work.

Reading the first edition of the book gives a real sense of the way Mr Millar, a Victorian plasterer, thought about and understood the skills of his trade. At times his writing style may seem to ramble slightly, but this adds to the feeling of being in conversation with him. The fourth edition carries on this conversation, but with George Bankart adding his 'voice' as he implores us to engage with the importance of craftsmanship. He obviously has a deep respect for William Millar, but is keen to highlight the shortcomings he saw in the move towards mass-production (symbolised by the Victorian ceiling rose), and wants to explain not only how the craft had been in the past but also how it could be developed in the future.

There would be little merit in trying to describe or analyse all the changes made in the fourth edition, but we hope that by highlighting a few we can give some insights into the differences between the two editions.

Chapter I, on the history of plasterwork, was originally written by George Robinson. It has been edited very slightly and more illustrations have been added, but still retains subjective views and prejudices from the first edition, including negative remarks about the Adam brothers and the 'death' of hand modelling. Chapter II (moved from Chapter XVI in the original), was originally entitled *Foreign Plasterwork* and has been renamed *Eastern and Continental Plasterwork*, possibly reflecting a slightly more enlightened view of the rest of the world!

The next three new chapters, on lime-stucco, modern plasterwork and modelling in relief, are pure Bankart, and give a real sense of his passion and interest in hand modelled plasterwork. He uses them to illustrate and explain his commitment to Arts and Crafts ideals.

Chapter VI is on tools (moved from Chapter XXI in the original), and has additional illustrations and notes. This is followed by two chapters on materials, all brought up to date with more photos and drawings. As one reads on it becomes clear that, while still retaining much of Millar's text and illustrations without alteration, Bankart has inserted sections into the original chapters to make them more contemporary. He assumes less background knowledge from his readers and adds further explanation where he believes it will help plasterers and others who want to understand the mechanics of plastering.

A good example of this is in Chapter XV, where a description headed *Renovating Old Ceilings* (page 243), which comes from the first edition, is then followed by a new section called *For Renovating Old Ceilings* (pages 243 and 244), which gives a detailed description of how to save an old ceiling using plaster and scrim to reinforce it from above. The chapter ends with an illustration (page 272) showing how this method works, and a further treatise (page 273) on saving historic decorative plaster.

In this same chapter there is an illustration (page 249) entitled 'Typical Victorian Centre Flower "Horrors" in Plaster'. Bankart does not hide his disdain for Victorian ceiling roses, or the period they represent. While understanding his plea, we need to remember that his views on design and production, although heartfelt and challenging, are as much a reflection of his time as the ceiling roses are of the nineteenth century. His views on 'mass-production' and the importance of 'hand craft' are pertinent to current debates about sustainability, but we should bear in mind that 'beauty is in the eye of the beholder' and that the passage of time can also give value to objects.

Chapter XI, *Exterior Plastering and Sgraffito*, is another completely new chapter added by Bankart. This method of decoration (also spelt Scraffito) involves applying contrasting layers of coloured plaster to a moistened surface, and then scratching away parts of the top layer to produce an outline pattern or drawing. The art of sgraffito (early examples of which can be found in Bavaria and Italy) was introduced into Britain during the late nineteenth century, and this chapter reflects the enthusiasm in the early twentieth century for this technique.

Bankart continues to update the content right through to the penultimate two chapters on *Compositions* (XVII and XVIII). This encompasses gesso, papier-mâché, carton-pierre, and an assortment of other products, and can be a very useful research reference when faced with the repair of such materials. Knowing that alternative, and sometimes novel, materials were used in decorative plasterwork from the latter part of the eighteenth century onwards is important. If, for example, decorative features have been formed using a glue binder they may be more susceptible to damp than plaster (and even become 'soggy' to the touch), but may simply solidify again once the ceiling or wall dries out. Unfortunately if the glue stays damp too long, it may encourage or sustain mould growth.

The last chapter, on quantities, weights and recipes, contains fascinating practical information on proportions and sizing of materials, including the coverage achieved using different plasters. There are explanations of the measures used, but as many are no longer in common usage it can be difficult to immediately translate them into modern terms. The description of the wide palette of materials that was available to plasterers at the time is a salutary reminder of how limited our own knowledge really is. We can only hope that the republishing of this book will begin to inspire a revived interest in the techniques and tricks of the trade that have been forgotten. There is a brief entry on 'Wages' (page 321), which reflects on the shortage of skilled plasterers in the 1920s, due to the First World War. Fortunately for Bankart, he did not know of things to come, with another World War and the subsequent de-skilling of the plastering trade.

The book finishes with an Appendix, outlining developments in American plastering, which offers some fascinating insights. This includes descriptions of new techniques and alternative materials, including a surprising reference to plasterboard (page 333). We are also told about the use of brightly coloured external stucco, developed by a Mr O. A. Malone of the Californian Stucco Products Co, which is referred to as 'Jazz plaster', much loved by Hollywood film stars. This is the beginning of the Art Deco movement, which started in Paris in 1925.

Sadly George Bankart, who seems to have been intrigued by the idea of coloured external stuccos, did not live to see the spread of this new fashion. He died in Welwyn Garden City, England, two years later in 1929, aged 63. His life was dedicated to promoting the ideals of craftsmanship and his legacy can clearly be seen in his books. The Arts and Crafts movement owes a great deal to a man who sought to develop and encourage the art of the plasterer.

At the time of writing this introduction, Jeff Orton is in America visiting the American College of the Building Arts in Charleston. He has been discussing *Plastering Plain & Decorative* with the students, and it seems particularly appropriate to conclude with their observations on the fourth edition. Their comments reflect on the challenges we face on both sides of the Atlantic.

> At a time when speed of production takes precedent over quality of craftsmanship, mass-produced, pre-fabricated building materials have become the standard of current building practices in the United States. This has resulted in a sharp decline of artisans in our country. We, the plaster students of the American College of the Building Arts in Charleston, South Carolina, have a unique opportunity to revive the traditional building methods of the past. William Millar's writing on the

trade provides us with an invaluable resource for guidance and inspiration. Millar not only specifies the proper techniques of plastering, but in the revised fourth edition George Bankart exhorts students to self-expression and artistic exploration. In the chapter *Modelling and Design in Relief* (page 74), he encourages students to develop their desire to create decoration and ornamentation:

> *By studying old work and Nature at the same time - by absorbing inspiration from both, by uniting that knowledge of both in developing our own ideas with good taste, judgement, simplicity of arrangement, variation, industry, and practice, the student must surely acquire and cultivate the art of decorative design for himself...But he must be content to learn.*

We are grateful to the students Cody Donahue, Michael Lauer and Bethany Costilow for their thoughts and observations. For more information on the American College of the Building Arts visit www.buildingartscollege.us

Jeff Orton & Tim Ratcliffe
(February 2009)

Jeff Orton (Plasterer) C.R.P., A.P.C., M.P.C.G.

Jeff Orton served a full plastering apprenticeship from 1963 to 1968 with a traditional family firm, and gained a 'First Class' in the Craft level City and Guilds, followed by a 'Distinction' in the Advanced Craft City and Guilds Final Examination. He is registered with the Worshipful Company of Plaisterers (CRP) and is also an Associate of the Worshipful Company of Plaisterers (APC). In 1981 he attended the San Servolo Architectural Conservation Course for Craftsmen in Venice. He is a member and past chairman of the Plasterers Craft Guild, and is currently a committee member of the Building Limes Forum. Following twenty years repairing and reinstating plasterwork in historic buildings, for the National Trust, English Heritage, etc, as well as private clients, he is now involved with the NHTG (National Heritage Training Group) and is committed to raising standards and encouraging a better understanding of traditional plastering skills.

Tim Ratcliffe (Architect) B.A., DipArch, A.A.B.C.

Tim Ratcliffe was awarded a 'Lethaby' travelling scholarship by the Society for the Protection of Ancient Buildings (SPAB) in 1987 and has also worked as a labourer for a number of specialist plastering and conservation contractors. He worked for two architectural firms specialising in historic building work (Rodney Melville & Partners and Donald Insall Associates) before setting up in practice with his wife, Jan, in 2000. Based in Oswestry, they work and give advice on churches, houses, castles and old industrial buildings in the Midlands and North Wales.

Yours faithfully

W. Millar

PLASTERING
PLAIN & DECORATIVE

Demy 4to, cloth, lettered. **30s.** *net*

ENGLISH DECORATIVE PLASTERWORK
OF THE RENAISSANCE

A Review of its Design during the Period from 1500 to 1800

BY

M. JOURDAIN

AUTHOR OF "ENGLISH FURNITURE AND DECORATION," ETC.

Comprising over 100 full-page Plates of Elizabethan, Stuart, Georgian, and Adam ceilings, friezes, overmantels, panels, ornament, detail, etc., from specially taken Photographs, and from Measured Drawings and Sketches. With an Illustrated Historical Survey on Foreign Influences and the Evolution of Design, Work and Names of Craftsmen, etc.

The beauty and high standard of English Plasterwork has only been begun to be realised of late years, and is even now not fully appreciated. It represents the full course of Renaissance modelled ornament, and enshrines much of the finest achievements of English craftsmanship. The selection here reproduced has been chosen with great care and judgment from many hundreds of photographs, including the fine extensive series of Mr G. P. BANKART, and gives complete designs, with many large-scale representations of the detail of the modelled ornament. The work will commend itself to all interested in Decoration, and in the productions of English art, and will be both attractive as a review and invaluable for reference.

" The arrangement of this book seems altogether admirable ; it combines a lucid survey of the subject with a wealth of detailed research which will be of inestimable value to the serious student. This book should bring to the notice of both the practical craftsman and the student of historical ornament the finest examples, many hitherto unpublished, of what was essentially a native product. Not the least interesting section of the book is the list of plasterers, largely compiled from original contemporary documents. The plates are excellently chosen and reproduced."—*Spectator.*

" The book becomes a very instructive survey of the best examples in each architectural period, illustrated by measured drawings, original designs by architects and craftsmen, and a great wealth of photographs. Indeed, it covers the field so completely that this volume, with its excellent index, is a dictionary of the subject as well as an able, critical, and historical essay."—*Manchester Guardian.*

PLASTERING
PLAIN & DECORATIVE

A PRACTICAL TREATISE ON THE ART AND CRAFT, INCLUDING FULL DESCRIPTIONS OF
MATERIALS, PROCESSES AND APPLIANCES, AND AN ACCOUNT OF HISTORICAL PLASTERING

By WILLIAM MILLAR
Plasterer and Modeller

*Edited and Remodelled, with new Chapters on Lime
Stucco, Modelling and Design in Relief, Modern
Plasterwork, Compositions, Etc.*

By GEORGE P. BANKART
Architect and Decorative Craftsman

*Author of "The Art of the Plasterer," "Plaster-
work Construction," "Plasterwork Design," Etc.*

FOURTH EDITION, REVISED & ENLARGED
*With Numerous Practical Diagrams, and 278 Illustrations
from Photographs on 125 Plates, mostly new to this Edition*

LONDON
B. T. BATSFORD LTD., 94 HIGH HOLBORN

PLATE I
[*Frontispiece*

COLESHILL, BERKSHIRE. Detail of Ceiling and Frieze in Saloon.

EDITOR'S PREFACE

IN revising this volume for the Fourth Edition, whilst fully appreciating and cherishing the Author's wide experience and teaching as a practical plasterer and skilled mechanic, it has been endeavoured, as far as possible, to condense, to clarify, and to rearrange the text and illustrations into a more useful and portable form, at the same time limiting the pages strictly to the Art and Craft of the Plasterer.

New chapters have been added on " Stucco-Duro " or " Lime-Stucco Plasterwork," " Modelling and Design in Relief," and " Modern Plasterwork in England."

The illustrations have been revised and many new ones added in a manner that it is hoped may prove interesting and serviceable.

For plasterwork generally, as an art and as a craft, technically and historically, great importance is attached to the Historical Account (Chap. I.), which every plasterer is urged to read, study, and remember to his advantage.

Since Mr Millar first penned the text of " Plastering Plain and Decorative," methods of building have undergone considerable change, affecting both design and construction. Architecture has reawakened to new life, inspired to some extent by the traditions of the past, whilst combining and developing new methods of construction with materials convenient to present-day use.

Mr Millar happened to live and work mostly during a period of transition, when plastering was a mechanical trade and not a decorative art. " Ornamental " plastering of a kind was done, and in profusion, but the design and modelling of plaster ornament at that time held little of the traditional decorative spirit of the past, and was misdirected so far as true *decorative* qualities were concerned.

Fibrous plaster casting from moulds in this country involved much labour in its earlier days in comparison with the process as worked at the present time. Plaster casting was then more extensively done from moulds of wax, or from plaster reverse moulds combined with inserted wax moulding pieces for enrichments.

Of late years, also, there has been a great increase in the number and variety of patent materials of all kinds, especially slabs for use on partitions, for wall coverings, etc. Though these are not strictly plastering, they are so nearly allied to the craft that a brief description of some principal varieties, with other special recent materials, is necessarily included.

EDITOR'S PREFACE

Experience and competition have produced change of methods, simplified processes, and a saving of time. For these reasons some of the processes described in detail and generally practised in the Author's life-time have gone out of use and given place to simpler and cheaper methods and materials. Since the latter part of Queen Victoria's reign the true quality of plaster as a decorative material has been better recognised and appreciated for its granular nature and its soft qualities of light and shade. The technical qualities of sixteenth and seventeenth century work have been studied and realised and the principles applied to modern circumstances in modern ways.

The technical qualities of modelling and working various materials and the poetry of pattern-making have been more closely studied and applied to a better development of the processes of manufacture.

The hope, expressed by the Author in his original preface, that he might help to spread a knowledge of methods and a greater appreciation of and desire for a wider use and revival of his favourite art and craft, has been amply and fully justified and realised by thousands of his fellow-craftsmen ; and it is further hoped that this edition will bring the usefulness of the volume up to date, more particularly with reference to the development of the Art of plastering which, as differing from the purely mechanical aspect of the trade, has until recent years received less encouragement and attention than it deserves from public and craftsmen alike.

GEORGE BANKART

LONDON, *March* 1927.

NOTE OF ACKNOWLEDGMENT

THE greater part of the illustrations are reproduced from the Editor's and Publishers' collection of plaster photographs, the majority of which have been taken expressly by Messrs Lewis & Randall Limited, Birmingham. Most of the diagrams of mouldings, etc., have been specially drawn by the Editor and Mr G. E. Bankart.

Plates XV, *b*, XV, *c*, and XVII, *c* are from " Old Halls and Manor Houses in Yorkshire," by Louis Ambler, F.R.I.B.A., and Figs. 30 and 31 are from drawings by Sydney R. Jones in " Old Manor Houses," by Jones and Ditchfield. The subjects on Plate XXXIV are from the late R. Phené Spiers's " Architecture, East and West," and photographs by the late W. Galsworthy Davie appear on Plates XV, *a*, XVII, *a*, XVII, *b*, LXXXVI, *a*, XCIV, *c*.

Messrs G. Jackson & Sons must be cordially thanked for kindly placing at our disposal designs of Adam motives—reproduced on Plates XXX, XXXA, and CXXII—of which they possess the original boxwood moulds.

Mynheer Martinus Nijhoff, publisher, of The Hague, has kindly allowed the reproduction of the old Belgian interiors shown on Plates XXXIX, *b*, and XL-XLII, from his publication " Old Interiors in Belgium," by Sluyterman ; and to the kindness of Mr Edward Hudson of *Country Life* is due the inclusion of the photographs of interiors illustrated on Plates LXXIV and LXXVI, *c*. Plates XX, *a*, LII, *b*, and LII, *c*, are from photographs by Messrs Valentine & Sons, of Dundee, reproduced by their permission, and Plate LVII, *b* is from a photograph of Messrs Bedford, Lemere, & Co., London.

To Messrs Morris & Co. is due the inclusion of Plate LXXX, *d* and Fig. 28, designs for fabrics by William Morris ; and Mr Archibald Thorburn and Messrs Longmans, Green, & Co., his publishers, must be thanked for the reproduction of LXXVIII, *e* (the Heron), from " British Birds," Vol. II., and LXXIX, *b*, from " The Naturalist's Sketch Book."

Photographs of subjects from the Victoria and Albert Museum, South Kensington, are shown in Plates LXXXI, *a*, LXXXIV, *a*, XCV, *a*, CI, *c*, and CXVI-CXIX, by kind permission of the Board of Education ; and acknowledgment must be made to the authorities of the British Museum for Plates XCII, *a* and XCIII, from the William Twopeny Collection ; Plate XCVI, *b* from " The Sculptures of the Parthenon " ; and Plate XCVII, consisting of reliefs in the Assyrian Collection.

The andirons designed by the late Ernest W Gimson (Plate LXXXIII, *a* and *b*) are reproduced by the sanction of Mrs Gimson, from the " Gimson Memorial Volume."

NOTE OF ACKNOWLEDGMENT

The Editor would like to thank various architects and fellow-craftsmen, especially Sir R. Lorimer, Messrs Joseph Armitage, Arthur Glover, George Jack, T. Stallybrass, and Heywood Sumner, for contributing examples of their work.

He is indebted to many manufacturers for permission to include valuable practical material relating to their specialities and processes. The brief Appendix on " Recent Developments in American Plastering " is due to the interest and energy of Mr George Cole, plasterer, of Alhambra, California, who has supplied a large quantity of interesting material, of which we wish it had been practicable to make a more extended use. In addition, we must thank the manufacturers concerned : Mr O. A. Malone, President of the California Stucco Co. ; the Plasterers' Association of Southern California for their Standard Plastering Specification ; the Portland Cement Association of Chicago for the Specification of Portland Cement Stucco ; the Nephi Plaster Manufacturing Co. of Utah for the Directions for Plastering ; and the United States Gypsum Co., Chicago, for the Notes on Oriental Stucco. Mr Cole has obtained permission for the inclusion of the Table of American Estimating Plastering Costs. To the Goldblatt Tool Co., of Kansas City, U.S.A., is due the illustration of their tools, which appears on Plate CIII, *b*.

A PREFATORY NOTE

MR MILLAR has asked me to say for him that which he finds somewhat difficult to say for himself, and I think the simplest way of doing this will be to explain in the fewest possible words how and why we made each other's acquaintance, and what came of it. Mr Millar came to a lecture I gave at the Society of Arts on " Decorative Plasterwork," a subject in which I felt much interest, and one on which I had previously written and spoken. Shortly afterwards he sought me, telling me of his craft-work and of his proposed book on plastering, upon which he had then been long engaged. For this he asked for such literary help as I could give him. I found in him a craftsman who delighted in his craft, and one who, whilst yet in his prentice days, finding that, unlike most other handicrafts, plastering had no text-book or manual, set before himself the ambition of writing one. Following his father's wholesome advice (himself a plasterer and a descendant of a long line of plasterers), he set himself to " learn his trade first " ; but whilst doing this he kept collecting facts and laying the foundation of the work he has at length achieved. Fortunately he had what is becoming in these versatile days the *rare* advantage of a rigorous apprenticeship, and bettered his instruction by learning more and working through the United Kingdom, even extending the sphere of his labour to Paris. Keeping his eyes open, he acquired a very extended knowledge of the direct ways of his trade, and taking notes of all the processes he came in contact with, he accumulated an extensive craft knowledge in the byways of it. These he extended by well-directed reading, and better still by observation and reasoning upon what he learnt ; inventing new methods, trying new materials, viewing both sides of the questions of the trade, now as workman and now as master, until he thoroughly fitted himself for the task he never lost sight of, and about 1880 commenced formulating his book. And now troubles came upon him—ill-health, misfortune, domestic afflictions, and last of all a fire, which not only bereft him of house and home, but burnt his treasured manuscripts and drawings and all he had written for his book. But Mr Millar, like a true Scot, without repining at the inevitable, set to work again, rewrote his manuscript and remade his drawings. Even yet an envious fate pursued him, for after making arrangements for their publication, and after they had been for many months in the hands of his intended publisher, that gentleman failed, without having made any progress with the production of the book.

The present publisher having undertaken to bring his book before the

PREFATORY NOTE

world, Mr Millar has carefully gone through the manuscript again, altering it, adding to it, and bringing it quite up to date. As for me, I have simply revised it for the press, in fulfilment of a promise I made long ago, finding, however, no alteration needed in the technical portion. Rarely have I made anything beyond verbal alteration, and that as small as possible, leaving Mr Millar to describe in his own language the processes he is so thoroughly familiar with. For the historical *résumé* he had accumulated an immense amount of matter, from which I have freely drawn, supplementing it by other information learned from my own studies, and chronologically arranging both; but the value of the work is entirely due to his own labours, and I heartily congratulate him on its final achievement after such arduous struggles. I wish it all the success his perseverance deserves and its thoroughness should command, and I trust that such success may encourage other craftsmen to write their own " shop knowledge " as intelligently and intelligibly as Mr Millar has here done that of plasterwork. To his own craft it is a life's legacy; to the younger members it will be an invaluable text-book; to the elder ones, a permanent pleasure. To my own profession, and to all others interested in so useful and so decorative a pursuit, it will prove a lasting book of constant reference.

GEO. T ROBINSON.

LONDON, 20*th February* 1897.

AUTHOR'S PREFACE

THAT this book may help to spread a knowledge of methods of working in plaster, a
greater appreciation of and desire for its wider
use and revival, is my earnest wish. Should this
be realised, my reward will be in the consciousness
that I have been the means of forwarding the study
of my favourite art and craft.

WILLIAM MILLAR.

CONTENTS

Plastering—Plain & Decorative

CHAPTER I

PLASTERWORK GENERALLY: A GLIMPSE OF ITS HISTORY

By G. T. Robinson, F.S.A.

Plastering—Prehistoric—In the Dawn of History—In Early Egypt—Amongst the Greeks and their Colonies—Roman Work from the Commencement to the Decline and Fall of the Empire—Its Oriental Development—In the Middle Ages—In the Renaissance —Its Culmination in the Sixteenth Century—Its Decorative Growth in France and England—Under Francis I and Henry VIII—Under the Stuart Dynasty—Its Decline under the Hanoverian Influence—Its Low Condition at the End of Last Century—Its hoped-for Revival.

Plastering is one of the earliest instances of man's power of inductive reasoning, for when men built they plastered : at first, like the birds and the beavers, with mud, but they soon found out a more lasting and more comfortable method, and the earliest efforts of civilisation were directed to plastering. The inquiry into it takes us back to the dawn of social life, until its origin becomes mythic and prehistoric. Into that dim, obscure period we cannot penetrate far enough to see clearly, but the most distant glimpses we can obtain into it show us that man had very early attained almost to perfection in compounding material for plastering. In fact, so far as we yet know, some of the earliest plastering which has remained to us excels, in its scientific composition, that which we use at the present day, telling of ages of experimental attempts. The Pyramids of Egypt contain plasterwork executed at least 4,000 years ago (some antiquaries, indeed, say a much longer period), and this, where wilful violence has not disturbed it, still exists, in perfection outvying in durability the very rock it covers, where this is not protected by its shield of plaster. Dr Flinders Petrie, in his " Pyramids and Temples of Gizeh," shows us how serviceable and intelligent a co-operator with the painter, the sculptor, and the architect was the plasterer of those early days, and that to his care and skill we owe almost all we know of the history of these distant times and their art. Indeed the plasterer's very tools do yet remain to us, showing that the technical processes then were the same we now use, for there are in Dr Petrie's collection at University College, London, hand floats which in design, shape, and purpose are precisely those which we use to-day. Even our newest invention of canvas plaster was well known then, and by it were made the masks which yet preserve on the mummy cases the lineaments of their occupants.

The plaster used by the Egyptians for their finest work was derived from burnt gypsum, and was therefore exactly the same as our " plaster of Paris." Its base was of lime stucco, which, when used on partitions, was laid on reeds laced together with cords, for lathing, and Mr Millar, who has examined a fragment in Dr Petrie's collection, finds it practically " three coat work," about three-quarters of an inch thick, haired, and finished just as we do now.

Plaster moulds and cast slabs exist, but there does not appear any evidence of piece moulding, nor does any evidence of the use of modelled work in plaster exist. That some process of indurating plaster was thus early known is evidenced by the plaster pavement at Tel-el-Amarna, which is elaborately painted. This floor is laid on brick; the first coat is of rough lime stucco about 1 in. thick, and the finishing coat of well-haired plaster about one-eighth inch thick, very smooth and fine, and showing evidence of trowelling, the setting out lines for the painting being formed by a struck cord before the surface was set, and the painting done on fresco. It is about 60 by 20, and formed the floor of the principal room of the harem of King Amenhotep IV, about 1,400 years before Christ, that is, between 3,000 and 4,000 years ago. Long before this, plastering of fine quality existed in Egypt, and so long as its civilisation continued it aided the comfort of the dwellings of its people and the beauty of its temples.

Nor was it merely for its beauty and comfort that plasterwork was used. Even then its sanitary value was recognised, and the directions given in Leviticus xiv. 42-48, which was probably written about 100 years before this date, show that the knowledge of its antiseptic qualities was widely spread, and the practice of it regarded as a religious duty.

Unfortunately there is no direct evidence that the adjacent Assyrian powers of Nineveh and Babylon used plasterwork. Possibly the fine clay brought down by the rivers of the Euphrates and the Tigris sufficed for all their purposes. Their records are in it; their illustrations on the sculptured walls of their palaces are in stone, their painting is glazed on their bricks, and for them there seems to have been but little need for plasterwork; nor do we find until the rise of Grecian art anything relating to our subject.

Very early in Greek architecture we find the use of plaster, and in this case a true lime stucco of most exquisite composition, thin, fine, and white. Some has been found at Mycenæ. We know that it existed in perfection in Greece about 500 years before the Christian era. With this the temples were covered externally, and internally where they were not built of marble and in some cases where they were. This fine stucco was often used as a ground on which to paint their decorative ornament, but not unfrequently left quite plain in its larger masses, and some of it remains in very fair preservation even to this day. The Temple of Apollo at Bassæ, built of yellow sand-stone about 470 B.C., has on its columns the remains of a fine white stucco.

Pavements of thick hard plaster, stained, of various colours, were common in the Greek temples. One of these, that of the Temple of Jupiter Panhellenius at Ægina, built about 570 B.C., is described by Cockerell as existing in the early part of this century, in good condition, though the temple itself was destroyed; and I have seen at Agrigentum, plastering existing in perfect state though scarcely thicker than an egg-shell, on the sheltered parts of a temple built at least 300 years before our era, whilst the unprotected stone was weather-worn and decayed.

What care the ancient Greeks bestowed on their stucco may be inferred from Pliny's statement that in the temple at Elis about 450 B.C., Panænus, the nephew of Phidias, used for the groundwork of his picture " stucco mixed with milk and saffron, and polished with spittle rubbed on by the ball of the thumb, and," says he, " it still retains the odour of saffron." Lysippus, the first of the Greek " realists " in sculpture, was the first we hear of who took casts of the faces of living sitters about 300 B.C., so the art of plaster casting must have advanced a good deal by that time, as he made presents of copies to his friends. Afterwards we read of many sculptors who sent small plaster

PLATE II

PORTION OF LOW RELIEF STUCCO CEILING, TOMB IN THE VIA LATINA, ROME. (FIRST CENTURY.)

PLATE III

(*a*) A Bacchic Scene in Stucco-duro, from a Vaulted Ceiling in a Roman House in the Garden of the Villa Farnesina.

(*b*) Stucco Decoration, Great Baths of Pompeii. (First Century a.d.)

models of their works to friends. These were, however, probably carved in the plaster rather than cast.

Whether the Greeks used stucco for modelling is a somewhat doubtful point amongst antiquarians. From certain passages in classic writers I am induced to think they did. Pausanias who describes the temple at Stymphalus, an almost deserted and ruined city when he visited it about 130 A.D., describes the ceiling of the Temple of the Stymphalides, built about 400 B.C., as being " either of stucco or carved wood," he could not decide which, but his very doubt would imply that stucco or wood were equally common. Now this ceiling was ornamented with panels and figures of the harpies—omens of evil, half woman and half bird, with outspread wings. He also mentions a statue of Bacchus in " coloured stucco." Of course, these are not definite proofs of early Greek stucco modelling, but as the city of Stymphalus had decayed and become depopulated before 200 B.C., there is certainly presumptive evidence of the ancient practice of the art. Again, figures of unburnt earth are mentioned in contradistinction to those of terra-cotta, and sundry other allusions to plastic work occur which lead to the opinion that quite early in Greek art this mode of using plaster began. At any rate, we know that it was early introduced into Grecia Magna —the earliest Southern Italian colony of the Greeks ; and as colonists invariably preserve the customs and traditions of their fatherland even long after they have fallen into disuse in their native home, we can have no reasonable doubt but this art was imported rather than invented by them. Thence it spread to the Etruscans of Middle Italy, a cognate people to the Southern Greeks, by whom both plain and modelled stucco was largely used.

The practical Etruscan element firstly constructed the roads and the sewers, and gave health to Rome. The Latins added to their territory until it embraced half of Europe, giving wealth to Rome, and not till the luxury and comfort thus created did the artistic element of the Greek come in, giving beauty to Rome, and the day of decorative plasterwork approached its noontide glory, making Rome the attraction of the world. The absorption of Greece as a Roman province took place B.C. 145, and the loot of it began, giving an enormous impetus to Roman art. Thousands of statues were brought to Rome, and to be deemed a connoisseur in things artistic or a patron of the arts became the fashionable ambition. But it was not until the century just preceding the Christian era that it became especially noteworthy. Of course, there is hardly anything left to us of the very early plasterwork of Rome. The constant search for some new thing was inimical to the old. Old structures were pulled down to make way for new, which in their turn gave way to newer, and until the age of Augustus we have but little of the early work left. Strabo, who visited Rome about this time, complains of the destruction caused by " the numerous fires, and continued pulling down of houses rendered necessary, for even pulling down and rebuilding in order to gratify the taste is but voluntary ruin " ; and Augustus, who boasted that " he found Rome of brick and left it of marble," in replacing the brick with marble destroyed the plaster-work. How that plasterwork was wrought we shall learn more from Vitruvius, who wrote his book on architecture about 16 B.C., and dedicated it to the emperor, " in order to explain the rules and limits of Art as a standard by which to test the merits of the buildings he had erected or might erect."

Now Vitruvius was a man who had travelled and seen much. He was with Julius Cæsar as a military engineer in his African campaign in 46 B.C., or ten years after Cæsar's invasion of Britain. Afterwards he became a designer of military engines, what we should call head of the Ordnance Department, and also a civil engineer, persuading himself that he had a pretty taste in architecture, just as though he were an R.E. of to-day. Thus he had a practical and also an artistic training, and here is what he says on matters connected with plasterwork in Book VII, Chapter II.

On tempering lime for stucco : " This requires that the lime should be of the best quality, and tempered a long time before it is wanted for use ; so that if any of it be not burnt enough, the length of time employed in slaking it may bring the whole mass to the same consistency." He then advises it to be chopped with iron hatchets, adding that " if the iron exhibits a glutinous substance adhering to it, it indicates the richness of the lime and the thorough slaking of it." For cradling out and for ceiling joists he recommends " the wood to be of cypress, olive, heart of oak, box, and juniper," as neither are liable to " rot or shrink." For lathing he specifies " Greek reeds bruised and tied with cords made from Spanish broom," or if these are not procurable, " marsh reeds tied with cords." On these a coat of lime and sand is laid, and an additional coat of sand is laid on to it. As it sets it is then polished with chalk or marble. This for ceilings. For plaster on walls he says : " The first coat on the walls is to be laid on as roughly as possible, and while drying, the sand coat spread thereon. When this work has dried, a second and a third coat is laid on. The sounder the sand coat is, the more durable the work will be. The coat of marble dust then follows, and this is to be so prepared that when used it does not stick to the trowel. Whilst the stucco is drying, another thin coat is to be laid on ; this is to be well worked and rubbed, and then still another, finer than the last. Thus with three sand coats and the same number of marble dust coats the walls will be solid and not liable to crack." " The wall that is well covered with plaster and stucco, when well polished, not only shines, but reflects to the spectators the images falling on it. The plasterers of the Greeks not only make their stucco-work hard by adhering to these directions, but when the plaster is mixed, cause it to be beaten with wooden staves by a great number of men, and use it after this preparation. Hence some persons cutting slabs of plaster from ancient walls use them for tables and mirrors " (Chapter III).

You will see by these remarks the great care taken through every process, and how guarded the watchfulness over the selection of materials, and you will also note the retrospectiveness of Vitruvius's observation. how he felt that the work done before the frantic haste of his own time was the better : very much as we find now. Time is an ingredient in all good work, and its substitute difficult to find.

There are other " tips " contained in Chapter III which are worth extraction, as, for instance, his instructions on how to plaster damp walls. In such case he primarily suggests a cavity wall, with ventilation to ensure a thorough draught, and then plastering it with " potsherd mortar," or carefully covering the rough plaster with pitch, which is then to be " lime whited over," to ensure " the second coat of pounded potsherds adhering to it," when it may be finished as already described. Further, he refers to modelled plasterwork, which he says, " ought to be used with a regard to propriety," and gives certain hints for its appropriate use. Speaking of pavements " used in the Grecian winter rooms, which are not only economical but useful," he advises " the earth to be excavated about 2 ft. and a foundation of potsherds well rammed in," and then a " composition of pounded coals, lime, sand, and ashes is mixed up and spread there-over, ½ ft. in thickness, perfectly smooth and level. The surface then being rubbed with stone, it has the appearance of a black surface," " and the people. though barefoot, do not suffer from cold on this sort of pavement." Now all this bespeaks not only theoretical knowledge, but practical observation and experience, and was written nearly 2,000 years ago, from which you can surmise how far advanced practical plastering had then become. This written evidence is almost all we have of the work of Vitruvius's own time, for even of the time of Augustus hardly anything remains to us, as the great fire of Nero utterly destroyed the greater part of the city in the year A.D. 64, and almost the only authenticated piece of plasterwork done before or during his reign is the Tabula Iliaca, a bas-relief of the siege of Troy, still preserved in the Capitol Museum at Rome.

That this was modelled by Greek artists is proved by the fact that its inscriptions are all in Greek language, and by some it is considered to be of very much greater antiquity.

Plate III, *a*, shows a good example of the character of modelled stucco which prevailed about this period. This is a small portion of a large surface of plaster which was on a vault cut through in making the excavations for the canalisation of the Tiber at Rome. There were many compartments of various sizes, and the modelling is of an exquisite delicacy. Casts of these you can see in the Victoria and Albert Museum at Kensington, and some of the smaller cartouches are almost as fine as cameos. In the same valuable museum you will find a series of arched tiles of very bright red, on which small subjects have been modelled in stucco, forming a very pleasing and suggestive combination. These are from an Italo-Greek tomb, and of the early part of the first century. Of about the same date is the example given on Plates II and IV, *b*, from the vaulted ceiling of a tomb in the Via Latina at Rome, the walls of which are covered with some very delicately modelled arabesque ornament. Both these are evidently the work of Greek artists. The more Roman method is shown in Plate III, *b*, from the Great Baths of Pompeii, which must have been executed before the year 79 A.D., when the city was buried by the ashes thrown up in an eruption of Vesuvius, and with it perished the natural philosopher and historian, Pliny the elder, who tells us that " no builder should employ lime which had not been slaked at least three years," " and that the Greeks used to grind their lime very fine," and that they beat it with pestles of wood. The very eruption which destroyed Pompeii preserved it to us, for the light scoria which fell upon it covered up the most delicate work, and it is now a museum of decorative plasterwork and decorative art generally, for there stucco treatments abound. Not only did it decorate, but it preserved the fragile and inflammable structures by its fireproof coating. The ordinary plaster was evidently prepared according to the prescription of Vitruvius, the sand coating or arenatum he describes being here formed of decomposed lava or volcanic sand, the final coat laid on being very thin, less than one-sixteenth inch in the best work. When colour was used it was chiefly fresco, done whilst the plaster was moist. Sometimes the colour was even mixed with the plaster, and every variety of plastering skill was called into service—scagliola, gesso, sgraffitto, impressed and relieved work—for Pompeii was evidently a city of plasterwork ; but I am afraid the " jerry-builder " was born before much of Pompeii was built, and then, as now, he relied upon the plasterer to cover up his iniquities.

There was more solid construction at Herculaneum, which was destroyed by the same volcanic eruption, but there, unfortunately, lava, hot and semi-fluid, was the overwhelming substance, and thus the more delicate fabrics perished. Of course, much of the work thus destroyed was of earlier a date than that of the catastrophe, though unfortunately we have no record of its technical history ; as far, however, as classic times are concerned, plasterwork became an artistic aid, reflecting the general tendency of the times. During Constantine's reign, on his transfer of the capital of the Empire to Constantinople, what little building was then done resulted in that Byzantine style of stiff, formal, plastic art which, though of archæological value, presents nothing pertinent to the present subject. Julian, " the Apostate," reverted from Christianity and became a pagan about 380 A.D. He had amongst his household gods a statue of Apollo, under the outstretched hand of which he daily bowed his head. Now this statue was of plaster (gypsum), but it was most probably sculptured in this material, rather than cast, as we find no traces of any replica, nor does any word equivalent to piece moulding occur in the language of this time. Henceforward very little was done throughout the Empire until a new Rome was founded, and for more than 1,000 years all relics of ornamental plasterwork were buried and wellnigh forgotten.

Materially, as a craft, it was debased; the old care in preparation had disappeared, and the drudgery of careless service replaced intelligent assistance to architecture and sculpture. As an art it was dead, buried under the ruins of the buildings it had adorned, and there we must leave it until we come to consider its resurrection.

There is, however, little doubt but that this Eastern removal of the Empire spread the art into the Far East, and it is probable that the over-enriched plasterwork of India, Persia, and other parts of the Indian Empires which are in question (a question we cannot yet enter fully into, owing to the very little knowledge we possess of their archæology) is largely due to the dispersal thus effected. The Arabian and Moorish results of this were brought back to the western world by the Moors in the early part of the thirteenth century, to whom we owe the splendid plasterwork of the Alhambra (described in Chapter II).

During the Middle Ages plastering existed only as a craft, and its highest function was to prepare a surface to be painted on. Sometimes it was used as an external protection from the weather, but rarely was it employed for direct adornment. Sometimes small ornaments were carved in plaster of Paris, but it played no important part in decorative art, excepting, perhaps, as gesso, though this belonged rather to the painter than the plasterer; nor was it until the commencement of the Renaissance in Italy that it showed any symptoms of revival.

With the commencement of the fifteenth century, old learning and old arts began to be studied, literature leading the way, as it always does, and their study was enormously facilitated by the discovery of the art of printing, and the consequent multiplication of the copies of the lore heretofore locked up in old manuscripts. We can glean somewhat of what was the state of the plaster-worker's art at that time by glancing at some of the old recipes which have been handed down to us in the notebooks of the artists of that dawning time. Amongst the foremost of them was Cennino-Cennini, a painter born about 1360, a pupil for twelve years of Agnoto Gaddi, of Florence (who died in 1378); towards the end of his long life Cennini wrote a book compiled from his notes of all recipes and directions for the conduct of all artistic processes known to him, and this book he finished on 31st July 1437—unfortunately dating it from " the debtors' prison at Florence." He also gives us directions " how to take casts from the face of man or woman," which is much the same as our modern process, and was doubtless that of Lysippus; but he quaintly remarks that " when you take the cast of a person of high rank such as a lord, a king, a pope, or an emperor, you should stir rose water into the plaster, but for other persons it is sufficient to use cold water from fountains, rivers, or wells." In taking a cast from this mould he advises the addition of a little pounded brick. In this there is as yet no reference to piece moulding, and it is very doubtful if these processes were then known. The nearest approach to such a suggestion is contained in the instructions " how to take a cast of the whole figure of a man." " In such case you must let the person stand upright in a box, joined together lengthwise, which will reach as high as the chin. Let a thin copperplate be placed against the shoulders, beginning at the ear and reaching to the bottom of the case, and bind it with a cord to the naked person, so as not to injure or press into the flesh. Cut four copperplates like this and join them together like the edges of the case. Then grease the naked person, put him directly into the case, mix a large quantity of plaster with cold water, and take care to have an assistant with you; and while you pour plaster into the case in the front of the man, let the assistant fill the back part at the same time, so that it may be filled to the throat. Let the plaster rest until it be quite set and dry, then open the case, separate the edges of the case from the copper bands with chisels, and open it as you would a nut. Withdraw the naked person very gently, wash him quickly with clean water, for his flesh will be red as a rose. With regard to the face, you may

PLATE IV

(a) ROMAN STUCCO-DURO PANEL, NOW IN THE VICTORIA AND ALBERT MUSEUM.

(b) STUCCO VAULT, TOMB IN THE VIA LATINA, ROME.

PLATE V

(*a*) and (*b*) Early French Renaissance Stucco Decoration, from the Palace at Fontainebleau.

do that another time." I do not expect a chance to cast from a living face would occur after such a process.

This may, I think, be taken as a merely theoretic instruction, showing more desire than facility, but is sufficient to show that piece moulding was not known to Cennini, if indeed practised by anyone at his time. In another recipe he gravely bids anyone wanting to take a cast of himself to spread a bed of wax about 9 in. deep on the dining-table and then lie down upon it, taking care not to disturb the mould when he gets up. From this mould he takes a plaster cast, and then carefully lies down on his other side and completes the mould ! ! Comment is unnecessary, and it is only from their negative value that these casting recipes of Cennini are worth remark, showing that the desire for such a process was greater than its achievement. The real utility of his recipes, in a positive direction, are those in which he treats of gesso and other painter's usage of the plasterer's material. Of lime stucco he says nothing, and all his remarks relate to plaster obtained from gypsum found at Bologna, or Volterra, whence comes that fine white translucent alabaster of which small figures, vases, and models of buildings are made to this day. A more practical recipe, and one relating to stucco, is found in the Marciana MS., which is preserved in the Library of St Mark at Venice, and was written about 1503.

This is headed as " tried by Master Jacopo de Monte St Savino, the Sculptor." " Admirable stucco for making and modelling figures and for colouring them, and it resists water. Take of finely pounded travertine 5 lbs., and if you would have it finer and more delicate, take fine marble instead of travertine, and 2 lbs. of slaked lime, and stir and beat them well together like a fine paste, and execute what works you will with it, either by forming it with your hands, or in moulds, and dry it in the shade. And if you wish to colour it white, when the work is dry enough to be tolerably firm, but not quite dry, grind white lead with water in the same way as colours are ground, and the flour of sifted lime, and apply it with a brush, and it will be very white and will effectually resist water. And if you wish to colour it with other colours, let the work dry perfectly and then colour it ; but these colours will not resist water like the white. If, then, you wish the colours to resist water, apply on the work the above-mentioned composition and paint with oil-colours."

This brings down the notice of our subject to the period of Raphael and the great revival of stuccowork, before considering which we must first cast a backward glance at some evidences of pre-Raphaelite use of it. We have actual evidence of its use by Donatello, who practised it, and it is on record that he used pounded brick and glue with his stucco, and from this many of his stucchi pass as terra-cottas. No doubt his object was to avoid the risk and distortion by baking his clay model. There is a group of the " Entombment " over the sacristy door in the Church of St Antonio at Padua, which was formerly considered to be in terra-cotta, but is now proved to be of this brick-dust stucco. There are medallions of the Four Evangelists in true stucco in the sacristy of San Lorenzo at Florence. In the Victoria and Albert Museum there is a large stucco plaque with a low relief of the Virgin and Child, and many others are known. Now, Donatello died in 1466, proving that in the first half of the fifteenth century stucco was making progress. In the same museum there is a very fine relief of the Virgin and Child surrounded by angels, exhibiting very marked Gothic features in its accessories. This has the date 1430 attributed to it. There, too, you will find many busts of very excellent modelling and great technical skill, all done with the grey stucco. Indeed, there is plenty of evidence that with the advance of the revival of all the arts, stucco was yearning to take its wonted place beside them. Bramante, the chief architect of his day, was uncle to Raphael, and inspired his nephew with an enthusiastic love for architecture and archæological research. He, Vasari tells us, invented " a mixture of lime " with which to decorate the exterior of his houses with festoons and friezes of foliage, and one of his last works was the building, in 1513, of Raphael's own house, which was decorated with stucco made according to the recipe from the Marciana MS., Jacopo Sansovino being one of the stucco modellers there employed. Bramante died in 1514.

Other experimenters were at work in other parts of Italy, for the endeavour to revive the lost art of modelling in stucco was becoming general, and in Bologna Alfonso Lombardi had achieved a pre-eminent success in the renewed art. Not only did he model many portrait busts in stucco, and amongst them that of Emperor Charles V, which he did whilst the emperor was sitting to Titian for his portrait, but, aspiring to greater things, he executed a large group of the death of the Virgin in a very hard stucco, which was so admired by Michelangelo, himself a stucco-worker, that on seeing it he exclaimed, " If this stucco could only become marble, it would be bad for the antique statues." Lombardi modelled many other statues in Bologna which were larger than life, all executed in the grey lime stucco, and Cicognara styles his figure of Hercules as the finest colossal statue of the century. About the same time Andrea Verrochio really founded the art of piece moulding in Venice, and brought the casting of plaster to such a pitch of perfection that reproductions of ancient and modern works were easily obtainable, and thus formative art secured an impulse the movement of which still continues.

In 1509 Raphael came to Rome, and was in 1515 appointed by Leo X Director and Inspector of the search for the buried remains of Ancient Rome ; and for this purpose determined, in 1518, to unearth the remains of the Golden House of Nero, then supposed to be the Baths of Titus, and which for 500 years had been buried under their own decay. Here was a great discovery and surprise. Not only were there found painted chambers, fostering the new growth of " grotesque " ornamentation, so-called from its abounding in the newly unearthed grottoes, but, more cherished than all else, abundance of modelled stucco decorations, which had survived still better their long entombment, astonishing Raphael and his attendant, Giovanni da Udine, by their hardness and brilliant whiteness. This discovery was most opportune, for the decoration of the Loggia of the Vatican (Plate XLV) was just then under consideration, and Udine set himself to work especially to find out the process and the manipulation. He says he made many experiments and reinvented the process ; but as Raphael, who was not a Latin scholar, had just then had a special translation of Vitruvius into Italian made for his own study, I am disposed to think this also was exhumed about the same time. Be this as it may, the newly found stucco-duro became at once the rage. By his last testament Raphael left the completion of his decorative works to Giulio Romano and Gio. Francesco Penni, who, for the stucco portion of these, allied themselves with Giovanni da Udine, its reinventor, and continued the work at the Villa Madama, then being built for Cardinal de Medici, a cousin of Leo X, who succeeded him as Pope in 1523.

You can form an idea of what the modelled stucco here was (Plate LIX, a) by examining a very beautiful model of it which you will see in the Victoria and Albert Museum ; but of the vastness of the villa and the richness of its surroundings it would, in a short notice, be impossible to give you an impression. Unfortunately it was partially ruined before it was completed, and suffered from the barbarities of the soldiers during the sack of Rome by the French in 1527. That drove Udine to Florence, where he was much employed by Cosimo de Medici and Michelangelo, but in his old age he returned to Rome, working to the last on the Loggia, on which, as a stucco-worker, he began, and where he died in 1564. He is buried in the Pantheon, close by the tomb of his loved master, Raphael, and, as says his biographer Vasari, " we may believe they are now met together in eternal blessedness."

Giulio Romano went in 1524 to Mantua to carry out work (Plate XLVI) for Duke Frederic Gonzaga, which Raphael had, before his death, promised to undertake, and there raised up an important school of stucco-workers, who we shall see influenced the whole of Western Europe. Pierino del Vaga, painter and sculptor, who was one of Raphael's staff of stucco-workers, having begun life as a " hawk boy," went to Genoa, where he founded a great school under the patronage of the Doira family, but returned to Rome when peace was restored, and worked on the Scala Regia and many of the principal rooms in the Vatican. Jacopo Sansovino, one of the first essayers of the new-found art, went to Venice, where he fostered it, making many statues and other large works, training up a large school there, and in it his most celebrated pupil, Alessandro Vittorio—a man to whom nothing was impossible. He was, in fact, too facile. Some of his work in the Palazzo d'Albrizzi in Venice are evidences of his ingenious and daring skill. Of a less hazardous and more restrained character is the vaulted ceiling, shown on Plate VI, *a*, from the Ducal Palace at Venice, executed about 1570, but each example of his skill is wonderfully varied, and in all phases of decorative art he was an exuberant master.

The school which Udine had founded at Florence produced great results : Vasari, the biographer of so many artists, went there to work on the Pitti Palace in 1555. There are many grand ceilings in this same palace, with marvellous stuccowork designed either by Vasari or the architect Ammanato, and executed by the school Giovanni da Udine established. But the most interesting example of external work, as demonstrating the perfect composition of the material and its great durability, is shown in the present state of the pillars of the courtyard of the Palazzo Vecchio there. These were done in 1566 under Vasari's direction, and as the names of good workmen are as worthy of record as are those of good designers, I, in praise of their honest and perfect workmanship, give them here. They are—Pietro Paulo Minocci, who afterwards settled in Parma, where he did much good work, of which some still exists ; Ricciavelli da Volterra, who afterwards joined himself to Pierino del Vaga at Genoa and in Rome, and ultimately came to England ; Sebastiano Tadda, whose relative Francesco was a noted worker in porphyry ; and Leonardo Marignalli, of whom I have not been able to trace anything further. Their monument is in their work, which you will find on plaster in Florence, and which, after 500 years, hands down the record of their craft almost as sound as the day they did it. With what they did it demands particular attention, and by a fortunate accident we have in a notebook still preserved in the Bodleian Library at Oxford, kept by Pirro Ligorio, a joint architect and coadjutor with Michelangelo for St Peter's at Rome, and which contains the exact recipe written just about this time : " Take," says he, " 3 parts of pounded Parian marble, easily got from among the ruins in Rome and from broken statues ; add 1 part of lime which is to be perfectly slaked by letting it lie in a heap covered with pozzuolana and exposed to the sun and rain for at least a year. The lime is to be made from pure white marble, not from travertine, or any other stone which is full of holes and yellowish in tint ; mix a day before with sufficient water on a tile floor. The first coat to be mixed with coarsely pounded and the finishing coat with finely pounded white marble." Now let us examine scientifically the rationale of all this. Firstly, *the lime is pure carbonate of lime* ; it was naturally burnt with wood fuel, and consequently was free from all those sulphurous and other deleterious compounds inseparable from coal firing. The air-slaking of it prevented the too great absorption of carbonic acid which is obtained by the free use of water, and which rather retards than assists the setting of the stucco. Then the pulverisation of the unburnt mortar introduces a fine crystalline substance into this identical chemical composition when as yet amorphous in structure. These minute crystals induce the formation of a general crystalline structure until the final and most permanent form of all mineral substance is achieved.   Thus the wisdom of the ancients achieved that which is only just dawning on the modern world of science, and the as yet but partially understood question, *why lime sets*, is full of thought seed for scientific inquiry—seed for us to propagate and so to carry still further the lore and practice of the plasterer, and to cultivate it into fruitful knowledge.   You will have remarked the absence of hair in any of these old formulæ ; the rapidly induced crystallisation seems to have rendered this unnecessary, for the introduction of any animal substance into plaster is an unscientific error which these old plasterers avoided.

After this digression which these Florentine plasterers have brought about, let us return to Mantua, where we left Giulio Romano in 1524.   He there did works in painting and stucco (Plate XLVI) which were renowned throughout Europe, and his school of stucco-workers achieved such a reputation that Francis I wrote to Duke Frederic Gonzaga, praying him to send him some young man able both as a painter and a stucco-worker to assist him in decorating his new palace at Fontainebleau.   This

FIG. 1.—Enriched Moulding, Gallery of Apollo, The Louvre, Paris.   (Louis XIV Style.)

was in 1536.   After conference with Giulio Romano, the duke sent him Francesco Primaticcio, the son of a wealthy Bolognese merchant, whom a love of art had seduced from the ways of commerce.   He gathered round him a large staff of modellers, of which he became superintendent, and together they, according to Vasari, " did the first stucchi ever executed in France."   If the pure white stucco is meant, this was true, but there was in France a considerable attempt to model in the ordinary plaster before this, and many of the fine Gothic-hooded chimney-pieces in the chateaux are modelled in plaster on wooden cradling.   At the Gros Horloge at Rouen there exists some well-modelled plaster, and there is evidence of the existence of a school of ornamental plaster-workers in the valley of the Seine some years before Primaticcio's advent.   At Fontainebleau, however, he did most noble figure work, much of it being considerably over life-size, such as you see in Plates V and VII, *a* ; long graceful figures, which formed the canon for the sculptors of the French school of Goujon, Pilon, and their followers.

It is, of course, here impracticable to trace the varied course of plastering in France, but a few typical examples will enable the characteristic forms of the decoration to be grasped.   Plates XLVIII and XLIX, in Chapter III, are of the Louis XIV style, and the usual enriched laurel leaf bands are shown in detail in Figs. 1 and 2.   The Louis XV Rococo is represented by Figs. 3 and 4, from Versailles ; the more restrained feeling of the Louis XVI appears in Plates VII, *b*, VIII, and IX, while the classic Empire is exemplified in Plate X.

PLATE VI

(*a*) STUCCO CEILING, THE DUCAL PALACE, VENICE. (A. Vittoria, 1570.)

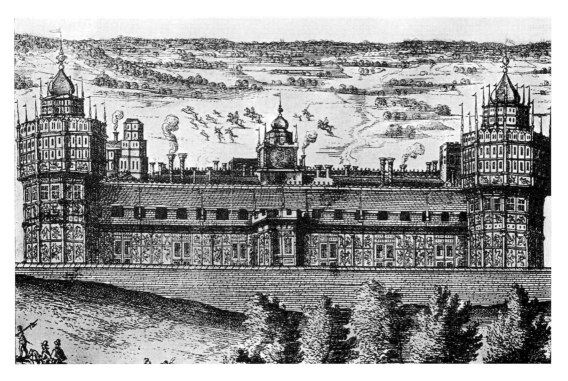

(*b*) NONSUCH PALACE, SURREY.

From the engraving by A. Hoefnagel.

PLATE VII

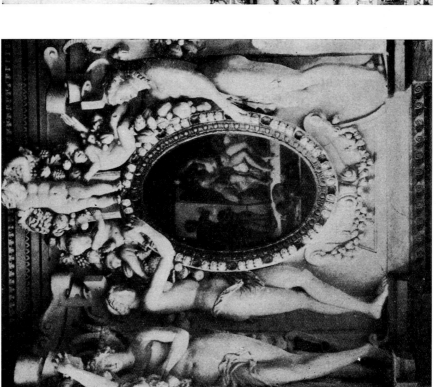

(a) STUCCO DECORATION, PALACE OF FONTAINEBLEAU.
(Primaticcio, 1536.)

(b) LOUIS XVI CEILING, DIPLOMATIC SALON, THE
ADMIRALTY, PARIS.

PLATE VIII

CEILING OF THE SECRETARY'S ROOM, PALAIS-ROYAL, PARIS.
(LOUIS XVI STYLE.)

PLATE IX

WALL DECORATION, HOTEL DE MME. DE BOISSAE, BORDEAUX.
(LOUIS XVI STYLE.)

Of course, if Francis I would thus emulate the arts of Italy in their then most fashionable phase, his great rival, our Henry VIII, could not be outdone by him. Already Cardinal Wolsey was busy fostering the Renaissance in England, and Henry sent, through his ambassadors, for those who could outvie the Italians in the service of the French king. By these means he collected many artists of renown. Amongst these were Luca and Bartholomew Penni, brothers of that Giovanni Francesco Penni whom Raphael left fellow-executor with Giulio Romano. Luca, who preferred painting to plastering, did not stay long here, but deserted the king and went to join Primaticcio in France, for plasterers who could model in stucco were the subject of much diplomatic correspondence in those days. Bartholomew was here at any rate until 1539, as records of payment to him are recorded in that year. Gerome of Trevisa, who, Vasari tells us, "made many ingenious devices and one honourable house for the king's use," came, and was so much admired by King Henry VIII that he gave him a stipend of 400 crowns a year. He was killed at the siege of Boulogne in 1544. Nicholas of Modena left Primaticcio, from whom he was receiving 20 livres a month, and came to help us. There was also Toto del Nunziato, whom the old account books call Anthony Toto and who was a wax modeller at Florence, whence " sundry merchants carried him off to England, where he made all manner of works for the king, and particularly the principal palace." Now this principal palace was that of Nonsuch (Plate VI, *b*), which was so-called because it had no equal ; it was built at Cheam, between Sutton and Epsom, but unfortunately not a vestige of it now exists.

FIG. 2.—Part Ceiling, Hotel Dangereau, Paris. (Louis XIV Style.)

It was a very large and sumptuous pile, containing two quadrangles, and built in the half-timbered style, then prevalent in England ; it was never quite finished before the king's death, but existed for more than a century, sufficiently long for record of plasterers' work to have been taken by those who admired it.

The Duke of Saxe-Weimar, who saw it in 1613, tells us that " the labours of Hercules were set forth on the king's side, the queen's side exhibiting all kinds of heathen stories with naked female figures " ; and John Evelyn, who saw it in 1665, says : " I took an exact view of the plaster statues and bas-relievos inserted between the puncheons of the outside walls of the court, which must have been the work of some celebrated Italian. I much admired how it had lasted so well and entire from the time of Henry VIII, exposed as they are to the air, and pity it is they are not taken out and placed in some dry place—a gallery would much become them. They are

FIG. 3.—Ceiling, The Medal Saloon, Versailles. (Louis XV Style.)

mezzo-relievos the size of life. The story is of heathen gods, emblems, and compartments." You may form some idea of them by turning to the illustration of Primaticcio's work at Fontainebleau. Unfortunately we had not the white marble here to mix with the lime, so we could not obtain the crystalline quality that preserved the old Italian stucco. We learn from a manuscript note by P. le Neve that "it was done with rye dough very costly." This would dry very slowly and give toughness to the stucco

FIG. 4.—Versailles, Ceiling of the Queen's Bedroom.

whilst being modelled. The writer tried it and found it pleasant to work with, and it dries a beautiful old ivory colour. Having thus brought the classic art of modelling in stucco into the English Renaissance, it will be well to pause awhile and take a brief backward glance at what English plastering was before the advent of this new fashion.

What the state of plaster working was before the Romans, under Julius Cæsar, came, we have no knowledge. We know that the ancient Britons used houses built of hurdles plastered inside and out with mud—the old "wattle and daub," in fact, much of which is still done in the West of England. Of course the Romans brought their arts with them, and during their 400 years' stay introduced the arts and luxuries of the capital, as the numerous ruins of their buildings show. The Anglo-Saxons plastered many of their buildings inside and out, as the illumination in their MSS., and some evidences of actual work, including perhaps the plasterwork on Anglo-Saxon masonry at the Church of Avebury in Wilts, demonstrate. The Normans were a highly skilled and civilised people, but we have no written records of how they plastered ; that they did so is proved by existing pictures showing painted walls of great richness, which could only be done on a finely wrought field. All this was, of course, the ordinary lime stucco, for the use of " plaster of Paris " or calcined gypsum was unknown in this country until the time of Henry II, who, on a visit to Paris in 1254, so admired the superior whiteness and fineness of the walls that he introduced it here. But plaster or lime stucco was as yet in England only considered as a structural necessity and not as a decorative adjunct. That its fireproof qualities and sanitary influence were known is shown by the edict of King John, who, after the great fire which destroyed the timber-built London Bridge in 1212, issued an edict that " all shops on the Thames should be plastered and whitewashed within and without. All houses which till now are covered with reed or rush, let them be plastered within eight days, and let those which shall not be plastered within that time be demolished by the aldermen and lawful men of the venue (overseers). And let all houses in which brewing or baking is done be plastered within and without, that they may be safe from fire." At Clare, in Suffolk, is an old house (Plate XII, a), with some very fine plasterwork modelled in relief, with figures and scroll-work, formerly stated to be fifteenth century, but undoubtedly much later. In 1519, Hormann, in his " Vulgaria," says : " Some men will have their walls plastered, some pargeted and white limed, some rough cast, some pricked, some wrought with plaster of Paris." In fact, the plasterer's and pargeter's art and craft had now become of such importance that it was formed into a separate Guild and Company in London in 1501 by Henry VII, who granted them " the right to search and try and make and exercise due search as well, in, upon, and of all manner of stuff, touching and concerning the art and mystery of pargeters, commonly called plaisterers, and upon all work and workmen in the same art."[1] However, in the Middle Ages occasional use was made of plaster beyond the plain coating of walls, of which mediæval builders were very fond. This may be seen in the two vaults at Chester Cathedral (Plate XI). Bishop West's Chapel at Ely has a deep-ribbed ceiling slightly Renaissance in feeling, elaborately mitred, without bosses (Plate XI, c).

It is noteworthy that here pargeters are " commonly called plaisterers," but in earlier times plasterers were commonly called pargeters. Parging was then plastering, and I am inclined to think that when the larger surfaces of the walls admitted the use of the " rule " and the " float," the distinction began. We still parge a chimney-flue,

[1] This charter, having been frequently renewed with varying powers, still exists, but the only trade function the Company now performs is the granting of £25 annually to the successful candidates in the examinations conducted by the City and Guilds of London for Technical Examination.

PLATE X

EMPIRE DECORATION IN THE SALON, HOTEL DE GRAMMONT, PARIS.

PLATE XI

(c) BISHOP WEST'S CHAPEL, ELY.

(a) and (b) PLASTER VAULTING, CHESTER CATHEDRAL.

PLATE XII

(a) HOUSE AT CLARE, SUFFOLK. (MID-SEVENTEENTH CENTURY.)
(Details on Plate XCI)

(b) PART OF FRIEZE, PRESENCE CHAMBER, HARDWICK HALL.

PLATE XIII

(*a*) STUCCO-DURO FRIEZE, RUINS OF OLD HARDWICK HALL.

(*b*) PART OF FRIEZE, PRESENCE CHAMBER, HARDWICK HALL.

FIG. 5.—The Drawing-room, Westwood Hall, Yorkshire.

in which neither rule nor float can be used, but only the trowel. In the old timber-framed houses the want of truth in the carpentry compelled the plaster to be laid with the trowel, hence we say they are pargeted, not plastered, and the modelling which so frequently enriched them was done with the trowel, and still bears the name of pargetry. We have thus seen how the taste of the time was prepared for the introduction of the plasterers who worked in the Italian mode introduced by Henry VIII. These kept continually coming until the death of their royal master, and having found the way here remained for many years after. Thus we have a De Rudolfi here in 1550, who was most probably a relative of Bartholomew Rudolfi, who worked in Venice and Padua, where he married the youngest daughter of Titziano Minio, also a stucco-worker. She likewise prosecuted the art, and is the only female stucco-worker I have met with any account of. Rudolfi and his wife took service with Sigismund II, King of Poland, leaving their only (?) son here. Leonardo Ricciarelli, one of those who worked at the Palazzo Vecchio at Florence, came here in 1570, and Luca Romano, who had worked with Primaticcio at Fontainebleau, came here after Primaticcio's death, and I have found his name as employed in England in 1586.

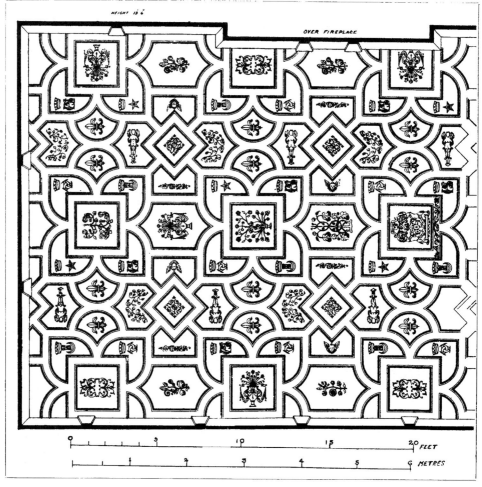

FIG. 5A.—The Drawing-room, Winton House, Haddingtonshire. (J. Baillie *del.*)

PLATE XIV

(b) Peartree House, Great Yarmouth.

(a) 4 South Quay Street, Great Yarmouth.

PLATE XV

(a) THE DRAWING-ROOM, WAKEHURST PLACE, SUSSEX.

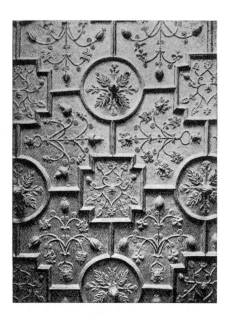

(b) BAILDON HALL, YORKSHIRE.

(c) LEES HALL, THORNHILL, YORKSHIRE.

PLATE XVI

(a) BISHOP KING'S HOUSE, OXFORD.

(b) ST PETER'S HOSPITAL, BRISTOL.

PLATE XVII

(*a*) and (*b*)
PANELS, SPEKE HALL, LANCASHIRE.

(*c*) HAWKSWORTH HALL, YORKSHIRE.

PLATE XVIII

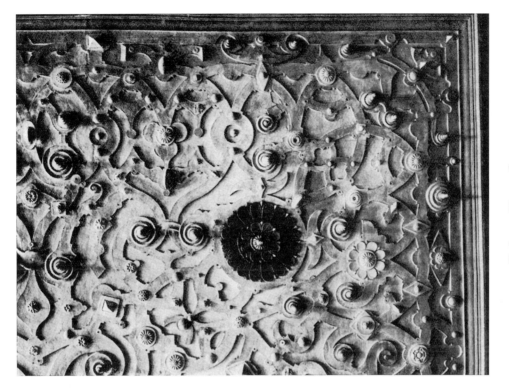

(b) LYME HALL, CHESHIRE.

(a) GREAT ST HELEN'S, LONDON, NOW IN THE VICTORIA AND
ALBERT MUSEUM.

PLATE XIX

TWO CEILINGS, MORAY HOUSE, CANONGATE, EDINBURGH.

PLATE XX

(*a*) THE DRAWING-ROOM, GLAMIS CASTLE, SCOTLAND.

(*b*) THE STAIRCASE, HOLYROOD PALACE, EDINBURGH.

PLATE XXI

(b) 135 FISHPOOL STREET, ST ALBANS.

(a) SPARROW'S HOUSE, IPSWICH.

PLATE XXII

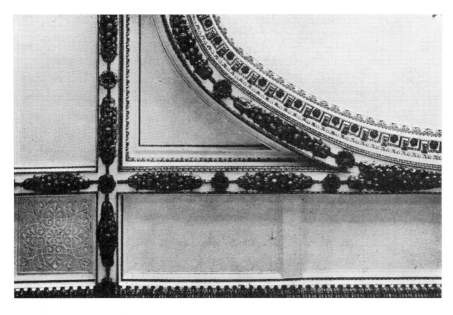

(*a*) LEES COURT, KENT. NOW DESTROYED.

(*b*) THE HALL, COLESHILL, BERKSHIRE.

PLATE XXIII

(*a*) THE STAIRCASE LANTERN.

(*b*) CEILING OF A SMALL ROOM.

ASHBURNHAM HOUSE, WESTMINSTER.

PLATE XXIV

(*a*) BOTOLPH LANE, CITY OF LONDON.   NOW DEMOLISHED.

(*b*) CUMBERLAND HOUSE, PALL MALL.   NOW DEMOLISHED.
(M. Brettingham.)

PLATE XXV

(*a*) St Clement Danes, Strand, London.

(*b*) St Mildred, Bread Street, London.

The English plasterers quickly learned the operative lessons these Italians taught, though they never learned the skill of their arts of design; nor indeed was this necessary. The exigencies of English houses were different from those of Italian palaces, so they fitted their work for its purpose—that of covering a flat ceiling in a room of moderate height with a suitable plastered decoration. That this lesson was early learned is shown by some notes we have of the career of Charles Williams, the first English plasterer of whom we have any record as a practiser of the new art. He wrote in 1547 to Sir John Thynne, then engaged in building his house at Longleat, in Wiltshire, offering his services in supplying internal decorations upon " the Italian fashion "; and among the papers at Longleat are two letters from Sir William Cavendish and his wife (Bess of Hardwick), begging from Sir John the use of this " cunning playsterer," to do work for them at Hardwick Hall. There is but little doubt the fragment of the frieze (Plate XIII, *a*) still remaining on the wall of the old house is his handiwork. If so, the " Italian fashion " he wrote of is more applicable to the handicraft than the design, and it is not improbable that the great frieze representing a stag hunt which yet adorns the Presence Chamber (Plates XII, *b*, XIII, *b*, LII, *a*, *b*, *c*) was executed by those who had studied under his direction. During the short and troubled reigns of Edward VI and of Queen Mary, when England was in the throes of the internecine strife of politics and religion, but little decorative work was done, nor until the long and more prosperous time of Queen Elizabeth did the English plasterer have the opportunity of showing his prowess.

He had not attempted to vie with the more artistically educated foreigners, but had evolved for himself an especial decoration of his own, based in some degree on the familiar groining which had strengthened and ornamented the stone roofs with which he was familiar. The ceiling of the bay window in the Banqueting Hall, Hampton Court, may be said to have been the foundation of the radiating pendentive system of ceiling which followed and developed in many ways during the next century. Geometric rather than freehand designs were his first essays. These at first consisted of interlacing squares, having radial ribs from their intersecting points, and as he grew bolder in his work these radial ribs became arched, and from their junction depended a pendant more or less ornamental, such as you may see copied, in the Victoria and Albert Museum, from a ceiling at Sizergh Hall, Westmorland, where you will find it in conjunction with fine Renaissance inlaid woodwork. These ceilings sometimes had colour and gilding, and Edmund Spenser sings in his " Visions of Bellay " of halls where

> " Gold was the parget, and the ceiling bright
> Did shine all scaly with great plates of gold,"

and the plasterer and the painter were united, not only in their work, but in their person—so much so, indeed, that the elder Company of the Painter-stainers was compelled to appeal to the Parliament in the latter years of the queen's reign to restrain the plasterers from using oil-colours, and they were ultimately, after considerable discussion during two Parliaments, confined to the use of distemper painting only. But it was not the encroachment of the Plasterers' Company by painting alone which depleted the trade of the painter-stainers. The purity of the white stucco then introduced, and the decline of the mediæval sense of colour in favour of this white homogeneous purity, had its effect also, and this was enforced by the richness of the plastering introduced.

Generally, the regular early Renaissance ceiling (Plates XIV-XIX, Figs. 6-10) had close-set interlacing ribs forming geometrical patterns, the panels or angles often set with birds, animals, floral or abstract devices. Often the rib itself holds a little

FIG. 6.—The Old Library, Bramshill, Hants.

FIG. 7.—King James's Bedroom, Knole, Kent.

FIG. 8.—Plaster Frieze in the Great Chamber, Aston Hall, Birmingham.

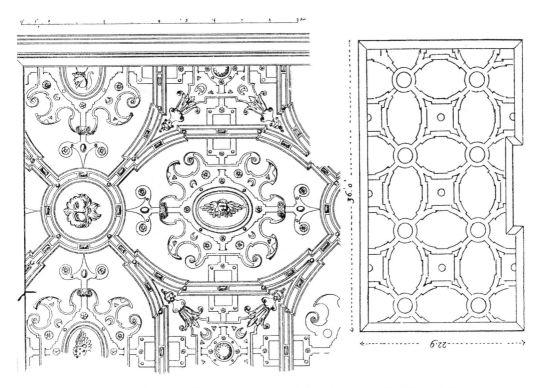

FIG. 9.—The Great Chamber, Aston Hall, Birmingham.   (W. Niven *del.*)

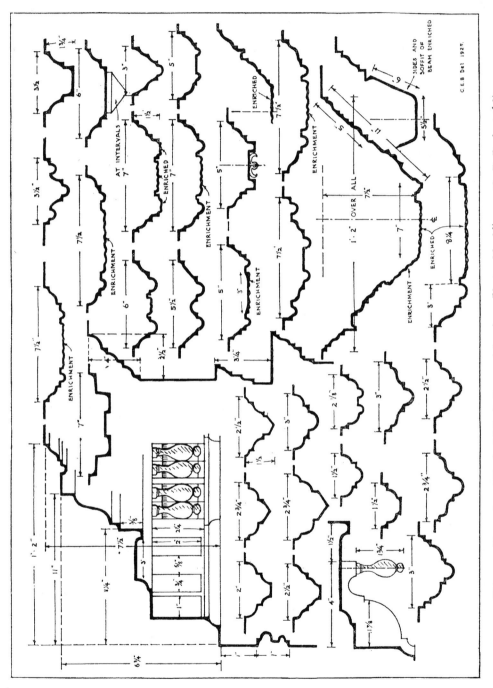

FIG. 10.—Examples of Typical Elizabethan and Jacobean Plaster Mouldings.   (G. E. Bankart *del.*)

delicately modelled band of ornament, as in Plates XVI and XVIII, *a*. Pendants hang sometimes from salient points, as in Plate XVII, *c*. The whole effect is rich and lively, but it is not often that we find modelled floral ornament of the quality seen in the panels at Speke (Plates XVII, *a* and *b*, LXXXVI, *a*, LXXXVII, *c*). The later strapwork and larger panels of Jacobean times are seen at Aston Hall (Fig. 9), and typical early Renaissance mouldings in Fig. 10. The geometric arrangement was not always confined to straight lines. Curvilinear, interlacing, and knotted forms were introduced, as at Wakehurst (Plate XV, *a*). As the art grew, even the geometric basis was abandoned, and a free adaptation of scroll-work of very large dimension was adopted (Plate XVIII, *a*). The ceiling was not sufficient for the plasterer, but his art encroached on the walls, and a deep frieze, filled with relief ornament of figure work and emblems, extended itself between the wainscot and the main cornice, as at Aston Hall (Fig. 8) and Crewe Hall (now demolished), where some of the friezes were nearly 6 ft. deep, and the Hardwick Hall example, before quoted, is 11 ft. deep.

External walls were sometimes covered with pargetry, like the cottage at St Albans (Plate XXI, *b*); and the string-courses, cornices, and other external architectural features were covered with plaster—in fact, there is hardly a single county in England or Wales which does not yet retain the evidence of the artistic powers of the plasterer. Some places, notably the older towns, once commercial centres but now somewhat decayed in wealth, have by that absence of growth preserved much of their wonted glory for us, such as Yarmouth, which abounds with rich plasterwork of the character you will see on Plate XIV.

The early years of James I were very fruitful ones to the plasterer, and in Bramshill House, Hampshire, built in 1603, there are several ceilings, one of which is shown in Fig. 6. One of the largest mansions of this time is Audley End, Essex, where many rooms exhibit a very varied design. This house was built by Thomas Howard, Earl of Suffolk, between 1603 and 1616. One ceiling with modelled groups of fish gives its name to the " Fish Room." One room has a singularly convoluted pattern, with wrought pendants at the principal points. This design was a favourite, for there are several versions of it existing, as at Charlton, Wilts., and Lyme, Cheshire (Plate XVIII, *b*), helping to prove that these ornamental plasterers travelled from place to place, taking their patterns with them. But the triumphant example of the plasterer's work here is found in the library, a large room 60 ft. by 30 ft. There is a variety of detail throughout the whole, no formal repetition, but a rhythmic balance is maintained, giving it emphasis and a cadence, and I know of no other ceiling of this date so pure and so restrained. A much richer one, though not so graceful, is found in the state bedroom of Brentford House. Of the external modelled work done at this time, it may suffice to mention the fine old house at Maidstone, which bears upon it the date of 1611. Bishop King's House at Oxford, 1620, the George Inn at Audley End, Sparrow's House, Ipswich (Plate XXI, *a*), and abundant instances exist to prove its popularity.

In Scotland, English patterns seem to have been appropriated, for they all belong to this epoch, and there does not appear to be any evidence of a national growth in Scotland, such as exists in England.

Probably the earliest of these Scottish examples is that of Craigievar, Aberdeenshire, which dates from 1611, when the castle was purchased by William Forbes, who " having made much wealth by trading in Denmark," " he plaistered it very curiously," adapting the usual pattern, common in many parts of England, to the arched and groined ceiling. Similar ceilings exist at Moray House, Edinburgh, two of which are shown on Plate XIX. Both of these examples show the ribs enriched with modelled ornament, and give excellent impressions of the effect of this treatment. A little later example of a

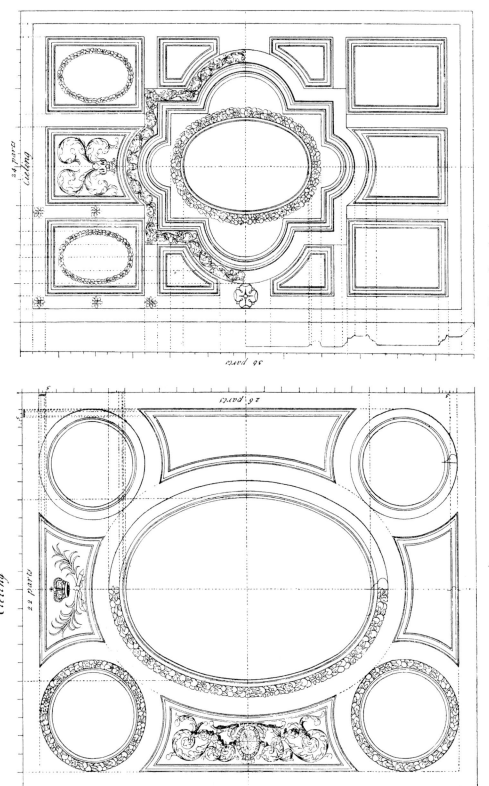

Fig. 11.—Designs for Later Renaissance Ceilings. (Batty Langley.)

similar pattern comes from Winton House, Haddingtonshire, done about 1620 (Fig. 5A). The design and details of all these three are so similar that it is more than probable

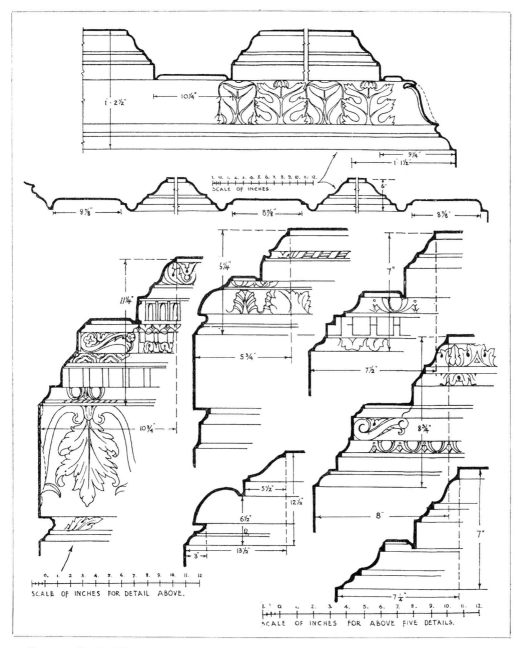

FIG. 12.—Typical Plaster Mouldings, Late Stuart and Queen Anne Period. (G. E. Bankart *del.*)

that they are all the work of the same school of plasterers, whether they be Scottish or English. At Pinkie House there are many plainer ceilings, partaking in form the character of those found in the houses pulled down in Lime Street,

London, proving that there was little or no difference between the two halves of the kingdom.

Under Charles I the old style of his father at first prevailed, and so late as the Survey of the Manor of Wimbledon in 1649 we read of a room in which " above the wainscot is a border of fret or parge work wrought; the ceiling is of the same fret or parge work "; and many of the older houses yet there remaining have good illustrations of this survival of the older character. Yet the advance in the study of Renaissance architecture under Charles I, greatly due to the influence of Inigo Jones, reduced this redundance of ornament, and ceilings of a plainer character, but still retaining the ribbed formation, prevailed. The revolution in style carried out in a few years may be appreciated by comparing the first examples of the later Renaissance (Plates I (*Frontispiece*), XXII, and XXV) with the Elizabethan work of Plate XIII *et seq*. The wide compartments and ornament concentrated into modelled bands and scrolls are seen at Forde Abbey, and also Coleshill (Plates I (*Frontispiece*) and XXII, *b*), the latter formerly ascribed to Inigo Jones, but now known to have been the work of Roger Pratt. Ashburnham House, Westminster (Plate XXIII), is also an early work by Inigo Jones or John Webb, and Lees Court, now burnt, a curious house of Louis XIII type (Plate XXII, *a*). The richer and more vigorous modelled ornament which came towards the end of the seventeenth century may be studied on Plates XXII, XXIV, *a*, LIII, and LV. Mouldings of this richest period (1670-1720) appear in Fig. 12. The unsettled state of the kingdom, and the Puritanic worship of plainness which set in and continued during the Commonwealth, were well nigh destructive to both, nor until the Restoration of Charles II was either enabled to revive.

Born of a French mother, passing his youth chiefly abroad, the king returned to his native country without any love for its national arts. The older or the wealthier families were requisitioned, and ruined during the past troubles by one side or the other, and not unfrequently by both, so there was but a mere tradition of the old art left, yet sufficient remained to resuscitate it in a new fashion. This was enhanced by Sir Christopher Wren's visit to Paris in 1665, where he particularly noticed the plasterwork done by Van Ostel and Anoldino, " plaisterers who perform admirable works at the Louvre," and refers to " the marble meal as the old and still the modern way of stuccowork in Italy." The art at this period adopted floral motives, and the illustration (Plate XX, *b*) is an excellent specimen of the plasterer's art of the time. This is from Holyrood Palace, where it forms the ceiling of the principal staircase, and is about 24 ft. square, consequently the figures in the angles representing Fame, Glory, Force, and Power are rather more than life-size. The floral wreathings are full of the most delicate and beautiful modelling. Two " English plasterers," Halbert and Dunserfield, are paid for this work in March 1679. In the Church of King Charles the Martyr at Tunbridge Wells is a very good ceiling with a large hemispherical dome, and an adjacent ceiling bears two dates, 1682 and 1690. These were done by John Weatherell and Henry Doogood, who were paid £190 for their work. Similar plasterwork, evidently by the same hands, was done at Groombridge Place, in the vicinity. Of course there is not much in London of the early part of Charles's time—the Great Fire destroyed the old, and the Great Plague arrested the new; but there is a very beautiful specimen in St Mildred's Church, Bread Street (Plate XXV, *b*). Once it had a band of cherubs circling round the foot of the dome, but these have been removed.

One of the most remarkable monuments of the plasterer's art in external work is " Sparrow's House," at Ipswich (Plate XXI, *a*). In the house itself there is very interesting internal plasterwork, together with some good work of earlier date, in an exterior court, but its chief effect is on the main front. Here we have coarse modelled groups of the four quarters of the globe, with their emblems, together with a large figure of

PLATE XXVI

(a) SALOON CEILING, HOLKHAM, NORFOLK.

(b) THE SALOON CEILING, HOLKHAM, NORFOLK.

PLATE XXVII

(b) The " Dog and Heron " Ceiling, Bouchier Mansion, Micklegate, York.

(a) Rococo Ceiling, Whitehall Gardens, London.

PLATE XXVIII

THE DINING-ROOM, LANSDOWNE HOUSE, BERKELEY SQUARE. (Robert Adam.)

PLATE XXIX

(b) END OF THE DINING-ROOM, BOWOOD HOUSE, WILTS.
(Robert Adam.)

(a) THE DRAWING-ROOM, 20 MANSFIELD STREET, LONDON.
(Robert Adam.)

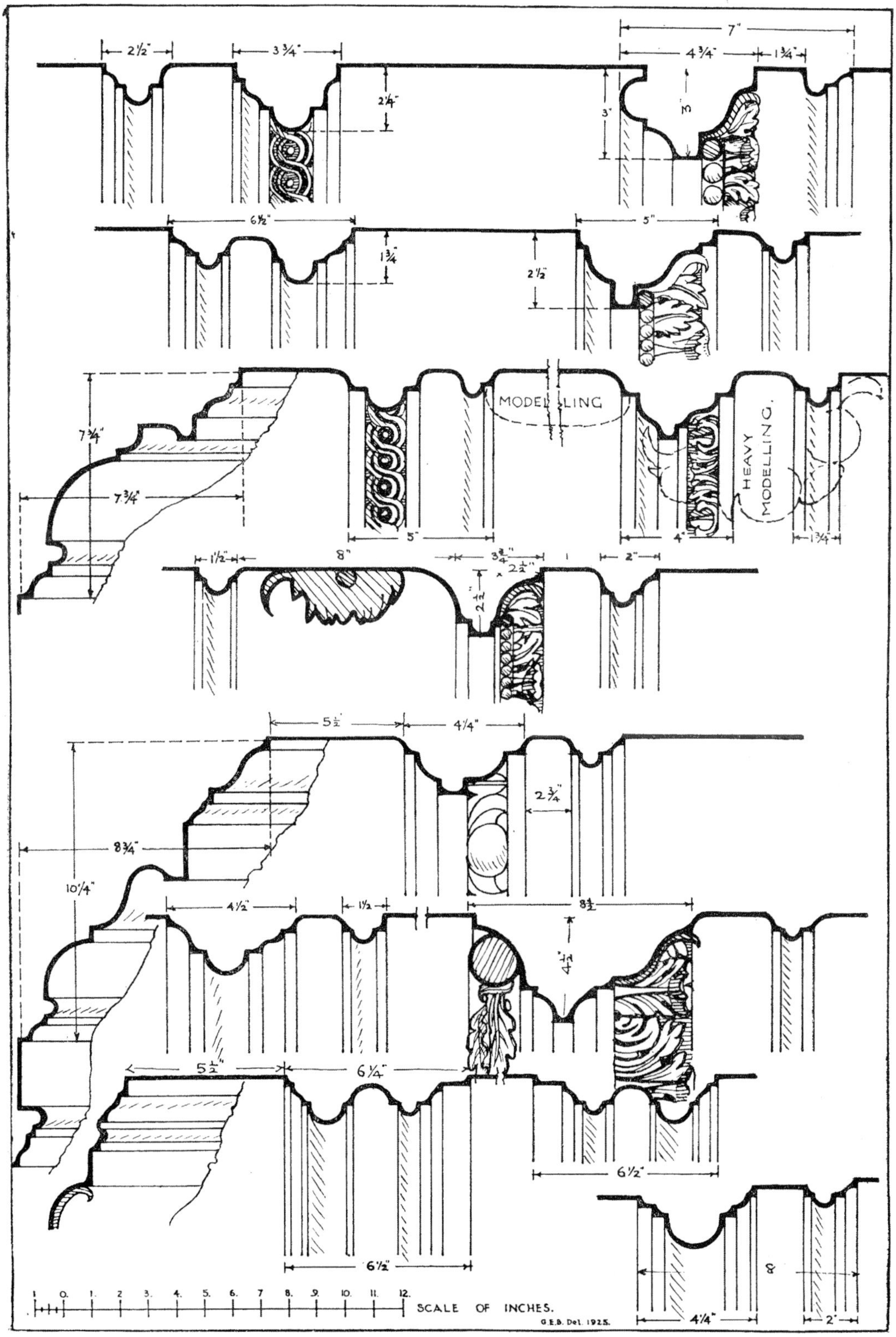

FIG. 13.—Typical Georgian Plaster Mouldings.   (G. E. Bankart *del.*)

Atlas bearing the globe itself.   There are festoons of foliage, S. George and the Dragon, a grand escutcheon of the royal arms, processional and pastoral scenes, making this well-preserved house veritably a national monument; and Ipswich is worthy of a plasterer's pilgrimage, as he will find much other evidence of the past history of his art and craft in this old port.

French fashions, however, reigned supreme during the latter portion of the Stuart dynasty, and the influence of the style of Louis XIV made itself prominent not only on the ceilings, but on the walls, where raised plaster panels with ornamental heads and bases began to prevail.

The so-called Georgian style of the Palladian architects of the second third of the eighteenth century is seen in Plates XXIV, *b*, XXVI, and LVII.   Ribs are again shallower and ornament more formal and repetitive, if not of a cold type.   For Georgian mouldings, see Fig. 13.   Under French influence the ceilings became divested of other panelling than a broad margin surrounding it, filled with flowing ornament, and often with rounded or incurved angles; the cornice became of small importance, the frieze had disappeared, and a deep cove, plain or ornamental, replaced both.   A good example exists at Drum House, Midlothian, where there is also an example of the later and richer form of this phase.   The ceiling of St Martin's in the Fields, by Arturi and Bagutti for James Gibbs, is a banal example of decadent rococo, and contrasts unfavourably with the vigorous early native work at St Clement Danes (Plate XXV, *a*).   Arturi and Bagutti were then the principal workers in modelled stucco in London, and were greatly employed by Gibbs, for whom they worked at Twickenham and at Cambridge; he deemed them "the best fretworkers" in England.   At Cambridge they were assisted by Denston, a Derbyshire plasterer, who afterwards did much work of this character throughout the Midlands.   The true French character of the rococo style will be found on Figs. 3 and 4, illustrating the ceilings of the queen's bed-chamber and the Salon de Medailles at Versailles.   As the Louis XV style followed that of Louis XIV, a more flowing and less architectural distribution of ornament took place, and the plain field of the ceiling became a more important feature, the ornament being driven into the corners and in the centres, such as you will see in Plate XXVII, where are illustrated a ceiling called from the centre panel subject the "Dog and Heron" at York and a London rococo example.   Other York ceilings of this type appear on Plate LVIII.   In such as these the trophies and medallions, taken from the illustrations of such works as "La Fontaine's Fables" and other works of French origin, were frequently introduced in cast plaster, to the detriment of the plasterer's art, as the moulds were, like their subjects, imported also; nor were these the only cast portions, but the repetitive curves, "mutton chop bones," as they used to be called, were cast in sizes, and used to form the principal cartouches and leading lines, until their monotony called forth Isaac Ware's satire upon them, "A ceiling straggled over with arched lines and O, C's, and C's and tangled semicircles may please the light eye of the French, who seldom carry their observation further than a casual glance," and further tells us that "the French have furnished us with abundance of fanciful decorations for these purposes, little less barbarous than the Gothic."   Chippendale, Lock, and even Batty Langley (Fig. 11) brought out books of designs for plasterers and carvers, setting a very reprehensible fashion, too much followed nowadays, by divorcing designs from craft, and by no means improving either.   The plasterer's art thus became thoughtless and absurd, having no specific character of its own, and the dilettanti would have none of it.   Simple purity became grateful to them because it was not ridiculous.

The very ruins of old Rome, which two centuries before had given such an impetus to the plasterer's art, led to its extinction, for about the middle of the eighteenth century there was a keen interest for the exhumation of the buried antiquities of Rome and

FIG. 14.——Designs by M. A. Pergolesi, 1768.

27

their study ; and the publication of such works as Cameron's " Baths of the Romans," Ponce's " Bains de Titus," together with the host of works treating of Roman architecture, now had a transforming effect. In this process the Scotch Adam brothers were predominant. The Adam manner is a compost from several sources, and the four ceilings of Plates XXVIII and XXIX show its shallow relief and delicate " liney " classic ornaments, griffins, and figure panels. Plates XXX, XXXA, and CXXII give a collection of Adam ornamental motives from Messrs G. Jackson & Son's original moulds. Adam mouldings have been drawn on Fig. 15. Exceedingly pretty, the style pleased the public taste ; their elements were simple and were easy to design ; and being full of work they gratified their maker ; and with here and there a cast cameo or a painting by Cipriani or Angelica Kauffmann, they were refined and delicate, such as you will find that from the Queen's room in Old Buckingham House ; but very little work was left to the art of the plasterer. He chiefly cast the models another artist had made, for when his ornament became so monotonously repetitive there was no reason why he should model it separately. If you examine the ceilings from Pergolesi's design for a wall decoration (Fig. 14), you will at once see how small amount of variety there is in the elements of their composition. And now it is no longer the plasterer who adorns the house—it is the " compo man "—again an Italian—so that the race and the place which caused the resurrection of plaster modelling caused also its death.

It may be thought I have in this short sketch of the long history of " Plaster Work, Plain and Decorative," dwelt too much on the higher development of it, but you must recollect that the higher development brings up the lower with it, and that all rise alike, so that in getting the best of one you get the best of both. Therefore, as time and space preclude the writing of an exhaustive history, I have only roughly outlined some of the prominent features of its interesting past. The principal object of this chapter is to show what great artists have aforetime been the votaries of art in plasterwork, and to induce those of our own day to try and revive the higher ambitions of the craftsmen of an art and craft which has such an important history, to raise it again to its former eminence, and to be no longer content with covering the sins of the " jerry-builder " with a charitable but very plain coat of indifferent plaster.

PLATE XXX

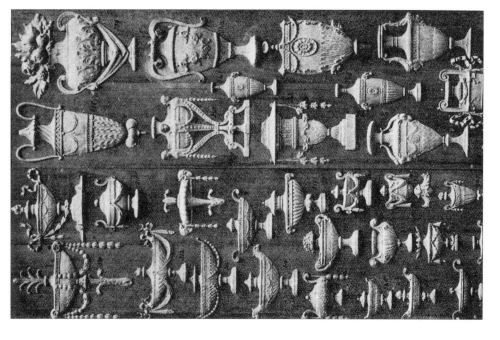

VASE MOTIVES, FROM THE ORIGINAL ADAM MOULDINGS.

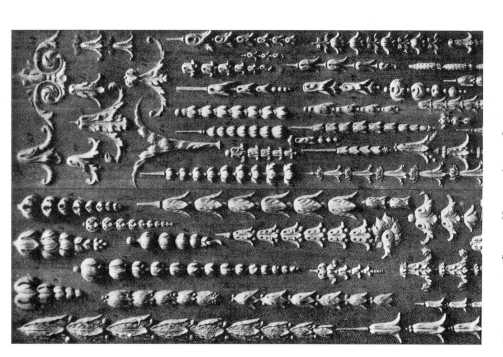

EXAMPLES OF COMPO HUSKS, ADAM STYLE, FROM THE ORIGINAL MOULDS.

(*Vide also* Plate CXXII)

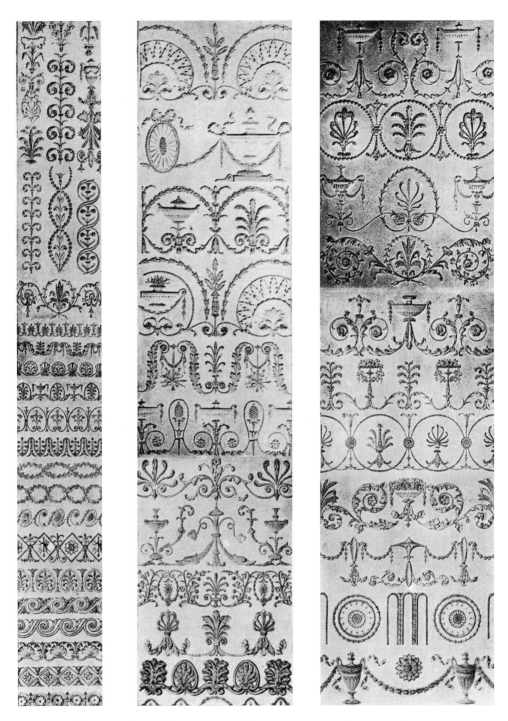

TYPICAL ADAM ORNAMENTAL MOULDINGS FROM ORIGINAL CASTS.

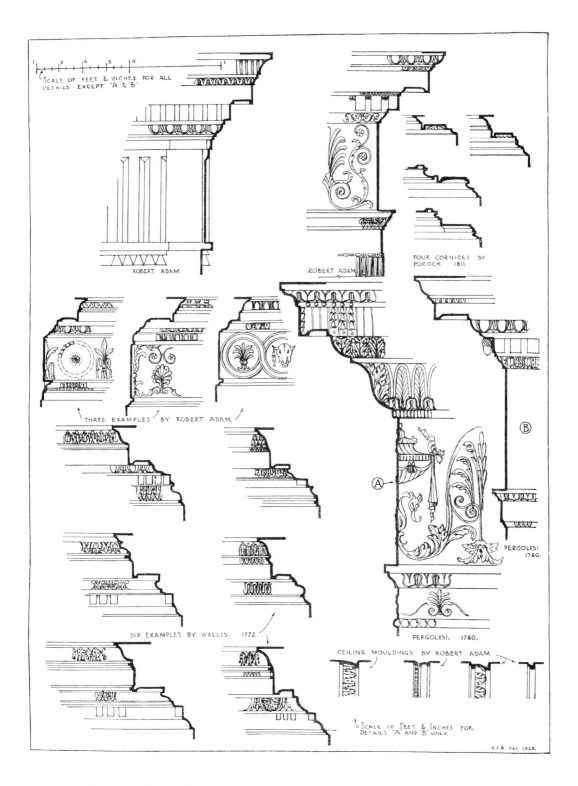

FIG. 15.—Typical Plaster Mouldings, Adam Period. (G. E. Bankart *del.*)

CHAPTER II

EASTERN AND CONTINENTAL PLASTERWORK

Saracenic—Persian—Spanish and Moorish—Indian (One-Coat, Two-Coat, and Three-Coat Work)—Chinese—Italian—French—German—Austrian—Belgian—Russian.

Saracenic Plasterwork.—Saracenic or Arabian architecture dates from the time of Mohammed in the seventh century. "Saracen," meaning Eastern, was the universal designation of Moslems in the Middle Ages. The word conveyed the two ideas of oriental and mediæval. Saracenic architecture spread to Syria, with Damascus for its centre. Another form of it is seen in Morocco, Persia, Armenia, and even Turkey in Europe. This architecture is commonly distinguishable by the " horse-shoe " arch, and is of supposed Eastern Christian origin.

The Mohammedan law placed limitations upon the character of all ornament, whether for mosaic, marquetry, or stuccowork. The image of any living thing, vegetable or animal, was forbidden and excluded. Curves, angles, and interlacings were often lavishly coloured, and formed the basis of such ornament. The lines, curves, and angles gradually assumed a species of tracery, or interlaced strapwork with inscriptions. Domes and minarets were surface decorated with geometrical patterns cut in stone, plaster, or wood, beautifully coloured and gilded. The mosque at Medina, A.D. 622, had partitions made of wattles and plaster. The Mosque of Ibn Touloun, Cairo, begun A.H. 263 and finished A.D. 878, has a court surrounded by arcades of painted arches resting on plastered brick piers. The capitals, like the rest of the building, are plastered and enriched with buds and flowers. The spaces between the arches are partly filled in with windows and engaged columns. The surfaces are enriched with a series of plaster rosettes worked by hand, and the inner parts with a knop and flower pattern. Plate XXXI, *a*, shows some of the arcading. The wall plaster in places is broken away, but the whole is in fair preservation, after exposure for 1,000 years.

The decorative borders in the *Mosque of Ibn Touloun* are the earliest known examples of the geometric designs and scroll-work so characteristic of Saracenic ornament. Excepting the grilles and fountains, the mosque is of burnt brick, plastered inside and out. The domes are usually of brick, each tier being laid a little within the lower one to take the curve, and plaster coated to conceal the irregularity of the brickwork. Wooden frames support the light plaster domes in a similar manner to modern fibrous plaster framework (Plate XXXI, *b*). The dome surfaces are ornamented variously. Some have intricate geometrical settings from star centres, others with horizontal bands of zigzag or chevron. Others are fluted, and some covered with arabesques of large outline, forming a diaper (Plate XXXII, *a*).

The *Sultan Hasan's Mosque* has some plaster decorations, and friezes of " Kufic " or of Arabic writing. Plate XXXII, *b*, shows some typical work and dome construction from the *Mosque of El Nasireeyeh*.

The *Mausoleum of Kalaum* (A.D. 1284) is perhaps the best example of plaster ornament in Cairo. The borders of the arches supporting what was once the dome, the borders of the clerestory windows above, and other decorations, are of stucco, delicate and lace-like. A central bud surrounded by leaves is developed until scarcely recognisable. The designs are chiefly a broad treatment of large foliage in a scroll-like continuous pattern.

The earlier mosques are decorated with plasterwork, varied and rich. The *Azhar*, built in 971, has stucco modelled Kufic friezes and arabesque ornament, chiefly surface work, applied and modelled with tools while moist, not cast. The difference is very great, the softness of the hand work contrasting greatly with the crudeness of the cast work.

In mosques and houses the ceilings are most beautiful. Coffered ceilings are formed by half-round wood beams, which sometimes show. In houses the outline of

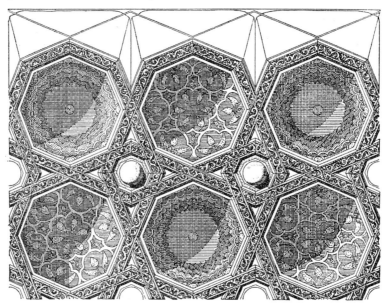

FIG. 16.—Portion of Ceiling, Mosque of Sultan Kalanoun, Cairo.

the beams is often preserved to within a couple of feet of the end, when stalactites mask the transition to the square. The beams are covered with canvas saturated with plaster. The panels between are divided into small coffers, similarly plastered, painted red and blue, with gold and white to give light. This work is not done *in situ*, but is fixed up when finished. One custom was to nail thin strips of wood on the joists in geometrical form and cover thinly with stucco, into which " dies " of arabesques and floral enrichments were pressed while soft, and afterwards painted and gilded. The colours were mostly blue and red. Part of a ceiling from the *Mosque of Sultan Kalanoun* (fourteenth century) is shown on Fig. 16. The conjunction of the ceiling with the wall is formed by a stalactite-shaped cornice, as shown on Fig. 17. The material used for this ornament is a composition of palm-leaf fibre. Willows, flax tow, and canvas are often found in Egyptian plasterwork.

The plasterers of the East were proficient in coloured and impervious plasters. An example is the red stucco in one of the chambers of the Pyramids, about 4,000 years old. The ancient cisterns at Alexandria are covered inside with thick red stucco impermeable to water.

In Cairo, plaster is curiously used in the windows of mosques and houses (Plate XXXIII). Over the niche of a mosque and over the lattice woodwork of a meshrebiya in a house, one sees the characteristic stained-glass windows. In houses they are generally set in a row of eight or nine in slight wooden frames over the lattice. The Victoria and Albert Museum has eleven of these windows. They have a wood frame about 2 in. by 1 in., forming a rectangle about 30 in. high by 20 in. broad. The frame is filled with an arabesque, floral, architectural, or inscriptional design in open plasterwork, filled in with painted glass, very simply made. Plaster was poured into the frame, the design cut out, and the glass fixed with plaster on the outside and the window put in place, flush inside the wall, in a slight wood frame with a flat architrave or margin outside to conceal the joints. Buttons keep the windows from falling inwards. The art is in shaping the perforations forming the design. Their shape and slant are regulated according to their height above the spectator. The thick plaster setting of the bright little facets of glass gives the light a shaped appearance of singular charm. The material is fragile, but could be considerably strengthened by the insertion of twisted galvanised wire in the outer edge of the plaster when soft. A twisted wire is

FIG. 18.—Plaster and Glass Window, Cairo.

FIG. 17.—Cornice, Kalanoun Mosque, Cairo.

three times as strong as a straight wire of equal thickness. Fig. 18 shows one of these windows, the original of which, with others, is in the Victoria and Albert Museum.

Fig. 19 shows part of a frieze and two windows from *Mosque del Daher, Cairo*.

The influence of Saracenic ornament extended to Turkey in Europe. Turkish ornament was a modification of Arabian and Saracenic. The decoration of the dome of *Soliman I, Constantinople*, is of exceptional beauty. A feature of Turkish colour decoration is the predominance of green and black.

Persian Plasterwork.—Very little is known of ancient Persian methods of building. The Saracens invaded and conquered Persia in A.H. 16 (A.D. 636), in the reign of the Caliph Omar, but the Persian Empire, which extended to the Oxus and Indus, was not conquered till the reign of Moawia. When the Saracens invaded Persia they found magnificent buildings.

The *Palace of Chosroes* contained great halls finely decorated in stucco. Bagdad was founded by the Caliph Mansur.

The *Djuma Mosque at Ispahan*, built by the same caliph, is richly plastered.

The *Mosque of Mesdjid-i-Shah*, built by the great Shah Abacs I, is decorated with highly-gilt plasterwork. There are numerous mosques, palaces, and monuments with stalactite domes, cornices, niches, and minarets all plastered. Some are further enriched with plaster and enamelled tiles.   The domes, niches, and stalactite enrichments show wonderful power and variety.

Mud houses are plastered with " kahgill," soft mud and chopped straw.   Mud houses are sometimes ornamented inside with hand-worked gatch or gypsum, highly

Frieze and Two Windows, Mosque del Daher, Cairo.

FIG. 19.

finished.   In the *Palace of Chium* the sun-dried bricks were covered with stucco arabesques.

The Persepolitan ornaments imitated at *Feruz-Abad*—an ancient *Palace of Fars* (ancient Persia)—were plaster throughout.   The extensive use or abuse of stucco decoration is a feature of Arab architecture.   Stucco, when fresh, being soft and malleable, enables craftsmen to show dexterity of hand in delicate quillings, gofferings, fillets, beadings, etc. ; but there is the danger and often abuse in mere dexterity.

PLATE XXXI

(b) THE DOME AND MINARET, MOSQUE OF IBN TOULOUN, CAIRO.

(a) DECORATED ARCHES, MOSQUE OF IBN TOULOUN, CAIRO.

PLATE XXXII

(a) DETAIL OF DOME AND MINARET, SHOWING PLASTER ENRICHMENTS, MOSQUE OF KAÏT BEY, CAIRO.

(b) DETAIL OF MOSQUE OF EL NASIREEYEH, SHOWING PLASTER ENRICHMENTS.

PLATE XXXIII

(b) PLASTER DECORATION ON OUTSIDE OF HOUSE CALLED
BEYT-EL-TCHELEBY, CAIRO.

(a) PLASTER DECORATION ON OUTSIDE OF HOUSE CALLED
BEYT-EL-EMYR, CAIRO.

PLATE XXXIV

(b) Doorway of Private House, Cairo.

(a) Vault in Vestibule of Mosque of Sultan Hassan, Cairo.

Plaster of Paris, or "gatch," is hideously used in Persia for the execution of prisoners. A hollow column is erected over a hole or well about 2 ft. deep, into which the prisoner is put, and plaster emptied in in boxfuls, alternating with water; the gatch swells, and as it sets, stops the blood circulation, causing excruciating agony and lingering death. After death a plaster capital is fixed on the column, covering the prisoner's head.

In Persia the plasterer was a most skilled artificer, and was usually made general supervisor. In England the general foreman is more often the carpenter. In Persia the plasterer was supreme among craftsmen—the work of other building crafts is covered and ornamented by him. The interiors and exteriors of many buildings are decorated with gypsum plaster. Persian plasterers cannot run mouldings. They daub the plaster on until thick enough, and work it down and shape the mouldings with gouges and drags. Holy Writ, describing those who cry "peace where there is no peace"—"they do but daub the walls with untempered mortar"—illustrates the practice of Persian plasterers at the present day. They gauge their plaster in a pannikin of water in very small quantities and work in the hands, rolling, squeezing, and drawing it out as a glazier does oil putty—until the initial setting power is killed. The mass becomes slightly flexible, is dashed on the walls and ceilings, spread and repeated until the proposed work is roughly massed up, when it is worked as already mentioned. It might be thought that this plaster would never set or become harder. It does, however, become very hard, due to reaction set up by the peculiar nature of the crude gypsum, and absorption by the brickwork. The plaster used for the ornamental work is mixed with a vegetable juice, to retard the setting, and applied *in situ*.

Persian plasterers erected a pavilion in the Paris Exhibition of 1878. There was in it an interesting stalactite dome ceiling. The Persian method of setting out such a ceiling is as follows: The floor below is levelled with ashes or sand, on which plaster 1 in. thick is floated and made fair. On this the ceiling is set out, the lines being struck with a cord blackened with charcoal, as our plasterers do in white on ceilings. V-shaped grooves, following the black lines, are incised in the plaster. When finished, the chippings are swept off, the floor oiled with hot melted suet, and a coat of plaster is laid which later forms the lowest plan of the ceiling. When set, it is taken up in sections, cut into shapes defined by the projecting lines, and fixed with gauged plaster, supported with wood and reeds. The large pendant stalactites are fixed with plaster, supported by iron chains, encased in plaster. The stalactites are made by hand. The next floor plan is then cast, cut, and fixed, until the series is completed. The arch, somewhat like the four-centred Tudor arch, is set out with a chalk line. A pin to fit the perforation of the reel is fixed in the centre of the small radius, and on this the reel is fixed. A pencil is placed through the loop at the end of the line, held by the hand, and moved as the line unrolls, until it reaches the centre line. The same process is gone through for the reverse side.

Spanish and Moorish Plasterwork.—Spanish plasterwork is distinct in character. It is generally carved, flat in relief, and admirably adapted to the material and the atmosphere of the country. The characteristic honeycombed ceiling and diapered wall surfaces are interesting. The Moorish diapered walls and arabesque stuccowork, originating from Damascus, is a link between the ancient work and the Italian Renaissance.

As already mentioned, Mohammedans were forbidden by creed to represent human or animal form in ornament. Thus restricted, they produced designs known as "arabesque" ornaments. They superimposed the enrichments and stalactite pendants. Their geometric tracery is either interwoven with "Kufic" or African inscriptions. One beautiful example of Spanish plasterwork is in the *Alhambra of*

Granada, the palace of the ancient Moorish kings of Granada, commenced in 1248 by the Sultan Ibn-ul-Ahmar, and finished by his grandson, Mohammed III, about 1314.

Plate XXXV. *b*, shows a portion of the *Court of the Lions in the Alhambra* (so-called from the fountain in the centre supported by these animals). It is a parallelogram of 150 ft. by 50 ft., surrounded by a portico with pavilions at the end. The portico and pavilions have 128 columns, supporting arches of delicate and elaborate workmanship, and of various colourings, now somewhat lacking. A small part of the ceiling between the walls is shown. The cusped (Plate XXXVII, *a*) and pendentive arches are excellent examples of the plasterer's art and craft.

The ceiling of the *Hall of the Bark* is a wagon dome of elaborate length. It is supported at each end by pendentives against the great arches. Fig. 20 shows the formation of these pendentives, which are constructed mathematically of numerous plaster prisms united by their contiguous lateral surfaces, of seven different forms proceeding from primary figures on plan. They are the right-angle triangle, the rectangle, and the isosceles triangle, A, B, and C respectively in No. 1 (Fig. 20). In these *aa, ab, ac* are equal, *ba* is equal to *bb*, and the vertical angle of the isosceles triangle (C) is 45°. B has one form in section, A three, C three, the latter being a rhomboid formed by the double isosceles triangle, as No. 3. The curves (X) of the pieces are similar, so that a piece may combine with others on either side. They are thus open to combinations as various as are the seven notes of the musical scale. The letters on the plan (No. 2), elevation (No. 4), and section (No. 3) correspond.

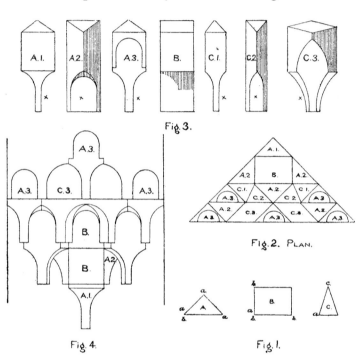

FIG. 20.—Setting out Plaster Prisms for Pendentive Ceilings.

The conical ceilings of the *Halls of Justice, Abencerrages*, and *Two Sisters*, also the column capitals and arches, are all plaster prism construction. Nearly 5,000 prisms construct the ceiling of the Two Sisters; although of plaster, with some pieces of reed, they are in perfect preservation. This pendentive construction shows the possibilities and effects of simple elements.

Arabesque work is done in pin-point stucco, mostly carved and brightly coloured in the primary hues. Arabesques on the walls are mostly handworked. The process was simple. Preparatory to applying the decoration, the naked walls were divided by horizontal or vertical lines, such as artists employ in producing pictures. Inter-

PLATE XXXV

(a) FRONTAGE TO THE PALACE OF RAJAH BHALDWUN SINGH, AT GOBARDHUN, INDIA.

(b) THE COURT OF THE LIONS IN THE ALHAMBRA, SPAIN. (MOORISH.)

PLATE XXXVI

(b) NORTH PORTAL OF THE ALCAZAR, SEGOVIA, SPAIN. (MOORISH.)

(a) MAURESQUE FAÇADE TO THE ALCAZAR, NOW THE HOSPITAL, SEGOVIA, SPAIN.

secting segments of circles were drawn over these, that the artist might work with quickness and surety. The Moorish artist used the compass, which, however, was not the usual two limbs of metal, but a fixed measure tied by a string.

Typical fretted patterns from the *Alhambra* are shown on Plates XXXV, *b*, and XXXVII, *a*. The arches of the fish-pond are of perforated plaster ornament and inscriptions in Kufic characters.

The Moors made beautiful use of plaster. The patterns are such as the stonework of the later fifteenth or early sixteenth century. Mr G. E. Street, describing Moorish plasterwork, says, " Plaster may be used truthfully and artistically, and without any approach to the contemptible effect which the imbecility and dishonesty of the nineteenth-century designers of plasterwork have contrived to impress on almost all their productions." The walls of the façade of the Alcazar and other buildings in Segovia are diapered in plaster (Plate XXXVI). They are generally tracery patterns, slightly in relief, repeated to produce a diaper. This decoration was very popular in the fourteenth and fifteenth centuries. Mr Street's opinion was that diaper work " was executed with a frame cut to the pattern, so as to allow of the ground being cut back slightly, leaving the pattern lines formed in the original face of the plaster. This kind of decoration seems legitimate, and here, owing to the care with which the plaster had been made and used, it had stood remarkably well, though most of the patterns (that he saw) had evidently been executed in the fifteenth century." On the front of the *Alcazar Hospital* (Plate XXXVI) these plaster patterns are carried all over the walls and round the towers and turrets of the angles, the smallest possible amount of wrought stone being used.

Madrid, a comparatively modern city, has little plasterwork of importance, but there is a growing tendency to paint a diaper over plaster fronts like thirteenth-century work. Philip II, when building the Escurial at Madrid, sent for the Italian stuccatore Pellegrino to do the plaster decorations. Pellegrino, a compatriot of Primaticcio at Mantua, gave a Renaissance character to the work.

Toledo possesses many rich and interesting examples of plasterwork. A synagogue founded there in the twelfth century, seized in 1405, and dedicated by the Toledano to Sta. Maria la Blanca, has some good plasterwork (Plate XXXVII, *b*). Eight horse-shoe arches spring from octagonal columns and capitals in brick, finished with plaster. The capitals are elaborate and slightly varied. Moorish stucco decoration was of fine quality, carved like stone, and rarely stamped or moulded. There is endless variety of design, which is often undercut.

The façades of many buildings in other towns have their plaster surfaces incised with patterns. Some of the work is coloured.

Indian Plastering.—The history of the plasterwork in India is rather obscure. There is abundant evidence of plaster craftsmanship in palace and temple in India.

At Kandahar, walls of rooms were plastered with gypsum. Cornices were stamped with arabesque patterns in the moist plaster, on which coarsely pounded talc or ground glass was dusted. During daylight the talc often shone like frosted silver ; by lamplight it sparkled like diamonds. In Northern India, lime known as " kankar " is mixed with burnt brick, which is ground to powder, in place of sand.

In the Ganjam district of Madras, native builders rarely use sugar (cheeney) in building mortar. In Chunam, plasterers use a considerable quantity of it. They gauge 100 lbs. of slaked shell lime, the white and yolk of 16 eggs, 1 gallon of fresh buttermilk, 25 lbs. of fine sifted clean sand, 1 lb. of fresh butter, 1½ lbs. country sugar, and 50 lbs. of water, thoroughly mixed together and placed in a covered tub for three days before use. This plaster will take a high polish, is like marble, and will stand washing. Native plastering is done in one, two, or three coats.

One-Coat Work.—Plaster of 1 part of shell lime and 2 parts of clean river sand is well mixed, knocked up with a wooden beater, and allowed to stand. When used it is again knocked up with jaghery and water ($\frac{1}{2}$ lb. of jaghery to each gallon of water). The plaster is trowel laid, floated with a wooden rule, and finished with a wooden rubber, the face of the work being sprinkled with water containing shell lime. The rubbing is continued until smooth. Indian one-coat work is barely $\frac{1}{2}$ in. thick.

Two-Coat Work.—The first coat is laid rough as just described, but without lime water. After one or two days the second coat is laid on the half-dry plaster. The second coat has 3 parts of shell lime to 1 part of fine white sand, gauged with the jaghery water. After standing it is ground on a flat stone with a small stone roller until reduced to a very fine paste, and laid about $\frac{1}{8}$ in. thick with a broad wooden hand float, floated with a trowel, and polished with a crystal—or smooth stone—rubber. It is afterwards dusted with finely powdered ballapam (soapstone or steatite) from a cloth or muslin bag, to further whiten and polish. Only so much is laid as may be polished in the day. It hardens too much in a night to polish next morning. The plaster is dusted and polished until quite dry. Several men polish, in order to complete in the one day. Drying is further hastened by wiping with soft cloths.

Three-Coat Work.—The first coat is done as for two-coat work, and allowed to dry. The second coat stuff, 1 part shell lime to 1 part of well-washed river sand, is beaten up in a wooden box or trough. After damping the first coat, the second coat is laid $\frac{1}{4}$ in. thick with a wooden hand float, and hand floated until consolidated and even. The third coat stuff is made in two lots. First, 4 parts of shell lime and 1 part of well-washed white sand, mixed with jaghery water, are ground between some mortar and slab to a very fine putty paste, and let stand. In an earthenware jar the whites of twelve eggs and half a gallon of whey and curds are well mixed. To this half a gallon of the putty paste is added and rubbed together until thoroughly mixed to a fine thin paste, which is then covered up and let stand. Pure lime, finely ground, is gauged with water in a trough and stirred until creamy. It is kept covered in readiness. The first gauge is stirred, spread on the second coat barely $\frac{1}{8}$ in. thick with a broad hand float, gently floated to lay fair and firm, brushed over with the lime cream, which is first floated gently with a hand float and afterwards with a trowel, until firm, and then polished with a crystal or white pebble, after being rubbed with steatite. The crystal is about 3 in. long, $1\frac{1}{2}$ in. wide, and is perfectly smooth. Frequent dusting with the powdered soapstone accompanies the polishing until dry. Moisture is wiped off with soft cloth. This marble-like plaster or stucco is extremely durable and proof against all the variations of the Indian climate.

Success, of course, depends on the proper quantities and gauging, especially the third coat, its being carefully floated, the polishing, and the absorption of moisture by cloths. Process and proportions vary slightly throughout India as elsewhere.

Steatite or soapstone, finely powdered, has been used for walls and ceilings. It polishes well, is of pearly grey tint, is hard, non-conductive, non-absorbent, and washable. When subjected to heat, moisture, or chemical fumes, it does not smell or discolour with age.

Ground glass for sparkle on plaster is sprinkled over a damp cloth. The cloth is turned over for surplus of dry glass to fall off. The glassy side of cloth is applied to the moist ceiling plaster, the underside being pressed so that the glass is embedded in the plaster, and the cloth removed. Glass cubes of varying size, form, and colour are hand pressed into the soft plaster. This combination of coloured surfaces and glitter is purely oriental.

For induration and protection of plaster exposed to inclement weather, boil 3 parts of linseed oil with one-sixth of its weight of litharge, and 1 part of virgin wax.

The plaster surface must be quite dry before the composition is applied hot with a brush. This recipe is frequently used in India.

An example of Indian plaster is shown on Plate XXXV, a.

There is an interesting story of Indian plastering. When in India since the Mutiny, Mr Lundgrun was sketching in the Punjab. Overtaken by storm, he sheltered in an unfinished tomb, the ceiling of which had been newly plastered, and was still soft. A native came in, and with three laths measured the length and width of the ceiling. Cutting the ends of the laths into different shapes, somewhat like modelling tools, standing on a tub, he set out lines on the ceiling and modelled an elaborate design in the soft plaster. Greatly interested, Lundgrun stayed until the plasterer left. To his interpreter, remarking that this plasterer was the cleverest he had ever met, the interpreter surprised, replied, " He is an idiot." Lundgrun rejoined, " I have been an artist for forty years, and could not do such a thing." The interpreter said, " His father was a clever man ; he could do five patterns. He had three sons ; one could do three patterns, one two, and this idiot can only do one."

Chinese Plasterwork.—In China, bricklayer and plasterer are the one man, who is also modeller and designer of enrichments. He produces his work without drawings, creates cornucopiæ over windows, designs and models enrichments of foliage and flowers ; arranges birds and fish on rain-pipe heads ; executes panelling in parapets and cornices by hand without straight-edge, running rule, running mould, or such mechanism. He is an artist ! Ornament is all modelled *in situ*, direct. To protect exterior plasterwork until set, a cage (tap pong chong) of bamboo is erected round the whole building. A thatching of leaves shelters the stuccowork from destructive rainstorms. An ornamental feature of their stucco façades is the ventilating apertures near the cornice. These communicate with flues opening into the roof, if there are plaster ceilings. Ventilators pierce the slope connecting walls and ceiling, an inclined plane, of the rake of the roof, lathed upon slender battens and joists. Lath and plaster partitions are sometimes made. Boarded divisions are the custom. A setting coat of internal plaster has shreds of white paper in place of hair. Their lime sets very hard. The Chinese like to tint their plaster blue. Stone mortar (shia fooi) is lime mixed with coarse grit. Lime mixed with red mud is laid on brick.

Italian Plasterwork.—So much has been written historically and technically on this subject by Mr G. T. Robinson in Chapter I, that little need be said here, except to refer back to the photographic illustrations, Plates XLIV, a, XLV, and XLVII, all of which are new to this edition.

Italy was mother of plasterers. In his " Glimpse of the History " (Chapter I), Mr Robinson tells of Italy's glories ; how her sons went throughout Europe carrying their art with them. Throughout her troubles, her ancient traditions and processes prevailed. In almost all her towns there were plasterers who repaired stuccos. The art of the Renaissance dwindled but survived. In 1851 an English architect sketching in the Campo Santo at Pisa, found a plasterer lovingly repairing portions of its old plasterwork injured by neglect. Of him he inquired concerning the nature of the lime he used. So soft and free from caustic qualities was it, that the painter could paint on it in true fresco a few hours after it was repaired, and the modeller used it like clay. Until the day the architect was leaving, no definite information could he extract. At a farewell dinner a bottle of wine softened the way to the old man's heart. The plasterer exclaimed, " And now, signor, I will show you my secret." Rising from the table the two went off into the back streets of the town. Taking a key from his pocket, the old man unlocked a door and they descended into a large vaulted basement, the remnant of an old palace. There, amongst planks and barrows, the architect dimly saw a row of large vats or barrels. Going to one of them, the old man tapped it with his key. It gave a hollow sound until the key nearly reached the bottom. " There, signor, there is my grandfather ! He is nearly done for." Proceeding to the next, he repeated the action, saying, " There, signor, there is my father ! There is half of him left !" The next barrel was nearly full. " That's me !" exclaimed he. At the last barrel he chuckled, finding it more than half-full : " That's for the little ones, signor !" The architect learned that it was a custom of the old plasterers, whose trade descended from father to son, for many generations, to carefully preserve any fine white lime, produced by burning fragments of pure statuary, and for each to fill a barrel for his successors. This they turned over from time to time, let it air-slake in the moist air of the vault, and so provide pure old lime for the future with which to preserve and repair the old work they venerated. Further inquiries showed that this was a common practice in the old towns. Thus the value of old air-slaked lime recorded some 1,800 years before, was preserved as a secret of the trade in Italy, while the rest of Europe was advocating the exclusive use of newly burnt and hot slaked lime. Was there ever, until the middle of the last century, a plaster image seller who was not an Italian ? At the present time nearly all the " formatori " or piece moulders working for the majority of European sculptors are of Italian nationality or descent. Chiefly by them has the nation craft been maintained.

When, after the long European wars of the eighteenth century, Italy had rest and recovery, the first industrial revival was felt by her plasterers. There were then, as now, more workmen than work ; they emigrated to neighbouring countries. Most of the plasterers in the Riviera, in the southern provinces of Germany and Austria, are Italians who go and return with the swallows to earn the wage their own country cannot afford them.

No sooner was the new kingdom founded than revival began. Sgraffitto (Chapter XI, Figs. 67, 68) saw new life in Florence and Rome. In 1890 endeavour was made to revive the style of the old modelled ceilings, once the pride of Venice. Baron Guggenheim, an antiquary and a dealer, deeply investigated the subject and described the process to Mr Robinson, thus : " The materials were stone lime, slaked for three or more years, and ' marmarino,' that is to say, marble dust from Carrara, pounded very fine into an impalpable powder, and most carefully selected and dried in an oven, with which to cover up the lime, which was then left for another year to gradually mix itself with the marble. It was then tempered into a paste until it was equally plastic as the clay of a sculptor, and with this you could model with equal ease. When partially set, you dust the model over with the finest marmarino, and when quite dry, brush it and wash it off." Heavy masses were cored with mortar lightened by reeds, coke, charcoal, and other light substances.

The Italian plasterers did great things with coloured stucco. Several ancient Roman baths exhumed in England in the nineteenth century were lined with a fine red impervious stucco. This material was also used for floor surfaces, proving that the colours were durable and the stucco hard. Coloured wall plasters, in fine preservation, have also been found in ancient Roman villas exhumed in England.

Remarkable are the ceilings of five circular rooms, designed by Michelangelo, Bartolomeo Ammanati, Baldassare Peruzzi, and Algardi, executed in the sixteenth century, at the Palazzo Mattei (1564) (Plate XLVII) and the Villa Pamfili (1644) in Rome.

Stucco for decorative purposes is said to have been reinvented by Margaritoni, who died in 1317. Italian stucco was old lime putty mixed with fine marble dust, and in some cases fine sand and hair. The mixture was frequently turned over and well beaten with sticks. Water was added at each turning, the mixture laid on brick floors to absorb moisture, and again taken up and beaten until the mass was plastic,

PLATE XXXVII

(b) PORTION OF NAVE, CHURCH OF STA. MARIA LA BLANCA, TOLEDO. (MOORISH.)

(a) MOORISH DETAIL AT THE ALHAMBRA, SPAIN.

Plate XXXVIII

Seventeenth-Century Rococo Ceilings

(a) At Schloss Tyttlsburg, Austria.

(b) At Schloss Neuwartenburg, Austria

smooth, tough, and cohesive. A small proportion of burnt gypsum was added. The gypsum was burnt in a similar manner to lime, instead of in an oven. The stucco set in ten or twelve hours, according to the gypsum used, attained great hardness and durability, and was for this reason called *stucco-duro*, or hard stucco. It was principally used before the introduction of lead or wooden moulds, and was mostly modelled *in situ* by hand, although also pressed into short moulds. Vittoria (a pupil of Giacomo Tatti) pressed the plastic stucco *in situ* with lead or wooden stamp dies. The rough form was thus defined by the die and the detail completed by hand. When the detail was large or repeating, the stucco was put into the moulds and worked up by hand after being fixed.

The plain stucco surfaces were usually done in three coats, the materials for each coat varying slightly. The first coat was of ordinary coarse plaster, the floating coat contained a larger proportion of lime, and the finishing coat was of rich lime, slaked for several months, beaten until homogeneous, and mixed with ground Carrara marble or with gypsum. Equal quantities of ground marble and putty lime were made into a stiff paste, again well beaten and toughened, and laid about ⅛ in. thick, scoured, and trowelled smooth.

French Plasterwork.—Much French decoration was carried out in papier-mâché. The decorations in the Council Hall of Henri II, the Louvre, the rooms at St Germain, and the Hotel des Fermes, etc., are examples. Carton-pierre has also been extensively used for the same purpose. The most notable examples were in the Tuileries, the Palais Royal, and portions of the Louvre. Stucco appears to have been used in France, according to the authority of M. Viollet-le-Duc, by the Carlovingian builders, A.D. 752 to 986, both for inside and outside relief decoration and for painting upon. A genuine example was the little Church of St Germigny-des-près (Loire), which dates back to the early ninth century. The stucco walls of this church were once engraved and painted, but, with the exception of the archivolts and columns inside the central steeple, the work has mostly disappeared. The early method of these builders was to raise rough walls of quarry stone, conceal the irregularities with a stucco coating, on which " chisel-lore and sculptors cut out or modelled ornaments based upon the patterns on Eastern tapestries. The large capitals of the old Narthex of St Remi of Reims, and those in the apse of the Church of Issoire,[1] are baskets of stone, covered with figures and ornaments in stucco. At a later period stuccowork was nothing but the delicate application of ornaments, trellis, and flowered chequerwork, on even surfaces to soften the bareness." Modelled plaster or stucco was revived in France early in the sixteenth century. Good examples are at the Grosse Horloge at Rouen, executed about 1530, and the Manoir of Yville-sur-Seine. Stucco chimney-pieces and wall decorations of considerable merit are to be found in many parts of France, especially in the vicinity of Toulouse. Typical illustrations of this work are shown in Plates V and VII, *a*, and Figs. 1 to 4, from Versailles, the Louvre, and elsewhere. There is excellent decorative plasterwork in the Louvre, executed by Van Ostell and M. Arnoldin, at Versailles, and many of the chateaux of France. Plaster of Paris has been the prevailing material for both plain and enriched façades for ages. Victor Hugo, in the " Hunchback of Notre Dame," punningly remarks in the description of Paris, that " our fathers had a Paris of stone ; our children will have a Paris of plaster." Typical examples of old French plasterwork from Versailles are shown on Figs. 3 and 4 ; other illustrations are given in Plates VIII, IX, XLVIII, and XLIX.

French architects sometimes use plaster where one would little suspect. For instance, in the Bibliothèque Nationale, Paris, the coffers and ornamental work above

[1] Illustrated in " A Short History of Art," Dr A. Blum and R. R. Tatlock (Batsford).

the piers in the hall are of plaster. In the Church of the Holy Trinity, the massive pillars separating the galleries from the body of the church are of plasterwork, harmonising so completely with the stonework that few persons would take them for stucco. The ceilings of many secular buildings are painted imitations of plaster mouldings and ornament.

With regard to plastering generally, there are two methods employed in France. One is similar to our system of forming concrete floors and walls; a centering of wood is formed lineable with a proposed ceiling, and the gauged plaster poured on from above. Partitions are made in a similar way. Another method is common to Paris, but far behind our own; the work is fairly good, but the waste of material is very great. For a plain ceiling, say 10 ft. by 12 ft., two plasterers and two labourers will be employed. The plaster is turned out on the floor. The labourers, supplied with boxes which will hold about two bushels, half-fill two of them with water and add plaster until of right consistency. The boxes are then placed on the scaffold, and the plasterers begin to mix with their left hands and with a trowel of brass, shaped like a gauging trowel, 5 or 6 in. wide, tapering to 4 in., and 7 or 8 in. wide. The narrow end is cut straight, to fit the corners of the box, and leave it clean when the plaster begins to set. When gauged, they splash the plaster on the part to be covered. By this time the plaster in the box stiffens, so they place it on a hawk of peculiar construction, having a handle about 9 in. long. The board is about 18 in. by 11 in. wide, and the longest edges are clamped by strips of hardwood. They place sufficient stuff on this to manipulate conveniently, press the stuff against the part to be plastered, spread it about with the flat face of the hawk, and work the hard edges to and fro until the work has an even surface. Two plasterers use from each box until empty, by which time the labourers or " companions " have supplied fresh boxes. This continues until they have covered the whole area flush with a narrow screed, formed by filling to a straight-edge bearing on dots of the required thickness. After this they straighten the surface by scraping off with a toothed drag all the bumps inevitable by their process. The drag is a steel blade 8 in. long, toothed on one edge and straight on the other. An iron bow with handle is fastened to each end of the blade. With the toothed edge they scrape down inequalities to a fair surface. The scaffold becomes covered deeply with waste plaster, in which they tread about until the labourers shovel it off the scaffold. They then use the straight edge of the drag and scrape the surface smooth.

Any two English plasterers could do the work of these four men with more skill and less time, without waste. They form mouldings with running mould and running rules in neat plaster; for mitres they fill the intersection with gauged plaster, and with plane-like tools shave the stiff stuff down to a mitre, as a mason would do. Plasterers in Paris are masons, or have been allied to them in their training. They form one body for all general purposes. The Government recognise them as one trade, no doubt on account of similarity of method. The material, rightly or wrongly, permits this treatment. It is plaster of Paris always, with rare exceptions. Parisian plaster is wholly different to ours. When gauged, ordinary French plaster is loosely granular, soapy in working, and easy to cut and drag.

Not only is interior work done in this Parisian plaster. External work with cornices, architraves, pediments, pilasters, columns, and all other architectural parts and details are executed in this same plaster. This is strange to English plasterers. According to our insular experience, plaster will not stand exposure. In Paris, houses built of rubble stone are faced with plaster, which remains good for many years. Should it fail, it is easily and cheaply renewed.

It is a common occurrence to see the fronts of large buildings or houses being replastered; although the fronts are but little smoke begrimed, they are stripped of the

PLATE XXXIX

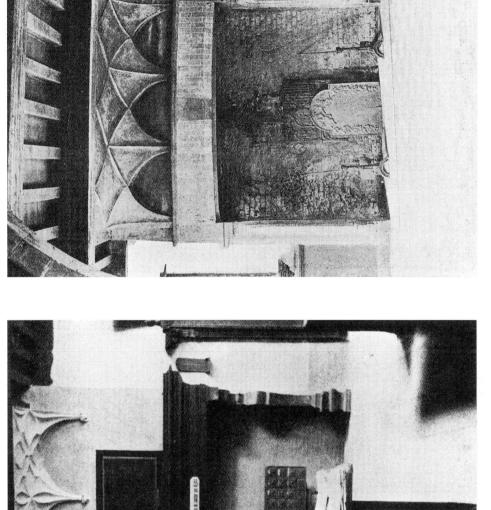

STUCCO VAULTING.

(a) AT MUSÉE PLANTIN, ANTWERP.

(b) IN THE OLD ABBEY AT AUDENAARDE, BELGIUM.

PLATE XL

(*a*) EARLY VAULTED CEILING IN A HOUSE AT LEYDEN, HOLLAND.

(*b*) CEILING IN THE HOSPITAL OF ST JOHN, BRUGES.

PLATE XLI

(*a*) ROCOCO CEILING IN THE BALLROOM OF A HOUSE AT THE HAGUE, HOLLAND.

(*b*) VAULTED PLASTER CEILING IN THE "BAROQUE" STYLE, ABBAYE DE 'T PARK, HEVERLÉ, BELGIUM.

PLATE XLII

(b) VAULTED PLASTER CEILING IN THE HÔTEL DE VILLE, GHENT.

(a) VAULTED CORRIDOR IN THE CASTLE OF AMERONGEN, HOLLAND.

entire plastering and done anew like soft white stone. No paint is applied to these fronts, and the cost thus saved pays for replastering, and thus having a new front for another series of years. Lime, sand, and hair, as we use them, are nearly unknown to the French. Where the expanding plaster might be expected to crack, as over cornice bracketing, etc., French plasterers use large quantities of tow in core, which they lay about and mix in the plaster.

Carved Plasterwork.—In and around Paris many large mansions have entrances, halls, and staircases decorated with carved plaster done *in situ*. The material is prepared and manipulated in a way peculiar to us. Composed of coarse plaster and finely ground lime, it is worked up in the manner of the Persian plasterers as described on p. 33, laid on the walls and ceiling and trowelled level. When partially dry it is dragged fair ; the ornamental parts are carved like soft stone. When perfectly dry it is rubbed down with a fine sandstone, and then resembles stonework. This work becomes exceedingly hard and is very durable, but it is practically mason's work and comparatively modern, and is not a legitimate artistic method of handling a plastic material, which, for decoration, should be added to a prepared surface, *not* subtracted or carved.

German plasterwork more nearly approaches English work than that of other Continental nations. The Government takes a keen interest in materials and methods, and encourage fire-resisting construction. Floors protected with plaster have given the best results. Neat plaster is used for slab work, also ordinary plastering on a network of wood rods and iron, or iron alone. This is quite feasible, bearing in mind that the conductivity of common plastering, compared with firebrick or building brick, is as 26 to 66, and that ordinary plaster on metal lathing, well embedded, will resist intense heat for a considerable time.

Plastering in Germany is usually on reeds instead of wood laths. Plaster slabs are used considerably for internal plastering. The Germans manufacture fine Portland cement. Years ago, London plasterers went to Berlin to construct concrete houses and plaster house fronts with Portland cement, since when German plasterers have been fairly proficient in Portland cement work.

The German Government encouraged in every way the induration of plaster casts to resist wet and inclement weather for exterior plastering. Their methods are described hereafter.

German Mortar.—Some years ago the Society for the Promotion of Prussian Industry offered a prize for the best plaster for brick walls. The conditions imposed were : (1) That the composition should not be affected by the weather, and should present an even, smooth surface when applied, becoming neither cracked nor loose by exposure to sun or frost ; (2) that the composition should take a uniform and durable colour by application, the colour to penetrate either through the mass, or to at least a depth of one-tenth of an inch from the surface ; (3) that although the cost of this composition might exceed that of ordinary painted plaster, it should be cheaper than " stucco lustro." The silver medal of the Society, supplemented by a money prize of £75, was awarded to Ambroselli, a mason of New Barmin (near Wurzen), after his plaster composition had been offered to the Society, and stood a practical test of several years' exposure to the weather. No new principles or materials were in the composition ; but its application demanded great skill of workmanship and careful selection of ingredients. The wall surface must be of hard, well-burnt bricks, free of marl, and thoroughly dry. The materials are lime and sand, specially cleansed, and entirely free from all impurities. Three different plasters are prepared from three qualities of sand. One of the most difficult applications (although in principle bad architecture) of sandstone dressings is given as follows : The brickwork itself should be of the desired profile for uniform laying on, the wall surface to be well damped with water. The first coat is made of one-third of lime, slaked for at least a fortnight, and two-thirds of very sharp sand. After thorough mixing, one-fourth of the bulk of Portland cement is added. The composition, after being prepared and well mixed, is applied wet to the surface of the wall as evenly as possible. To prevent air-bubbles or cracks, time must always be allowed between the layings on for the mortar to set, the profile having been roughly shaped with mortar No. 1. A finer mass (No. 2), composed of 2 parts lime, 2 parts fine sand, 0.12 part Portland cement, and colouring liquid necessary for the desired tint, all stirred together, follows mass No. 1. Two coatings of No. 2 mortar in ordinary work suffices to produce the profile required. For very fine work a third coat is used, composed of 1 part very fine sand, 1 part fine-sieved lime, 0.5 part fine-sieved Portland cement, with colouring matter to dry the tint desired. Test experiments should be made beforehand with complete intermixing of the ingredients. Divide the laying-on area into so many days' work. Each portion must be begun and finished the same day, as touching up cannot be done after a certain lapse of time.

The above directions emphasise the necessity of very careful selection, mixing, and manipulation of plastic materials, even those for common everyday use, and show that, with care, good and enduring plaster for exterior purposes can be made from lime and sand with a little Portland cement. The colouring matter being an ingredient of the finishing coat, wears more uniformly and durably than a painted surface. The mixing of colour in the finishing coat has long been common in England ; also the gauging of Portland cement with lime mortar.

Austrian Plasterwork.—In Vienna the house façades are generally faced and enriched in stucco. As in Italy, the workers hand down their traditions from generation to generation. The stucco is made of white lime matured in water a long time, with Danube sand. Coarse grit is used for floating in one coat, and the finest grit for the finishing. Their proportions of lime and sand vary, according to the work in hand and the condition of the walls. The materials are proportioned by guesswork and judgment of fitness, according to how the plaster leaves the fingers after dipping. Portland cement and hydraulic lime have been tried, but Austrian plasterers seem unable to use these materials satisfactorily. Figure work is largely indulged in everywhere and in every part of a façade where the human figure can find a place. The Austrian stucco and cement façades stand well. They are washed and coloured with distemper made and used by plasterers as soon as they show dirt, and look bright and clean. Women, mostly barefooted, are employed as plasterers' labourers in Vienna.

The Austrian Government encourage science and education. The Museum of Applied Art and Technical Art Schools have special modelling and plaster-casting rooms.

Plate XXXVIII shows illustrations of Austrian ceilings of interest, typical of their work in the rococo style.

Belgian plasterwork somewhat resembles the French work. Carton-pierre and fibrous plaster are used extensively in their modern decorative work.

Plate XXXIX shows a very characteristic feature in Belgian houses, of plasterwork ornament covering the brick cove or arch supporting the fireplace hearth of the room over. These are usually done in very slightly hollowed planes, forming saucer or dish-like spaces between the intersecting continuous vaulting lines. The idea perhaps arises from the basis of the Moorish or Saracenic stalactite origin, but is only very slight facial decoration, instead of constructive work. It is, however, very charming, quaint, and decorative.

Plates XL, XLI, and XLII show typical examples of ceilings, which are usually very simple in design. This system of decoration generally partakes of a softly moulded

PLATE XLIII

(b) EXTERIOR PLASTERWORK ON HOUSES ON THE PONT DU
LAITAGE, GHENT.

(a) PLASTER DECORATION ON THE FAÇADE OF A HOUSE
(BELGIUM).

PLATE XLIV

(a) RENAISSANCE CEILING IN STUCCO IN THE DUCAL PALACE AT VENICE.
(The Painted Medallions are by Veronese.)

(b) STUCCO CEILING IN THE BAROQUE STYLE, SCHLOSS ROSENBORG, DENMARK.

rib at a little distance from the wall, breaking out at the corners into some intersecting geometrical shape, and continuing straight between the corners, although sometimes shaped centrally between.

Danish Plasterwork.—An illustration is given in Plate XLIV, *b*, of a ceiling in the Schloss Rosenborg, Copenhagen, dating about the end of the seventeenth century.

Russian Plasterwork.—Plasterwork in Russia is somewhat limited. The country and the smaller towns have mostly wooden buildings. Decorative work in plaster was introduced by Vladimir, who built Vladimir and other towns in the eleventh century, assisted by craftsmen from Greece and Italy. Kiev, once the capital of Russia, has its important buildings ornamented with plaster decoration. Ivan III imported foreign artists for the adornment of the buildings of Moscow, about 1490. Peter the Great engaged artists and artificers from all the art centres in Europe to decorate buildings in St Petersburg, the new capital, founded in 1703 (now Leningrad). All the important works in plaster have been done by or under foreign artists. There were numerous lime works on the Ishora River and in the Peterhof district, and many Portland cement factories about the country. They also manufactured plaster from gypsum, in several large factories in St Petersburg, where it was burnt out of the natural gypseous stone. The plaster manufacturers cast and painted their plaster figures and ornaments, the colouring being very artistically executed. The greater part of the plaster produced was used for stuccowork on buildings.

CHAPTER III

LIME-STUCCO PLASTERWORK (STUCCO-DURO) IN PRINCIPLE AND PRACTICE

By G. P. BANKART

PREVIOUS editions of this volume have dwelt but slightly on this branch of the plasterer's art. The "Introduction" by the late Mr G. T. Robinson (Chapter I) refers to the subject historically only, and Mr Millar gave some accounts of the stucco material by various authorities. The art and craft of the stucco-worker, from a practical standpoint, has been omitted from previous editions. Mr Millar's skill lay in other processes which are fully explained by him throughout this volume. The art of stucco-working was then non-existent: it had been dead as an art since before the introduction of the style of decoration designed by the Adam brothers.

The process of casting undercut relief modelling from gelatine moulds was introduced, improved, and sufficed for the production of that kind of plaster decoration throughout the latter part of the nineteenth century and up to the present time. No better material or process had been available for the reproduction of clay modelling in high relief with undercut detail. This process is still the best known for work requiring much repetition, but it is not Art. No attempt had been made to analyse or to manufacture the old lime-stucco material of the great Italian era, or to revive the art of working it. Until the last few years there had been no sign or thought of a revival of the only right process of modelling the undercut decoration of the period from Charles I to the Georges. Had the material and craftsmen been forthcoming at the time of the arts and crafts revival, the genuine old process might have seen new life sooner. The desire was there, but the process and the lime stucco were not. Instead, new life was given to low relief decoration in plaster of Paris. The desire to revive something of the type of undercut plaster ceiling decoration of the later English Renaissance has been and is still alive, and although the modern gelatine process (Chapter XIV) of reproduction meets modern demands to some extent, it is incapable of giving the genuine effect of the old hand-modelled lime-stucco process. The gelatine process cannot be regarded, at best, as anything but a poor substitute and a modern makeshift.

The lime-stucco process and material, like every other, is open to right and wrong use. Like other fine crafts and arts, its decadence came through a long period of abuse and degradation. Artists there are who speak against it now as not being plasterwork, but "carving." More correctly, this criticism applies to the modern imitative high relief ornament rather than to the old lime-stucco ornament which is perfectly legitimate craftsmanship. They do not understand it. The masterpieces of ages disarm all arguments against it and its revival and unsuitability to modern needs and modern construction. The same arguments applied to stone or wood carving, metal work, or jewellery would be held up to ridicule. It has to fight against prejudice and hustle.

The object of this chapter is to investigate the art in its various historical modes

44

and developments, and to show something of the various processes of working the stucco material, the composition of which is dealt with at length towards the end of the chapter.   No more permanently beautiful plastic material than lime stucco has ever been made or used for relief decoration.   No more supple and responsive material has ever been manipulated by plasterers.   The fact that it can be regulated and retarded in its setting to any degree desirable, without injury or detriment to its ultimate hardness or degree of refinement, alone is sufficient justification and advocacy for its great superiority over all other plasters, without exception.

It is unnecessary in this chapter to repeat the history of its use, fully treated in Mr Robinson's " Introduction," Chapter I.   It is very necessary, however, to know how it differed from other kinds of plaster and plaster decoration, and why.   It is necessary to realise that the extreme facility and simplicity of its manipulation was, and is, its virtue as a durable and permanent medium for artistic expression in modelled relief, leaving little to be desired ;   that rightful usage had everything to do with its employment by great artists ; wrongful usage brought about its downfall.   It cannot be expected that a durable medium and process which allows an artist every freedom and licence of personal expression and artistic development, can be used, even with repetition, as cheaply as a plaster whose chief virtue is its adaptability to cheap and mechanical reproduction.   Nor would it be sane for a moment to compare it with the cheap, mechanically pressed, skin-like imitation plasterwork which the uninitiated public are content to substitute and accept for real plaster decoration.

If beauty of design and quality of workmanship have any value at all, no right-minded person could tolerate any form of sham for work where beauty of design and genuine workmanship are combined in reality with due reticence.   Herein lies a danger common to craftsmen and little guarded against by the majority.   This danger is in the form of a tendency to do too much through uncontrolled enthusiasm : the tendency to imitate Nature rather than to be inspired by her, *i.e.*, to be decorative : the tendency to lose restraint, reticence, rhythm, and simplicity.

Plastic art, like every other, needs wise restraint in many ways.   That essential to design is the dividing line between Art and imitation ; between the decorative element and naturalism ; between the easy use of one's medium, quite simply and " decoratively," bearing in mind that imitation of Nature is not possible in any material, nor is it decoration or design.   Decorative design is a music of form (instead of sound) inspired from Nature through the brain and imagination, and in no way an imitation of her.

" Design " is the inventive harmonious arrangement of lines, forms, and masses, pleasurable for their own beauty, often (though not essentially) inspired from, or suggested by some natural form, and developed in such manner as to enhance the quality and beauty of the material in which it is done.   Its mission and purpose are to be beautiful at least, inspired from Nature, not imitative of her ;   wholly creative, a poetical interpretation of form through the imagination, the mind, and the hand of man.

It may be constructive design (as architecture) or decorative design (as ornament) subservient to " architecture."   Decorative design may be said to be a language of pleasurable and harmonious arrangement of lines, forms, masses, and colour, to fill a given space or take a certain shape, possibly inspired by Nature, but with intelligent and appropriate technical handling of the material used, to show to the utmost its natural quality and what can be done with it.   It should be more than a giving of pleasure to the eye ; it should be a reposeful appeal to the mind, through a gratification of the senses of sight and feeling.

It must be emphasised again and again that there is danger ahead for the inexperienced designer who, for inspiration, goes to Nature only.   The temptation is strong to copy natural form and growth outright in work.   There is even hope in such oversight, hope of healthy reaction with experience, skill, and right guidance to realise what decoration is.

This principle applied to plaster decoration means that soft, fragile, and easily damaged plaster, such as plaster of Paris, should be low in relief, soft in modelling and in definition; that hard plaster, such as good lime stucco, may have any relief desired, with sharpness of edge, crispness of definition, delicacy of surface detail, and depth of " undercutting " or overlaying to hold shadow compatible with reason, because the process of building up piece by piece and the ultimate hardness of the lime plaster permit greater licence with due and reasonable restraint, although it is safest and best to keep the bulk of the modelling homogeneous throughout, should there be much projection of relief.   This consideration really brings us to the pith of the subject, viz., how much or how little depth of hollow or overlapping of built-up detail is legitimate and advisable for the right development of the material in its truest form of Art.   This is a point of great importance ; it is just as important to the stucco modeller to know how much he may overlap his detail, as to the carver to know how much he may undercut his with advantage.   It must not be forgotten that good lime and marble stucco become ultimately harder than stone or marble, whereas the process of the carver in cutting away and undercutting his relief in granular stone (which in most cases is softer than lime stucco) is a weakening process, and we think less legitimate. The misunderstanding, where it exists, is in the failure to realise the excessive hardness that good lime-stucco plaster acquires with time, and the superiority of the process of building up detail bit by bit, constructionally, over that of cutting away, and the risk of fracture that attends it.

We can best realise this by seeing how the Italian and other craftsmen gave decorative form to stucco-duro.

The stucco modellings of the first half of the first century (A.D.) were all very slight in relief, extremely beautiful in design, and delicate in modelling ; masterpieces of plastic art, which cannot be praised too much (see Plates II-IV, XCVI, a, XCIX). They are typical examples of the perfect use of plaster, particularly for a soft and easily damaged plaster.

Plates XLV-XLVII show some work of the sixteenth-century revival in Rome, at the Vatican, and the Villa Madama (Plate LIX, a), by the school of painters and plasterers Raphael had working under him.   The work was based to some extent on the first-century discoveries, and in like manner is entirely decorative, in very moderate relief, and masterly in conception, in design, and in execution.   Careful examination will show that in the relief treatment much drawing was incised with the metal tool.   Plates XLVI and XLVII show some modelled detail to a comprehensive scale.   There are plaster casts at the Victoria and Albert Museum which should be very carefully studied and copied by plasterers interested in modelling.   There are also full-size cartoons, painted, of the corridor pilaster faces, showing the modelled work and the painted work in combination.

Let us go a step further and examine modelled stucco ornament having more relief and some little undercutting.   What development do we find there ?   It became gradually more architectural in its main lines, more constructive in its decorative setting, more pronounced in strength of relief, yet well controlled within mouldings, self-contained, and well maintained in the general shape and bulk of its own masses.

Unlike the earlier work, which was almost entirely surface decoration, the stronger architecture required stronger mouldings, stronger and richer modelling, more pronounced light and shadow, or " colour " (Plate XLVII).   This call for more pronounced relief led to the separate modelling of small parts, lump by lump, leaf by leaf, and the packing and the fixing of them into a shaped bed prepared to receive them, or on to a level bed or groundwork without mouldings.   In either case the general lines, the mass

PLATE XLV

PAINTED STUCCO DECORATION OF THE ITALIAN RENAISSANCE IN THE CORRIDORS OF THE VATICAN, ROME.

PLATE XLVI

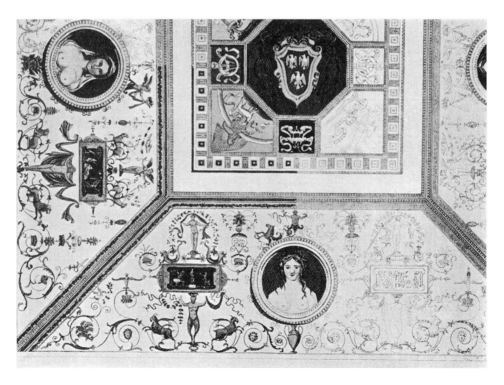

ARABESQUE DESIGNS FOR CEILINGS WITH PAINTED MEDALLIONS IN THE DUCAL PALACE
AT MANTUA, ITALY.

or contour, the architectural form, and the compactness of bulk were well developed, well maintained, and perfectly modelled.

It is at this period that the Italian stucco art reached its purest and best form. The human figure was at this time, and for long afterwards, used nobly, reticently, and decoratively in relief, in alto-relief, and in the round, as in Plate XLVII. All that was beautiful and possible was done in this lime stucco, until exuberance and extravagance of design, of form, and detail were lavished upon the decoration of Italian buildings. The craft lost restraint, dignity, and nobleness in exuberance of ornament, in very weariness of detail, and of detached, writhing figures. It gave place to a too close imitation of Nature, to excessive movement in place of repose.

It lost the more decorative function for want of restraint ; became prolific, superabundant, commonplace, and comparatively worthless (compare Plates VI, *a*, XLIV, *a*, with Plates XLV-XLVII).

It is necessary to call especial attention to the compactness and disciplined order in the setting of the separately made lumps, fruits, leaves, and other detail of this best Italian period.

Some examples of the lime-stucco art in France by Italians now claim attention. We find much the same handling, much the same architectural control of lines, spaces, and bulk. The detail is equally refined, equally decorative, and equally compact in arrangement, control, and continuity of section in the modelled bands and mouldings, *cf.* Figs. 1 and 2. Plates XLVIII and XLIX are from Fontainebleau, and illustrate stuccowork done for Louis XIV. Notice particularly how crisp, refined, and well defined is the modelling. Notice also how the lines of the modelling are arranged to help and emphasise the sectional shape of the moulded and enriched bulk, without being deeply undercut.

This "clean" drawing—moderation of relief, crispness of definition, sharpness of edge, and smoothness of finish—is all quite sound and good in principle and practice, because lime stucco is a smooth plaster to work and, when set, hard enough to be durable, without risk of any but wilful damage. Imagine, for a moment, all this done in a soft plaster, produced by mechanical means ! The result would be quite different ! Assuming that it can be produced, it would deteriorate in definition and become dulled in the process of casting, because the mould becomes heated and worn. The attempts of this age to produce mechanically in soft plaster the technical definition and sharp, deep-set modelling of the Italian relief ornament in lime stucco-duro have been vain. It would, however, be quite proper in soft plaster to model a surface ornament in comparatively low relief if the groundwork of the modelling partock of the sectional bulk required (Figs. 1 and 2). That is quite different to the parody of highly relieved, deeply overlapped, and interlocked modelling of some of the Italian and English Later Renaissance work which we illustrate and examine later in this chapter.

The work at Nonsuch Palace, carried out by Italian modellers for Henry VIII, has already been mentioned and illustrated (Introduction, pp. 11, 12, and Plate VI, *b*).

The next thing we have, and perhaps the best piece of lime-stucco modelling now remaining in this country, is the frieze decoration of the walls of the ruins of old Hardwick Hall, by Abraham Smith (Plates XIII, *a*, LX, *b*). This work is perfectly good and interesting decoration. It was followed a few years later by another modelled and coloured frieze in the adjoining Hall (Plates XII, *b*, XIII, *b*, and LII, *a*). This later frieze is admirable of its kind and very decorative, though inferior in design and workmanship to the earlier one. Other friezes and coves of very inferior design are shown in Plate LI. White marble dust and lime, however, proved too expensive and difficult to obtain for general use in this country. The shortage resulted in the plasterer's art taking, for a time, a different development, as mentioned in "The Historical

Sketch," describing the native character of the work in other plasters during the reigns of Queen Elizabeth and James I, up to the time when the great architect, Inigo Jones, again revived the lime-stucco art, though in a manner different to its earlier use in this country, after his travels in Italy.

The English work of this period, as regards the modelling, was not quite so refined and perfect as that of Italy and France, from which it was inspired.

Compared with the stucco modelling of a later date, the treatment of the modelled detail of the Inigo Jones and Webb style has more of the best Italian spirit in its compactness of mass and severity of form (Plates I (*Frontispiece*), XXII, XXIII, L, and LX, *c*). As time went on, change and development came with it. Modelled detail became less compact. Fruit, flowers, and leaves became more loosely grouped together, or in lumps or masses, with variety in the kind of relief and with sometimes a spiral treatment of the stemwork. Plate LI shows this development.

The modelling gradually assumed a native character. Later on, by degrees, the modellers, left more to themselves, began to lose the sense of architectural fitness and restraint, and tried to imitate and copy Nature in her accidental tangle, straggling growth, and limitless variety of form. They became naturalistic instead of decorative, and were very clever indeed, but sheer mechanical cleverness is not the function of decorative art, which is only worthy and pure when it is the reflection of man's delight in beautiful arrangement for its own sake.

There is an old French proverb that " Lime at a hundred years old is still a baby," and an old Scotch (mason's) proverb that " When a hundred years are past and gone, then gude mortar turns into stane."

The air-slaking prevented too great an absorption of carbonic acid, which is obtained by the free use of water, and which rather retards than assists the setting of stucco.

The pulverisation of the unburnt mortar introduces a fine crystalline substance into this identical chemical composition when as yet uncrystallised or formed in structure. The minute crystals induce the formation of a general crystalline structure, until the final and most permanent form of all mineral substances is achieved. Hair was absent from the old formulæ.

The rapidly induced crystallisation seems to have rendered this unnecessary, for the introduction of any animal substance in stucco was avoided in early times.

One more formula ! Baron Guggenheim asserts that " Marmarino," or Carrara marble dust, finely powdered into an impalpable powder and very carefully selected and dried in an oven, was used to cover up the lime, and left for another year to gradually mix with the marble (air-slaked) ! It was then tempered into a paste until as plastic as sculptor's clay. When partially set, you dust the model over with the finest " Marmarino," and when quite dry, brush it and wash it off. The heavy masses were cored with ordinary mortar lightened by reeds, coke, charcoal, and other substances. Vitruvius and Pliny give similar recipes which simply mean that everything depended upon the very careful selection, burning, slaking, and age of the limestone, which must have the largest possible proportion of pure carbonate of lime. Everything depended, also, on the burning in a kiln with wood fuel, at a temperature watched and regulated by a skilful kilnsman, and afterwards air-slaked for at least three years and mixed with the finest white dust of statuary marble. Various ingredients are given at different dates and places for " fattening " the stucco, for retarding the setting, and regulating shrinkage and cracking, viz., rye dough or flour, gluten of rice, a slight proportion of burnt gypsum (plaster of Paris, or sulphate of lime), wort of malt, etc., hog's lard, curdled milk, fig juice, and albumen, etc.

Elm bark and hot barley water (tannin and size) were mixed in the stucco of

PLATE XLVII

STUCCO DECORATION OF THE INTERIOR OF DOMES, PALAZZO MATTEI, ROME.

PLATE XLVIII

DETAIL OF STUCCO CEILING IN THE THRONE-ROOM, PALACE OF FONTAINEBLEAU.
(STYLE OF LOUIS XIV.)

PLATE XLIX

STUCCO CEILING IN THE QUEEN'S BEDROOM, PALACE OF FONTAINEBLEAU.
(STYLE OF LOUIS XIV.)

PLATE L

DETAIL OF PLASTER ENRICHMENTS TO THE STAIRCASE CEILING, ASHBURNHAM HOUSE, WESTMINSTER. (MID-SEVENTEENTH CENTURY.)

Justinian's Church of the Baptist at Constantinople ; at Rockingham Castle, melted wax ; Eleanor's Cross, Charing Cross (thirteenth century), the white of eggs and strongest wort of malt with the lime, and Calais sand ; in Edward II's time, 1324-27, wax and pitch in stucco and mortar ; in India, " jaghery " or " goor " (a very coarse sugar) with their shell lime (which takes a polish). It is probable that the use of sugar passed from India to Egypt and Rome, and that malt and other saccharine or glutinous matter were used.

Sugar enables water to absorb fourteen times more lime than plain water would do, but it causes shrinkage and cracking, which needs correction by other means.

The stucco of Knossos consists chiefly of (89 per cent.) pure rich carbonate of lime, with no hydraulic properties.

With 2 per cent. of magnesia		and a small amount of gypsum.	This lime was slaked in water and allowed to stand a long time.
,, 4 ,,	,, iron and alumina		
,, 4 ,,	,, silica		
,, 1 ,,	,, sulphuric acid		

In this early stucco no marble dust was used, but it is most likely that ground unburnt limestone powder was used in both coatings at Knossos, and in the undercoating only at Tiryns. The marble dust was not used until a much later period. The stucco of the Palace of Tiryns is almost identical with that of Knossos.

Hydraulic limes (which are not so suitable) contain a much smaller percentage of carbonate of lime : 78.45 Abathau ; 59.61 Barnstone ; 58.4 Warmsworth. The Hurlet and Campsie (Scotch) limes—90.40 (lime), 1.50 (silica)—are very good ; the Irish limestone is purer still in carbonate.

The slaking of lime varies according to the kind employed ; slaked lime is hydrate of lime (lime chemically combined with a definite quantity of water).

There are three methods of slaking lump lime : by immersion, sprinkling, and air-slaking.

Immersion is best for rich fat stone limes, to keep them plastic. They gain strength under water. Pliny says the Romans used this method, keeping for three years before use, but this lime was probably used for internal (and not external) use.

Sprinkling is often very imperfectly done. The lime lumps should be broken into small pieces, placed in layers 6 in. thick, uniformly sprinkled with water through a rose end, or watering can, afterwards covered with clean sand, left for twenty-four hours, and turned over and riddled.

The sand retains the heat developed and ensures slaking throughout slowly. The amount of water must be carefully regulated. Water will not dissolve more than $\frac{1}{2}$ grain of lime to 1 oz., or two small teaspoonfuls of water. Too much water will give a useless paste. Too little water will make a dangerous powdering lime. Different limes require varying quantities of water, but an average quantity might be said to be about $1\frac{1}{2}$ gallons of water to 1 bushel of lime. Water must not be added after slaking has begun, nor must the mass be disturbed until time has been allowed for general slaking.

In England three weeks is usually the time allowed for cool lime. Hence results. Hot limes are not suitable for plastering, and are allowed three months, say, for mortar for building purposes. When mortars of these hot limes are used the unslaked particles go on slaking and blistering for a long time, drying up the moisture and leaving only a friable dust in the joints. This sufficiently explains the wisdom of the old Roman law, compelling at least three years' seasoning before use.

Pliny's statement that it was an ancient practice to beat mortar for a long time with a heavy pestle before being used, means that the stucco material was thoroughly incorporated, the compound of lime and silica being taken from the outside of the sand and incorporated with the mass. It helps it to consolidate more quickly, and toughens it greatly.

A labourer in the editor's employment remembers beating lime for stucco with a flail with a steel end. The experienced plasterer generally uses the lime putty at the furthest end of the pit from the sieve. It is best, finer, and works more smoothly. Putty is run through a finer sieve than slaked lime for stucco. Some authorities say that lime should be exposed to the weather; but this was not the case with the Roman limes, which were kept in covered pits and in dark and damp cellars. The reason is that, if exposed, it absorbs the atmosphere and carbonic acid gas, which carbonates it and causes it to lose its causticity and binding and hardening nature.

The top of the lime putty works dry, scaly, short, and inert. That from the middle is oily and tenacious.

There is much difference in the nature and quality of lime. Chalk lime is the most useful for stucco. It is the most pure, rich, and fat, and is produced from limestone containing the largest proportion of carbonate of lime. It is also the most plastic and smooth working. International experience shows that the poorer common limes make the best mortar and show quicker setting properties, whereas rich fat limes never " take bond " except in so far as they return to their original condition of carbonate by the reabsorption of carbonic acid from the atmosphere and the slow evaporation of the admixed water. Without evaporation the mortar remains soft. With too rapid evaporation the mortar falls to powder. This accounts for the clouds of dust one sees during the pulling down of old buildings. Pure fat lime easily slakes, and is less liable to blister than other limes. It doubles its bulk when slaked, and can be reworked again and again without injury.

Lias and blue lias lime, so called from the colour of the stone, is variable in quality, feeble in nature, and often hydraulic, and made into Portland cement. It is, from the amount of clay contained in it, unsuited for stucco, containing as much as from 10 to 30 per cent. of clay and 38 per cent. of carbonate of magnesia, and a low proportion of carbonate of lime. The clay gives hydraulicity in proportion to its amount.

As regards the burning, much is now left to chance. Improperly burnt or " dead burnt " lime will not slake with water, only half of its carbonic acid being expelled.

This basic compound, on the addition of water, instead of forming hydrate of lime and being converted into a fine impalpable powder with the production of considerable heat, is changed into hydrate and carbonate with little heat.

With hydraulic limes containing much silica, dead burning may arise from the limestone having reached too high a temperature, whereby a partial fusion only of the lime formed has been produced. Eminently hydraulic limes require burning at as low a temperature as possible. Pure limes subjected to excessive heat tend to combine less with water than the same properly calcined. Caustic limes combine with water with great energy, evolving great heat. The great secret was the slow and thorough slaking and maturing like wine, the mixing, the thumping (to toughen and thicken), and the spreading on of each coat very thinly over an under thin coating of like material that had thoroughly evaporated the carbonic acid it had contained.

The hardness of each coat was due to this thin spreading, whether worked as a coat, in low relief, high relief, or in the round. The principle was the same for all.

We must, of course, take climate into consideration in regarding even the old Roman and Italian stucco. The chief cause of the premature decay of external stucco is presence of clay, loam, muddy earth, or decayed animal or vegetable matter in the silicate or in the lime.

PLATE LI

(a) Detail of Modelled Wreath in the Saloon, Groombridge Place, Kent.

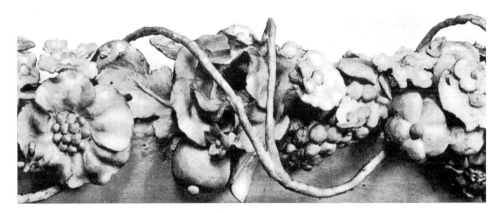

(b) Detail of Border round Staircase Lantern, Brickwall House, Sussex.

(c) Detail of Decoration around Staircase Lantern, Brickwall House, Sussex.
(Late Seventeenth Century.)

PLATE LII

(a) PORTION OF MODELLED AND TEMPERA-PAINTED FRIEZE ON WALLS OF PRESENCE CHAMBER, HARDWICK HALL, DERBYSHIRE. (EARLY SIXTEENTH CENTURY.)

(b) and (c) DETAILS OF THE " CHEVY CHASE " FRIEZE, FROM ST MICHAEL'S MOUNT, CORNWALL. (SIXTEENTH CENTURY.)

My own stucco, made for modelling, was as follows :—

The lime is fat lime, about nine years old.

This is first dried, then crushed, and put through a very fine sieve ; then mix dry :—

Two parts lime to—
{
1 part marble dust.
1 ,, rye flour.
1 ,, kaolin (china clay).
}

One part plaster of Paris is added to 3 of the above mixture to prevent cracking. Thoroughly mix in a dry state. In making up for use, form a ring of the dry mixture on a slab.

Two solutions are used.

" A " solution : composed of ½ lb. *Althæa officinalis* radix (marshmallow root) to 1 gallon of water.

" B " solution : ½ lb. gum acacia (gum arabic) to 1 quart of water.

Take 3 parts of " A " to 1 of " B " and mix up into the powdered material until it takes the consistency of dough, or paste, or plumber's putty ; work and pulverise it thoroughly with trowel and wooden mandel, until thoroughly pliable, smooth, fat, and clean working. Allow to stand for a day and retrowel thoroughly before use. It can be kept soft for a week in a wet cloth ; but it is better made up fresh, and used thinly, and newly made.

Are we for ever to be compelled to use the comparatively rubbishy modern plaster for our buildings, when we could have stuff as good and durable as the old stucco ? The greatest abuse of the material seems to be in the fact that we ignore it completely, when we might be doing excellent and durable work with it. Anything can be done with stucco ; therefore, I suppose, it is open to the danger of abuse. In capable hands it may be used as simply, easily, readily, and as unconsciously as a good pastry cook makes nice pie crust, or as a modeller fingers his clay ; with this difference, the clay will dry and tumble off, the stucco will remain permanently clean, crisp, and fine as left from the fingers, or from the tool, or trowel, or the mould, and get harder and harder every day, month, and year, as time goes on.

As to the mannerism and personality of handling and expression of form in our design and detail, it is for each one to decide according to his convictions.

Now that we know the composition of lime stucco and how to make it, we may turn our attention to modelling with it in various ways. We have already illustrated in a general way various old examples of modelled lime stucco of Italy, France, and England.

We are now concerned with right and wrong ways of modelling with it.

We may, if we choose, model with it just as with modelling clay, direct on to the finished plaster, ceiling, or wall, building up the relief pellet by pellet until complete. We have the satisfaction of knowing that, unlike the clay, the stucco will not dry and tumble off, but that it will harden and remain permanently and exactly as it leaves the fingers or the tool of the modeller. All the little irregularities, overlappings, or under-cuttings which the plasterer so dearly loves to remove from a plaster cast or a clay model to prevent adhesion of mould and cast, all the little subtleties, technicalities, and accidents of surface or of touch, remain fresh and living for ever as on an artist's canvas. Two or three simple illustrations of this are given in Plates L, LIV, and LX. A more vigorous treatment of modelling with lime stucco, from the great frieze at Hardwick Hall, Derbyshire, is shown in Plates XII, *b*, XIII, *b*, and LII, *a*. The frieze appears to have been modelled throughout with metal tools. The tree trunks and branches are quite soft and round in relief, but the leaves are flat, quite plain of surface, square edged, and somewhat undercut.

The other detail appears to have been modelled straightway on to the wall ;

portions have come away entirely, and the surface has been replastered and painted to harmonise at some later date.

A chemical analysis of a fallen portion revealed that the stucco was composed of local lime (air-slaked) and a small proportion of fine grit.

This frieze and the portions that still remain exposed to the varying climate since 1598 on the walls of the " Giant's Chamber " of the ruins near by (Plates XIII, *a,* and LX, *b*) are quite the purest and best examples of lime-stucco modelling of the kind in this country.

Plate LII, *b* and *c*, shows part of a much narrower, although similar, kind of modelling, done *in situ*, at St Michael's Mount, Cornwall. The next development of the art, belonging to a later date, brings us face to face with the period when the parts were modelled (and cast) quite separately and put together afterwards. That most of the parts—the leaves, flowers, fruit, etc.—were designed and modelled individually and distinctly, there can be no shadow of doubt, although in some ceilings, perhaps, the smaller leaves and the small repeating moulding enrichments may have been pressed with a die or even cast and bedded up in small pieces.

Granted that we make all the parts strong, simple, and decorative in form, how should they be placed and arranged to be rightly decorative, reposeful, and safe ? It would not be reposeful to feel that they might drop off the ceiling at any moment. There must be the sense and feeling of proper attachment (homogeneity) to the groundwork, *i.e.*, to the ceiling itself. It must be felt to be a part of the ceiling proper ; not a thing in itself. How then should they be placed to be legitimately and truly decorative, beautiful, strong, and serviceable ?

In the first place, they should not be made up on sticks. A case in point is illustrated in Plate LIII, from *Kilmainham Hospital, Dublin*. Blackthorn twigs were embedded in the stucco flowers and leaves and in the stucco foundation supporting them. In the middle of the nineteenth century it was found that the sappy blackthorn supports had dry rotted ! Thus the ceiling was in a dangerous state. It was taken down, and alas, " reproduced "—in " carton-pierre " ! ! ! That was not good decorative workmanship. There should have been for each separate piece direct support, both from the plaster bed at the back and also a bond from each neighbouring piece.

Perhaps the first conclusion to be drawn is that the belts of ornament should be modelled to maintain a given contour somewhat in the manner of Plates L and LVI, and Fig. 21. The whole of this work is homogeneous and strong, the contour well maintained and compact, the detail highly decorative and beautifully contrasted by the slight surface modelling. In like manner is the modelling of the oval at *Groombridge* (Plate LI, *a*), as also the ceiling circle in Plate LIV, *a*, from *Eye Manor*, and the stucco ceiling work at *Holyrood Palace* (Plates XX, *b*, and LV), *Caroline Park* (Plate LVI), *Kellie Castle* (Fig. 21), *Ashburnham House* (Plates XXIII and L), and many other such instances.

At a later period, say from the middle to the latter periods of Sir Christopher Wren's work, the modelled detail became looser and more open in arrangement, less compact, more " naturalistic " in tendency, less constructive, and therefore less decorative. Stemwork, weak and liable to damage, was wound and cork-screwed in and out and round about the loosely arranged and less securely held belt of modelled work, and other work such as we find at Brickwall, Northiam, and elsewhere became a tangled growth, a marvel of modelling and skilful workmanship, beautiful and wonderful in itself, but beyond the realm of strictly good and legitimate " decorative " art (see Plate LI).

Many other examples of the kind might be given, but these will suffice to illustrate the climax that soon afterwards led to excess and extravagance of meaningless

PLATE LIII

DETAILS OF CEILINGS AT THE ROYAL HOSPITAL, KILMAINHAM, DUBLIN.
(EIGHTEENTH CENTURY.)

PLATE LIV

(*a*) DETAIL OF PLASTER WREATH, EYE MANOR, HEREFORDSHIRE.

(*b*) PLASTER ROSETTES FROM ACKLAM HALL, YORKSHIRE.

PLATE LV

DETAIL OF CEILING IN THE FOURTH ROOM, HOLYROOD PALACE, EDINBURGH.
(SEVENTEENTH CENTURY.)

PLATE LVI

DETAIL OF CEILING AT CAROLINE PARK, NEAR EDINBURGH.

PLATE LVII

(a) DETAIL OF CEILING IN THE STONE HALL, HOUGHTON.
(MID-EIGHTEENTH CENTURY.)   (William Kent.)

(b) PLASTER DECORATION IN THE DRAWING-ROOM, EASTON NESTON HALL,
NORTHAMPTONSHIRE.   (Nicholas Hawksmoor.)

PLATE LVIII

(b) Ceiling at York, in the Rococo Style.

(a) Ceiling over the Staircase, Wilberforce House, Hull.
(Eighteenth Century.)

PLATE LIX

(b) VAULT OF GREAT STAIRCASE, THE LOUVRE, PARIS. (Jean Goujon.)

(a) STUCCO ARABESQUE ORNAMENT, IN THE VILLA MADAMA, ROME.

PLATE LX

(b) STUCCO-DURO FRIEZE DECORATION FROM THE RUINS OF OLD HARDWICK HALL. (EARLY SIXTEENTH CENTURY.)

(a) ROMAN LOW RELIEF MODELLING FROM THE VILLA FARNESINA.

(c) DETAIL OF SALOON CEILING AT COLESHILL, BERKS.

True elevation of half of one side

FIG. 21.—Detail of Ceiling in Vine Room, Kellie Castle. (Sir R. S. Lorimer *del.*)

and restless curvature, and its consequent reaction in the form of severe architectural detail, modelled very harshly, as Plates XXVI, XXVIII, and LVII.

The rococo stucco ornament of the middle eighteenth century was a different reaction (Plates XXVII and LVIII). This developed into a meaningless restlessness, sprawling of form, and ultimately to the low relief decoration of the brothers Adam (Plates XXVIII and XXIX), who took their inspiration from the tombs of the Appian Way, etc. (see Plates II, IV, etc.).

Let us revert to this period of lime-stucco modelling when each leaf, flower, fruit, etc., was made individually, and put together afterwards. Let us analyse what is said against this work. It is said that " it is not plasterwork " ; it is " carvers' work " ; it is " liable to damage " ; that " it harbours dust and dirt."

Let us admit at once that the lower relief treatments of lime-stucco modelling are everything that can be desired in plastic art ; but let us not deceive ourselves as to the legitimacy of this other form of stucco decoration. The first two objections we have already disposed of. The third objection is that " it is liable to damage." An examination of dozens of examples will show surprisingly little damage. It would be interesting to know if decorative work in other materials, done at the same date, has come down to us undamaged, or less damaged. We think not. Marble, stone, wood-carving are all less hard in substance, equally liable to damage ; more so in process of working. Good lime stucco is harder than marble and more durable.

" It harbours dust and dirt ! " This cannot be denied, but are we to sweep away from the realm of Art all craftsmanship that does so ? Such criticism is chillish, ridiculous prejudice !

In the chapter on modelling some slight reference has been made to the sources of inspiration for design. The general design or " lay-out " of the main abstract lines of a ceiling depends largely on considerations and circumstances ; that may to a ready and recipient mind suggest influence, and control the general idea or conception, though not necessarily so. Central lines—of windows, chimney-pieces, projections, recesses, and other forms and details—influence and help the imagination towards a happy arrangement of symmetrical lines and compartments. Beams, columns, pilasters, and other projecting constructional features (unless concealed) may do a great deal to control the main lines of a design. Beyond this and with this must be considered the general design of the rest of the room—the size and the height of the room, the design of the walls, chimney-piece, windows, and other features, that may have some scale relationship to the ceiling and its lay-out. Beyond this, fancy, knowledge, and experience do the rest. The imagination is free within prescribed limits. A glance through the old examples will show that the general main lines, on plan, were mostly quite simple and symmetrical in arrangement, no matter how elaborate or simple the detail. This characteristic particularly applies to the time when the main lines were of modelling in high relief and rich detail, even if portions of the groundwork, such as spandrel and panel surfaces, were in much lower and more quiet relief. Here the designer will need control, dignity, refinement without pettiness, rhythm, contrast, " balance," and those qualities of combined imagination, judgment, and technique that make up the small word " artist." There are no laws of design. No two ceilings need be alike any more than any two meadows in spring. Each may be different in a hundred beautiful ways ; different in conception, different in plan, different in detail, in personality, in every way. Here lies the great fascination of an artist's life, of an artist's work—to be doing something always fresh, always different, always beautiful, for his work has no right to existence unless it be so.

PLATE LXI

(*a*) AT EARLSHALL, FIFESHIRE.

(*b*) CEILING OF CEDAR ROOM, EARLSHALL, FIFESHIRE.
(Sir Robert Lorimer.)

PLATE LXII

DETAIL OF RELIEF MODELLING FROM MODERN OVERMANTEL AND FRIEZE.
(G. P. Bankart.)

CHAPTER IV

MODERN PLASTERWORK IN ENGLAND

By George P. Bankart

A consideration of modern plasterwork brings us up against a much misunderstood and disregarded question, viz., that of " styles " that waxed and waned centuries ago.

The nineteenth century produced a great amount of imitation, mechanical reproduction, and open forgery, which was and still is supplied on demand by the public.

Admiration or fancy for antique examples of old work then became (and still remains) a form of idolatry which, in its narrowness, developed into incapacity for regarding any work for its own true merits. On the contrary, and to its great detriment, our natural aptitude for a National Architecture as a creative art was left (and still is) far behind the sister arts in throwing off the shackles of " periods " or " styles " that have lived out their time and served their purpose ; but liberty is apt to grow into licence, and licence to run wild, which danger attends those who would be free from the imitation of " styles " and copying of stereotyped periods of past fashions in architecture.

The " reproduction " of past examples may serve the commercial purpose of tradesmen who, by reason of their commercial responsibilities, are compelled to bow without reserve to their customers' slightest expressed wish, and who are thus limited to business-like methods. It does not occur to or trouble them that they are defrauding future generations. Nevertheless, it indicates a lack of imagination and incapacity to design.

Man's architecture and its attendant " decoration " has always, in the past, shown evolution—as Nature does in all things. All living Art is related to that which came before. It never was, until the last century or so, a repetition or make-believe of some good old " has been "—as it is largely with the plasterer's craft to-day. Enterprising " Art " firms, whose main objective is to profiteer by pleasing their patrons (who admire and desire copies of past styles), do not understand the fact that the habitual copying of old examples stifles evolution, or any healthy growth of good modern development in design and craftsmanship.

For the past few generations the prevailing custom has been to copy (by quite unsuitable methods) favourite " styles " or " periods " of decoration known as " Elizabethan," " Georgian," " Adam," " Louis XIV," " Empire," and so on. Why ? Because for the above reason the then present-day invention was crushed and listless. This is the doing of the "dilettante" in matters of Art ; the work of the dabbler conjointly with the quack commercial salesman who manufactures sham art—who pulls genuine Art to tatters—who copies, imitates, reproduces, and perpetuates false " taste " (and mental poverty) in wicked use of wealth.

It is not the case with the sister poetic arts as it is with Architecture and

Decoration. It should not be so with the latter. If a patron commissions an artist to paint a picture, he does not ridicule himself by instructing the artist to paint it in the Holbein style, the Reynolds style, the Turner style, or the David Cox style—nor is a musician instructed to compose in the Beethoven style, or the Handel style. On the contrary, both are free and unshackled to work out their own individuality. By long study of past and experience of modern Art and Music, both artists have acquired a strong individuality of their own. So with the poet, the novelist, the playwright, all of whose interpretations are modern. In like manner a lady does not order her new dress or hat to be made in the " Elizabethan " or " Georgian " or " Empire " style ; she takes very particular care to have it " up to date "—*modern*. So does a man with his tailor and new suit. And yet these most particular persons, in this respect, are the worst offenders concerning the style of a new house, decoration, or furniture. Why don't these stylists go about in the clothing of these periods ? It would be just as ridiculous !

There are architects and others who profess contempt for certain " styles " of architecture and decoration, also for plaster decoration in particular, if modern. These gentlemen's conception of their " profession " is in too deep a rut to get out of. Some architects despise modern decoration in any form of relief, because they are stylists. Modern low relief is called by them " Elizabethan " ; modern high relief is termed " Georgian " ; some lose their hearts to the " Adam " style, which is but an anæmic admixture of Pompeian plus classic Greek.

Some show prejudice for " Georgian " and predilection for " Empire." This inconsistency may be the outcome of a cosmopolitan race. All " styles " of ornament are legitimate and good and beautiful in their day, their place, their method. All are in turn equally " fashionable " and absurd to-day ; parrot-like in cleverness—but architectural bastardy. Craft cleverness, but—craft paralysis ! Is there to be no history for present-day architecture and decoration ? No honour for the architect but the O.B.E. ; and no fame for the plasterer to leave to posterity but mechanism ? The building public may some day regard the architect and craftsman of their own time as they do the portrait and landscape artist, the poet, the novelist, the dramatist ; they may demand from them good modern architecture and good modern decoration, apart from " styles " or " periods," as they now insist on good modern clothing.

One knows so well the national lethargy, " conservatism," indifference, and how each thinks any change on his part would " make no difference " ; that because things are as they are, they must go on. This spirit is too common and retarding to this age, but it is very prevalent, particularly in the art and craft of building and decoration.

There are, however, signs of change bearing on the design and execution of buildings to-day. Very healthy signs—bearing on the design and execution of plaster decoration to-day.

Many very worthy and skilful plasterers, who have plied their trade honourably and well all their lives, may naturally protest—" What has all this to do with plastering ? What has change to do with the plastering trade ? Plaster is plaster ! I was taught my trade as an apprentice ! What I don't know about it, no one can teach me now ! It has always been the same since I have known anything about it ! It was no different in my father's time, or my grandfather's ! " Precisely so. That is quite true of the trade. That is the point. Those few generations knew plastering only as a trade ; a branch of the building trade—a very important branch too. Is this not true ?

This may be an oversight. It will come—soon, or later on. It must come if—if the plasterer's craft is ever again to be a craft such as it was—in the sixteenth and seventeenth centuries. The trade was not in the nineteenth century a great art or craft as we know it was in Italy, in France, in England, and in every country of Europe

PLATE LXIII

(*a*) CEILING IN A HOUSE AT KENSINGTON BY THE LATE E. W. GIMSON.

(*b*) BEAM AND FRIEZE, THE DRAWING-ROOM, WILLERSEY, GLOUCESTERSHIRE.
(G. P. Bankart.)

PLATE LXIV

(*a*) Vaulted Cast Fibrous Ceiling, Canons Park, Edgware. (G. P. Bankart.)

(*a*) Bedroom Ceiling, Ardkinglass, Scotland.

PLATE LXV

(*a*) THE DINING-ROOM, AVON TYRELL, WILTSHIRE.

(*b*) THE DRAWING-ROOM, AVON TYRELL, WILTSHIRE.

(W. R. Lethaby and E. W. Gimson.)

PLATE LXVI

(*a*) THE BILLIARD-ROOM, "WOOD," DEVON.
(G. P. Bankart.)

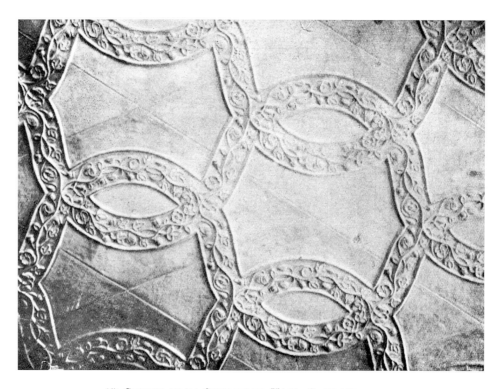

(*b*) CEILING FROM SKETCHLEY HALL, LEICESTERSHIRE.

and Asia in the centuries gone by. These times, fashions, and customs have gone by, never to be revived. Let them be honoured and cared for—as such. Times, fashions, and customs have changed—circumstances, people, and "tastes" have changed. Buildings, building materials, and methods have changed greatly—and will go on changing. The plasterers' trade still remains a "trade," chiefly; but it is gradually becoming more than this—it is gradually, through the efforts of a few men, coming back to its own. There are some who will not understand this. There are some who will, viz., those who are skilled craftsmen and artists as well as skilled mechanics. To understand the modern "Arts and Craft" movements, one must know what "Art" is.

"What is an 'Art'?" "Art" is a much misunderstood word; a word too commonly used (or rather misused), like "religion," in speech and in practice. "Why should plasterers be artists?" Why not? It is, or was, a great Art. Art is not a form of "swank," as some think. Art is not "affectation," as many make of it. It is not in the imitation, copying, or reproduction of old work—because it is fashionable. That is craftiness. It is not anything "handsome," "pretty," "ornate"—or shabby-fine.

Some persons maintain that "Art" can be done without; that it is unnecessary to life or existence. Some kinds can.

Art is a way of doing things well, and legitimately—and beautifully; it is "the expression of man's delight in creation" and creating, whether it be the making and shaping of a tea-cup, a table, a house, or anything he makes for his own and his fellow's use and pleasure. It is a degree of mentality above the primitive "animal" state. "Fine Art" appeals to the emotions—"decorative Art" appeals to the sense of repose or rest. One can drink just as effectively from an ugly tea-cup as from an "artistic" one. A common deal table is as serviceable as a shaped oak or mahogany table. An ugly suburban villa is as habitable as (and often more so than) an "artistic" house. Apparently, that may be so, but *not* in reality! Many persons know nothing different. Accustomed as some are to a certain type of common ugliness, peculiar to the Victorian era, a different state is unknown to them; a better state does not exist for them, or appeal to an unawakened sense of sight, or of touch. Habit makes them content and happy. Anything different is unseen, unknown, "unnecessary"—superficial, misunderstood, and mistaken for—"Art."

It is very necessary, indeed, to understand this aspect of life and art. By way of illustration, suppose that two very young children are taken away from their parents, surroundings, and influence, and brought up in two distinctly different spheres. Suppose that one child is associated always with commonplace ugliness, ignorance, and the usual accompanying influences, not necessarily "low"; suppose that the other child is associated with nice things, refinement, pleasant or beautiful surroundings, not necessarily costly. Allowing even for any unknown hereditary development, what a mental contrast there must be between those two "souls," even before they reach maturity. Bring children up in refined or nice surroundings, however plain, and see the difference.

"What has this to do with plastering?" It has everything to do with it. Plasterers please note. Those who decry "Art" as unnecessary; those who are content (if not proud) to live the ugly villa life (as "good enough for them")—in homes with the usual ugly patterned papers on walls and ceilings, with mirrored chimney overmantels, ugly upholstered and "anti-macassared" furniture, fluffy wool mats, sham lace curtains, oil-cloths with gawdy patterns, and gay carpeted floors, etc. Why do you always have patterned papers on the walls of your rooms? Why? "Because" (you say) "the plastered walls are so smooth, and so cold, and so un-

interesting. We must have something to make it comfortable to live with." That is
the invariable answer to the question, and it is true ! If this is so, why does the plasterer
make the walls so smooth, and cold, and uninteresting that his work should at once be
covered up with insanitary germ-holding paper ? Is it because he thinks it cleaner and
harder than good plastering, less dust-harbouring, less germ-absorbing, and more
hygienic ? Is this the reason at all ? Is this object and work of his to be defeated by
obliterating the skilled plasterer's work with wall-papers—that harbour dust-germs,
insects, sour paste odours, and infection ? The " swell " wall-papering is done for no
other reason than to satisfy an inherent desire for something nice to live with, some
comfort for eye and nerve, some unsupplied " homeliness "—said by these same persons
to be " artistic "—" unnecessary " to existence.

People don't like it. Architects don't like it, but they don't give it a thought
and let it pass, so it goes on being done. They paste something with a pattern on it—
a patterned paper, or a stamped-pulp of some kind—geometrically panelled in small
" pretty " patterns. This is not recognised as the shadow of a once living and common
tradition of the plasterer's art, viz., the old, moulded-rib panelled and modelled plaster
ceilings. The people cannot live with or put up with your smooth plaster. A cheap
make-believe satisfies them, and takes the place of what the plasterer builder has long
since ceased to give them. The desire is inborn, is inherent. Ever so little would do.
Some little " quality," or inequality, of surface (at least) would help to satisfy the eye,
to soothe and interest, to kill the " bareness " and " coldness."

Take one other modern illustration, perhaps unthought of by most persons—the
" pier glass," the Victorian " pier glass " or chimney-piece mirror, and the wood
" furniture " chimney-piece overmantel—common everywhere. Why ? To supply
another once living tradition of the plasterer, viz., the chimney overmantel of plaster !
The central feature of every " home " was, and still is, the hearth and the wall space
over. The chimney overmantel was as frequent and interesting, when plastering
was an art, as the modern (Victorian) pier glass is now uninteresting, and damnably ugly !

This is the result of the plasterer's art being allowed to lapse into mechanism only.
The public do not like mechanism only. They cannot live with it. They cover it with
wretchedly patterned wall-paper.

How very much nicer it would be to return, in some nice, simple, modern form
to this traditional feature over the fireplace, the plaster overmantel, in place of the
modern chimney-shelf nightmare of tawdry little pot nicknacks, called " ornaments,"
which the women of the house must have. Why ? Because there is a useless shelf
which must have something on it.

A plaster overmantel done in a small modern house is shown in Fig. 22. The
chimney-shelf is not wanted—is really very unnecessary, particularly so in bedrooms—
in these days. It is only a dust-collecting excrescence, and might advantageously and
economically (from a labour-saving point of view) be done away with.

Plaster is a nice enough material. That it be studied and used naturally and
beautifully is all that is expected of it, and asked of the modern plasterer.

Let it not be (wrongly) called " artistic " to make it look nice, and be nice. It is
not so when it is too mechanical, when it is carried too far, when it is made to look
like something else, when it is made almost as smooth as ivory, when it is falsely
modelled and wrought smooth and sharp like carved stone, wood, marble, or any other
non-granular material that will take (and retain) a sharp edge because it is hard.
Plaster will not do that to retain it. It is not honest plasterwork when it does not
look like what it is, viz., plaster ; a soft, easily damageable granular material ; because
cold mechanical smoothness does not appeal to any sense of " homeliness " or comfort.

Who is to blame for this ? Plasterers are not to blame ; the trade is not to blame. It is due to enforced habit throughout a century when all graphic art but pictorial art was dead. Mechanical plastering was the outcome. Who can alter this condition as existing now ? Architects and their quantity surveyors who design and control the erection of modern buildings, can see to it, if they will. Many are doubtless too much engrossed in the " business " side of building to trouble about such a matter, or to alter it.

There are other changes and influences bearing greatly on modern plasterers' work, viz., change of materials, change of methods, change of construction. " Patent " plasters or cements now commonly used chiefly for solid plastering (these were quite unknown to sixteenth and seventeenth century plasterers) are excellent materials, properly used, for good modern decorative purposes—Keen's cement, Parian cement, Portland cement, and " fibrous plaster " (it would be better termed " reinforced plaster ").

Instead of " running " mouldings on the ceilings or walls, and inserting solid-cast short repeating pieces of ornament, the whole thing is now " laid down " on the bench in clay by preference, or in plaster. Then a mould of plaster (or gelatine if undercut) is made, and casts taken off in plaster, reinforced with " scrim " and wood, in lengths of, say, 8 to 10 ft., or in slabs, say, up to 10 ft. square, which are finally secured to timber or iron cradling around the steel construction.

Not that this is advantageous from an artist's point of view, but it is a system of building which has come to stay, and it should be labour and time saving from an economical point of view. Fibrous plaster casting is open to very excellent results, to bigger and broader schemes of design, to greater speed in production and execution ; but, like all good things, it is also very open to wrong use, and to bad workmanship in the hands of indifferent workmen or unprincipled " business " men.

The fibrous plaster process, rightly made use of, has at least the advantage of enabling a designer to get away from " littleness " ; from small repeating panel arrangements (which the ancient " solid " process necessitated) ; to develop larger, broader, and freer conceptions ; to make the work away from the site (if necessary), although this is not necessarily advisable or advantageous.

Gelatine moulds should not be resorted to if one of plaster is possible. Although gelatine gives sharpness of surface definition and clean light and shadow (if required), it has a disadvantage, viz., that of producing too markedly unequal castings, blistered casts, often distorted modelling, and of sometimes doing great injustice to the refinement and labour bestowed on the modelling.

The construction of modern buildings very greatly concerns the design of present-day plasterers' work. The employment of steel stanchions and girders in place of solid stone or brick walls and beams of timber, the substitution of reinforced concrete or patent fireproof floors for wood joists, opens up a field of design and construction altogether different from the old work, excepting in one respect, viz., that plaster is plaster, and is still used, and also that it should be treated as such in the form of castings, surface ornaments, and other ways.

Opportunities for fine design are thus offered that never before existed. Many rooms are now larger and higher than of old ; some are immense. Beams often have greater girth and longer span than in the case of wood beams. Flat ceiling spaces—free of interruption—are often much more extensive in area. Vaulted ceilings are more easily constructed, more frequent, and often very large. Lighting by day and artificially differs much from what it was a few years ago, and has great bearing on the successful treatment of modern ceiling decoration.

" Taste " (wrongly so called) has changed. " Taste " is a sensual word irrelevant to Art—synonymous with luxury—a word used chiefly by " superior " persons who create their own standard of " taste " and regard it as " a matter of opinion " ; a species of refinement peculiar to their standard of intelligence.

In reality the word has a coarse, indefinite meaning, indicating ornateness or lust of eye and pride. " Taste " has become " fancy," " predilection," " fashion "—among the newly rich. But this state is reacting on itself in a desire for spontaneous Art— Art inherent from the past without being its slave.

The decoration of a room is a thing to some extent apart from necessity. A room may be architecturally beautiful and dignified without resort to decoration of any kind. Ceilings, cornices, friezes may be of wood or other material, plain or carved, painted or left from the tool. Walls may be panelled, tapestried, painted, or otherwise treated.

The ceiling is but accessory : a flat covering or canopy to the room : a thing entirely interdependent on the design of more important parts. The ceiling of plaster should take its place with the rest and play its part accordingly. It should not predominate or overwhelm, but should be quiet, refined, and reticent, whether of wood, stone, or plaster.

Plaster, however, has been favoured by the gods because of its cheapness, its humbleness, its warmth, its readiness of use, its sound-preventing qualities, and its adaptability.

More often than not, the ceiling of plaster is better plain than otherwise—or nearly so—in contrast and as a relief to the richness of the walls or furnishings, as a plain blue sky may be to the richness of a garden in the glory of summer, or to a sunlit city with a wealth of architectural splendour.

There are instances in which the plasterer has a claim beyond his skill as a mechanic to be called upon to ply his material as a vehicle of Art ; to exercise his handicraft as an artist.

This should not be regarded as an invitation for the display of a " base imitation of other men's high breeding " in other media of Art ; on the other hand, he should give of his own in a manner in which the gods intended that a humble and malleable material such as lime and sand should be honoured and used to give covering, pleasure, and repose to his fellows. How beautifully this has been done in the past is well known, and partly illustrated in this volume. Primitive and unskilled some of it may have been, but it has its lessons for us. Much of it holds our admiration now.

A few illustrations of work done by modern British plasterers of the present generation are shown with this chapter. They are not given as examples of skill, or as standards to copy or imitate, but to show that some really genuine modern work is being done, without pretence or presumption. They are varied in design, treatment, and interest. They maintain the old traditions of the craft without copying its forms or patterns, and all are distinctly modern in design.

They are given also to show what, at least, is within the easy reach of the present-day journeyman plasterer to think out and do in a similar way for himself (if he will) with endless variety, and no small amount of happiness and profit.

These general views may be taken as supplementary to some of the illustrations in larger detail, in the chapter on " Modelling and Design in Relief," although they are not specially referred to in the text. They show work of various kinds and methods as follows : Plates LXI, a, and LXXXVIII, b, are instances of the design being drawn on the ceiling; the leaves and grapes were cast loose and applied to the " floating coat surface " where required, the stems being later modelled in coarse plaster and finished in white plaster and lime putty with a small tool; the skimming coat was added last.

Plate LXIII, b, is an illustration of shallow beam casings, cast fibrous throughout

PLATE LXVII

(*a*) THE MUSIC ROOM.

(*b*) THE DRAWING-ROOM.

"PURSE CAUNDLE," MILBORNE PORT, SOMERSET. (G. P. Bankart.)

PLATE LXVIII

(*a*) VAULTED CEILING, " ROSSDHU," LUSS, SCOTLAND.

(*b*) ENLARGED DETAIL OF ABOVE. (G. P. Bankart.)

PLATE LXIX

BEDROOM CEILING IN ROOF, ROWALLAN CASTLE. (Sir R. Lorimer.)

PLATE LXX

(b) PLASTER GABLE, GREAT GLEN, LEICESTER.

(G. P. Bankart.)

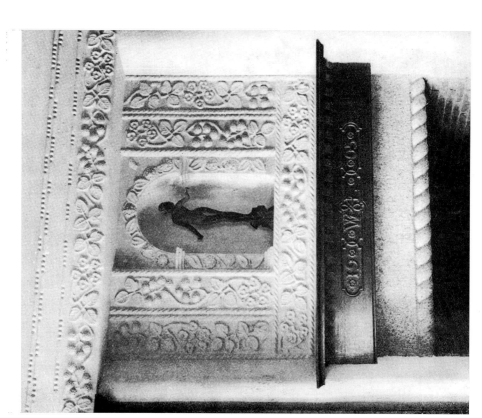

(a) MANTELPIECE AT "WOOD," DEVON.

PLATE LXXI

PLASTER BAYS, WHITE HOUSE, LEICESTER. (E. W. Gimson and G. P. Bankart.)

PLATE LXXII

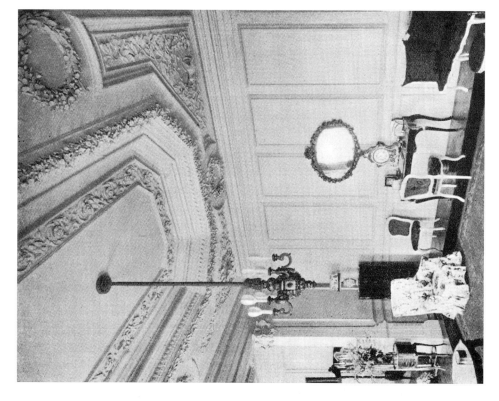

Two Modern Ceilings in Lime Stucco, Acklam Hall, Yorkshire. (G. P. Bankart.)

PLATE LXXIII

THE CORRIDOR, ST AGNES'S HOUSE, BRISTOL. (The late J. D. Sedding.)

PLATE LXXIV

THE DINING-ROOM, LITTLE RIDGE, TISBURY, WILTS. (T. Stallybrass.)

the ends of beams, and abutting into a modelled frieze, the ceiling panels between beams being quite plain solid work, to give contrast to the softly enriched beams and frieze.

Plate LXIV, *a*, shows a vaulted ceiling with simple straight bands of soft modelling (without mouldings) cast fibrous throughout in slabs and strips.

Plate LXVIII, *a* and *b*, shows a somewhat similar barrel-vaulted ceiling of alternating panels, cast fibrous throughout and fixed up in large slabs and strips.

Plate LXVI, *a*, shows a ceiling done in "solid" plastering. The modelled bands of surface ornaments were cast in short lengths, and "let in" to form very soft interlacing surface bands of white on white around and over the central feature—the billiard table. The cornice (a very simple one), of wavy and beaded mouldings, is placed flat on the wall, projecting only its own thickness. The modelling of the ceiling bands is kept well up to the bounding edge lines, so that mouldings are unnecessary.

Plate LXVI, *b*, shows a ceiling worked in clay, cast in plaster, and fixed up in square slabs. The interlacing ribwork was softly modelled in clay (in repeating sections).

Plate LXX, *a*, shows a very simple treatment of a room with a narrow modelled and beaded cornice only. The same strips of ornament are cut to form a chimney-piece overmantel over the fireplace, framing in a plain coved niche, with a very narrow enrichment around.

Plate LXX, *b*, shows exterior work to a pair of gables, done to form a meshwork, in Portland cement; the lozenge-shaped panels between enrichments are rough cast.

Plate LXXII shows two ceilings worked with lime stucco *in situ* and (in the old Italian principle) to harmonise with the old ceiling of the main room.

Plate LXXIII shows a very interesting cloister ceiling at Knowle, Bristol, in which a double width of rose enrichment on either side is slightly tilted (giving the suggestion of a flat vault); single widths of the same pattern connect the side belts at intervals, between the windows. Only a very short piece of modelling forms the repeat of this ornament.

Plates LXXIV, LXXV, *b*, and LXXVI, *c*, show ceilings worked entirely *in situ*, in large soft beadings.

CHAPTER V

MODELLING AND DESIGN IN RELIEF—AS SPECIALLY APPLICABLE TO PLASTERER'S WORK

By George P Bankart

This chapter is particularly addressed to the journeyman and apprentice plasterer who would model and design decoration as a part—and an important part—of his trade.

On the subject of modelling in general, much has been spoken and written. Of the branch of the subject as applied to decorative plastering, little has been said. It should be understood that this chapter applies distinctly to the plasterer's craft. Every craft has its own particular character, technical bearing, and development, and not the least important is the training of plasterers to model. For generations past (owing to altered conditions) the plasterer has ceased to model, and the modeller to plaster. This is not as it might be. History shows that wherever and whenever the plasterers' art flourished, plasterers were artists as well as mechanics.

There is no more pleasurable material to model with than lime stucco, plaster, or clay. The subtle qualities and the ease with which they may be used have been the making and the undoing of the craft.

It has too long been customary for the apprentice plasterer to be trained only as a mechanic and to follow this calling as a means of livelihood only. For this reason the absence of any ability to model is not surprising. With the present reawakening of the arts and crafts, this condition of the trade should soon be a thing of the past.

There is a healthy and actual desire for good quality plaster decoration. Although plain " solid " plastering must predominate, the modelling of plaster is increasing in demand.

The interest attached to the plasterer's trade is far greater now than it has been for generations, therefore a knowledge of modelling should be acquired by those who would be artists.

On such men the future honours of the craft will depend.

The technical qualifications of the modern plasterer as a skilled mechanic are much greater now than ever before. As plastering was once a great and spontaneous art, so it must be again some day, although in a different way.

The mastery of any subject, or of any art, lies in the thorough understanding of its elements.

It is therefore most important and necessary that the novice should first of all learn what his material is, what can be done with it, and how. No less important is it that he should know how to manipulate his plaster as a medium or vehicle of art without wrongly using it, because the downfall of plastering as an art came about from this cause, viz., the gratification of indulgence in vulgar ornament.

The true function of plastering lies not only in coating rough wall and ceiling surfaces, but in decorating those surfaces beautifully. The plasterer does not need to be a " sculptor."

Modelling and sculpture are widely different in their nature and technique.

Modelling is the building up of form.

Sculpture is the reverse : the cutting away of a more or less hard material with a chisel, or sharp tool.

The difference of the two processes is frequently ignored or wilfully abused by experienced modellers and carvers, who are apt to disregard technique for speed or effect.

This technical negligence arises from ignoring and undervaluing the great importance of the very functions, the *elements* of subject, by student and teacher alike. It may be through a desire to acquire skill hastily, or, a more common fault, to arrive at a result by any means, no matter what the medium may be.

Let us at least, then, understand our medium from the outset. The object of this chapter is to put within the plaster student's reach principles and processes that should help him to model decoration in a straightforward way by simple and direct means. It should help to develop and cultivate his observation, his judgment, and individuality, for it is in this that the making of an " artist " begins.

Good drawing is the foundation of all good modelling. To draw well is essential to the plasterer who models, not only to train the eye and the observation to see, but to interpret impressions whether on paper, in clay, or in plaster.

The plasterer student, although occupied daily at the bench or building, would be wise to follow up his day's work with some drawing and modelling with pencil and clay, until " ideas " begin to come. Those in towns have some advantage in night-school classes, where training of a kind may be had ; but even there the modelling of plaster decoration is seldom rightly understood.

Students attend these classes too often in a general way, without a definite object in view. They consequently acquire a general knowledge, instead of concentrating on particular technique. " Concentration " is essential to success in any subject. Serious thought, application, and devotion must be given to a subject to command success. Spare time with pencil and notebook in the fresh air of the country lanes and fields, or in buildings of antiquity, museums, and art galleries, will be remunerative, if one would gather in material, knowledge, and inspiration.

A common danger of Art school training is that a student is apt to be led away from the special technical training he desires and study necessary for particular craft work. Art school committees and principals necessarily run to earth Government grants, and in doing so sacrifice specialisation of craftsmanship to general methods unnecessary for some students, but necessary to the fulfilment of the departmental curriculum and the winning of " grants " and " results."

The plasterer modeller does not need a " general " Art school training ; but he should cultivate a good idea of line and curvature. In drawing let him cultivate a good, clear, free, firm pencil outline, with sufficient suggestion of pencil line-shading to answer his purpose for clear notation and memoranda. He has no absolute need for perfection of drawing, shading, atmospheric perspective, etc., as the pictorial artist has ; he is better without it. Nor is it necessary or advisable for him to copy slavishly in clay, or laboured pencil-shading, plaster casts of carvings, or of natural objects, or examples of craft work other than his own, no matter how beautiful. Such is the custom of some Art school teaching. What he *does* need to know, in addition to his trade mechanism, is how to draw from still objects of life sufficiently for his purpose, how to model and build up clay in relief, or in the round, with a dry, clean hand (not with wet fingers and sponge as so commonly taught), and how to model in plaster or cement with the trowel and small metal tools.

The plasterer student cannot have too simple a training from the beginning, if only properly and wisely directed for his special mission. The genuine student is always a student, always ready, always receptive, reflective, and inventive ; but life is too short for ordinary men to become proficient and expert in more than one great craft, although " there is only one Art."

Let us for a moment examine the nature of the material or medium with which he is to work. Plaster is, or should be, sulphate of lime, or carbonate of lime and marble dust or fine sand, with or without hair and other ingredients to hold and bind it together and to regulate its speed in setting.

It is a soft material, to be applied as a covering in a semi-liquid condition, whether " decoratively " or otherwise does not matter. The principle of addition by degrees is what he needs to remember. Its most easy and natural means of working is by addition, not by subtraction. In this lies its technical virtue as an artist's medium. The abuse of this qualification has always brought about its degradation and extinction. Nature never intended that it should be carved in imitation of marble or stone ; when it is so treated the softness and frailty of its nature are unequal to what is expected of it, and comparative failure results.

To the plasterer decorator who models, the whole realm of Art and of Nature is open for reference, inspiration, and pleasure. It is a peaceful and restful occupation to those who will have it.

Cultivate a memory of the appearance and shape of things. Memory may be greatly helped by the use of a sketch-book, or even a camera, if discreetly used as an aid only to visual memory. The former is the better by far.

It is surprising how the habitual use of the sketch-book increases the pleasure of observation. It makes one realise how many persons " have eyes and see not." The practice of this habit of observation and notation brings to our notice numberless details and things that would otherwise probably escape attention. Further development of observation and memory may come by trying to draw simple things from memory, and afterwards correcting the impressions from the object. After a time anything and everything may be mentally stored thus. To him who creates, nothing comes amiss, for such a man raises himself above his animal-self and becomes spiritual.

Students should cultivate another invaluable habit : that of keeping in touch with the past, with men who have lived and worked in bygone ages and bequeathed to posterity, at least, their work for our guidance. It may be that the best that has been done cannot be beaten—cannot be done again. Be this as it may, we cannot *ignore* their work, methods, thoughts, and experience expressed in words and deeds without infinite loss to ourselves and our own work.

If we are to progress we must to some extent live with the past as well as with the present, and learn from the past how our predecessors did their work ; we may adapt their principles to modern conditions and construction in our own way to our present needs, and try to do things of our own, based on past experience, as the craftsmen of the Middle Ages did. Old work interests us, fires our sense of sight and feeling. Old books inspire thought and fire the imagination. Old examples of craft work show us how to do things—how to express Nature in work—how to express our own ideas in various ways.

The modern plasterer student who has liking enough to pursue his work as an " art " in addition to his craft, cannot and must not expect to learn as did the apprentice of the Middle Ages—directly from his master and associates. Trade mechanism he will certainly learn with industry, but the art of modelling and designing he must, under modern conditions, acquire chiefly in his leisure time, and apply and cultivate it in the workshop or on the building as opportunity offers. To this end the student will be well advised always to carry a sketch-book in his pocket. He should constantly

PLATE LXXV

(*a*) DETAIL OF LOW RELIEF MODELLING, WHITE HOUSE, LEICESTER.
(E. W. Gimson and G. P. Bankart.)

(*b*) THE DRAWING-ROOM, THE KNOLL, LEICESTER. (G. P. Bankart.)

PLATE LXXVI

(c) LITTLE RIDGE, TISBURY, WILTS. (T. Stallybrass.)

(a) DETAIL OF CAST MODELLING.

(b) DETAIL OF MODELLING IN KEEN'S CEMENT

IN SITU, INGLE CEILING, SKETCHLEY HALL. (G. P. Bankart.)

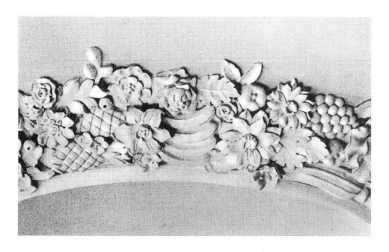

Fruit Modelled (Loose) in Clay, Cast in Plaster of Paris, and Bedded up in situ round a Rough Lime Plaster and Sand Core.

Enlarged Detail of Modelled Band.

Detail of Vine-leaf Border to a Modelled Panel.

PLATE LXXVII

MODERN FIGURE AND FLOWER FRIEZE, EXETER (5 ft. deep).
(G. P. Bankart and Arthur Glover.)

note down " memoranda," with measurements, of any interesting examples of old work he may come across, either from actual work, from photographs, pictures, or drawings, also from Nature, and in doing so analyse what is noted down to help his memory of it: for instance, plans of ceilings (or portions of ceilings) in skeleton lines with (figured) sections of ribs, beams, cornices, mouldings, make sketches of overmantels, frieze and rib patterns, modelled work, and bits of detail to as large a scale as convenient to the size of the notebook, and as clearly as possible.

Very little shading, if any, is necessary, but figured measurements and written notes, as in Figs. 22-24, are helpful. As the student is interested in his work, so will he store his memory and notebook with innumerable sketches and notes from Nature and other sources, for use and reference. It is always to hand when required.

When noting down suggestions from Nature, try to recall some example of old work; try to see or transpose into material what is being noted down from Nature. It is instructive to compare Nature's modelling with man's interpretation. Compare some flower, leaf, fruit, bird, animal, or whatever else may be selected, with some good representations in plaster. Whatever natural object is studied and sketched

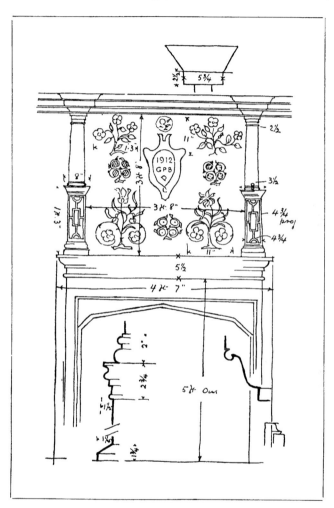

FIG. 22.—Overmantel, Borde Hill.

for decorative use should be given as little perspective as possible. To be serviceable for decorative setting in relief perspective is not needed. Examples of such sketch notations are given in Figs. 25 and 26. Sketches made for pictorial use and those made for decorative purposes, such as we are here concerned with, are entirely different in kind.

The designer and modeller of decoration should always look for and never lose grip of any decorative setting or bearing of natural objects. This exists in the harmonious arrangement of form and detail; in its adaptability to expression in the material, as opposed to its accidental arrangement or pictorial representation. In

FIG. 23.—Sketch-book Notes of Gallery Ceiling, Burton Agnes.

other words, a decorative artist should accustom himself instinctively to see everything as it may be, or should be, translated into the solid material in which he works.

Gradually, almost imperceptibly, is thus acquired a gift of selection and arrangement of form and detail expressible in relief; by a particular process—in our case by modelling in clay or plaster—to be reproduced by casting (in plaster) from a mould of either plaster or gelatine. Process and method have an important bearing on this question of interpreting Nature into material form—by mechanical means or otherwise.

For example, a student might perhaps observe and sketch a bird—a stork or crane. The untrained eye and mind of an ordinary person would see it merely as an interesting

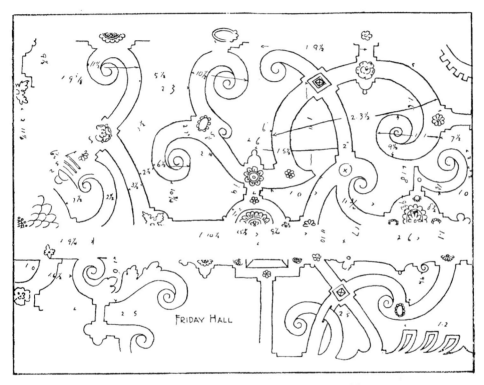

FIG. 24.—Sketch-book Notes of a Strapwork Ceiling.

or beautiful living being. The painter would see and paint its glory of natural form, colour, and perspective amidst the intricate beauty of natural surroundings.

But not so with the decorative artist. His privilege it is to interpret his impression poetically into a design. He sees principally the outline, the character, the attitude of the bird, the abstract grouping and harmonious arrangement of feathers, the anatomy, structure, and lumping-up of those parts arrangeable into (modelled) relief. It would be futile to attempt to express minute feather detail; so he instinctively looks for the main form and detail as it may be decoratively expressed (Plate LXXIX, a). He models it decoratively, to fill perhaps a panel, with sticks, leafage, and boughs, pleasingly and inventively arranged (Plate LXXIX, c).

Note that the form is "built up" (not cut away) and the surface detail added. The carver would get this form and detail by cutting away, and it is expressive of his process that his cuts are sharp and clean.

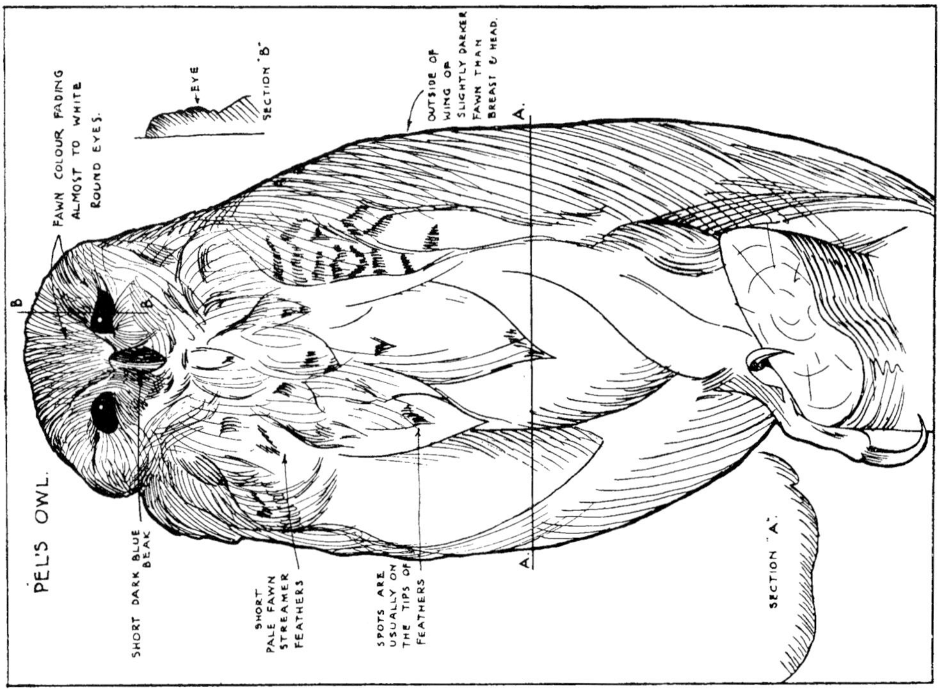

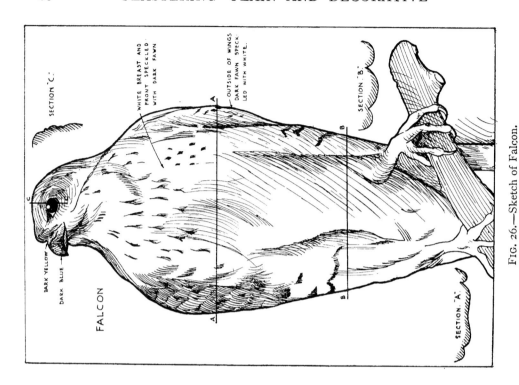

FIG. 26.—Sketch of Falcon.

FIG. 25.—Sketch-book Note, Pel's Owl.

PLATE LXXVIII

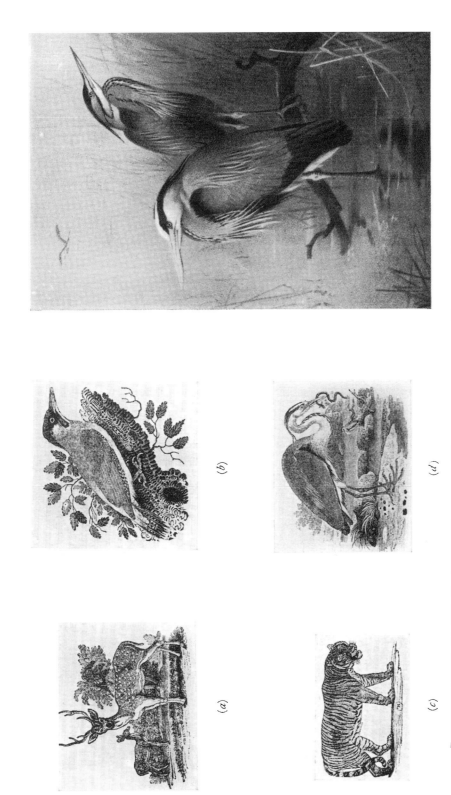

(a)

(b)

(c)

(d)

REPRESENTATIONS OF THE DEER, THE TIGER, THE WOODPECKER, AND THE HERONS AS MOTIVES FOR PLASTER MODELLING.
(The large Herons by Archibald Thorburn, F.Z.S. The four small subjects from Wood Engravings by Bewick.)

PLATE LXXIX

(a) AN EAGLE MODELLED IN PLASTER. (George Jack.)

(b) SKETCH OF A PEREGRINE FALCON.
(A. Thorburn *del.*)

(c) DECORATIVE RENDERING OF THE HERON
DESIGN (*see* Plate LXXVIII) IN LOW
RELIEF MODELLING. (George Jack.)

PLATE LXXX

(d) HONEYSUCKLE DESIGN FOR A FABRIC.
(William Morris.)

(c) PHOTOGRAPHIC NOTE OF
HONEYSUCKLE.

(b) DETAIL OF MODELLED HONEY-
SUCKLE IN PLASTER.

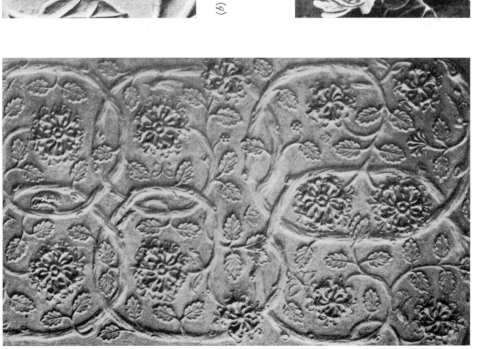

(a) HONEYSUCKLE IN MODERN PLASTER.
(G. P Bankart.)

PLATE LXXXI

(b) MARQUETRY PANEL OF FLORAL DESIGN FROM THE TOP OF A CHEST. (*Circa* 1690.)

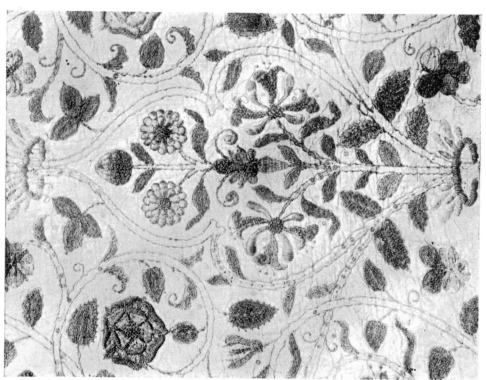

(a) NEEDLEWORK PANEL WITH A FLORAL DESIGN OF HONEYSUCKLE.

PLATE LXXXII

(*a*) MODERN PLASTER OVERMANTEL, SHOWING THE APPLICATION OF THE
ROSE AND PINK IN DECORATIVE DESIGN. (G. P. Bankart.)

(*b*) PHOTOGRAPHIC NOTE OF
CARNATIONS.

(*c*) INLAID DESIGN WITH THE PINK AS
PRINCIPAL MOTIF.

(*d*) DETAIL OF CLAY MODEL, SHOWING PROGRESSIVE STAGES
OF WORK. (G. P. Bankart.)

PLATE LXXXIII

(c) DETAIL OF LOW RELIEF PANEL IN LIME STUCCO. (G. P Bankart.)

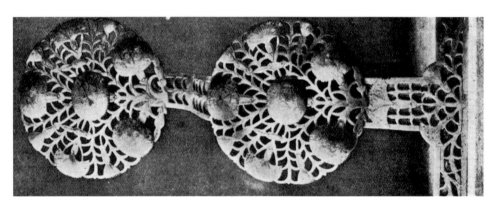

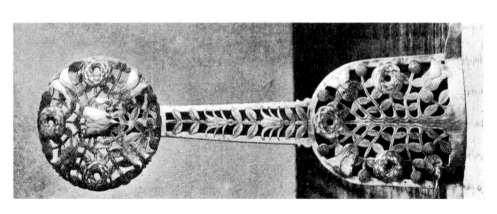

(a) and (b) ANDIRONS, WITH ROSE AND PINK MOTIVES INTRODUCED INTO THE DESIGN. (Ernest Gimson.)

PLATE LXXXIV

(b) MODERN EMBROIDERED FABRIC, SHOWING THE INTRODUCTION OF CONVENTIONAL FLORAL MOTIVES.

(a) NINETEENTH-CENTURY CHINTZ, SHOWING A NATURALISTIC "ROSE" DESIGN.

PLATE LXXXV

(b) PHOTOGRAPHIC NOTE OF ROSES.

(a) DETAIL OF MODELLING IN CLAY, ROSE PANEL. (G. P. Bankart.)

Take the instance of a honeysuckle flower and leaf; in Nature one sees them as Plate LXXX, c; an example of old plaster modelling interprets them as Plate LXXX, b; in the sketch-book one may note as in Fig. 27.

None of the decorative interpretations are pictorial representations such as the painter would see and give. They are, nevertheless, " honeysuckle " flowers and leaves variously interpreted. They are modelled in flat relief on a flat plane, to withdraw easily from a mould of plaster. They express the decorative idea without strain of imitation. The flowers, leaves, and stemwork fill the space harmoniously, i.e., with rhythm, symmetry, pleasant line, form, light, and shade. It is " decoration," or reposeful inventive arrangement. To illustrate the contrary, try to model a spray of any plant as Nature grows it. The decorative sense is not gratified, because pleasurable arrangement, fitness, and control are absent. It becomes at best but a very poor representation of Nature. Material and method fall very short of adequate imitation and do not satisfy the mind restfully.

The worthy decorator or modeller unconsciously knows that his material, clay or plaster, cannot possibly imitate Nature exactly. He acknowledges this shortcoming —limitation—gives his impression, gives the best his material is capable of doing easily, and arranges line and form to gratify his sense of order and beauty. The needlewoman, for instance, arranges her honeysuckle in forms and lines to suit her stitchery (Plate LXXXI, a); the wood-carver with sharp-cut delineation. The weaver does it (Plate LXXX) to suit the " warp " and " woof " of his loom.

So with the carnation (Plate LXXXII). In Nature, as Plate LXXXII, b, the plasterer models it as in Plate LXXXII, a. The blacksmith hammers his plate and cuts and chases it, as Plate LXXXIII, b; the wood inlayer as Plate LXXXII, c; the embroidress as Plate LXXXIV, b; and the wall-paper stainer as Fig. 28. All are " decorative "; none are pictorial, imitative, or deceptive; all are interesting and beautiful—of their kind, because they are technically right.

Refer for a moment to the meaningless, undecorative arrangement of lines and patterns of the typical Victorian chintzes and wall-papers, worked out from Nature's accidental arrangement. The difference is at once apparent (Plate LXXXIV, a) —" Naturalistic " !

Concerning modelling, there are some points of technical importance to which care and consideration should be given, not only by beginners, but by modellers, if they are not already too deep in the rut of bad habit. It is best at first to model in clay and afterwards in plaster. The latter process we will consider later.

The first consideration is that the clay shall be of proper consistency, i.e., not too stiff to spread easily, or too sticky to the fingers. If too wet the more it is " worked " through the hands, the better it will become—for modelling with. It is impossible to model properly with clay that is not exactly right.

The clay ground should be, if anything, slightly firmer than that for modelling with, for obvious reasons. The modeller should know how to keep his work in condition during his absence without in any way spoiling his previous day's work. This is a common oversight with modellers.

Students and modellers are most careless and reckless concerning this. Any soaking wet cloth thrown on to the model is " good enough " for some. One of the most disheartening things is to find work on which care and pains have been bestowed softened to a pulp, or injured by the pressure of a too wet or heavy cloth ; or, on the other hand, too much dried, or even cracked by neglect. There is no greater sign of indifference and slovenliness than this.

In the case of relief models, two or three pieces of wood nailed to the frame of the groundwork in the form of an inverted V or roof, or projecting straight out if on an

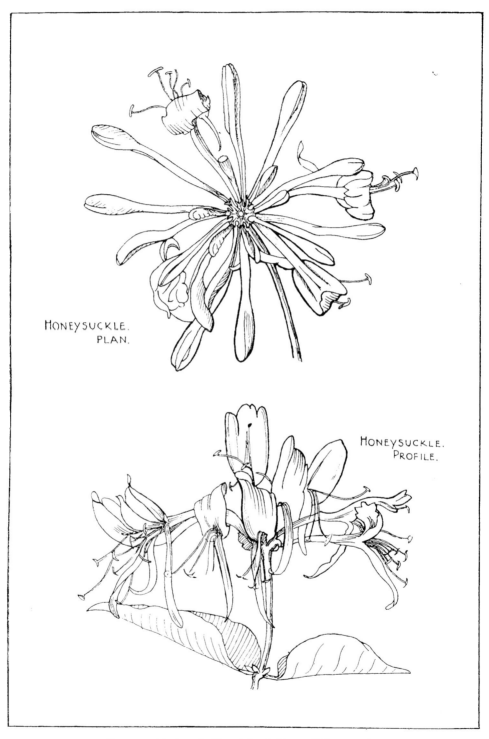

FIG. 27.—Designer's Sketch-book Note of Honeysuckle.

easel, will keep the damp cloth from contact with the modelling and the moisture in the clay from evaporating, which is all that is needful. A piece of damp blanket and American cloth stretched on to a rough wood frame and placed over the model will be found effectual, particularly in the case of models in the round.

We cannot too often repeat that modelling is the reverse of carving. It is rightly

FIG. 28.—Design for Embroidery, by William Morris, Carnation Motive.

a process of gradually building up the form, by laying one piece of clay over another until the proper relief is arrived at. Each piece added should be formed by the fingers to the shape required before being put on, and so by addition the final result is arrived at.

Many modellers, so-called, arrive at the result by a process of cutting away and building up. This is a method resorted to by many " carvers " who model, which is bad in principle.

In starting a model, know clearly beforehand what you wish and intend to do, and do it, straightforwardly and with decision. Another bad practice is working with a wet sponge and moist finger. For good plaster ornament this habit is particularly objectionable, as it leaves the surface of the clay smooth and shiny.   Plaster being naturally a soft, dull material, takes a too smooth and shiny surface when cast from such a model.   Each piece of clay added is best laid on spread, and at the edges blended into the clay around, rather than by smearing, wiping, rubbing, etc., which produce a shiny hardness of surface.

Plasterers are mostly concerned with relief modelling, which is quite unlike modelling in the round.   In the latter case one has to study the model from every point of view. There are various treatments of relief modelling.   Plasterers are mainly concerned with two kinds, which, for convenience, we will refer to as " low relief " and " undercut relief."   Low relief decoration is that kind of flat surface modelling which grows out of or belongs to the background, in the manner of the Elizabethan plaster ornament (Plates XIV-XIX).   This kind of relief is somewhat bevelled or spread at the edges to withdraw easily from a mould of plaster without sticking to the mould or breaking. The relief may have almost any projection, from that of a coin to about an inch or so. It is necessary sometimes, however, to undercut more or less the modelled outline when lighting is difficult, and decided definition of form is necessary, and to cast such models from moulds of gelatine.   The projection from the background to the extreme surface of the modelling varies considerably, according to circumstances.   The principle of foreshortening and contrasting of planes applies throughout.

It is less easy to do (at first) than relief in the round, but a little patient and intelligent study of the best old examples, combined with practice and judgment— more especially where figure-modelling is concerned—should soon be productive of good results.   Low relief modelling is the more legitimate work for reproduction in plaster of Paris, by virtue of its softness of texture and its easy manipulation.

When about to begin a low relief, panel, or repeating band of ornament, prepare a background of clay, $\frac{3}{4}$ in. to 1 in. thick, on a rough board foundation edged with strips of wood to keep the clay of equal thickness.

Into this wooden tray or framework the clay should be laid to the thickness of the boundary strips, and ruled off fairly level with a straight-edge from the strips on either side.

If the groundwork must be slightly curved or bevelled in profile, a drag or template should be shaped to the curve required and passed over the clay surface.

The streaky scratches and irregularities should then be worked away, and a fairly smooth and even surface left on which to draw and model the design.   The rough surface of the boarding will form a good key for the clay to adhere to and keep the air from working in between the clay and the boarding, and thereby drying and cracking the clay groundwork, which must be kept in good condition.

When this has been done, draw on the clay the outline of the design to be modelled, as Plate LXXXII, d.   Lay on the clay, first in the parts in lowest relief.   Always gradually build up this relief, pressing the pieces of clay on to and over those beneath. Do not smooth off or wipe out the overlapping edges of the numerous pieces of clay until the relief is generally fairly well arrived at.   Plate LXXXVII, c, shows a similar treatment in lime stucco instead of clay, worked from the fingers.

This done, the overlapping edges may be softened off by spreading, welding, and pressure of dry fingers or thumb.   Use the fingers and thumb only wherever and whenever possible ; use the modelling tool as seldom as possible.   A beginner should copy some nice pieces of old plasterwork, or plaster casts of such, until he can handle the clay fairly freely and get something of the simple feeling of the old modelled ornament.

For instance, leaves, flowers, fruit, or bits of conventional ornament of various kinds might be " copied," not slavishly or necessarily to the same size, but perhaps slightly larger or smaller than the example.   This will prove serviceable

PLATE LXXXVI

(*a*) DRAWING-ROOM CEILING, SPEKE HALL.

(*b*) DECORATIVE APPLICATION OF THE ROSE. (William Morris.) (For a Fabric.)

(*c*) DETAIL OF A ROSE DESIGN IN OLD PLASTER.

PLATE LXXXVII

(c) DETAIL OF PLASTER CEILING FROM SPEKE HALL, INTRODUCING VARIOUS ROSE MOTIVES.

(a) and (b) DETAILS OF ROSE PANELS, CARVED IN WOOD. (Joseph Armitage.)

PLATE LXXXVIII

(*a*) DETAIL OF TUDOR ROSE, BRIARY CLOSE. (G. P, Bankart.)

(*b*) AN EXAMPLE OF MODERN DESIGN, WITH THE VINE MOTIF,
COTTINGHAM GARDENS. (G. P. Bankart.)

PLATE LXXXIX

(b) DETAIL OF VINE MODELLING, COTTINGHAM GARDENS.

(a) MODERN SPANDREL, ACKLAM HALL, YORKSHIRE.
(*Vide* also Plate CXI, *a*.)

SPANDREL TREATMENT.
(G. P Bankar.)

training for the judgment of eye and hand. Do not model from carved marble, stone, or wood, or from casts of carving, unless you are doing so as a study of carving only. The technical character of such work, however beautiful, is quite different from that of good modelling, as modelling for plaster.

The writer has frequently seen students set to do this at schools of Art. The teachers at these establishments do not usually know, or appreciate, or demonstrate the technical differences of materials and processes as necessary to give the full value and quality of the material in working out a design. Many instructors do not know this matters. So long as a student acquires skill in copying whatever is placed before him, that is sufficient for the average art school teacher. Students are thus often innocently misguided in a general training, without direction towards any ultimate goal. This is very wrong.

For instance, a student in modelling from a carving of, say, stone or wood, uses the modelling tools, cuts and carves at the clay, and thus lays the foundation of a habit not only bad in principle for a " modeller " but one that is seldom pointed out to him, or checked. Carving is carving; modelling is modelling, or should be so. Whether it be for reproduction in gold, silver, bronze, lead, plaster, or other material, the technical handling of the clay (or wax) should vary according to the material fineness required.

After copying some good plaster relief ornament, the student should have learned something of the simple formation, setting, flatness, and softness of modelling of the old plasterwork; also, he will probably have found that his fingers are his best tools.

He should have learned something of the relative planes of projection, soft outline, light and shade, and convention of form in low relief decoration as modelled and produced by the plasterers of the sixteenth century.

He will have found out the importance of careful drawing, the variation in tone or " colour " of different strengths of relief, the necessity of building up to produce flat decoration on a flat ground, avoiding foreshortening and perspective, which is not permissible in flat decoration. All form should be flat—mostly in profile or full front view. There should be contrast in relief, in symmetry, or balance of setting and grouping of the forms.

The avoidance of perspective and foreshortening in flat decorative work cannot be emphasised too much. To " go to Nature for study and ideas " is a metaphor open to, perhaps, too literal interpretation by some persons who try to copy her arrangements pictorially. This is a common and fatal error. Good decoration and naturalistic representation are two widely different methods of expression. No better illustrations of naturalistic decoration can be given than the paperhangers' pattern books of the middle Victorian period and even of the present time. An illustration is given on Plate LXXXIV, a, of " naturalistic " flowers and leaves.

The same fault is common in much modern embroidery and in printed and woven fabrics and carpets. It is an entire misconception and misinterpretation of the term " to hold the mirror up to Nature," etc.

In studying Nature for decorative purposes, one should look for suggestions only, for suggestion and perfection of form and detail, for guidance, for inspiration. But the making of good decoration lies beyond this, in the selection and adaptation of Nature's suggestions poetically—by pleasant arrangement—or " invention," rhythm, metre, and balance.

Take a natural spray of roses, as Plate LXXXV, b. Compare it with an interpretation in plasterwork (Plates LXXXV, a, LXXXVII, c, and LXXXVIII, a); the one is naturalism, the others decoration. Examine the detail of a natural flower or leaf, as Plate LXXXV, b. Take a flower or leaf from a piece of old modelled plaster, as in the above decorative instances.

The same interpretation of the pleasure of invention or arrangement is shown in each case. In each instance it is differently interpreted, differently expressed; but in each instance it is plaster ornament in flat relief. In each instance the modelled relief is bevelled outwards to withdraw easily from a mould of plaster and not invite damage.

Plate LXXXVII, *a* and *b*, shows the rose applied to wood-carving in low relief. In these the difference of texture, the sharp, clean cutting of the chisel, the crispness of definition that the hard wood necessitates, the flatness of the relief, the undercutting and the granulation of the wood, all go to enhance the quality of the work and of the wood. But this treatment would be very wrong, in plaster or clay modelling.

Plaster cannot give this technical definition and crispness; even if it could be given in the clay model to some extent, it would be dulled in the process of reproduction. It would look wrong, and be wrong when done.

Another interpretation is shown in Plate LXXXI, *b*, of the adaptation of Nature to wood inlay. Here we have a clean-drawn silhouette expressed by cutting out thin, flat pieces of wood, laid into the surfaces of another wood groundwork. The principles are the same, but the method and process of technique are different. There is no relief of any kind; the interpretation depends entirely upon good silhouette form. These few illustrations are necessary to explain and enforce the right application of natural form to pure decoration in various materials.

The student may ask, " What is decoration ? " " What is ' ornament ' ? " The best answer is the experience of art workers who have devoted their lives to the patient analysis and practice of such matters.

Ornament may be defined as a language or poetry of form. Decoration is the art of expressing beauty of rhyme in some material. It is the art of adorning and beautifying materials with convention and " decorum," *i.e.*, in a manner best suited to enhance the quality of material—the blending of handwork and beautiful arrangement of form. It is not the mere copying of " old styles " or of Nature. It means a combination of the choice of good and suitable materials with a power or gift of arranging beauty of form for a special place and purpose, with sound good workmanship; a proper degree of " finish," fresh thought, imagination, or " design."

Once understand these principles underlying the word " design "; rid the mind of the nonsense of keeping up " styles " and " periods " of design, and then a student may safely set about modelling variations or rearrangements of some nice old examples from casts, photographs, or drawings. This is entirely different from " copying," and may lead to invention, or " design." Let him take some good example that he really likes, adapt it, and vary it, first in one way and then in another, until it resembles (without being like) the original, and the veil over the mystery of " design " will gradually lift, but—remember—design will only come by designing.

Most design has been based on precedent, and must always be in the making of a thing—may be resembling but different to something that has been done before. It may begin so, but not necessarily !

Motives suggested by Nature may creep in by degrees, but one may always safely seek inspiration and guidance from some example known and felt to be really good, varying it and developing it in our own way, so long as the technique is natural and suitable.

By this means—by studying old work and Nature at the same time—by absorbing inspiration from both, by uniting that knowledge of both in developing our own ideas with good taste, judgment, simplicity of arrangement, variation, industry, and practice, the student must surely acquire and cultivate the art of decorative design for himself. How else can he hope to do it ? But he must be content to learn. He must reach his

PLATE XC

(c) A Mitred Panel and Detail of Border to Central Section of the Ceiling in the Queen's Bedroom, Holyrood Palace, showing a Delicately-Modelled Foliated Design.

(a) A Pheasant.   (b) A Squirrel and Hedgehog.
Modern Panels against Floral Backgrounds.
(George Jack.)

PLATE XCI

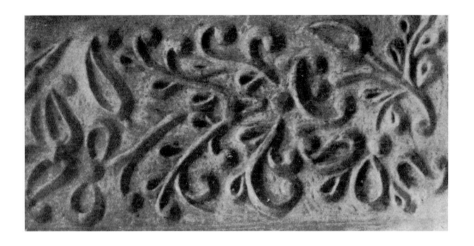

DETAIL OF TWO MODELLED PARGETTED PANELS, CLARE, SUFFOLK.
(MID-SEVENTEENTH CENTURY.)
(For General View of the House *vide* Plate XII, *a*.)

result, his ideal, by " building up " little by little, piece by piece, using good judgment and " taste "—not by concealing his process, but by showing the process and method by which he arrives at the result in his handiwork. Work that shows the process—the technique—is always interesting.

Try a panel something like Plate XCVI, *a*, but alter it in your own way. Do a short repeating length of a continuous border or frieze, something like a good old one you may know of. Some fanciful birds may be introduced, perhaps, at certain intervals where, as lumpy forms, they may " space " nicely with other lumps in the pattern, and so on.

The sketch-book, as an aid to memory and to imagination, has claims upon us. Each note or sketch should be a memorandum of some character, quality, or form which we may require for reference ; we never know when. One note may remind us, perhaps, of a pleasing piece of detail, or of modelling ; a peculiarly interesting pattern, or a plan of some ceiling design, moulding, or pendant ; or it may be a sketch of an interesting vault, a beam design, a chimney overmantel ; or a piece of outdoor plasterwork ; a panel between the windows of a house, or under the eaves gutter. The sketch-books should include notes and studies of animals, birds, fish, innumerable things of this kind, from life and from other sources. Book after book should be filled —not for show, but for use—as the storehouse of the mind.

Nothing affords greater variety and interest in decorative design than the introduction of living form ; the shapes of various birds and beasts ; but a casual interest in these is not sufficient. Students cannot hope to have that intimate knowledge of the habits and moods of these creatures which those closely associated with them possess ; they can, however, observe and note down enough information as to shape and characteristics to work from—to model form.

Without vitality and character animal forms are dull and meaningless in decoration. The selection of an attitude or action is a matter of great importance and interest. Avoid excessive action and insipidity, although strength and emphasis of action yields character in one's work. It is safer and more useful to suggest attitude rather than action or energy expressing actual movement. The representation of extreme action and motion is the work of the pictorial or emotional artist—what is called " fine art." We are here concerned with " applied art."

The importance of making a special study of character and movement in animal and bird life, as also in the human form, cannot be overrated. It is not always easy and convenient for townsmen to do this, although excellent opportunity for animal and bird life study is afforded at the Zoological Gardens, aquariums, etc., etc.

Photographs may be helpful if accompanied by some anatomical knowledge from life, for one must have constructive knowledge of detail and sections of parts to be able to shape them.

The wood engravings of animals by Bewick are very excellent illustrations of the kind of drawing invaluable for decorative purposes. They should be well studied by students, especially those who are prevented from studying from life.

Four studies from Bewick, such as may be useful for decorative purposes, are given in Plate LXXVIII, *a* to *d*. Very elaborate drawings are neither needful nor advisable. Note down nicely and clearly the main outline and masses, as nearly as possible in the position required to fill the space, if the study is being made to occupy a given space. Only a suggestion of detail (to be studied independently) is necessary. Sections through various parts, as illustrated in Figs. 25 and 26, written notes relating to various planes, foreshortenings, colourings, etc., will be valuable and helpful, as illustrated in the sketches referred to.

Cultivate a constant habit of observation and reflection in these matters in going about anywhere and everywhere. Follow and watch subjects in the streets and lanes; for instance, the movements of a horse, a dog, or other animal such as may be required, and as far as possible note on paper or commit to memory such details, parts, and actions as one may be working on.

Full size or large scale drawings are helpful sometimes in working out an idea; but it is better to work direct in clay or plaster than to needlessly absorb time and energy that should be devoted to the model. It is hardly to be expected that all can do this, but there are plasterers well known to the writer who do so, and more! There will be others, many others, who will rise above their purely trade calling and do likewise. To such belongs the key of life and of greater achievement. It is no difficult achievement. It is one rather of gradual and happy self-education, open to any intelligent operative plasterer whose future is in his own keeping. What has been before, in less favourable times, will happen again in a better way to those who possess the wish and the will to raise themselves above the dross of everyday life.

It is for them to see and do things out of the ordinary humdrum of mere " Trades Unionism." Were they to organise, to legislate, and to " strike," not only against ill conditions of employment, but against ill conditions of craftsmanship, ill conditions of training, ill conditions of education for their special and natural sphere of life, how much happier would be their daily work!

It is for the younger generation to honour and to resurrect their craft, to raise it to the very high position it has several times held amongst the sister building arts included in the term architecture. This is no dream, no impossible task. Men have done it, and are doing it in many instances. Their work is excellent and original " as far as anything can be original " of its kind. These men *live* in a new realm (of thought and work) in comparison with their older selves. The whole world belongs to them. The fields are their gardens, the woods are theirs, and are peopled as they choose. For them the hedgerow banks are embroidered with the inimitable wealth of floral beauty—the cowslip, the primrose, the bluebell, the wild orchid, the tufted crowtoe, the little blue-bird's eye, the wild strawberry, and—the emblem of storm and sadness—the simple white anemone. The power and inspiration of " design " comes best to him who in the course of a country ramble can see arrangement and suggestion in this aspect of Nature.

It will come to him who can see rhythm and poetry of form in the tangle of the honeysuckle or of the " wild rose in the hedgerow growing "; to him who can see pattern in the carpeting of the spring woods and of the meadows, or in the tufting of the lawn with snowdrop, crocus, saffron, stells, and daisy.

It will come to him who can see decorative *motif* in the birds of the air, in the animals and fruits of the earth, and " things that move in the waters."

Design comes to those who can see " ogres " in tree trunks and cherubs in children's faces, to those who can " see " a wreath in the laurel bush by his door, or a crown of thorns in the briar near by.

Many there are who, in the heat of a summer's day, may seek coolness under some spreading oak or leafy shade, but few are they who can see or do delight in the pattern of leaf and stem as set against the sky. To those who can it spells " design." Many there are who delight in looking from a bridge into the flow of a trout or salmon stream. There are those who can see pattern in the rush, the swirl, likewise elsewhere in the mighty prancing of " Neptune's horses."

" Rubbish! " some of you will say. " This is not for such as us. This is not for the journeyman plasterer. This is not possible in a trade like ours! " Oh, yes it is, plasterers—one and all; it is not rubbish; it is all very true and real. It is all very possible to any one of you. It has been the life of the " common lot " in times gone by. It is the life of some of you now, and it is for each one of you to decide for himself, *now*, whether he will have it or not. *Make no mistake about it.*

The old Italian plasterers modelled and coloured the corridor vaults and domes of the Vatican (Plate XLV) with trellis work inspired from their vineyards and pergolas of vine and rose. Are there no hop fields and rose pergolas within the reach of us for inspiration?

The ancient Chaldeans took inspiration from the heavens and all around. They made ceilings like the sky, pavements like the sea. The constellations of the planets as they moved (known as the twelve Zodiacs) they knew and watched as we do the dial of a clock; and much more inspiration than this (the outcome of their natural lives) did they work into the decorations of their domes and ceilings. The sun, the moon, and the stars they placed in emblem in their vaulted roofs, in the same order as the real luminaries in the heavens. The Egyptians often figured, with zigzag lines, the " Goddess of the Sky " stretched out across the arch of the dome. All the recurring patterns of the ancient and classical world were founded on the diaper, square or round. All their borders or friezes were formed either by tufts of flowers growing side by side, their tendrils sometimes touching, sometimes interlacing; or by scrolls wherein there was no continuous growth, but only a " masking " of the repeat by some spreading member of the pattern. But, when Gothic took the place of old Classic form, the change was marked (in pattern designing) by the universal acceptance of continuous growth as a necessity of borders and friezes, and in " square pattern work " this growth was the general rule in all the more important designs. Of this " square " continuous pattern work there are two principal forms of construction: the branch formed on a diagonal line and the net framed on variously proportioned diamonds.

These main constructions were, as time went on, varied in all sorts of ways, more or less beautiful and ingenious; and they are, of course, only bounding or leading lines, filled up in all sorts of ways. Yet sometimes the leading lines are not drawn, and we have left a sort of powdering in the devices which fill up the spaces between imaginary lines.

The principle of the continuous line and its elaboration was an invention of the later Eastern age, which, once invented, we cannot drop if we would. It must always remain a subordinate part of architecture and decoration. All borders should be made up of several members, even when narrow, or they will look bald and poor. Turning the corner of a border is sometimes not easy to do, and will test a designer's skill; but it is better turned to run on, rather than be stopped by a rosette at the corner.

It is good and reasonable to make use of flowers in all ornamental work. Those natural forms most familiar and most delightful to us from association, as well as from beauty, are good for the purpose. The rose, the lily, the tulip, the pink, the pansy, the poppy, the columbine, the snake-head, the vine, the oak, herbs, and trees all serve our purpose better than queer, strained, and uncouth forms. If we cannot be ourselves with these simple things we can do nothing with outlandish ones, although much can be done with lines and lumps and dots geometrically set.

A few words about " style " must suffice before we turn to the subject of the human figure.

If " Art " belongs to its own particular time and " nationality," it should be so especially with the art of pattern designing and modelling. We must not suppose that a new style can be built up suddenly out of the apathy and wreckage amidst which we live, without help from the Art of past ages. We must study without copying past Art if we are to create. We must study all styles having real life and growth in them. For the others a passing glance will suffice. Beyond this, we must try to do our own, as our predecessors did.

So far we have only considered and concerned ourselves with modelling decoration in clay for reproduction and repetition from moulds of plaster.

There are other forms of modelling in decorative relief perhaps more interesting, more free, and broader in principle than the making of a short piece of clay modelling for mechanical repetition by casting, at a minimum cost, although not necessarily so.

Let us take an instance where it is desired to cover a large surface all over with a flat, modelled design, say of grapes, vine leaves (Plate LXXXVIII, *b*), and stem-work (Plate LXXXIX, *b*), or roses, leaves, or any such similar growth such as shown in Plates XVII, *a* and *b*, LXXXVI, *a*, and XC, *c*. There are various and equally nice ways of doing this. Let it be done on the ceiling or wall itself. It may be as well first to sketch out the idea quite roughly on paper, laying down the lines of the main stemwork design, and afterwards indicating the branch-off stemwork, with some suggestions of the filling in and clusterings of roses, leaves, and buds, or of grapes, leaves, and tendrils, etc., etc. When the main idea is thus conceived, draw the design (first in charcoal) on the finished ceiling or wall surface, afterwards dusting out and redrawing as may be necessary, until it looks right in scale, rhythm, and filling from every point of view. When this is done, model (in clay) two or three sizes of roses, buds, leaves, or bunches of grapes, leaves, and tendrils (or whatever the *motif* may be) to the right degree of relief; mould in plaster or gelatine, and cast (in plaster of Paris) a quantity of each kind with only an edging of background. The charcoal drawing on the plaster should be finally corrected and firmly and clearly drawn in. The next thing to be done is to cut away the skimming surface of plaster down to the floating cast, wherever a leaf, flower, stem, or bunch of grapes, etc., comes, and to hack and roughen the surface to form a good key for sticking up these individual details or pieces of plaster, which may be done after brushing away all plaster dust or loose grit, and properly sprinkling the plaster groundwork with water enough to stop suction.

The next point is to gauge some plaster of Paris and lime putty and to stick up the roses, leaves, grapes, etc., etc., on to the prepared groundwork. It is advisable in doing this to support each little cast from the scaffolding with a lath or stick (padded at top) until securely set. This may be done quite quickly all over the area to be decorated, afterwards filling in the surrounding joint space, so that each cast properly belongs to the background, appears to grow out of it, and is properly bevelled and softened off all round (Plates XVI, *a* and *b*, and LXXXVII, *c*). When this is done, or whilst it is being done by an assistant, the stemwork should be roughed in. If the relief has any bulk it may be roughly cored in with ordinary lime and sand plaster, some tow or canvas, and afterwards worked over and finished with plaster of Paris retarded in its setting with size water, or any other retardant, to give time for finishing up smoothly, or it may be done with Keen's or Parian cement.

By this process a large surface may be covered beautifully, quickly, and inexpensively after some little experience. In this manner were done, in England and in Scotland particularly, some of the most beautiful plaster ceilings of the Elizabethan period (Plates XII to XX) and some very excellent modern ones (Plates LXIII and LXVIII). It is most fascinating work and not necessarily difficult to do. One point should be carefully noted : the cast leaves, flowers, grapes, etc., that are stuck up to the plaster surface, may be treated in one of two different ways : they may be attached only on to the groundwork, showing an undercut and serrated outline, and with a three-quarter round or slightly undercut stemwork, as the old lime-stucco panel backgrounds were often filled (Plate XC, *c*, Holyrood), or they may be inserted into the groundwork (without being undercut) and bevelled and well softened off all round the outline (Plate LXXXVII, *c*). For low relief work in plaster of Paris this latter is much the nicer and altogether more decorative treatment. For stronger relief work round a pronounced moulded core, either straight or circular, the fruit, flower, and leaves may be modelled and cast loose and stuck up round a rough core.

The former treatment is more excusable if the leaves and parts are cast in lime stucco, or some very hard white cement, and applied in the decoration of a high room which, perhaps, may not be too well lighted and requires greater definition of drawing and light and shade and relief. There is, in this kind of attachment, always a hesitating feeling of insecurity ; of its not being a part and parcel of the groundwork ; of its tendency to approach rather too near to the naturalistic to be pure decoration.

Another and still more interesting and artistic method of *in situ* decoration is to draw the design on the prepared plaster ceiling or wall and to model the stemwork only, as last described. To do the leaves, flowers, etc., a plaster die may be made from the clay models and pressed into shaped dabs or pats of wet plaster or Keen's cement, which have been placed (a few at a time) on the ceiling where required. Each of the several dies must be propped up from the scaffolding below with a padded stick or lath until set ; afterwards the sticks and dies may be removed and the background cleaned and made good. The leaves and roses in Plate LXXXVIII, *a*, were done in this manner. This process, if anything, gives rather a cleaner, smoother, and sharper definition to the work as a whole than the method last described, as the surface of the dies must be clean and smooth not to adhere to the cement, and the pats, before being surface veined only with the dies, shaped with a small metal tool.

In the old work occasionally we find another application of the die applied in rather a different manner, viz., pressed right into the soft finishing coat, as a wooden " pat " is pressed into butter, leaving a pressed pattern on a recessed background which is shaped roughly to its general outline (see Fig. 29).

Another and still more genuinely beautiful decorative process is to model the whole of the relief work *in situ* with metal tools. This, of course, requires more skill and experience than either of the two partially mechanical methods just explained. It needs also quickness of hand, decision, and a ready knowledge of form and design, combined with the aptitude and resourcefulness of an artist to turn accident to good account. To do this in Keen's cement, or any good " fat " white cement, gauged to retard the setting somewhat, gives a result that cannot be acquired by any other means : freedom of design, variety of detail (although this may easily be overdone), freshness, crispness of technique, rapid and " stick " workmanship, and happy labour withal. Time, of course, is absorbed by reason of the absence of mechanical repetition, but experience, knowledge of what is to be done, and smartness of manipulation soon reduce time and cost to within the reach of practical politics.

Undoubtedly the most beautiful and interesting process of all is that of modelling relief direct *in situ* with lime stucco, as explained fully in Chapter III on " Lime-Stucco Modelling," pp 51-4. All that is necessary to say here is that it is like modelling in clay direct on to the ceiling or walls, the actual modelling remaining permanently, just as it leaves the fingers or tool. This lime-stucco work, whether in low relief or otherwise, is the consummation and perfection of the plasterer's art. Often clay " modellers " exclaim : " If we could only model in clay direct on to the finished surface, and know that it would remain permanently in position just as it leaves the fingers, instead of having it spoilt by reproduction, how fine it would be, how much more encouraging, how comforting to know and to feel that one's actual work would be seen, appreciated, and valued—as an Art ! " This is what takes place with lime-stucco modelling.

It is a great thing to realise (as it may be realised by) modelling direct from the fingers in lime stucco " exactly as with clay," adding and spreading each pellet or portion by degrees until finished, with the great satisfaction of knowing that it will remain to posterity as it is.

We cannot pass on here without a few words relating to opportunities plasterers may have of doing interesting decorative modelling on the outside walls of buildings. In the old days this work was in certain districts and localities no exception, but the rule. Even quite ordinary, simple cottages whose walls were of wattle and dab, rough brick or

FIG. 29.—" Butter Pat " Ceiling Ornament.

stone, or of timber framing, were protected outwardly (and inwardly) with a covering of plaster to keep out the cold wind and wet in the bad seasons and keep the inside cool in the hot weather. This particular plaster, or " parge " as it was called, was made of lime and sand, hair, straw, and possibly stable urine, road scrapings (containing ground stone grit and horse manure), and a proportion of fresh cow dung, all thoroughly mixed and incorporated until it became tough and leathery and practically weather-proof. With this the walls were covered, and very frequently decorated, either with modelled work (Fig. 30, Plates XCII, b, and XCIV, a), combed patterns (Fig. 30, Plate XCIV, b), pricked work, or trowel point work, or geometrical panel work left by plastering the last coat round wooden templates temporarily fixed up, to leave slightly recessed or projecting shapes on the wall surfaces (Fig. 31, Plate XCIV, c).

PLATE XCII

(*a*) PLASTER DECORATION OF GABLES AT MARL HOUSE, BRENCHLEY, KENT.

(W. Twopeny *del*.)

(*b*) PARGETTING FROM HOUSE AT WYVENHOE, ESSEX.

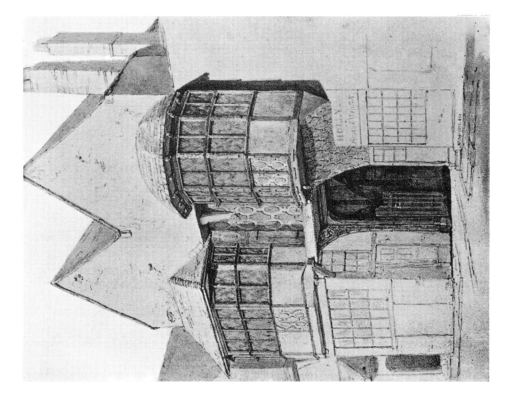

(b) Modelled Panels over Porch at the George Inn, Salisbury.

(W. Twopeny *del.*)

(a) Exterior Stucco Decoration on a House at Banbury, Oxfordshire.

Plate XCIII

PLATE XCIV

(c) PARGETTED HOUSE AT STEVENTON, BERKS.

(a) MODELLED PARGETTING, EARLS COLNE, ESSEX.

(b) COMB PATTERN IN PARGETTING, IPSWICH.

PLATE XCV

(*b*) FIGURE OF DAVID. (By Michelangelo.)

(*a*) ENLARGED HEAD OF DAVID, FROM MICHELANGELO'S STATUE.

PLATE XCVI

(*a*) ROMAN STUCCO BAS-RELIEF IN THE VILLA FARNESINA.

(*b*) A SECTION OF THE STONE FRIEZE OF THE PARTHENON. (In spite of the low relief the sculptor has shown, by use of perspective, four horsemen riding abreast.)

PLATE XCVII

(*a*) and (*b*) A SIMPLE BUT EXPRESSIVE TREATMENT OF COCKS, HENS, AND PIGEONS IN BAS-RELIEF (ASSYRIAN).

(*c*) ASSYRIAN CARVED BAS-RELIEF OF LIONS.

(*d*) A HERD OF DOES, CARVED WITH IMPRESSIVE SIMPLICITY IN BAS-RELIEF (ASSYRIAN).

Occasionally some of these sunk panels would hold a small piece of modelling (Fig. 30), such as a rosette, fleur-de-lis, geometrical patera, or simple heraldic forms ; or they would frequently be picked out in bright pale ochres or earthy colours—greens, yellows, and reds.

A sunk geometrical design in a gable (Fig. 31, Plate XCIV, *c*), a strip partly up the rake of a gable (under a barge board), between two windows, a modelled panel over an entrance porch (Plate XCII, *a*), along a projecting beam (Fig. 32), or over the whole exterior surface of a wall (Plate XCII, *b*), were all quite usual occurrences. It must not be forgotten that all this work was spontaneous and customary. It was all done in the quiet daily routine of the builder's life in those days, without the instruction and the supervision of a

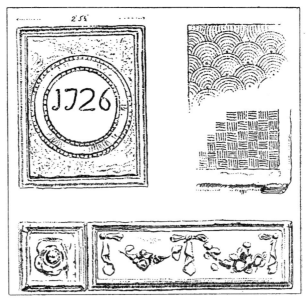

FIG. 30.—External Plaster Details (Pargetting), Herts., Essex, and Suffolk.

" professional architect." Some of the walls merely had the " rough casting " (and it was rough cast and not a wretched sand dusting in those days) scraped off in places to show a pattern or panelling ; or the ordinary parge plaster would be roughly floated on and left in quite a primitive manner, very unlike the horrid mechanical and uninteresting smoothness of modern external cement work, for which there is no excuse but apathy. All this is possible again in our own day and in our modern materials, grey or white Portland cement, even if we are too lazy to make a good parge plaster ; or it can be done in ordinary good lime and sand plaster with a gauging of Portland cement, particularly in application to the new and future system of ferro-concrete buildings.

FIG. 31.—Berkshire Pargetting.

No less important or interesting were the inside walls and chimney overmantels, quite apart from the ceilings. So may and should they be again. What can be more delightful on the wall over the hearth round which the family life is centred than simple modelled borders, forming panelled frontals, perhaps quaintly pilastered on each side, or recessed, or niched in the centre ? Others there are with merely a little moulded cornice at top, or a simple moulding enclosing (down to the ground) a broad, flat space of wall, sprigged or patterned round a central shield with monogram, motto, or date (Fig. 22, p. 65). In the larger homes armorial bearings, crests, personal devices, and such like matter were clustered together 'twixt shelf, ceiling, and pilasters.

A wall feature of such importance is open to endless variety of treatment of design, from the simple and variously inexpensive arrangements of short strips of cast enrichments (Plates LXII and LXX, *a*) to the modelling of a decorative subject panel, such as that illustrated in Plate LX, *a*. More important and extensive are the lime or marble stucco overmantels in the palaces and houses of Italy and France, as Plate C.

The design and modelling of the human figure in decoration has never until lately come much within the range of the British plasterer, although it should do so. It would be futile in a chapter of this nature to attempt anything beyond a few notes on so large a subject, which would require a volume in itself, embracing, as it does, anatomical study (a science in itself), without which knowledge any figure modelling would be superficial. The study of the human figure, whether in the round or in relief, must be structurally and anatomically correct, quite apart from the design and clothing of the figure. It is important that this should be realised from the outset. The figure is the crowning art of mankind. It combines scientific knowledge with artistic capacity of no small degree, and with both of these, literature and history. It is not a matter of inspiration

FIG. 32.—Band from Wyvenhoe, Essex.

only or even of ability to produce beautiful surface form. It is a life subject, in more senses than one, which must be rightly studied from the commencement and pursued step by step with intelligence, intentness, and good judgment before entering fields of fancy and imagination. It is a fascinating study, an Art which must be built up on a foundation of knowledge.

The course of study advocated by those artists most highly qualified to teach should begin with modelling in the round from a cast of some well-recognised masterpiece of sculpture such as Michelangelo's " David " (Plate XCV, *b* and *a*), coupled with an anatomical knowledge of bones and muscles ; mouth, nose, ear, and eye should also be studied separately and individually.

Carefully drawn or modelled studies of one's own face (by the means of a mirror) will be found helpful practice. Then should follow a careful and thorough study of a head, combined with the anatomy of the skull, the grouping of the muscles of the face, with notes on the diversity and variety of main characteristics.

To study the head well, copy a bust or two from a cast of some fine example (say by Donatello or Michelangelo), in which the anatomy is clear and the masses plainly modelled, clearly expressed, and easily understood. The greatness of those antique masterpieces is their marked decision and apparent simplicity. The contours of the modelling are in reality so delicate, refined, and subtle that to copy them may have results of great importance. For a beginner to model a head without knowledge of its anatomy would be like designing a building without knowledge of construction (see Plates XCV and CI, *c* and *d*).

Constructive knowledge of the figure is most vital to progressive work. We must understand something of Nature before we can interpret her. Personal or individual interpretation or expression in Art must not be confused with affectation or eccentricity. A clearly pronounced personality is a gift of Nature that falls to the lot of few. Affectation (or eccentricity) is deplorable ; " originality " so-called never existed, and never can be anything more than personality of interpretation, *i.e.*, experience expressing itself in its own way.

The study of the head from life may follow that from the plaster cast. If possible the guidance of a capable figure modeller or instructor should be obtained. Instruction cannot be acquired so well from printed matter, although there are very excellent practical books on the subject of figure modelling by Professor Lanteri, Mr Albert Toft, and drawings by Mr Hatton and Mr J. H. Vanderpoel. Study of the figure must proceed on gradual and methodical principles.

The study of the body must follow that of the head in a similar manner ; by the same gradual process, step by step, limb by limb, bone by bone, muscle by muscle ; the hand, the foot, the arm, the leg, the torso, and the back ; the treatment of hair ; then the figure from Nature ; posing and draping the figure, contrasts of lines and surfaces, comparative proportions, and—the skeleton.

All this, and more, must be studied in the round, preferably under the patient and sympathetic guidance of some one who is a good modeller and gifted with the art of imparting knowledge to others. Modellers of the human figure seldom excel in other branches of industrial art, such as purely decorative design and modelling of ornament. Students trained to model and design the human figure are usually so exclusively concentrated on the study of the figure that other decorative motives are almost invariably beneath their attention to a degree of contempt. This was not so with the great modellers and sculptors of the fourteenth and fifteenth centuries. Few art school or academy students have much idea of decorative art (floral ornament, animals, etc.) apart from " the figure." On the other hand, I have known students possessing a fine sense and grip of decorative art who have had this sense completely annihilated by two or three years' academy training with the human figure. Plate CI, *a* and *b*, shows the work of a modeller who ruined academic training.

The design and modelling of decoration other than the figure is simple in comparison, less complex, and quite different, although accessory to " the figure " and to architecture. The lack of this other simple decorative instinct accessory to the design and modelling of the human figure has produced much mediocre work by figure modelling. Until comparatively recent years, neither the controlling and governing spirit of architecture nor any decorative element was combined with the figure, with very few exceptions. Compare Plate CI, *a* and *b*, of the nineteenth-century academic school with Plates XCV. CI, *c* and *d*, the work of fourteenth and fifteenth century masters.

In the earlier work is combined equal delight in the figure and the decorative. To model and design the figure decoratively, in relief, is a gift of the gods, the most difficult aspect of plastic art. The slighter the relief, the greater the difficulties become.

Model the figure in relief following a good grounding in " the round." There is no cut-and-dried law for relief modelling. There are some generally accepted principles from which good relief work cannot escape.

Relief may vary from the flatness of a coin to a full round attached to a background. The degree depends on the situation it is to occupy, on the strength and character of the surroundings, on the degree of light, the direction from whence it comes, and other considerations. The object of relief work is to enrich a flat surface ; to suggest (rather than to assert) some form, decoratively, in a more or less flat manner. Unlike the superficial process of the painter, the intention is to express in material a surface design in flat relief without perspective.

The term " relief " emphasises the flat character of the work, some form standing out from a background to which it belongs and is a part of. The object is to enhance, to adorn, not to assert. It may be a surface embellishment only, or it may conceal construction; it should never be imitative of Nature, as a picture. This is not always sufficiently realised.

There is always a tendency to lose the flat press, to recess too deeply or unequally, to project too variously. There should be rather a general flatness of surface throughout, as though a mould had been dropped face downwards and the detail afterwards modelled into the flattened surface.

This flat effect of planes must be got by the addition, not by cutting away, as so often recommended. Sculptors do this, but it is not legitimate modelling, but carving. The main bulk of relief should be built up to slightly less than required, the surface detail being added; not incised, or removed with the wire tool.

Good plaster relief should not be restless or predominate. Its duty is to be reticent and subservient to architectural lines framing it.

We are dealing with modelling as especially applicable to good decorative reproduction in plaster. This is most important. Modelling is modelling, no matter what material it is to be reproduced in. There are, however, other ways of working for other purposes.

The production of sketch " models " for carving from in marble, stone, or wood is another matter, technically quite different. In this case carving and cutting away are necessary and limited according to material hardness or softness, fineness or coarseness, grain and other circumstances that control technique of carving of the figure in relief. Assume that a flat board with a framework round it has been provided, clay filled in level, and the outline of a figure design drawn carefully on this clay surface.

The first thing some modellers do is to cut down to the background, set back the planes required in medium relief, gradually getting plane behind plane.

This may perhaps be the easiest way, but it is not modelling. It is not sculpture. It is better for the modeller (who is not a sculptor) to set his planes forward instead of back, add or block in the various planes, one on top of the other, by degrees. Good results have even been obtained by dropping the relief flat on its face on the floor, if not too large.

The next thing to consider is the surface of the bulk on to which detail has to be added. When once thoroughly grasped in principle, it can be done simply and beautifully, as a worn coin, the surfaces in relief having comparatively little modelling or undulation.

As in drawing, it is best to go for a good well-drawn silhouette or outline. The modelling of surface detail is of secondary importance. This may be so slight as to be practically flat, provided that the outline or silhouette is beautiful in design, drawing, and modulation.

This is better seen, perhaps, in antique reliefs where the surface modelling is rubbed off and the outline mass has been left. The explanation of this is to be seen in the modelled and carved reliefs of Donatello, Della Robbia, Settignano (Plate CI), also in the plastic reliefs of the first half of the first century A.D. (Plates II, IV, XCVI, a, and XCIX). The necessity for proficient drawing is apparent at a glance.

The beauty and delicate form of surface modelling are useless if the light and shade and relief of silhouette are not right.

Nor is relief drawing confined to outline. Surface detail claims careful and subtle drawing and modelling, so slight, sometimes, as to be hardly noticeable, excepting in a certain light. Hence the advisability of modelling work in the lighting it would have when placed in position. It is well to see the work under various lights, coming back in the end to the lighting it will have in its final and permanent position.

PLATE XCVIII

(b) Stucco Figure Modelled in Low Relief from Villa Farnesina (Roman).

(a) A Sacred Group in Coloured Faience, by Luca della Robbia, the Arch Enriched by Figured Panels of Various Fruits and Flowers.

PLATE XCIX

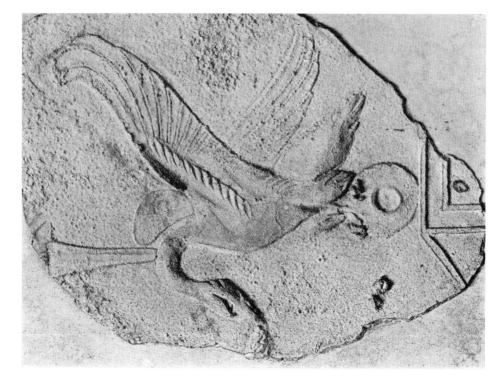

STUCCO FIGURES MODELLED IN LOW RELIEF AND ADAPTED TO A GENERAL DESIGN FOR A FRIEZE, FROM VILLA FARNESINA (ROMAN).

PLATE C

Two Modelled Stucco Chimney-pieces, Palace of Fontainebleau.

PLATE CI

(c) A FIGURE IN LOW RELIEF BY DONATELLO, in which detail is almost entirely eliminated to give full effect to the classic precision of outline.

(a) and (b) TWO EXAMPLES OF VICTORIAN SCULPTURE FROM THE GREAT EXHIBITION, 1851. The somewhat "fussy" detail and exaggerated sentimentality of the poses disguise a feeble and over-emphasised design.

(d) A PLAQUE IN LOW RELIEF BY LUCA DELLA ROBBIA, showing a sensitive treatment of detail subordinated to a finely-balanced ensemble.

Whether the relief be slight or full the principle is the same, viz., to arrive at a harmonious arrangement of form and grouping of light and shade.

The relief may be so subtle in parts as to have little or no difference of surface. Unless the silhouette be pleasing and beautifully set up first, no surface detail, however beautifully modelled, can redeem it.

Low relief modelling, especially that of the figure, requires great concentration of attention throughout to the end. It is unlike modelling in the round when, should the attention tire in one part, the model may be turned round and another part worked on. In low relief work every part requires undivided thought, attention, care, and concentration.

Of relief work generally, let the student study for himself the extremely decorative, beautiful, and yet simple Assyrian relief carvings (Plate XCVII), the Roman stucco models of the early first century (Plates II, IV, XCVI, *a*, XCIX), and the bas-relief carvings from the Parthenon frieze (Plate XCVI, *b*)—all in the British Museum, London. These are all that relief work ever can be. Particular attention should be given to the wonderful and superb quality of drawing throughout, but it must be noted that they are sculpture and not modelled work. Although the same in principle, they are different in method.

Little need be said here with reference to modelling the figure in high relief (*alto relievo*), or in the round. Both are beyond the sphere of the plasterer, although practised to perfection by the Italians of the fifteenth and sixteenth centuries (Plate XCV). Such a treatise would require a volume in itself, and years of study. This is one of the most difficult and formidable arts a man can set his hand and heart to.

Such a treatise profusely illustrated by photographs and diagrams has been given in three volumes of inestimable value by Professor Lanteri, of the Royal College of Art, South Kensington.

All serious students with ambitions beyond the sphere of the decorative art of the plasterer should possess these volumes, for no better, no clearer, or more progressive treatise on modelling has ever been given for the guidance of students. Another valuable but less detailed book on the subject has been written by Mr Albert Toft. In these volumes all that can be said has been said explicitly and perfectly.

CHAPTER VI

TOOLS AND APPLIANCES

Plasterers' Tools, Appliances, and Plant—Labourers' Tools—Scaffolding—The Worshipful Company of Plasterers—The Plasterers' Craft.

THERE is an old saying, that " a good workman is known by his tools "; and another, that " a bad workman always complains of his tools." Whichever may be the more correct does not much matter. What does very much matter is that a good workman should have a good " kit " and know how to take care of it. A thorough knowledge of tools can be had only by long practice in the workshop and on the scaffolding.

A man may have hundreds of tools and be neither an artist nor a good mechanic. On the other hand, he may have few tools and be both. The wisdom of the first saying is revealed more in the way the tools are used and kept than in their number, whereas a " duffer " can do little or nothing with the best and most ample kit in the world.

Among the plasterers' relics found by Dr Flinders Petrie at Kahun, in Egypt, were two hand-floats, now at University College, London. One is $3\frac{3}{4}$ in. long and $1\frac{7}{8}$ in. wide, rounded at both ends, and slightly convex on the sole. The handle is the length of the sole, as our modern panel-floats, and the whole float is cut in the solid. The other is longer and has evidently been used for the rough coat. The sole projects beyond the handle, more at one end than at the other, somewhat like our modern skimming hand-floats. This is also cut out of a solid block. Both were smeared with mud plaster as their owner had left them; they are the oldest known plaster tools in the world, and were used for plastering B.C. 2500.

Fig. 33 illustrates plasterers' tools, plant, and appliances : A is the stand, B the gauge board, and C the platform, nailed on the bottom rail of the stand; No. 1 is a laying trowel with a double " shank "; 2, laying trowel with a single " shank "; 3, panel trowel; 4, margin trowel; 5, gauging trowel; 6, small gauging trowel; 7, large gauging trowel; 8, a hawk; 9, ordinary hand-float; 10, cross-grained hand-float; 11, skimming-float; 12, joint rule with stock; 13, small joint rule with stock; 14, small joint rule without stock; 15, moulding knife; 16, plaster chisel; 17, level; 18, chalk-line and reel; 19, fine drag; 20, coarse drag; 21, scratch drag; 22, bradawl; 23, tool brush; 24, large tool brush; 25, duster; 26, flat, wide stock brush; 27, four-tufted stock brush; 28, hand-float for cement work; 29, panel-float; 30, fining-float with round end; 31, fining-float with splayed end; 32, water pot; 33, plaster plane; 34, lath hammer; 35, fine hand sieve; 36, gauge pot; 37, mitre box; 38, square; 39, compasses; 40, plumb rule and bob; 41 and 41a, scratches; 42, combined square, triangle, and level; 43, broom; 44, pail; 45, tool bag; 46, water measure; 47, tool box; 48, darby; 49, plaster box stand; 50, plaster box; 51, angle-float; 52, concrete rule; 53, gauge rule; 54, nippers; 55, traversing rule; 56, feather-edge rule; 57, saw; 58, splash brush.

Plate CII reproduces the photograph of a set of plasterers' tools of rather different composition. It is interesting to compare the varying forms, which in the photograph are of more recent make. Plate CIII, *b*, gives a series of American types from a toolmaker's catalogue.

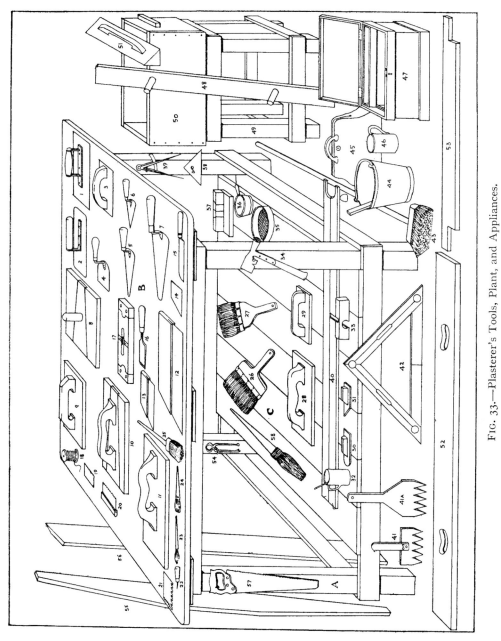

FIG. 33.—Plasterer's Tools, Plant, and Appliances.

Banker.—A banker is used for gauging large quantities of material, the gauging being done with shovels. They were in general use when hawk boys did all the gauging for plasterers. Bankers are made about 5 ft. long and 4 ft. wide, with boards 6 in. high on two sides and on end.

Brushes.—Good brushes are formed with hog bristles nailed or bound on wood handles with string, copper wire, or metal bands. Cheap brushes are formed with grass fibre, etc. The principal brush is the stock brush, which varies slightly in size and form. In some districts a brush having three or four tufts tied with string or wire is used; in other districts a flat, wide brush bound with leather and nailed is preferred. Tool or sash brushes are used for mitring, stopping, and general shopwork. Fibrous brushes are generally home made. The hair is about 4 in. long, and tied on to a handle about 6 in. long, $1\frac{1}{2}$ in. wide, and $\frac{1}{2}$ in. thick. After the string is tied it is saturated with hot glue. A hot iron is afterwards passed over the glue to bind the hair together. Employers usually supply stock brushes (for whitewashing only) and all shop brushes; the men find stock brushes and tool and water brushes for building work.

Brooms are made of split whalebone or metal wires, and are used for keying plaster-work, sweeping scaffolds, paving works, etc. They are supplied by the employers.

Calipers are compasses with curved legs suitable for measuring the inside and outside diameter of bodies. Hardwood calipers are made with a movable centre, so that proportions may be enlarged and reduced. Large calipers and compasses for workshop use are usually supplied by employers.

Compass.—An instrument consisting of two movable legs for describing arcs or circles, etc.

Chalk-line.—A long fine cord, on a reel, for setting out and striking long lines on a flat surface.

Cradle.—A wood frame made to a desired concave curve and lathed and plastered. It is used as a ground in forming, running, or moulding circular work. If the curve is convex, the frame is called a " saddle."

Drags are tools with toothed edges, usually made of thin steel plate of various sizes and forms, for dragging surfaces straight or smooth, rough, and keyed for another coat of material. A piece of an old tenon-saw blade, about 6 in. long, makes a handy drag. A scratch drag is for keying the back of castwork before the material is set. A useful size is 4 in. long and 2 in. wide. The teeth are made about $\frac{1}{4}$ in. wide, $\frac{1}{4}$ in. deep, and $\frac{1}{4}$ in. apart. A smaller set of teeth are made on the ends for scratching narrow parts. The teeth should be undercut to give a good key.

Files and rasps of steel are used for finishing running mould plates and for cleaning up plaster and carton-pierre. Coarse rasps are used for fining concrete work. Employers usually supply files and rasps.

Floats and rules for spreading plaster on walls and ceilings vary in size and form, and should be made of well-seasoned pine, free from knots.

Angle-float from 2 to 3 ft. long, 3 to 4 in. wide on each face, formerly used in making internal angles true and square, but is now, unfortunately, obsolete.

Concrete floating rule, similar to a parallel rule, about 1 in. thick, 6 in. wide, and of various lengths, with two hand holes to give power to the worker when floating concrete, which is mostly done by beating with the edge of the floating rule.

Darby (48, Fig. 33).—A blade or sole, 3 ft. 6 in. to 4 ft. long, 4 to 5 in. wide, $\frac{1}{2}$ to $\frac{3}{4}$ in. thick, with two handles, each about 5 in. long and 2 in. in diameter, nailed or screwed on the back of the blade at about one-fourth of the length from each end. The darby is used for floating bays between screeds on walls and ceilings, and in some instances for floating setting stuff to a fair surface, before hand-floating and trowelling. In Scotland it is called a " slack-float." Darbies are generally supplied by employers.

Feather-edge (56).—A wood rule, generally about 5 ft. long, 5 in. wide, and 1 in. thick, with one end cut to an angle of 45°, and one side splayed to an edge about $\frac{1}{16}$ in. thick, used for working and cleaning out angles, etc.

PLATE CII

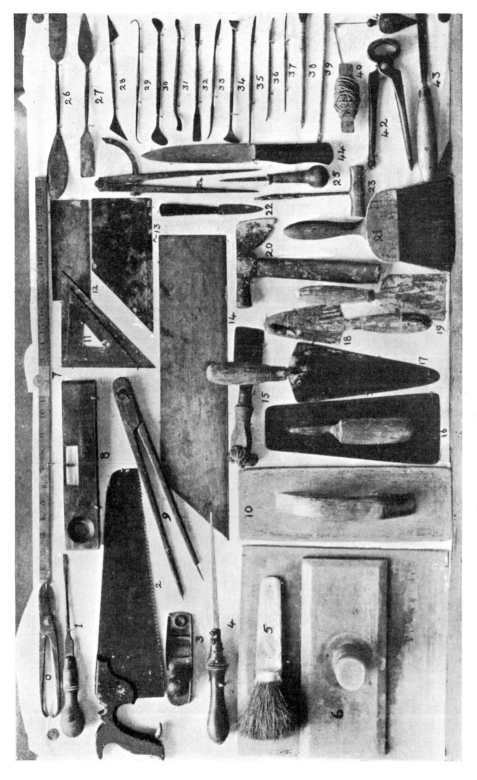

PHOTOGRAPH OF TYPICAL PLASTERER'S TOOLS.

o. Scissors for cutting zinc.
1   Screwdriver.
2. Saw.
3. View from above of small plaster
    plane.
4. Saw.
5. Splashbrush.
6. Hawk.

7.   Two-foot folding rule.
8.   Spirit level.
9.   Large wood pencil compasses.
10. Wood hand-float.
11. Two metal set-squares.
12 ⎫
13. ⎬ Set of joint rules.
14. ⎭

15. Chisel.
16. Metal hand-float.
17. Large gauging trowel
18. Gauging trowel.
19. Margin trowel.
20. Lath hammer.
21. Dusting brush.
22. Moulding knife.

23. Gimlet.
24. Steel dividers.
25. Bradawl.
26-39. Set of small steel plasterer's tools.
40. ⎫ Plumb bob and line.
41. ⎭
42. Pincers.
43. Chisel.
44. Trimming knife.

PLATE CIII

(a) PHOTOGRAPH OF A SET OF MODELLER'S TOOLS.

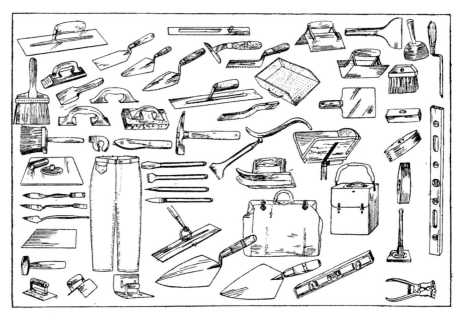

(b) TYPICAL CURRENT AMERICAN TOOLS.   (The Goldblatt Tool Co., Kansas City.)

Floating Rules (55, Fig. 33).—For floating screeds and ruling off and forming fair surfaces between screeds and flanking in bays ; vary from 8 to 20 ft. in length, 4 to 7 in. in width, and 1½ to 2½ in. in thickness. The back edge is tapered towards the ends, to decrease the weight, give a counterpoise at the middle, and thus more power to the worker.

Gauge rules (53) are straight-edges with sinking at one or both ends. A double gauge rule has a sinking at each end and is used for forming sunk surfaces. A single gauge rule has a sinking at one end and is used for forming raised surfaces, such as the plinth of a skirting.

Grooved Rule.—Considerable physical strength is required when working a long floating rule. In some positions it is difficult to hold, and apt to slip out of the hands or cramp the fingers. To prevent these evils, a rule made like a floating rule, but having a groove on each side about 2 in. wide, ½ in. deep, and 1 in. from the back edge is useful. To give grip, power, and freedom when working, and decrease the weight of the rule, the size and position of the grooves vary according to the size of the rule and the requirements of the worker. Two holes, each about 1 in. in diameter in the sides, prevent warping, and are handy for hanging it up by. The plan and section of a grooved rule is shown in illustration Fig. 58, p. 162.

Parallel rules of various sizes are used for levelling and for setting out parallel lines. A useful size is 9 ft. long, 6 in. wide, and 1 in. thick.

Levelling Rule.—A long parallel rule with a wood fillet, on which a level is placed for guidance when levelling ceilings, etc.

Plumb Rule.—A rule with parallel edges, a centre line and an opening at one end to allow the lead-bob to work. It is used to " try " and adjust uprights.

Running rules (in Scotland " rods ") are made in long lengths, about 2½ in. wide, ½ in. thick (planed on all sides and edges), as guides or bearings for running moulds, for fences, and many purposes for scaffold and shopwork.

Straight-edge.—A long rule with a straight edge, used for testing the flatness of surfaces.

Screed rules are generally 2½ in. wide, 1 in. thick, and in long lengths as screeds for laying concrete, or for giving a square edge or thickness to plasterwork.

Thickness rules are similar to screed rules, for a given thickness.

Traversing Rule.—A floating rule about 6 ft. long for forming screeds of gauged putty or setting stuff, for running mouldings on, known as a *justing rule* in Scotland and a *sweeting rule* in the North of England. Employers find all floats and rules.

Hand-floats are many and various. Panel and mastic floats are made of hard wood. All other kinds are made of yellow pine. None are so suitable to the worker as those made by himself. The float most generally used is a hand-float, about 10½ in. long, 4½ in. wide, and ¾ in. thick.

Cross-grained float is about 11 in. long, 4½ in. wide, and 1 in. thick. The sole is cut with the grain crossways, that the sides may cut the work freely and last longer. On the upper surface a dovetailed groove is cut, measuring ¼ in. deep, 2 in. wide at one end, and tapering to 1¾ in. wide at the other. A hardwood bar is made to fit the groove, and on the bar the handle is fixed with screws. The bar strengthens and prevents the sole from warping. Cross-grained floats are used for scouring the setting coat of good three-coat work and for making angles square and clean. Float soles soon wear thin, and it is desirable to keep a few in stock that they may get well seasoned.

Skimming-float, from 12 to 14 in. long, 4½ in. wide, and ½ in. thick, is used for laying setting stuff and cements.

Panel-float, used for laying and smoothing gauged stuff in panels, also for mastic ; is made of beech, pear tree, or other hard, light-coloured wood, which will not stain the white plastic material.   The soles are about 6 in. long, 3 in. wide, and $\frac{1}{2}$ in. thick; the top edges are splayed.

Fining-floats, varying from 3 to 6 in. long, from 1 to 3 in. wide, and from $\frac{1}{8}$ to $\frac{1}{4}$ in. thick, are used for fining Portland cement mitres, cornices, panels, etc., and where larger floats cannot be used.   Workmen provide their own wood hand-floats.

Iron-floats (usually cast in one piece) are used for ramming and beating concrete.

Gauge.—A wood measure cut to a given length, for setting out equidistant spaces and marks accurately and expeditiously.

Gauge boards and stances are grounds for gauging plastic materials on. Composed of boards generally about 3 ft. 6 in. long, 3 ft. 3 in. wide, and $\frac{3}{4}$ in. thick. Two cleats are nailed across the back.   A diagonal cleat fixed between them prevents the board from warping.   Stances, to support the boards, are made with four legs, each about 2 ft. 6 in. high, a top rail fixed on all sides flush with the leg tops, and another rail about 6 in. from the bottom.   The lower rail should be boarded over as a platform (as shown at C on Fig. 33) for tools, etc., not in use.

Gauging boards for concrete (about 9 ft. square and 1 in. thick) are made in two halves, to be easily moved; strong cross cleats project about 6 in. on one side of each half, to fit together and keep the halves in position.   The halves are sometimes held together with hinges.

Gouges and chisels, similar to those of wood-carvers, are used for carving, cutting, and cleaning up plaster, cement, and carton-pierre, etc., but their use should be extremely limited and not allowed to infringe in any way upon the province of the modeller.   As explained elsewhere, plaster was intended by Nature to be modelled or cast, and not to be carved.

Groovers (of various lengths), made of beech or other tough wood, are used for forming grooves in concrete surfaces.   A useful size is 2 ft. 6 in. long by 4 in. wide by 1 in. thick; one edge is splayed on both sides into a flat V shape.

Rollers, for indenting concrete surfaces (for a good foothold), are made of brass, with a series of projecting pins.   The usual size is about 8 in. long and 4 in. in diameter.

Jointers are small rollers, about 2 in. long, plain or corrugated, for indenting the marginal edges of concrete slabs; one side of the roller has a rim about $\frac{1}{8}$ in. projection for indenting a line.

The above three tools are employers' plant.

Hammers.—A plasterer's hammer (34) has a steel head, one end having a hatchet blade (with a slot for extracting nails) and the other (the driving end) a hammer head indented to prevent slipping.   A wood handle is fixed into the shoulder of the head. It is used for lathing and general scaffold work. *A mounter's hammer,* for driving French nails and needle points when mounting composition, carton-pierre, etc., is similar to an upholsterer's hammer. *A hammer with a flat round head* and a short handle is used for piece moulding. *Knapping hammers,* as used for breaking stones, are employed for breaking foundation materials for concrete.   Knapping hammers are supplied by employers; lathing, mounting, and moulding hammers by the workmen.

Hawk (8, Fig. 33).—The board on which plaster is held, usually of pine, is about 11 to 12 in. square, $\frac{5}{8}$ in. thick, splayed at the back about 4 in. wide, to leave the edges about $\frac{3}{8}$ in. thick.   A dovetailed groove (about $\frac{3}{8}$ in. deep by $3\frac{1}{2}$ in. wide, diminishing to about $\frac{1}{4}$ in.) is made in the centre of the board, across the grain of the wood, and a bar to fit the groove.   Though usually made of pine, beech or other hard woods give greater strength.   The handle, of pine, about 5 in. long by $1\frac{1}{2}$ in. in diameter, is sometimes turned, with a slight swell in the centre, and a knob at the end is fixed on the bar with one thick screw, so that it may be taken off at pleasure.   If fixed permanently with three fine screws (the heads flush with the bar), the bar and handle can be withdrawn in one piece and will serve for three or four boards. A clumsy way is to fix board, bar, and handle in one piece, by two or three nails through the boards into the bar and handle. There is a " hinged hawk," grooved as first described, cut with a fine saw down the centre of groove and hinged about 1 in. from the ends flush with the surface of the groove, to keep the halves together. The bar and handle slide into the groove and keep the hawk rigid. A leather or rubber collar on the bar will protect the joints of the forefinger and thumb from damp and friction. American hawks are from 12 to 14 in. square, sometimes of sheet iron with a wood handle. Hawks should be light, strong, and damp-proof, for holding stuff and for gauging small portions of stuff, provided by the workman.

Hod.—The hod varies in size and form, according to locality. The London hod is the smallest, the American the largest, the Scotch the " happy medium " in size. The London hod box is about 16 in. long, the sides 9 in. deep, and will hold about two-thirds of a cubic foot of mortar, or about forty hods to the cubic yard. The American hod box is about 2 ft. 4 in. long, the sides 1 ft. deep. The Scotch hod box is about 1 ft. 10 in. long, the sides 11 in. deep. The shank, 3 ft. 3 in. to 3 ft. 9 in. long, is fixed a little in front of the centre of the box with a flat round block behind it and an angle stay in front. A hod of this size will hold 1 cub. ft. of mortar weighing 110 lbs. ; the weight of the hod (8 to 14 lbs.) added, the labourer carries over 1 cwt. in each load of coarse stuff. One cubic foot of coarse stuff (allowed to this size of hod) equals twenty-seven hods to the cubic yard. Hods are labourers' tools, sometimes provided by employers.

Joint rules, made of hard wood such as pear tree and boxwood, were used for mitring before steel plates were introduced. For long mitres, joint rules of pitch pine, feathered on one side, one end cut to an angle of 75°, and seasoned with linseed oil, work clean and smooth. Joint rules are now made of sheet steel in various lengths, 3 to 4 in. wide and about ⅛ in. thick ; one end is cut to an angle of about 30° ; the acute angle and one side is splayed about one-third of the width of the rule, leaving a moderately sharp, straight edge. Scotch joint rules have a thinner plate, let in (about 1½ in.) to a hard wood, mahogany or oak, " stock," about 3 in. wide by ⅜ in. thick, fixed by two or more rivets. This wood backing or "stock" stiffens the plate, is more agreeable to the touch, and less liable to cramp the fingers than a thin, cold, steel joint rule.

Knives.—*Building knife* blades are about 6 in. long ; *trimming knives* from 4 to 7 in. long. *A small knife* about 3 in. long, ground on both edges to a sharp point, is useful for trimming the curves and eyelets of small perforated ornaments. *A canvas knife* is thin and broad, with a square end, similar to a cobbler's knife. *Moulding knives* are from 9 to 15 in. long. *Composition knives* are about 18 in. long, with a handle at each end.

Larry (or **Drag**).—A three or four pronged rake, with a handle from 6 to 9 ft. long, for mixing hair with coarse stuff and knocking it up for use. *A rake,* similar to the larry, has a plain blade instead of the prongs, and is used for making setting stuff, etc.

Level.—A spirit level, the companion of the square and compass, is, as its name implies, for laying levels and proving horizontals.

Mitring tools (Fig. 34A), or *small tools* of various sizes and shapes, of wrought iron or steel, are used for mitring, moulding, cleaning out, stopping and modelling ornaments. They vary in length from 7 to 11 in. The principal one has a leaf or spoon-shaped blade at one end and an oblong rectangular blade at the other. The barrels should be octagonal in section and thick at the centre. A round barrel is apt to turn or slip ; a small one to cramp the fingers. 1, a small tool with a square end and a leaf end, is used for mitring and stopping ; 2, a small spade tool with one end square and the other a trowel or spade-shaped, is useful for laying and pressing gauged stuff on the back of the cast and for many purposes; 3 is a large mitring tool with a leaf end and a square end; 4, another mitring tool with a pointed leaf end and a round leaf end, for mitring, bedding, and cleaning out; 5, a double square-ended small tool with one blade 1¼ in. wide, 2 in. long, and the other ¾ in. wide by 1¾ in. long, is useful for laying and finishing narrow spaces, cleaning out when fixing blocks, and for work where the margin trowel is too large. Bone tools, hollowed to fit different sized beads, were once used for beads when mitring. A few tools with the blade end straight and the other curved, having the edges serrated, are useful for working circular work, or where the plaster is full. They are commonly called " scratch tools."

Scratch Tools.—Fig. 34B shows various scratch tools: 1 is one of many gouge tools, for carving mitres and cleaning up; 2 is a double-ended scratch tool, curved for working down mitres and circular work; useful for cleaning up and for modelling cement or plaster *in situ*; 3, 4, and 5 are scratch tools useful for circular mitres and other work; 6 is a stopping tool with a leaf end and a spear end, one edge of which is serrated and the other plain; useful for many purposes.

Pails, of galvanised sheet iron, to hold about 4 gals., are usual. Wood pails, to hold 3 gals., are used in some districts. Putty pails have an extra handle on the sides. Employers provide pails.

Pinchers or **nippers** of steel for extracting nails, twisting wire, etc., are provided by workmen.

Radius Rod.—A wood or metal rod for running circular mouldings. A running mould is fixed at one end of the rod and a hole made in, or a metal plate fixed on, the other end to fit a centre pivot. In Scotland it is known as a *gig-stick* and in some districts as a *trainer*.

Planes, for levelling down and smoothing plaster surfaces, should have toothed blades.

Saws, about 18 in. long, are used for cutting running rules, mouldings, etc. A fine-toothed saw is best for fibrous plaster. Employers provide saws for shop work only.

Scaffolds are temporary erections of timber and boards to work from and place materials and tools on. In Scotland, plasterers erect their own scaffolds. For ordinary sized rooms the uprights, called " slipheads," have a slot at the top to receive the needle or transom. The scaffold has battens 7 in. wide by 2½ in. thick, placed about 7 in. apart. In England, regular scaffolders are employed. The transoms are tied on poles with cords; the scaffold is clad with boards 9 in. wide by 1½ in. thick, laid close together.

Scratch.—An implement generally of pine, about 14 in. long, 7 in. wide, and ½ in. thick, with teeth about 3 in. long, the points about 1¼ in. apart. A simple and effective scratch may be made by fixing four laths together and tapering the points. Good and durable scratches may be made of thin metal plates, or strong wires inserted into a wood handle. Employers supply scratches.

Screen.—An upright sieve about 6 ft. long by 3 ft. wide, with sides 6 in. deep. It is fixed at an angle of about 45° for screening lime and sand which are dashed against the wires; the finer parts pass through, leaving the coarser parts on the inside. Screens being " plant," are supplied by employers.

Plaster small tools, similar to mitring tools, are useful for shop work. A few extra shapes are required for cleaning up originals. Brass small tools are useful for cleaning up plaster, and are generally made by the user out of brass rod about ¼ in. thick, cut a little longer than the length of tool, to allow for cutting off ends, which generally split while being beaten out flat. File the ends to the desired shape. The barrel is filed to octagonal form to prevent them from turning in the fingers. Waxed string wrapped round the barrel will give a soft, easy hold. Fig. 34C shows a set of small tools for working plaster. They are made largely in Paris, and extensively used for general shop work.

Sieves or **riddles** of varying size and fineness are used for running and riddling lime and washing sand. A *riddle rest* is used in some districts to carry the weight of the riddle and lime. It is rapidly moved backwards and forwards by one man, while another fills it. As the lime forms into heaps, they move back a little, until finished. *Putty sieves* have a fine wire or hair mesh on a wooden frame with two handles. *Punching sieves* (used in some districts for making setting stuff) have a wooden frame about 2 ft. square by 7 in. deep, on which a strong, fine steel wire mesh is fixed. A wooden punch (like a large hand-float for both hands) is used to punch the putty and sand through the mesh into a tub, on which the sieve is placed.

Squares (set squares), of wood or iron, of various size, are useful, particularly one about 1 ft. each way. Being triangular in form, the 45° angle is useful for mitre joints. They are sometimes made with a level or small plumb-bob attachment, or with both, and are useful in forming small works plumb and level. One about 6 in. is useful for return mitres, etc. *Wood squares*, about 3 ft., are required for large work on ceilings, bench, and other work. Employers provide large squares ; plasterers provide their own small ones.

Templates (circular running rules and screeds) are cut out of pine boards to the desired curve. *Plaster templates* are used for running clay profiles, etc.

Tool Box.—Usually about 18 in. long, 14 in. wide, and 12 in. deep (inside measurements). A movable tray 5 in. wide by 2½ in. deep, placed on runners inside the box, is useful for holding small tools. The box is usually carried by a strap fixed to the handles. " American cloth " bags are useful for keeping tools. In some districts tools are simply tied up in an apron.

Trowels, of various shapes and sizes, have each their own particular use. Tyzack, of London, is a noted maker of plasterers' tools, his trowels being in general use throughout the United Kingdom.

Laying Trowel.—The most important of its kind. A constantly used tool for the plasterer, about 10½ in. long and 5 in. wide. The plate is made of the best steel, light and flexible. The " shank " is riveted on to the plate with three (sometimes four) rivets. Some trowels have two shanks (without tangs), one at each end, made with a flat round head with a countersunk hole, to receive screws or a long rivet.

Polishing Trowel.—A half-worn laying trowel. The edges should always be straight and parallel, or nearly so. Parallel edges work truer than tapered edges.

Margin Trowel.—Is used for laying and polishing margins, styles, or spaces where a larger implement could not be employed, similar to a gauging trowel, but the edges of the blade are parallel and the end cut square. The blade is about 3½ in. long by 2½ in. wide. The handle is shorter than that of a gauging trowel.

Angle Trowel.—A novel tool for finishing internal angles ; is similar to a margin trowel, but has the two side edges of the blade 1 in. deep, turned up at right angles to the blade, perfectly square, and the points of the turned up sides cut back at an angle of 45°

Panel Trowel.—Used for setting small panels ; is similar to a laying trowel, but the blade is thin and springy, and is about 5 in. long, 3 in. broad. The handle is slightly shorter than that of a laying trowel, for easy working in small and deep panels. A good panel trowel can be made out of an old laying trowel.

Gauging Trowel.—For gauging small portions of stuff on a gauge board or hawk, and for laying stuff on mouldings, mitres, etc. The most useful blade is about 6 in. long by 3 in. wide at the heel or handle end, tapering to a narrow point at the other end. The shank and blade are sometimes made separately and riveted together ;

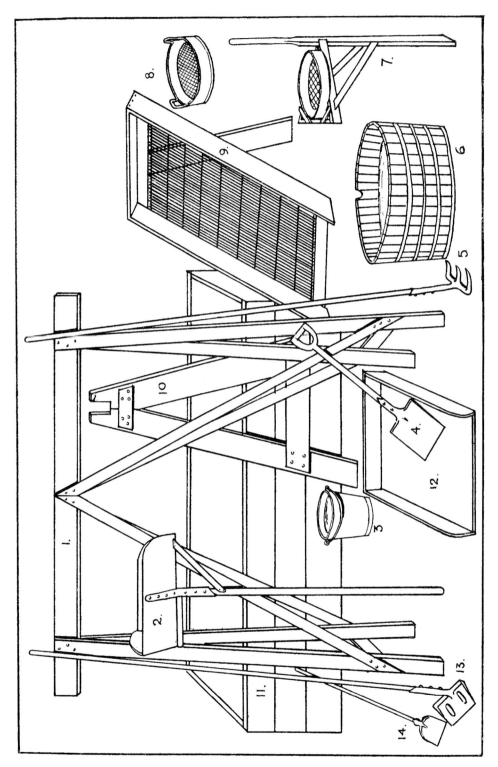

FIG. 34.—Plasterers' Plant, Labourers' Tools, and Scaffolding.

more often than not they are forged in one piece. The wooden handle is bored to receive the tang of the shank, and partly filled with powdered resin and plaster. The tang is made hot and pushed in; the heat, melting the resin, forms with the plaster a strong cement, securing the tang and handle.

Laying Gauging Trowel.—Similar to, but much larger than, the ordinary gauging trowel; is used for laying gauged stuff on large mouldings and for bedding large plantings. The blade is from 7 to 9 in. long by from 3 to 3½ in. wide at the heel end, tapering from 1½ to 2 in. wide at the point. The *small gauging trowel*, generally an old one which has been worn small, and ground to a sharp point, is used for stopping small holes, scraping and cleaning rules, etc. *The handles of gauging trowels*, now generally made of ash, with deep brass ferrules, were formerly made of mahogany or ebony.

Tubs.—Vary in size (according to requirements). For holding water, washing sand, slaking lime, etc. An old spirit cask cut in half makes two good tubs.

Plate CIII illustrates a set of wire and boxwood modelling tools, caliper compasses, syringe, and sponge.

Plasterers' Plant, Labourers' Tools, and Scaffolding.—The annexed illustration (Fig. 34) shows plasterers' plant and labourers' tools: 1. Scaffold trestle, also used as a hod-stand, as shown. 2. The hod. 3. Putty pail. 4. Shovel. 5. Larry for coarse stuff. 6. Water tub. 7. Riddle rest. 8. Putty sieve. 9. Sand screen. 10. Sliphead. 11. Putty slack box. 12. Banker. 13. Putty rake. 14. Hawk boy's server. This latter tool is now obsolete, and is only given as a relic of the past. (See description in Chapter XIX, p. 321.)

Cleaning Plasterers' Small Tools.—Plasterers usually clean their small tools with a piece of wood dipped into setting stuff or brick dust. This brightens but wears them more than working with them, scratches the surface and spoils the edges. They should be cleaned daily when in use by wiping them thoroughly dry. *Rust destroys them.* If dried when done with, they will *keep clean and smooth*. Some plasterers make their own small tools out of old files or fencing foils. A deep black polish can be given to all small tools as follows: Boil 1 part of sulphur in 10 parts of oil of turpentine; this produces a brown sulphurous oil. Warm the tools, brush the hot solution slightly over them, and heat over a spirit lamp or slow fire until black polished. Tools thus polished should not be scrubbed, but wiped clean and dry after use.

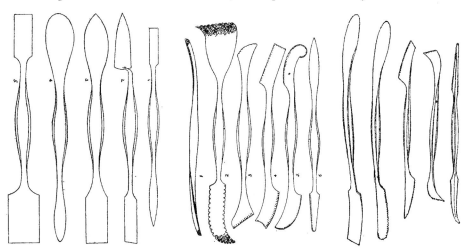

FIG. 34A.—Mitring Tools.   FIG. 34B.—Scratch Tools.   FIG. 34C.—Small Working Tools.

CHAPTER VII

MATERIALS

PLASTER OF PARIS: Manufacture, Boiled Plaster, Baked Plaster, Quick and Slow-setting Plaster, Tests, Chemical Properties, Setting Qualities, Colour, Compressive and Adhesive Strength of French Plaster—LIMES: Hydraulic, Lias, Chalk Limes, Rich versus Short Limes, Scotch Limes, Irish Limes, Calcination, Slaking and Tests—MORTAR: Grinding Coarse Stuff, Lime Putty, Protection of Lime Putty, Setting Stuff, Haired Putty Setting, Lime Water—HAIR: Ox Hair, Fibrous and Sawdust Substitutes for Hair—SAND: Pit, River, and Sea Sands—MASTIC: Scotch and London Mastics, Mastic Mouldings, Hamelein's Mastic, Mastic Cement—Stearate of Lime—" Pytho " Plaster.

Plaster of Paris.—Gypsum, from which plaster of Paris is made, is a sulphate of lime, and is so named from two Greek words—*ge*, the earth; and *epsun*, to concoct, *i.e.*, concocted in the earth. In Italy it is known by the name of gesso; in Scotland it is called stucco; in America it is known as calcined plaster; and in the English trade as plaster. The term "plaster" will be used herewith. The writings of Theophrastus and other Greek authors prove that the use of plaster was known to them. A stone, called by Theophrastus gypsos, chiefly obtained from Syria, was used by the ancients for converting into plaster. Gypsum is mentioned by Pliny as having been used by the ancient artists, and Strabo states that the walls of Tyre were set in gypsum. The Greeks distinguished two kinds—the pulverulent and the compact. The latter was obtained in lumps, which were burnt in furnaces and then reduced to plaster, which was used for buildings and making casts.

Gypsum is found in most countries—Italy, Switzerland, France, Sicily, the United States, and some of the South American States, also in Newfoundland and Canada. The latter is said to have the finest deposits in the world. It is found in this country in the counties of Derbyshire, Cheshire, Nottinghamshire, Cumberland, and Westmorland. The finest gypsum is called " alabaster," and is soft, pure in colour, and fragile. This white, translucent material is a compact mass of crystalline grains, and is used for making small statuary, vases, and other ornaments. Gypsum is found in immense quantities in the tertiary strata of Montmartre, near Paris. This gypsum usually contains 10 per cent. of carbonate of calcium, not always in intimate union with the sulphate, but interspersed in grains. This sulphate gives the Paris plaster some of its most useful properties. Pantin, near Paris, has large beds of gypsum, one bed being horizontal and over 37 ft. thick.

The term " plaster of Paris " was mainly applied to it because gypsum is found in large quantities in the tertiary deposits of the Paris basin. Another reason is that lime and hair mortar is seldom used in Paris for plasterwork, plaster of Paris being used for most kinds of internal and external work. Plaster is known in the colour trade as *terra alba*. Plaster of Paris was known in England by the same name as early as the beginning of the thirteenth century. The gypsum, in blocks, was brought from France, and burnt and ground here. It continued to be burnt and ground by

96

the users until the middle of the present century. The burning was done in small ovens and the grinding in a mill, sometimes worked by horse-power or more often by hand.

Plaster is the most vigorous, as it is the oldest, vehicle for carrying down generation after generation the masterpieces of art with which the golden age enriched the human race. For reproductive uses, plaster enables youth to contemplate antiquity in its noblest achievements. To-day plaster is revolutionising industrial art for us, and in all probability for those who are to come after us. Plaster, lowly and cheap, but docile and durable, is the connecting agent with this greatest of men's endorsement in the past. Plaster thus employed in duplicating works of marble, pottery, and metal work is to-day extending the finest industries, modern and ancient. Plaster in some climates has great lasting properties. The Egyptians covered their granite sometimes, and sandstone always, with a thin coating of " stucco." The Greeks coated even their marble temples with stucco, and these portions are now in better preservation than the unprotected masonry, particularly at Agrigentum in Sicily.

The fire-resisting properties of plaster of Paris have long been known and utilised. It does not lose its cohesive power when raised to white heat and then drenched with water ; but when highly heated for a considerable time it is not always to be trusted under the action of water, which washes away the calcined matter.[1] Its strength and fire-resistant properties are greatly augmented by metallic wires or other stiffening substances being embedded in it, as in the case of some of the patent plaster slabs now on the market.

Manufacture.—The gypsum is got by blasting and by crowbars and picks. The only preparation which it undergoes before calcining consists in chipping and cleaning the outer portions if earthy, which would give the plaster a bad colour. The finest and whitest gypsum is selected for fine plaster, the darker and coarser being used for coarse plaster. There are two processes for manufacturing plaster in this country, viz., " boiling " and " baking."

Boiled Plaster.—By the boiled process the gypsum, after being quarried, is broken by means of a pulveriser and then carried by an elevator into a hopper, from which it is conducted down again by a spout to a pair of millstones, the feed being regulated by means of a small spindle attached to the cross-bar of the stones, which, in revolving, are made to agitate the spout and cause the gypsum to fall in a regular stream between the stones. After grinding, the gypsum is again elevated into hoppers, which supply a large open pan or boiler to a depth of about 3 in. The pan has large flues underneath it, heated by a furnace at one end. The gypsum is kept in agitation on this boiler by means of a pair of rakes attached to a spindle, which revolves by machinery. After it has been on the boiler for about an hour and a half, the powder becomes agitated by the heat, and small volcanic-like eruptions take place through the water of hydration being driven off. At the expiration of about three hours, the powdered gypsum becomes more dense and sand-like, lying heavy on the scrapers or rakes. This is termed by the makers as " just caught," and an experienced plaster boilerman knows by the way the powder hangs when it is ready. As soon as the latter is complete, a slide which forms one of the side plates of the boiler is drawn, and the plaster is thrown off by the circular motion of the scraper. It is then left to cool, and afterwards bagged up for commerce.

The waste of gypsum in evaporation and dust, which takes place in the process of boiling, is about 25 per cent. Boiled plaster is fine in texture, works very freely, and when set is not liable to warp. It is also generally more reliable than baked, from the fact

[1] In his report on the great Baltimore fire, Mr Edward Atkinson states that plaster of Paris, used in blocks or otherwise, utterly failed under the high and long-continued heat.

that each molecule is properly treated and the material alike throughout. If the powdered gypsum is left too long on the boiler it will burn, and will not set for a considerable time, if at all. It will also be very " chalky," and if not boiled enough it will be weak, so that the greatest care and experience is necessary in the boiling.

Baked Plaster.—For the baked process, several methods of heating the gypsum are adopted. A flat kiln or oven, so constructed that the fuel is never in contact with the stone, is generally used. The kiln is raised to a low red heat, when the firing is discontinued and the kiln charged with lumps of gypsum. The heat is then gradually increased. After about sixteen hours the gypsum has lost its water of hydration, and after grinding becomes plaster. The kiln is sometimes worked continuously and is heated by flues carried round the kiln. When this method is adopted it is necessary to observe that the temperature does not rise too high, and that the plaster is drawn as soon as the water has been evaporated. Great experience is required in this process (which is simply one of dehydration), for although, when the temperature is kept within proper limits, the plaster possesses the power of reabsorbing water with avidity, this power is diminished if the gypsum be overheated. When subjected to a red heat, the gypsum increases in density, and if this temperature be continued it gradually assumes the character of natural anhydrite, which has totally different properties to those of plaster. It is safer not to drive off the whole of the water rather than to risk exposing the gypsum to too high a temperature, as the retention of a small portion of moisture does not prevent the plaster from reabsorbing the water that has been driven off. The time required for burning depends greatly upon the quantity and hardness of the stone in the kiln. It is considered to be sufficiently baked when the plaster is of an oily nature and adheres to the workman's fingers.

Quick and Slow Setting Plaster.—M. Landrin, in giving the results of his long-continued studies relative to the different qualities of gypsum, states that the more or less rapid setting of plaster is due to the mode in which it is burned. Its properties are very different when prepared in lumps or in powder. The former, when mixed in its own weight of water, sets in five minutes, while the latter under similar conditions takes fifteen minutes. The reason probably is that plaster in powder is more uniformly burned than when it is in lumps, which tends to prove the fact that, when the latter is exposed longer than usual to the action of heat, it sets more slowly. Gypsum prepared at a high temperature loses more and more of its affinity for water, retaining, however, its property of absorbing its water of crystallisation. Plaster heated to redness and mixed in the ordinary manner will no longer set ; but if, instead of applying a large quantity of water, the smallest possible portion is used (say one-third of its weight), it will set in ten or twelve hours and become extremely hard. To prepare good plaster, it should not be burned too quickly to drive off its moisture and for its molecules to lose a part of their affinity for the water. If plaster is exposed to heat until it has only lost 7 or 8 per cent. of its moisture it is useless, as it sets almost immediately. If, however, the burning is again resumed, the substance soon loses its moisture, and if then exposed to the air it very rapidly retakes its water of crystallisation, and absorption continues more slowly. It then sets slowly, but attains great hardness.

Testing.—The quality of plaster may be tested by simply squeezing it with the hand. If it coheres slightly and keeps in position after the hand has been gently opened, it is good ; but should it fall to pieces immediately, it has been injured by damp. Although plaster does not chemically combine with more than one-fourth of its weight of water, yet it is capable of forming a much larger quantity into a solid mass, the particles of plaster being converted into a network of crystals, mechanically enclosing the remainder of the water. Sulphate of lime (plaster of Paris) is soluble in water to the extent of about 1 part in about 450, the solubility being but little influenced by temperature. It is on account of this solubility in water that cements which have to a large extent plaster for their basis are incapable, in this raw state, of bearing exposure to the weather. The setting of plaster is due to hydration, or its having but little water to take up to resume a state of consolidation. Plaster is used with hydraulic limes to stop the slaking and convert the lime into cement. These are then called " Selenitic."

Setting Qualities.—In 100 parts of gypsum there are 46 of acid, 32 of lime, and 22 of water. Good plaster should not begin to set too soon, and it should remain for a considerable time in a creamy state. When once set it should be very hard. Plaster should set slowly to give time for manipulation, but principally because one which sets quickly and swells never becomes so hard as the slow-setting material.

Colour of Plaster of Paris.—The quality of plaster cannot be determined by its colour, that being regulated by the gypsum ; but, all things being equal, the whitest and hardest generally yields the best plaster. But as the exception proves the rule, it may be mentioned that the Cumberland plasters (such as Howe's) are of a delicate pink tint, of a very fine grain, and exceedingly strong when gauged. This pink plaster is much appreciated by many plasterers for making originals, as owing to its fineness and density it is very suitable for cleaning or chasing up models taken from the clay and also for durable moulding pieces. One of the whitest plasters in England, which is also very close in texture, is that manufactured by Cafferata. For cast work the colour of plaster is of small moment, because the cast work is sooner or later covered with paint and, moreover, unfortunately daubed over with distemper, or, worse still, with whitewash. Coarse plasters are darker in colour than fine. Coarse plasters of a sandy nature, which rapidly sink to the bottom when put in water, contain too much silica, or improperly burnt gypsum, or are derived from a bastard gypsum, and are generally of a weak nature.

Compressive and Adhesive Strength.—The compressive resistance of properly baked plaster is about 120 lbs. to the square inch when gauged with neat water, and 160 lbs. when gauged with lime water ; thus showing that lime water hardens and improves the affinity of plaster. The adherence of plaster to itself is greater than to stone or brick. The adhesion to iron is from 24 to 37 lbs. the square inch.

French Plaster.—A considerable quantity of French plaster was formerly used in London, but owing to the English plaster being now more uniform in quality and cheaper in price, the use of the French material is somewhat limited. A considerable quantity of gypsum is imported to Bristol from France. The stone is manufactured at Bristol and has all the superior qualities of French plaster. This is known as " Bristol plaster." Benvenuto Cellini preferred the French plaster to that of Italy, his own country. In Paris various kinds of gypsum mortars are in general use, raw gypsum and other materials being often intermixed. They also contain free carbonate of lime, according to the degree of heat to which the raw stone has been subjected. The Hôtel de Plâtres, in Paris, affords a good illustration of the constructive uses to which plaster can be put, some of the blocks being about a hundred years old.

Limes.—Lime is one of the most important materials in the building trades. Limestone is the general term by which all rocks are roughly classified which have carbonate of lime for their basis. They are obtained from many geological formations, varying in quality and chemical properties. The carboniferous consists of nearly pure carbonate of lime. In the limestone of the lias, carbonate of lime is associated with silica and alumina (common clay) in proportions varying from 10 to 20 per cent. The best kinds are obtained from Aberthaw, Rugby, Barrow-on-Soar, and other districts in England ; Arden, Fifeshire, and other places in Scotland ; and Calp and Larne in Ireland. Carbonate of lime is found in a state of chemical purity in rhombohedral crystals as Iceland spar. It is also found in six-sided prisms, known to mineralogists as arragonite. Its purest form as a rock is that of white marble. Coloured marbles contain iron, manganese, etc.

The lias strata consist of a thin layer of hard limestone separated by another of a more argillaceous character, or shale, containing various proportions of carbonate of lime. The lias districts extend from Lyme Regis to the north-east of Yorkshire ; the limestone in the counties of Warwick, Dorset, and Leicester. In the chalk districts of Kent and Surrey there is in the upper chalk a soft kind of comparatively pure carbonate of lime, and in the grey chalk lying below it there is a carbonate of lime of a harder description, having a small proportion of argillaceous matter.

Hydraulic Limes.—Hydraulic limes are those which have the property of setting under water or in damp places, where they increase in hardness and insolubility. The blue lias lime formation is that from which hydraulic lime is principally obtained in England, and it is found over a wide area—at Aberthaw and at Rugby, where it is also manufactured into Portland cement. This lime, while it has excellent hydraulic properties, can hardly be classed as a cement. The stones which produce these limes contain carbonate of lime, clay, and carbonate of magnesia. The clay plays an important part in giving hydraulicity to the lime, consequently this power is greater in proportion to the amount of clay contained in the lime. The proportion of clay varies from 10 to 30 per cent. Lime containing clay is not so easily slaked as pure lime, does not expand so much in doing so, and therefore shrinks less in setting.

Lias lime (called " blue lias," from the colour of the stone from which it is produced) varies much in quality and is generally of a feeble nature, but is sometimes of a hydraulic nature. M. Vicat divides them into three classes—feebly hydraulic, ordinary hydraulic, and eminently hydraulic. " Those belonging to the first class contain from 5 to 12 per cent. of clay. The slaking action is accompanied by cracking and heat. They also expand considerably, and greatly resemble the fat limes during this process. They are generally of a buff colour." Those of the second class contain from 15 to 20 per cent. of clay. " They slake very sluggishly in an hour or so without much cracking or heat, and expand very little. They set firmly in a week. The eminently hydraulic limes contain from 20 to 30 per cent. of clay, are very difficult to slake, and only do so after a long time. Very frequently they do not slake at all, being reduced to a powder by grinding. They set firmly in a few hours and are very hard in a month."

A natural hydraulic lime, known as " Arden lime," is found in the West of Scotland. This lime is obtained from what appears to be a sedimentary limestone formed by being deposited from water which held it in solution. It is very fine grained and contains few fossils, and scarcely the trace of a shell is to be seen, except at the top and bottoms of the four divisions, in all from 9 to 12 ft. thick. When first worked, the stone was slaked in hot kilns, but now this is effected by grinding. According to the " M'Ara " process, the " lime shells " from the kiln are ground in the same way as the clinker of Portland cement. Beginning with a stone breaker, the lime passes to a pair of chilled crushing rollers, and finally to the millstones, after which the powder is carried by screw conveyor and elevator to a rotary screen, 12 ft. by 4 ft., covered with wire-cloth, which retains and returns to the millstones any residue in excess of the required fineness. Sifting is a very important factor in the process, as it is scarcely possible to have the millstones so perfect that they will not pass a few particles.

The residue of imperfectly ground lime will doubtless slake when mixed with water, but at long or uncertain periods. Fine grinding is therefore a necessity. The setting properties are not fully and safely developed unless the whole is finely pulverised. With regard to fine grinding, the expense to the manufacturer is increased in proportion to the fineness, so much so that to reduce the lime down to a residue of 15 per cent. instead of 35 per cent. will quite double the cost of grinding. Against this, however, a reliable natural cement is obtained. On the other hand, if coarsely ground, the covering capacity and subsequent strength of the mortar or concrete is very much less. This hydraulic lime, tested on the same lines as for Portland cement, has a tensile strength per square inch at seven days of from 80 lbs. to 100 lbs. ; at one month from 150 lbs. to 200 lbs. ; at six months from 350 lbs. to 400 lbs. ; and at three years from 600 lbs. to 700 lbs.

The setting and hardening are mainly due to crystallisation, caused by the action of water on the silicate of lime, as shown hereafter.

The following is a chemical analysis of hydraulic limes :—

TABLE I.—ANALYSIS OF HYDRAULIC LIMES

	Lime.	Silica.	Alumina.	Oxide of Iron.	Magnesia.	Water, Carbonic Acid, etc.	Authority.
Aberthaw blue lias	78.45	9.35	6.25	Trace	...	5.70	H. Faija, 1885.
Barnstone	59.61	20.61	6.98	4.01	2.25	6.54	J. B. Dyer, F.C.S.
Warmsworth Cliff (Yorks.) magnesian	58.4	0.50	...	1.4	38.6	1.1	F. Hudson.

Chalk lime is a term used principally in London for fat lime. Fat lime is produced from limestone, which is nearly pure carbonate of lime. It is also known as " pure lime " and " rich lime." As it has little setting power and is easily dissolved in water, it is unfit for any purpose requiring strength or in situations exposed to the weather.

Rich versus Short Limes.—The general practice is for lime producers to show their lime as rich as possible by analysis. Users prefer a rich lime, as it makes a more plastic and better working mortar with the usual quantity of sand. It has been shown by experiments, many and varied, and extending over a long period, by the most eminent authorities, French, German, and English—the most prominent among them being Smeaton—that this preference should be exactly reversed, and that the poorer common limes make the best mortar, and, in a comparatively short time, show some slight setting power, whereas the very rich limes never " take band," only in so far that they return to their original condition of carbonate by the reabsorption of carbonic acid from the atmosphere and by the slow evaporation of the added water. If that does not evaporate, the mortar remains soft. If the water evaporates too quickly, the mortar goes to powder, a result noticeable by every one who has seen the removal of old buildings and the clouds of dust caused thereby.

Some of the stone from which fat lime is produced contains a proportion of sand, which is an impurity, therefore yielding an inferior substance. This, though cheaper, is less economical than pure lime, as it increases its volume less when slaked. Pure or fat lime should only be used for solid plastering, as it is easily slaked, and therefore less liable to blister than most hydraulic limes. It expands to double its bulk when slaked, and may be left and reworked time after time without detriment.

Scotch limes, the Hurlet and Campsie series, have reputations handed down for generations. The analysis of the lime of the Hurlet and Campsie Alum Company gives the following proportions : Carbonate of lime, 91.40 ; carbonate of magnesia, 3.40 ; carbonate of iron, 2.07 ; bisulphide of iron, .41 ; alumina, .60 ; silica, 1.00 ; phosphoric acid, .10 ; coaly matter, .80 ; water, .10.

Irish lime, used in the West of Scotland for finishing work, is slaked by immersion. The Romans are said to have prepared their limes thus. "Lime putty," slaked by immersion for a longer or shorter period than three weeks before being used, should be laid on very thinly, and produces a hard surface skin. This is largely due to the thinness of the floating coat, absorbing carbonic acid from the air. This skin should become harder than the undercoat of plaster.

This process of preparing lime and laying it in thin coats, with considerable time between the coatings, is conducive to hardness throughout.

Calcination.—"Lime-burning" is done in various ways. Whether done in the simplest way, or in kilns, on scientific principles, quality and quantity much depend upon the experience of the kilnsman. Only by constant observation is the man capable of judging when the proper temperature has been reached. A correct opinion can only thus be formed of the effects set up by any disturbing causes influencing the working of a kiln, viz., its size, shape, quality of fuel, and atmospheric conditions. Kilns vary much in different districts ; they are usually inverted cones or ellipsoids, into which layers of limestone and fuel are alternately thrown. When worked continuously as "running" kilns, the lime is periodically withdrawn from below, fresh quantities of fuel and stone being supplied at the top. Improperly calcined or "dead burnt" lime will not slake with water. This may be due to insufficient burning, when the limestone has only been changed into a basic carbonate, *i.e.*, two parts of lime and one of carbonic acid, one half only of its carbonic acid having been expelled. The basic carbonate, on the addition of water, instead of forming a hydrate of lime and being converted into a fine and impalpable powder, attended with the production of a large amount of heat, is changed with little elevation of temperature into a mixture of hydrate and carbonate. In the case of hydraulic limes containing considerable silica, "dead burning" may be due to subjecting the limestone to a too high temperature, producing a partial fusion of the silicate of lime formed, thus choking the inner pores of the stone and retarding the further evolution of carbonic acid. Eminently hydraulic limes require careful calcining at the lowest temperature practicable ; hence lias lime has been imperfectly calcined. Pure limes subjected to excessive temperature show less tendency to combine with water. Caustic lime unites with water with energy, evolving very considerable heat. Water poured on well-burnt lime generates heat rapidly, the lime hissing and crackling, the mass quickly becoming "slaked" lime.

Slaking.—Slaked lime is chemically hydrate of lime, CaH_2O_2, or lime chemically combined with a definite quantity of water. In "slaking," 28 lbs. of lime combine with 9 lbs. of water (a proportion of nearly three to one) to form 37 lbs. of solid hydrate of lime. The water thus loses its liquid condition, and heat is developed during the slaking. In England burnt lime, before slaking, is known as "lump lime," and in Scotland "shells."

Slaking is most important in making coarse stuff and lime putty. Unless carefully and thoroughly done, the material resulting is liable to blister or "blow." Blisters may not show until a considerable time has elapsed. There are three methods of slaking "lump lime"—by immersion, by sprinkling with water, and by absorbing moisture from the atmosphere. Rich limes may be slaked by immersion and kept plastic, gaining strength under cover or water. The Roman laws forbade the use of lime unless kept for three years. Rich limes may be slaked with water sufficient to reduce it to a thick paste. Lump lime should be broken small, placed in layers about 6 in. thick, and uniformly sprinkled with water by means of a large watering-can. It should be quickly covered with sand or graded quite twenty-four hours before being turned over and riddled. The sand retains the heat and enables slaking throughout the mass. Unslaked lumps may be transferred to the next heap for slaking. The quantity of water must be properly regulated. Over-watering would produce useless paste. Insufficient water would produce a dangerous powder lime. Slaking is frequently done very imperfectly, portions of the lime slaking long after use. Special care and sufficient time must therefore be allowed for slaking.

Limes require variable proportions of water; the average is about a gallon and a half to every bushel of lime. No water should be added or the mass disturbed after slaking has begun. In most parts of England lime for coarse stuff is generally slaked by immersion and run into a pit, the sides of which are usually of boards, brick, or sand, the lime being put into a large tub containing water. When slaked, the lime is poured from a pail through a coarse sieve. It is sometimes made into a large oblong box, having a grating at one end to run off the lime and prevent the sediment from passing through.

In preparing lime for plasterwork, the general custom in the North of England is to slake it for three weeks before use, a particularly cool lime being selected, or blistering will deface the work when finished. While all this precaution is taken for plastering, the lime is slaked and made up at once, and it is frequently used within a day or two for mortar. But this is not all. Limes unsuitable for plasterwork, " hot limes," which plasterers are sometimes obliged to use, must be slaked for not only three weeks, but months before use, and then are not safe from blistering, and are mostly used for building purposes. In the South of Europe it is the custom to slake lime a season before it is to be used.

Mortar.—This is a term used for various admixtures of lime or cement, with or without sand. For plasterwork it is usually composed of slaked lime, mixed with sand and hair, and is termed " coarse stuff," and sometimes " lime and hair," also " lime." In Scotland the " coarse stuff " is generally obtained by slaking the lump lime (locally termed " shells ") with a combination of water sprinkling and absorption. The lime is placed in a ring of sand, in the proportion of 1 of lime to 3 of sand, and water is then thrown on in sufficient quantities to slake the greater portion. The whole is then covered up with the sand and allowed to stand for a day; then turned over and allowed to stand for another day; afterwards it is put through a riddle to free it from lumps and allowed to stand for six weeks (sometimes more) to further slake by absorption. It is next " soured "—that is, mixed with hair ready for use. Sometimes, when soured, the stuff is made up in a large heap and worked up again as required for use. This method makes a sound, reliable mortar. In some parts lime slaked as above is mixed with an equal part of run lime. The latter method makes the coarse stuff " fatter," and works more freely. All slaked limes have a greater affinity for water than the mechanically ground limes.

Grinding is beneficial in making mortar with any kind of limestone. It thoroughly mixes the materials, increases adhesion, adds density, and prevents blistering. Where there is a mortar mill, either ground or lump lime can be used, and coarse stuff may be made in the proportion of 1 part lime and 3 parts sand. The lime should be thoroughly reduced and incorporated, and should not be ground for more than thirty minutes.

When grinding lime in a mortar mill, sand may be dispensed with, excellent results being obtained by substituting old broken bricks (if clean and well burnt), stone chippings, furnace cinders free from coal, or slag. The materials used must be perfectly clean. A thorough incorporation of all materials is most essential in slaking and mixing for coarse stuff, whether by hand or machine. The sand or other material used should be tested by washing in a basin of clean water and sifting through a fine sieve. If there is an undue residue of clay, fine dust, or mud in the water or sieve, the whole of the aggregate should be washed or rejected. Lias lime should be mixed dry with sand and damped down for seven or ten days, to ensure slaking. It should not be used fresh for floating or rendering. Pure or rich limes are not so well adapted as hydraulic limes for outside work, or for exposed or damp places. Mortar should be well tempered before using. The ancient practice of beating the mortar for a long time just before use was not only to ensure a thorough mixture of materials, but to consolidate the mass by thoroughly incorporating in it any compound of lime and silica. Well-beaten mortar sets sooner and becomes harder than that otherwise made. Hydraulic lime mortar should be mixed rapidly, thoroughly incorporated and freshly used, otherwise the setting properties deteriorate.

Pure limes may be rendered hydraulic by mixing with calcareous clays or shales, altered by heat so that the silica contained to some extent becomes soluble. In good coarse stuff each granule of sand is coated over with the lime paste so as to fill the interstices ; the lime paste is to hold the granular substances in a concrete form. If too much lime paste is present it is called " too fat " ; if the lime paste is insufficient it is " too lean " or " poor." The quality may be tested with a trowel ; the " fat " will cling to the trowel, while the " lean " will run off like wet sand. The coarse stuff may be tested by making briquettes and slowly drying ; if good, it will stand great pressure ; if bad, it will not ; in some cases it will fall to pieces. Some coarse stuff will appear " fat " on the trowel, but it may be the fatness of mud, not the fatness of lime, as the sand may be adulterated with fine screened earth. When made into briquettes and dried, it will easily break and crush ; or, if put into water until soft, the earthy matter will show. Fine screened dry earth is not objectionable, but wet dirt or mud should be rejected. Lime increases in strength by the addition of sand ; Portland cement is weakened by it. Of four samples of mortar mixed with 4, 6, 8, and 10 parts of clean-washed sand to 1 part of ground lime respectively, all set hard. When placed in water, that having 4 parts of sand expanded and went to pieces ; those with 6, 8, and 10 parts of sand remained whole, and hardened. A small proportion of brick dust added to mortar will harden and prevent its disintegration. Good proportions are 1 part of brick dust, 2 parts of sand, and 1 part of lime ; mix dry and temper as usual.

Hydralime is hydrated lime in its best form. It is in the form of a dry powder, made by scientifically treating quicklime with sufficient water to satisfy its chemical affinity. It is produced from lime made from chalk and is supplied in two forms, viz., grey for mortar, white for plastering.

Hydralime for Plastering.—Hydralime white is hydrated lime made from white chalk lime. It is a bone-dry white powder entirely free from any impurities.

When mixed with water a plastic paste or putty is formed, which can be used at once. It therefore saves the tedious, old-fashioned task of " running " that is necessary with lump lime, which has to be " run " and kept for some weeks to ensure perfect slaking.

By dispensing with the task of " running " lime, time and space are saved. The latter consideration is important. It is sometimes inconvenient to find space for a " putty-lime bin " necessary for slaking lump lime for plastering.

Being scientifically hydrated, there is no possibility of " pitting " or " blistering," and there is no waste.

Delivery.—Hydralime is loaded in sacks containing 84 lbs. net each = 2.27 bushels = 2.265 cub. ft.

It can be stored in the same way as cement, and it will keep for an indefinite period under ordinary conditions.

It can be mixed as required. *The best results are obtained by mixing overnight for use the next day.*

For Plastering

For rendering—

Hydralime	1 part by volume.
Sand -	4 parts ,,

For finishing—

Hydralime	1 part by volume.
Fine sand	1 to 1½ parts by volume.

If more rapid setting is required, hydralime may be gauged with Portland cement or plaster as follows :—

For rendering—

Hydralime	2 parts.
Sand - -	8 ,,
Portland cement - -	1 part.

For finishing—

Hydralime	2 parts.
Sand -	3 ,,
Cement or plaster -	1 part.

Lime Putty.—Lime putty is prepared as run lime for coarse stuff, put through a finer sieve into a box or pit. In the latter case the interior should be plastered with coarse stuff to prevent leakage and keep the putty clean. The best lump lime should be used, and the putty allowed to stand at *least three months* before use. Lump lime for coarse stuff, putty, and setting stuff is often run into one pit. The putty at the end farthest from the sieve being the finest, is retained for putty and setting stuff, and the remainder for coarse stuff. Putty left for months unprotected during the progress of the building, absorbs carbonic acid gas, becomes carbonated, and loses some of its causticity or binding and hardening properties.

Protection of Lime Putty.—It may be kept indefinitely without injury if protected from the atmosphere, and should be protected from the air.

Old Roman limes were kept in covered pits. If a small portion is taken at the top it will be found dry, scaly, short, and inert ; that in the middle, up to the carbonated stuff, will be oily and tenacious. That farthest from the sieve is the finest and best for mitring.

Setting Stuff.—Setting stuff is lime putty and fine, sharp, well-washed sand. The proportions of sand and lime vary with the kind of lime and work, the average being 3 parts of sand to 1 of putty. Various proportions are given for different works. Setting stuff is used for finishing off lime plastering. The putty is usually mixed with a larry on a platform of scaffold boards, or in a bin, the sand being first washed through a sieve of the desired mesh. In some districts, setting stuff is made by pressing the putty and sand through a " punching sieve " into a tub. Setting stuff is less liable to shrink and crack by allowing the stuff to stand and partially harden after mixing ; then, by knocking up, it reduces the risk of shrinkage and cracking with (preferably lime) water and a shovel and larry. During evaporation it should be covered up and protected from dust and atmospheric influence, and used as soon as " knocked up." Setting stuff may be tinted by mixing with various ingredients. (See " Setting and Coloured Stuccos," p. 99.)

Haired Putty Setting.—Haired putty was used considerably for setting where lime was strong or hydraulic, the composition being fine lime putty and well-beaten white hair, thoroughly mixed to toughen and prevent cracking. So much hair was added in some instances that the setting coat, when broken, appeared like white felt. This is now seldom used. A prominent plasterer of Shrewsbury, who occasionally used this material during alterations at Cound Hall, erected about a century ago, stripped from the floating a piece of haired putty setting about 4 ft. by 2 ft. and ¼ in. thick, which he rolled up like felt, with but little injury. This shows the toughness and flexibility of haired putty setting, also the lack of tenacity, for it to strip thus. This is probably due to slight knowledge of the nature of the material and its manipulation, or to a common evil, viz., the unkeying of the floating, and laying the setting coat on a dry, absorptive surface. Haired putty setting is usually inseparable from the floating and very adhesive.

Lime Water.—Lime water, used as a wash, will harden plaster casts, as also the surface of setting stuff, when scouring and trowelling same.

Hair.—Hair is used as a binding medium, to give cohesion and tenacity. It should be ox hair, but is sometimes adulterated with the short hair of horses. Good hair should be long, strong, and free from grease and impurities, obtained dry in bags or bundles. It should be well beaten with two laths, to break up any lumps and separate the hair. This must be thoroughly done, or the hair will have no binding power and cause soft, weak spots in the plaster when laid. Many failures are due to this cause. Human hair is sometimes used for jerry work. Goats' hair is often chosen in America. In Scotland, hair is obtained direct from the tanners' yard, fresh and wet. This is much the best, is stronger, and mixes freely. Never mix hair with hot lime, and not with mortar, until nearly ready for use. Wet or hot lime weakens hair, especially if dry. Coarse stuff on lath work needs more hair than on brick or stone. For stuff made in a mill, add the hair last thing. Excessive grinding injures it.

Fibrous Substitutes for Hair.—Hair substitutes have been experimented with, conclusive tests being made with plaster briquettes or plates, containing respectively manilla hemp, sisal hemp, jute, and best goats' hair. The ends of the plates were supported, and weights suspended from the middle. That mixed with goats' hair broke at 144½ lbs. weight, the jute at 145 lbs., the sisal at 150, and the manilla at 195. In the latter case the hemp cracked rather than broke, and though cracked in the centre, the lower half, suspended, held to the upper half by the manilla. In the other instances the two parts of each plate severed entirely. In another experiment with two barrelfuls of mortar, each of equal portions of sharp sand and lime, one barrel was mixed with a measure of manilla hemp and the other of best goats' hair, with the usual quantity of water, and stored in barrels in a dry cellar. On examination nine months later, the hair mortar crumbled and broke, little hair being visible, the bulk having been consumed by the lime; the mortar containing hemp showed great cohesion, requiring effort to pull it apart, the hemp fibre showing little evidence of injury by lime.

Sawdust Substitutes for Hair.—Although sawdust has been and is still sometimes used in plaster and mortar, *it cannot at all be regarded as a legitimate or proper plastic ingredient, and should be avoided.* Sawdust as a substitute for hair, for sand in mortar for wall plastering, makes a cheap additional aggregate for coarse stuff. Sawdust mortar for external plastering stands rough weather and frost. The sawdust should be used dry. It can be used with plaster for both run and cast work, and is useful for the breaks of heavy cornices. It is strong and light for handling. Some sawdust requires soaking or washing, and it is apt to stain the plaster. There have been patents in America of sawdust plasters. One was equal parts of lime and plaster and sawdust. Another, $4\frac{1}{2}$ parts slaked lime, $4\frac{1}{2}$ parts sawdust, 1 of plaster, $\frac{1}{4}$ of glue, and $\frac{1}{18}$ of glycerine, with a little hair. Kahl's patent plaster is 35 per cent. sawdust, 35 per cent. sand, 10 per cent. plaster, 10 per cent. glue, and 10 per cent. whiting.

Sand.—Sand is the siliceous particles of rocks containing quartz, produced by the action of rain, wind, wave, and frost, and may be classified as calcareous, argillaceous, and metallic. It varies in colour according to the metallic oxides contained. Quality is of prime importance. Its function is to induce uniform shrinkage during setting, hardening, or drying. Irregular shrinkage causes cracking. Sand is also a factor in solidity, hardness, and cheapness. There are three kinds—pit, river, and sea sand, containing impurities such as loam, clay, earth, and salts, which necessitate washing, especially for finishing coats. Pit sand is sometimes clean, sharp, and angular. River sand is fine grained, less sharp than pit sand, but good for setting stuff. Sea sand varies in sharpness and size, and should be washed free from salt particles. Sand is necessary to give body and hardness to an otherwise too soft and plastic material. The coarser, sharper, and cleaner, the better. Coarse particles allow carbonic acid to penetrate into and harden mortar. In the case of cement, sand only lessens the aggregate cost, and in the majority of sands strength is reduced out of all proportion to saving. Brunel, in making the Thames Tunnel, was so convinced of this that he used pure Portland cement in the arches. General Pasley recommends pure cement only for arduous work.

Nature and Quality of Sand.—Sand varies so much in quality that 1 part of an inferior or clayey sand may reduce the strength of mortar as much as would 3 or 4 parts of clean, sharp, granitic sand. This is well proved in the test made with "standard sand," a pure siliceous sand sifted through a mesh of 400 holes per sq. in., and retained on one of 900.

For lime plaster sand should be hard, sharp, gritty, and free from organic matter. For coarse stuff and cement floating it should not be too fine. Good sand rubbed between the hands will not soil them. Salt in sand and water does not impair the strength of mortar, but effloresces in white, frothy blotches on plaster surfaces, and the mortar is liable to retain moisture.

Fine grained sand is best for hydraulic lime, coarse grained for fat limes. Sand, like the aggregate for concrete, should vary in size and form. *For coarse stuff*, fine and coarse sand are best, for lime will receive more sand in that way without losing plasticity, and make a harder and stronger material. With plenty of fine and a scarcity of coarse sand, the mixture should be 1 of coarse to 2 of fine. With plenty of coarse and a scarcity of fine sand, 1 of fine to 2 of coarse, the proportion of sand varying with the kind and quality of lime or cement, and the purpose, and is given under various headings. Barytes is sometimes substituted for sand. *Silver sand* is used for *Portland cement* work of light colour and fine texture. Silver sand is chiefly obtainable from Leighton Buzzard. Arnold's silver sand is extensively used in London for cement work and sgraffito.

Mastic.—Mastic was formerly used where Portland cement is now employed. It is still used in Scotland and the North of England for pointing the joints between window frames and walling. Mastic is waterproof, heat-resisting, and adherent to stone, brick, metal, and glass.

Scotch mastic is composed of 14 parts of white or yellow sandstone, 3 parts of whiting, and 1 part of litharge, mixed on a hot plate to expel moisture, and sifted to exclude coarse particles. It is then gauged with raw and boiled linseed oil, in the proportion of 2 to 1. The sandstone is finely powdered before being mixed. The surface to be covered must be first brushed with linseed oil.

London mastic is prepared as follows : 100 parts of ground stone, 50 parts silver sand or of fine river sand, and 15 parts of litharge, all dried and mixed and passed through a fine sieve, until it resembles fine sand. This will keep any length of time, if dry. When required for use, it is gauged with equal proportions of raw and boiled linseed oil, until of the consistency of fine stuff. It requires long and frequent beating and kneading ; in fact, the more it is " knocked up," the better it works. To ascertain its fitness, smooth a portion with a trowel. If the different materials show separately or in spots, the kneading must be renewed until of even texture. Fifteen parts of red lead increase its tenacity.

Mastic Manipulation.—Walls are prepared for mastic by raking the joints, sweeping clean with a coarse broom, and saturating the brickwork with linseed oil. Plastic screeds, 1 in. wide, guide in floating plumb and level. When laying the mastic, press firmly on and pass the floating rule over the surface until straight and flush. Cut the screeds out and fill the spaces with extra stiff mastic. Finish the whole surface with a beech or sycamore hand-float, leaving a close and uniform texture. Mouldings should be roughed out with quick-setting cement and the running mould muffled, allowing $\frac{1}{4}$ in. for the mastic coat.

Hamelein's Mastic.—This mastic consists of sand and pulverised stone, china, pottery, scharff, different oxides of lead such as litharge, grey oxide, and minium, all reduced to powder, and pulverised glass or flint stone, the whole being intimately incorporated with linseed oil. *The proportions are as follows :* To any given weight of sand or pulverised pottery ware, add two-thirds of the weight of pulverised Portland, Bath, or any other stone of the same nature. To every 550 lbs. of this mixture add 40 lbs. of litharge, 2 lbs. of pulverised glass or flint stones, 1 lb. of minium, and 2 lbs. of grey oxide of lead ; the whole to be thoroughly mixed and sifted, the fineness of the mesh depending on the purpose required. Use as follows : To every 30 lbs. of mastic add 1 quart of linseed oil, and well mix by kneading or with a trowel. As it sets quickly, only the quantity required for immediate use should be mixed. All surfaces to be plastered with this material must first be brushed with linseed oil.

Mastic Cement.—Mix 60 parts of slaked lime, 35 parts of fine sand, and 3 parts of litharge, and knead them to a stiff mass with 7 to 10 parts of *old* linseed oil. The whole mass must be well beaten and incorporated until thoroughly plastic. This mastic cement takes a fine smooth surface by trowelling, is impervious to damp, and unaffected by atmospheric changes.

Stearate of Lime.—This is used in America as a finishing coat to resist damp. It is a mixture of 1 bushel of lime, 20 lbs. of finely-chopped suet, and boiling water added until the ingredients are mixed to the consistency of lime putty. The lime and suet are placed in a barrel, boiling water is poured on, and the whole worked together by a revolving shaft with arms at its lower end (similar to a " pug-mill "), until the mass is thoroughly incorporated. Stearate may be applied hot with a brush ; two coats should suffice. Suet chemically changes when mixed with the lime, forming a durable compound impervious to water. It is excellent for stone, brick, or concrete, and will take any tint by adding stain.

CHAPTER VIII

MATERIALS (*Continued*)

Manufacture—CEMENTS—Portland Cement, Super-Cement, White Portland Cement, Water-proofing Cements, Slag, Roman, Martin's, Keen's, Parian, Robinson's—SELENITIC : Hydraulic Cements and Plasters, Granite, Sirapite—LATHING : Expanded Metal, Jhilmil, Bostwick, Johnson's, Patent Metal Sheet Lathing, Patent Reed Lathing, Slate Laths, Hy-rib.

Cements.—The earliest known patent for cement was obtained in 1677 by Kendricks Edisbury, for " a certaine sort of Plaister of an Extraordinary Hardness called ' Glassis ' which may be used instead of Freestone for paving of Floors and Water Mills for grinding corn." There is a long specification protecting the inventor and his exhibition, but not a word about the materials or process. Inventors were not bound to disclose their process and method of manufacture. Cements are composed of finely ground lime or other substances, which may be used alone or mixed with other materials, to set on the addition of water. They are usually divided into natural and artificial cements. Roman cement, plaster of Paris, and similar cements are natural cements ; Portland cement, slag, and similar cements are artificial cements.

Portland Cement.—Portland cement is a British invention, having been introduced and patented by Joseph Aspdin, a bricklayer and plasterer of Leeds, in 1824. His son, William Aspdin, was one of the earliest makers of Portland cement, having a manufactory at Wakefield. He later associated himself with Messrs Maude, Son, & Co., and in 1843 started a manufactory at Rotherhithe, on the banks of the Thames. Aspdin also obtained a patent in 1825 for a concrete of lime, road scrapings, etc., for an artificial stone. In 1852 his son William obtained a patent for an improved method of manufacture of Portland cement. Portland cement is a careful combination of carbonate of lime, alumina, and silica. This combination can be arrived at from waste products such as the slag from iron districts, alkali waste from the soda and other cognate manufacturers. The materials from which it is generally made are chalk and clay, or mud. Its advantages are—its hydraulic properties, great strength and its continually increasing strength, and its power of carrying large proportions of sand or other aggregate when made into mortar or concrete.

The cement best known in this country is made from Thames and Medway chalk and estuary mud. At Newcastle and Hull there are factories which combine a local clay with chalk from the London district, the resulting cement being of excellent quality. In some localities the denser limestones are used in the absence of chalk, and hard shales instead of clay. In the Midlands excellent Portland cement is produced from stones and shales of the blue lias formations. In blast furnace districts, slags containing nearly the same constituents as Portland cement are used, but not in the same proportion. Great caution is necessary, as blast furnace slags differ much in their composition. When care is taken that the constituents exist in suitable proportions, a very good cement results.

The two chief processes of manufacture are the wet process and the dry process. The former is adopted for materials which can be reduced to a perfectly homogeneous creamy mixture technically termed " slurry," by treatment in a wash-mill with an excess of water. The chalks and clays of the London district are thus treated. The dry process is used for materials which are too hard to be treated in the wash-mill

The Associated Portland Cement Manufacturers Ltd. now mature cement by hydration during manufacture, and render prolonged storage unnecessary.

The object of aeration is to render slower setting, sometimes of an importance. Furthermore, some cements, especially the very finely-ground ones, are so quick in setting when new, that if used immediately they would set before manipulation could be completed.

Magnesia in Portland Cement.—A Portland cement containing more than 3 per cent. of magnesia is not desirable. A high proportion of magnesia acts inertly, while the rest of the cement sets. After a time the magnesia hydrates and sets very hard, which considerably increases the bulk with a consequent destructive effect in work. Magnesia is hardly ever present harmfully in Thames and Medway cements, but it occasionally bulks largely in those of the Midlands.

Magnesia calcined at a low temperature renders Portland cement more durable and able to withstand the salts of sea water. The temperature of calcination is important, for magnesia calcined at a high temperature has a most evil effect upon the durability of Portland cement, in consequence of its uniting with water to form a hard hydrate, an increase of volume at the same time taking place. In the case of over-calcined magnesia this hydration takes place only after prolonged contact with water. In some cases where made from dolomitic marl, which sets very hard and is apparently satisfactory, disruption of the cement and destruction of the buildings in which it had been employed showed the practical effect in a year or two. The indurating effect of ammonium salts is disputed by some, but they are, nevertheless, used by several patentees in artificial stone.

Magnesia Cement.—Magnesia was formerly merely calcined and made up with water. Calcined magnesia is now carefully slaked and subsequently exposed to the action of carbonic acid gas, much in the same way that plasterers dry and harden new plaster by burning coke in closed rooms to liberate carbonic acid gas. The new substance is used as a cement. When mixed with marble dust, an artificial dolomite is obtained.

Effects of Age on Cement.—Practical experiments fully determine the effect of age on Portland cement in a dry state. As cement gradually absorbs moisture and carbonic acid from the atmosphere, chemical changes occur in it such as when it is gauged for use. The longer the cement is kept, the greater will be the changes and consequently the extent of deterioration. Ultimately a cement may become quite useless. Portland cement should be used within six months of manufacture, after then it deteriorates. If protected from atmospheric influences it will keep better and longer.

To Set Quickly.—Various materials and methods have been used to hasten the setting of Portland cement, more especially for cast work and for paving. A common method for cast work is to place the newly filled moulds before the fire. This should *never* be done. The heat withdraws the moisture which is necessary for the proper setting of the material, thus causing the work to become more or less friable. Dry heat will dry the cement, which is different from causing it to set. Moist heat is advantageous ; it hastens setting and hardens the cement. Urine is sometimes used to hasten setting. Besides being offensive, it causes efflorescence on the surface. Warm water for this purpose is disappointing, unless care is taken to regulate the temperature.

For jelly moulds it is disastrous. Soda dissolved in water and added to the gauging water is often used to hasten the setting of Portland cement casts, but it sometimes causes the work to blow and crack. This may be partly corrected by heating or roasting the soda on a hot plate before dissolving in hot water, allowing the solution to thoroughly cool, and sieving through muslin to free it from sediment. Mix with the gauging water and regulate as for size water and plaster, exposing the solution to the air for not less than three months before use. Portland cement mixed with a solution of calcium chloride rapidly acquires great hardness. Setting begins in three or four minutes, with a rise of temperature up to 158° F. Cement mixed with calcium softens immediately in water, but air-dried for eight or ten days may be immersed without detriment. Damp air has no influence upon the mixture. For hardness and quick setting, cement may be used *neat*. For general purposes, cement and sharp sand in equal proportions is best.

Setting.—The chemistry of setting is rather vague. It has not been clearly demonstrated what part each constituent of Portland cement plays in its setting. That the lime and silica are the greatest factors is certain, but the action of the rest is somewhat uncertain. Iron and alumina are only of indirect service. Soda and potash (which combine with silicic acid to form silicates of soda and potash which are in that form soluble in water) act as " transferrers of silicic acid to the lime." The setting times of Portland cements vary according to manufacture, freshness or staleness, and gauging. The time may vary from ten minutes to ten hours. Slow-setting cements are preferable. Before beginning large work, the time of setting should be tested and noted by gauging pats of neat cement and placing them in the air. If a pat can be indented by a moderate pressure of the thumb nail after two hours, it may be considered slow setting. The " initial set," that is, when it commences to stiffen, and the " set hard " should be timed. The initial set indicates the time limit between the gauging and laying. The addition of sulphuric acid or 2 per cent. of plaster retards the setting, but accelerates the maximum strength.

Hardening.—The hardening or induration of Portland cement is but imperfectly understood. Various theories have been advanced, but causes are somewhat obscure. A portion of the calcium oxide formed by calcination reacts upon the clay and converts it into a compound easily decomposed by acids. When water is added, this compound and the excess of calcium oxide react upon each other and produce a solid, stone-like " silicate." At a comparatively low temperature lime is converted into silicate of lime. A high temperature induces the formation of aluminate of lime, and finally of a double silicate of alumina and lime. This double silicate of lime and the aluminate of lime, on the addition of water, form hydrated silicates and aluminates, which set by crystallising. The hardness and non-absorptive qualities of Portland cement are due to its structure being laminated, while that of other cements is globular, the results being that the Portland cement particles touch at all points, admitting no interstices for water, while the reverse condition would be the case with cements where the particles were globular. Hardening results from the formation of a chemical compound of lime and silica. If Portland cement is made up with a strong solution of carbonate of ammonia, no hardening takes place. If hydrate of lime is added, the cement hardens.

Influence of Light on Portland Cement.—That light has influence on cement has been shown by dividing a quantity of newly made cement into three parts, exposing part A to the air and full light, B to the air and diffused light, C in darkness and excluded from the air. After six months, A made a weak mortar by absorbing $38\frac{1}{2}$ per cent. of its weight of water, and was crumbly. B with $33\frac{1}{3}$ per cent. of water made a mortar which was too adhesive to the trowel, and it did not yield any of its water. C with $33\frac{1}{3}$ per cent. of water made an excellent mortar, easily gauged, and it relinquished some of its water. After setting for twenty-eight days the relative strengths were :

A, 3; B, 37.9; C, 44.6. These tests show that cement should be covered over with boards, or kept in bags until required for use.

Super-cement is an improved and more efficient form of Portland cement. It is produced by adding catacoll to the Portland cement clinker during the process of grinding in the place of an approximately equal quantity of *raw* gypsum usual in ordinary Portland cement. The essential ingredient of catacoll is tannic acid. The results obtained can only be accomplished through the combination of tannic acid with gypsum in certain definite quantities, and the subsequent intimate grinding with clinker in the tube mills.

Catacoll itself has no more cementing value than the raw gypsum it replaces. It occupies no greater volume. It is anything but a water repellent.

The strength and qualities developed in super-cement concrete are derived from the reactions which occur between the mixing water and the constituents of the clinker. The function of tannic acid as catacoll in the super-cement is to facilitate these reactions and ensure them more completely than in Portland cement.

Super-cement used with ordinary intelligence makes better concrete than ordinary Portland cement, but under present conditions it is more costly.

White Portland Cement — " Sandusky." — This cement is used in the same manner as ordinary Portland cement, from which it differs only that it is pure white. To produce white concrete or white artificial stone, the cement should be mixed with white sand, crushed white quartz, ground marble or ground white limestone.

White Portland cement is used for reinforced concrete work, window sills, mouldings over windows, concrete pillars, doorways, steps, railings, etc., which are plastered with it, and for plastering brickwork. White Portland cement will be found suitable for the following purposes :—

Stucco.—One part white Portland cement mixed with 2 to 3 parts crushed marble or white sand, will produce a strong, rich mortar which will adhere to new brick, metal lath, plaster board, etc. It can be used as a finishing coat over stuccowork. The face of this mortar, after it has set hard, should be washed off with dilute muriatic acid to remove any stains caused by impure water. It will give a sparkling and pure white wall.

Interior Decoration.—For staircases, panels, reliefs, floors, pure white floors, wainscoting, etc., use 1 part white Portland cement and 2 parts marble screenings or white sand, applied as a top coat before the base has reached its final set. Sand which is not clean will stain the work.

Statuary.—It is a good substitute for plaster in reproducing statuary figures and groups, for galleries of casts, or exterior or interior decoration. For such work mix 1 part white Portland cement with 2 parts ground white limestone, crushed marble, or white sand. Mix dry until thoroughly incorporated, add water, and again mix to the consistency of thick cream. Use plaster or gelatine moulds. Keep moist for a week, allow surface to dry, then wash with dilute muriatic acid (1 part commercial muriatic acid, 4 parts water). Apply with a brush *having no metal*; wash with clean water; scrub the surface with a house scrubbing brush.

For monuments, vaults, columns, urns and plot kerbs, fountains, seats, railings, steps, walks, and gateways, use with white crushed marble, gelatine or plaster moulds; wash off the finished work with dilute muriatic acid to produce a sparkling white.

From its entire freedom from colouring ingredients, white Portland cement is absolutely stainless, and may be used safely in laying up stonework of any kind. It is particularly adapted for outside work, and will be permanent in pointing up joints between blocks or slabs of white marble, limestone, or brick.

Swimming baths may be plastered with white Portland cement.

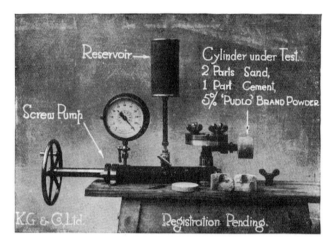

(*a*) Apparatus for Testing Strength of Plaster (Pudlo).

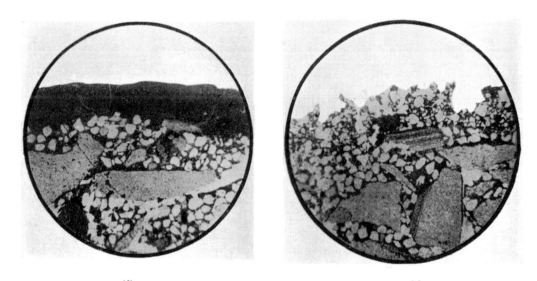

(*b*)   (*c*)

Ordinary Concrete (*b*) Treated with " Pudlo " Waterproofing Powder ; (*c*) Untreated. (Photomicrographs.)

PLATE CIV

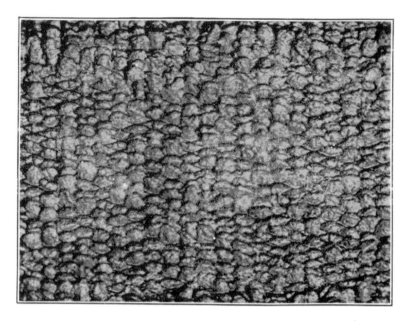

(a) DETAILS OF PLASTER, SHOWING "KEY" OBTAINED WITH
EXPANDED METAL LATHING.

(b) METAL GROUNDS BEFORE PLASTERING, AND PLASTERED ONE SIDE:
WITH DOOR FRAMES, AND TEMPORARY STRUTTING AND RAILING.

Waterproofing Cement—Renderings and Washes for Walls.—It is sometimes necessary to render the walls of a structure with a plaster material that will be waterproof, or at least repellent to water or damp.

This waterproofing is sometimes attempted by producing various insoluble precipitates by the admixture with the dry cement of materials such as soft soap, alum, potash, and other substances, which go right through the mass. Mineral oil is sometimes mixed with cement mortar to repel the water, but not animal or vegetable oils, which are apt to decompose with the production of free fatty acids. All oils thus used are detrimental to the strength of the cement.

There are various patent compounds on the market advertised under fancy names which give different degrees of efficiency, but they consist largely of oils, fats, soaps, or solutions of salts of some kind. So far as is known, most of these preparations are *not* successful when exposed to water under a high, or even low, pressure. Most have an injurious effect upon the cement by reducing its strength considerably—a very important point. Some compounds consist essentially of calcium carbonate, calcium soap, alum, oil, fat, or wax in powder form, to be mixed dry with cement before water is added, or in a paste or in a liquid, to be mixed with the water before gauging the cement.

Other water-repellent compounds consist of mineral oils, sodium silicate solutions, or solutions of silico-fluorides of sodium or other metals.

Silico-fluorides of zinc, magnesium, and aluminium are classified and sold under the name of " fluates." There are other solutions of acids and salts, viz., oxalic acid, and alum or zinc sulphates, all of which are for brushing into the surface of concrete and mortar to fill the pores with insoluble compounds ; *they are only to some extent effective for the protection of stone, plaster, and brickwork.*

There are some proprietary " waterproofing " compounds of a different type. They consist of a mixture of finely-powdered iron and a soluble salt which, in the presence of water, produces rapid rusting. The material is made up into a paste with water, and rubbed with a stiff brush into the surface to be treated, in two or three applications. Properly applied, it has been found to be of value where the brown, rusty colour is not objected to.

Cement renderings and concrete structures may be waterproofed integrally or superficially by materials known as " repellents " and " densifiers."

Plasterers are not much concerned with " repellent " waterproofers which are usually applied to an existing surface.

Repellent waterproofers may consist of wax dissolved in a light-bodied oil ; the oil carries the wax into the surface pores, where it is deposited as the oil passes inwards by absorption. The effect is not permanent. Hot weather inclines to melt and extract the wax from the surface ; it then is scoured away by the weather and thus gradually becomes ineffective.

A true waterproofer must be *incorporated* with the cement in the formation of renderings or concrete ; such densify the mixture and prevent the formation of voids and capillary pores. It is very necessary that the sand or other aggregates should be hard and non-porous, and graded with such proportion of cement as will fill up all interstices. Besides being coarse and well graded, they must be thoroughly washed and cleaned of impurities and loam which would form a pervious film around the particles of aggregate and prevent perfect adhesion of the cement. Thus water would percolate through minute ducts.

The waterproofing of the cement used thus should render the mass impermeable.

Finely-divided powders of inert materials such as slate, hydrated lime, or china clay, intended or used for filling up voids in cement mixtures, cannot be compared for efficiency with the use of a complete chemical waterproofer mixed with the cement. The best result that can come from an inert void-filler is to supply the deficiency of cement required to fill the interstices of the aggregate, which could be better done by using a greater proportion of cement or by a more careful grading of the aggregate, to minimise the voids. Inert materials cannot increase the natural waterproof degree of Portland cement. Although neat cement is nearly waterproof, it is *not entirely so* under ordinary working conditions. Neat cement mortars invariably crack and craze.

Water for Mixings.—When Portland cement is mixed in the laboratory, the required amount of water can be limited to that sufficient only for the hydration of the cement. This may be about 8 per cent. by weight of the dry cement. In actual working, the time required for mixing with so small a proportion of water could not be allowed, and cements so gauged would be too stiff to manipulate.

All cement mixtures as actually used in practice have water greatly in excess of that required for the hydration of the cement. This excess of water remains inert and occupies space. When the water dries out, the pores honeycombing the mass permit percolation of water.

A well-known waterproofing powder mixed with the Portland cement creates a re-action with the constituents of the cement, and an entirely new substance is evolved which fills up the voids in the cement matrix. By its lubricating action, the particles of aggregate become closely packed, perfectly dense, and the mixture is then impervious to damp.

Sand.—A cement waterproofing medium cannot counterbalance the evil of unsuitable sand or other aggregate, or insufficiency of cement. Warning must be emphatic against the use of too fine a sand. When Portland cement and water are mixed, each grain of cement becomes gelatinous and unites with those cement grains in contact with it. Thus a homogeneous mass is formed. If in a rendering mixture of, say, 3 parts of sand to 1 of cement, the sand grains are of the same fineness as the grains of Portland cement, it would be absurd to expect homogeneity in the mixture. The grains of cement cannot surround and fill in the spaces between the grains of sand which are of equal size, and outnumber them by 3 to 1.

A perfect cement rendering should be a miniature concrete, the sand grains being graded from $\frac{1}{4}$ in. mesh gauge down to " fine." Washed Thames sand is excellent for renderings to be waterproofed.

Cracks.—Hair cracks are objectionable in cement stucco. They are regarded by some persons as unavoidable in a cement finish. They may chiefly be attributed to a too rich mixture of cement, aggravated by excess of water or perhaps the use of too fine a sand. As in lime plastering, the lack of intelligence or proper effort by a callous workman may produce cracking, if the rendering stuff is not adequately con-solidated. Over-trowelling of a surface breaks up initial setting, brings to the surface an excess of neat or " fat " cement, which forms a surface film which " hair cracks."

The desire to make cement stucco " weather resisting " at times induces the use of too much cement. Also a " fat " mixture will take a sharp arris and " run " smoothly. The addition of " Pudlo " brand waterproofer to 2 or 3 parts of sand and 1 of Portland cement forms a weatherproof stucco, and gives a plasticity otherwise only attained by an excess of cement. Stucco so composed and properly applied will be perfectly weathertight and remarkably free from hair cracks.

Preparing Walls.—The execution of cement stuccowork must commence with a right preparation of the wall surface. If the wall is of brick, the joints must be deeply raked out and the surface of the bricks well chipped to give a key. The wall must next be thoroughly drenched with *clean* water to prevent any absorption of moisture from the waterproofed first coat of cement to be applied.

The second coat of waterproofed cement mortar should be applied immediately the first coat is set sufficiently to hold it. A perfect bond between the two coats results. When once the waterproofed cement first coat has set hard, being waterproof, it has no suction and consequently less bond. The work must be kept *damp for several days after being finished*, by repeated sprinklings with clean water. This is especially necessary where waterproofed cement work is exposed to hot sunshine or drying winds. If Portland cement work dries out too quickly it loses strength and waterproof qualities.

Efflorescence.—Ordinary cement plastering is subject to the formation upon its surface of fine white crystals (known as " efflorescence ") which sometimes collect to a thickness of $\frac{1}{2}$ in. or even more. This trouble is occasionally accompanied by an erosion of the surface where it occurs.

Efflorescence may be due to the presence of soluble salts in the cement, in the sand, in the water used for construction, or in the brickwork behind the rendering. Salts are dissolved by the water used in constructing the building, or perhaps in the case of a damp wall, by the water which causes the dampness.

This water, carrying with it salts in solution, travels to the interior or exterior surface of the wall, and when the saline water passes through the porous cement rendering and evaporates, the salts are left upon the surface in the white powdery form which is the symptom of the trouble.

Efflorescence cannot occur upon the surface of waterproof cement work, because the moisture containing the salts in solution cannot pass through it.

The advent of waterproofed cement has brought within the province of the plasterer the cure of walls damp from causes other than exposure to the weather, work that has formerly been done by other craftsmen. In deciding upon the remedy, we have to consider details of construction not usually concerning the plasterer. We will now consider these new methods after touching upon the treatment of ordinary damp walls.

Damp Walls : External and Internal Treatments.—In treating walls damp from exposure to rain, the remedy may either be applied on to the outside surface of the wall in the form of waterproofed cement stucco or rough casting, or on to the interior surface of the wall by removing the old damp lime plaster and replacing it by a rendering of waterproofed cement. The advantage of exterior treatment is that the wall is kept dry. External treatment prevents damage which occurs from action by frost.

The *disadvantage* of external application is that it prevents evaporation of moisture in the wall outwardly. Evaporation can then only occur from the inside face of the wall, and this takes time. The advantage of exterior treatment is thus not apparent immediately. The cost of scaffolding outside high buildings may be a serious item, and possibly external treatment be undesirable for architectural reasons. The remedy is to remove the damp interior lime plastering, rake out the joints of the fabric, wet the wall and replaster with 2 or 3 parts of clean, sharp, coarse sand to 1 of Portland cement, with from 3 to 5 per cent., by weight, of the waterproofing powder added to the cement. The surfaces of all indoor cement renderings, whether waterproofed or not, should be skimmed with lime plaster to absorb any condensation of atmospheric moisture.

Dampness in walls is often due to the absence of a horizontal damp course. In such cases dampness is continuous throughout the wall, being worst at the bottom. With such a wall, attempts to cure were at one time made by inserting a new horizontal damp-proof course, at considerable disturbance to the wall and great expense. Walls once damp often remain a source of illness and trouble in other ways. Decorations placed upon them stain and perish. Wall surfaces that are damp owing to the absence of (or to defects of) damp courses, can be cured by substituting a rendering of waterproofed cement for the old interior lime plaster, as shown in Fig. 35.

The old lime plaster must be removed from the bottom of the walls to 2 ft. or

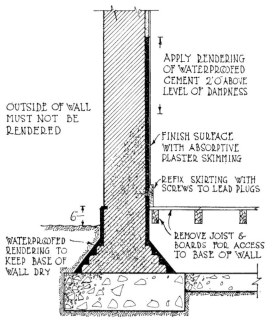

APPLY RENDERING OF WATERPROOFED CEMENT 2'0" ABOVE LEVEL OF DAMPNESS

OUTSIDE OF WALL MUST NOT BE RENDERED

FINISH SURFACE WITH ABSORPTIVE PLASTER SKIMMING

REFIX SKIRTING WITH SCREWS TO LEAD PLUGS

6"

WATERPROOFED RENDERING TO KEEP BASE OF WALL DRY

REMOVE JOIST & BOARDS FOR ACCESS TO BASE OF WALL

SECTION OF WALL WITHOUT A DAMPCOURSE SHEWING TREATMENT WITH WATERPROOFED CEMENT

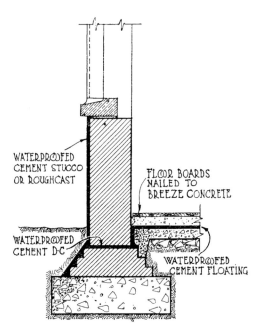

WATERPROOFED CEMENT STUCCO OR ROUGHCAST

FLOOR BOARDS NAILED TO BREEZE CONCRETE

WATERPROOFED CEMENT D·C

WATERPROOFED CEMENT FLOATING

SECTION THROUGH NEW WALL SHEWING OUTSIDE TREATMENT WITH WATERPROOFED CEMENT

FIG. 35.

more above the dampness, and the walls afterwards rendered *down to the foundations* with sand and waterproof cement. A suitable mixture is 2 or 3 parts of sand to 1 of cement and 3 per cent. of " Pudlo " brand waterproofer. The wall *fabric* will remain damp, but the dampness cannot penetrate the new rendering, and the inside wall surface and the room will be perfectly dry. When earth abuts on to a wall a vertical damp-proof covering of waterproofed cement and sand may be effectively substituted for asphalt or for slates usually bedded in ordinary cement mortar. For very damp ground the rendering should consist of 2 parts of sand to 1 of cement and 5 per cent. of waterproofer.

Floors. — Granolithic paving and floors are frequently laid by firms who " specialise " in them ; they are properly plasterers' work. A mistake commonly made is the use of unscreened granite chippings carrying quarry dust. Fine dust, from the crushing of the granite, weakens the cement and gives a friable and dusty floor.

Granite is more hard-wearing than cement. The best wearing floor has a surface composed almost entirely of granite aggregate. Any excess of cement over that required to *fill only the voids* between the granite chippings will separate the chips of aggregate and expose superfluous cement and produce a floor with a wearing surface inferior to one with less, but still sufficient, cement.

Two defects are common to granolithic floor surfaces, viz., (1) lifting from the concrete bed, (2) cracking. The former may be detected by a hollow sound when tapped or walked upon. Such a surface, of course, has no support and may break up under a weight, or blow, or crack. No layer applied to a surface of concrete previously laid should therefore have a less thickness than $1\frac{1}{2}$ in.

The concrete bed should be thoroughly chipped, washed clean, and then slurried over with a grout of neat cement immediately before the granolithic floor surface is laid, and great care is needed to clean the bed. It often happens that the laying of a floor surface is deferred until after the wall and ceiling (lime and hair or patent) plastering has been done.

In such cases the concrete bed will be covered with a film of material which will prevent the adhesion of the concrete and granolithic layers. The only remedy then is to continue hacking the concrete bed until a clean, new, rough key is exposed over the entire surface of the concrete bed.

Floor cracks can be greatly minimised by limiting the amount of water used in gauging the " grano " to sufficient only to produce a workable mass. Avoid any excess of cement. Keep the finished floor *damp* by a covering of wet sawdust, kept wet by repeated soakings, until the cement has thoroughly set.

Cracking may be due to expansion and contraction set up by absorption of water and its subsequent evaporation. Concrete mixtures expand and contract when wetted and dried. The U.S.A. Bureau of Standards state that the complete saturation with water of concrete specimens tested by the Bureau, caused expansion equal to that which resulted from their temperatures being increased by 1,000° F. This disposes of the old theory that granolithic floor cracks were chiefly due to movement originating from changes of temperature. The makers of " Pudlo " brand waterproofer claim that by stopping absorption their material eliminates the chief cause of cracks.

Freedom from cracking is certainly a qualification of properly laid and water-proofed granolithic surfaces, now frequently used for flat roofs in place of asphalt. The lesser amount of water used in gauging waterproofed concrete has also much to do with this result. The lubricating action of the waterproofing material gives a plasticity frequently obtained in ordinary concrete by an excess of water, the rapid evaporation of which promotes a shrinkage that sets up internal stresses before the material attains much strength. These stresses result· in minute cracks which increase as the concrete dries.

Joints.—It is important to execute all cement work continuously with as few joints as possible. Joints in rendering should never occur at, or near, any angle of a wall. Each coat of rendering should be continued *beyond* an internal angle, a joint being made about 2 ft. away from it. The following rendering coat would be carried in the opposite way round and jointed on the return wall 2 ft. from the angle. All internal angles, horizontal or vertical, must be slightly rounded or coved. Sharp angles are weak and apt to crack.

Joints, whether of waterproofed cement renderings or concrete, should never be straight. The edge of an unfinished rendering or of concrete should be ragged and splayed to a long rough chamfer, which upon resuming work should be washed over with a slurry of neat cement containing 5 per cent. of waterproofing powder and followed by the new concrete or rendering before the slurry dries.

Number of Coats.—Horizontal renderings should always be made in one coat. Vertical renderings should not exceed $\frac{3}{8}$ in. in thickness per coat. A 1 in. rendering of three coats would therefore require a bare thickness of $\frac{3}{8}$ in. each coat.

Renderings (Finishing).—Waterproofed cement facings to outside walls should be finished with a wood float. Inside walls finished in cement are also better left with a floated finish. A granular surface does not show surface condensation so much as a trowelled finish.

Condensation.—A more certain cure of surface condensation is to skim with porous lime plaster on top of the last coat of waterproofed cement. The following specification is recommended :—

" Rough render the walls, using cement and sand with the addition of ' Pudlo ' brand waterproofing powder mixed to the specification suitable for the situation. Thoroughly scratch the rendering to give a key and follow on with a second coat, when first coat is set enough to hold it. Scratch the second coat as before and let it harden. If only two coats of waterproofed cement are necessary, give a coat of ordinary cow-haired lime plaster (' coarse stuff '), say 3 of sand to 1 of lime, to which add at the time of application a little plaster of Paris to hasten the setting and assist adhesion. Score this coat from a nail float in the usual manner to receive a final skimming coat from a wood float when the mortar is hard enough. Do not trowel the surface, as this would consolidate it and reduce the absorptive properties. The best finishing coat to prevent condensation depends largely upon the qualities of the lime and sand used, which vary considerably in different districts. The following proportions have been found from exhaustive tests to give excellent results :—

" 3 parts of lime putty run from Buxton or other pure chalk lime.

" 6 parts of washed sand.

" 1 part of plaster of Paris (to be added at the time of using)."

There are many other kinds of waterproofed Portland cement work that concern the plasterer. For instance, the construction and reparation of basements, garage pits, and manholes, in flooded land ; reservoirs and tanks, wells in polluted soil, flat roofs, and so on.

Various specifications for the use of waterproofed cement are given in a handbook of cement waterproofing issued by Messrs Kerner-Greenwood & Co. Ltd., of King's Lynn. The reader is referred to this source for detailed information respecting the use of the cement waterproofing powder (" Pudlo " brand) which this firm manufactures. (See also Plate CIIIA).

Slag Cement.—An example of the use of waste products is in the manufacture of cement from iron furnace slag. Another example is the use of crushed slag as an aggregate for fine cement. Slags are not all fitted for conversion into cement. Some have not the necessary ingredients in suitable proportions ; others have an excess of sulphur.

Manufacture.—In 1850 mortar was made by mixing slag with lime. Melted slag (run from the iron furnace) subjected to a powerful jet of air or steam, produces slag wool, or silicate cotton, now used for many purposes. Further improvements reduced slag to slag sand. Slag sand ground with 5 per cent. of lime, makes a good mortar which sets within twenty-four hours. There is a process for converting slag sand into cement. The slag is screened, about 25 per cent. (by weight) of slaked lime is sieved and added, thoroughly amalgamated, and ground together through a " homogeniser " (a revolving drum partly filled with metal balls about 1 in. in diameter). In this drum the slag and lime particles are crushed to pass through a sieve of 32,000 holes per square inch. These molecules are mechanically brought into the closest possible contact, thus producing a " floury-silky " powder. This treatment would improve ordinary Portland cement. The process of " homogenising," as compared with simple mixing, is a vast improvement in the quality of the slag cement. The tensile and compressive strength are thereby almost doubled. The average weight is about 90 lbs. per bushel. Specific gravity is 2.73 against 3.10 for Portland.

Fineness.—Slag cement is finer ground than Portland cement. A sample of slag cement tested left no residue at all on a sieve of 1,600 meshes per square inch, 1 per cent. on one of 3,870, 5 per cent. on one of 5,800, and 14 per cent. on one of 32,200 meshes.

Uses.—Slag cement gauged neat is more plastic and works " fatter " than Portland cement. It requires from two to five hours to set. When set it is white. It is well adapted for casting and is useful for plastering. Its adhesive strength, its unequalled fire-resisting properties commend its use for concrete stairs, floors, and roofs. It was used in the construction of the harbours and docks at Skinningrove, Yorkshire.

Roman Cement.—A hydraulic cement so-called from its resemblance to the mortar of Roman buildings, is made from the septaria nodules of the London clay formation in the Isle of Sheppey. The septaria of Harwich produced a similar cement. A similar material is also found in the Bay of Weymouth, Calderwood in Scotland, in Yorkshire, Burgundy, and Russia. It consists of detached nodules of dark-coloured argillaceous limestone, with veins filled with calcareous spar. Its colour is sometimes blue and sometimes brown or red, due to the presence of oxide of iron.

Martin's Cement.—Martin's cement was the first reliable white cement with a gypsum basis. It consists of a mixture of alkali and acid with gypsum. According to the specification, 1 lb. of strong alkali (pearl ash) is dissolved in 1 gal. of water, and then sulphuric acid is added ; the gypsum is soaked in this solution, then it is calcined and ground to a fine powder. Hydrochloric acid is sometimes added to prevent alkaline reaction. The cement is creamy in colour, sets very hard, is chiefly used for walls, dados, and skirtings, works cleanly and freely, and can be painted or papered over directly after being finished. There are three qualities—coarse, fine, and superfine.

Keen's Cement.—Keen's cement was patented in 1838 by J. D. Greenwood and R. W. Keen. Keen's cement is obtained by soaking the best plaster of Paris in a solution of 1 part of alum to 12 parts of water, at a temperature of 95° ; after three hours the mass is removed and dried. It is then baked a second time to eliminate the water of combination, after which it is carefully ground. It is manufactured in three qualities —coarse, fine, and superfine. The latter is white. This cement can be worked to a very hard and smooth surface with polish. It is useful for internal decorations, columns, and architraves, and is a good hard plaster for walls, skirtings, etc. It can be painted on or papered over within a few hours of being finished. When used for pathways, the rendering coat should be formed of the coarse quality of the same material, or Portland cement.

Parian Cement.—Parian cement was patented in 1846 by J. Keating, a London scagliolist. According to the specification, the cement is made by dissolving 5 lbs. of borax (borate of soda) in 6 gals. of water, also 5 lbs. cream of tartar in 6 gals. of water, and mixing together. The gypsum stone or plaster is then immersed in this solution. The mixture is afterwards calcined and subsequently carefully ground. Parian cement is so-called from its supposed likeness to Parian marble. Parian cement works more freely than Keen's or Martin's cements and has greater tensile strength than either. Briquettes having a sectional area of $2\frac{1}{4}$ in., at the end of fourteen days give the following results : Martin's, 580.7 ; Keen's, 585.8 ; Parian, 642.3. Parian cement sets rather quickly for general use ; it has the property of *resetting after being worked up a second time.* This would not be possible if the cement had fairly hardened. If it has become stiff it may be used again by adding water. It is an excellent finishing coat on a floating of Portland cement, as a preventive of damp on walls ; also for hospital walls, as it is non-porous and a smooth face can be worked, making the walls washable. On account of its great hardness, Parian cement is used for work such as beads, arrises, skirtings, etc. It is valuable for any work liable to damage by contact, for chimney-pieces, pedestals, etc., and can be painted or papered over as soon as finished. Coarse Parian for floating purposes can be rendered more dense and hard by adding a solution of white china clay in the proportion of 7 lbs. of clay to 1 cwt. of cement, gauged with about 28 lbs. of water. A solution of white clay in lesser proportions can be used to render the work closer in texture for setting purposes and give a semi-polish.

Robinson's Cement.—Robinson's cement was patented in 1883. It has a basis of gypsum with an admixture of tincal (an imported material) and alum, in about the proportion of 45 lbs. of tincal and 15 lbs. of alum to 1 ton of gypsum, all finely ground together and treated in a particular manner. The gypsum used is nearly white and very hard, which gives greater strength to the cement when set. It is fireproof and has a dense, hard surface. The cost is less than Keen's or Parian cement and rather more than ordinary plastering. As with other cements and limes, the sand to be mixed with it must be clean, dry, and sharp. The cement and sand are mixed dry in a gauge box, sufficient water being added to gauge them. The cement must *not* be knocked up a second time. Walls must be thoroughly brushed and wetted before the first coat is applied. Laths should not be more than ¼ in. apart. The first coat is scratched, and the second finishing coat may be laid on at once. The finishing coat should be gauged in pails, and thinner than ordinary setting stuff. The cement should soak a few minutes before using. It may be used for cornices and for castings. It is non-absorbent. For setting fibrous plaster slabs, the soffits and the ceilings of concrete stairs and floors, it is better than gauged putty or setting stuff. It is good for repairs and for alterations and additions; the work can be finished in one operation, and be painted, distempered, or papered soon after setting. No. 1, for finishing coat on walls or ceilings, whitewashing mouldings, castings, and tile fixing; it is pure white and can be polished to a beautiful surface; No. 2, for first coating, with sand according to requirements. The proportion of sand varies, but 2 to 1 for ceilings and 3 to 1 for walls and partitions may be safely recommended for good work.

Selenitic Cement.—Selenitic derives its name from the chemical term for gypsum, viz., selenite. Patent selenitic was invented by General Scott in 1870. Selenitic cement sets quickly and forms a good groundwork for white cements. It is usually made by gauging about 5 per cent. of plaster (at the time of using) with any hydraulic lime, lias being the best. Lime may be selenitised by an admixture of sulphuric acid, or a small proportion of any sulphate. The effect of sulphate on lime is to arrest slaking, to quicken its setting, to increase its strength, and to enable a large proportion of sand to be used. Selenitic is prepared for plastering either by means of a mortar-mill or a tub. If in a mortar-mill, pour into a pan two full-sized pails of water, gradually add a bushel of selenitic, and grind to the consistency of a soft lime putty; then throw into the pan about 5 bushels of clean sharp sand, hard burnt clay ballast, or broken brick, which must be thoroughly incorporated. If necessary, water can be added during grinding, which is preferable to adding an excess of water to the prepared lime before adding the sand. The water and selenitic must be mixed together first, and where the improved style of self-discharging mortar-pan is used, it is better to mix the selenitic and water in a tub (as explained hereafter), adding the paste to the sand or other aggregate proportionately as required. If prepared in a tub, pour in six pails (18 gals.) of water, and gradually add 3 bushels of selenitic, keeping it well stirred until thoroughly mixed with the water to the proper consistency. Form a ring with half a yard of clean, sharp sand, into which pour the mixture from the tub. The whole gauge should then be turned over three or four times and well mixed with a larry, and water added as required. The tub should be able to contain about 40 gals. An oblong box or trough with a sluice may be used. Selenitic should be kept in a dry place until used. Plastering with selenitic cement on brick or stonework may be floated like Portland cement. This requires no hair. For plastering with selenitic cement on lath-work, pour in six full-sized pails (18 gals.) of water and 3 bushels of selenitic, adding from 9 to 12 of clean, sharp sand and 3 hods of well-haired lime putty. When a mill is used the haired putty should not be put in the pan until the mixing of the selenitic and sand is nearly completed, and should only be ground until the haired putty is mixed. Long grinding destroys the hair. This gauge will answer well for all classes of lathwork, if the sand is very sharp. Nine bushels of sand (3 of sand to 1 of selenitic) will answer well for first coating the lath, and 12 bushels of sand (4 of sand to 1 of selenitic) for floating after the first coat is set. For common setting, the ordinary method of finishing with putty lime and washed sand may be adopted. When a selenitic face is required, the prepared selenitic may be first passed through a fine sieve to avoid blistering, and used in the proportion of 4 pails of water, 2 bushels of selenitic, 2 hods of lime putty, and 3 bushels of fine washed sand. This may be used in the same way as trowelled stucco, viz., well hand-floated and trowelled to produce a hard surface. The latter method of working selenitic is preferred by the workmen; putty lime makes it work "fatter" than by adding plaster only, which works "short" and "heavy." Selenitic should *not* be used with gauged stuff for cornices, angles, or screeds.

Patent Selenitic Blue Lias.—Manufacturers of this material advise the following for plasterers' and bricklayers' work: 1 bushel of selenitic lime requires about 6 gals. of water (two full-sized pails).

Method of Preparing in a Mortar Mill.—1. Pour into the pan of the edge runner three and a half full-sized pails of water. 2. Gradually add 2 bushels of selenitic lime, and grind to a creamy paste. 3. Throw into the pan 10 bushels of clean, sharp sand, burnt clay, or broken bricks, ground until thoroughly incorporated. Over-grinding of burnt ballast or broken bricks causes cracking. Water can be added in grinding, preferably to an excess of water before adding the sand.

When a mortar mill is unavailable, a plasterer's tub, holding 30 or 40 gals., or a trough with outlet or sluice, may be substituted.

Method of Preparing in a Plasterer's Tub.—1. Pour into the tub four full-sized pails of water. 2. Add gradually to the water 2 bushels of selenitic lime; stir well until thoroughly mixed to a creamy paste. 3. Form 10 bushels of clean, sharp sand into a ring, pour in the selenitic lime from the tub through a 16 by 16 mesh sieve (to avoid clods), and add water as necessary; turn over two or three times, and well mix with the "larry" or mortar hook.

The above mixtures are suitable for bricklayers' mortar for first coat of plastering on brickwork. Plastering on brick can be floated (or straightened) in the coat and requires no hair.

Selenitic Lime for Plastering on Lathwork.—To the above quantities of water and selenitic lime, add only 6 or 8 bushels of clean, sharp sand and 2 hods of well-haired lime putty, the hair being previously well "hooked" into the lime putty. When a mill is used, the haired putty should be ground just sufficiently to ensure mixing. Longer grinding destroys the hair too much. Lime putty should be run some time before it is used, to avoid blisters. It will answer equally well for ceilings and partitions. If the sand is very sharp, use only 6 bushels of sand for rendering on the lath, and when sufficiently set, follow with 8 bushels of sand for floating or straightening.

When no mill is used, make up a fat, coarse stuff with plenty of long hair, and mix with the selenitic lime and sand, in the proportion of 1 part of coarse stuff to 3 parts of selenitic and sand. Well "larry" the whole together. Chalk lime putty should be run at least one month beforehand.

Setting Coat and Trowelled Stucco.—For common setting or finishing coat, ordinary chalk lime putty and washed sand may be used. If a very hard face is required, selenitic lime, passed through a 24 by 24 mesh sieve, may be used in the proportions of 3 parts of lime putty, 2 parts washed sand, 1 part selenitic lime. This should be first well hand-floated and then well trowelled.   A very hard surface is thus produced.

The workmen should have suitable measures for the lime and sand, to ensure proper proportions.   Want of care leads to unsatisfactory results.

It is very important to thoroughly stir the selenitic cement in the water before mixing it with sand or other ingredient.   This is the *only* point of difference from ordinary mortar preparation.

Selenitic lime should *not* be used with gauged stuff for cornices, screeds, etc.   Sand and other ingredients should always be clean and free from loam.

Selenitic lime must be kept perfectly dry until made into mortar for use.   One day's supply only should be gauged at a time.   The supply required for the roughing or backing coat should be prepared overnight.   The setting or finishing coat should be made at least three hours before required.

Finely ground burnt clay (ballast) or cinders, or stone chippings, as a substitute for sand, in whole or in part, may be used advantageously for every description of work.

In fine weather selenitic plastering on walls may be finished as above, as two-coat work, in twenty-four hours, though two days are preferable.   Ceilings may be floated soon after the application of the first coat, and set in forty-eight hours ; much depends on the state of the atmosphere affecting the drying.

Selenitic cement mortar, with 5 parts of sand, will set harder and more quickly than common mortar with 2 or 3 parts of sand.

Selenitic blue lias is very superior to that prepared from the ordinary grey lime, etc. for all purposes.

Cost.—The cost of selenitic is less than 25s. per ton in London or Liverpool.[1] One ton of selenitic will cover 200 yards of plastering, consequently it is one of the cheapest of plasters.   It may be used in lieu of Portland cement for backing, especially if followed and finished quickly with Keen's or Parian facing for painting upon.

Selenitic is quite suitable for exterior use, but the work must be protected from the wet for some time and worked to a smooth face.

Mouldings require coring with great nicety and uniform thickness.   If " dubbing out " has to be done, use Portland for the dubbing and face with selenitic.

If work is protected from the rain while soft, it will dry out a light stone colour and become very hard.   Rain will clean the face of the work and improve it.

To ensure success is as follows :—

    1. A uniform thickness of, say, 1 in.

    2. Clean, sharp sand, free from silt.

    3. Mouldings to be run up fat and smooth.

    4. The plain face backing put on in fine, shingly, sharp sand, left rough and true.

    5. A facing of sharp sand and selenitic gauged half and half, straightened, faced, and scoured-up two or three times, and then trowelled to a smooth face, care being taken not to trowel fat off face.

    6. Joint with a smooth jointer while material is soft, not too deep.

Selenitic will stand frost ; it is suitable for window sills, jambs, etc.   It will bleach with the weather and look clean.   It must be done on a brick core, 1 in. thick.   The backing may be gauged 2 of clean, sharp, well-washed sand to 1 of selenitic.   The next day the finishing may be put on and faced up smooth.   Arrises sharp and true to be left with the trowel (not the wood float).   The selenitic must be fresh, in no way air slaked or stored in a damp place.

If more than 1 in. in thickness is necessary, the backing should be dubbed out and left for a couple of days.   Not more than 1 in. must be put on at a time, lest

---

[1] Spring 1927.

it should "heat." If so, considerable expansion will occur. To prevent this expansion it is necessary to put on a little at a time, allowing time for setting between each dressing. In summer, work should not be exposed to the sun's heat, or it will dry out a Portland stone colour. A finishing coat should be $\frac{1}{4}$ in. thick, gauged half silver sand and half selenitic, left smooth from the trowel.

Selenitic Clay Finish.—Ground selenitic clay improves mortar and renders it more hydraulic. The following proportions are good : 1 bushel prepared selenitic, 3 bushels prepared selenitic clay, 2 bushels washed sand, 1 hod of chalk lime putty, and 13 gals. of water. The mixture must be well gauged, well laid, floated true, twice hand-floated, and finally trowelled to a good fair face. For outside work, use from 5 to 6 bushels of sand to the same proportions of other materials. Selenitic plastering has been used for many large works throughout the world.

Hydraulic Cements.—Hydraulic cements and plasters set and harden under water. They generally consist of silica and caustic lime. Clay and magnesia increase their consistency and strength. Smeaton's search, preparatory to building the Eddystone lighthouse, for a mortar capable of resisting the sea is of much interest. His discovery was the genesis of the manufacture of Portland cement. Smeaton did not invent any particular cement, but he was first to discover that the hydraulic properties of lime *depended upon combination with clay*. To this circumstance the serviceableness of cement is due and the marvel of hydraulic engineering.

General Pasley says of Smeaton : " Of all the authors who have investigated the properties of calcareous mortars and cements from time immemorial to the present day, our countryman Smeaton appears to me to have greatest merit ; for although he found out no new cement himself, he was the first who discovered, in or soon after the year 1756, that the real cause of water-setting properties of limes and cements consisted in a combination of clay with carbonate of lime, in consequence of having ascertained by a very simple sort of chemical analysis that there was a proportion of the former ingredient in all the natural limestones which, on being calcined, developed that highly important quality without which walls exposed to water go to pieces, and those exposed to air and weather only are of comparatively inferior strength. By this memorable discovery Smeaton overset the prejudices of over 2,000 years, adopted by all previous writers, from Vitruvius in ancient Rome to Belidor in France and Semple in this country, who agreed in maintaining that the superiority of lime consisted in the hardness and whiteness of the stone, the former of which may or may not be accompanied by water-setting or powerfully cementing properties, and the latter of which is absolutely incompatible with them."

Granite Plaster.—Calcined gypsum is the basis of granite plaster. The raw material is specially treated to yield a hard and quick-drying plaster for interior work. It is a substitute for ordinary lime and hair plastering. It permits rendering and floating in one coat and setting the same day. The work may be painted or papered two days after finishing. Granite plaster is delivered in sacks ready for use. It should be gauged in a box with water. No more material must be gauged than can be used in one hour. Granite plaster is excellent where time is limited. Its fire-resisting properties are valuable.

Sirapite.—Sirapite plaster has a basis of selected hard gypsum. It is perfectly hygienic, free from glue or organic compounds, and absorbs very little water. It has been used for many years with uniform success for all classes of work, especially in hospitals, asylums, Government and public buildings, etc., as a substitute for lime and hair plaster. The material is easily gauged and applied, requiring only the addition of sand and water. It supplants ordinary lime plaster in point of speed in working, hardness, and durability. Its cost is about that of ordinary lime plastering. Two coats only are needed, the second following the first in twenty-four hours. Sawn or cleft laths may be used. The former give a more uniform surface and require less material. Sirapite is gauged in a " banker " as for ordinary cement. On brickwork, gauge with 3 parts clean sand and a small proportion of lime putty to 1 part sirapite. On lathwork, a gauging of 2 parts of sirapite to 1 of sand, with a little lime putty, is best. The laths should be nailed $\frac{3}{16}$ in. apart. The finish is usually gauged in a pail of water, allowed to settle, and the surplus water poured off. It is laid and trowelled off as for gauged putty and plaster. Excessive gauging or prolonged trowelling should be avoided. For metal lathing mix sirapite and common hair plaster half and half for a first coat.

For uneven walls and other reasons sirapite is often used half and half with common lime plaster, or on lathwork with common hair plaster. The work is kept thin and is done in two coats. It is finished quickly and makes excellent work.

Sirapite plaster can be safely used on Fletton bricks. With the special precautions given by the makers there is no discoloration of the plaster which often occurs with these bricks.

Sirapite is largely used on metal lathing and steel sheeting. Dr Gerald Moody, F.I.C., F.C.S., of the Central Technical College, South Kensington, conducted some experiments in March 1905 as to the action of sirapite on such lathing, and his report concludes as follows : " My analyses show that neat sirapite is entirely free from any acid constituent. From a chemical point of view, a material having such a composition as sirapite, and used, either neat or mixed with lime putty, would be expected not only to be non-corrosive of metal, but to actually protect bright sheets of iron and steel from rusting. In order to investigate this question, a number of perfectly bright sheets of iron and steel and of ' expanded iron ' were partly covered with sirapite plaster and then exposed to an atmosphere charged with much moisture and acid vapours. After seven days' exposure the uncovered parts of the metal were thickly corroded and pitted with rust ; whereas on removing the plaster from the covered portions of the sheets the metal thus laid bare was found in every case to be bright. Direct observation therefore confirms the conclusion, deduced from a consideration of the chemical composition of sirapite, that sirapite has no corrosive action on metal ; but that, on the contrary, its effect is to prevent the rusting of iron and steel."

Sirapite is most convenient and economical for all kinds of plastering repairs. Like all gypsum plasters it should not be used in permanently damp places such as basements where no proper damp course is present. The walls should be dry before being coated. Applied to Portland cement concrete, the work should be dry before the sirapite is put on.

Wood Lathing.—Wood lathing is used on wood joists, studding, etc., for plasterwork on ceilings and partitions. Plastered partitions were introduced about the end of the sixteenth century. Lath wood is straight-grained wood ; the outsides of fir trees are split into laths. Red Baltic timber makes the best laths. Lath rendering or splitting was formerly done entirely by plasterers, and was a profitable source of employment during winter months. Lath driving or nailing was also allotted to them, but owing to the subdivision of labour, lath-splitting and nailing in most large towns has become a branch trade, although it is in some places still done by plasterers. Laths were formerly all made by hand. A large quantity, however, are now made by machinery. The latter are known in the trade as " sawn laths." An old method of lathing was done by sawing broad timber into thin boards about $\frac{1}{4}$ in. thick, and in width from 3 in. upwards. The boards were split in position to give a key. Samples of this class of work are still to be found when repairing old plasterwork. Laths are now made chiefly from Baltic or American timber. This should be specially selected, cut into lengths, and split by wedges into " bolts," with a dowel axe into " fittings," and with a " chit " split into " laths."

Laths are usually purchased by the load, bunch, or bundle. A bundle of ceiling laths is computed to contain 500 lineal ft., but in many parts of the country they are still reckoned by the long thousand or 1,200 ft. ; hence a bunch will contain 100 4-ft. laths and a bundle will contain two bunches, and will cover 7 yards superficial. A standard bundle should contain seven score 3-ft., six score 4-ft., and five score 5-ft. laths. These terms and quantities vary according to locality. Machine or sawn laths are superseding hand-made laths. Those split by hand give the best work. They

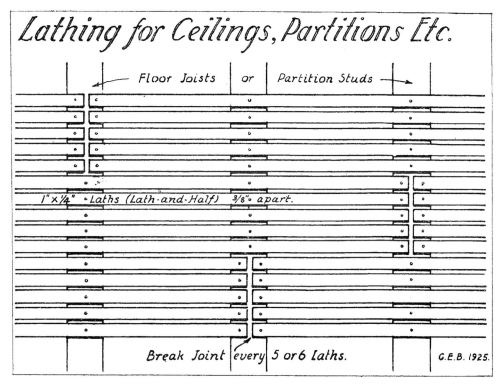

FIG. 35A.

split with the grain of the wood, are therefore stronger, and less liable to twist than machine-made laths. Cast-iron nails are used for common work ; wrought nails in high-class work. Galvanised wrought-iron nails prevent rusting. Laths should be selected in lengths best suited to the spacing of the joists from centre to centre, and should be fixed about ⅜ in. apart. In common work the ends overlap. In good work they should butt against each other. This is termed " butt work." They should also break joint in bays every 3 or 4 ft. in width, to give a better key and prevent any cracking of the ceiling or wall along the line of joists, as shown in Fig 35A. When ordinary laths are used, the studding and joists should never exceed 14 in. from centre to centre. The thickest laths are used for ceilings, lath and a half for partitions, and battened or studded walls for good work. Single laths are used for ordinary work, stoothed walls, or partitions. All timbers over 3 in. wide should have fillets or double laths nailed along the centre and the laths nailed to them. This is done to give a better key to the plaster, and is known as " counter-lathing." Reeds, wickerwork, slates, and wire have been used as substitutes for wood lathing. Wire and metal sheet lathing are now preferred for fire resisting and material saving. The by-laws of the London County Council require " all laths used for plastering to be sound laths free from sap, but iron or other incombustible laths, wire netting, or other suitable materials to the satisfaction of the district surveyor, may be used."

Expanded metal lathing plays a very important part in the plastering of modern buildings, and is a paramount necessity in all large buildings.

The expanded metal lathings as made by The Expanded Metal Company Limited (London and West Hartlepool), are made from mild steel sheets. They give an ideal key for plaster ceilings, steelwork encasing, solid and hollow partitions, exterior walls, and other work. Two types are manufactured and known to the trade as—

" B B " Expanded Metal Lathing.
" Expamet " Expanded Metal Lathing.

" B B " expanded metal lathing (Fig. 36A) is made in sheets 9 ft. by 2 ft., from 26, 24, and 22 gauge mild steel, in weights varying from $2\frac{1}{4}$ lbs. to $3\frac{3}{4}$ lbs. per yard super.

" Expamet " expanded metal lathing (Fig. 36B) is made in sheets 6 ft. by 2 ft., 7 ft. by 2 ft., and 8 ft. by 2 ft. 3 in., from 24, 22, and 20 gauge mild steel, in weights varying from $3\frac{1}{2}$ lbs. to 5 lbs. per yard super.

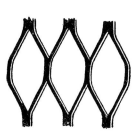

" Expamet " lathing, the older type, is made on a vertical cutting machine. The " B B " lathing is a new invention made on rotary machines, which run at a much higher speed and produce more cheaply than the vertical machines.

FIG. 36A.—" B B " Lathing.

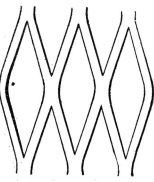

FIG. 36B.—" Expamet " Lathing.

" B B " expanded metal lathing is recommended most. It was designed to combine all the best properties. The meshes are a small diamond shape. From their shape and size a minimum quantity of plaster is required, and very little material is wasted.

Both lathings are coated with a mineral oil during manufacture and dipped in asphaltum paint.

Unpainted lathing is unsuitable for plasterwork; lathing required for other purposes may be uncoated.

Metal lathing can be galvanised, but is more costly.

" B B " expanded metal lathing can be made from galvanised blank sheets; but the edges of the strands are uncoated.

It can be obtained also in the form of corrugated lath; the standard corrugations are 1 in. wide by $\frac{1}{4}$ in. deep overall, are contiguous and run the long way of the mesh, viz., the long way of the sheet.

Generally both kinds are suitable for all purposes to which metal lathing can be applied. All of the meshes are suitable for hair plaster. The " B B " and $\frac{1}{4}$ in. meshes are best for hairless plaster.

The 26 g. weight is for solid partitions, steelwork casing, and similar work.

Nothing lighter than 24 g. lathing is advisable for ceilings and similar work ; 26 g. " B B " is good for small plain ceilings.

For heavily ornamented plaster ceilings and other work, tiling, mosaic, and exterior work, the heavier lathings are more suitable.

Painting, etc.—All metal accessories, clips, hangers, ceiling bars, tension rods, and lathings used with plasterwork must be painted. Where excessive moisture is apprehended, galvanised lathing, *if not back-plastered*, is best.

Spacings.—For ordinary plain, horizontal, and sloping work—

No. 250 may be used at spacings up to 12 in.

Nos. 252, 1, and 26 for spacings up to 14 in.

Nos. 254, 91, and 93 for spacings up to 16 in.

Nos. 92 and 94 for spacings up to 18 in.

Fixing.—Metal lathings should be fixed securely, long way of the sheet across the bearers, to ensure a level and rigid ground for plaster. The strands of the sheets should slope in one direction ; for vertical work they should slope inwards and downwards.

The lathings should be fixed at intervals— not more than 4 in. for the lighter, or 3 in. for the heavier—by staples or nails to woodwork, or wire clips to steelwork (Fig. 37), and wired together at similar intervals between supports. The sheets must overlap not less than one mesh where they join. Sheets should be bent to give a proper " key " for the plaster. Overlaps must not be made at angles or curves, but about 2 ft. beyond.

Galvanised slice-cut staples 1 in. or 1¼ in. long are intended for woodwork. No less than 18 g. galvanised soft iron wire is required for tying. Special lathing clips are made for clipping the lathings to flat ceiling bars, cradles, etc.

To clear the lathing from the face of joists, studs, etc., for a good plaster " key," a small round rod or a strip of hard wood should be clipped or stapled on to the face of the structural member.

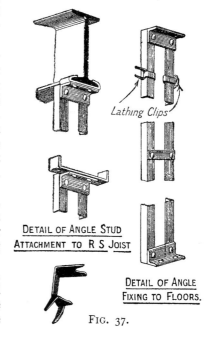

Lathing Clips

DETAIL OF ANGLE STUD
ATTACHMENT TO R S JOIST

DETAIL OF ANGLE
FIXING TO FLOORS.

FIG. 37.

Plasters for Expanded Metal Lathings.—Ordinary lime and hair mortar, plasters with a natural basis (such as suitable quarry or river sand), or those gauged with Portland cement, which tend to preserve metal, are recommended for use with expanded metal lathings.

Plasters and mortars containing ground ashes are unsuitable. Boiler ashes, cinders, or other materials containing corrosive chemicals must be avoided ; in fact, plasters and mortars containing sulphates, chlorides, or other corrosive ingredients should not be used on metal lathings.

Lime and hair mortar is cheap, efficient, and fire-resisting.

Plaster should be mixed " stiff " and applied without excessive pressure. If too much pressure is used, the lathing in a bay newly plastered will spring or give to the trowel and the newly finished plaster fall off. Pockets or holes must not be left in the body of finished work. The moist air returned by them is liable to set up corrosion of the metal.

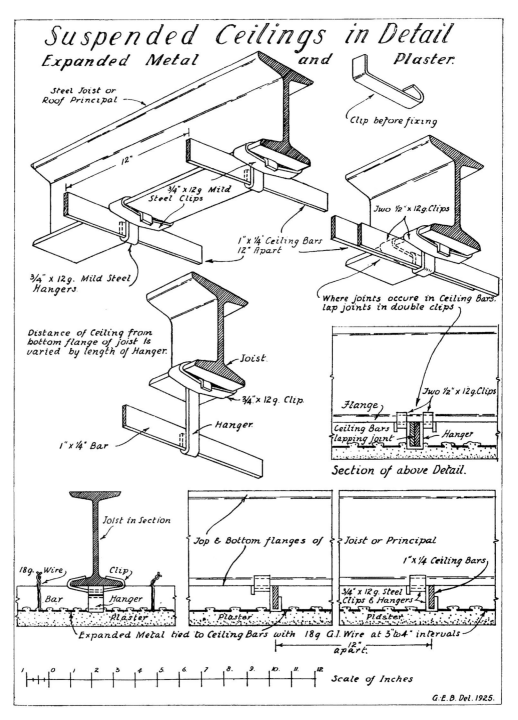

FIG. 38.

Plaster may be applied in two coats. The total thickness upon properly fixed lathing need not exceed ½ in. Three-coat work, ¾ in. thick, is more usual.

The water used for gauging must be fresh, clean, and unpolluted.

Render.—Lime and hair mortar, for interior " first " and " second " coat work, should be composed of 1½ parts of clean, sharp, coarse river or pit sand, 1 part of thoroughly slaked lime, and not less than ½ a part of Portland cement ; for exterior work there should be not less than 1 part of Portland cement. The first coat at least should be mixed with long cow hair, free from grease, dirt, and other impurities, in the proportion of not less than 1 lb. of hair to 3 cub. ft. of mortar   Plate CIV illustrates the back of rendering coat, showing the " key " obtained by inter-expanded metal lathing.

Finish.—Any plaster may be used safely for " finishing " interior work. Keen's cement is recommended for high-class work. Portland cement should *always* be used for finishing exterior work.

Solid Partitions.—For interior solid partitions a quick, hard-setting plaster

SECTION THROUGH FLOOR AND CEILING.

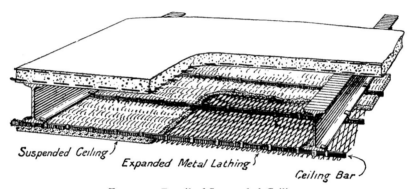

Suspended Ceiling.   Expanded Metal Lathing.   Ceiling Bar.

FIG. 39.—Detail of Suspended Ceiling.

is best.   Granite plaster " render " is good for a first coat, " brick " for second, and " finish " for final coat work.

Decorating.—The pores of plasterwork should not be sealed in any way, such as by painting or decorating in oil colours, *until the building is thoroughly dry.*

Suspended Ceilings.—For spans of up to 8 ft., flat steel bars, of suitable section, are suspended on edge from the floor joists, etc., at intervals according to the weight of lathing and plaster to be used, by means of purpose-made mild steel hangers, as shown in Figs. 38 and 39.

The section of bar to be used depends upon the kind of work to be done ; for ordinary *plain* work the following have proved satisfactory :—

For spans up to and including 4 ft.				Bars $\frac{3}{4}$ in. by $\frac{3}{16}$ in.		
,,	,,	,,	,, 5 ,,	,, $\frac{7}{8}$,, ,, $\frac{3}{16}$,,		
,,	,,	,,	,, 6 ,,	,, 1 ,, ,, $\frac{1}{4}$,,		
,,	,,	,,	,, 7 ,,	,, $1\frac{1}{4}$,, ,, $\frac{1}{4}$,,		
,,	,,	,,	,, 8 ,,	,, $1\frac{1}{2}$,, ,, $\frac{1}{4}$,,		

For spans of over 8 ft. use angle or tee supports at, say, 6 ft. centres, and from them suspend the ceiling bars.

Where bars join they should overlap, at least 2 in., in a hanger. In wall-end bays they should be pinned not less than 2 in. into the masonry. In corridors and places where the spans are not too long, intermediate support is not necessary. The bars may be pinned at their ends into the brickwork, etc. In long bays it is wise at the half-span to tie a bearer bar on top of, and at right angles to, those on edge, to maintain them in a vertical plane.

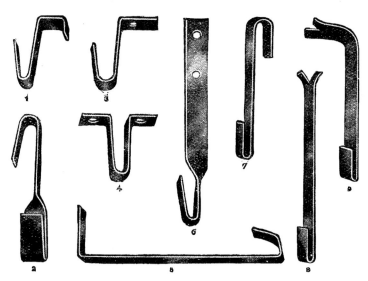

FIG. 40.—Lathing Accessories in Suspended Ceilings.

Hangers (Fig. 4 o) should be secured by screws to timber joists; attached to R.S.J.'s by means of mild steel clips, bent over tie-members of roof trusses, and pinned into concrete beams. The bars should be fastened *in* the hangers with wire, and at lapped joints, to prevent the metal grounds from rising.

Metal lathing should be fixed to the ceiling bars with clips, or galvanised soft iron wire, as described previously. The ceiling grounds are then ready for plastering.

Wall casing or deafening is constructed by setting holdfasts into the wall vertically at about 4 ft. centres and horizontally according to the weight of the lathing to be used. The holdfasts are holed or hooked at the outer end to receive flat vertical bars, which are either bolted or wired in position. Lathing and plaster is applied as before described. Details of construction are shown in Fig. 41.

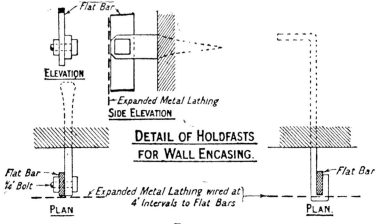

FIG. 41.

Thin Walls, Partitions, etc. (Plate CIV, *a*, *b*).—Metal grounds for solid walls, etc., may be formed of expanded metal lathing fastened to $\frac{3}{8}$ in. diameter steel rods, or other suitable sections, placed 12 in. to 15 in. apart.

Tension rods are fixed tautly at their ends with screws to timber, hangers or spikes to concrete, and clips to steelwork; in some cases it suffices if their ends are bent round structural members, as in steel frame buildings.

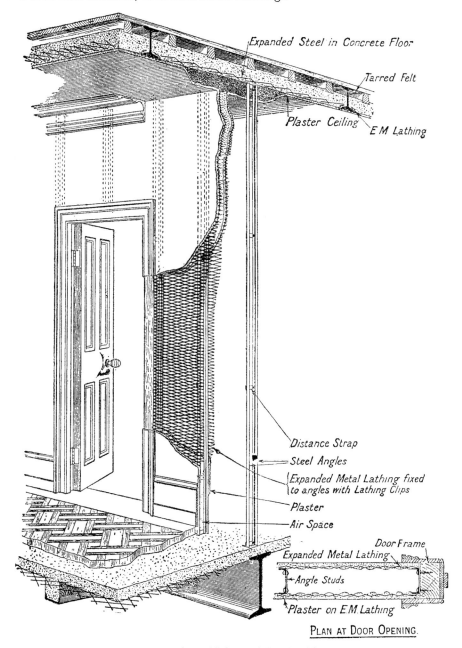

FIG. 42.—Details of Hollow Walls, Partitions, etc.

Upright rods may be sprung and grouted into holes in the flooring at bottom and top, particularly in new buildings.

Frames for doors and other openings should be fixed in position before the metal grounds are commenced, and a rod fixed to each side of the frame.

When the metal groundwork is completed, it must be temporarily strutted and railed half-way up on one side to keep it in a vertical plane.

The first or " render " coat should then be applied on the opposite side, $\frac{1}{2}$ in. thick, and allowed to set hard previous to the second coat being applied. When the two coats are set, the temporary supports may be removed and the reverse side floated. The finishing coat is applied in the ordinary way.

Timber dado and picture rails, panelling, etc., may be fixed direct to the plaster with wire nails, or they may be blocked apart and fixed to the metal grounds before the plaster is applied.

Interior solid partitions are built only $1\frac{1}{2}$ in. thick. Usually they are 2 in. thick. Exterior solid walls are generally made $2\frac{1}{2}$ in. to 3 in. thick.

Hollow Walls, Partitions, etc. (Fig. 42).—The metal grounds for hollow walls, etc., are formed of expanded metal lathing fastened on *both* sides to steel studs spaced from 12 in. to 18 in. apart.

The studs are formed of two angle bars connected at intervals by distance straps and by angle foot and head pieces, which are holed for the studs to be fixed to flooring, etc. If the studs are to be fixed to steelwork, a clip is riveted to the foot and head pieces for attachment.

Other and cheaper studs, stamped out of thin steel sheets, may be substituted. Some studs may be sprung into holes drilled into the flooring at bottom and top, or fixed there by spikes, staples, etc.

Overall thickness is regulated by the length of the cross straps and pieces in the built-up stud and by the width of the web in the other studs ; 6 in. is a usual overall dimension ; $\frac{3}{4}$ in. of plaster is enough for the interior skin ; $1\frac{1}{4}$ in. for the exterior.

It is wise to back-plaster lathing in exterior work and thus embed it. The additional plaster need not increase the overall thickness of hollow walling, and adds but little to the weight.

EXPANDED METAL AND PLASTER PARTITIONS FIXED TO TIMBER JOISTS, FIG. 43.

Fig. 43 illustrates a sketch with details of fixing $\frac{3}{8}$ in. tension rods with galvanised iron staples, and the application of expanded metal lathing to them. For solid partition work inside buildings a quick, hard-setting material such as granite plaster is best. In such cases for the first coat or rendering, a coat of granite plaster should be used, " brick " for the second coat, and finish for the last coat. The pores of the plasterwork should not be sealed or stopped by painting or any form of oil-colour application until the work is thoroughly dry.

EXPANDED METAL AND PLASTER PARTITIONS FIXED TO STEEL JOISTS, FIG. 44.

Metal groundwork for walls of solid plaster is formed of expanded metal lathing, properly secured to $\frac{3}{8}$ in. diameter steel rods or other varying suitable sections, placed about 12 in. to 15 in. apart.

Tension rods should be fixed at their ends with screws to timber work, hangers or spikes to concrete work, and clips to steelwork ; in some cases it is enough if their ends are bent round the structural members, as in the instance of steel-framed buildings.

Frames for door and other openings must be fixed in their place before any metal or groundwork is commenced, and a rod should be fixed to each side of the frame.

When the metal groundwork is done, it should be thoroughly well strutted and railed temporarily, at half the height on one side to keep it vertical whilst the plastering is being done.

The rendering coat should then be put on from the opposite side, $\frac{1}{2}$ in. thick, and

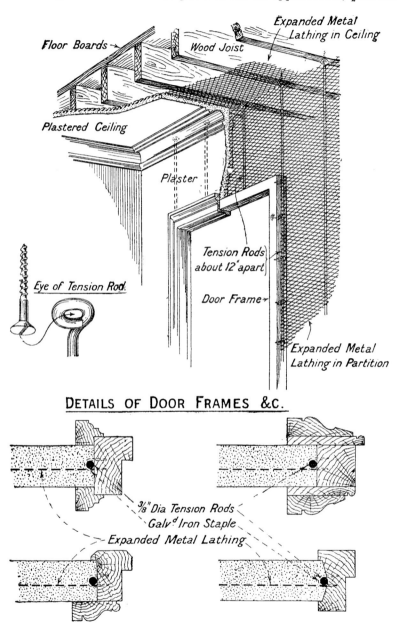

FIG. 43.—Details of Solid Partitions fixed to Timber Joists.

this must be allowed to set hard before the second coat is applied ; when both of these coats are set, the supports may be removed and the other side supported ; the finishing coat is then put on in the usual way.

Picture rails, dado rails, panelling, etc., or any woodwork, may be fixed direct on to the plaster with wire nails, or they may be blocked apart and fixed to the metal groundwork before the plaster is applied.

Solid partitions are built sometimes only 1½ in. thick, but usually they are 2 in. thick; exterior solid walls are generally from 2½ in. to 3 in. in thickness.

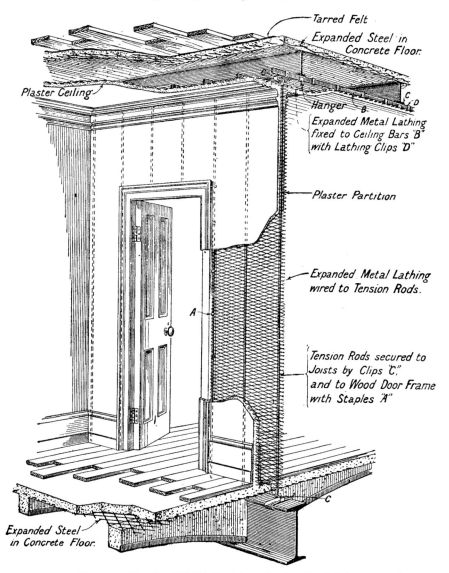

FIG. 44.—Details of Solid Partitions fixed to Steel Joists.

For solid plaster partitions on expanded metal, the metal groundwork should consist of ⅜ in. diameter steel tension rods, fixed tautly to the flanges of the steel floor and ceiling joists with clips, to concrete work with hangers or spikes, or to timber work by screws, all depending upon the construction of the floor and ceiling. Tension rods should be placed from 12 in. to 14 in. apart. The expanded metal is then tied securely

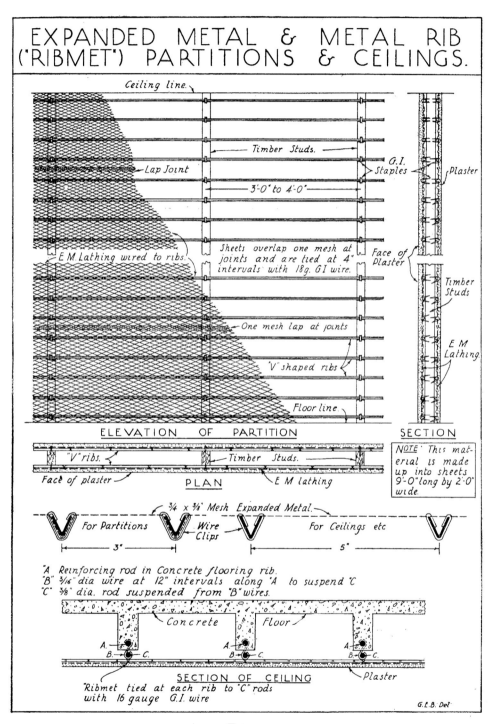

EXPANDED METAL & METAL RIB ('RIBMET') PARTITIONS & CEILINGS.

Ceiling line.

Timber Studs.

Lap Joint

G.I. Staples

Plaster

3'-0" to 4'-0"

Sheets overlap one mesh at joints and are tied at 4" intervals with 18g. GI wire.

E M. Lathing wired to ribs.

Face of Plaster

Timber Studs

One mesh lap at joints

E M Lathing.

"V" shaped ribs

Floor line.

ELEVATION OF PARTITION

SECTION

"V" ribs.

Timber Studs.

Face of plaster

PLAN

E M lathing

NOTE: This material is made up into sheets 9'-0" long by 2'-0" wide.

¾ x ⅜" Mesh Expanded Metal.

For Partitions

Wire Clips

For Ceilings etc

3"

5"

"A" Reinforcing rod in Concrete flooring rib.
"B" ³/₁₆" dia wire at 12" intervals along "A" to suspend "C"
"C" ⅜" dia. rod suspended from "B" wires.

Concrete   Floor

A   A   A

B — C   B — C   B — C

SECTION OF CEILING

Plaster

"Ribmet" tied at each rib to "C" rods
with 16 gauge G.I. wire

G.E.B. Del.

FIG. 45.

to such tension rods at 3 in. to 4 in. intervals with soft galvanised iron wire of no less gauge than No. 18, and securely stapled to any timber work, such as door or window frames, with 1 in. or 1½ in. galvanised staples. The metal sheets should be fixed with the long way of the mesh horizontal, and the sheets, which are made in specified widths, should lap over each other at joints not less than one mesh and tied at 4 in. intervals throughout the lap joint.

Joints should never occur at an angle or on a curve. Door and window frames or other similar woodwork should be fixed in position before the metal grounds are commenced, and the tension rods fixed to each side of the frame. When the metal work is erected it must be supported up to half its height by temporary timber strutting on the one side and by railing to keep the metal work quite vertical.

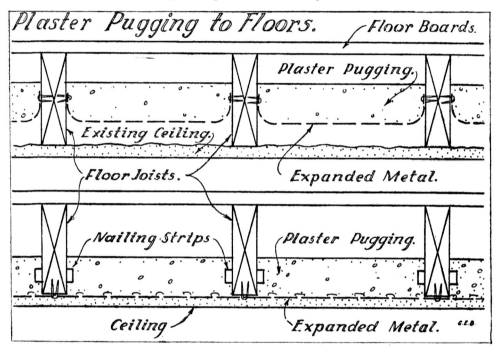

FIG. 46.

The steel clip and method of fixing the ceiling bars to the joists and the expanded metal, wired or clipped to the ceiling bars, is shown in Fig. 38.

Expanded metal and metal rib ("Ribmet") partitions and ceilings. Fig. 45 illustrates clearly a very serviceable and recent development of the use of expanded metal and metal ribs for partitions and suspended ceilings.

A plan, elevation and section of part of a partition are shown with a detail which explains the fixing of the mesh in connection with the metal ribs and studs.

The supplementary section of suspended ceiling with metal rib and expanded metal hung from reinforcing rods in the concrete flooring seams is self-explanatory, and can be strongly recommended if properly executed as intended by the manufacturers.

Pugging.—Pugging (Fig. 46), which is sometimes called deafening, is placed between the joists in timber flooring and between the studs in timber partitioning, with the object of preventing the passage of sounds, smells, etc., from one room to another. Practice varies so far as its thickness is concerned, but 1 in. seems to be a recognised minimum ; and, generally, pugging is suspended midway between the floor boards and ceiling in a floor, and midway between the two lath and plaster skins in a stud position.

Expanded metal lathing and coarse plaster, breeze concrete, slag wool, or similar material laid upon it are often used for the purpose and give excellent results. The lathing should be fixed with the long way of its meshes from support to support ; it may be bent at its ends and stapled or nailed direct to the sides of the joists or studs ;

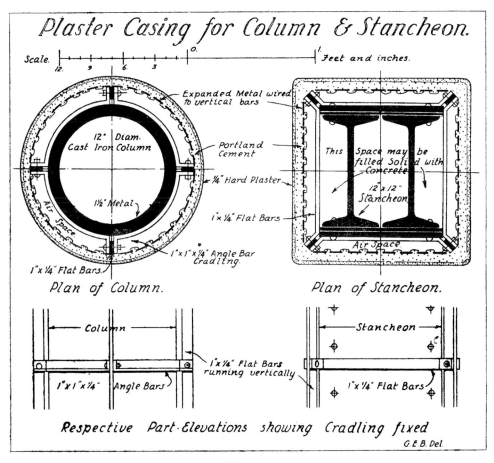

FIG. 47.

or it may be fixed to wood fillets nailed along the sides of the joists or studs. In some cases of flooring the lathing has been fixed to the soffit of the timber joists, fillets nailed along their sides, and breeze concrete laid on the lathing ; in that way the lathing acts as permanent centering for the concrete and as a base for the plaster ceiling ; the wood fillets being buried at, say, the centre of its depth, help to support the concrete.

Composite Flooring on Timber Joists.—In the alteration or reconstruction of buildings having timber floors, it is often desired to replace the floor boards with sand and cement, fine concrete, or other composite flooring, and at the same time to retain the existing timber joists ; likewise, for new buildings such floorings may be desired. It can be built satisfactorily by fixing heavy expanded metal lathing on top of the joists and laying the decking on it ; with the object of preventing dry rot in the timber, it is advisable to lay between it and the decking, tarred felt, bitumen sheeting, or some such reliable preservative.

Steelwork Encasing, Expanded Metal Lathing, and Plaster.—Fire-resisting is inefficient unless all structural steelwork is properly encased and protected from fire risks.

Structural Steelwork Encasing.—The covering of columns, stanchions, girders, joists, etc., and the forming of false work with " Expamet " to receive plaster or concrete, varies according to conditions and requirements.

For *plasterwork*, the lathings and sometimes the lighter weights in ¾ in. mesh " Expamet," such as No. 38, are used. For *concrete* encasing, formed with temporary centering, the lighter weights in 1½ in. mesh " Expamet," such as No. 6, are recommended.

In many cases lathing is wrapped simply round the steelwork, secured in position when necessary, and wired together at lapped joins and then covered with plaster. A better system is to use metal cradling, such as ¼ in. or ⅜ in. round rods, bent to the shape of the steelwork and secured in position, to which the lathing is tied to give the plaster a better " key " (Fig. 47).

In high-class work, the encasing should be in one body, not less than 2 in. thick, obtained as follows :—

For Plaster Finish.—By fixing the lathing 2 in. from the face of the steelwork, filling in the space with concrete, and covering the lathing with plaster.

For Concrete Finish.—By using temporary centering and filling in the concrete encasing, with 1½ in. mesh, " Expamet " at the centre of its thickness.

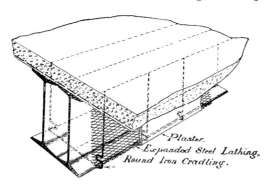

FIG. 48.—Detail of Girder Encasing.

Column Encasing.—In Fig. 47 is shown an arrangement for encasing a column or stanchion. Quadrant clips with holed lugs, made from flat steel bars, are fixed round the column or stanchion, and vertical flat bars are bolted in between the lugs. To these bars the lathing is wired or clipped, the space between the column and lathing is filled in with concrete or left vacant as may be desired, and the lathing is covered with plaster. If concrete filling is to be used the lathing should be fixed in courses of, say, 2 ft., and the concrete filled in nearly to that height, before the next course is placed in position. The lathing thus will act as permanent centering and save the expense of temporary timbering.

Where concrete filling is used the clips and bars may be omitted, as the lathing can be bent to the required shape, placed round the column, and tied with wire at the lapped join ; but it must be held in position while the concrete is packed behind it. If this method be adopted, the lathing in each course should be left protruding above the concrete, so that the overlapped sheets may be wired together.

By this arrangement a square stanchion may be encased to represent a round column, or a round column to represent a square, hexagonal, or other pillar.

False Columns.—It is obvious that, with a skeleton frame of vertical bars and horizontal bands, a false pillar can be constructed, as is shown in Fig. 42 and elsewhere.

In such cases, angle or " tee " bar uprights are to be preferred to flat bars, and the horizontal bands should be fixed on their outer faces, the lathing being attached with the long way of its mesh vertical.

Girder Encasing (Fig. 48).—For boxing-in exposed girders, etc., not more than 12 in. on side or soffit, expanded metal lathing can be wrapped round the beam and secured by staples, tenter hooks, or spikes to the underside of the floor above ; or, preferably, it can be wired to $\frac{3}{8}$ in. round rod cradling fixed at 12 in. to 15 in. centres along the beam, as shown below. In the first system the long way of the mesh in the lathing should be vertical on the sides and in the second it should be horizontal. For larger section beams, in high class and heavy work the second system should be used.

" **Jhilmil** " **steel lathing** is made in sheets 72 in. by 24 in. and 72 in. by 18 in., which are easily cut. The patentees claim that the perforations, by virtue of their arrangement, give a firm key with a minimum of plaster passing through them, combining a maximum economy of plaster with strength and fireproof qualities.

Various patterns are adapted for wrapping round girders and columns, and for fixing on rough wood planking, etc., for bridging ceiling spaces, etc., and for partitions.

" **West's** " **lock-woven mesh** for flooring columns, beams, etc., is a mechanically woven fabric, formed of main or tension steel wires and secondary or transverse steel wires, having an elastic limit of 64,000 lbs. and an ultimate strength of 89,000 lbs. per sq. in.

The Bostwick Patent Fireproof Metal Lath.—The Bostwick patent metal lath is an American invention, and is extensively used in that country. In England it has given every satisfaction. This metal lath makes a strong fire-resisting foundation, little liable to crack from settling of walls or deflections of ceilings. Plaster is firmly keyed and cannot be detached. A plasterer can, in a given time, lay more than double the yardage on this lath than on wood lath, and plaster will cover nearly twice the area because the surface of the metal lath is even and unyielding. The openings being uniform, guarantee a stronger key, without waste of mortar behind the lath. The cost is little, if any, more than with wood lath, due to the economy of material and labour. This lath is easily and quickly fixed. For fixing to iron, special clasps are made.

Johnson's Patent Galvanised Wire Lathing.—A wire netting, $\frac{3}{4}$ in. or smaller mesh, is laid on strips of varnished hoop iron and fixed with staples edgeways, across the joists. The netting is spread on this backing and stapled to the joists.

Patent Metal Lathing Sheets.—These are sunk and dovetailed on both sides, and, having serrated edges, form a double key for the plaster.

Helical Metal Lathing.—This is made of flat steel wire or ribbon twisted and woven to a convenient size and to any length. The stock size is 10 ft. 6 in. by 2 ft. 6 in. It is fixed by hooks.

Patent Reed Lathing.—A German patent, a webbing of reeds or rushes secured by wires. Ceilings are constructed by first nailing a close, and afterwards an open webbing to the joists. Both kinds of webbing are made in rolls of 20 square yards, in widths of from 1 to 2 yards. Reeds were the forerunners of wood laths in England, and were used in plasterwork long before the Christian era.

Slate Laths.—Slate lathing was introduced more than a century ago, and was once largely used in Manchester. The laths were made of waste slates of good quality, which had been spoilt in cutting or were too narrow for slating. They measure from 12 in. to 18 in. long, and are of various widths.

" **Hy-Rib,** " as manufactured by the Trussed Concrete Steel Company Limited, is made from the very best quality steel sheets. It is claimed that owing to the rigid stiffening ribs which are formed in the material in the process of manufacture, far less framing is necessary in the body of the structure. The type of lath takes plaster very rapidly with little waste.   Sheets are supplied in lengths up to 12 ft. ; the standard width of the sheet is 12 in.

Outer ribs are made to interlock, so that any width can be built up.   The sheets also overlap at the ends.   In this manner any required height can be attained. " Hy-Rib " is supplied in three gauges—28, 26, and 24.   For suspended ceilings and similar work, 30 gauge is often used.   " Hy-Rib " obviates the use of timber centering ; concrete flows through the lath of the material sufficiently only to afford a good key for plastering on to.

" Hy-Rib " walls and partitions are light, strong, fire-proof, quickly erected, and need be only 2 in. thick.

Suspended ceilings, boundary walls, tanks, reservoirs, culverts, etc., are equally well treated, as also steel hooping for circular columns.

Wall or building board is a dependable lining for walls and ceilings.   One important factor in its use is the frame to which it is applied.   Rigid and level joists and studding, and good carpentry in all additional framing parts, have an important effect on the finished work.

The studding must be so placed that *all the edges of the wall board can be nailed down*.   If wall board be used over old work, the surface must be evened by using strips of wood or waste strips of wall board.

In nailing the panels, a $\frac{1}{8}$ in. space should be left between the joints to allow for possible expansion of the timber behind, or for a fractional expansion of the board itself. Special care should be taken round windows and doors.

The board should be nailed through the centre of the sheet, at the top, in order to be hung square.   Then $\frac{3}{4}$ in. common brads should be nailed down the centre about 6 in. apart.   This enables the person erecting to smooth out the board on both sides.   Then the edges should be nailed (using 1 in. French nails) about $\frac{1}{2}$ in. from the edge and at about 3 in. intervals.   Work from the middle to each corner.

For ceilings, if only one man is erecting, it is usual to support one end with a T-shaped support to hold the panel temporarily.

Panelling.—Although the arrangement of panels depends upon individual taste (and the effects are almost endless), there are really but four basic designs.

Almost all boards can be supplied in 32, 36, and 48 in. widths, and in lengths from 6 ft. to 16 ft., and some makers supply a 24 in. wide sheet.   These different sizes afford numerous combinations.

The simplest, and perhaps the best, method is to divide into sections by false beams and then work a design similar for each section, thus producing panels within panels.

Decoration.—It is not advisable to put paper over wall board, and this is not necessary, as it is far better to fix moulding strips (which can be stained) and to paint the board with two coats of an oil paint.   With improvements in paint and a large variety of tints, the only difficulty is the choice, which will give no trouble to the decorator with a colour sense.   A good oil paint gives excellent results and enables the boards to be sponged down.   Varnishing size is applied in the manufacture of most wall board ; but give, after fixing, a first coat of size mixed with a little of the colour of paint to be used. Moulding strips should not be less than 2 in. ; narrower strips are apt to look insignificant.

A decorative strip should never be placed where there is no joist or where no frame is behind the panel.

In decorating, the brad holes in the panelling should be punched in and stopped with putty, or with a filler made of 3 parts plaster of Paris and 1 part dextrine, of putty con-sistency.   If the latter is used it should dry for twenty-four hours before paint is applied.

Stencilling, hand-painting, and graining can be reproduced on wall board.

" S X " Board.—This has a white mat surface, and is prepared wood fibre compressed into layers, cemented to form panels about $\frac{3}{16}$ in. thick, possessing rigidity and strength. As a lining material it is light and tough, while a special sizing preparation, incorporated with the fibres in manufacture, is stated to make it moisture resisting. The stock boards are made in 32, 36, and 48 in. widths, and in lengths from 6 ft. to 16 ft. They are easily cut with a fine tooth saw. One advantage as an alternative to plaster is that a house lined with the boards can be occupied immediately, and any interval for drying is obviated. Distinctive decorative effects may be obtained by dividing into panels the structural outcome of the moulding strips over the joints. The manufacturers guarantee that no waste paper or similar matter is used in " S X " board, which does not split or crack when handled or nailed, and is permanent. Furthermore, ceilings and walls of it are resistant to vibration. It should be painted or distempered at least once before fixing cover strips. No preliminary treatment is necessary before applying the decorative material, and the mat surface itself produces an attractive effect. These boards are made at Thames Mills, Purfleet, Essex.

"**Fiberlic**" (Macandrews & Forbes Ltd.) is made from a tough, strong, fibrous root. Rigid, close-grained, and hard, it is durable, fire-resisting, sound-deadening, and a non-conductor. Any handy-man can erect it, and it is often adopted as a rapidly applied substitute for lath and plaster on walls and ceilings. It can be painted or coloured as soon as fitted, and by panelling decorative effects are obtained. The material composing " Fiberlic " passes through three stages : (a) the conversion of the root into pulp ; (b) the formation of the pulp into thin sheets ; (c) the assembling of the sheets into the finished board, with the process of rendering all the layers waterproof. Every particle of the material is sized before being built up. " Fiberlic " can be cut with a fine tooth cross-cut saw or chisel, or can be scored through with a sharp knife against a straight-edge. The desiccation or " cooking " of the fibres during the initial stages so completely destroys living organisms that the finished product is free from any likelihood of developing dry rot or fungoid growths.

"**Beaver Board**" (The Beaver Board Co. Ltd.) is a Canadian product, and consists of pure wood fibre pressed into large panels, slightly exceeding $\frac{3}{16}$ in. thick. The panels are resistant to moisture, and are made 3 ft. and 4 ft. wide, and of 8, 9, 10, 12, 14, and 16 ft. lengths. The material is laminated, and weighs a little over $\frac{1}{2}$ lb. per sq. ft. The spruce logs are shredded into fibres, and these are " meshed " by machinery into thin sheets, four cemented together comprising the boards or panels. These are seasoned, and after the front and back surfaces receive single and double coatings respectively of patent sizing, so that when the front is painted each side is covered and protected. "Beaver board" may be employed where lath and plaster is generally used, as in finishing walls, partitions, and ceilings. For brick walls fix battens about $1\frac{1}{2}$ in. in width to the brickwork at required distances to receive the boards. For wood partitions the boards are nailed direct to the studs, and for ceilings fixed to the joists. Each board should be nailed on all four edges as well as intermediately. For applying to concrete walls or ceilings beneath concrete floors, the method is as for brick walls. In nailing to supports, allow for expansion by leaving about $\frac{1}{8}$ in. between adjacent edges. This space must be covered by a strip of wood, plain, sunk, or moulded, not less than $1\frac{7}{8}$ in. wide. By employing wider strips than this minimum and placing studs or battens in a prearranged scheme, good decorative effects are produced. Ordinary paint or distemper may be used as a finish.

"**Venesta**" **ply panels** (Venesta Ltd.) are of wood, and contain neither fibre nor pulp. Each panel has three layers cemented together, which not only renders it unshrinkable and unsplinterable, but greatly increases its strength. " Venesta " panels are light and hygienic, and may be fixed to brick walls, partitions, old plaster, or ceilings. For brickwork, rough deal battens about $1\frac{1}{2}$ in. by $\frac{5}{8}$ in. are nailed to the wall to take the panel edges where they meet. The panels are secured with ¾ in. fine nails, and the joints covered with thin strips or mouldings fastened with small-headed nails. For partitions or ceilings no battens are necessary, the panels being nailed direct to partition studding, floor joists, or ceilings. The panels possess a clean, smooth surface which readily takes distemper, paint, or enamel. The many sizes kept in stock will help the designer to get good effects of panelling without waste. " Venesta " plywood also offers advantages as a material for door panels. The increasing difficulty of obtaining solid fit seasoned wood may be overcome by this material, which obviates replacing shrunken and split panels. Venesta supply various classes of plywood in door-panel sizes, or in stock sizes from which they can be cut. It can also be obtained faced with mahogany, figured oak, etc., for any scheme of decoration.

" **Vi-Board** " is a series of building boards of various applications. In " Simplex " or 1-ply form, the board is homogeneous and durable, made from paper pulp and denatured wattle bark, with waterproof adhesives. This is used for wall panels or ceilings, as it is easy to fix under cover strips, and does not warp. Simplex boards, made in stock sizes of 9 ft. 10 in. by 3 ft. 11 in., may be sawn or planed, need no priming before painting, and can be polished a rich brown. " Duplex " grade consists of one ply of Vi-Board, or Violeum (by itself used as floor covering), and one of asbestos cement, glued together. It is suitable for wall panels, partitioning, and ceiling, can be nailed or screwed to wood, brick, or concrete, and is of value in damp positions. Its decorative treatment is as for Simplex. Vi-Board " Triplex " is a 3-ply board of either (a) 2-ply Vi-Board and 1-ply asbestos cement in the middle ; (b) 2-ply asbestos cement and 1-ply Vi-Board in the middle ; or (c) 1-ply Vi-Board, 1-ply asbestos cement, and 1-ply Violeum. Vi-Board Triplex (c) is used as complete flooring (combining flooring and floor covering), and is laid on joists with overlapping joints by nails or invisible screws. It may also be used as skirting board. Duplex and Triplex are supplied in sheets 8 ft. by 3 ft. 11 in., 6 ft. by 3 ft. 11 in., and 6 ft. by 3 ft., can be cut with a fine saw and fitted with close joints. The (a) and (b) qualities are adapted to partitioning or ceilings, and are fire, heat, and sound resisting, impervious to dry rot. Vi-Board " Veneered " (surfaced with various woods) is another form used for panelling and similar work. " Violeum "—the floor covering—may be laid on wood floors, when it is pinned with invisible brads like linoleum, or can be glued to concrete floors. It is stated to harden with age, wear well, and be waterproof when polished. The sheets are 9 ft. 10 in. by 3 ft. 11 in., and are readily cut and laid as linoleum. For hospitals, rounded Violeum skirtings are obtainable. Vi-Board " Weatherproof " is made in 1, 2, or 3 ply, and is suitable for outside building work, hoarding, etc. The manufacturers (Vi-Board (Sales) Ltd.) point out that this quality, with no covering, has withstood seven years' exposure without deterioration.

" **Celotex** " **insulating building board** is made from sugar-cane fibre, long, hard, and of great strength. No adhesive constituent is introduced, its strength depending on the fibre interlacing. Its resistance under Hunt tests is 373 lbs. per sq. in. It is waterproofed throughout, and combines sound deadening, insulation, shock absorbence, with extreme lightness. It provides a base for plaster, stucco, or rough-cast, and can be fixed to a damp brick wall. Celotex serves the double purpose of centering and surface finish to reinforced concrete flooring. " False work " and centering of this material adheres to the concrete, and when the scaffolding is removed the flush ceiling can be papered, plastered, distempered, or painted. It is used for exterior and interior finish, for partitions, ceilings, roofs, and inside linings. Other uses include theatre scenery, boxes, and hard tennis courts, as a veneer filler between rubber surface and concrete base.

" **Ten Test** " wall sheathing consists of selected spruce and pine wood pulp, with other ingredients to increase strength. It is compressed into sheets, cut to 8 ft. by 4 ft., and reduced to a thickness of $\frac{7}{16}$ in. The material has a mat surface on one side for paper, paint, and distemper adhesion ; on the other, a special finish for adhering to stucco and plaster face ; it weighs 12 oz. per foot super. While " Ten Test " may be applied to the lining of internal walls and ceilings, its capacity for cohesion renders it of service for external work on the construction of bungalows, garages, pavilions, etc. It does not warp or crack, is weatherproof and considerably soundproof. National Physical Laboratory tests show its heat conductivity about the same as cork. The standard sheets are " flameproof " only, but can be supplied " proofed," so that they will not smoulder.

Gyproc fireproof plaster wall board is manufactured with a core of hydrated gypsum set hard and reinforced with surfacing material. It is a wall of gypsum constructed of the material of the finest of walls, and comes to the builder ready for use. The lathing, plaster mixing, and plastering itself are done. All that remains is to nail the wall board to the supports. It cuts like timber, is clean to handle, and rapidly and easily applied. There is no waiting for drying. When the sheets are nailed up the rooms are ready for decoration. The boards can be papered, painted, distempered, or panelled. It is fireproof, a splendid insulator against heat, cold, damp, noise, and vermin. It is rigid and cannot warp, crack, or buckle, and is permanent and durable. Gyproc is suitable for exteriors and interior walls and ceilings, and is supplied in convenient lengths. Full particulars from Evans, Osgood, & Co. Ltd., Dashwood House, 69 Old Broad Street, London.

American Plastering.—In conclusion, space only permits us to make a glancing reference to many patent plastering and partition materials which have been produced in recent years in the United States. Particulars of these can be obtained from the advertisements in any American architectural journal or magazine, and the manufacturers are always ready to give full information ; none of these, however, are in general use in the United Kingdom.

Recently a new system has come into use in which colours are introduced, and this is suitable for both interior and exterior work. By its use the co-operation of the decorator or painter is eliminated. In addition there has also been introduced a type known as improved Mexican and Spanish plastering, and also a form called " Jazz " plastering, in bright colours. The older plaster craftsmen are not by any means fond of this type of work, but it has gained a good deal of popularity, and it is reported that some of it of a highly decorated type has a fine effect. Further information on this and other American materials and practice will be found in the Appendix, p. 323.

CHAPTER IX

OF DECORATIVE CEILINGS GENERALLY: SOLID WORK

Panelled, "Figured," and Ribbed Ceilings—Rib Brackets and Lathing—Floating Panelled
  Ceilings—Setting Out Panelled Ceilings—Panel Mouldings—Coffered Ceilings—Planted
  Panel Mouldings—Setting Ceilings—Lime Putty Finish—Hard Finish—Fine Finish—
  Cement Finish—Portland Cement Ceilings—Fibrous Plaster Ceilings—Working Plans
  of Panelled Ceilings—Classic Panelling.

MUCH time and thought must be devoted to the decorative aspect of plasterwork, which
cannot be separated from the technical or mechanical without injury to the art and the
craft as such.

Plasterers should have a thorough practical knowledge of their beautiful art.
The illustrations of this volume prove what plasterers have done in the past in both
design and execution. There are good practical plasterers and modellers to-day able
and skilful if opportunity were offered them. Supply would follow demand. The
subject of decoration as applied to plastic art is immense, and absorbingly interesting
from every aspect. The deplorable part about it is that most journeymen are content
to follow the trade as mechanics only, because they must; because the time is not yet
ripe for sweetening their labour and life with a great art, of which we speak at greater
length in Chapters III and V   Students should collect sketches and information of fine
examples to be found in all parts of the three kingdoms.

Panelled Ceilings.—" A panelled ceiling " is one whose whole surface is broken
up into lesser spaces, coffers, or bays by beams, girders, or shallow ribs (Plates XI-XIX,
XXV-XXVI, c). Ceilings enriched with mouldings are known in the trade as " figured "
and " ribbed " ceilings. A " figured ceiling " is one having small mouldings, designed
in geometrical figures. A " ribbed ceiling " is one with rib mouldings on the intrados
of arches or circular ceilings; the term is also used of flat ceilings having circular
mouldings. " Decorative flat ceilings " is a term applied to those with flat surface
modelled ornamentation, but without rib mouldings.

Rib Brackets and Lathing for Panelled Ceilings.—Large ceiling mouldings
such as coffers, caissons, or mock beams, when worked solid, require a bracket and
lath foundation for the plasterwork. Spike and rope brackets are generally used for
ordinary ceiling mouldings, girthing up to 12 or 20 in. Any width of moulding may
be secured by two or more rows of spikes. Rib mouldings 6 in. to 9 in. deep have been
run on such brackets. Where mouldings are wide and deep, the floating should be
cut to the lath work, but before the spikes are driven, to give a key to the bracket,
freedom for driving, and proper cleaning and damping of the lath work. Before the
ceiling lathing is begun, small joists or strong quartering should be fixed where required,
to receive the spikes. Lath work for panelled ceilings should be sound and strong
to carry the rib mouldings. For wood lathing, double lath is best. Metal lathing is
not only strong, but practically fireproof. It is not economy to use inferior materials

for this or any kind of work.   Rib and cornice brackets may also be formed with metal lathing.

Floating Panelled Ceilings.—Panelled ceilings need sound foundation work in the first coat and the floating coat, the former on strong well-seasoned laths, securely nailed, or on corrugated metal laths, or expanded wire netting   The first two coats should be of strong-haired, well-tempered coarse stuff.   It is most important, where rich or fat lime is used, that each coat should stand as long as possible before the next· one is laid.   Lime plaster laid in thin coatings, with considerable time between them, hardens well.   Each coat needs long exposure to the carbonic acid in the atmos-phere before being covered.   It is a common practice to place a coke fire in the centre of rooms to hasten the drying of plaster.   The carbonic acid gas given off by the coke hardens, while the heat helps to dry.   For good work or heavy mouldings, coarse stuff should be gauged with $1\frac{1}{3}$ parts of strong coarse plaster.   The floating surface must be level and straight.   Cornice screeds must be formed all round the ceiling, levelled by lath dots, proved by a parallel ceiling rule.   Narrow screeds are formed 4 ft. to 6 ft. apart across the ceiling, and ruled flush with the main screeds, the intermediate spaces filled in and ruled flush with the screeds.   Gauged work should not be hand-floated with water, which with the working tends to kill the plaster.   The work should be left moderately rough, as a key for the running screeds and setting stuff.   If the ceiling has few mouldings, gauged putty running screeds (for the running mould to bear on) are formed where the mouldings are required.   For numerous mouldings it is best to make the whole ceiling smooth, level, and straight, into one entire screed : by filling up the rough places with soft gauged coarse stuff, floating smooth with a rule worked over the stuff in every direction, testing with a long straight-edge, and finishing with a hand-float.   Size water must be used in gauging, to allow time for proper ruling and floating.

Another good method is to leave the floating straight, if rough, by working the floating rule flat on its face with a zigzag motion to take off excess stuff.   Smooth surfaces should be roughened with a coarse broom before the stuff is set, or, if set, with a rough drag, afterwards brushing off loose particles.   While the work is green, form narrow screeds between the main screeds, and from these, others about 10 ft. or 12 ft. apart, over the ceiling area ; fill in the intermediate spaces and rule off flush.   Before this is done the screeds should be tested with a long straight-edge, to see that all are lineable.   Where possible, lay and rule off from the main screeds, make true and smooth with a straight-edge worked in all directions, make good any defects with soft stuff, and finish with a hand-float.   For the above process use setting stuff, made of $\frac{1}{10}$ part of well-beaten white hair, gauged with size water, and $\frac{1}{3}$ part of fine plaster.   All ruling and scouring must be completed before the stuff is set.   When mouldings are to be run and mitred, key the haired coat with a sharp drag.   Dust the surface and leave the frayed hair loose and rough to ensure a good and strong key for the final coat.

Setting Out Panelled Ceilings.—A knowledge of elementary geometry is useful for setting-out purposes to ensure speed, proficiency, and accuracy.   The " rule-of-thumb " man wastes time, temper, and energy through lack of this simple knowledge.

For simplicity the main centre lines of the pattern should be set out in single line or " skeleton " form first, showing the form and position of the mouldings bounding the panels ; the " working lines," from which the mouldings are formed, come next. There are three necessary kinds of setting-out lines, viz., " centre lines," " width lines," and " radial lines."   The centre lines or half-width of the mouldings from which measurements are made and taken come first in importance.   The width lines, representing the width or bed of the mouldings, are necessary to show the intersections, for guidance in cutting out of floating coat, and planting on the mouldings.   Radial lines necessary for some designs are struck lengthwise, crosswise, or diagonally, to give radius centres and angles of mouldings, also to test squareness and accuracy. There are three kinds of working lines, viz., " screed lines " at the nib and slipper bearings of the running mould to guide in forming the running screeds, for sunk panels and beams, or where the ceiling is left rough from the floating. " Rule lines " show the position and guide in fixing the running rules. The space between one of the width lines and the rule line is equal to the width of the bearing part of the slippered side of the running mould. " Template lines " guide the fixing of templates and trammels. Good guidance for this purpose may be had by indicating centre marks and angle points, from or on the centre and radial lines. Similar marks and points should be made on the template, the corresponding marks being brought together when fixing. The various lines should be struck in different colours : black (charcoal or burnt wood) for centre lines ; red (ochre or chalk) for width lines ; yellow (ochre) for radial lines ; and brown (umber) or white (dry plaster) for the screed, rules, and template lines if on a surface where it will show. Width and rule lines should be taken from centre lines with a " mould gauge," cut from a piece of running rule, to width of moulding plus the slipper of running mould. Rebate one end the length of slipper and mark the centre of the remaining part. Lay the centre mark on the gauge to the centre line on the ceiling, mark the ceiling at one end of the gauge and at the inner end of the rebated part for the widths. A mark at the outer end of the rebated part will give the rule line. The coloured lines should be struck with a chalk line. Measurements, repeat lengths, and widths are more accurately and quickly marked off from a " gauge," or wood lath.

Run the cornice first. From the outer members the measurements for the panel mouldings are taken ; some rib or panel mouldings spring from or intersect with the main cornice. Always measure or set off from the *centre line* of moulded ribs, *not* from outside lines. Neglect in such a matter has caused serious trouble. The same principle applies equally much to ceilings with beams or sunk panels. Rule and other working lines should not be made until all skeleton lines have been proved correct, when they may be made, and the running rules fixed.

Solid " Run " Mouldings.—Panel or rib mouldings may be either "run" *in situ* or planted, after being " run " on a bench or running board, and cut to the proper lengths to mitre. If there are no wood brackets, the floating coat should be cut down to the lath work to key the mouldings. For deep moulding, spike and rope bracket is best. The stuff for roughing out should be extra haired and strong gauged. The running mould must have a muffle plate, which is an extra plate cut about $\frac{1}{8}$ in. within the profile of mould plate, and screwed over mould plate to run a rough core or muffle, over which the finer material is finished. After this roughing out is done, the muffle plate is removed and the mouldings finished with the mould plate. This is cheaper, quicker, and better than a plaster muffle, especially when running in white cements. When several men are working a moulded ceiling, sets of running moulds are necessary —one cut to the muffling line and another to the finished line. All the moulds must be " horsed " alike in size and form, to exactly fit the running rules and screeds. Where there is little space for working the running mould, plant on the short or segmental pieces. Mouldings run *in situ* are stronger than those planted on.

Cofferings and deep panel mouldings should be bracketed and lathed. The soffits, or centre of the brackets, take the screeds from which parallel running rules run the mouldings on each side. Sometimes an enrichment is inserted between the mouldings ; the screed then forms the bed. To assure a level and uniform depth, level from the main screeds with a rule and wood gauges. Bracketed panel surfaces should always be levelled before moulding. Brackets sometimes need cutting at the intersections for the mould to run past for doing long lengths.

Planted Mouldings.—Small, numerous, short mouldings, circular pieces, small or intricate panels, are best " planted." The mouldings may be either cast, or " run down," *i.e.*, run down on a bench or running board, instead of on the ceiling. Mouldings, run *in situ*, are termed " run." Mouldings may be " run down," cut in lengths, and mitred ready for planting ; or cast in plaster or cement. Reeds were used for strengthening. Fibre and wool are now used instead, and are lighter and stronger than solid mouldings. The planting or fixing of mouldings needs care, accuracy, and thoroughness. Whether " run down " or cast, they must be well keyed and cross scratched on the bed, and correspondingly on the ceiling. The fixing stuff should be haired putty and fine plaster in equal parts, with enough size water to retard the setting. This gauge, stiffened with dry plaster, is useful for filling in deep undercuts and giving strength. Spread the soft stuff on the keyed parts and on the ceiling, applying the cast to the ceiling ; work quickly but gently backwards and forwards into position to expel air globules or superfluous stuff, and unite the surfaces. The inter-sections must be tested with a straight-edge or rule, to mitre with the adjoining piece. Heavy pieces may be further secured by a screw or two to the joists. Nails or thin rules fixed at one side of the moulding guide the fixing. These ceilings are usually " set " before the mouldings are drawn out and painted on, in which case rule lines are not required, and hair should not be used in the soft fixing stuff. Superfluous stuff should be cleaned off immediately with a square-ended wooden tool, and the joint stopped and softened off with stuff of the same colour and plaster as the cast. White hair should be used for fine work. Black hair is coarser than white and more noticeable on the surface.

Setting Panelled Ceilings.—The setting or finishing coat requires care in selection, manipulation, and method, each having individual merit. The terms generally used are " putty finish," " hard finish," " fine finish," and " cement finish," as follows :—

Lime putty finish is the cheapest ; a gauge of 3 parts of fine putty with 1 of fine plaster is the cheapest and most common finish ; but it will not stand scouring, and a true and uniform hard surface is not easily obtained. Unless quickly trowelled before set, the surface is apt to peel, while excessive trowelling kills the plaster and renders the surface soft. It is best laid fair with a hand-float and afterwards laid smooth with a trowel, each coat, and the trowelling and polishing off following in quick succession and being carefully brushed before set.

Hard Finish.—The best work requires " fine setting stuff " made with finer sand and lime putty than that ordinarily used. The sand must be washed through a fine sieve until clean and free from all foreign matter. The putty should be run through a fine hair sieve several months in advance, covered up, and protected from dirt and atmospheric changes while maturing. The proportions vary, according to the quality of the lime, from equal parts of both to 1 of putty with 2 or even 3 of sand, thoroughly well mixed, frequently worked, and beaten. A punching box is excellent for this purpose. If procurable, 1 part to 3 parts of marble dust may be added when ready for use to bind and harden the stuff. Gauge 1 part of fine plaster to 3 parts of fine setting stuff, lay with a skimming float, rule fair with a straight-edge, and scour with a panel-float quickly and lightly. Use soft gauged stuff to fill up small holes. Trowel at once, use water sparingly, and finish by brushing diagonally, crosswise, and length-wise, first with a damp brush and afterwards with a semi-dry brush. When finishing small panels with gauged stuff a keen perception of the suction and setting power of materials is necessary, also dexterity and lightness of touch.

Fine Finish.—The stuff for this is as last described, with one extra part of silver sand, used neat, *i.e.*, without plaster. A portion is mixed with $\frac{1}{10}$ part of well-beaten white hair, for " scratch coating," which lay with a skimming float. Over this, while green, lay a coat of unhaired fine setting stuff, rule with a straight-edge lengthwise, crosswise, and diagonally (both ways), scour up the surface *without* water, and fill up small holes with soft stuff. After a rest, for shrinkage, scour up three times with water, and trowel continuously until smooth, hard, and unimpressionable on the surface.

FIG. 49.—King Charles's Room, Winton House, Haddingtonshire.

Hardness may be known by a clear metallic sound given off by contact of the trowel on the surface. The sound becomes clearer as hardness increases. The surface may then be gone over with a soft, damp brush—not wet—crosswise, diagonally (both ways), and lengthwise, and finished with a semi-dry brush. This surface will be true, hard, brilliant, and fit to paint on. When dry the gloss disappears, leaving a good surface for paint or gold.   Hardness may be further increased by scouring and trowelling with lime water, and pure water for brushing off.

Cement Finish.—Ceilings are sometimes finished with Parian or other cement, in

FIG. 50.—Perspective View of Plaster Ceiling in King Charles's Room, Winton House, Haddingtonshire, 1620. (*v.* next Fig. for Working Plan.)

which case the foundation coats should be gauged with a coarse quality of the particular cement selected, as advised under their respective names.

Portland Cement Ceilings.—Ceilings exposed to damp or atmospheric moisture, such as porticos or open corridors, may be rendered damp-proof and durable by mixing Portland cement and coarse stuff for the foundation coats, and neat Portland cement, or combined with setting stuff, for the final coat.   Metal lathing gives a safe foundation ;

or wood double laths, nailed with 1¼ in. wrought-iron galvanised nails. The laths should be of best red Baltic, well seasoned, strong, in narrow widths, and fixed no less than ⅜ in. apart for a strong key ; or, better still, for the stuff to press between and envelop the lath work.

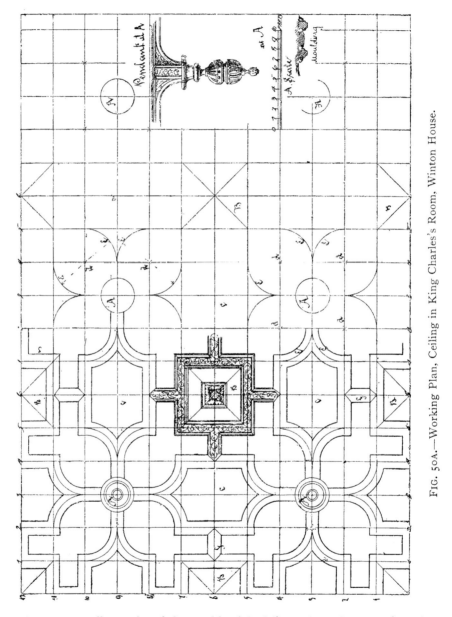

FIG. 50A.—Working Plan, Ceiling in King Charles's Room, Winton House.

The coarse stuff must be of thoroughly slaked lime, clean sharp sand, and strong long hair, all well tempered and seasoned by time.   When required for use it should be retempered with a larry and an extra proportion of hair for the Portland cement to be added. Gauge 5 parts of this stuff with 2 of Portland cement for the first coat, and 3 parts of coarse stuff with 1 of Portland cement for the floating. The finished coat should be 2 parts of setting stuff gauged with 1 of Portland cement, laid, scoured, and trowelled as for hard finish. The panels may be more smoothly and expeditiously finished with " limed cement." Add 1 part of well-slaked fine lime putty to 3 parts

FIG. 51.—Detail of Plaster Ceiling, Careath House, Ayrshire, 1847. (With Working Plan.)

of Portland cement to make the finishing stuff "fat," plastic, easy to work, and to increase the density. Rough out the mouldings with the material used for floating, and finish with 2 parts of Portland cement and 1 part of fine lime putty. Sift the cement through a very fine sieve, gauge moderately stiff for the first coat, and run off with soft gauged stuff to mould smooth. This recipe produces an anti-damp plaster for work in exposed positions.

Fibrous Plaster Panelled Ceilings.—"Fibrous plaster" is now chiefly used for ceilings. Panels and mouldings are made in one piece and cast in large sections.

Large "fibrous plaster" slabs may be decorated with low or high relief ornament and screwed to the joist or to concrete. "Fibrous" cast mouldings may also be screwed on to "solid work." Fibrous plaster is light, dry, quickly fixed, and paintable soon after being fixed. Solid lime plastering will always remain staple for permanent purposes.

Panelled Ceiling (Winton House).—A perspective view, complete plan, and setting-out plan of part of a ceiling in Winton House, near Edinburgh, is shown in Figs. 49 and 50. It is a good example of old hand-wrought plaster. The ribs and panels are decorated with modelled foliage, heraldry, etc., and pendants cover the intersecting ribs at intervals. The frieze is interesting in its arcaded form. This, with the ceilings shown on Plate XIX, is a typical example of Scottish plaster-work, 1620-30. The same details are used at Pinkie House and Moray House, and no doubt the same plasterers worked at all three houses. The geometric arrangement is common to many English ceilings of this and earlier date. No records or definite evidence other than the work itself exist to show the methods used by the old plasterers in the numerous mansions where they worked, but they could model well,

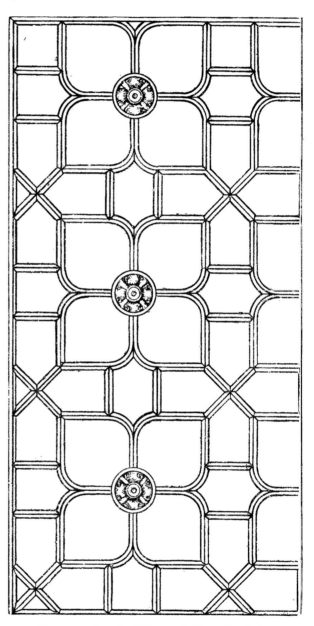

FIG. 52.—Detail of Plaster Ceiling, Beeslack, Midlothian, 1855. (See opposite.)

they were careful geometricians, and they knew how to select and work their materials as artists with good effect and enduring workmanship.

A working plan of this ceiling design is given (Fig. 50A) to show the setting out and working. The design is contained in the square A, A, A, A. The panel B is the centre ; the square is subdivided into six smaller squares each way, or thirty-six squares in all, which form the repeat. The lines marked 1, 2, 3, 4, 5, 6 repeated, over the whole ceiling area, give the rib centre lines, the centres of the panels B and C, the pendants A, A, A, A, and the centres (*d*) of the segments (*e*). The diagonal lines in the B panels, giving the fixing points for the centre, may be extended to prove the intersections of the panels and the centres of the pendants A. The working lines follow this skeleton setting out, after which the running rules should be fixed, to run the longitudinal mouldings from end to end of the ceiling. Rules should be fixed for longitudinal mouldings to be in hand together, the roughing out and finishing to be done throughout in each case, to save constant change of muffle and materials. Rules may be in 10 ft. or 12 ft. lengths, fixed the length of ceiling, excepting on a ceiling having pendants. Long lengths of moulding are best run first, but much depends on circumstances and design. When the longitudinal mouldings are run, the rules should be removed and fixed for the transverse mouldings. The circular ribs (*e*) and the short straight ribs (*f*) are run on a bench, cut into lengths, mitred, and planted on. The ribs to the pendants are run on a cradle and planted on. If there are no wooden brackets on the ceiling, set

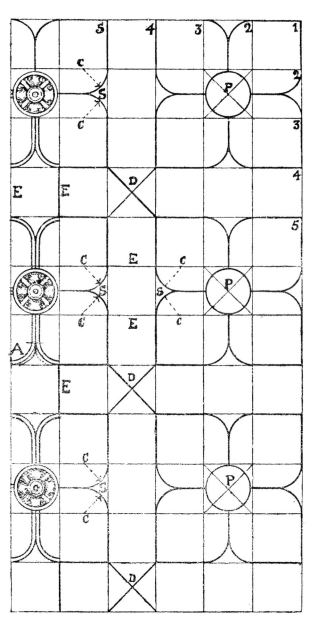

FIG. 52A.—Plaster Ceiling, Beeslack, Midlothian, 1855. (Working Plan.)

them in position on a cradle, piece-mould, cast, and plant on in one piece. An iron pipe or bolt (threaded at the ends) must pass through to secure the pendant. Cast and fix the four leaves and the pendants to complete the ceiling.

Fig. 51 shows the plan of a ceiling design. All this work would now be done in large fibrous plaster sections, cast on the bench in a workshop and afterwards screwed up; not run solid in plaster on the ceiling. Nevertheless, the old process is sometimes resorted to, and is therefore given. One-half shows the centre lines and radial lines, and

Octagons and Squares.

Hexagons of Lozenges.

Squares with Guilloche Borders.

Squares and Hexagons forming Octagons.

Octagons, Hexagons, and Crosses.

Hexagons and Triangles.

Lozenges with Guilloche Borders.

Squares and En-wreathed Circles.

Squares and Stars with Rosettes

FIG. 53.—Methods of Coffering Ceilings. (Classic Type.)

the other half shows the centre and width lines. The semicircular ribs from the centres at A are here run first. Straight mouldings are easier to mitre than circular ones, hence the reason. They are run a little *beyond* the line of mitre, for the joint to be cut out of the solid, the straight bit being run and mitred up to the circular mitre joint. The short straight pieces are run on the bench, cut to mitre, and planted up.

The semicircular ribs are run from a " radius pin " (R.P.) or block of wood 6 in. square and ½ in. thick, with a hardwood pin 2 in. long and ½ in. diameter through the centre, like a miniature hawk.   This is screwed to the ceiling, the true centre being obtained by keeping the angles lineable with the centre lines.   A hole to fit the pin is made in the radius rod for running the circular ribs.   The " radius pin " is far better than working from a centre pin fixed through the lath work, which breaks the lathing and floating and is not reliable.   When the circular ribs are done, rules are fixed to run mouldings B, C, and D from point to point, and later on mouldings E and F.

The short lengths, G, H, and I, are run on the bench and planted on.   With a few exceptions, solid run mouldings over 1 ft. long are done *in situ*.   The square pateræ, shields J, or ornaments are cast and fixed up, their positions and centres being ascertained on the radial lines.   Pendants P are cast and planted.   Their positions and centres are found by temporarily fixing four nails in a circle line previously made on the ceiling, or by four quarter marks cast with the pendants and by ranging them with the intersecting lines.

If accurately cut to size and mitre, very little " stopping " will make good the joint. Figs. 52 and 52A give the plan of another rib ceiling.   The method of setting out is similar to the other designs already described.   The figures at the side and end indicate the skeleton and centre lines of ribs, which form equal-sized squares over the ceiling area. The repeat design is between the lines 1 and 5.   Diagonal lines D, drawn from the angles of the squares, give the diagonal ribs and centre of pendants.   The centres C, for the segmental ribs S, are half-way along the small squares ; small segmental ribs are run on the bench, cut to exact size, mitred, and later on planted on to fit close and intersect accurately.   The working lines being set out, fix the running rules and run the longitudinal mouldings, and afterwards those going crossways, as before explained. Plant on the short cross ribs E, the diagonal ribs D, the segmental ribs, and the pendants last.   Run as much work as possible *in situ*, for strength and expedition. All " planting " means extra labour.   Very short ribs *only* should be run on the bench and planted.

Classic Panelling.—Nine examples of panelled ceiling work, from designs by Sir William Chambers, are shown in Fig. 53, for general guidance.

CHAPTER X

RUNNING DIMINISHED AND CIRCULAR MOULDINGS

Diminished Columns—Diminished Floating Rules—Column Trammel—Constructing Diminished Plain Columns—Setting Out Flutes of Diminished Columns—Constructing Diminished Fluted Columns—Forming Diminished Fluted Columns by the Rim and Collar Methods—Diminished Fluted Pilasters—Panelled Coves—Pressed Screeds—Diminished Mouldings—Double Diminished Mouldings—Running Double Diminished Mouldings—Diminished Rule Method—Top Rule Method—Cupola Panels and Mouldings—Panelled Beams—Trammel for Elliptical Mouldings—Templates for Elliptical Mouldings—Plasterer's Oval—Circular Mouldings on Circular Surfaces—Trammel Centre.

Diminished Columns.—The diminishing of columns is an interesting if somewhat difficult operation, requiring great care not to exaggerate the entasis or curve. This may commence very gradually from the base to the capital, or the column may be of equal diameter, one-third of the length up from the base, and then diminish for the remainder of its length. Two methods are given to show how this may be done, more particularly to show how to set out the diminished floating rules, rather than to define the swell or diminution of a column.

Diminished Floating Rules.—The instrument used for shaping a diminished column (plain or fluted) is a floating rule (Fig. 54), with a cutting edge to the diminished contour of the column. This rule is used to determine the central position of the astragal and base mouldings (which act as bearings when ruling off the floating stuff and the final coat) to obtain a true and uniform diminution and a fair surface. Fig. 54 shows one method of setting out diminished columns and rules. To set out a rule for a column that diminishes two-thirds of its height, draw a perpendicular line equivalent to the centre line of column; set out the upper and lower diameters as in 1a. The right half shows the constructional brick core, the plaster (dark shaded), and the floating rule in place. A floating rule for columns requires an iron template to cut the plastic stuff off clean and true, and to stand wear. The left half of the elevation shows the lines and divisions for obtaining and setting out the entasis.

To diminish the column, divide the height into three equal parts, then at the lower third, 5, draw a semicircle equal to the lower diameter of the column. Divide the upper portion of the column into four equal parts, as at 1, 2, 3, and 4; draw a line parallel with the centre line from 1 at top of column to 1 on the semicircle. Divide the remainder of the semicircle into four equal parts, which give the diminishing points. From these points draw lines parallel to the axis of the column to the corresponding figures or up the column. At these intersecting points fix pins or nails, bend a flexible strip of wood or metal to them, and draw the curved line. Transfer the line on to a board to be used for the floating rule. This method requires the curve to be drawn by hand; a trammel is used for a column with a diminished curve from base to top of shaft.

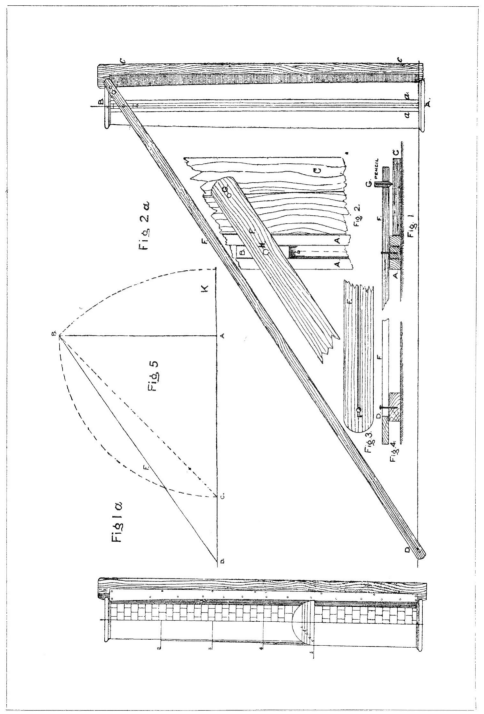

FIG. 54.—Column Trammel and Floating Rule.

Column Trammel.—A column trammel is simple in construction, and when carefully made and used gives a graduated curve from the lower to the upper diameter of the shaft. No. 5, reduced to half scale of No. 2a (Fig. 54), explains clearly how to obtain point D.

The centre pin on which the trammel slides while working, which is reduced half on the scale of No. 2a, the letters corresponding. Set out the centre line AB and the base line AC as described in No. 1a, extending it indefinitely. From A as a centre with the radius AB, describe the arc BC; from C as a centre and with CB as radius, describe the arc BK; add the distance AK to the base line at C, which gives the point D.

The trammel should be set out full size, as just described, on a wall or a clean floor. To construct the trammel take two rules, each the length of the column, 2 in. wide and 1½ in. thick; fix one on each side of, and parallel to, the axis line, about 2 in. apart, to form a groove B. The rules AA should be thicker than the floating rule board to allow the trammel pencil to run freely on the board (see section No. 1). This forms a permanent groove, a smooth channel for the sliding block to work in.

No. 2 is an enlarged sketch of the top end of the groove rules AA, the groove *b*, the sliding block B, the pin H, the radius rod F, the pencil G, the board for the floating rule C, and the entasis line. No. 1 is a section of the above. No. 2a shows the column trammel and finished floating rule C. The radius rod should be about 2 in. wide by 1 in. thick, and a little longer than from D to B, plus the half diameter of base of the shaft. The sliding block B, about 4 in. long and as wide and deep as the groove *b*, should be smooth, to slide freely from end to end of the groove. In the exact centre of the block fix a round nail H, so that it will run immediately over the axis from end to end. Bore a hole in the radius rod to fit this pin, and from the centre of the pin set off on the rod exactly half the diameter of the base of the column, which will give the pencil point G. A hole to receive a pencil must be made in it. At the other end of the radius rod, cut a slot wide and long enough to work the centre pin at D (see Nos. 3 and 4).

The block under the radius rod (No. 4) is to keep the rod level with the rules and sliding block shown on No. 1. To ascertain the length to cut the slot, place the rod along the line AD, with the pencil point at the outside base line of the column, and mark on the rod where the centre pin D comes; then place the pencil end of the rod at the top diameter, and mark the rod again at the centre pin D; this will give the length required. Having made the trammel, provide and place on both sides a stout board and one edge for the floating rule C. Place it up against the rules *a, a*, keeping the planed edge outwards, and parallel with the axis or centre line of the column. The planed edge may be used as a straight-edge to plumb by when fixing the top and bottom rims or mouldings, which are the guides and bearings when floating the column. Place the sliding block in position, lay the radius rod over the centre and sliding block pin, keeping the rod on the base line DA, and the pencil in its place; then slide the rod upwards to the top, keeping the pencil point upon the board, the line given being the diminishing edge of floating rule, which is cut out, the edge being strengthened by a strip of sheet iron nailed on the board. This is especially useful for floating diminished fluted columns or pilasters, the thin and sharp edge allowing the flutes to be more easily formed. The diminished line of the metal plate is also formed with the trammel.

The trammel, once made, may be used for setting out any column or floating rule lines of less size than the original one, the only alteration needed being to correct the point D to the size of the proposed column, and the shortening of the radius rod. The floating rules should be long enough to bear on the base and necking mouldings, but usually they are shorter, bearing on the cast or run rims at the top and bottom of the shaft.

Constructing Plain Diminished Columns.—Plain diminished columns and pilasters are formed with a diminished rule shaped at the ends to bear and run on the necking and base mouldings (termed rims), or on collars, the making of which are described in connection with diminished fluted columns.

To Set Out the Flutes of a Diminished Column.—Fig. 55 explains how to set out the flutes of a column. No. 1 is the half plan of a column: A the plan of the flutes at the base, and B at the top of the shaft. No. 2 shows a part elevation of the column with the various parts marked. No. 3 shows the plan and centres for setting out the flutings for the different orders with arrises or with fillets. A column may be divided into twenty, twenty-four, or twenty-six flutes, according to the order to which it belongs. Two different sorts of flutes are used. One is worked to an arris and sunk down in different depths, one is described by the fourth part of the circle, one by the sixth, and others by the half-circle, as shown at C, D, E (No. 3).

The square or fillet of the second kind is equal to one-third part of the flute. It will be seen in No. 2 that two lines are shown at the top of the flutes. The lower one shows how the flutes finish when the fourth and sixth depths are taken, and the top line when the half-circle is taken together with the fillets. Flutes intersecting with an arris usually belong to the Doric order, and those with fillets to the other orders. The fillets or lists at the top

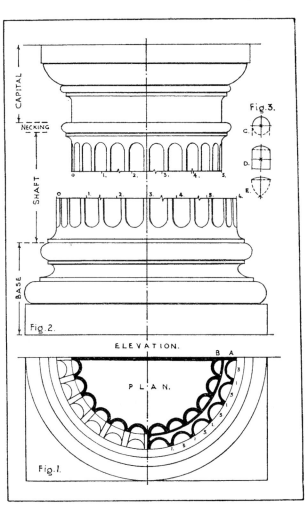

FIG. 55.—Diminished Fluted Columns.

and bottom of the column serve to divide the shaft from the cap and base mouldings, are known as the upper and lower or horizontal fillets, and in architecture as "cinctures." The hollow members or cavettes at the top and bottom of the shaft are termed "apophyges."

Constructing Diminished Fluted Columns.—The formation of diminished fluted columns by means of a running mould has been a somewhat vexed topic among plasterers. In this, an ounce of practice is worth a ton of theory. Flutes diminish in depth as also in width.

The difference in depth at the base and the top of the shaft is shown at A and B, No. 1, Fig. 55.

The foregoing method of running flutes is slow and tedious, the worst part being that they are not true segments ; in fact, the methods mentioned are more or less inaccurate and unsatisfactory.

The cement and sand should be mixed in the proportion of one of the former to five of the latter. This gauge has sufficient binding power and strength for this purpose, and is not liable to expand or contract in wet or dry weather. This process is useful for small work, and makes a good job when cleanly cast and neatly fixed. The necking with the capital and the base may be fixed before or after the shaft casts are fixed, according to circumstances. The shaft casts are best formed in a reverse casting mould, as described in Chapter XVI, p. 279.

After many years' experience and observation, it is felt that the true form of a diminished fluted column (composed in Portland or similar cement and constructed *in situ*) is best obtained by hand, with the aid of cement rims or plaster collars and a diminished floating rule. The two methods hereafter given for forming diminished fluted columns by hand are simple, speedy, and accurate. They are on one principle, and each may be used as circumstances require : one is termed the " rim method " and the other the " collar method."

Forming Diminished Fluted Column by the Rim Method.—First make models of the half circumferences of the astragal or necking and base mouldings, each having about 4 in. of the fluted shaft, as shown in Nos. 1 and 2, Fig. 55. To make the models, cut a mould plate to fit each of the full-sized mouldings, and then shaft and " horse " them with radius rods, run a little over one-half of each circumference in plaster, and cut them to the exact half circumference. Set out the flutes, cut them out, and form the returned ends as shown on No. 1. A is the plan at the base, and B the plan at the top of the shaft. The returned ends of flutes are shown on elevation No. 2. Add a square plinth to the base as on plan No. 1 ; complete the model. Piece mould in plaster and cast as many half astragal and bases as required. The materials for the casts must be for the shaft. Clean and wet core of the column, fix astragal and bases in position, and with the diminished floating rule prove if they are central and the fillets lineable with each other. A plumb rule applied to the back edge of the floating rule will show if the astragal and base are concentric and parallel with each other. These half casts fixed together on the shaft are termed " rims." This done, fill

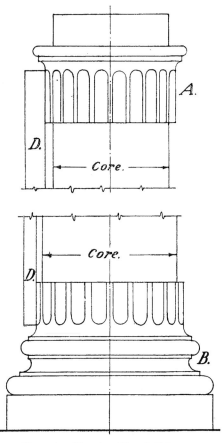

FIG. 56.—Floating Fluted Columns. (Rim Method.)

in and rule off with the diminishing floating rule the intermediate space on the shaft, using the rims as bearings and guides for forming the fillet line of shaft.

The " rim method " in **Fig.** 56 shows the brick core shaft with the astragal rim A, the base rim B, the diminished floating rule D, all in position for floating the main or fillet surface of the shaft. The method of using a diminished flute rule for the flutes is illustrated in the " collar method." This being done, the flutes are cut out to diminished rule.

A second diminished floating rule is required to form the back surface of the flutes. This can be quickly made by laying the first rule flat on the floor, and from this, with compasses, describe the back line of the flute on another board, which is afterwards cut to the desired line. This rule is used as a long joint rule to form the flutes, and should be worked with uniform pressure, the men at top and bottom working the rule together with a circular cutting motion. The flutes are fined down by a small float, semicircular in section. For extra large columns three floats should be used—cut to the top, middle, and bottom sections. These floats may vary from 5 in. to 7 in. in length, according to the height of the column. If a smooth surface is required, cover the floats with fine felt, leather, or rubber, and finish smooth with short joint rules or with flexible busks. The cast parts of the shafts should be keyed with a drag, so that the whole shaft may be fined to give uniform texture and colour, and avoid a surface joint of the cast and the fined work.

A modification is as follows : Cast the lower fillet of the shaft and the base mouldings separately ; use the fillet as a bearing when floating the shaft, as already described, and fix the base after the shaft is fined. This method is useful for large columns, gives more freedom for working the shafts, and the bases are less liable to injury.

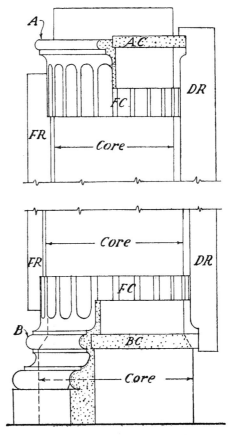

FIG. 57.—Floating Fluted Columns. (Collar Method.)

Running of Diminished Fluted Column by the Collar Method.—Run a plaster collar AC (Fig. 57) about $1\frac{1}{2}$ in. wide to the diameter of the top fillet of the shaft, the thickness being the space between the core and the face of fillet. Cut the collar in halves and fix them on to the core, keeping the under side level with the top of the proposed fillet of the shaft. Run another collar to fit the fillet at the base of shaft and fix the upper side of this one level with the bottom edge of the fillet at base of shaft, This being done, make two plaster models of the flutes, one for the top and one for the bottom of the shaft, each about 3 in. wide, and in thickness according to the brick core, the diameter being taken about 1 in. beyond the returned ends of the flutes at either end of the shaft. Set out and make the model as described for the first method, casting with plaster instead of cement. Fix the casts in position and lay and rule off core with the diminished floating rule from the plain collar bearings, these forming the main contour of face of the vertical fillets and the top and bottom horizontal fillets of the shaft. Use the diminished flute floating rule and the plaster models of the flutes as bearings for the flutes. Cut out the fluted collars, fill in and rule off the spares, form the returned ends of the flutes, and fine the whole shaft while the work is green. Cut out the fillet collars and fix the astragal and base mouldings to complete the column. This method entirely dispenses with the joints between cast and floated work of the other method, and allows the shaft to be fined in one operation.

The method of running diminished fluted columns with the aid of collars is illustrated in Fig. 57. AC is the top fillet collar, BC the bottom fillet collar, and FC, FC, are the top and bottom flute collars fixed on the brick core of the column. DR is the main diminished floating rule in position for forming the main contour or fillet face of the column. The rule is rebated at the top for a bearing on the top as well as on the edge of the collar. It also forms the profile of the top and bottom horizontal fillets, and the curved parts of the shafts below the top and above the bottom fillets.

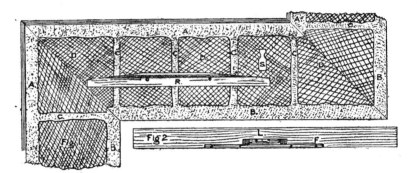

FIG. 58.—Levelling Rule. (Floating Cover.)

FR is the flute rule in position when floating the flutes. The ends of the rule are shown bearing on the back surface of a flute, the astragal moulding A, and part of the shaft are shown to indicate the position of the fillet collar AC; the base moulding B and part of the shaft also show the position of the bottom fillet collar BC. These collars form a bed for the astragal and base mouldings; when removed they leave true joints.

For small columns the above methods of forming the fillets and flutes may be modified thus : Fill in the spaces on the shaft between the collars (or the rims) and rule them off as described ; when the stuff is firm (but not set) set out the fillets and flutes on the floated surface, cut out the flutes by hand with gouges and drags, and fine as described.

In the case of very high columns it is difficult to work a floating rule the whole height in one operation ; in the case of columns 20 ft. to 30 ft. high, or higher, it would be impossible. In such cases divide the column into two or more sections and cut the floating rules accordingly, two or more plaster collars about 3 in. wide, the exact circumference of the column at the point of division being required. The collars are temporarily fixed as screeds, and after the filling in and ruling off are done, they are cut out, the spaces filled in, and the entire surface fined in one operation. Three or more floats, as already described, are required for the fining of high or massive columns.

The conclusion to be drawn is, that diminished fluted columns are best done by

PLATE CV

(b) RUNNING THE MOULD CASTING OF A DIMINISHED COLUMN IN FIBROUS PLASTER.

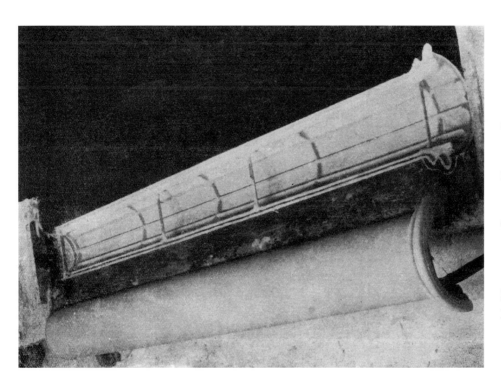

(a) MOULD AND CAST IN FIBROUS PLASTER.

working them by hand, with the aid of diminished floating rules and cast or run bearings. The first or rim method will be found useful for many purposes ; but the collar method, with the addition of intermediate collars for extra high columns, is the best for general use.

Plate CV gives two photographs of the process of making the mould for a diminished column in fibrous plaster : (*a*) shows the cast in the mould, and on the left a cast removed from the mould ; (*b*) running of the mould.

Diminished Fluted Pilasters.—Pilasters bear an analogy to columns in their parts, have the same names and standard of measurements, and are diminished and fluted on the same principles.

Panelled Coves.—Fig. 58 shows the elevation of a levelling rule as used for levelling dots for ceiling, beam, or crown screeds. This is similar to an ordinary parallel rule, but with the addition of a fillet F, nailed flush with the bottom edge to form a ledge to carry the spirit level L. The levelling rule is applied on the dots to test if they are level ; this is proved by inspecting the spirit level ; if one dot is too full, it must be depressed until the levelling rule is level.

Diminished Mouldings.— Mouldings that diminish in width and projection (" double diminished mouldings ") are less common than those that diminish in width only. To diminish in width is a simple process, worked by a " triple slippered " running mould and two running rules fixed to form a diminished space, as described hereafter. The success of a regular diminish in projection depends to some extent on the profile of the moulding. Small members, especially at the sides, are more difficult to

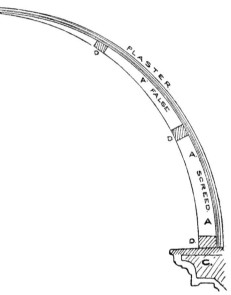

FIG. 59.—Section Double Diminished Mouldings. (False Screed Method.)

diminish than large ones, especially one with plain deep fillets at the sides. Three methods are given for running double diminished mouldings on curved surfaces.

Double Diminished Mouldings—False Screed Method.—By this method the diminish in projection is obtained by false screeds, and in width by a diminished rule, fixed on the centre of the bed of enrichment. Fig. 59 shows the section of a vertical moulding on the plaster or floated surface inside a dome. C is the main cornice from which the inner line of the dome springs. The D's are dots, used to regulate the diminish of the false screeds. The various thicknesses and positions of the dots are obtained by setting out the full size section on a floor, or to scale. If the section is elliptical, dots should be placed at short intervals. There is no marked transition in the curve of a true ellipse ; they should therefore be at fixed intervals. When the surface has been floated, diminishing dots D are placed at each side of the intended moulding in their required positions, beginning above the cornice C and going upwards in rotation. No dot is needed at the top. The spaces between the dots are filled in and ruled off from the dots, as bearings, with curved rules or templates. When ruling the top bay of the screed, the top end of the rule bears on the original floating at the crown or extreme point, this being the true thickness of the screed.

Fig. 60 shows the plan and elevation of the work. No. 1 shows the process, No. 2 the finished work. AA shows the false screeds, BB the brackets, CC the diminished running rule. To make the rule, plane one face of a pine board about $\frac{1}{2}$ in. thick and of sufficient length and width for the desired purpose. Draw a centre line from end to end, from which set off the width at each end; extend the diminished width lines from end to end, and then plane the running edges to the diminished lines. In order that the rule may bend to the curved surface, saw-cut the back or bed face, make the false screeds as already described. The centre screed for the running rule is made with the help of a template and a slipper on either side, to run on the false screeds, the centre or cutting edge of the template being the depth of the proposed screed. The surface of the bracket is laid with gauged stuff and finished by working the template. This done, fix the diminished rule C on the centre of the screed. The running mould E on the plan is made with the slippers, bearing on the centre screed and against the running rule, and on the side false screed. The slippers must be segmental on the running edges to fit the circular screeds. A short slipper at the nib gives freedom and ease for running, and the mould is not so liable to cut the screeds. When the moulding is run on both sides, take off the running rule, cut the false screeds down to the floating, make the sides good, and fix the enrichment. No. 2 shows the plan and elevation of the finished moulding and enrichment. A, on the plan, shows one side of the moulding before the false screed is cut off, and G shows the screed cut off and the member made good to the floating. The diminish from the bottom to the top of the moulding is shown at B, and by the profiles of the cornice on the plan and elevation. The bed and section of the enrichment is shown at F, on plan. As this enrichment is diminished (in width and projection), the whole length must be modelled.

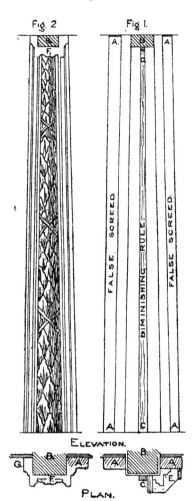

FIG. 60.—Diminished Mouldings.

Running Double Diminished Mouldings —Diminished Rule Method.—This method is similar to the first described. It is well adapted to running mouldings without enrichment in the centre, the bed being used as a screed for the running rule, the whole moulding being run in one operation. The diminish in depth is obtained by two running rules, diminished in thickness. The diminished thickness of the rules is obtained as described for the false screeds in the preceding method. Saw-cut the backs of the rules to bend them to the surface of the dome. These rules replace the false screed of the first method, form the fillets of the outside members, save cutting down the screeds, and making good. The diminish in width is effected by drawing a central line on the bed of the proposed moulding; from this line, at each side, set out half the width of the moulding and the bearing parts of the running mould at each end of the moulding. From these marks draw lines from end to end. On these lines place nails every 2 ft. to 3 ft. apart, as guides for the running rules. Place and fix the rules outside the nails and extract the nails, leaving the diminished space and bearings free. Use a triple-hinged mould with a slipper at each side to close up while traversing the diminishing space. The stock should be rebated to run on the rules. The mould plate must fit the greatest width of the moulding, care being taken that the depth at the outer members is the same as for the top. The ends of the inner slippers and the adjoining parts of the stock are cut to allow both parts to work freely when the mould rakes, as in Fig. 61.

The extra depth of the square outside members is formed by the running rules. The rules at the top should be about $\frac{1}{2}$ in. thicker than the depth of the outside fillets, to allow for the necessary bearing for the running mould. The ends of the stock bearing on the inside of the rules must be rounded off to run freely when the mould closes up in running up the diminished space.

The various parts of the running mould are shown in Fig. 61. No. 1 shows the mould in position at the bottom or widest part of the moulding; R shows the running rules; S the slippers; and H the hinges connecting the halves of the stock to the slippers. The hinge connecting the mould in the centre is fixed on the opposite side

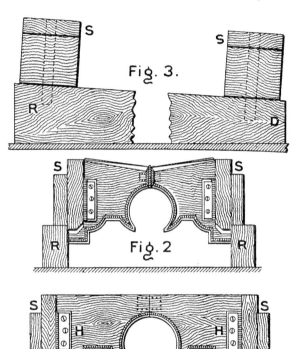

FIG. 61.—Running Mould and Rules for Diminishing.

of the stock, as indicated by dotted lines. No. 2 shows the mould when at top of the moulding. The thin seams at centre and sides of the moulding, caused by the joints of the mould and rules, are cleaned off by hand. The defect of both methods is that the diminish lies in the fillets of the outside members of the moulding. The difference between the diminished and the regular members will be noticeable on the adjoining vertical fillets of the cavettos. The defect may be remedied by working the members down by hand, after the moulding is run, to reduce the depth of the fillets and throw the difference into the cavettos. A line should set out the diminish desired on the fillets as guides in working.

Running Double Diminished Mouldings—Top Rule Method.—Running double diminished mouldings by a "top rule" is another method. The diminish in width is obtained as previously described (see Nos. 1 and 2, Fig. 62). No. 1 shows the running mould M and the slipper rules R at the fullest end of the moulding. No. 2 shows the running mould and rules at the diminished end. The diminishing depth is obtained by a "top rule," which is fixed on two blocks BD at either end of the moulding, as at No. 3, which is an elevation of one side of the running moulds at the springing and diminished ends of the moulding, also the running rules. B is the fixing block at the springing end and D that at the diminished end, upon which

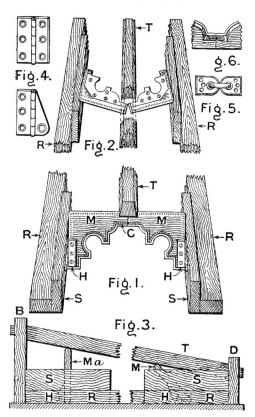

FIG. 62.—Running Mould and Rules for Diminishing.

the top rule T is fixed to the desired diminish. It must be wide enough for a bearing for each half stock, M, of the running mould, and fixed over the joints of the mould, as at T. The slanting top rule causes the running mould to gradually cant over when drawn from the vertical position at the springing end of the moulding to the diminished end (see No. 3), thus forming the diminish of the moulding. Ma shows the end section of the stock in its vertical position at the springing end; M is the slanting stock at the diminished end of moulding. The dotted lines indicate the part of the stocks inside the slippers, and the angular dotted line at H the splayed side of hinge. S is an outer elevation of one slipper at each end of moulding, and R is the slipper running rule. The running mould (No. 1) is somewhat similar to the triple hinged running moulds previously described, with two important exceptions, namely, the hinges at the centre and sides of mould.

The side hinges must be cut across on one half, and the angles rounded off, leaving only one screw-hole to reduce friction, and allow the hinge to turn on a screw fixed on the slipper—the use of which will be seen hereafter. An elevation of a hinge, before and after being cut, is shown in No. 4. The hole in the lower cut half is used, as the nearer the "turning points" are to the running ground or screed, the less the bearing edges of the running mould rise as the mould cants over. This hole must be enlarged to take a short, thick screw to give strength. This part of the hinge works on the *head* of the screw.

The hinges being shaped, screw them to the lower edge of stock and slippers of the running mould, the half hinge with three screw-holes to the stock, and the part with one screw-hole to the slippers, as at H, No. 1, to allow the stock of the mould to cant from its base. When screwing the cut side of the plate to the slipper, allow just sufficient play for the hinge to turn smoothly but firmly on the screw. The centre hinge connecting the halves of the stock M is formed with two pieces of metal. Round off the inner ends to allow them to turn, drill a hole one-third the width of the plate near the rounded ends, and more screw-holes for fixing purposes at the square ends, and fasten the plates together with a flat metal ring or stout copper wire. The ring should be the size of the hole, with play for the plates to turn either way as the mould tilts (see Nos. 2 and 5). Screw this hinge to the inner side of the stock C, No. 1. An enlargement is shown at No. 6. Round off the outer edges of the stock to allow it to cant over easily. The diminished depth and width, *as drawn*, are exaggerated to show the parts and method clearly.

The diminishing depth is drawn about two-fifths and the width about one-third. The diminishing depth should not be overdone, as the running mould, assuming an angular position on plan and section, forms the vertical parts of the members in a slanting line, and the horizontal parts out of level. These defects become more pronounced at the diminished end of the moulding. Make the top member level and fair by hand; but as it entails much labour to remedy the defects of the other members, this method should only be used for small mouldings where the diminish is slight. The seam on the top member is cleaned off and made good by hand.

Cupola Panels and Mouldings.—In setting out and forming cupola panels and mouldings, the method given on Fig. 63 will be found useful, whether done in " solid " or in " fibrous plaster." To draw an octagonal cupola, as in No. 1, take AB (the width of one side of the octagon) as the base line. From the centre erect the perpendicular line DC, draw the lines CA and CB, giving the triangle ABC the plan of an eighth part of the cupola. The section (No. 2) is the quadrant of circle ABC over the plan. Divide half the base line, AB on plan, into seven parts, as figured, six of which will make two panels and the seventh the border. The same divisions must be marked on the section line AB, as follows : Take for the bottom margin four parts, as on plan ; place them on the section line from the base to No. 1, and draw a line parallel to base line of plan ; measure the length of the two central lines marked 2 2, and place it on the section for the second panel. From thence draw another parallel line, measure the length of the two central lines 3 3 on plan, the square height of the third panel, and so on to No. 8, as shown on plan and section.

The elevation of the octagonal cupola (No. 3) is set up as follows : First draw the base line AB on plan equal with the base line AB of the profile ; on this set up the centre line DC, and draw the parallel lines as shown by GG, etc. Take half the length of each line, figured on plan, and set off on each side of the centre line (No. 3) until the length of every panel is fixed. From these lines and points the skeleton lines of the panels are fixed, the inner divisions being brought over to the number of panels contained in the manner shown in No. 3. The same rule applies to No. 4.

If the arch soffits are panelled, they are usually uneven in number, having a centre panel ; on the quadrant EF (No. 2) the panels of the soffit are divided. Soffits of lesser and of greater breadth are shown at MN, sections being shown at the top of each.

The construction of such plasterwork depends on the design and scale of the panels and mouldings. For example, if the panels are large enough to work a running mould, run the sides of the panels ; but if too small, cast and plant on the moulding. In some cases the lower panel mouldings may be run, the smaller panels above should be planted on, the intersections only requiring to be stopped. If the mouldings are long enough to be run, the brackets must be cut down at the intersections to let the mould pass. Whichever method is used, the surface must be floated to the curve to form a true bed for the mouldings. The surface must be floated smooth enough for a screed without using gauged putty, as described for panelled ceilings. The groundwork for floating is formed by a screed on the base AB and the top margin at C, and from these as bearings, screeds on the vertical styles, from which the panel surface is floated. It is sometimes difficult to float the panel surfaces uniform in depth and curve.   A floating rule cut to clear the brackets cannot get into the angles and float the whole surface; but this may be overcome by placing dots in the angles, or narrow screeds from angle to angle and ruling off with a gauge rule cut to the required depth and bearing on the screeds.   Rule off the vertical screeds with the segmental rule, on which pieces of board of the desired depth and length are fixed, and rule off the intervening spaces with short curved rules.

A better way is to cut an angular floating rule to fit the curve from A to *a*, and float all the panel surfaces in a line from border to border in one operation. This angular rule is set out as described for angle brackets, and must suit the longest line of panels. The rule must be shortened. to fit each set of panels. The mouldings being diminished in width, are run from a centre screed as described for domes. The screed is formed by a floating rule cut to curve anglewise. In some cases a twin slippered running mould is used, forming also about 1 in. of the panel surface as a ground for floating. When large paterae are used, cast the ground surface with them to avoid floating and setting. The octagonal panels in No. 4 are done in the same way ; when the vertical and horizontal mouldings are run, plant in the diagonal sides of the octagons. Where square panels form the design, run the mouldings from a centre pin and block with a radius rod running mould. Run the section of the soffits of the arches with a radius rod running mould, fixed on a radius board, and plant on the cross styles or mouldings at K and L. A small portion of the arch curve should be run for a ground on which to model the

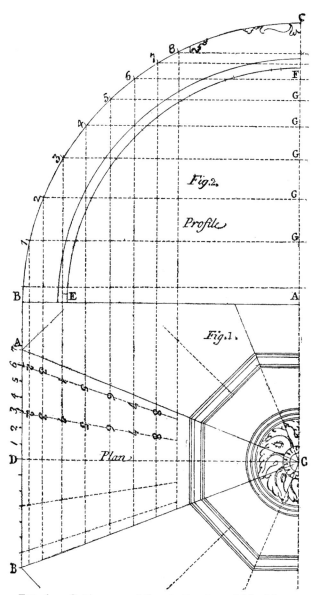

FIG. 63.—Setting out of Cupola Panels and Mouldings, and Soffits of Arches.

enrichments. Fibrous plaster is best suited for the construction of decorations of cupola linings.

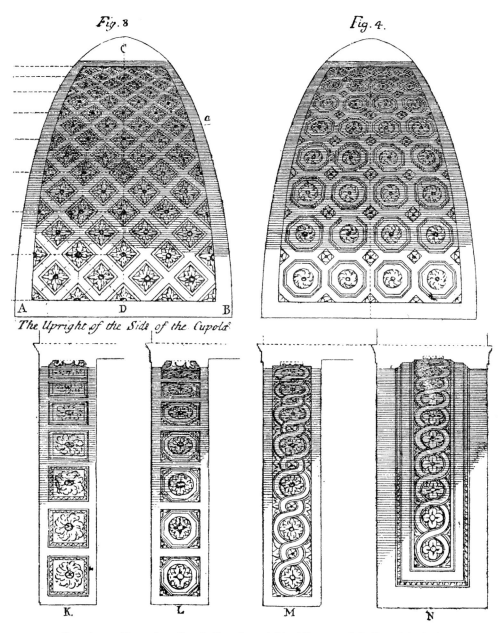

FIG. 63A.—Plastering Cupola Panels and Mouldings, and Soffits of Arches.

Panelled Beams.—When panel beams have sunk mouldings on their sides and soffit, they may be run in two parts.   Form screeds on the sides and centre of the soffit. If the side mouldings have more girth than those on the soffit, run them from rules on the side of the beam, the nib bearing on the style or soffit. If the style and soffit mouldings are small, run all mouldings in one mould. If the styles are broad, run the moulding on the sunk soffit from a rule in centre of soffit. The latter way is most general. The short mouldings are run separately and planted in. Fibrous cast mouldings now replace much run work.

Beams of considerable length should have a " camber," to allow for any settlement that may take place and to correct optical illusions of sagging centrally.

Trammels for Elliptical Mouldings.—Trammels are often used for running elliptical and oval panel mouldings, and for forming the lines when setting out oval templates. Trammels are made of wood and metal. A simple way of making a trammel (for small work) is to sink two grooves at right angles in a hardwood board (termed the plate), about 7 in. long, 5 in. wide, and 1 in. thick. The grooves are about $\frac{1}{2}$ in. deep and $\frac{1}{2}$ in. wide. Two hardwood pins are then made to fit the grooves. They

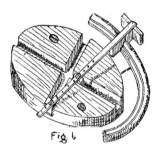

Fig. 1

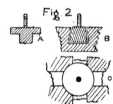

Fig. 2

FIG. 64.—Trammels.

have collars to bear on the surface of the plate. The upper part is made round to fit the centre holes of the rod. Fig. 64 shows a template and pins. No. 1 is a view of a template with the two pins, rod with the running mould attached in position, and a part of a moulding. No. 2 shows various sections of pins A is the section of the pin as used in No. 1, and C is the plan of the pin at the intersection of the grooves. B is the section of a dovetailed pin used for another form of trammel. The rod is made to any desired length so that it may serve for various sized ovals. The average size for this kind of trammel is about 1 ft. 6 in. long, 1 in. wide, and $\frac{1}{4}$ in. thick. A series of holes, $\frac{1}{4}$ in. in diameter (to fit the head of the pin), is made about $\frac{1}{8}$ in. apart on the flat side. The first hole is made near one end of the rod and continued down the centre for about 15 in., leaving the blank space for screwing on to the running mould. A pin is now laid into each groove, and the size of the desired oval is obtained by regulating the length of the rod at each diameter by means of the holes. The pin in the short groove is the point from which the length of the oval is taken, and the pin in the long groove for the width. The trammel is fixed on the running board by means of two or more screws, as shown. This size of trammel can only be used for oval mouldings from about 10 in. to 36 in. at their longest diameter, therefore large sizes are required for larger ovals.

A trammel for running large ovals (say from 6 ft. to 10 ft. at the major diameter), if made solid, as shown in No. 1, would be too heavy and cumbersome for fixing on ceilings where the mouldings are run *in situ*. A lighter kind, termed a " cross " template, is made as follows : Cut three flooring boards, one a little less in length than the longest diameter of the proposed oval, and two less than the short diameter. Lay them down on a floor in the form of a cross (similar to the grooves in No. 1), and fix and brace them together. Four angular braces will hold them together and allow the whole to be fixed on the ceiling. On the centre of this ground make two lines at right angles to each other, and from these set out the width of the desired grooves at the ends and intersections, and then fix wood fillets, each about 1 in. thick and 2 in. wide, to the marks, thus forming the grooves. In order to prevent the pins dropping out of the grooves when the trammel is fixed face downwards on the ceiling, the inner sides of the fillets should be splayed to receive dovetailed pins, as shown at B, No. 2. This may also be effected by fixing running rules on the fillets to overlap about $\frac{1}{4}$ in. over the groove space, thus forming rebated or square grooves. The pins are made with shoulders to fit the grooves. In both modes a linch-pin must be inserted in the trammel-pin to prevent the rod dropping.

Various methods are employed for running oval panel mouldings on flat ceilings. The most useful are wood or plaster templates. A trammel is not good for running wide, oval panel mouldings, as the mould is apt to jump and cripple the junction of the curves.

Templates for Running Elliptical Mouldings.—An ellipse is derived from a diagonal section through a cone by a plane obliquely through the opposite side, and the nearest approximation to this curve must be obtained by continuous motion. There is no instrument so adapted to producing this form as a trammel. Given the length and width of same, or both diameters on the face of a board, make a groove $\frac{1}{2}$ in. deep and 1 in. wide, central with the two diameters, 2 in. of the extreme size at the cardinal points of ellipse. On a radius rod laid along the longer half diameter, mark centre point of ellipse, which gives the position of one pin. Move the rod along the lesser diameter, and with end at extreme point, mark off centre as before. Through these marks on the rod fix pins into small blocks to slide in grooves, the block carrying pin for the longer diameter to run in the shorter groove, and that for the shorter diameter to run in the longest groove.

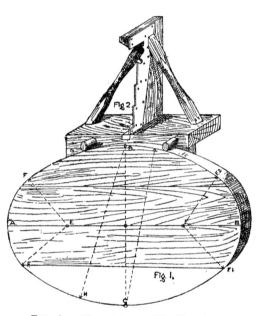

FIG. 65.—Template and Pin Mould for Elliptical Arches.

Plasterer's Oval.—Fig. 65 shows a method of setting out an incorrect form of ellipse; or, an oval having the major axis one-third greater than the minor one. It shows a template and pin running mould in position for running an elliptical arch moulding. The template (No. 1) should extend below the springing line of arch, so that the mould can run down to the spring of arch and save mitreing. The template for running the arch should extend to the shaded part; in the example the curve has been continued to show how to set out a template from which a complete oval moulding having its major axis one-third greater than its minor may be run, setting out as follows : Draw the line AB, the greater diameter, to the desired length ; bisect it, erect the perpendicular line CD, the lesser diameter a third less than the line AB. Bisect each half of the line, which will divide the line AB into four equal parts and give the centres EE, which are the centres for describing the ends F to F and F1 to F2. From the centres C and D describe the flat curves F to F1, and F to F2, which complete the oval. It is better to set out the template by trammel, as the junctions of the segments are always more or less crippled.

No. 2 shows a " pin mould " in position for running an elliptical arch moulding.

This mould has two hardwood pins in the bearing face of the slipper. The pins bearing on the edge of the template being apart, allow the mould to take any variation of curve without "jumping."

Before running mouldings on oval arches or windows, the centres and running rods shculd be tested for the mouldings to intersect accurately and avoid jumps where the curves change.

All centre pins should be level with each other and equidistant from the centre. The outline and intersections of the moulding can be tested by fixing pencils on the outer and inner lines of the running mould, and passing the mould over the screeds, so that the pencils will mark the two lines. This complicated method is of little use.

Templates are used for running most elliptical panel mouldings. Plasterers may make their own templates or running rules by substituting fibrous plaster casts for wood as follows : Setting out a quarter of the oval panel, cut out or run a temporary plaster running rule to fit the inner line, allowing space for the slipper of running mould. Cut a reverse running mould to the section required (about 1 in. thick and 3 in. wide), run a quarter length of oval, and after making true end joints, make four fibrous plaster casts, which lay and fix to complete the full oval, or run the whole *in situ* and in one operation with a trammel or radius rods, according to the size of the panel. Strong, stiff-gauged plaster or white cement should be used for the running rule, to resist friction on the running moulds.

Circular Mouldings on Circular Surfaces.—No. 1 (Fig. 66) shows the section of a cove, the external angle rib moulding C, and the panel rib moulding D, which spring from the weathering of a cornice moulding and intersect with a longitudinal moulding at crown of cove. The section of the horizontal moulding is shown at G, and that of the panel moulding over D, the external rib being that of the panel moulding doubled. Where circular and straight mouldings intersect, run the circular mouldings first, so that the whole can be run, the intersection mitreing on the straight moulding. Some-times this is not advisable. If the crown or longitudinal moulding, as at G, No. 1, is the lower member of a large moulding intersecting with smaller cove mouldings, run the straight moulding first and cut away enough of it to let the nib of the circular running mould pass. In this example there would be very little mitreing to do, it being a mitre butting up to the back circular moulding. The external rib moulding C is best run with a jack template. The circular panel mouldings (one-half is shown at D) may be run in three parts, using a sledge-slippered running mould on a hinged radius rod, the two straight parts being run from running rules, or the whole moulding at one operation by a fibrous plaster template, as already described.

A circular panel between such ribs would be run with a raised centre block, as on plan and section at MD, No. 2 ; the use of this will be seen later.

The section of a large cove and cornice is shown at No. 3 on Fig. 66. The main mouldings are the longitudinal mouldings at top CH on section, and the moulding JM, above the dotted line, and the vertical rib mouldings JM to CH. The main ground of cove shading on section springs from the weathering of main cornice at JM and terminates at H (No. 3). The crown moulding CH is shown without a lathed bracket, so that the section of intersection with the rib mouldings will be more clearly understood.

When floating, screeding, and running the cove mouldings, care must be taken in setting out and horsing the running moulds and screeds that all the mouldings will intersect properly. When crown and rib mouldings intersect at right angles, as at CH, the intersection is easy ; but if the ground is not so the outer members out of a square or perpendicular, as at WB, the intersection is not so easily made. The transition or intersection of the circle with the straight mouldings is sometimes formed in the

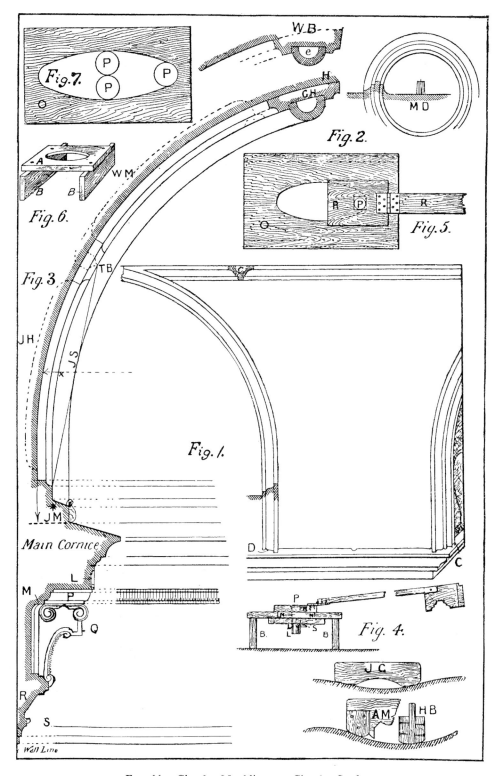

FIG. 66.—Circular Mouldings on Circular Surfaces.

bed of the enrichment, as at *e*, WB. Lack of care in setting out running moulds or in forming screeds will cause incorrect intersection, and the mouldings will have to be cut out and mitred, inserted and " humoured."

The main mouldings should be run first; circular mouldings on circular grounds are more difficult than mouldings circular on section only. The main mouldings being run, cut off the inner sides from the nib of the running mould to pass when running the circle panel mouldings. Mitre these parts and make good after the circular panel mouldings are run. In order to avoid stuff falling on run parts, work from the top downwards, and cover up any parts with sacks or paper while running any intermediate work. Run crown and rib mouldings on screeds on the bed of the centre enrichment.

Run ribs in two parts—one running mould will do for both—from a parallel running rule in centre of section, as at DK. Run the crown moulding in a similar way, with two running moulds, cut for the inner and outer sections. The foot moulding may be run in one operation, or in two sections, to such size and form, the main running mould for either being horsed to run on a nib screed and a slipper screed, the latter on the weathering of cornice, on which is a parallel rule, which may also be used as a slipper rule for running the foot moulding and as a nib rule for cornice.

The method of running the mouldings has been described in reverse order to practice, to make the method of screeding more clear. The screeds are based on dots at convenient places. For the crown moulding, place screed dots on the brackets across the bed of enrichment, each level crosswise, as also from end to end cove. As the mouldings form the base of the enrichment, the dots and screeds should be of gauged coarse stuff for a sound foundation. All screeds for work of this class should be of gauged stuff. Place the first dots on the crown bracket, one at each end of cove, keeping them level each way. Intermediate dots, according to the length of the cove, are made lineable and level with the former. Then screed and rule off with a long floating rule. A narrow screed is then similarly made on bracket of foot moulding. This screed must be on a member, on the plane of enrichment bed, as a bearing for forming the rib screed, which also acts as a nib screed for running the lower part and a slipper screed for the upper part, the joint between being set by hand.

Where size permits, the whole foot moulding may be run in one operation from a slipper screed on the weathering and a nib screed on the inner surface of the cove. In this case place dots at the foot of each rib, as bearings for rib screeds. The screed on the weathering must be level from end to end. Rule off the rib screeds with a rule cut to the segmental section, using the screeds or the dots as bearings. Screeds for the nibs of the crown, rib, and foot running moulds must be made and used for floating the cove surfaces between the panel mouldings. Spandrel surfaces are screeded and floated as described for cupolas. The running rules for the crown and foot mouldings must be equidistant and parallel, and tested with a rod cut to exact length, as also the rules or the vertical ribs, setting out each centre on the crown and foot screeds from end to end of the cove. This, if accurately done, is a guide for fixing each rib rule vertically. Test with a plumb bob from the top marks and a large set square at the bottom marks, or with eye judgment.

The main mouldings being run, cut off the inner side where the circular panel moulding intersects, for the running mould nib to pass in running the circular panel mouldings. Make up screeds at the top, bottom, and sides with a gauge rule bearing on the run work. A circular running mould is then cut to run a part of the inner ground of the panel, and is horsed with a slipper on the outside, the inner screed not being required.

Circular mouldings on circular grounds require special methods, to intersect accurately with other mouldings. A circular moulding on a segmental ground is not a true circle on plan.

The curve at spring and crown would partake of a flat-trend form of an oval. This may be avoided in one way by raising the centre pin by a block. In the circular panel at JH, on the section No. 3, the chord line JS is taken from the arris of the member of the moulding touching the corresponding member of foot moulding, and up to the same member above, at TB. If the centre pin be on the surface indicated by the dart at JS, the radius rod would form a true circle on the horizontal line, but the circle would be flat at the vertical line. If the centre was raised, say to X, the radius rod would decrease the diameter of the circle at the horizontal line, but it would extend the diameter at the vertical line. To run the moulded circle true and to intersect with the square panel mouldings, the exact height of the centre and length of the radius rod must be regulated until the cardinal points on the horizontal and vertical lines are touched. An oval panel may also be run thus : Make a flat template to the desired size, lay it on and project the outline on to the curved ground, and lay a plaster template on the ground.

Trammel Centre.—An oval moulding may also be run with a radius rod worked from a small oval trammel centre, fixed in centre of oval. To make the trammel centre, set out the oval to a scale on a board, cut it out, and fix on two blocks to raise the centre. The centre pin, held in position between sliding boards, works on the rim of small oval. Sketches at No. 4, Fig. 66, show section of trammel centre with radius rod and running mould attached. B, B are the blocks raising the centre board N, N, the width of oval opening in centre board. The centre pin is round up to the centre board, but square through sliding board R, attached to rod. The pin cannot rise because of the sliding board S, further secured by a linch-peg L, through centre pin. The radius rod, hinged to sliding board, enables the mould to rise and fall to the curves. Fix the hinge under the radius rod and on top of the sliding board at R, really a part of the radius rod.

No. 5 shows the upper side of the centre boards, the sliding board and end of radius rod R, and centre pin P. Here the hinge is on top of radius rod. No. 6 shows the centre board A, the blocks B, in perspective. No. 7, a plan of centre board, shows the centre course of centre pin P, round edge of oval centre.

Mouldings segmental or elliptical in form and plan, or diagonally set on arched or coved surfaces or on concavo-convex surfaces, need special running moulds, for the slippers and nibs run accurately on the screeds and produce mouldings without " jumps." The sledge slipper is particularly useful and reliable for working on curved surfaces without broken lines. JG (Fig. 66, bottom right-hand corner) shows a sledge slipper on an irregular curved surface. The " bull-nose nib " is rounded off to give a small bearing surface. A side section of a bull-nose nib is shown at AM and an end view at HB. A nib to fit any curve is made with a metal ball working inside a cup, the end of the cup being cut away to allow the ball to work on the screed.

Any decorative work may be executed either by modelling *in situ* or by moulding and casting. It is often advantageous to work *in situ*, but the modeller must judge the expediency of doing so, according to circumstances of time, cost, and materials.

With the exception of the small enrichments in cornice, the ornamental work, human and animal, may be most effectively modelled *in situ*, or made up with part cast and part wrought stucco leaf and flower after the manner of the old seventeenth-century Italian work in England, or modelled in clay, cast, and fixed afterwards. Work done in this way may be properly studied, the defects adjusted, and variety of design and detail given ; but the labour and expense, of course, must be considered, although it is not always of paramount importance. Work modelled *in situ* sometimes costs less than work cast, according to the design and treatment.

In the first method, work modelled direct minimises labour and cost; in the second method—cast work—the piece has to be modelled, moulded, cast, and fixed. In the examples given and in most works of this kind, the work has to be modelled in sections, some of which have to be separately moulded, cast, and fixed, thus increasing cost. Cast work is economical where there is a considerable amount of repeat. Work modelled *in situ* should have the advantage over cast work, in that it is fresh and the direct work of the modeller, and not reproduced elsewhere.

PLATE CVI

(a) MODERN COLOURED SGRAFFITO DECORATION AROUND WINDOW IN ST JOHN'S CHURCH, MILES PLATTING, MANCHESTER.

(b) MODERN COLOURED SGRAFFITO DECORATION IN ALL SAINTS' CHURCH, ENNISMORE GARDENS, LONDON.

Heywood Sumner.

PLATE CVII

FIGURE DESIGN FOR A PANEL IN COLOURED SGRAFFITO,—DAVID AS SLINGER.
(Heywood Sumner.)

CHAPTER XI

EXTERIOR PLASTERING AND SGRAFFITO

By G. P. BANKART

Sgraffito or " Graffito "—Fresco—Buon Fresco—Fresco Secco.

Sgraffito or " Graffito " (Italian for " scratched "). — Scratched decoration is the most ancient mode of surface decoration employed by man. The primitive, inarticulate savage expressed himself by this simple form of writing in hieroglyphics, the proem of the civilised arts. The term was applied to scratched or incised decorations upon potter's clay whilst soft. A case of pottery ornamented by scratched ornaments of this type is in the Victoria and Albert Museum. Probably early Italian mural decorations of this manner followed in the fifteenth and sixteenth centuries by covering the fronts of buildings with an intonaco of black plaster, which was covered, whilst fresh, with white stucco, to which cartoons were transferred and the outline " hatched " over with a graving iron to expose the coating of black underneath. The whole work was then gone over with a black or darkly tinted water-colour in very fluid condition. This elementary form of " sculpture " or " engraving," not altogether unlike a kind of " stencilling " in appearance, but, of course, entirely different from it, ran parallel to its sister art of the stucco-worker, and was an equally legitimate, beautiful, and durable form of plastic decoration in its earlier and more simple form. The substitution of colour for black and white robbed the art of some of its purity and freedom compared with the latter, due to the preparation of cartoons and their transference to the plaster surface by mechanical means in contrast to direct drawing. The term is now employed for decoration scratched or incised in plaster before set. It may be used for both external and internal decoration. Figs. 67 and 68 show examples of Italian sgraffito work in Italy. Examples may be seen at the Choir Schools of St Paul's Cathedral, the School of Music (near the Albert Hall), and at the Science and Art Schools, South Kensington. The latter work was done experimentally by students (1871) from designs by T. W Moody, and covers an extensive wall surface. In a few instances only the colours used have faded, due, no doubt, to experiment. Examples of modern English design, by Mr Heywood Sumner, are shown on Plates CVI and CVII.

Some of the work is low relief rather than sgraffito, being deeply cut, the final coat being plastered instead of washed on. Deep cutting sometimes gives a harsh appearance to the design, prevents the water from running off the walls, and catches dirt. In true sgraffito the cut or scratch should be exceedingly slight. The above work is darker than at first, but perfectly distinct and sound.

This is evidence that sgraffito does not suffer materially from atmospheric change. Sgraffito was extensively used in Italy and has spread throughout Europe to this country, which it reached in Henry VIII's time. Its limited use in Great Britain may be due to an idea that it might not resist our climate, or prove too expensive ! Examples have proved the contrary. Vasari says of it : " Artists have another art, which is called graffito. It is used to ornament the fronts of buildings, which can thus be more quickly decorated, and gives greater durability and resistance to rain, in consequence of the etching on the wall being drawn in colours. The cement (stucco) is prepared and tinted, and forms the background, and is subsequently covered with a travertino limewash, the lines being afterwards scratched in with an iron stilus." " Backgrounds are obtained by the entire removal of the surface wash." Vasari tells how strong projecting shadows for foliage, fruit, and grotesque figures may be obtained by adding stronger shades of colour to the background. In some backgrounds colours in monochrome are added as fresco, which is simple after experience has taught the difference of tint, wet and dry. Gilding is used in parts when the sgraffito is perfectly dry. Properly manipulated, external sgraffito will resist all weathers; it is very hard, much less porous than stone or brick, will wash, and in cost compares well with other forms of decoration.

FIG. 67.—Italian Renaissance Graffito from Rome.

The late G. T. Robinson, speaking of combining sgraffito with fresco, says: " In my own practice as an architect and decorator I have, during the last fifteen or twenty years, used sgraffito somewhat extensively for both external and internal adornment, and most of that which I have done is still in perfect condition, even in grimy London. The mode adopted has nothing new in it; in fact, Vasari's instructions hold good to this day, *excepting that I use ordinary materials, and find the simplest the best.* The wall is prepared in the ordinary way. A rough coating of Portland, mixed with three times its quantity of good sharp sand, is, for external work, laid on and finished with a roughened surface, by stubbing it with an old birch besom, leaving it barely $\frac{1}{2}$ in. from the finished face. For internal work the ordinary ' pricking up ' suffices. When this is dry, a thin coat of selenitic lime, mixed with the desired colouring matter for the background, is floated over it. This background may be black, ' bone-black ' being used; red, for which you may use Venetian or Indian red, or the ordinary purple brown of commerce, singly, or mixed to produce any tone you may desire; yellow, produced by ochres or umbers; blue, by German blue, Antwerp blue, or any of the commoner blues, avoiding cobalt ; and these colours you may use to any degree of intensity or paleness. When this coat is nearly dry, you skim over it a very thin coat of pure selenitic lime, which dries of a parchment colour and generally suffices. If you want a pure white lime, use a moderate quick-setting one, as stiff as you can work it, and as each variety of lime has its own individual perversity, I can give no general direction, and would advise the beginner to stick to selenitic, which is always procurable. You have, of course, prepared your cartoon. This is pricked and pounced as for any other transfer process, and then with an old, well-worn, big-bladed knife—for there is no better tool—you can round all the outlines, and with a flat spatula clear away all the thin upper coat, leaving the coloured ground as smooth as you can. If your plaster is not quite dry enough for the two coats to separate easily, wait a little longer, but not too long, for that is fatal. By the time you have cleared out your background the plaster will be in a good condition to allow you to cut out the finer parts of the design, such as the folds of the draperies, or the finer lines of the faces or of the ornament. Use your knife slightly on the slope, and if you want to produce half-tones, slope it very much ; but, as a rule, the more you avoid half-tones and the simpler and purer your line, the more effective your work will be. Recollect, above all things, you are making a design and *not* a ' picture,' and you must never hesitate, for to retouch is impossible. Sometimes it may be desirable to gild the background, and you can then carve or impress it with any design you choose. It occasionally happens you want to give some semblance of pictorial character to your work when it is small in scale and near the eye, and then you can proceed as though you were cutting a woodblock.

" By cutting out your ground colour in places and plastering it with that of another colour, you may vary any portion of it you desire. You can also wash over certain parts of your upper coat with a water-colour if you desire, combining fresco with sgraffito ; but, as a rule, the broader your design and the simpler your treatment of it the better. It will be seen that this process is very available for simple architectonic effects, and for churches, hospitals, and other places where large surfaces have to be covered, it is the least costly process that can be adopted. It has also the great advantage of being non-absorbent, and it can be washed down at any time. At Messrs Trollope's establishment in London there is a specimen which for two years was fixed up outside their heating apparatus chimney, exposed to all weathers, under the adverse circumstances of rapid changes of temperature, and it was naturally encrusted with soot. It has simply been washed, and presents a very fair illustration of how enduring this mode of decoration is and how well fitted for the external decoration of town buildings. The artist is untrammelled by difficulties of execution, but he should bear in mind that the more carefully he draws his lines and the simpler he keeps his composition, the more charmed with the process he will be, and the better will be the effect of his work."

Mr Heywood Sumner records his considerable experience of sgraffito as follows : " Rake and sweep out the mortar joints, then give the wall as much water as it will drink, or it will absorb the moisture from the coarse coat, as it will not set, but merely dry, in which case it will be worth little more than dry mud. Care should be taken that the cement and sand which compose the coarse coat should be properly gauged, or there may be an unequal suction for the finishing coats. The surface of the coarse coat should be well roughened to give a good key, and it should stand some days to thoroughly set before laying the finishing coats. When sufficiently set, fix your cartoon in its destined position with nails ; pounce through the pricked outline ; remove the cartoon ; replace the nails in the register holes ; mark in with chalk spaces for the different colours, as indicated by the pounced impression on the coarse coat ; lay the several colours of the colour coat according to the design, as shown by the chalk outlines ; take care that in doing so the register nails are not displaced ; roughen the face in order to make a good key for the final coat. When set, follow on with the final surface coat, only laying as much as can be cut and cleaned up in a day. When this is sufficiently steady, fix up the cartoon in its registered position; pounce through the pricked outline; remove the cartoon; and cut the design in the surface coat before it sets; then, if the register is correct, cut through to different colours, according to the design, and in the course of a few days the work should set as hard and as homogeneous as stone, and as damp-proof as the nature of things permits.

" When cleaning up the ground of colour which may be exposed, care should be taken to obtain a similar quantity of surface all through the work, so as to get a broad effect of deliberate and calculated contrast between the trowelled surface of the final coat and the scraped surface of the colour coat. The manner of design should be founded upon a frank acceptance of line and upon simple contrasts of light against dark or dark against light. The following are the proportions of the various coats :—

" Coarse coat—1 of Portland cement to 3 of washed, sharp, coarse sand. The Portland cement should be of the very best make, and *not* used fresh from the kiln, when cracks are sure to manifest themselves, particularly if uneven of surface.

" Colour coat—$1\frac{1}{2}$ of air-slaked Portland to 1 of colour, laid $\frac{1}{8}$ in. thick. Distemper colours are Indian red, Turkey red, ochre, umber, lime blue ; lime blue and ochre for green ; oxide of manganese for black. In using lime blue, its violet hue may be overcome by adding a little ochre. It should be noted that it sets much quicker and harder than the other colours named.

" Final coat internal work—Parian air slakes for twenty-four hours to retard its setting, or Aberthaw lime and selenitic sifted through a fine sieve.

" For external work—3 selenitic and 2 silver sand.

" When finishing, space out the wall according to the scheme of decoration, and decide where to begin, and give the wall in such place as much water as it will drink ; then lay the colour coat, and leave sufficient key for the final coat. Calculate how much surface of colour coat it may be advisable to get on to the wall, as it is better to maintain throughout the work the same duration of time between the laying of the colour coat and the following on with the final surface coat ; for this reason, that if the colour sets hard before laying the final coat, it is impossible to get up the colour to its full strength wherever it may be revealed in the scratching of the decoration. When the colour coat is quite firm and all the shine has passed away from its surface, follow on with the final coat, but only lay as much as can be finished in one day. The final coat is trowelled up and the design is incised or scratched out. Individual taste and experience must decide as to thickness of final coat, but if laid between $\frac{1}{8}$ in. and $\frac{1}{12}$ in., and the lines cut with slanting edges, a side light gives emphasis to the finished result, making the outlines tell alternately as they take the light or cast a shadow."

Another method which I have used in sgraffito for external decoration was done entirely with Portland cement. This material, for strapwork or broad foliage, or where minuteness of detail is unnecessary, will be found suitable for many places and positions. Three colours may be used if required, say black for the background, red for the middle coat, and grey or white for the final coat, as desired. The Portland cement floating can be blackened by smithy ashes as an aggregate, and gauging with black manganese, for a thin coat. Red may be obtained by adding 5 to 10 per cent. of red oxide ; white by gauging the cement with white marble dust, or with whiting or lime, the grey being the natural colour of the cement. The first coat, when laid, should be keyed with a coarse broom ; the second coat laid fair, and left moderately rough with a hand-float. The suction of the first coat should give sufficient firmness for a third coat to be laid (without disturbing the second) before the second is set hard. The second and third coats may be used neat, or gauged with fine sifted aggregate as required. The outlines of the design may be pounced, or otherwise transferred to the surface of the work, and the details put in by hand. The thickness of the second coat should be about $\frac{3}{16}$ in. and the third coat about $\frac{1}{8}$ in. The thickness of one or both coats may be varied to suit the design.

The plates here given are taken from old engravings, and give a very fair idea of the black and white work of the best period. Such methods, which have been practised for ages, may be safely taken as a basis for modern work, and developed in a modern way according to the ability and aptitude of the interpreter.

Fresco.—The plasterer is closely allied to the artist painter. He has always

FIG. 68.—Example of Graffito from Rome.

to be in readiness to plaster the wall for the artist. Owing to the alliance with distinguished artists and the various methods of preparing and using the plaster materials, I am induced to give a few notes, also extracts, from writers of authority. Fresco is a mode of painting with water-colours on freshly laid plaster while it remains naturally wet. The colours incorporate with the plaster, and drying with it the work becomes very durable. It is called "fresco" either because it was originally used on buildings in the open air, or because it was done on fresh plaster. Fresco is an ancient art, mentioned by Pliny. Dr Flinders Petrie found some remarkably fine specimens on floors and walls at Tel-el-Amarna which reveal the state of the art 3,300 years ago. Fine frescoes were discovered in the ruins of Pompeii. In one of the principal houses the plaster walls are adorned with theatrical scenes; in an inner room is the niche often to be seen in Pompeian houses. The frescoes on the walls consist of floral dados.

Above this is a whole aquarium with shells, plants, birds, and animals. They are all executed in their natural colours, and are naturally and gracefully drawn. Michelangelo's beautiful fresco on the ceiling of the Sistine Chapel in the Vatican is grand both in conception and execution. It measures 133 ft. in length by 43 ft. in width. Raphael's frescoes in the Vatican, Farnesina Palace, etc., are wonderfully fine, and may be regarded as the high water mark of Cinquecento decoration. Raphael was assisted by Giovanni da Udine and Giulio Romano, who were also artists in stucco. There are two large frescoes by Maclise (each 45 ft. long and 12 ft. high) in the House of Lords. The fine frescoes executed by the late Lord Leighton in the Victoria and Albert Museum, South Kensington, are admired by all classes of art lovers.

For fresco or buon fresco the lime has to be carefully run, and the sand should be white, clean, and of even grain, being well washed and sifted free from impurities or saline properties. Silver sand is preferred by some artists. The older the putty lime, the better the results. The lime is slaked in a tub and then run through a fine wire sieve into a tank, and after being covered up, is left for three months. It is then put into the tub again and re-slaked, or rather well worked and run through a fine hair sieve into earthenware jars or slate tanks, and the water which collects at the top drawn or poured off, the jars or tanks being covered over to exclude the air. Lime putty in this state will keep for an indefinite time without injury. A large quantity of old putty for fresco purposes is, or was lately, kept in the cellars of the Houses of Parliament. The proportions of the putty and sand will vary somewhat according to the circumstances and (particularly) according to the quality of the lime. From 2 to 4 parts of the sand to 1 part of putty is usual. Marble dust alone is sometimes used in place of sand, and also with sand in equal parts. Every difference of lime and sand found in various localities should be considered and tested before using. A soft sand is quickly dissolved by a strong lime, and a plaster made of this is fit for use sooner, and will deteriorate more quickly than a plaster made with a less powerful lime and a harder sand, or with marble dust.

The wall surface to be plastered must be well scraped and hacked, the joints raked out and brushed, and the whole surface well scrubbed and wetted. The rendering is done with the best possible prepared old coarse stuff. If the walls are rough or uneven they should be first pricked up and then floated. In any case the surface is left true, and with a rough face, to receive the finishing coat. Portland cement or hydraulic lime gauged with sand, also gauged with coarse stuff, has been used where the walls were damp (damp is fatal to fresco), or if exposed to the atmosphere. When Portland cement or hydraulic lime is used, the work should be allowed to stand until thoroughly dry to allow any contained soluble saline efflorescence to come to the surface. This is brushed off with a dry brush, and a few days are allowed to elapse to see if there is a further efflorescence. When this is all extracted and swept off, and the artist is ready to commence, the wall is washed with a thin solution of the fine setting stuff and then laid about $\frac{1}{8}$ in. thick with well-beaten, worked, and tempered fine setting stuff. It is then rubbed with a straight-edge and scoured with a hand-float (using lime water for scouring) until the surface is true and of a uniform grain. Most artists prefer a scoured surface without being trowelled. No more surface should be covered than can be conveniently painted in one day. While the plaster is still soft and damp, the cartoon is laid on and the lines and details pounced in or indented by means of a bone or hardwood tool. Should the finishing coat get too dry in any part, it can be made fit for work by using a fine spray of water. The method of plastering and the gauging of materials may slightly vary according to the desire of the painter and the kind of fresco in hand. The following is taken from an old manuscript in the Soane Museum, dated 1699 :—

" 1. In painting the wall to make it endure the weather, you must grind colours with lime water, milk, or whey, mixed in size.

" 2. Then paste or plaster must be made of well-washed lime, mixed with powder of old rubbish stones.   The lime must be often washed till finally all the salt is extracted, and all your work must be done in clear and dry weather.

" 3. To make the work endure, stick into the wall stumps of headed nails, about 5 or 6 in. asunder, and by this means you may preserve the plaster from peeling.

" 4. Then with the paste, plaster the walls a pretty thickness, letting it dry; but scratch the first coat with the point of your trowel longways and crossways, as soon as you have done laying on what plaster or paste you think fit, that the next plastering you lay upon it may take good key, and not come off nor part from the first coat of plastering; and when the first coat is dry, plaster it over again with the thickness of half a barley-corn, very fine and smooth.   Then, your colours being already prepared, work this last plastering over with the said colours in what draught or design you please—history, etc.—so will your painting unite and join fast to the plaster, and dry together as a perfect compost.

" *Note.*—Your first coat of plaster or paste must be very haired with ox-hair in it, or else your work will crack quite through the second coat of plastering, and will spoil all your painting that you paint upon the second coat of plastering; but in the second coat that is laid on of paste or plaster there must be no hair in it at all, but made thus : Mix or temper up with well-washed lime, fine powder of old stones (called finishing stuff), and sharp grit sand, as much as you shall have occasion for, to plaster over your first coat, and plaster it all very smooth and even, that no roughness, hills, nor dales be seen nor scratches of your trowel.   The best way is to float the second coat of plastering thus : After you have laid it all over the first coat with your trowel as even and smooth as possible, you can then take a float made of wood, very smooth, and 1 ft. long and 7 or 8 in. wide; with a handle on the upper side of it put your hand in to float your work withal, and this will make your plastering to lie even; and lastly, with your trowel you may make the said plastering as smooth as can be.

" 5. In painting, be nimble and free; let your work be bold and strong; but be sure to be exact, for there is no alteration after the first painting, and therefore heighten your paint enough at first; you may deepen at pleasure.

" 6. All earthy colours are best, as the ochres, Spanish brown, terra-vert, and the like.   Mineral colours are naught.

" 7. Lastly, let your pencils and brushes be long and soft, otherwise your work will not be smooth; let your colours be full, and flow freely from your pencil or brush; and let your design be perfect at first, for in this there is no alteration to be made."

Fresco Secco.—Closely allied with the genuine fresco (fresco buono) is another kind called fresco secco (dry), or mezzo (half) fresco.   The plasterwork for fresco secco is similar to that used for fresco buono.   It is allowed to stand until thoroughly dry. The surface is then rubbed with pumice-stone, and about twelve hours before the painting is commenced it is thoroughly wetted with water, mixed with a little lime. The surface is again moistened the next morning, and the painting begun in the usual way.   If the wall should become too dry it is moistened with the aid of a syringe.   There is no fear of joinings in the painting being observable, and the artist can quit or resume his work at his pleasure.   Joinings are distinctly noticeable in the frescoes in the loggia of the Vatican.   Fresco secco paintings are heavy and opaque, whereas real fresco is light and transparent.   While the superiority of fresco buono over fresco secco for the highest class of decorative painting is unquestionable, still the latter is suitable for many places and forms of decorative paintings.   The head by Giotto in the National Gallery, from the Brancacci Chapel of the Carmine at Florence, is in fresco secco.

CHAPTER XII

MODEL AND RUNNING MOULD MAKING

To Draw a Truss—To Make a Model of a Truss—Hinged Running Moulds for Diminished
    Models—To Make a Keystone—To Set Out and Make a Corinthian Column Capital—
    To Make a Pilaster Capital—To Make Composite, Doric, and Tuscan Capitals—To Set
    Out and Make Ionic Capitals and Entablature—To Draw the Ionic Volute—Centre
    Flowers—Cast Enrichment Mitres and Abutments—Running Moulds—Running Moulds
    for Enriched Cornices—Twin Slippered Mould—Arch Radius Mould—Hanging Moulds
    —Notes on Running Moulds.

Truss Consoles and Modillions.—To design and draw a truss or console bracket,
such as illustrated in Fig. 69, requires the knowledge and skill of an architect, and to
produce one the skill of a modeller. It is now usual for this to be drawn full size by the
architect, modelled in clay, and for the plasterer to produce it by casting in fibrous
plaster from a jelly mould, as described elsewhere (Chapter XIV). There is no binding
rule for either the design or proportions of an architectural feature of this nature, nearly
every instance varying according to the taste and gift of design on the part of the
architect.

The example given illustrates one stereotyped form of bracket, the proportions of
which are figured, but they must by no means be taken as a standard of excellence.
One or two approximate proportions may be noticed, however, for guidance, as being
those found in good examples, although not strictly applicable. The thickness of the
scroll is usually that of the pilaster it is fixed upon.

To Make a Model of a Truss (Fig. 70).—For the sake of variety, a different
design of a truss from the above is given to illustrate the method of making trusses,
which are usually divided into three parts, viz., the "body" or main part, the "cap,"
and the "foot leaf." The latter in some districts is termed a "frog leaf."

The common method is to cut two profiles out of a plaster slab, fix them on edge,
run the front mouldings, and model any ornament. There are various ways of doing
this, but the following is expeditious and accurate :—

Make a set of five thickness rules, equal in thickness to the outside members of
the truss, and in length to the length and width of the truss, as shown by the A's (Fig. 70,
No. 1). Fix the centre rule on a smooth board, trace the outline of truss on the board
each side of the rule, and fix the rules touching the outline as shown. Make up between
outline and rule with clay strips B, held in place with clay or plaster, where shaded.
The clay strip may be laid slightly back from the line rather than up to it, to allow
trimming. The thickness rules give the desired thickness of the sides of the truss,
and with the clay strips form fences for the liquid plaster ; a common way is to trace
the outline on a plaster slab, which is cut into two pieces, each being cut to the traced
line ; the bottom scroll being weak, is apt to break in cutting. The other process saves
plaster and labour, and allows an iron or galvanised wire "leg," W and W, to be
inserted at and strengthen the narrow part. Oil the spaces C and C, fill in with plaster,

insert the wires W, W, and rule the surface off. When set, clear away rules and clay, take up and place the casts together on their back edges against a fixed rule to prevent movement when trimming the outer edges, which must be true, smooth, and square. A file is useful for this purpose. After trimming, lay them flat on the board, mark the inner lines (by pricking or pouncing from the drawing) indicated by the dotted line on No. 2, and sink the sides as No. 3. If the scrolls rise above the face of band, they must be worked up. Place the sides on edge, as No. 4, hold them in position by rules A, secured with clay or plaster. Fix wood or plaster stays inside, and two or more cramps at B and B (see No. 5 of cramp). Form a foundation of laths D, D, deep enough for a good thickness of the face moulding. To ascertain this, place the running mould in position, mark each side; draw a line parallel with outline of bracket from end to end. These are some guidance in cutting the keying and fixing the laths with plaster, gauged with lime putty water, after shellacing the sides to stop the suction. Shellac is quicker, cleaner, and better than water, and does not weaken the plaster. A plaster surface overcharged with water gives as bad fixing as a dry surface.

FIG. 69.—Drawing a Classic Truss and Cornice.

After lathing, run the face mouldings and bed for enrichments. No. 6 shows the running mould for the former, F, F ; Nos. 7 and 8 that for the latter ; at C (No. 8) where the stock bears on the edges and outside surfaces, it should be cut square, not splayed. Cut the metal plate short at the ends, leaving enough to form the inner arrises, and prevent it from cutting the plaster bearings when running. Run the face moulds quickly and with few gauges, to avoid swellings and jumpy mouldings. Muffle the running mould, block out the moulding with gauged plaster (in one gauge), and

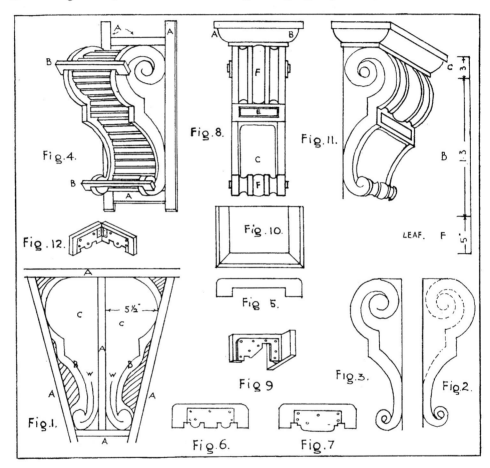

FIG. 70.—Making the Model of a Truss.

finish with neat plaster. An experienced man might run the moulding by dragging the gauged stuff down (to counteract swelling) while a boy gauges the neat plaster for finishing. The success of this lies in blocking out and running the first two gauges, following up with the neat plaster before the other swells. Plaster gauged with lime putty water takes shellac less evenly than neat plaster. Make up the ends and work the sunk panel E (No. 8) by hand. Make the cap and temporarily fix in position. To make the cap, cut a running mould to section, with a bed for the enrichment, as No. 9 ; run a length of moulding, cut, mitre, and fix together, as shown on plan of cap (No. 10). Fill the bed in with clay and run profile with a wood or plaster template A (No. 8), ready for modelling at B. Shellac the whole thing and model all enrichments. For large caps a short piece is modelled and moulded, casts made and fixed, and the mitres formed. For small work the whole enrichment and mitres may be modelled. If only a few trusses are required, mould direct from the clay ; if the model is for stock purposes, waste mould, cast an original with a background, and retouch. Plasterers are usually too free and indiscreet in the use of metal tools when " cleaning up " ! (See reference to this in Editor's preface and elsewhere.) If a truss diminishes in width, run the face moulding with a hinged running mould, made as follows :—

Hinged Running Moulds for Diminished Models.—Hinges enable a mould to lessen in width in running a diminishing moulding ; both halves close or open uniformly when being worked up and down an acute angle space formed by two running bearings. A mould side-hinged only cannot run at right angles with centre line of moulding, as it lifts up ; each moulding varies in width and profile, the rake becoming more acute and pronounced as the moulding diminishes.

Cut the mould plate to the moulding section at its greatest width. When roughly shaped, cut the plate through the centre, place the halves together in a vice, and file both equal and true. Fix the half plates on separate stocks and hinge them centrally, as Fig. 70, No. 12,

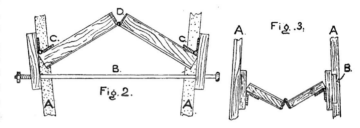

which shows the mould at its narrowest. Clean the seam off by hand, unless an enrichment covers it up. Slippers are unnecessary in small examples, but the stock must overlap the sides of truss, the rebates acting as slippers, and must square at the bearings, to run smooth and true without cut-ting.

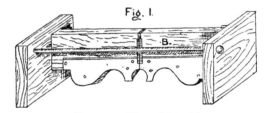

FIG. 71.—Hinged Moulds.

A hinged running mould for large or special work needs a slipper at each end, connected to the stock by hinges.

To Make a Keystone.—A keystone is chosen by way of further illustration of a face moulding diminishing in width. A model is made as for a truss, using a hinged mould for the face moulding.

When cutting and horsing the plate of a running mould for the face of a diminished model, allow thickness for the truss sides, the upper edges acting as bearings and the sides as running rules. No. 1, Fig. 71, shows a mould rebated each side of moulding to allow a bearing on the edges of the sides of the model and the slippers bearing on the sides. No. 2 is a plan showing the mould in its narrowest position, A being the edges of the model sides, C the hinge connecting slippers and stock, and D the centre hinge of stock. A flat, diminished moulding would be more easily run if the slippers worked between running rules, better regulating the expansion and contraction of the running mould, in which case the side edges of model are part of the face moulding : hence the slippers bearing against the sides of truss.

Where the moulding is wide, it is sometimes difficult to work the slippers quite squarely, which will cause the two halves of the moulding to be unequal in profile.

This may be avoided by inserting a ½ in. iron rod, with a round head at one end and a screw nut at the other, through the slipper at B, Nos. 1 and 2. When the mould is in position at the widest part, screw the nut tight up to slipper.

Take hold of the rod centrally with the right hand, bear down on the mould with the left, and draw the running mould towards the diminished end. Thus the slippers will slide parallel with each other, the halves of the mould collapse regularly, and the moulding be equal in profile. The holes in slipper must be large enough for the rod to work freely as the mould narrows. No. 3 is the plan of a hinged mould with the slippers bearing against running rules A, A, for running a moulding on a wall or cove. Equal-sided mouldings, column flutes, etc., graduated in projection and in width may be run with a rule diminished on upper edge, fixed to suit the diminish in width, a fillet B being screwed to each slipper as a rebate, bearing on the upper inner edges. This is only practicable where the moulding sides butt against a stile, to cover the unequal projection of the outer members.

To Set Out and Make a Corinthian Column Capital.—Fig. 72 is taken from Palladio. More skill and labour are required to make a plaster model of a Corinthian

FIG. 72.—Corinthian Capital.

cap than for perhaps any other detail of the plasterer's craft. The most expedient and usual way now is to set out and model in clay or plasticine one quarter or half of the capital on a shellaced plaster bell and abacus, to jelly mould, cast fibrous and put together, four quarter casts making up the whole cap. The old-fashioned way was to model one leaf and one volute, waste mould and piece mould them, back and front, cast and put them together in innumerable pieces. Like all other strictly architectural features, this capital should, properly, be set out full size by the architect, whose profession it is; but more often this is deputed through the master modeller and his journeyman to the foreman plasterer, who prepares the groundwork for the modeller to work upon. Failing the learned architect's drawing, set out a complete full-size section and plan. The "vase" or "bell" is that part between the necking and abacus, the bodyground for the leafage. Run the "astragal" or "necking" moulding, and about 1 in. of shaft, with the bell, for a guidance and judgment in modelling the cap. (For scagliola or polished work the bell is cast without the necking, which is made with the shaft, the joint being less easily seen above than below it.) Fig. 73 is a setting out of a Corinthian cap. In practice a half plan suffices, and that sub-divided, the quarters applying to cap or pilaster, as right-hand subject. The quarter plans of the column cap A and pilaster B show the diameter line, the volutes, leaves, abacus, and plan of shaft with flutes at necking, which is omitted for clearness. Pilasters are sometimes, though rarely, insular or square; usually they only project a fourth or fifth of the column diameter. A half pilaster cap is usually modelled, so that for either two halves a fourth or fifth part may be utilised, the latter by stopping off the mould. To set out the cap, divide the neck diameter of shaft as on the right-hand subject. The abacus angles are cut off to detail. The radius is the length between the angle points E, E. For the abacus, run a segmental length of moulding, cut, mitre, and fix it on half of plan. The left-hand subject is a quarter skeleton elevation C (above), a section of bell and abacus at the centre. The lip of bell usually projects about 7½ parts from the finished line.

In setting out the section of bell (the core of the cap), leave space for the thickness of the leaves. The surface line of the first row of leaves should range with the shaft face below necking. Their thickness depends on the size and detail of the model,

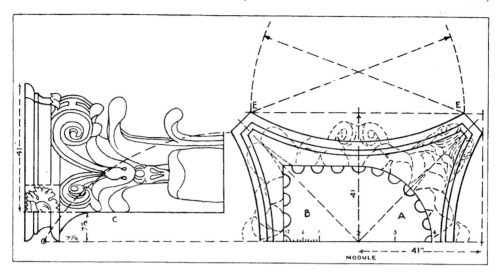

FIG. 73.—Setting out Columns and Plaster Caps.

¾ in. being a fair average thickness for a cap 12 in. diameter. Much, of course, depends on the character of the modelling. The raised edges of the Greek foliage appear higher in relief than the rounded-off edges of Roman examples, even when both are alike in thickness. Horse the mould upside down for ease and freedom in running the bell. Fix radius rod lineable with mould plate, so that the centre plate will line with centre pin and give an accurate centre. If placed at the side of the wood backing, the radius is neither so true, nor can the mould mark the upright lines for the enrichments on the bell. To construct a bell, fix on a moulding board wood block centre A, Fig. 74, the height of the mould, core all round G with old bricks or plaster, and fix with gauged plaster, leaving 1 in. space between core and running mould. The core should come about 1 in. over the centre line as a bed for the plaster. Fix a wood template (as a muffle) on the running mould, cover the core with gauged plaster, and finish with the muffled mould. The position of the bell during the fixing of enrichments is shown at H. The bell is fixed on the abacus before the en-

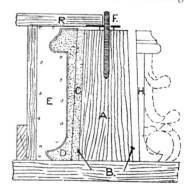

FIG. 74.—Section of Bell and Running Mould for Corinthian Column Capital.

richments, which—with the exception of those covering the joints of the two halves—are fixed in the shop before being placed on the column shaft.

When the core is finished, brush it over with clay water to prevent the bell from adhering, and drive in two or three nails outside the centre line to keep it firm while being run. It is wise to draw a half plan of column on the board before fixing the wood centre, dividing the half circle into eight parts, to be later marked up the bell for guidance in spacing the leaves. Lines from the centre should be produced on the board beyond the bearing part of the slipper to prevent them from obliteration whilst running the bell. Fix the pin exactly central, or the lines will be useless. The centre is found by placing (two) set squares at side of the half cap line and proving the centre on the block, with a straight-edge bearing on the upright edges of the set squares, reversing them to the quarter lines and trying them again. When the bell is run, place the running mould with the mould plate in position in a line with the lines on the board. Mark the upright (leaf) division lines from neck to lip, the mould plate for guidance. Take the bell off the core and saw through at centre lines. Run the abacus moulding as before described, and fix bell on it.

FIG. 75.—Composite Capital from the Arch of Titus.

To Make a Pilaster Capital.—Run the bell from the mould used for column cap. Horsing it to run flat, run enough straight moulding, cut to the lengths for front and sides, place upright on a board on which the plan of bell has been set out, fasten together with plaster, make good the mitres, fix the abacus, shellac the whole cap, and model.

The most expeditious process now customary is to make a jelly mould from the clay model and cast in fibrous plaster, as described in Chapter XIV, pp. 217-240. The previous method, now obsolete, was to waste mould the various parts of clay model, cast clean up, and piece mould them with either wax or plaster, or both combined, cast again, and make up round each bell in a most laborious manner which no plasterer would now be permitted to do.

To Make a Capital of the Composite Order (Figs. 75 and 76).—The composite order, as its name implies, is a combination of the Corinthian and Ionic, and was received into the regular number of orders by the Romans. Its capital consists, like the Corinthian, of two ranges of acanthus leaves on the vase, but instead of stalks and branches, the shoots appear small as though flowering, adhering to the vase and rounding with the capital towards its middle. The vase proper terminates upwards by a fillet, over which is an astragal and an echinus, from which the volutes roll out to meet the tops of the upper leaves on which they appear to rest. A large acanthus leaf is bent above the volutes as if sustaining the corners of abacus, the flower between the volutes being differently set to that of the Corinthian example. (Compare Fig. 72 with Fig. 75.)

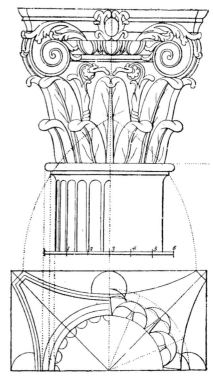

FIG. 76.—Plan and Elevation of the Composite Capital.

Some composite capitals have animals and human figures in addition to the foliage. The composite like the Corinthian capitals are made as described. Fig. 76 shows a skeleton plan and elevation to scale with the centre from which the abacus is struck, at the intersection of the dotted lines. Only one volute need be modelled and one leaf of each size. Since the introduction of gelatine the model may be moulded and cast in one piece. Capitals of the Doric and Tuscan order are comparatively simple in construction, and with full-size drawings there should be no difficulty in making models of them.

To Set Out Ionic Capitals and Entablature. —There are several types of Ionic capital. In some the abacus is square and plain, in others it is curved each side, and others have two faces only curved; the flanks are different in conformation, both vertically and horizontally. This capital usually has no necking. In some a swag depends from the eye of the volute. Whatever the form of the Ionic capital, it may be made in a similar manner to the foregoing.

In the antique examples the extraordinary projection of the ovolo makes it necessary either to bend it inwards towards the extremities to pass behind the volutes, or (instead of keeping the volutes flat in front, as they commonly are in the antique) to twist them outwards till they give room for the ovolo to pass. Le Clerc thinks the latter the best, and reduces the projection of the ovolo to ease the difficulty.

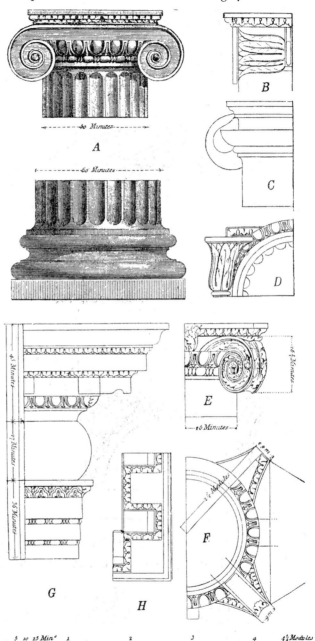

FIG. 77.—Plans, Elevations, and Sections of Ionic Capitals and Entablature.

This takes place also with the ovolo and angular Ionic volutes; it is therefore advisable to open or spread the volutes enough for the ovolo to pass behind.

Fig. 77 shows scale elevations, plans, and sections of Ionic capitals, columns, and entablature, with figured proportions. A is an elevation of column, base, and capital, the abacus of which is square on plan, D; see the profile C and the end B. A quarter Ionic capital, with angular volutes and abacus, is shown at E and on plan at F. The intersection of the diagonal lines, which spring from the angles of the abacus, gives its centre and radius. Ionic entablature is shown at G, the frieze being swelled or cushioned. A plan of soffit is shown at H.

The Ionic capital, Fig. 78, shows diagrams of Ionic column and pilaster capitals, viz. :—

No. 1. An elevation of one face of capital.

No. 2. Quarter plans of a circular and square column with capital projection.

Fig. 79 shows the volute in elevation to larger scale, showing the setting out.

Between the two parts (Fig. 78) is shown a scale of one diameter, half of which is divided into six parts, to which are added three parts on each side for the projection of capital. Draw a line in centre of column horizontally and vertically for the upper part of capital. Give half a diameter for its height, AB; divide it into three parts, as marked on left hand above; take one-third for the abacus, which divide into two parts and the upper half into four, of which give three to the ovolo and one to the lift of the abacus. Divide the height BC into eight parts, two of them give the ovolo H, one the bead I, which answers to the eye of the volute, and half one of the parts gives the lift K. This done, form the volute from its several centres, as in Fig. 79. As the height of the volute is divided into eight parts, the breadth of it must be seven parts (see Fig. 79).

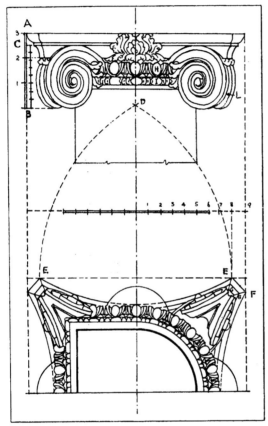

FIG. 78.—Ionic Column and Pilaster Capital.

To draw the plan No. 2 (Fig. 78), take five parts of the diameter for the solid or diminished part of column at necking. From the profile of the upright face of capital draw the projection of ovolo, bead, and lift, and mark them on the plan. If fluted, there are twenty-four flutes, to form which, divide the quarter plan of column into six parts, which will give the centre of each flute. Then divide half a sixth into four parts; take three parts for half the diameter of the flutes and draw them semicircular; the spaces between the flutes will be one-third of a flute; the eggs and darts are of the same number, and answer the same divisions. The flutes of the pilasters and square columns must be the same as to the round columns, viz., seven in number, divided from the middle ; at the corner of each pilaster there remains one-third for a bead.   Then form a square at the extreme projection of the capital ; take off at each corner diagonally one-sixth of half the diameter of column (at base) ; from the corner of the remaining length mark the intersection at D ; from this centre draw the segments or cavities of the abacus EE ;   set off cornerwise one-sixth for the two members of the abacus F ; divide it into two parts and give one part to the narrowest part of abacus GG ;   join the inner and outer corners by a line and return the members of the cavity ; the greatest projection of the volute L falls plumb with the lower part of abacus G, as shown.

To set out the spiral lines of the Ionic volute (Fig. 79), take the line AB and divide

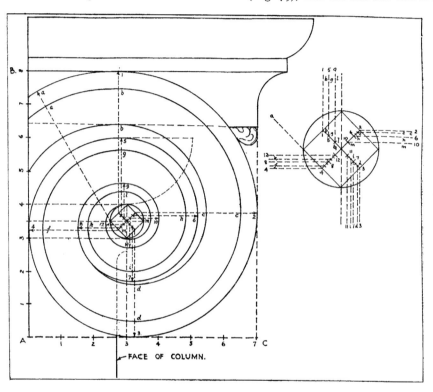

FIG. 79.—Setting out and Method of Drawing the Ionic Volute.

it into eight parts, the fourth being the size of the eye of volute, which divide into two parts for the centre, then draw AC at a right angle to AB, and mark on it seven of the divisions of AB, which give the breadth of the volute ; the upright line on the third division gives the centre of the eye, then draw the diagonal lines through the centre of it.   Parallel to these diagonal lines describe the inner square, in which draw the cross lines from side to side divided into six parts for the centres, as shown in enlarged diagram of eye, where the centres are marked 1, 2, 3, etc.   From these centres draw lines parallel to the sides of outer square extended on each side.   Fix point of compass in centre 1 with the radius 1, and draw the large quadrant 1 to 2 ;   change compass to centre 2, and with the radius 2—2 draw the quadrant 2—3, and so on, to the number of centres until the spiral line touches the upper part of the eye.   The inner spiral runs parallel to the outer from AA to centre 3, and the breadth of the fillet formed by them is half of one of the divisions of the vertical scale AB.

The second spiral is marked A, B, C, D, etc., as also the centres belonging to it.

Centre Flowers.—The central ceiling feature (Fig 106), known by this name during the early and mid-Victorian era, was perhaps the lowest form of degradation to which the plasterer's trade in this country ever descended, and to which it succumbed ;

but the degradation did not stop with this feature only ; it embraced the whole trade. In spite of this fact and the extreme badness of the design, the modelling and the method of manufacture of these things, we feel that we cannot pass over the subject without giving reason for its deletion from this edition.

The fashion of their use in this country prevailed throughout an era when all decorative art was non-existent, when engineering was in the ascendancy, when art became pictorial only, craftsmanship became mechanism, and the architect little better than a draughtsman. When this is borne in mind, and the fact that the process of its manufacture is now obsolete (or nearly so), little further need be said. The various parts were cast separately and made up in many pieces, from front and back wax moulds, the seams of the perforations being trimmed off with the

FIG. 80.—Cast Enrichment Guilloches and Frets.

knife. The fibrous plaster and gelatine process has done away with this laborious wax process for ever, and the substitution in most places of electric light for coal gas has further wiped out the centre flower which was the crowning ventilating feature to the gas chandelier. Plates VIII, XVII, XLVII, XLIX, and especially Plate CVIII, show earlier examples of central ceiling ornaments in England and France, and what might have been made of them under more favourable and refined conditions of taste ; and Fig. 106 shows two examples of the general type of centre flower as it was known when this volume was first written. The contemptible and deplorable " design " which the nineteenth-century workers in plasterwork gave to all their productions was perhaps the worst form of artistic imbecility ever perpetrated.

Cast Enrichment Mitres and Abutments.—Mitres for cornice enrichments are generally modelled *in situ* for large work, or if they are few in number. If small or of short repeating patterns, as the guilloche or numerous mitres, it is expedient to model the mitre, mould, cast, and plant it. To successfully mitre a well-designed and modelled band of ornament re-quires the judgment and resourcefulness of an artist. In many old examples of running patterns each mitre works differently, unless the design is arranged for all to be alike, the space in between taking a design of short repeat as in Plate CIX. It is the function of the artist to take advantage of and to give interest to such opportunities, for which no law or rule can be laid down. Some in-stances are quite simple ; others not so easy, according to the design ; but in most cases the general metre and rhythm of the pattern should be carried round into the mitre. In the case of geometrical pat-terns, as the guilloche

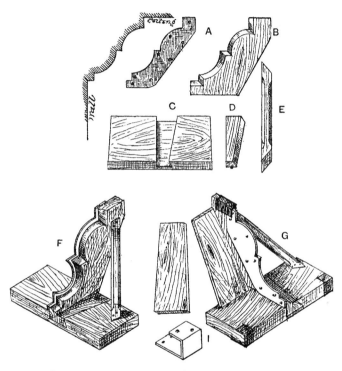

FIG. 81.—Method of Making a Running Mould.

or fret, the pattern should continue as simply and legibly to the eye as possible, as in Fig. 80 ; but circumstances vary in almost every instance, indicating an " art " requiring cultivation at every turn of the plasterer's career. (Plates CIX and CX give some old and new examples of mitre treatment, which vary in almost every individual case.)

Running moulds are used to form mouldings in soft plaster, and usually consist of five parts, viz., the plate, stock, slipper, wedge, and handle. The construction, or mounting, is termed the " horsing." Some running moulds have " splash-boards " and " metal shoes." The general practice is to cut and horse the mould in the plasterer's shop. Running moulds, formerly cut out of beech, boxwood, pear tree, or some hard wood, are now cut out of sheet zinc for lime, plaster, and white cement work, or sheet iron for Portland cement work. In " horsing " or forming the various wood parts, the wood should be planed on all faces before being used. The stock B (Fig. 81) of pine wood, $\frac{1}{2}$ in. to 1 in. thick, according to size, is cut a little wider than the plate for strength. The top bearing on ceiling is the "nib," and the bottom bearing on the wall is the "toe." Lay the plate on the wood for guidance in scribing the profile. Cut the nib and toe flush and square with the ceiling and wall line, and the profile $\frac{1}{16}$ in. less than plate profile, and splay the edge to allow any coarse particles in the materials accumulating at the plate to free the running edge. The stock B should be set back $\frac{1}{8}$ in. for cement and sand mouldings, to allow space for coarse particles.

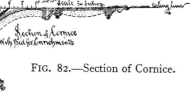

FIG. 82.—Section of Cornice.

Cut the bottom end of stock square with the toe, and $\frac{1}{2}$ in. deep to fit into the slipper. The slipper C should be square on both sides and edges, with a groove $\frac{1}{2}$ in. deep across the centre, the side next the plate being cut square down and the other side slantwise and dovetailed for a wedge. The stock is thus stronger and truer than in the modern way of nailing it to the slipper. The slipper should not be longer than twice the projection of the cornice; or the plate and stock cannot run into the angles, and a long mitre will result. The wedge D must fit the groove; the handle E, a square piece of wood with the hand part spoke-shaved off, leaving about 2 in. square at the ends, should be long enough and fixed to clear the mouldings, with ample room for the worker's fist. Fix one end near the nib to resist pressure and vibration when running the moulding. Large running moulds need other stays to support the weaker parts and to ensure rigidity and squareness of the stock. Fix the plate on the stock with tacks or screws, set up the other parts and wedge tight, keeping the toe of stock flush with the running edge of slipper. A couple of nails inserted at the junction will secure the stock to the slipper. Keep the nails back from the running edge to clear the running rules. When fixing the handle, apply a set square to the slipper to plumb the stock, which, unless square with slipper, will not give the true profile. F shows the complete mould. When running any quantity of mouldings, if the screeds are hard, protect the wood bearings of the running mould by shoes I on the nibs of zinc, or leather on the slipper. A slow-setting or soft material requires a splash-board $\frac{1}{2}$ in. thick, as at G, to catch any dropping stuff.

G shows the complete mould with the splash-board, shoes, and slipper. A splash-board is also useful for running mouldings with a greater projection on ceiling than wall.

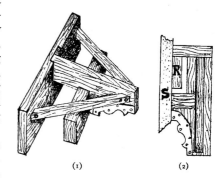

FIG. 83.—Twin-Slippered Mould.

Running Moulds for Enriched Cornices (very little used since the introduction of fibrous plaster casting).—When cutting a mould plate for an enriched cornice, allow a bed for the enrichments. If the top enrichment is on the ceiling, allow a matrix for same on the mould plate for the thickness of casts. Beds for enrichments, such as egg and dart bed moulds, should have straight beds with the angles cut off, leaving enough thickness for bedding the cast, as shown in Fig. 82. The dotted surface shows the inserted casts, the front line shows the finished profile, and the back line the bed. In fibrous work the whole enrichment is cast in one piece.

Twin-Slippered Mould.—No. 1 (Fig. 83) shows a running mould with a twin

PLATE CVIII

(*a*) PENROSE ALMSHOUSES, BARNSTAPLE.

(*b*) and (*c*) BISHOP LLOYD'S HOUSE, CHESTER.

THREE EXAMPLES OF TREATMENT OF A CENTRE FEATURE IN
EARLY RENAISSANCE PLASTERWORK.

PLATE CIX

JOINTED MITRES FROM BROUGHTON CASTLE, OXFORDSHIRE.

slipper used only where one bearing is possible, in the case of a moulding adjoining old work, or a skirting under. For the latter purpose the inner slipper is shorter and thicker than the outer one, forming a nib for the mould and a counterpoise for the outer slipper. The slippers and the stock must have space between them for a running rule. A section is given at No. 2, showing the running rule R on the plaster screed S. Let the stock into the outer slipper in the usual way, and rebate for the inner slipper. Two handles, nailed to both slippers, stiffen the mould.

Arch Radius Mould.—Fig. 84 shows a radius mould for running archivolt and panel mouldings in one operation on an arch. A, No. 1, is a section of arch and panel moulding springing with the arch at B, S is a running screed, M the mould, R the radius rod and centre plate, B the radius board, and P the radius pin. No. 2 shows front face of extreme end of radius rod, centre plate with its half eye, which easily apply to and remove from the centre pin. When the mould is above the spring line of arch the weight comes on the centre pin, but if continued lower than this line, the leverage downwards calls for a full eye fitting the centre pin exactly, otherwise the moulding may vary from a true circle, unless firmly held up to the centre pin after passing the horizontal line. The plate should

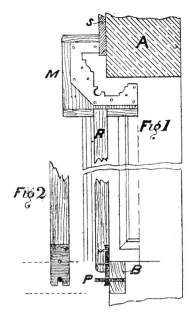

FIG. 84.—Arch Radius Mould.

be fixed on the back face of radius rod in line with the surface of arch, the face of radius board on which the centre pin is fixed being identical.

Hanging Moulds.—When running a large rib or beam moulding on a cove, the

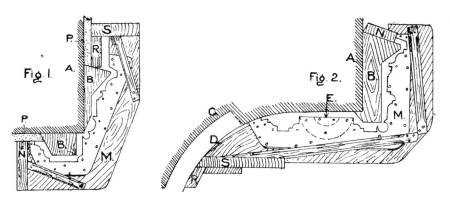

FIG. 85.—Hanging Running Moulds.

mould being unsupported, tends to drop away. This may be obviated by a " hanging mould," which is made by using two slippers on the mould. The upper or wall slipper (termed the runner slipper) is so made that it will clear the face of the running rule and bear on the upper edge of the running rule fixed on the vertical or top screed. The lower slipper (termed the nib slipper) is fixed at the nib of the mould and bears on the soffit or horizontal screed.   Sections of the various parts of this mould and a hanging mould for a crown moulding are shown in Fig. 85.   A, in No. 1, is the constructional work or wood framing, B the brackets, P the vertical and horizontal plaster screeds, R the running rule, and M the running mould.   Two handles on one side are usual for such moulds and two on each side for large moulds.   S is the running slipper, N the nib slipper, generally only half the length of the running slipper.   The mould runs more easily thus than if on the nib only.   No. 2 is the section of a longitudinal moulding at the crown of a cove, run from a rule on the cove.

No. 2 illustrates the method.   The moulding is run from a main running rule R and a nib rule N.   A is the constructional work, B the lath bracket, M the running mould, and S the slipper.   Large mouldings are run in two sections.

Notes on Running Moulds.—Running moulds should be horsed with well-seasoned wood, or the slipper will swell when running the mouldings and throw the mould out of square, especially with large moulds.   All the woodwork should be planed, to clean easily after each gauge.   Rough wood retains matter which makes furrow lines and roughness in the moulding.   Swelling is prevented by brushing the wood with paraffin oil.   Zinc or copper is best for the mould plate for white cement mouldings.   When running mouldings in neat plaster, the running mould must be strongly " horsed " to resist the swelling of the plaster.

CHAPTER XIII

MOULDING AND CASTING

The Plasterer's Shop—Plaster Box—Squeezing Wax—Moulding Wax—Clay Squeezing—
Clay Piece Moulds—Plaster Waste Moulding—Moulding from Life—Plaster Piece
Moulding—Modillions and Blocks—Model Making of Balusters—Plaster Piece Moulding
Balusters—Casting Balusters—Oiling Plaster Moulds—Solutions for Moulding and
Casting—Gauging Plaster—Plaster Casting—Hollow Casts—Strong Plaster for Casting
—Casting White Cements—Casting Portland Cement—Water-Seasoned Plaster Moulds
—Casting Cement Mouldings (Waste Mould Process)—Pressed Cement Work.

The plasterer's shop should be dry and well lighted and contain a large gas ring
capable of heating twelve to fifteen pailfuls of gelatine at one time. A section through
a water-jacketed jelly pot of this capacity is shown in Fig. 87. Good and sufficient
benches are indispensable ; they should be about 2 ft. 8 in. high, and convenient for
a man to stand well over his work. All benches should be made about 12 ft. long by
8 ft. wide, if convenient to the size and arrangement of the workshop. All benches
should be of one level, for convenience of connecting together for working very large
models. Fig. 86 is a working drawing showing the construction of a plasterer's bench
for ordinary fibrous plasterwork or other casting ; this applies to tables 12 ft. by 12 ft.,
although this particular example is 12 ft. by 6 ft. The plan, section, and elevations
explain themselves. A large tank for clean water for gauging is necessary. A size
water tub and a slush tub are necessary. Slush tubs should be placed at the sides of
the gauging box, for convenience in washing out pails and bowls. Other requisites are
a quantity of running rules, thickness rules, a mitre box, two or three squares from 12 in.
to 5 ft., compasses, jack-plane, chisel, saw, vice, shears, and files. Strips of modelling
clay are useful for fences when moulding large circular work or making cases. Pails,
oils, shellac, soap, gelatine, and a jelly pot are necessary. Plaster boxes are important.
A good yard attached to the shop is necessary where possible. The yard should contain
tanks for water, bins for putty, setting stuff, coarse stuff, sand, crushed granite, and
other aggregates ; storage for scaffolding and general plant ; an enclosed shed for
plaster sacks, scales, canvas, and fibrous laths.

Plaster Box.—Fig. 88 shows a self-feeding plaster box of new type. The plaster
keeps dry and clean, and is easily got at when gauging. The inside size is 3 ft. by
3 ft. by 1 ft. 3 in. The open trough in front (sloping) is 8 in. deep and 9 in. projection.
The front stops short of the bottom, to allow the plaster to fill the trough. The division
separates the fine plaster from the coarse. The shelf underneath is for holding the
buckets whilst gauging the plaster ; they are normally placed underneath on the front
of the box ; more than one man can gauge at the same time. The slush tub, a water
tub, and size water tub should be placed at the ends, as shown in Fig. 88. This shows
a number of improvements on the older form. No lid is required, as the bags of plaster
are generally stored and tipped into the box from the sides. Ordinary 3-gal. zinc pails
are used for gelatine pouring, and common zinc wash-hand bowls, with handles for

gauging the plaster for small castings. For large castings the plaster is better gauged in a pail and taken out as required by the operators.

Fig. 89 shows a plan, elevation, and sketch of a canvas bin usual to the modern fibrous plasterer's workshop, all figured complete.

Workshop Plan.—Fig. 90 shows a useful plan of the general arrangement of a workshop, which, however, must be varied considerably according to the shape of the shop itself. The illustration speaks largely for itself; it is advisable to have one bench 12 ft. by 12 ft., with one or more benches 12 ft. by 6 ft., with a 3 ft. passage between. Wherever possible, side benches should be arranged 3 ft. wide at the end on one side, with, in a convenient place, a canvas bin, plaster storage bench, plaster box

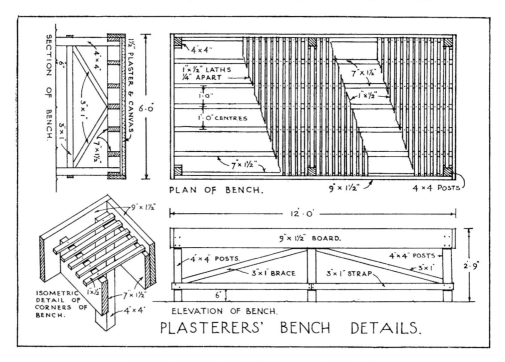

Fig. 86.—Working Drawing of Plasterer's Bench.

and zinc for slush tubs, size water tub, and tub for clean water for gauging, all convenient for the benches. The zinc for the tubs should have a drain to the street. At the opposite end should be a space for storage of timber, laths, etc., to be used in the fibrous casting. A glazed office should be arranged in a convenient place for supervision of the whole workshop, with a bench for a drawing board and a side bench for drawings, as indicated on the plan. Where top light is possible it is always advisable.

Squeezing Wax.—Until recently wax was used for taking impressions of models of varying degrees of relief. The surface of the model was dusted with French chalk to prevent adhesion and discoloration. Where several pieces were required for one model, the joints would be dusted and the whole area cased with plaster to keep them in position. The squeeze was then filled in with plaster and a replica of the model produced. There were various recipes for making squeeze wax, the following being respectively English, French, Belgian, and Austrian recipes :—(1) $\frac{1}{2}$ lb. of pure beeswax,

½ lb. of lard, and 1 gill of linseed oil ; melt over a slow fire, sprinkle in 1 lb. of flour, whilst stirring, pour the whole on to a slate or bench, and knead all together ; if the wax is too sticky add flour, and knead until properly pliable. (2) 1 lb. of beeswax, 1½ lbs. of lard, and 1 gill of olive oil ; dissolve over a slow fire, and add sifted whiting until properly pliable, and knead as before. (3) ¾ lb. of beeswax, ¼ lb. of Burgundy pitch, and dissolve over a slow fire, and add ¾ pint of olive oil ; stir gradually equal parts of flour and fine sifted whiting until of proper thickness ; turn out on to a slab and knead until pliant, adding whiting as required ; the more it is kneaded, the better it will be. (4) Two parts of beeswax, 1 part of suet, and 1 part of turpentine ; dissolve, and add fine whiting as before. If tinted wax is preferred, add yellow ochre, Paris white, green, or vermilion, according to taste. Paraffin wax mixed with olive oil and whiting, prepared as above, was also used. " Plasticine " is now largely substituted for wax, with equally good results, for taking squeezes of relief work of any kind.

Moulding wax was, until after the publication of this book, chiefly used for making moulds for plaster casting. It consisted of 1 part pure beeswax and from 1 to 2 parts of powdered resin, dissolved in a metal pot, over a slow fire or on a hot plate. The wax was not allowed to boil, as its nature is thus destroyed and rendered hard and brittle. The proportion of resin used varied, according to the quality of the wax.

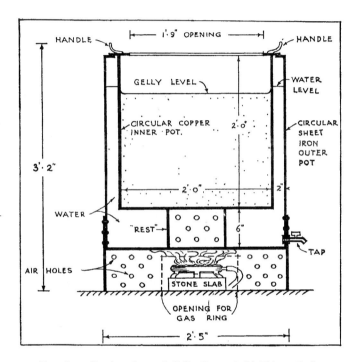

FIG. 87.—Section through Jelly Pot to hold Fifteen Pails.

Rich wax carries more resin than poor wax, which is improved by adding from 1 to 3 oz. of mutton suet, or best white tallow, to the pound of wax. After frequent use, wax becomes " short," and often retains small pieces of plaster, clay, wood, etc. It can be cleaned by thinning, with extra heat, and pouring through a hot sieve. Old and short wax may be improved by adding new wax and tallow. When a hot plate is used, the pots should be broad and shallow, to heat a large surface, say 14 in. diameter and 6 in. deep, of block tin or copper with handle each side and a wide lip, for the wax to flow freely. For ordinary small work a common saucepan was used, and where steam was available it was used for melting wax or gelatine, in which case the pots were deep and placed in an iron jacket or tank. Wax may be dissolved by hot water like gelatine. Wax or jelly thus melted is more uniformly heated and lasts longer. To know the proper temperature for pouring, oil or wet the finger and dip it into the wax. If it can be borne comfortably, the wax is in good condition for pouring over the model.

If the wax be too cool, a skin will form on the surface, or it will become crinkly and unfit for moulding.

Clay or Plasticine Squeezing.—Clay is used for temporary moulding, where it is inconvenient to use plaster, wax, etc. The model is dusted with French chalk, or brushed with turpentine or paraffin oil, to prevent adhesion. The clay must be

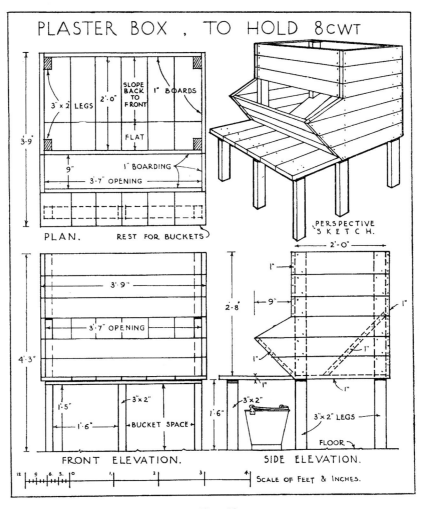

FIG. 88.

well tempered, beaten, and rolled into sheets until smooth. It is then pressed over and into the work with the fingers, in close contact with the model. Press the clay uniformly, to avoid blebs or creases on the surface of the clay. If the first piece of clay is insufficient to cover the work, cut a clean joint and lay another sheet of clay up to that already laid, and continue until covered. Leave the back of the clay rough as a key for the gauged plaster case to be laid on, and float the back of case with a wet board, so that it will bed flat on the bench. Plasticine may be used instead of clay, if preferable, as above.

Clay Piece Moulds.—A clay piece mould is used where portions are too undercut to draw away in one piece. After squeezing, as before described, back up with stiffer clay, cut joints where clay pieces are necessary, and brush with turpentine or paraffin oil before the next piece is laid. Continue until all is covered, and make a plaster case to keep all together.

Plaster Waste Moulding.—Waste moulding is used for clay models " on the round " where only one cast is needed. The term arises from the process of breaking or wasting to get at a cast. If the clay is firm it can be thinly coated with shellac and oiled with a soft, fine brush, but not enough to injure the modelling. Just sufficient oiling gives freedom in moulding without fear of injury to the model when fixing the

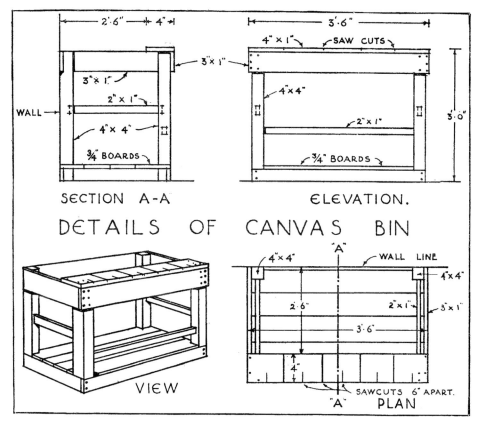

FIG. 89.

clay fences. The clay model should not be dry enough to shrink, and if firm should not require shellac. Allow for extracting the clay when moulded by making a plaster piece at the back of model, where plain, or by back and front moulds. To mould a bust, beat a sheet of clay 1 in. thick and cut it into strips 1 in. wide for fences. Place one fence on the head in the form of an oval tonsure or ring, large enough for the hand to extract the clay when the mould is finished. If the fences are laid slanting outwards, the piece will draw without further splaying. Each coat of plaster is tinted a different colour, to distinguish it from the other when chipping the mould from the cast. Tint the water for the first coat of plaster red or yellow ochre, to distinguish it from the second coat. Gauge soft and throw with the hand, spoon, or gauge brush over the mould (excepting inside the clay fence), until $\frac{1}{4}$ in. thick. When the tinted

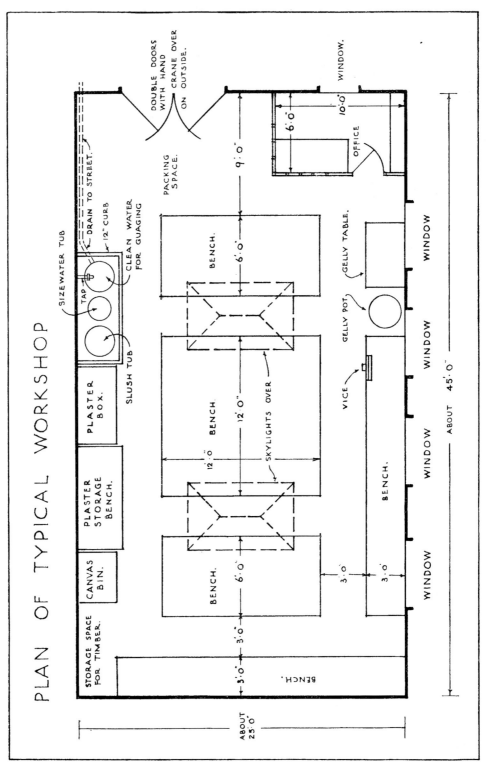

FIG. 90.

PLATE CX

(*c*) GUILLOCHE MITRE, HOLKHAM HALL, NORFOLK.
(William Kent.)

(*a*) DOUBLE MITRES (RUNNING FLORAL DESIGN).

(*b*) SINGLE MITRE.

(*d*) DOUBLE MITRE.

PLATE CXI

(*a*) PLASTER CEILING RIB AND MOULD (*vide* Plate LXXXIX, *a*, FOR FINISHED DESIGN).

(*b*) MOULDS OF MODILLIONS.

(*c*) ENRICHED CORNICE SHOWING MODILLIONS. (G. P. Bankart.)

gauge is set, brush the surface over with clay water, to prevent the next coat adhering to it. Next, gauge, allow to stiffen, and lay a second untinted coat about $\frac{3}{4}$ in. thick. When set, remove the clay fence, trim the edge, cut two or three sloping joggles, and brush with clay water. Gauge plaster enough and cover the oval part level with the top of other section. When set, sprinkle the mould with water. Insert the point of a chisel at the joint and prize off the top piece, thus leaving an opening for extracting the clay ; separate the mould from the stand, and from the opening underneath and at top extract the clay from the mould, clearing the centre until the clay gets thin, when it will peel from the mould. Wash inside with water and a soft brush, then with soap water, and again with clean water. Replace temporarily in the crown piece, secure with cord or plaster ready for filling. Gauge and pour into the mould plaster enough to cover about $\frac{1}{8}$ in. thick, turn and shake it to cover the interior surface, return any surplus plaster to the basin, turn the mould again, pour the plaster again into the mould, and it will thus cling better. Repeat this process until the cast is thick enough. To separate the mould from the cast is a delicate operation. The tinted plaster acts as a signal for caution when chipping the inner mould, to avoid injury to the cast. With a blunt chisel and mallet chip away the outer coat of the mould, then carefully chip or pick off the tinted coat until the cast is clear and clean.

Another way for waste moulding such models for gelatine moulding is to clay fence across the whole bust, dividing the model into back and front moulds, keeping the front one the larger. Begin the clay fence at the base and work upwards. Let the fence line take the angle of the shoulders up to the edge of the ear and the middle of the head. Do the same process on the other side, the fences meeting at the top. The clay fences should be about $1\frac{1}{2}$ in. wide, laid flatwise rather than on edge, until $1\frac{1}{2}$ in. thick, allowing $\frac{1}{2}$ in. for gelatine and 1 in. for plaster case. Great care must be taken not to impress the clay model in laying the fences, which can be secured by pins or fine French nails, the pin holes being stopped afterwards. When practicable, the fence should be on the front half, and after the back half has been covered with the two coats of plaster, the model may be laid on its back, the face being thus more easily moulded than if erect. Cut three or four oblong joggles into the plaster margin at each side ; brush with clay water ; fix a board or plaster ground at the base of model to prevent the plaster running over, and as a guide for the thickness of mould. The other half mould is then made as before described, and when set, saturated with water to stop all suction ; allow the mould to be opened and the clay extracted. To do this, lay the mould on the bench, back uppermost, insert three or four thin wood wedges between the joints, clear of the joggles, and drive them gently home until the back can be lifted off ; but first extract as much clay as possible from the end, to minimise resistance (by suction) to the back coming off. After dividing, washing, and soaping, a cast may be taken from each half for casing and moulding. The advantages of this system will readily be seen, everything being done more easily and quickly thus, and there is no cutting the jelly at the joints of the case as must be done when moulded in one piece. These moulds or cases keep together best for casting with a ring of hoop iron over each end of the mould, tightened up by wedges.

Moulding from Life.—Masks from life or death are often taken in plaster, also casts of various parts of the body required for models. Pliny states that Lysistratus, the sculptor of Sicyone, was the first to make moulds and masks from the living face, the date being about 328 B.C. Pliny's statement is probably correct as far as he knew ; but as already mentioned, Dr Petrie's recent discoveries prove that moulding from life was in use about 1300 B.C.

The novice may first try a hand by greasing it and smoothing down all hairs, and laying it in position on a moulding board. If the position of the hand hollows the palm, support with clay or rags and lay a margin of clay all round.   The mould need not " draw," as the flesh will yield to it.   Make with a round tool a few joggles in the clay margin, gauge the plaster with warm water (for less shock and quicker setting), and pour over the hand.   When set, reverse the hand, grease the palm, clay water the plaster margin, gauge more plaster with warm water, pour on, and when set part the back and front half moulds, and cast as already described.

Grease the hand as before and plunge it into a basin of gauged plaster.   When the surface is covered, place in the desired position, and as the plaster thickens, lay a strong thread on the wet plaster along the hand, down the middle finger, over the point, up the palm to the wrist, and another thread from the wrist to the thumb.   Put the remaining plaster all over sufficiently thick, and when nearly set, cut the threads through the plaster.   We thus have a piece mould.   When the plaster is set, the hand may be released.   By another method waxed thread may be laid on the hand where required, before the hand is greased if preferred ; the thread will adhere to the hand if kept motionless.

After experience with the hands, the face may next be tried.   The person should be recumbent, the ears stuffed with wool and the face greased, the eyelashes and brows covered with wax, clay, or thick pomade, the beard, etc., covered with thick clay paste.   Fix two quills in the nostrils with wadding or fine wool for breathing purposes, and tie a towel round the head and neck, close to the back of the ears, to prevent the plaster from running over.   Gauge one basin of plaster with warm water and another with strong alum water to set quicker, pour the former over the face, and as soon as set pour the latter over the first gauge, and when nearly set gently but firmly remove the mould.   The object of the second gauge setting first is explained above.   If the first gauge becomes set and any hair or eyelashes mixed with the plaster, the face might get injured.   The back part of the head may be moulded in a similar way before the front mould is removed, and a full face and head cast from it.   Be careful not to disturb or cover the quills when pouring the plaster, or the mould may spoil.   To mould an ear, the nose, or eye separately is good practice.   Limbs or the whole figure may be thus moulded with plaster and good casts obtained.   Usually one gauge is resorted to, but for preventing the hair from being injured, the above is best.   The alum water should be tested by gauging a small pat of plaster, and a small pat of the first gauge laid aside to judge the time of setting.   Two moulders are better for gauging, and give more confidence to the patient.   The eyes must be closed before the plaster is poured over the face.   If it is desired to have the eyes open in the casting, it is best to take a clay squeeze out of the mould and model the eyes from life.

Plaster Piece Moulding.—A piece mould derives its name from the process of forming a complete mould of a number of small ones placed together.   Piece moulds are for reproducing models that are " on the round," or are undercut, and where they cannot be moulded in one piece, or with " front and back " moulds.   The seams formed by the joints of the pieces have to be removed from a cast taken from a piece mould.   Plaster is better for piece moulding than any other material because of its quick setting powers, its unshrinkable and plastic nature, its fineness, and smoothness of surface.   The process is difficult to explain in print, and is an art requiring considerable skill, practice, and care.   A piece mould has numerous sections that can be removed independently from the model and cast.   They are kept together by a plaster case.   Where the pieces are large, few, and simple, they are bound together with string, wire, or hoop iron.   Roman joints or joggles keep the parts together.   A good piece mould has close and firm joints, takes to pieces easily, and is light and strong.

Only the best plaster should be used and, if possible, completed in one gauge, to ensure equality in setting, swelling, and strength throughout, a case requiring several gauges. Lime putty water added to the gauging water will strengthen the case, but should not be used for the pieces, or the oil will peel and "fur" when casting. A newly made or unseasoned plaster model should be seasoned with linseed oil or shellac, to stop the suction as described for seasoning plaster moulds. When piece moulding a new or unseasoned plaster model with plaster, a solution of soap will stop the suction and prevent adhesion to the model. Soap the first and adjoining pieces, and so on until complete. Stearic solution, already described, may also be used.

Models seasoned with linseed oil or shellac are oiled with sweet oil or suet solution, which can be brushed on very thin to advantage. The thinner the coat of oil, the better. Suet solution will not soil the model, but indurates and seasons the plaster. Joints should not be oiled, or they clog and widen, but soap solution prevents cohesion and gives fine, close joints.

Moulding knives, strong and long, are necessary for trimming joints, as described in Chapter VI, on "Tools and Appliances." A moulding hammer is used for tapping pieces to fit close to the model after trimming, to loosen when they adhere to the model, and for tapping the case when it adheres to the mould. A "moulding hammer" is shorter and heavier than a "lathing hammer," and being flat-headed, the piece is tapped with less force than with a light and narrow-headed hammer and with less fear of injury. A "joggler" made from an old stiff putty knife or old chisel, the end being rounded or V shaped, is used for sinking circular joggles; but for most work the point of a gauging trowel does well. A fine drag, a coarse drag, a dusting brush, and moulding boards or turnbats are also required.

Beat out a sheet of clay $\frac{1}{2}$ in. thick for "fences"; test the oil and solution before setting to work. The term "oil" or "oiled," used in describing the method of piece moulding, includes also soap and suet solutions, used for the parts described.

When moulding a model requiring many pieces, the size and shape of each should be decided by eye judgment and faintly marked on the model with a soft pencil; each piece must "draw," or something may fracture. The size of each piece must be regulated to "draw" freely. When they have been carefully considered and arranged, form each section, piece by piece. If the model is "on the round," say a pedestal or figure, work upwards from the base, the first tier of pieces supporting those above. Make a strip of clay $\frac{1}{2}$ in. square, lay it on the model to the line drawn, oil the surface, and lay the plaster as described. When set, take off the piece and trim the joint, and replace it on the model to fit close and true, tapping the back with the moulding hammer. Continue this work until the whole model is moulded. Then make the case in two or more parts, each to draw off the mould. The several pieces are bound with hoop iron, tightened with wedges, or tied up with cord or sash line. A case for flat work should be in one piece. Each piece should be numbered or marked. Joggles sunk on the backs give ease and speed in replacing each piece in the case and in keeping them in position. Small pieces are the more easily removed and show less suction than large ones; but that is no reason for making small pieces. The larger the model the larger the pieces, so long as they draw off the model. Clay models, piece moulded direct, require one or two thin coats of shellac solution before moulding. For carton-pierre casting, trim off the upper edges of each piece $\frac{1}{8}$ in. to $\frac{1}{4}$ in. deep; a flat V sinking thus formed and the converse raised part in the case, keep the pieces in position. This is applicable to all moulds, but if circular or "on the round," splay well to draw. Deep or thin parts on the model call for the plaster pieces to be strengthened with perforated sheet zinc, or wire inserted before set. The last or "closing piece" requires no trimming, and remains until the case is made.

In large work, arrange the pieces in sections, with a closing piece in each section, to ensure close and good joints. When the case is made and taken off, remove the

closing pieces first, and the others in the order (or the reverse) made. Each closing
piece should have a looped ring or " eye " of copper or galvanised iron wire inserted
in the centre as the plaster begins to set for pulling them off. Bend the wire over the
tapered handle of a medium-sized tool brush until the ends meet, twist the ends together
until there is a stem $\frac{1}{2}$ in. long, bend the ends in opposite directions at right angles to
the stem, and the eye is complete. So that they will draw, the eyes must be covered
with clay ; a sinking in the case thus formed is cut through and a hole made $\frac{1}{2}$ in. in
diameter. Remove the piece and the clay, and pass a piece of strong waxed string
12 in. to 15 in. long through the eye, leaving the ends equal in length. Offer up the piece,
pass the string through the holes from the inside, and tie outside over a piece of wood,
about 2 in. long and $\frac{1}{4}$ in. square, the edges notched to prevent slipping, and further

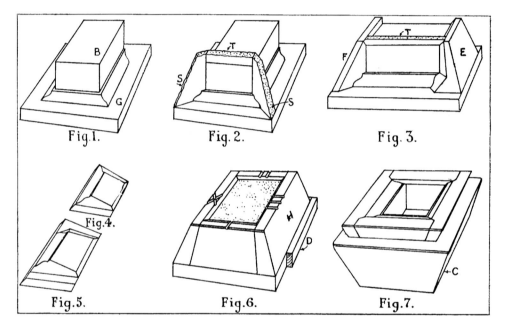

FIG. 91.—Plaster Piece Moulding a Modillion.

tighten by a wedge. Fill the mould, untie the string, remove the case, leaving the
piece on the model, the piece on the mould when moulding, and on the cast when
casting. Eyes are necessary for angle pieces or deep parts, where they do not hold in
the case or fall out while the mould is being turned over.

The angle of the piece joints when trimmed should not be too acute, but should
have just enough splay for the adjoining piece to draw. Too much splay gives sharp
edges and bad joints, and liability to chip.

Many joints might be cut square were it not for the swelling of the plaster in
mould and cast, which tightens the pieces together and makes it difficult to remove
them. Seams from the joints should be cleaned off the cast while " green," with
Dutch rush, fine scratch tools, fine riffles or files, and smoothed with fine flannel.
Fish skin is excellent for smoothing large surfaces, and resists water and wear a
long time.

To Plaster Piece Mould a Modillion or Block.—The method is illustrated
in Fig. 91. No. 1 shows the moulding piece. B is the block and G the ground. Beat

a clay sheet; cut strips 2 in. or 3 in. wide for vertical fences and 1 in. wide for the top fences. Make the end pieces first, one at a time (a smart man should do two with one gauging), the sides next, and the top last. Cut a narrow clay strip, lay it on one end of block; keep the slanting edge outwards, in line with the arris as at T, No. 2. Cut a wide clay strip to the height of block and top fence, fix it on one side at an angle of 45°, up to the arris, repeat on the other side, and trim slanting from 1 in. wide at top down to the ground, as at S, S. The arris must neither be covered nor left exposed; if covered, the piece will be short and the adjoining one will project over and damage it; if exposed, the same will result. This is most important. If the fences are carefully and accurately laid up to the edges and with the proper slope, the joints will require little trimming, and there will be no fear of fracture when moulding or casting. This applies chiefly to arris or undercut work, where it is not advisable to remove the piece to trim the joint. For general work fences may be $\frac{1}{16}$ in. outside the joint line, the plaster being afterwards trimmed true. A joint well trimmed with a good knife should be true and close, but clay is indispensable for the fence and rough work. Joints should be splayed only enough for the piece to draw clear; after oiling the piece and gauging, lay the plaster with a small gauging trowel or a spatula. The soft plaster may be slightly spread into deep interstices or angles with a tool brush, but should not be dabbed in, as the brush draws away some of the plaster, leaving air blebs on the surface. Spreading with the brush drives off the air and leaves a solid surface. Press the remainder of the plaster firmly and evenly into the space with the gauging trowel until the piece is of the required thickness. The side fences guide the thickness and the top fence the height. Smooth the back surface of the plaster before set, make good, and work fair with a drag after removing the piece.

Repeat the process at other end. While the plaster is setting, remove the first piece, trim the joints, and cut off the edges left by the side fences, so forming a square side or " shoulder " and a strong joint and interlock with the adjoining piece. The several pieces are thus kept from falling in the case. No. 4 shows the piece trimmed and jointed and its use in the complete mould, No. 7. This done, replace it and secure with a clay dot. Trim the other end piece as before, and form the side shoulders without cutting the joint of the projection formed by the mitre of the moulding. No. 5 shows the back end piece and No. 7 a plan of the shoulders.

To make the side pieces, lay a narrow clay strip on top of block, between the end pieces, as No. 3. F and E are the front and back pieces. Oil the side, lay the plaster, and trim and joint the top edge, which must be splayed to draw from the case, thus forming a rebate in the case (see No. 6). The thickness of the side pieces is regulated, as explained for the ends, by fixing a clay fence on the end pieces, projecting to the edges of the ground, and cutting to the slope for guidance when filling. Joggle each piece on top edge, as No. 6, with a knife, for guidance in returning each piece to the case and to prevent side movement. Make the joggles (figures are sometimes used) in the order in which they are to be placed in the case. With numerous pieces to a mould, time and annoyance are thus saved. In the example the pieces are marked in the order made; in practice the side pieces are placed first, otherwise it would be difficult to get them in afterwards.

Making the case completes the mould. In small work the top and case are made together in one piece to draw.

For intricate work this is not advisable, the case being liable to injury, in which event a new one can be made, but not as part of the mould. The case for the present example need extend only to within 1 in. of the ground, as at H, No. 6. This saves material and is useful when lifting the case. Lay a fence on the moulding board against the pieces, the thickness of the case, for guidance. If the case must extend to the ground, covering everything—as necessitated by small pieces in the sides of moulds—thickness rules must be laid around and away from the mould, on the ground edge, for regulating the thickness of the case, as at D. Hand holes, for lifting this case, are best formed by fixing a clay dot, say, $2\frac{1}{2}$ in. long by $1\frac{1}{2}$ in. deep, and the width of the fence. Where the ground extends beyond the pieces, dots similar to the above, fixed on the ground against the pieces, may also regulate the thickness of the case. Having fixed the fence at H, put a clay dot on top of each piece, clear of the joggles, for guidance as to thickness and for the escape of dust when brushing out the case. When the case is made the dots are removed, the original and the pieces oiled, and the plaster gauged and laid carefully (but quickly) by pouring some and laying the rest with a trowel, until all is formed fair. Level the top surface with a wet board, worked in circular motion before the plaster is set, and drag smooth the sides and ends, lift the case and the pieces, dust, make good surface defects, and shellac or oil ready for casting. No. 7 shows the mould complete with pieces and case.

If the face of the block is shaped or modelled, possibly more than one top piece may be required, regulated in thickness by the joints of the side pieces. No joint trimming being required, let the top piece remain, but make fair and smooth the top surface and edges with trowel and drag. The case for this is distinct from the top piece. Place a dot 1 in. wide, $1\frac{1}{4}$ in. deep on each corner of the top piece, $\frac{1}{2}$ in. from the edge, to regulate the top thickness of case and so that the cast and the pieces may be tapped through the holes, to loosen, and the cast brushed out as before described.

Plate CXI, *b*, shows photographs of moulds of modillions; *c* shows the finished modillions in their position in an enriched cornice.

To Make a Baluster.—Cast as before described for piece moulding. The model, circular on body, is done in three pieces, which are afterwards fixed together. The circular portion is turned in a lathe. The top and bottom squares or blocks of plaster may be cast from a mould made up of four rules. When fixing together, the plinths must be level and square and the body central. The inner surface of the plinths should draw from moulds. Models turned in wood are in one piece. Balusters, square or octagonal, may be run in one piece by fixing running rules on a moulding board to the desired plan, and with a twin-slippered mould running the sides vertically in one operation on a core fixed on the board as a bearing.

To Piece Mould a Baluster in Plaster.—The chief difficulty in moulding a spherical form, a plain vase, or round baluster is to divide the model into equal halves, so that the mould may be made in two profile pieces. The centre line is a guide for fencing the first side piece. The top and bottom blocks being square on plan, their diagonal angles serve this purpose, the method being shown in Fig. 92. A baluster is usually moulded in one end piece, E first and two side pieces. No. 1 shows a baluster, say, 2 ft. high; TP and BP are the top and bottom plinths, square on plan. Before the end piece E is made, a joggle 1 in. deep should be sunk in the top of model to keep the end piece in place while the side pieces are being made, and to key the casts for fixing purposes. This joggle may be either round or square, but it should be irregular at one angle, forming a distinguishing mark for ready replacement after trimming. No. 2 is a plan of the end piece and the raised joggle J, made by fencing the four sides flush to a thickness of $1\frac{1}{2}$ in. to 2 in., according to the size of baluster, allowing strength for the joggle sinkings. The fences being fixed, the model is oiled, the plaster poured, the surface levelled with the fences, and when set the piece is trimmed and the joggles sunk, but differing in form or number on each side, and well defined in depth and outline for strength of joint with the side pieces. A joggle broad of surface and shallow in depth is stronger than one narrow and deep. As they entirely support the pieces in the mould, strength is necessary. In some districts the end piece is made with the case, which also holds the side pieces in position, instead of a bottom hoop; but this is not so secure as a hoop and wedge. To proceed, lay the model and end piece longwise on a moulding board, keeping two of the plinth angles vertical, supported and held by clay at the angles B, B, No. 3. Put similar blocks at the top end, long enough

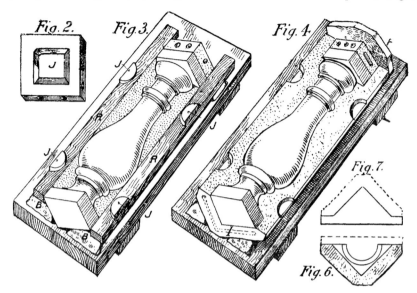

to support the model and the end piece. The clay blocks will also support the wooden rules R, R, which are partly side fences. The rules vary in width from $1\frac{1}{2}$ in. to 2 in., according to the size of baluster and the strength necessary for the mould. They must be fixed exactly to the arrises of the plinths and level with each other. Fill the space between the rules and the model to within $\frac{1}{4}$ in. of the surface of the rule with fragments of plaster, wood, or clay, pour the gauged plaster, and make the surface smooth and flush with the rules.

Make raised joggles on the rules with clay blocks $2\frac{1}{2}$ in. by $1\frac{1}{2}$ in. by $\frac{5}{8}$ in. thick, placed two on each fence, as at J. An angle iron for each end is cut and bent and inserted in the unset plaster $\frac{1}{2}$ in. from the ends of the side pieces, as indicated by the dotted line at I, No. 4, to strengthen the angles of the mould. The sides of the piece

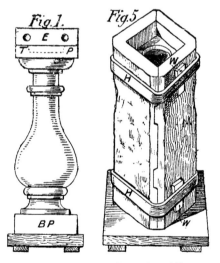

FIG. 92.—Plaster Piece—Moulding a Baluster.

are regulated by the edges of the side fences and the thickness at the angles, and the ends are regulated by sighting the ends of the model, or by fixing a wood or plaster fence at each end, as at F, No. 4. Flatten off the angles for the pieces to lie on the bench. Take up the side piece, the model, and end piece, turn over, and lay them on the moulding board, as No. 4, dust, oil, gauge, and lay the plaster, insert the angle iron, and form the sides as described ; take the pieces off the model and make good defects ready for casting.

A baluster square on plan is piece moulded as just described. Octagonal balusters require four side pieces, and if the sides are panelled, eight pieces. Modelled balusters require pieces to suit the design.

Casting Balusters.—Lay the open moulds on the bench, season, oil the pieces and place together (the end piece downwards) on a casting board or bench, as No. 5, Fig. 92. A band of hoop iron at top and bottom, H, H, tightened by means of wedges, W, W, will keep the pieces together, and the mould is then ready and in position for filling, after which rule the plaster flush with the top of the mould, and joggle the end of the cast for fixing purposes.

Oiling Plaster Moulds.—Plaster moulds are usually oiled with Russian tallow and sweet oil, or lard with or without sweet oil. Paraffin oil renders them more soft, clean, and free to work. Soft soap alone, also mixed with sweet oil, is preferred for some purposes. Plaster has a porous nature, contains lime, and is easily affected by soaps, fats, or oils. Fatty acids unite with lime, and the face of the mould and cast becomes sticky, dust accumulates, and by degrees crustation is set up. One part of finely separated stearic acid (or stearine) melted in a water bath and 5 parts of alcohol or benzine dissolved to a clear solution will clean this away. By shaking as it cools the acid will be obtained in a fine state of division, forming a kind of magma with the alcohol. Oil the mould with this, and as the alcohol evaporates a thin film will form on the mould. The next cast taken will be covered with a thin imperceptible film of non-adhesive stearate of lime. Stearic oil is also useful for gelatine moulds. Animal oils develop acids, vegetable oils become gummy. The admixture of mineral oil (preferably paraffin) will neutralise either condition. Moulds intended for two or three casts need only be saturated with water and oiled with soap solution.

Suet solution is excellent for models and piece moulding. It is made by dissolving fresh mutton suet by gentle heat, and adding paraffin oil to keep it soft and creamy when cold.

Soap solution is soft soap reduced with boiling water to a creamy condition. It is good for waste moulding, for the joints of plaster piece moulds, and other purposes. It should not be used for washing old or dry plaster moulds or casts, as it dries sticky and retains dust. They should be dry dusted, washed with warm water, wiped, and oiled.

Stearic impervious solution is good for piece moulding and for the moulds of figures, panels, etc. Clean, white, and sharp casts result from its use. A neutral soap of stearic acid and caustic soda is prepared and dissolved in about ten times its weight of hot water. Coat the models and moulds either by brushing with or immersion in the solution, which does not colour the moulds, but renders them impervious and enables washing, even with lukewarm soap water. Stearate of potassium is soluble only in hot water. Soap water leaves a dust-holding film on the surfaces of moulds ; so also does plaster impregnated with alum and stearine, or stearate of alumina in benzole. Plaster becomes impermeable to water if washed with a solution of oleic acid in benzine applied cold ; but soap water must not be used for washing, as it would take up the oleic acid. It is best to wipe with a cloth moistened with the acid. The stearic acid and caustic soda solution is best, and is good for waterproofing plaster.

Gauging Plaster.—Though quite simple, very few plasterers gauge plaster as it should be done. Plaster should be kept in a box as described at commencement of this Chapter. Gauging from a sack is slovenly, wasteful, and tiring. The water must be clean and fresh. Dirty water affects the strength, setting properties, and colour of plaster. For solid cast work the mould should be filled in one gauge to ensure equal expansion.

In fibrous work, or plaster gauged with size water, this is not practicable for large work. The proportion of plaster to water is about 2 lbs. to 1 pint for a gauge of medium stiffness; but this does not generally apply as a working rule; plaster has to be gauged in different degrees of stiffness for different purposes. To gauge a pail of plaster, fill it three parts full of clean water, lift the plaster with the hands, sprinkle it round about over the surface of the water until the plaster appears at the surface. This is the proportion of plaster and water necessary for ordinary fibrous work. Stir quickly with the hand, which enables one to feel and crush any lumps and inequalities, and to judge the consistency of the gauged plaster. For small gaugings a spoon is preferable for stirring. A creamy consistency, thick enough to run freely into the intricate parts of the mould, is best. Water added after gauging weakens its strength, due to extra stirring, which tends to kill the plaster. Many plasterers, when finishing the joints of cast work, use neat, fine plaster without size water, and kill the plaster by continuous working with the water brush. This is termed " killed stuff." Size water, as used for the cast, should be used for the joints. It retards the setting and hardens the plaster.

The bad practice of adding plaster to that already gauged creates additional heat and swelling, injury to the mould, and warping in the casts. Old or liquid plaster must not be added to a gauge. Lime water must not be used in fibrous work; it furs the moulds, weakens the casts, and causes adhesion to the mould and difficulty in extraction. Plaster soaked in water on the blade of a trowel sets hard. It will take up the minimum of water if not submerged too long, *i.e.*, when air bubbles stop rising, as there is no stirring and the setting properties are free. Plaster left in water for hours will set harder than if thinly gauged. The stiffer plaster is gauged, the harder it will set. Plaster gauged thin is too porous, has less strength and durability than that stiffly gauged. It is difficult to brush stiffly gauged plaster into crevices. Plaster should be quickly gauged and sparingly worked to be strong and durable.

Plaster casting has greatly improved in the last generation or two. The following is the most modern and effective way of producing good plaster casts :—

After greasing or oiling the mould, gauge the plaster and splash or brush it over the surface into the deep parts and angles, covering the whole surface quickly and uniformly, to expel the air and avoid blebs on the face of the cast. Do not dab with the brush, as it causes air blebs, makes the surface of the mould rough, works the oil into the plaster, and makes the cast difficult to take out of the mould. Do not blow the surface of plaster with the mouth or bellows, as doing so causes air blebs. The mould may be shaken and bumped to expel air blebs. If the plaster is properly brushed in it will suffice. When brushed in, for small solid work, pour the remainder and press in with brush or gauging trowel, rule off the upper surface flush with the back or rim of mould, and key the fixing surface; when set, take out the cast. Thick casts draw out of the mould less easily than thin or shallow casts. In the former case the mould, if small, may be turned face downwards and violently shaken, or the rim beaten. If the mould is large or heavy, lay it solid on a bench and gently prize up the cast with a chisel. For small enrichments place and make several, side by side, and fill them all in one operation. All casts should be trimmed before dry. Strengthen thin or tender casts with splints of wood or cane, reeds, rushes, string, canvas, or galvanised wire inserted in the plaster before set.

Hollow Casts.—Large casts should be hollow. The thickness depends on their size and on the purpose intended. Casts may be strengthened by inserting wood strips and canvas. Hollow casts may be produced by pouring part of a gauge into the mould, shaking and rolling the plaster into every part ; turn the mould until the surplus plaster shows signs of thickening, when it should be poured and the mould kept turning. Pour a second gauge before the first is set, and continue until the cast is sufficiently thick. If the mould is heavy or large, suspend it by ropes from the ceiling, or lay it on a bed of old bags or shavings to facilitate the shaking and rolling without injury.

Strong Plaster for Cast Work.—Plaster is sometimes gauged with glue water to retard the setting, to give time for manipulation, and the plaster to harden when set. It is useful for setting plain surfaces, but is impracticable for casting purposes. Sulphate of zinc added to plaster and glue neutralises slow setting and gives hardness when set. The proportions are from 3 to 5 lbs. of glue and $1\frac{1}{2}$ lbs. of sulphate of zinc to 100 lbs. of plaster. Dissolve the glue and sulphate of zinc in water and add the plaster when gauging This may be used for casting from gelatine moulds and for fibrous plasterwork.

Casting White Cements.—Superfine Keen's or other white cement is chiefly used for casting cement work. It should be gauged moderately stiffly, some of it being brushed over the surface of the mould, and the remainder laid and pressed all over with a sponge, to consolidate it. Extract with the sponge any surplus water which may accumulate on the surface. When the surface is formed, stiffen the gauge with dry cement, press it into the mould until full, rule off the surface, key the back, and allow it to set. When set, immerse the mould in water for a few minutes and take off the cast. Plaster, sulphur, or Spence's metal are occasionally used for moulds for white cement casting, and give sharp and white casts.

Casting Portland Cement.—Portland cement casts may be produced in two ways, *i.e.*, by the " wet process," or the " dry process." With a study of the nature of Portland cement, its aggregates, their gauging, and the seasoning and oiling of moulds, the casting is easier and more accurate. Portland cement castings, while strong, are sometimes disfigured with small surface cracks, caused by too much water in gauging and by improper seasoning of the moulds. Excess water, attracted by unequal suction, collects and percolates the weak parts of the mould, leaving minute spider-web fissures or fine lines : hence the necessity of well-seasoned, watertight moulds, and firm, thorough gauging. Excessive suction, set up by the plaster case of piece moulds, may be prevented by plunging the case in water until saturated, or by saturating the backs of the pieces, which prevents absorption from the cast.

For clean, small casts, use neat cement. Sift the cement for the surface coat through a fine hair sieve or a muslin bag. Fine ground cement gives quicker and sharper casts than a coarser cement, and for gelatine moulds should be used neat. Rough or sharp aggregates destroy a mould. Sand, plentiful almost anywhere and mostly used, should be sharp and clean. Granite, slag, stone, or brick, broken small and freed from dust, are good aggregates in the proportion of 1 part of Portland cement to 2 parts of aggregate. After seasoning, oil and brush the mould with " slip " (neat cement) ; gauge the cement, lay, press it into the angles with a stiff brush, and thicken with a trowel. Large casts should be hollow, to reduce the weight and to give a fixing bond. Strengthen angles and deep hollows by bedding broken brick, tile, slate, or old concrete before the cast is set, and large casts by partitioning in the hollows. Casts for constructive purposes should be solid, the centres being cored with broken brick or similar material.

All casts should be stopped and cleaned whilst wet, air dried for a day, and kept in water for three days at least, to harden and expose weak spots. Defects must be made good. When taken out of water, casts should be air dried for two or three days, according to the atmosphere. If discoloured, brush or wash the surface with a thin Portland cement solution before the surface is dry, and make good straight from the mould.

Water-Seasoned Plaster Moulds.—Water seasoning of moulds for Portland cement casts is cheaper and more expeditious than oil seasoning, and may safely be employed when only a few casts are required. As soon as made, saturate the back of the mould with water, and when fully charged wipe off any surface moisture, brush with paraffin oil or soap solution, and fill in the gauge at once. The process must be repeated for each cast. If properly gauged and laid, the cast will readily leave the mould clean, sound, and free from water cracks.

Casting Cement Mouldings (Waste Mould Process).—Circular mouldings with deep, narrow, undercut sectional forms cannot always be piece moulded; with gelatine the long, narrow, projecting parts of the mould get out of position. The cost of piece moulding is prohibitive for odd or a few casts. To run these undercut mouldings in Portland or white cement for planting purposes is slow, tedious, and expensive work. The " waste mould process " is less so. A mould or fence repels expansion, and so compresses and strengthens the work. The cement may be stiffer, and pressed and consolidated in a mould more than if laid on an open bracket or core. In the latter case the working, trowelling, and running disturbs and lessens the setting and hardening of the stuff! Portland cement mouldings deeply undercut require a run waste mould for each cast. With a reverse running mould, run a casting mould or, when practicable, use a fixed core. Season the mould with water, fill in the gauge, when set; take off the combined mould and cast from the core, and place in water for a day or two to harden the cast and soften the plaster. Remove the plaster with a mallet and chisel. Use the one core for each new mould.

Pressed Cement Work.—The dry cement casting process is called " pressed work." It is clean and expeditious work, and well adapted for casts, large or flat. Make the plaster piece mould, coat with shellac, and keep it dry; do not oil, but dust it with French chalk through muslin. Gauge 1 part of Portland cement and 2 parts of washed sharp sand, fine granite, slag, or stone, passed through a $\frac{1}{16}$ in. mesh sieve. No more stuff should be gauged than can be used in one hour. It is better to gauge enough at one time to fill the mould, large or small. Mix and gauge on a bench or a raised board with a planed board about 2 ft. long, 4 in. wide, and $\frac{1}{2}$ in. thick. Measure the sand, spread on the gauge board, and measure the dry cement and sprinkle it over the sand. Heap the mass in the centre of the board with the mixing rule, cut and draw in layers about 1 in. thick, and repeat until thoroughly mixed; when so, spread on the board in a layer from 2 in. to 3 in. thick and sprinkle a little water over it. Gather together, cut and draw backwards and forwards two or three times, sprinkling water until the mass is moist. Test a handful by squeezing. If it retains its form, it is fit to use; if it sticks to the fingers, it is not so. Use little water at first, and add gradually if the gauge is too dry. If one man works the mass backwards and forwards with the mixing rule and another sprinkles, the water is added more equally and the right consistency better arrived at. When the gauging is finished, lay a layer from 1 in. to 3 in. thick in the mould, according to its depth or the thickness required for the cast, and consolidate by beating with wooden punches and mallets. Add fresh layers, and beat and ram until the cast is flush with the rims of the mould. If the mould is large and flat it is important to consolidate the first layer by beating with a flat wooden mallet. If the mould has an ornamental surface or deep parts, well ram and then beat the stuff with a wooden punch and mallet by gentle but rapid blows on the punch along the surface of the loose layer.

The punches, of pine or other soft wood, vary in size from 8 in. to 12 in. long, and from $\frac{1}{2}$ in. to 3 in. square, according to the extent of the mould. Have the first layer thick. When ramming or beating deep or round parts, the punch should be smaller than the parts and rounded off.

When the first layer is thoroughly consolidated, roughen and key the top surface for the next layer ; lay another portion of the gauge and beat as before ; and continue thus until the mould is full above the edge of the mould, to allow for beating down solid. Work the surplus stuff off with a straight-edge flush with the mould. Scoop the centre of cast out where unnecessarily thick to save materials and weight, and for a good fixing bond. Take out the cast when pressed, but the stuff not being nearly set, has to be supported in the hollow parts with neat moist sand, carefully pressed in without disturbing the cast until flush with the top of the mould ; this will prevent a collapse of the cast when the mould is turned over. Sprinkle fine sand on the upper surface of the mould and cast, lay a strong board or slate on the top, gently move it backwards and forwards (to spread the sand and to give a solid bed for the mould and cast), hold the board firmly to the mould, turn both over together, and lay them carefully on the bench ; take the case and the pieces off the mould and press in the seams with a small tool or hardwood float. Great care is required when turning over the mould or when taking off plaster pieces, to avoid cracking or breaking the unset cast. Plaster pieces will leave the cast more easily if gently tapped with a hammer. A board for a large and heavy mould should have a narrow cleat on one edge (to prevent the mould from slipping whilst being turned over), and should be perfectly rigid, as any yielding or bending of the board will crack the unset cast. Old cistern or billiard slates are best, and old tiles or roof slates for small work. After the seams are pressed, allow the cast to stand an hour, more or less, according to the atmosphere, and sprinkle with water very gently, or the surface will be disturbed and spoilt. After a further stand of three or four hours, water the cast again more freely. Repeat at intervals for a day or two, until the cast is set and hard enough to handle ; then cover with water for not less than three days. A sponge or tool brush half filled with water is good for the first damping of small casts. Hold the brush or sponge near the surface, squeeze gently drop by drop until the whole surface is slightly damped. If the atmosphere is hot and dry, or the cement quick setting, press the seams in immediately the cast is taken from the mould. If allowed to dry, they cannot be pressed out, and will remain. The first damping must follow on immediately to prevent rapid drying and imperfect setting. An ordinary garden watering pot with a fine rose is best for sprinkling when gauging and watering casts nearly set.

Clean and hard casts are obtained by placing them, as soon as made, in a chamber charged with vapour, or in a moist atmosphere. Hot steam greatly accelerates setting and hardening. Pressed work requires fewer moulds than the wet process. One mould, kept dry and whole, should suffice for one man to produce any reasonable number of casts. Much depends, of course, upon the form of the mould ; more casts can be taken from a plain mould than from enriched modillion moulds, according to the skill of the mechanic ! A mould may be useless after thirty casts by unskilful handling, or good after eighty or ninety casts have been lifted. This method costs less than piece moulding, and as no time is wasted it is economical.

Where building stones are scarce, but sand plentiful and cheap, strong and durable building blocks may be produced quickly and inexpensively by hydraulic power.

CHAPTER XIV

GELATINE MOULDING

Gelatine : Its Use for Moulding.—The process of casting in plaster from gelatine moulds is troublesome to many (often to skilled) plasterers. It is regarded by some as more or less secret, which it is not. The process is not so old as might be imagined, having not yet attained its century. It is a branch of the plastering craft that is distinct in its technical manipulation, possessing great virtues open to abuse, combined with imperfections still open to remedy. Its virtues, properly understood and manipulated, lie in the reproduction of deeply undercut modelling, but, alas, with a certain amount of deterioration and loss of surface detail and crispness of edge, due partially to the chemical corrosion of the gelatine, to variation of atmospheric temperature, and to rough handling and ignorance on the part of the operators. Elasticity is at once its virtue and its drawback. The credit of introducing gelatine for moulding purposes is claimed by Mons. H. Vincent, who in 1850 produced six casts from one mould, which at that time was considered a wonderful achievement. The date of Mons. Vincent's first attempt with gelatine moulding is uncertain, but in 1847 J. Herbert, a London modeller, produced undercut cast work from gelatine moulds. R. Foster, a plasterer's shop hand, was the first to use gelatine in Scotland. The initial cost and trouble is more than repaid by the ready multiplication of undercut work.

A process so useful in the reproduction of artistic work was not likely to escape the Italians, who were then finding out the possibilities of gelatine moulding. They grasped the idea, and " flexible moulds " were used for casting busts, statuettes, plaques, etc. The Great Exhibition of 1851 was a revelation at the time. Samples of undercut plasterwork had been cast from gelatine moulds, and in the early days of the process only the most expensive was used, 4s. to 5s. per lb. being the usual price given. Gelatine costing less than one-half the above prices will last a considerable time and yield good cast work. Before the introduction of gelatine for moulding, plaster and wax were used for work in the round, and wax piece moulds for trusses and similar work.   Highly relieved work was cast separately and planted in the main casts. Perforated work was front and back moulded in wax ; soffits and friezes were moulded in wax and undercut by hand.   Piece moulding, front and back moulds, and under-cutting by hand are now replaced by the use of gelatine.   It is now much used for moulding ordinary cast work, whether relieved or not.   The originals being jointed, little jointing or trimming is required for the casts.   Gelatine moulds being more flexible than wax, less force is required to ease the moulds.   Wax moulds have the advantage of lasting longer and can be kept for an indefinite time, whereas gelatine moulds dry and become hard, and have to be remade for future use.   Unless the best gelatine is used and the moulds are properly treated and oiled, they will not produce clean, sharp, and true casts.

Gelatine Manufacture.—Gelatine is a superior kind of glue obtained from bones, hoofs, hides, cartilage, and fish skins.   It is extracted by means of acids, boiling and washing in lime water ; it is then strained, cooled, and dried.   The coarse form of gelatine obtained from hoofs, hides, etc., is glue ; that from skins is size.   The strongest known glue is that made from the skins and sounds of fish.   The Laplanders make a very strong glue from the skin of perch, for in this country fish skin decomposes before it can be dried.   The Laplanders put the skins into a bladder which takes the place of a water bath, and heat until a strong elastic glue results.   Common glue has great strength if it is not injured in the making by decomposition or overheating. English gelatine and Scotch glue are stronger and more elastic than the foreign materials.

Tests.—There are various tests for gelatine and glue.   If the taste and smell are unpleasant there will be little strength.   A simple test is to weigh a piece of glue, say, ½ oz., which has been in water for twenty-four hours, at a temperature of 50° F.   Glue swells from absorption of water ; colouring matter will sink.   When taking glue out of the water, weigh it.   The greater the increase in weight, the better the glue.   Common glue is made from bones.   Good glue is hard, clear (not necessarily light coloured), and free from cloudiness or flecks.   Bad glue will give off an unpleasant smell after being dissolved a few days, the odour being unbearable.   Good glue and gelatine will not dissolve in cold water.   They swell and assume the consistency of jelly.   The quality of glue may be tested by breaking.   If good, it will break hard and tough and be starry and irregular on the broken edge.   If poor, it will break easily, with a smooth edge.   Gelatine easily dissolved in cold water is not strong.   The best qualities merely swell in cold water, and must be heated to the boiling point to dissolve ; they absorb more water than the poorer qualities.   Gelatine, when dissolved, is " jelly," a term hereafter used generally.

Insoluble Gelatine.—Gelatine, after immersion in a concentrated solution of tannic acid, is less sensitive to the action of water.   Chrome acid or good chrome alum renders jelly insoluble.   Two parts of tannic acid to 100 parts of dry gelatine will resist the action of water.   A mould may be immersed for a few seconds in (or quickly brushed with) a solution of 100 parts water and 10 parts of bichromate of potash, and then exposed to the light or sun.   Compounds formed by tannic acid and by bichromate of potash are widely different.   Neither can be remelted.   Bichromated gelatine partly retains its flexibility, and is rendered still more flexible by the addition of glycerine. Bichromated jelly is insoluble in water, even in hot water, and in all known solvents. It may be advantageously used in jelly moulds for casting Portland cement, or other slow-setting cements.   Gelatine exposed to the action of formaldehyde in a gaseous state is rendered insoluble.   A solution of paraffin wax and paraffin oil applied on the surface of jelly moulds will render them impermeable.   Glue dissolved with skimmed milk (in the proportion of 1 lb. of glue to 3 pints of milk) will resist moisture. A glue which stands moisture without softening may be made thus Dissolve in 8 fluid oz. of strong methylated spirit, ½ oz. (each) of sandarac and mastic ; add ½ oz. of turpentine. Add this to a hot solution of glue to which isinglass has been added. Glue is rendered waterproof by the addition of a small percentage of caoutchouc dissolved in benzoline, naphtha, or chloroform. Half pint of spirits of wine and 1 oz. of rock candy to every 5 lbs. of glue will render it more flexible and also preserve it.

Preserving Gelatine.—Soft jelly may be hardened by adding 1 per cent. of alum, or ½ per cent. of sulphate of zinc. Nitric acid will prevent souring and quick drying. Carbolic acid will prevent it from turning mouldy or smelling disagreeably. Linseed oil enables jelly to resist damp. Brown sugar or treacle preserves and keeps it moist. Jelly that has been frequently used may be improved in strength by dissolving it with stale beer or vinegar instead of water. A small portion of pure beeswax will render jelly tough. Glycerine will correct its faults of drying, shrinking, or curling, and also make it tougher and more elastic. Glycerine for this purpose need not be purified. The commercial kind is quite suitable. Gelatine, new or old, should be kept in a dry place. Jelly soon decomposes in damp. The addition of a small quantity of salicylic or boracic acid will prolong its keep. Gelatine dissolved with vinegar instead of water is rendered tougher and more elastic. Vinegar is also a good preservative.

Indurating Solutions.—It is often necessary to indurate the surface of jelly moulds to render them impermeable to moisture and to better resist heat and the effects of continuous casting. For most purposes a " saturated solution " of alum will be found sufficient. A saturated solution is made by dissolving as much alum as the water will hold until a sediment of alum remains undissolved, *i.e.*, the water must soak up as much alum as it can possibly hold. Heat or slow boiling will hasten dissolution. Water overcomes the force of cohesion in certain substances and distributes their particles throughout its own volume, the solid form becoming entirely lost, and the result is called a solution. A solution is said to be " saturated " when no more of the solid will dissolve in it. " Sugar wash " is also used for indurating jelly surfaces. It is made by dissolving 1½ oz. of sugar of lead (acetate of lead—this is poisonous) and 2 oz. of brown sugar to 1 quart of strong solution of alum. The whole is dissolved by gentle heat and frequent shaking. When dissolved and cool, allow the sediment to remain, pour the clear liquid into a clean bottle, and keep corked when not in use. Dust the mould with French chalk and then wipe out clean with a soft rag or brush, to absorb any oil from the face of the mould ; oil would prevent the solution from penetrating into the surface. Then thoroughly saturate the mould with alum solution, or coat with sugar wash. If alum is used the solution may be freely brushed on the mould, or poured on and allowed to lie for ten or fifteen minutes, then poured out, and the mould wiped clean. It is then ready for oiling. If sugar wash is used, carefully brush it over the mould two or three times. If the jelly is soft or the surface becomes flaccid, correct by brushing with a weak solution of sulphate of zinc. Two ounces of linseed oil to each gallon of jelly will render it more waterproof.

Dissolving Gelatine.—Gelatine may be dissolved by means of a water bath. Two pots are required (the outer one for water and the inner for the jelly), like a joiner's glue pot on a large scale, having a lip to pour the jelly freely. The primitive plan of using two pails (one placed inside a larger one) to dissolve jelly is a waste of time, heat, and material. The open space between the pails allows the steam to escape, instead of confining it to melt the jelly more quickly. An old sack placed over the pail is sometimes used to confine the steam. The hot water should never be below the level of the jelly, as it takes longer to dissolve and may burn. Scotch plasterers have a good plan for melting jelly and wax at the same time. They use an iron boiler, about 3 ft. long, 2 ft. 6 in. wide, and 18 in. deep, having two openings on the top to fit a jelly pot and a wax pot. The openings may be used for either as required. Feed and waste pipes are connected at the top, and a hot water tap at the bottom. These boilers are built on a brick setting, having iron bars and a door similar to an ordinary copper. They can be made at most iron foundries, are cheap, durable, and keep the jelly or wax clean, free from burning and with a ready supply, and also provide hot water for general use. The jelly pot should be of block tin, as jelly leaves the sides more freely and is not liable to cake as it does on iron. An ordinary sized jelly pot is about 16 in. deep and 11 in. in diameter. A flange is fixed about 1 in. from the top to support the pot on the top plate of the boiler. The flange is about 1 in. wide at the back, and increases at the front to form a lip for pouring purposes. There should be a lid with a hole in it for the stirring stick. To keep out dirt and retain the heat, pots should be oiled before being used so that any surplus jelly will leave it clean. A jelly pot is shown on Fig. 87, Chapter XIII.

There are two ways of preparing gelatine for dissolving. The first is, to soak the dry material in clean, cold water until soft, swollen, and ready for dissolving. The time required depends upon the quality of the gelatine. Pour off the surplus water and keep it for thinning the jelly if too stiff, or for soaking more gelatine, or for making size water. The other way is to break the gelatine in small pieces, place them in the pot, pour hot water over it, and boil until dissolved. The quantity of water required may vary from a $\frac{1}{2}$ pint to 1 quart for each pound of gelatine, according to the quality. The first way is best and quickest; it retains the strength; excessive boiling weakens gelatine; to oversoak gelatine weakens it. When dissolving gelatine, stir occasionally to distribute any undissolved lumps. Gelatine should be dissolved at a temperature of 100° F. to 120° F. The temperature for remelting should not exceed 110° F. Prolonged heating or too high a temperature will cause it to lose its setting and elastic powers. Take the pot out of the water bath as soon as the jelly is dissolved, stir once, and allow to cool. If stirred again air will mix with the jelly and the mould will be full of small holes. When properly dissolved it should be of the consistency of treacle. When sufficiently cool to pour, the jelly will have a skin on the surface. Before pouring, make a hole in the skin, close to the lip, and another small hole opposite to allow air to escape and the jelly to run freely. When the pot is emptied the skin will hang to the side; remove this and remelt for size water. If the jelly is too hot when poured it is liable to stick to the model. Push a wet finger through the skin (care being taken to wet the finger first), and if not uncomfortably hot the jelly is ready for use

Glycerine renders jelly more elastic and moist. Each pound of gelatine requires from 3 to 6 oz. of commercial glycerine according to the quality of the former. Add the glycerine to the dissolved jelly just before the final stirring. When the moulds are used, cut them into small pieces and dry until wanted again.

After one or two meltings a few drops of carbolic acid should be added to each pot of jelly to preserve it. Some large moulds may require a dozen or more pails of jelly. In order that sufficient jelly for a large mould may be prepared, a deep galvanised iron tank, heated by gas stoves, is necessary.

Seasoning Plaster Models.—Seasoning is a process of hardening plaster and stopping any suction to prevent the adhesion of wax, sulphur, jelly, or plaster to the model. Models for wax and sulphur moulding need soaking in water only. Models for jelly moulding may be seasoned by coating with shellac " patent knotting." Linseed oil, paraffin wax, and French polish have also been used. Painting with shellac is cheap, clean, and quick. A good method is to immerse the " model " in a strong solution of borax, gradually heating it. This renders plaster hard and polishable.

Shellac Seasoning.—To make shellac varnish, fill a jar or bottle about one-third with dry orange shellac, adding wood naphtha until three parts full. Cover and stand it in a warm place until dissolved. This may be hastened by frequent shaking. Before using, try it on a piece of gauged plaster. If too thick it will peel or flake, when naphtha should be added. Two thin coats of shellac are better than one thick one. Models should be warm or dry before shellac is applied to them. A semi-dry and warm surface gives greater cohesion. A coat of linseed oil, laid before shellac is applied, hardens the surface. Shellac is useful for a variety of plastic purposes ; for general use it can be applied without any oil or drying preparations. " Shellac cement " is useful for sticking together small broken casts. This cement is simply shellac in a thick form, made by evaporation, or burning the superfluous naphtha in a tin or saucer.

Oil Seasoning.—Models of plaster may be seasoned by three or four coatings ·of linseed oil. The model must be dry before the oil is applied, or the oil and moisture will rot the plaster. Linseed oil gives a hard and smooth surface, but the process is slow for general work.

Paraffin Wax Seasoning.—Seasoning with paraffin wax is a quick process, and the models and moulds can be used at once. It hardens the plaster and renders the surface impervious to damp. The model is warmed and dissolved paraffin applied hot, quickly and evenly, or it will cake on the surface. The paraffin wax is dissolved by means of a hot water bath, as for jelly. This is safer, cleaner, and retains the strength of the wax better than if dissolved in a pot over a fire. A little paraffin oil added to the wax makes the solution work more freely. When cold the model can be rubbed with soft rags or cotton wool, which gives a smooth and polished surface. The finer the surface of the original, the finer will be the surface of the mould. Paraffin wax is used for other plastic purposes. It is a white, pearly, translucent substance. Though not affected by the strongest acids or alkalis, it is soluble in paraffin oil and turpentine. Its affinities are so feeble that it derives its name from this peculiarity. It has a lower melting point than spermaceti, wax, or stearic acid. The melting point varies from 110° F to 150° F

Seams and Blebs in Jelly Moulds.—Seams in moulds are caused by pouring the jelly too cold, also by insufficient space or ventilation for it to run freely. These faults can be avoided by proper manipulation. Blebs are caused by similar errors, but principally by imprisoned air. The air is expelled, and a better passage for the jelly obtained by pouring one or two tablespoonfuls of methylated spirit down the funnel just before pouring jelly on to large moulds.

Oiling Jelly Moulds.—When jelly moulds were first introduced their surfaces were painted or varnished to prevent corrosion from the heat and moisture of plaster in setting. Painting makes the mould surface coarse and blunt : it is a slow process, and spoils the jelly for remelting. Varnishes have been employed for rendering jelly surfaces heat and damp proof ; owing to the moisture of the jelly it is difficult to obtain a perfect cohesion of the two substances. Various gums, waxes, mixtures of stearine, spermaceti, wax, and oils have been used with varying success. Canada balsam thinned down with turpentine makes a good oil. One of the best and cheapest for this purpose is " gum oil."

Gum oil protects the surface of moulds, and no painting or varnishing is required. It is made as follows : Dissolve 4 oz. of gum damar and 2 oz. of paraffin wax together by gentle heating, and add 1½ pints of kerosene (the finest paraffin oil). When dissolved, pour into a bottle and keep corked when not in use. Pour only enough oil into a dish to last for a day, or, better still, use a ball oil pot. This oil is also good for oiling the model, as the jelly, when poured on, absorbs part of the oil, which renders the surface of the mould more durable and damp-proof.

Chalk oil is also good for jelly moulds and useful for other shop purposes. It is made by adding steatite (French chalk) to paraffin oil until of a creamy consistency.

Petroleum Oil.—Crude petroleum is excellent for oiling jelly moulds, especially if the jelly is old or has to stand excessive damp, as when casting with slow setting cements. Crude petroleum is about the best varnish renovator known. Having more body than paraffin oil, it gives greater protection against damp to soft or weak parts of jelly moulds. Crude petroleum is prepared for commercial purposes by settling, etc. The distilled products—kerosene oil, etc.—are valuable, and oilmen are not keen to market the crude oil, hence it costs as much as kerosene oil.

To Make a Plaster Case.—Plaster cases are for keeping the parts of wax or plaster piece moulds in position. A case for a jelly mould keeps the jelly in position and regulates its thickness and pliability. The jelly has to be poured through a hole in the case, and a space has to be provided for it. The space between the model and the case is the thickness of the jelly. Cover the surface of the model with a coat of clay before the case is made. This clay is termed " thickness clay " (because it regulates the thickness of the jelly), and is laid as follows : First cover the model or original with damp paper, so that the thickness clay will not adhere to, soil, or injure the model. Beat out a quantity of clay $\frac{1}{2}$ in. thick, cut into strips of convenient size, and lay them, piece by piece, on and round the surface of the model until it is completely covered of a uniform thickness. The sides and deep undercut places of the model require an extra thickness of clay, splayed out to allow the case to draw from the clay and from the jelly mould. The clay surface should be smoothed with the hands and water (not oil). A wet brush or sponge may also be used for this purpose. The smoother the clay and case, the better the jelly will flow and the mould leave the case when casting. When the clay is smooth, place conical clay dots on all the high points of the thickness clay. The dots should be about $\frac{1}{2}$ in. thick and about 1 in. high, or according to the intended thickness of the case. The dots form vent holes, and are guides for the thickness of the case. The vents allow air to escape when the jelly is poured in. Another clay dot, about $1\frac{1}{2}$ in. diameter, is required for a hole for the funnel, and placed conveniently for pouring the jelly at the lowest level of the model, so that the jelly, while being poured into the funnel, will force the air in the case out at the vent holes. When the clay dots are laid and smoothed, fix a clay, wood, or zinc fence round the outside edge of the model to regulate the width and thickness of the rim of the case. The rim of large cases may be strengthened by bedding rod or hoop iron in the plaster while making the case. Cases for large circular models may be further strengthened by placing a hoop-iron band on the outside of the rim. This will prevent chipping when turning the case over. Brush the whole with soapy water ; use oil only for the plaster ground of the model and any plaster pieces. Pour gauged plaster over the clay covering, flush with the dots ; make four or more plaster dots and float the points level with a wet board, so that, when the case is turned over, it will lie level on the casting bench. When the original is higher at one end than the other (as, for instance, a truss), the plaster dots for levelling purposes may be dispensed with and only the highest and lowest points floated. To keep such a mould level when casting, the low end should be propped up with a block. After removing the case, clean the surface, smooth and trim the vents, stop any holes, shellac the inside and a margin round the vents on the outside ; this completes the case.

Funnels are made of block tin or zinc, from 6 in. to 2 ft. long. A few from 6 in. to 12 in. long will be sufficient for ordinary work. The diameter at the bottom end varies from 1 in. to $1\frac{1}{2}$ in., and increases upwards to a diameter from 2 in. to 3 in. Clay and plaster funnels are insecure and a waste of time and material. Metal funnels are clean and cheap. Cases having deep sides require a rebated edge to support and prevent the jelly from slipping into the case. The sides of long, straight moulds need stiffening rules ; short or circular moulds with deep sides do not. The lip is made by beating out a sheet of clay, about $\frac{3}{4}$ in. thick ; cut strips about $\frac{3}{4}$ in. wide, holding the knife slanting for the first cut and upright for the sides. Two strips, each with a square and a splayed edge, are thus made. Place the strips on edge on the ground of the model, against the side of the thickness clay ; keep the splayed edges upwards and the acute point outwards to form a corresponding splayed lip in the case. This is quicker than cutting a lip after the case is made. (See the illustration of truss mould, Nos. 1 and 2, Fig. 93, and regard the jelly as thickness clay ; the formation and use of lips will then be better understood.)

In large models, where the space is thin, the jelly, when poured in, often runs slowly, causing crinkles or blebs on the mould's surface. This is partly due to the jelly cooling over a large space, to being reduced in thickness, and to air resistance. It may be avoided by forming a series of small channels in the surface of the case, each about $\frac{1}{4}$ in. wide and $\frac{1}{4}$ in. deep, from vent to vent, allowing a passage for the air and the jelly to run freely. Channels are best formed when making the case by laying V-shaped strips of clay on the thickness clay from vent dot to vent dot. Fibrous plaster cases, punctured to allow air to escape, are used for jelly moulds.

Cases.—Cases must be securely fastened down or the jelly will lift and spoil the mould. They are best secured by weighting down, or by wood struts from the ceiling to the case. Large work must be further secured by a coat of plaster and canvas over the joint of the case and the ground of the model. All joints should be covered with plaster or clay to prevent the jelly from oozing out.

Joggles.—Models and cases require corresponding joggles to keep in position. Unless the case is always put on right way about it will injure and chip the model. Joggles should be made on the ground of the model by scratching the parts required, and for a further key, drive a few tacks into the plaster ground, leaving them protruding. The joggles are then made to the desired form and size with gauged plaster and putty water. They form a sinking in the case, are not in the way, and allow the mould to be ruled off. If too small the case may slip.

Joggles should vary in size, shape, and place, to distinguish the placing of the case, to save time, and to keep the model from injury. Small models do not require joggles, but one end may be cut to a different shape, or have a sunk mark.

To Separate Cases.—Sometimes it is difficult to separate the case and the model without injury. This may be due to suction, through insufficient seasoning. If the plaster model is too large to be conveniently soaked before moulding, wash or brush with soapy water until the suction is stopped. Damp the case in the same way and dry before oiling. Seasoning with oil or shellac stops the surface suction only. Pouring jelly too hot, or irregular oiling, will cause jelly to stick. This should not arise with care, but may be cured by immersion in water until air bubbles cease to appear ; then place the model on a bench, insert flat wood wedges about 12 in. apart, and gently drive them home until the case lifts. Should the mould stick to the model, plunge the whole into water as before. Good jelly is not injured by temporary contact with water.

Gelatine Moulding.—The jelly, dissolved and cooled to the requisite temperature, is poured steadily into the funnel until it rises to the highest vent holes. These must be stopped with clay, as it works through them, and allowed to stand until cold or set. When sufficiently set, remove the funnel, cutting the jelly below. Remove the clay pats and cut off any projecting bits of jelly. Take off the case and the jelly protrusions and dust the surface (to prevent adhesion when casting) by dipping a dry brush into dry plaster and shaking the same over the mould, thus lightly sprinkling the plaster over the mould's surface. Brush off the superfluous plaster, remove the mould from the model, and place it in the inverted case. Wipe dry the model with a soft brush, soft rags, or paper, and brush with alum water or " sugar wash." Wipe the surface again, oil with " gum oil " or chalk oil, and leave ready for filling and casting.

To Jelly Mould a Truss.—Fig. 93 shows a method of jelly moulding a truss cap and leaf in one piece. In No. 1, A is the truss, G the ground, D the case, B the jelly, C a plaster piece, F the funnel, and e the vent holes. The plaster piece C is to limit the amount of jelly and allow the sides of the mould to be opened when casting. This plaster piece is used when there is a plain flat back to the model, before the thickness clay is laid. To make this, sink two or more joggles in the top of the truss cap (at C) to keep the piece in place when making the case and when casting. Lay strips of clay ¾ in. thick on the sides and top of the cap (keeping them close to the edge), oil the top or end of the model, and lay the plaster on (about 1½ in. thick at the bottom), tapering to the top to about 1 in. thick. Do the sides in the same manner. Then take off the piece and trim and splay the inner edges to draw off freely. The splay is shown on the top left-hand edge of C. Coat the piece with shellac, replace in position, and lay the thickness clay, keeping it flush with the edges of the piece as shown. Complete the case as before described. The case need not be taken over the end plaster piece, but as shown,

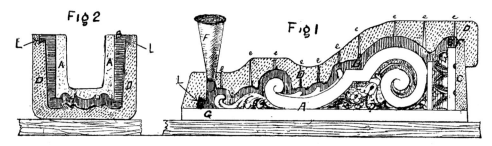

FIG. 93.—Moulding a Truss with Gelatine.

to leave a hand hold for lifting when casting. A lip, continued round the sides as at L, supports the jelly sides. Fig. 2, a cross section. shows the case, the jelly, the lips, and the cast, lettered as before.

To Jelly Mould a Bust.—Fig. 1, Plate CXII, shows a bust and base moulded and cast separately, and afterwards fixed together. They are generally moulded and cast in one piece. When the bust and the base are cast separately, the bust may be jelly moulded and the base piece moulded in plaster, to decrease the weight of the mould, give greater space for filling, and more freedom in casting. A plaster base mould gives a better result if white cement casts are required. Fig. 2 shows a front view of the bust on a moulding board, covered with thickness clay. The dark band round the bust is a clay fence, to divide the case into two parts and to keep the joints or seams clear of the features and ears. The case for the back half should be made first, so that the bust may be laid flat to form the front cast. If cased in an upright position the back makes a firm stay for casing the front. Fig. 3 shows the back case on the clay. At the top is the opening for the funnel, a guidance for cutting the jelly for the two halves of the mould, so that the jelly joints correspond with the case joints.

Joggles should be made in the thickness of the case, as the jelly is less liable to escape when the joggles are made on the outer edge of the case. The opening at top must be larger than the funnel, and to allow for a projection of jelly scum. Fig. 4 shows half the case, the joggles, and funnel hole. Fig. 5 shows the two halves of the case and mould tied together for casting. The rope is tied clear of the opening for

PLATE CXII

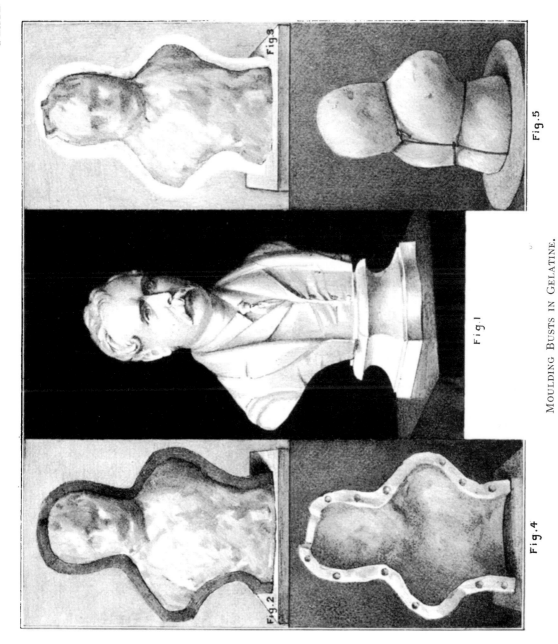

Fig.3

Fig.5

Fig.1

Fig.4

Fig.2

MOULDING BUSTS IN GELATINE.

1. Bust of the Author modelled by himself.
2. Model covered with thickness clay.   3. Model with thickness clay and back case.
4. Half-case.   5. The mould.

filling in the mould, enabling the mould to be hung, turned, or rolled when making hollow casts. The tension on the rope, caused by the weight of the hanging mould, keeps the joints tight.

Brushed Jelly Moulds.—A method of moulding employed by an American requires no case or clay fences, the warm jelly being brushed over the model until thick enough for a mould. I cannot venture on an opinion on this method, not having seen the process in work.

Compound Moulding Piece.—When numerous small casts such as beads, small bed moulds, etc., are required, fix a number of them on to a plaster ground and mould in one operation. The casts for moulding should be clean, sharp, and accurately jointed at both ends before being fixed, to save jointing afterwards. Two or more, if nearly uniform in size, may be moulded in the same way. When modelling, a joint in continuous ornament should be made to cut through stems and between other parts. The design must not be sacrificed to the jointing. Joint without interrupting a design ; avoid mutilation and distortion. This modelling is all in low relief (in no way undercut) and drawn from a plaster mould. Undercutting of the casts by hand, if necessary, and "touching up" should be done by a modeller. No case would be required for small models, only wood fences for the sides and clay fences for the ends. If a stock moulding piece is being made, the side and end fences may be cast on for permanence.

Stock moulding pieces are those kept for future use.

Moulding Undercut Clay Models.—Several jelly moulds may be taken from a clay model without fear of injury. The ground of the model should have flat-headed nails projecting above the surface to give a key. If the model is deep or there is fear of disturbing it, a case may be made after the jelly is poured on, by making a strong fence to retain the jelly. After the jelly is poured on, and cool, remove the fence, cut off any superfluous jelly, to allow the case to draw, brush with a solution of clay, and pour the plaster on. Cutting the jelly in deep places may be avoided by placing pieces of clay in the mould while soft, to displace the jelly, removing the clay pieces when the jelly is cool. Clay having little suction, jelly leaves the model easily.

Moulding White Models.—Sometimes a jelly mould has to be taken from a plaster or cement bust, or plaque, without discolouring the model. This may be done by carefully brushing the model with a solution of fine white Castile soap. It is best to mould when the surface is semi-moist and has a glossy face. No oil must be used, and the jelly must be new and clean. After the mould is taken off, wipe the model with a soft sponge and warm water and it will dry quite clean.

Moulding Casts.—Sometimes a few undercut casts are required from old work. In such cases it will be necessary to take a clean cast from the old work and shellac the same. Fix the cast on a plaster ground with thin plaster or soft clay to prevent the jelly from running under the cast. Fix a clay fence round it and mould with jelly in an open mould.

Open Jelly Moulds.—Jelly moulds do not always need a case. If only a few casts are required, fences will prevent the escape of the jelly. If the model is large or deep and much undercut, mould in one piece and afterwards cut the jelly to form a piece mould. Models with long flat surfaces should be moulded without a case. If circular casts are required, the mould can be bent to any curve, but there is much risk of distortion.

Straight Moulds.—When making long casts, such as panels, friezes, or mouldings, from a gelatine mould, it is sometimes difficult to keep the outer edges straight and level, owing to the swelling of a new jelly mould or the shrinkage of an old one. The edges are also liable to tear by frequent handling. Tacks or small nails driven through the jelly into the case answer for small work, if only a few casts are required. A reliable method is to strengthen the edges of the mould with laths, running rules, or " stiffening rules."

Glue Moulds.—In some workshops glue is used for moulding undercut models as a substitute for gelatine, and it is supposed to be cheaper. The first cost is cheaper, but not so in the end. Glue may be used for casting where work need not be fine or sharp. Glue moulds are generally coated with a paint of gold size, patent driers, white lead, and linseed oil, thinned down with turpentine. This paint is used for jelly moulds when casting Portland cement work, if the jelly is old or the cement slow setting. Models should never be oiled with sweet oil; it prevents cohesion of the paint and retards the drying. Some use composition of white lead, linseed oil, and turpentine for oiling the plaster model. The suction of fibrous models is best stopped by plunging them into water for a few minutes, or by sponging with soapy water, and then brushing the back with a thin solution of clay, to keep the moisture in the body, to prevent the suction of the porous plaster, and counteract the heat of the jelly. After this lubricate with chalk oil and the glue mould will leave the model quite clean. This use of lead oil is a slow and dirty process; it has to be washed off the original every time a mould is made. Painting is also a slow and dirty process. The paint peels with every third or fourth cast, and requires patching and drying. Painted moulds produce poor casts. Glue may be improved by adopting any of the treatments applied to jelly methods. Old glue, like jelly, is improved by using stale beer, vinegar or milk instead of water, for dissolving. Washing the face of the mould with paraffin oil before painting or varnishing indurates the surface. A limited number of casts may be obtained by using the best Scotch glue for moulds. Quick drying, elastic varnish gives better results than oil paint. The following are the best-known varnishes :—

Rubber Varnish.—Dissolve india-rubber shavings in naphtha in a close vessel by gentle heat (or a hot water bath), then strain the liquid off into bottles and keep them corked until required for use. Before varnishing the mould with this solution dust with French chalk, to absorb any surface oil or moisture which would prevent the varnish from adhering to the glue surface.

Copal Varnish.—One gill mixed with 1 oz. of patent drier, thinned with turpentine before mixing, makes a good solution. Dust the mould, varnish, and allow to dry.

Shellac varnish is made as follows : 100 parts water, 12 parts best hard shellac, and 4 parts of borax are dissolved together in a close vessel by gentle heat and with continued stirring. Cover the vessel and allow to cool, pour into bottles and well cork. This may be used alone, or mixed with a small portion of linseed oil and a few drops of turpentine. The whole mass well incorporated will dry in fifteen or twenty minutes. Glue and jelly moulds used for casting hot plaster or Portland cement are apt to become soft and sticky at the prominent parts. Allow the moulds to stand in a cool place until the dressing becomes firm, then revarnish or wash with bichromate of potash. Oil varnished moulds with chalk oil.

Soft Casts.—The surface of cast work from glue and jelly moulds is often soft, sticky, or spongy, caused by a hot plaster dissolving the surface of the mould, or weakening the paint on the glue and preventing the plaster from setting quickly. Soft cast surfaces are also caused by the use of plaster which takes longer to set on the face of the mould than at the back of the cast. Alum water accelerates the setting and hardening of the plaster and hardens the face of the mould. If plaster is extra slow in setting, or the glue weak, use extra strong alum water, or ordinary alum water. If this causes the plaster to set too quickly, add size water. From 1 to 2 per cent. of sulphate of zinc will neutralise the slow setting of glue. Sulphate of zinc will indurate a mould and harden the cast; a combination of the two materials gives still greater hardness to plaster, and is often used when casting fibrous plasterwork.

Spotty Casts.—All cast work is liable to be spotty, or to discoloration, especially if produced from a painted glue mould. This is due principally to sulphur or lime in the plaster drawing the oils from the paint and the glue to the face of the casts. If the plaster contains much sulphur, or the alum not cleanly dissolved, they will discolour the plaster. Inferior or impure oil will discolour casts. A little chloride of lime in the gauging water will prevent this. The proportions vary according to the plaster used, but are about 1 lb. of chloride of lime to 50 gals. of water.

Gelatine Casts.—Shop hands are sometimes called upon to mould and cast parts of the human body for surgical purposes. The following process of moulding in plaster and casting in jelly is practised at the Royal Infirmary, Edinburgh :—

Preparation of the Material.—Take of Nelson's or Young's best gelatine, say, 6 oz. (by weight), soak till soft and swollen, and dry slowly until just pliable. It has then the minimum of water necessary; melt in a water bath and add 6 fluid oz. of clear glycerine. When thoroughly mixed the material is ready. To render it opaque add, while still hot and fluid, small quantities of a thick paint made by rubbing up oxide of zinc in glycerine. A little vermilion will give a warm, life-like hue. The prevailing colour of anything can be given with water-colour as desired (tubes of moist water-colour sold at 2d. each will be found convenient). Several pounds of this may be made at once, and portions used as required.

Making the Mould.—Mould the part required in plaster of Paris in the ordinary way. Limit the casts to those moulds which can be removed from the body in one piece. When both sides are moulded at once, the gelatine cast is by no means easy to extract from the mould. After removal from the body, the mould must be slowly and thoroughly dried. If moist, the gelatine cast will soften; if too much heated, the plaster mould will crumble. Apart from thorough drying, no further preparation of the mould is needed; but for convenience the margins should be banked up with clay before casting.

Making the Cast.—Melt the prepared gelatine and glycerine and pour it into the dry, banked-up mould, being careful to rock (as a ship) the melted mixture backwards and forwards over the face of the mould to get rid of air bells. The heated jelly at first runs into the hollows, leaving the raised parts of the mould with a very thin coating. The operator must keep ladling up from the hollows, and as the jelly cools it will coat the upper parts.

Making a Plaster Bed for the Cast.—While the cast is still in the mould its reverse side must be covered with lint or wool, and this, in turn covered with plaster of Paris, either pure or mixed with cotton wadding, oakum, lint, wood wool, etc., made to fit into the hollows and elevations of the back of the cast, and when set, remove to be dried. The cast can be easily peeled out of the mould, and it will be found to be elastic. When placed upon its plaster backing the shape will be preserved.

To Paint the Cast as Required.—Use water-colour when a dry surface is to be imitated, oil-colours when the surface is moist. Water-colour may require several coats. Finally, an edging of black velveteen or other material will amend the irregular margin and give a finish.

The advantage of this method of casting is its likeness in appearance and texture to flesh. A great number of copies may be taken from the mould. The disadvantage is that it may not keep in good condition for more than five or six years, and the extra time required to cast in jelly instead of in plaster.

India-rubber Moulds.—India-rubber has been used for flexible moulds for undercut casts "in the round." In 1875 a patent was granted for flexible moulds.

According to specification, the model was coated with a solution of india-rubber in benzine. This soon dries, leaving a sticky surface, on to which layers of vulcanised rubber, about $\frac{1}{30}$ in. thick, cut into convenient sizes, are pressed, and repeated until sufficiently thick to resist inward pressure when casting. If the work is in the round, cut the mould at one side to release the model. If desired, the two halves can be securely joined again with rubber solution. The mould may be held in shape by a plaster case. Before the mould is used it must be vulcanised. This form of mould is good for plaster or cement casting. The moulds will keep for an indefinite time and are good for cement work, but the cost is prohibitive for ordinary commercial use.

Fibrous Plaster and Concrete for Fire-resisting Construction and

FIG. 94.—Front Section of Balcony.

Decoration.—This subject, being quite apart from that of gelatine moulding, may not appear to be in its proper place, but owing to the numerous and varied processes and materials that are used in plasterwork, it is confessedly difficult to give an exhaustive description of each subject under one heading ; therefore this, like others which are inseparable from other subjects, is given where occasion demands. Another reason is, that part of the sketches here given to illustrate gelatine mouldings also serve to illustrate the above subject. The various parts of fibrous plaster, concrete, and jelly moulding are shown in the following illustrations :—

Balcony Front.—Fig. 94 shows a section of a balcony front for a theatre. Part of the construction is shown to illustrate a method of combining concrete with fibrous plaster for fire-resisting purposes. The section shows some of the ironwork. A shows the end of a cantilever projecting from the main walls ; J the iron joist between the cantilevers. The ironwork is protected from heat and fire by concrete casing. Fixing bars E, or " fixing blocks " of specially prepared concrete, are placed at intervals, being laid in position on centering before the rough concrete is laid.

T is a section of half the top rail, formed of concrete and T iron. The rails are supported by iron standards. C is a fire-resisting, metal lathing partition, concreted on both sides, before the fibrous work is fixed. The metal lathing is fixed at the upper and lower edges into grooves in the concrete rail and floor, or the partition can be cast and fixed in position while the rail and floor are being formed. The rail can also be cast if required. When made *in situ* a wood frame or box is formed round the joist, the top being open for the concrete to be laid and rammed. The floor is formed in a similar way. The floor, partition, and rail may be in one monolithic body if required. This would necessitate extra framing, and a thicker partition for the concrete to pass freely between the framing to the floor. The main body of the floor is laid in the usual way. D indicates the floor boards fixed direct to the concrete to be less combustible, and to avoid a space which would harbour dirt, vermin, or foul air. The board D is movable, the channel underneath being for water pipes, electric wires, etc.

F shows the section through the fibrous plaster box front, indicated by cross hatching. The enrichments are here omitted, being shown on the casting moulds. G is part of the soffit, set out to cover the joint and fixed to the bar E. The rail H is of wood, rebated over the fibrous plaster (or of " carton-pierre," or " papier-mâché," stained, varnished, or polished as required). The fibrous plaster front is secured by screws to the fixing bars in the concrete. The weight of this

FIG. 94A.—Running Concavo-Convex Mouldings.

fibrous front is supported by the edge of the concrete floor requiring only screws at intervals in the three fixing bars to secure the front. The upper and lower mouldings are sometimes run in " solid plaster," and the enrichments cast in fibrous plaster, carton-pierre, papier-mâché, or composition. Fibrous plaster has the advantage of being lighter, of larger sections, and fixable with greater expedition than other materials not strictly plasterwork.

The fibrous front would be jointed at intervals where most convenient, according to the design. The foregoing details enable the general principles of construction and fixing to be understood. As regards the moulding piece, a running mould is usually cut to the full section FF. allowing a bed for the enrichments L at the top and bottom.

Concavo-convex mouldings, *i.e.,* concave one way and convex the other. This form of moulding is made on a plaster ground, having the contour of the concavo-convex frontal. The section of this ground is shown at A, No. 1, Fig. 94A, which describes the method of running a circular panel on an ogee surface, assuming that circular panel mouldings are here placed at intervals over the joints of the cast lengths. The ground is run with the running mould used for the main part of the model, but slightly altered, by fixing pieces of sheet iron or zinc on the model, one at the bottom to cut off the moulding D, to allow the running mould to pass and run on the section to a regular curve ; the other piece of iron is fixed at the top, as shown at E, for the same reason. The running mould for the circle moulding is constructed to fit the various curves by rounding the nib, and using a short and oval-shaped slipper with a small bearing. The radius rod works on a pin, which passes through the " slot," to allow the mould to take the up and down curves. A centre plate is fixed on the centre end of the radius rod. A centre hole is made to fit the centre pin. This plate is made of flexible metal (hoop iron will do), to yield with the rising and falling of the radius rod and mould. No. 3 shows the mould with the radius rod. The mould is shown in two positions (one on the concave, the other on the convex plane) of the ground in No. 1. B is the centre block and pin; C is the centre plate. The centre block is raised to equalise the height and depth of the two opposite curves. When running the mould the centre plate should be kept down on the centre block to obtain a uniform radius. The mould should be made to run about 1 in. off the background, the space shown by the line from B to A on No. 2. The remainder is made up by hand and by the aid of a template. After the circle moulding is run, the straight mouldings at each side of the circle panel are made to butt against the circle moulding as shown by the dotted lines at D and E. This is simply replacing what was taken off the original section, to allow the panel to be run on the contour, so that the panel casts will fit to the main cast. After this, part of the top rail should be fixed in position, as at H on No. 2. This gives a ground for modelling and moulding a grotesque clip, if required, and a better judgment and fitting for any modelling. Before modelling, the circle panel and the front should be placed upright.

Moulding Balcony Fronts.—The moulding process with jelly next claims attention. Fig. 95 shows a section through the moulding piece, jelly mould, and fibrous plaster case. A is the ground and B the moulding piece. The back section is identical with

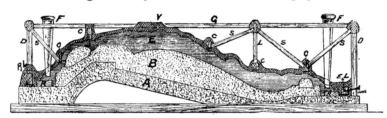

FIG. 95.—Section of Moulding Piece, with Jelly Mould of Fibrous Plaster Case, of Balcony Front.

the structural work of the balcony front, as shown on the previous illustration. The moulding piece can be made in two ways: first, by running a length of ground sufficient to take two or more lengths of the cast to be fixed on it, with space at each end for moulding purposes, equal to the thickness of the jelly and case. The groundwork cast with the modelling is moulded, and the casts made for the moulding piece fixed on to the ground, both ends being jointed. A second method is to make up the ground at the sides and ends of the original cast, to form a moulding piece. In most instances the back section need not be fitted accurately. This example illustrates the method of obtaining a good bed where required. A fixing point at the top and bottom of the cast is generally sufficient. The first method is similar to making a model for any small mould. Large clay models should be moulded direct from the clay to retain the modeller's technique and dispense with waste moulding and cleaning up. A novel method of moulding balcony fronts, or other long frontage moulds, is by the use of wood "stiffening rules" as a substitute for the "lips," generally formed in solid cases to keep the deep or long sides of jelly moulds in position, to produce straight casts.

Stiffening rules are used to stiffen or hold the sides of long jelly moulds in position, to prevent twisting or drooping, and to ensure true and straight casts. Stiffening rules form a part of the mould, but allowance for them must be made in making the case. They are from pine boards, about 1 in. wide by $\frac{3}{8}$ in. thick, should be planed and tapered on the sides that fit into the case, to enable the case to withdraw from the mould, and vice versa. When making the case, lay the stiffening rules on the ground, about ½ in. from each side of the model, and lay the thickness clay as usual, about 1 in. over the rules, leaving ½ in. bed in the case. E, in Fig. 95, is the thickness clay, R the stiffening rules, showing their positions and splayed outer edges. One side beds into the case, the other side and the greater part of the top is bedded into the jelly. These rules enable long or large jelly moulds to be better taken off the model with little risk of tearing the mould.

To Make a Fibrous Plaster Case.—Fibrous plaster cases are used for large moulds, being lighter than solid cases and more easy to handle. One vent is generally sufficient for a fibrous case, passage for the air being obtained by puncturing the surface, without fear of the jelly escaping. This process is cleaner and quicker than forming clay dots for the vents and stopping the vents when moulding. (See Fig. 95.)

Having laid the stiffening rules in position, the thickness clay, the clay dots for the funnels F, and the vent V are formed. The vent should be midway between the funnels. For a mould of 7 ft. long and 3 ft. wide, four funnels are better than two; the jelly is not so apt to cool and crease by travelling as when two are used. For a model of this section, funnels should be placed on both sides, so that the jelly may run up to the vent. If on one side only, the jelly would have to float to the top of the model and over the other side. This is bad practice, as the jelly running down is liable to retain some of the air and cause blebs in the mould; whereas, by flowing up, it forces the air out at the vents.

A fibrous plaster case being thin (⅛ in. to ¼ in. in parts), it is necessary to strengthen it with strong laths and for the mould to lie true on the bench when casting, two deep frame laths being required to support the case. These are laid from end to end of the case, are inserted while making the case, and secured by means of wood stays and rib laths, laid crossways, to bind and stiffen the longitudinal laths. They are fixed with plaster and canvas, and in some instances with screws or nails. The frame and rib laths should be nailed together before being inserted in the plaster and canvas. This makes a frame, which is laid on when making the case, and is stronger than if laid in pieces and fixed with plaster and canvas. After laying two coats of plaster and canvas (one coat will suffice for small cases), the rim laths RL and EL are laid, and the overlapping canvas turned over and brushed with plaster. The body laths C are laid and covered with canvas strips and plaster brushed. The frame laths D are next laid. Two ways of fixing are shown. One is laid on the rim lath RL, and is fixed with brushed canvas strips; the other is laid against the rim lath EL, and fixed with nails. The frame laths are further secured by rib laths G, placed at intervals about 3 ft. apart, and fixed with nails or brushed canvas strips, and further supported by the stays S. The upright stay L supports the lath beneath and offers a fixing for the angle stays to support the remainder of the body laths. The top points or bearings at the frame and upright laths, the vent and body lath, are made level. The fibrous plaster is indicated by cross lines. The rim body laths vary from ½ in. to 1 in. thick and from 1 in. to 2 in. wide, and the frame laths from ½ in. to ¾ in. thick, the widths as required. The plaster and canvas and the laths are laid and brushed as usual. When the case is removed it is cleaned and punctured by a fine sharp-pointed bradawl, stabbing from the inner surface, to leave the perforations clean and without ragged edges. The perforations are made at random, about 1 in. apart and near the highest points, or where vents would be made in a solid case. The case is then seasoned with shellac, the stiffening rules inserted, and it is ready for use.

Before laying the case on the model the stiffening rules must be temporarily fixed in the case beds, to prevent them from moving or falling while turning the case over and fixing it, or while the jelly is being poured. The rules are fixed with screws through the case from the outside, and are not easy to place truly on the ground of the model.

This done, the case is oiled, but not the parts of the stiffening rules bedded in jelly, as it would not then adhere to the wood, which would be rendered useless. The mould is made in the usual way, and when the jelly is cool the screws are extracted, the case taken off, and the rules are a part of the mould.

Casting Balcony Fronts.—A section of the casting mould is shown in Fig. 96.

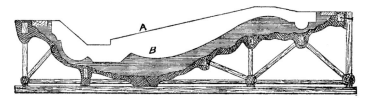

A is the ground line at the ends of the case, and from which the back surface is ruled off. B is a section line of front surface, the ornament being in the jelly thickness.

FIG. 96.—Section of Jelly Mould of Balcony Front.

The case, laths, and the stiffening rules correspond with those in the previous illustration. Fig. 97 is a section through the cast. A are wood blocks to support the· edges and to prevent the cast from warping while drying. The casts are made in the same manner as the fibrous cornices, but the laths are stronger to carry the weight of the larger casts. F are frame laths, 3 in. wide by ¾ in. thick. C a body lath, laid flat for fixing purposes. This, and the body laths B, are 2 in. wide by ½ in. thick. R is a bracket ¾ in. thick, cut to fit over the body laths, and placed 2 ft. or 3 ft. apart. The cast is strengthened by nailing the frame laths and the end brackets together to form a frame, which is placed on the mould after the plaster and canvas are laid. After this the canvas margins are turned over and brushed, and the body laths and the brackets laid in the frame. The whole of the woodwork is canvased and brushed with an extra thickness of plaster to better resist fire.

Casting in Large Jelly Moulds.—When filling in large jelly moulds for fibrous work, alum water must not be used in the "firstings." Alum water is only used for small work or for solid casts, to hasten the setting of the plaster, that the cast may be removed before the plaster generates heat. Alum increases the heat of plaster, and in large moulds requiring two or three hours to fill, would corrode the surface of the jelly. Heat is avoided by using size water in the "firstings," and time gained to lay and brush the canvas. The "firstings" must be stiffly gauged, only size being used to delay the setting until just before the "seconds" sets. Alum and size water combined are sometimes useful for this purpose.

Curved balcony fronts are usually segmental, or horse-shoe on plan. The expense of a separate moulding piece and mould for each curve may be avoided by making and recasing a

FIG. 97.—Section of Cast of Balcony Front.

straight jelly mould to fit the variation of curvature. When laying the thickness clay for the straight jelly mould, run the clay surface with a wood template fitting the section, bearing on the side grounds of the moulding piece and producing a uniform clay surface. Make the plaster case and any straight casts required. Then make the curved case with two templates, one to the upper and one to the lower radius. If both edges of the cast sprang from a straight line, one radius would answer for the two templates. For convex work the radius must be reversed. Having cut the case templates, fix them on edge. The distance apart is equal to the width of the straight case. Acute arches should be lathed or roughly cored with bricks at the extremities, to give thickness for the plaster cast. The space between the templates is filled in with plaster and run with a " bed template," the reverse section of the clay template, and bearing on the case templates. When the bed and sides of the case are run, varnish with shellac and transfer the jelly mould from the straight case to the circular one. The ends of the case are then made up to the mould with plaster. If the ends of the jelly mould, when curved, show acute points or are too thin to retain their forms, stiffen with plaster. The stiffening rules used in the straight mould may be bent to the curve of the circular case by saw-cutting the inner curve, and are useful (as fixing points for nails) to help in keeping the mould in place when laid in the circular case.

Where points of modelling project above the average line, the template must be worked close to them and the intermediate portions worked off by hand, then covered with thickness clay, cased, and moulded by setting. The projecting parts should be indicated on the rough core of the circular case, and clay blocks placed where marked deeper and wider than the part it is meant to receive, the upper surface of the blocks being lineable with the bed of the case. When the case is made, take out the blocks and lay the mould in. The projecting parts occupy the cavities formed by the blocks. The exposed jelly at the back of the case and the excess space of the cavities are covered and made up with plaster. If the projecting parts are deep, or the jelly thin, they should be made up with clay or filled in with plaster, before the mould is taken out of the straight case, to retain their form in the circular case, and while the cavities are being made up. By this process straight and circular casts (of any curve) may be made from the one mould. Another way is to cut off the points, mould and cast them separately, and afterwards fix them on the cast.

Interchangeable Moulds.—It is sometimes necessary to change parts of a mould where variety of detail in the main design is concerned. A separate and loose mould for each varying part is made and inserted in the main mould. A bed in the case and a space in the mould for the changeable part is formed before the case is made, by making a plaster " bedding piece " on the model to the size and bulk of the changeable part, allowing ample length and width. After the bedding piece is made, the thickness clay is laid close up to the bedding piece. The case is made, and when removed the bedding piece is taken out and moulded. The piece is then replaced on the model and the main mould made. The bedding piece is again taken out, leaving a bed and space for the changeable moulds. The mould of the bedding piece is filled in, the cast forming a ground for the modelling on. This is moulded a little thinner than the original for bedding purposes, laid in the main mould, and the mould, with the alteration, filled in. When the cast is taken out, the thin seam caused by the points of the inserted portion must be cleaned off. The mould of the bedding piece is used in this manner for each variation only when it is more convenient and cheaper than modelling the variations *in situ* on the finished casts, in plaster, with metal tools. The interchangeable models may, if wished, be cast separately and inserted in the main cast. This is sometimes more convenient, but care must be taken (when fixing the insertions) that the joints will not crack and open when subject to draughts and variations of temperature.

Combined Gelatine and Plaster Moulds.—A jelly mould combined with " plaster insertions " for moulding with large plain portions, or deep sides, where interchangeable parts are required, is sometimes advantageous. An example is shown in " truss moulding." The method is shown in Fig. 98. The model A is a section through the panel, and similar models do not require a plaster " moulding ground."

The original model is made and moulded. If a back section is required, a plaster block cut to the section is fixed at each end of the model, as at P, forming bearings for ruling off and a moulding piece without running a bed. Taking the length of the completed panel at 12 ft. and the depth at 5 in., a jelly mould down to the bench would be pliant, incline inwards of its own weight, and cause the sides of the casts to be wavy. This defect may be avoided and the jelly saved by using the plaster pieces B and D. Two formations are shown. The upper edge of the piece B is made above the level of the jelly point and sloped to the arris for the mould to draw. The raised ridge forms a corresponding groove in the case, acting as a joggle to keep the piece in place and prevent it from slipping inwards. The edge of the piece D is flush with the arris of the model, and held in position by round sunk joggles about 9 in. apart. The flush edge allows the jelly to lap the joint, so that if the mould should shrink in setting it would still cover the joint, whereas the raised edge forms a butt joint ; therefore, should the jelly shrink, the fluid plaster would run into the open joint and cause a seam on the cast. Similar pieces are made at the ends of the model. Should the side pieces break, the broken parts (being laid in the mould and being joggled) will keep in place and still be fit for use. Both methods are used for " plaster piece moulding," but the " flush edge," or joint C, is the best. When the plaster pieces are made the thickness clay is laid. Another use of stiffening rules is shown, illustrating a method of keeping a jelly mould straight and in position. It is useful for large moulds where delicate mouldings occur. In

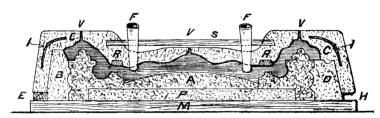

FIG. 98.—Section of Moulding Piece, with Jelly Mould, Plaster Pieces, and Case, for Panel.

the present example they are placed over the inner members of the panel mouldings at R, and are about $1\frac{1}{2}$ in. wide and $\frac{1}{2}$ in. thick, in suitable lengths, and are sloped on both edges for the case to draw. They are bedded $\frac{1}{4}$ in. in the thickness clay, allowing $\frac{1}{4}$ in. bed in both jelly and case. When bedded in the thickness clay the exposed part should be shellaced and oiled to prevent swelling and for the case to draw freely. When the case is removed, shellaced, and oiled, the unplaned rules are laid in the case (but not oiled, that the jelly may adhere) and temporarily fastened with screws.

The plaster pieces being strong and rigid, it is unnecessary to take the sides C down to the board or bench. Any depth or thickness is obtained by laying a rule up to the plaster pieces B, as at E. When the case is finished the rule leaves a grip for lifting the case, as at H. Large cases supporting heavy plaster pieces are strengthened by angle irons, as at I, about 3 ft. apart. Irons are also placed in each angle on plan. Wood stays, as at S, are put at intervals to stiffen the case for turning about. Cases for all moulds and plaster pieces should be made with a good inward slope, so that casts can be removed without turning over. Large casts are readily removed from an open mould by using " hand rules." The upper vents V should be 1 ft. apart and the lower ones 2 ft. apart, with one to each row at ends. The funnels F must be at the lowest parts, on each side of the centre if raised for the jelly to flow upwards, also in the centre of the lengths for the jelly to run both ways.

The foregoing description of methods and principles for the making of fibrous

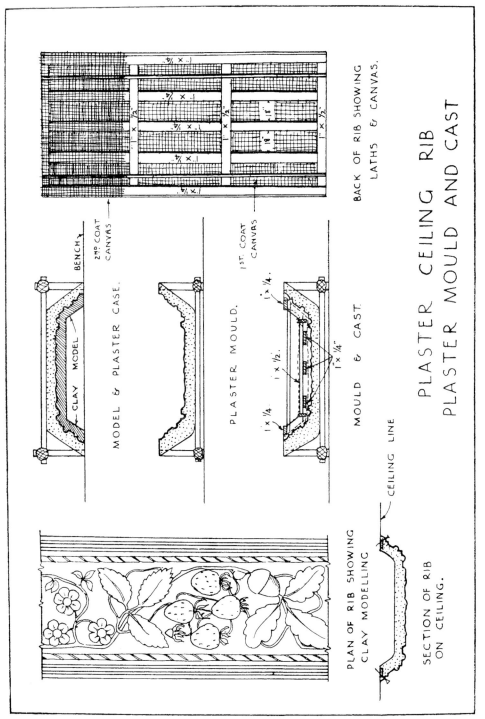

BACK OF RIB SHOWING LATHS & CANVAS.

BENCH
2ND COAT CANVAS

CLAY MODEL

MODEL & PLASTER CASE.

PLASTER MOULD.

1ST COAT CANVAS

1" × 1/4"

1" × 1/2"

1" × 1/4"

MOULD & CAST.

PLASTER CEILING RIB
PLASTER MOULD AND CAST

FIG. 99.

PLAN OF RIB SHOWING CLAY MODELLING

CEILING LINE

SECTION OF RIB ON CEILING.

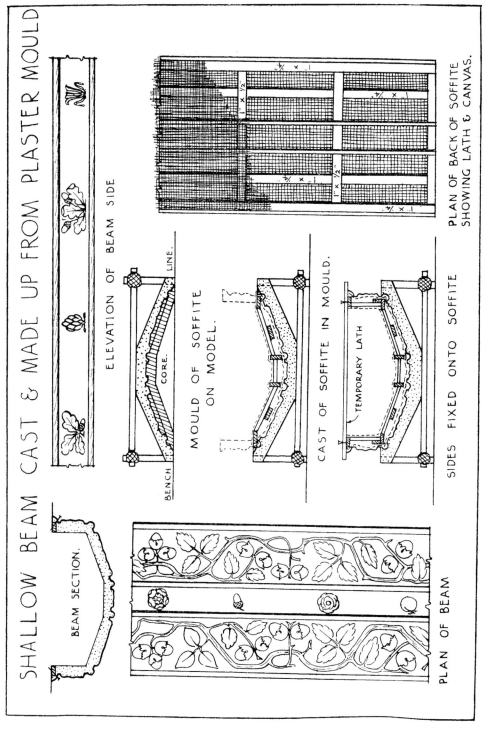

SHALLOW BEAM CAST & MADE UP FROM PLASTER MOULD

BEAM SECTION.

ELEVATION OF BEAM SIDE

MOULD OF SOFFITE ON MODEL.

BENCH.

CORE.

LINE.

CAST OF SOFFITE IN MOULD.

TEMPORARY LATH

SIDES FIXED ONTO SOFFITE

PLAN OF BACK OF SOFFITE SHOWING LATH & CANVAS.

PLAN OF BEAM

FIG. 100.

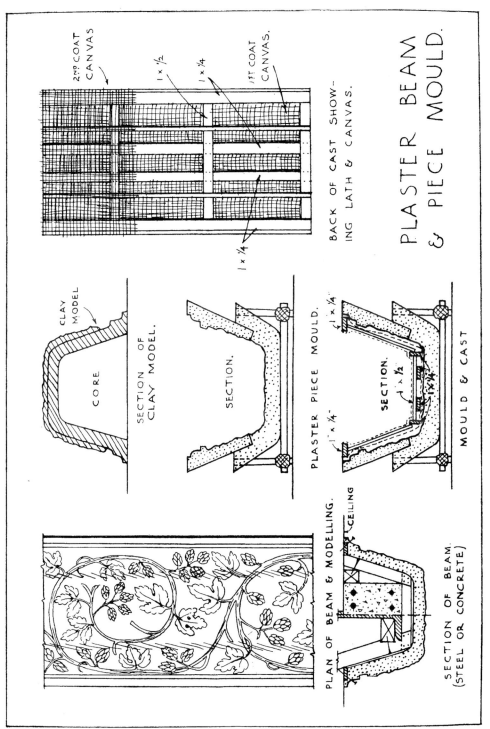

2ND COAT CANVAS

1 x ½

1 x ¼

1ST COAT CANVAS.

1 x ¼

BACK OF CAST SHOW-
ING LATH & CANVAS.

PLASTER BEAM
& PIECE MOULD.

CLAY MODEL

CORE

SECTION OF
CLAY MODEL.

SECTION.

PLASTER PIECE MOULD.

1 x ¼"

SECTION.

1 x ½

1 x ¼

1 x ¼"

MOULD & CAST

FIG. 101.

PLAN OF BEAM & MODELLING.

CEILING

SECTION OF BEAM.
(STEEL OR CONCRETE)

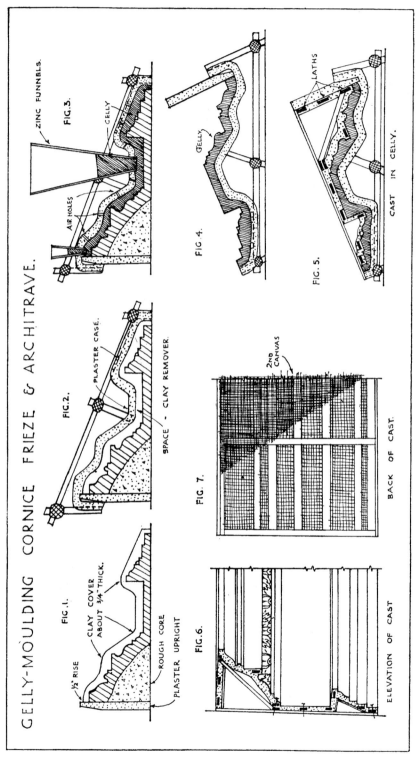

GELLY-MOULDING CORNICE FRIEZE & ARCHITRAVE.

FIG.1.

½ RISE
CLAY COVER ABOUT ¾" THICK.
ROUGH CORE
PLASTER UPRIGHT

FIG.2.

PLASTER CASE.
SPACE - CLAY REMOVER.

FIG.5.

ZINC FUNNELS.
AIR HOLES
GELLY

FIG.4.

GELLY

FIG.5.

LATHS
CAST IN GELLY.

FIG.7.

2ND CANVAS
BACK OF CAST.

FIG.6.

ELEVATION OF CAST

FIG. 102.

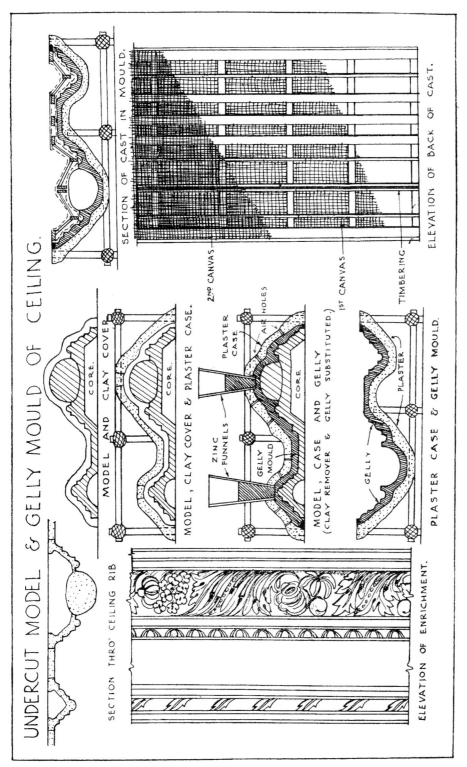

UNDERCUT MODEL & GELLY MOULD OF CEILING.

SECTION THRO' CEILING RIB

SECTION OF CAST IN MOULD.

ELEVATION OF BACK OF CAST.

2ND CANVAS

PLASTER CASE

AIR HOLES

1ST CANVAS

TIMBERING

CORE.

MODEL AND CLAY COVER.

CORE.

MODEL, CLAY COVER & PLASTER CASE.

ZINC FUNNELS

GELLY MOULD.

CORE.

MODEL, CASE AND GELLY
(CLAY REMOVER & GELLY SUBSTITUTED.)

GELLY

PLASTER

PLASTER CASE & GELLY MOULD.

FIG. 103.

ELEVATION OF ENRICHMENT.

plasterwork, viz., cases, jelly moulds, interchangeable moulds, combined jelly and plaster moulds, and fibrous plaster castings from them, are now universally put into practice for the production of modern fibrous plasterwork generally, whether plain or " ornamental," artistic or otherwise. The principles, once understood, are applied to the construction of all kinds of work—cornices, ceiling enrichments, beam casings, stanchions, columns or pilaster casings, modillion brackets, entire ceilings in sections, alcoves, domes, pendants, etc.

In supplement to the foregoing, further diagrams are given (Figs. 99-103) of some ceiling bands, ribs, beam sections, showing model, mould, case, cast, etc., under various shapes and conditions of the process of reproduction in fibrous plaster from plaster and jelly moulds. The latter is further referred to in Chapter XV on " Fibrous Plaster Moulds."

CHAPTER XV

FIBROUS PLASTERWORK

Patented and Introduced into England—Uses for Fibrous Plaster—For Renovating Old
Ceilings—Fibrous Plaster for Panelled Ceilings—Fibrous Plaster Nomenclature—
Materials—Cutting Canvas—Fibrous Plaster Wooden Laths—Size Water—Fibrous
Plaster Casting—Casting Plain Fibrous Plaster Columns and Pilasters—Casting Fibrous
Plaster Centre Flowers—Undercutting Fibrous Plaster—Fibrous Plaster Cornices—
Mitre and Joint Stops—Casting Fibrous Plaster Plain Cornices—Casting Fibrous Plaster
Enriched Cornices : Bedded Enrichment System—Moulding and Casting Fibrous
Enrichments—Casting Fibrous Plaster Enriched Cornices : Fixed and Cast Enrichment
Systems—Fixing Fibrous Plaster Cornices—Fibrous Plaster Measurements—Fire-
resisting Fibrous Plaster—Expanded Metal Lathing—Fibrous Plaster Decorative Sheets
—Muslin Plaster Casts—Tow and Plaster Casts—Rapid Plastering—Fibrous Plaster
Slabs—Fibrous Plaster Slab Moulds—Fibrous Plaster Slab Making—Setting Fibrous
Plaster Slabs—Fire-resisting Slabs—Combination Slabs—Patent Simplex Partition
Blocks—External Slabs—" Mack " Patent Fire-resisting Slabs—Reed Slabs—Grooved
Slabs—Perforated Slabs—Pugging and Deafening Slabs—Hardening and Damp-
proofing Fibrous Plaster Slabs—Litharge Oil—Fibrous Plaster Blocks.

Patented and Introduced into England.—Fibrous plaster was patented in 1856
by Leonard Alexander Desachy, a French modeller. The patent was for " producing
architectural mouldings, ornaments, and other works of art formed with surfaces of
plaster." The materials named are plaster, glue, oil, wood, wire, and canvas, or other
woven fabric. A part of the specification reads : " To facilitate the fixing of such
moulded surfaces to other surfaces, wires are, when required, laid into and between the
two or more layers of canvas. Flat surfaces are strengthened with canvas, wires, hooks,
or pieces of wood may be inserted whilst the plaster is in a fluid state." The specification
also includes the formation of solid slabs of plaster strengthened with two layers of
canvas in the centre. Desachy introduced the manufacture of fibrous plaster decorations
into London, where he employed a large number of hands, male and female. The
late Owen Jones, architect, and the author of " The Grammar of Ornament," was
the first patron of fibrous plaster. Desachy, after a precarious run of work, returned
to Paris. The business was then for a time carried on under the management of
J. M'Donald and R. Hanwell, respectively foreman and modeller to Desachy. When
Desachy retired from the business, he was pecuniarily indebted to Owen Jones, which
handicapped the efforts of M'Donald, and the business was eventually taken over by
a London firm, who acquired the then existing patents, and have since introduced many
improvements. Fibrous plasterworking is now open to all. Such is the history of
British fibrous plaster. It is an old saying, that " there is nothing new under the sun."
This may be safely applied to fibrous plaster, as the use of linen and canvas, in conjunction with plaster and glue, was known and practised by the Egyptians long before
the Christian era (as recorded in Chapter I).

While giving Desachy the honour of reviving the process and of introducing it into England, it is more than probable that he got the idea from some of the French writers—Reinaud, Prisse D'Avennes, Girault de Prangey, or others—who had very fully described and illustrated Egyptian arts and architecture. Coming nearer home, it will be found that canvas has been used for ages for another plastic purpose. Canvas and mortar were in everyday use in Great Britain up to the middle of last century as a heat-resisting plaster. It is still to a small extent employed in some districts, but its general use ceased after the introduction of Portland cement. Canvas was used as a binding power to prevent the mortar round wash-house coppers from cracking or expanding when subjected to heat. The mortar was composed of equal parts of haired lime and gritty road scrapings. Sometimes clay was substituted for the scrapings, but more often all the three stuffs were well worked together. The walls of the copper were rendered with this mortar and allowed to stand until the next day. Then it was floated with the same kind of stuff and, while soft, a sheet of strong, coarse canvas was laid over the mortar and pressed and patted with a hand-float into the mortar and then trowelled. I have found that this canvas plaster, after many years' wear and exposure to heat and damp, was extremely hard and tenacious when being pulled down for alterations.

"Fibrous plaster" is the term used for the manufacture of slabs, casings, and other forms by combining sulphate of lime, burnt or boiled gypsum, or plaster of Paris, with fibre composed of jute woven into an open-meshed canvas and strengthened or strutted with wood. It is chiefly used for casting purposes, as will be described in detail, from mould of plaster or gelatine. The castings, when made, are fixed into position with brass screws or nails, or secured to metal work construction with "wads" or bandages of canvas steeped in liquid plaster, which are wrapped round the metal and held until set hard and firm. This method of fixing is rigid and secure, and has never been known to fail.

Uses for Fibrous Plaster.—Fibrous plaster is an important branch of the plasterer's craft, and is now in great general request for the casing of modern forms of construction which, indeed, renders it essentially necessary and legitimate. It should not, however, be allowed to take the place of good "solid" plastering where this can and should be made use of in its own and equally legitimate place and manner. Its uses are so various that it has become general for works requiring lightness and rapidity of execution. It is fast superseding carton-pierre and papier-mâché, as it should, neither of them being properly plasterwork, but "compositions." Fibrous plaster is not only lighter and tougher than either, but it also can be made in much larger sections and adapted to more purposes. Large surfaces can be quickly covered without much preparation for fixing, as it is less than one quarter the weight of modern solid plaster, and it can, if required, be painted. Fibrous plaster was used in the Paris Exhibitions of 1878 and 1900 for the construction of the ceilings and walls of the principal edifices of the Exhibitions. Some of the panels were nearly 40 ft. square. The panels, with the enrichments, were composed of fibrous plaster, but tow was used instead of canvas or trellis cloth. In France it is known by the name of "*staff*," and the enrichments in their frames as *chassis en staff*. In the Victoria and Albert Museum, South Kensington, there is a large figure of Moses, taken from the marble original in the Church of San Pietro in Vincoli, Rome, executed 1541-53, by Michelangelo. This cast was made by the Desachy process, and weighs only 168 lbs. The ornamental plasterwork of the new Opera House in Paris has been made in *staff*. Fibrous plaster affords great facilities for the faithful reproduction of ancient or modern architectural or other works, either for temporary or permanent purposes. It was used for stage properties, notably for the column capitals in the Ducal Palace scene, when Miss Marie

Wilton produced " The Merchant of Venice " at the old Prince of Wales's Theatre. The caps for perspective purposes ranged from 3 ft. to 4 ft. 6 in. in height. The bells and the abacus and necking mouldings were composed of fibrous plaster and the enrichments modelled in plaster and tow. A combination of tow and canvas fibrous plaster (with iron wire instead of wood laths) was used for the ornamental parts of various built scenes at the Royal Theatre, Bradford ; also a fountain and other properties for Mr H. E. Abbey, when Miss Mary Anderson appeared as " Juliet," in 1884, at the Lyceum, London. Fibrous plaster has been successfully adapted for construction and decoration. It was used for constructing facsimiles of the temples of Saturn and Vespasian that stood near the " Roman Forum " in the grounds of the Italian Exhibition, London, 1888. The temple of Saturn, with its eight remaining columns and the entablature, was 33 ft. high. The temple of Vespasian, with its three remaining columns and cornice, was 38 ft. high, and was constructed from carefully measured drawings. After standing in the open air during the six months that the Exhibition was open, they were taken down, seemingly none the worse for the exposure, and sent to other exhibitions. For the casing of exhibition buildings all the world over, fibrous plaster has been used *ad libitum,* as also for the decoration of theatres, public and private buildings, and ships. Plaster and tow were used for modelling the Italian coat of arms, and a replica of the old Roman shield for the Exhibition Fine Art Galleries. The whole was made in the shop and then fixed in position. It is commonly used for triumphal arches in street decorations.

Renovating Old Ceilings.—Where old or cracked ceilings require strengthening and repair, fibrous plaster is admirably adapted. Old ceilings (that are loose and bagging down) can be renovated and held up without taking down the old plaster. A measured plan of the ceiling with the section of the main cornice and beam or other mouldings should be taken. From these measurements and profiles, a new design, or a copy of the old one, may be arranged to cover the old ceiling. The old work should be probed in places with a fine bradawl, to ascertain the positions of the joists and brackets. These positions are marked on the drawings, and corresponding laths for fixing purposes are laid in the new work while being made. The work should be made in convenient sections, with joints at the strongest and least noticeable parts. The design should, where possible, be arranged so that the joints are covered with mouldings and the screw holes with pateræ. Joints can also be made in the centre of the bed of enrichments, which is afterwards covered with the enrichment. With fibrous plaster enrichments made in lengths and fixed dry with fine nails, there is little damp or dust. Care must be taken to use only brass screws or nails when fixing fibrous plaster which is not quite dry, or situated in a humid or salt atmosphere, otherwise there is every risk of rust stains appearing and spreading everywhere a screw or nail happens to be. There is great risk even when the screws or nails are galvanised. This warning is given from experience on the coast, in one case necessitating the withdrawal of every iron fixing screw and nail, and the substitution of brass for the same, and the cutting out and making good of each stain. The salt seaside atmosphere was the cause of rust in one case. It must be remembered that plaster absorbs the atmosphere. The above precautions for the joints are especially requisite for work that has to be painted before being fixed. The joints in ordinary work can be stopped with gauged plaster or Parian cement in the usual way. The work is made in the plasterer's workshop, and when dry it is screwed on to the old plasterwork without disturbing the contents of the room or causing damp or dirt. The ceilings can also be painted and gilded before being fixed, if required, but are better done afterwards when possible.

For Renovating Old Ceilings.—Fibrous plaster is invaluable for the strengthening and repair of old solid plaster ceilings in which the wood laths have dry rotted away and caused the ceiling to part from the timbering above. Several very fine examples of Elizabethan ceilings on the verge of collapse have been saved and made secure by this means. The process has been to prop up the ceiling from beneath with planks, bearers, and scaffold poles, until the portions bagging have been brought up to the proper level. The work is then done from the top. After removing the floor boards immediately above, the accumulated rubbish must be cleared away and the rotten lathing removed. When this is done the hollows formerly occupied by the laths give a good rough " key " for grouting the top surface of the ceiling between the joists. This should be done with strong plaster of Paris, gauged with size, and lime putty. Whilst the grouting is wet, lay a layer of strong " scrim " or canvas between the joists. When this is thoroughly set, twisted wads of scrim steeped in plaster are fixed on the back surface at intervals of about 3 ft., the wads being looped over the wood joists or beams. The ends of the wads should be spread out on to the canvas about 12 in. and well dabbed down. It is not necessary to insert " butterfly " supports through the ceiling. When the wadding is set, spread another layer of canvas over the wads. The whole of the support is thus obtained from the back surface of the ceiling and the joists. When quite set, remove the planks and scaffolding, and the cracks caused by the bagging of the ceiling can be stopped with canvas packing and plaster and filled up.

The following illustrations of jute canvas or scrim are photographed large size from seven samples manufactured by Messrs Latto & Co., of London, and represent the meshes most generally in use (Plate CXIII).

For small castings Nos. 2, 3, and 5 are most suitable. For good general domestic work No. 1 is best, and for larger work Nos. 6 and 7 are made use of most.

Fibrous Plaster for Panelled Ceilings.—Fibrous plaster is now largely used for ceilings of all kinds, being cast in large sections and screwed on the joists, thus dispensing with the ordinary lath and plaster. " Finished face slabs " are also used in a similar way, the joints covered with fibrous mouldings or ribs, thus forming plain panelled ceilings at small cost. This method may also be used for covering and enriching plain or old ceilings without disturbing the existing lath and plaster. Fibrous plaster is now extensively used for casing wood or iron beams and girders ; the casing, plain or enriched, can be made, if necessary, the entire length of the beams, thus avoiding joints. Fibrous plaster is also used for casing columns and pilasters. Columns are made in two vertical halves and screwed together over the iron or brick core, and the joints then stopped.

It will be seen that fibrous plaster can be adapted for many purposes, and that its uses are unlimited for plain and decorative plastic work. It is also a good and ready substitute for wood casing and for decorating rough or constructional surfaces. Fibrous plaster, made in the shop and dried before being fixed, obviates delay by frost or inclement weather. Where time is a principal consideration this method has a decided advantage. Fibrous plaster will never properly take the place of the old-fashioned lath and plaster (or " solid work," as it is termed), but its utility for many purposes and places is fully recognised.

Fibrous Plaster Nomenclature.—Some of the existing terms used in connection with fibrous work are confusing, and apt to be mistaken for those used in the more familiar branches of the trade. It is therefore imperative for clearness and for future reference that each part and process should be properly named. Existing names that are not conflicting will be retained. Terms for unnamed parts and new names for old ones will be given with due regard to applicability and brevity. These will be readily understood by the present proficient workers in fibrous plaster.

Materials.—The materials for general fibrous plasterwork are plaster, canvas, size, and wood laths. Wire netting, galvanised iron wire, tow, jute, fibre, sawdust, reeds, slag wool, wood wool, Portland cement, slag, coke breeze, and other aggregates are used for special purposes. These are described under their respective headings. The plaster used for this work should be strong and slow setting. Coarse plaster, if strong and not sandy, may be used for some purposes, such as making up edges, also for parts of " fibro slabs." Canvas for fibrous plaster should be strong, coarse, and open meshed. It should be strong to resist stains and pressure ; coarse, so that the plaster will adhere to it ; and open, so that the plaster will go freely through the meshes when brushed. The size of the mesh varies from $\frac{1}{16}$ in. to $\frac{1}{8}$ in., according to the class of work in hand, the small mesh being used for fine or small casts, and the larger mesh for general work. A still coarser and more open kind is used for some kinds of fibro slabs. Canvas for fibrous plaster is generally supplied in the No. 3 quality and in 52 in. and 72 in. widths. Canvas is also known by the name of " scrim," and is principally made in Dundee, from specially prepared jute yarns, to resist the process of decay. The nature of the fibre from which the yarns are made necessitates careful treatment in the preparation, previous to spinning.

Cutting Canvas.—There is a knack in cutting canvas. Cutting by scissors is slow work. The canvas should be unrolled and doubled flat in as many plies as can be conveniently cut through at one draw of the knife. Some men cut through twelve thicknesses at once. It is generally done on a soft wood board, but it is cleaner and better done on a piece of plate glass bedded (with plaster) into a wood frame. The knife (sharpened on a rough sandstone) has a slightly toothed edge, which severs the meshing better than a fine edge. Sufficient canvas should be cut to last for a day or two.

Fibrous Plaster Laths.—These should be cut from " seconds " pine, redwood, or from any old wood that will not twist or warp. Laths are cut in various lengths and thicknesses, according to the size and weight of the work on hand, and must be left rough from the saw. To save time and confusion, the various kinds are named and described as required for the various works. Laths are used for strutting and strengthening the work, and also for fixing purposes.

Size Water.—Size water should be clean to ensure strength, and it is best when made with good glue and clean water. It should be tested by measuring a given quantity with a given quantity of clean water, and then gauging a small amount of plaster to determine whether it sets too quickly or too slowly. Suitable measures should be kept ready for measuring both waters. Cream of tartar is also used to retard the setting of plaster.

Fibrous Plaster Casting.—The process of casting fibrous plasterwork, although simple, requires care and method in manipulation. Great attention must be given to the gauging of the plaster and the time of setting noted. Never begin gauging until all the necessary canvas and laths are cut to the required sizes. When these are different, place each to hand in a separate place to save time and confusion. Place the cut canvas where it will be free from dust and plaster splashes. Cleanliness and care cannot be too strongly enforced ! Always cut more canvas and wood than is actually required for a day's work, in case of unforeseen incidents. The size water should be tested and timed. The annexed sketch (Fig. 104, No. 1) shows the mould of a plain panel with the laths and a part of the canvas in position. The panel is 3 ft. long, 1 ft. wide, and 1 in. thick, with a plain band 2 in. wide. M, M are the top and side of the rim of the mould. The mould's rims are the ruling-off edges. The side and end laths F, F are $1\frac{1}{2}$ in. by $\frac{1}{4}$ in. A $\frac{1}{4}$ in. space at each side and end should be allowed for plaster and canvas. The canvas is cut into sheets, allowing a margin of 4 in. wide at the sides and ends for turning back over the laths and on to the surface, as shown at C. This margin, when turned over, tightens a part of the surface canvas and binds the laths together. Two layers of canvas should be used for good class work. It sometimes happens that the thickness of a cast will not allow of both sheets being turned over. In such cases cut the second sheet to the size of the cast, with just sufficient margin to reach the outer sides of the laths. Care must be taken to cut the canvas at the external angles, so that it will lie flat over each lath, without increasing the thickness at the angles A. The small square pieces that are cut out of the angles are useful for covering lath joints and a variety of other purposes. If space permits, the angles of the canvas may be cut diagonally, as shown at B. The first lot of canvas and laths should be tentatively laid loose in the mould, to avoid mistakes. The mould is then carefully greased, great care being taken to use as little oil or grease as may be absolutely necessary to prevent adhesion of the plaster to the mould. It is a common practice to put on too much grease. A careless workman will often ruin a mould in this manner by partially filling up surface modelling with an over-abundance of grease, by scrubbing the surface of a mould when washing, or by rough handling in other ways. Then gauge as much plaster—without size water—as will cover the surface of the mould barely $\frac{1}{8}$ in. thick. This gauge is called " firsts," and is brushed over the mould to expel

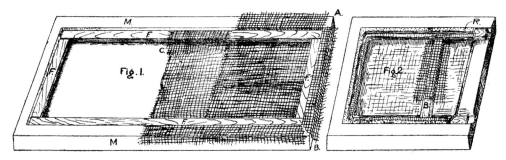

FIG. 104.—(1) Panel Mould, showing Filling in of a Fibrous Plaster Cast; (2) Portion of Mould with Cast nearly Finished.

the air. The next coat is called " seconds," and is gauged with size water to give time to lay on and brush the canvas before the plaster sets. The two gauges should be mixed at one time, so that the " firsts " will not be set before the " seconds " can be applied. When the " firsts " is slightly firm, or " tacky," a small portion of " seconds " is poured on and lightly brushed over the " firsts," so as to bind the two coats together, but without disturbing the thickness of the " firsts." For delicate work the " seconds " is gently splashed on with a tool brush. This tends to bind the two coats with less brushing.

Great care must be taken that the " firsts " is not set before the " seconds " is put on and brushed; also that the " seconds " is not set when the first sheet of canvas is put on. This is one of the great secrets of success in casting fibrous plaster. If the two coats of plaster are not properly incorporated, the " firsts " will be left in the mould. If the canvas is not properly worked and brushed into the " seconds," both will be left in the mould and the casts will be useless. Having properly laid and brushed the two coats, lay the first sheet of canvas, allowing the margin to lie over the rim of the mould. Press the canvas down into the angles at the sides and ends, also into any sunk parts of the mould with the fingers, beginning in the middle of the canvas piece, so as to work the air outwards and to prevent creases in the canvas. Then, using the fingers of the left hand for pressing the canvas more accurately into the hollows, with the right hand take a gauge brush, dip it into the gauge pot containing the " seconds," and brush all over the canvas until the surface plaster and the canvas are well knit together. The second sheet follows in a similar way, care being taken that the first is moist. If dry, brush it over with " seconds," to give a good binding key for the new sheet. If the size or shape of the mould necessitates several pieces of canvas to cover the surface, lay each piece to lap about 2 in. over the edge of the previous one. Make the joints of the second coat of canvas in the same way, but at the centres of the first coat pieces. Lapping and breaking the joints makes the cast stronger, thinner, and more uniform. The canvas margin that lies over the mould rim is left unbrushed with plaster until the laths are laid. The laths must be dipped in, or brushed over with " seconds," and laid in place, after the bed of each has been brushed with " seconds." Turn the canvas margin back over the laths and well press and brush into all angles. Do one side at a time and fold the external angles closely together. When the margins are finished, stiffen a little " seconds " with dry plaster and make up the edge of the cast flush with the mould rim, as shown at R (No. 2). Make the edges $\frac{1}{2}$ in. to 1 in. wide ; rule fair with the mould rims, and leave a smooth edge and a true bearing for fixing purposes. Strengthen casts with extra thick rims by placing the laths on edge, or by doubling the laths. Thick edges may be composed of strips of canvas dipped in plaster and brushed in position. Tow and plaster make a strong edging. Turn all canvas margins back over the rim laths, or on to themselves, to strengthen the edges before the plaster sets ; if set, the canvas will not turn over so freely, or fit the laths or angles. The plaster is also apt to lift from the face of the mould. Sometimes the canvas and plaster get above the level of the rim When this happens, trim the rim flush with a sharp knife after being set.

No. 2 shows part of a mould with cast, side laths, and made up rim of cast. B is a " body lath " with canvas strip unbrushed. Body laths are to strengthen large casts. Canvas strips should be cut wide enough to cover the laths, with about 2 in. on each side. When filling in large casts, more than one gauge of " seconds " may be required. Put aside a small portion of each gauge as a guide as to when the under coats are set. The cast must not be taken out till all is set, If the setting is properly timed by the size water, this is unnecessary. Fibrous casts containing a small body thickness of plaster are strong and flexible and with little or no expansion ; the casts are much more easily released from the mould than " solid " casts. The laths or canvas are brushed with " seconds." All classes of fibrous plaster are made on the foregoing method. As a further aid to the novice, the manufacture of ornamental castings in fibrous plaster is given hereafter.

Casting Plain Fibrous Plaster Columns and Pilasters.—Fig. 105 shows elevations, half-sections, and plans of a fibrous plaster column and pilaster. The plans show the placing of the laths at the base and neck of shaft, the same laths being indicated on elevations by dotted lines. The vertical laths should be $1\frac{1}{4}$ in. by $\frac{1}{2}$ in., the short laths $1\frac{1}{2}$ in. by $\frac{1}{2}$ in., 2 ft. 6 in. apart, and the intermediate laths 1 in. by $\frac{1}{2}$ in., placed " herring-bone " fashion.

The column would be cast in two halves, the entire length from bottom of base to the top of the first fillet of necking. Plans at base and necking of a pilaster are likewise shown. Pilasters vary somewhat in projection, but the usual proportion is either one-half or one-third of the width of shaft at its base. Three laths only are used vertically. A lath at the angles of pilaster is apt to shrink and crack the face of the plaster, and for this reason is better omitted.

Cross-bracing laths should be placed diagonally at about 2 ft. 6 in. spacing from under the $1\frac{1}{2}$ in. by $\frac{1}{2}$ in. edge lath to the opposite angle.

To Cast a Fibrous Plaster Centre Flower.—Circular ceiling ornaments known as " centre flowers " were extensively used and are still to be found in most

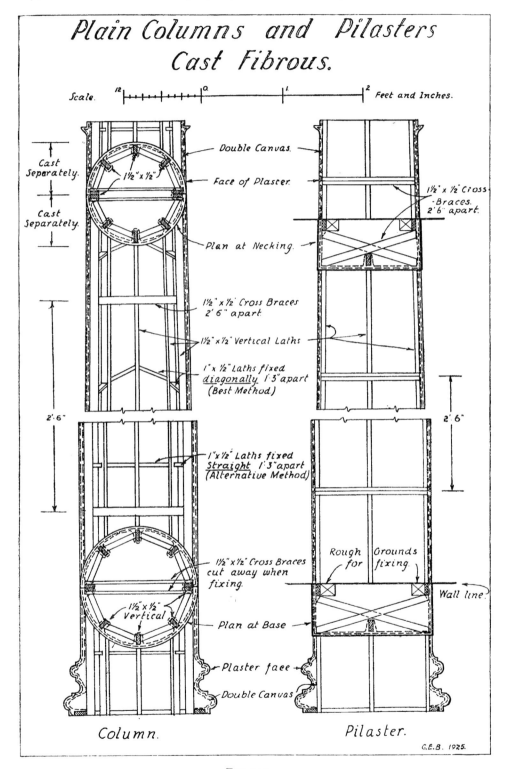

FIG. 105.

PLATE CXIII

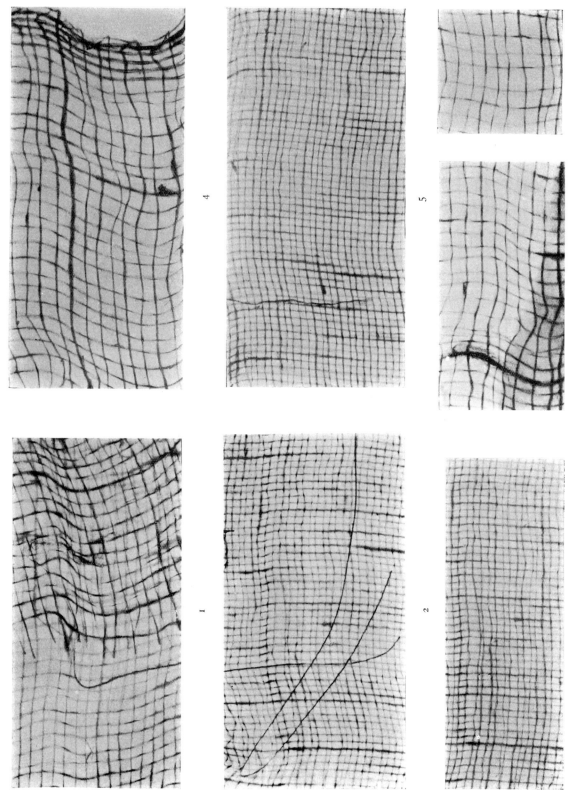

SEVEN EXAMPLES OF CANVAS, ENLARGED TO SHOW MESH.

PLATE CXIV

THREE EXAMPLES OF LATE AND POOR DESIGN. (FIRST HALF OF NINETEENTH CENTURY.)

(b) and (c) FROM ACKLAM HALL, YORKSHIRE.

(a) FROM MELTON CONSTABLE, NORFOLK.

houses of the Victorian era. The plasterer's trade was then at its lowest ebb, and devoid of every artistic sense or capability ; as most other branches of the building trade were, plaster "ornaments" at that time were irretrievably bad in design and modelling. The art and craft of decorations was then dead and putrid. All the same, a great deal of very elaborate work was made in plaster, and the "centre flower" was considered perhaps the crowning masterpiece of plasterer's work at that time. As the fault lay not so much with the plasterer as with the designer and modeller (two separate trades), and as the same part of the ceiling might under different circumstances have been as beautifully designed, modelled, and cast as it was done badly, we will

FIG. 106.—Typical Victorian Centre Flower "Horrors" in Plaster.

not altogether expunge a description of the process of casting from these pages. It is enough to say that with the revival of architecture the plasterer's craft also improved in taste, so that the "centre flower," as it was then known, has become a thing of the past, now rarely used and better forgotten. The average plasterer of to-day is sufficiently educated to know and feel this. But some abominations "die hard." For the guidance of students it should be explained that with the exception of the art of picture painting, most art was then dormant, if not dead. Any attempt at "decoration" was then (for the want of a better name) pictorial, or "naturalistic" in character. Mechanism was growing and pervaded everything. The aim of the plasterer, then, was to make everything as smooth, clean, and sharp as possible. Plaster ornament was not understood, apart from the mechanism of reproduction, which was done with a fatal and misdirected mechanical skill more suitable to glass cutting. Apart from this, "design" was not understood; the proper use of the material of plaster was not understood, and the result of all attempt to use it "decoratively" was consequently purely mechanical and artistically bad. "Bad" is a mild expression to use. Plaster "ornaments," such as "centre flowers" and cornices, were usually sharply carved from a draughtsman's "designs," either in wood or plaster, and then reproduced in plaster by casting. Fig. 106 and Plate CXIV give some general idea of the work of the period. This type of work was not modelled, as it should have been, in clay. Clay may sometimes have been used, but when it was, the process of carving was applied to its shaping. The following description of making and casting from a mould of wax

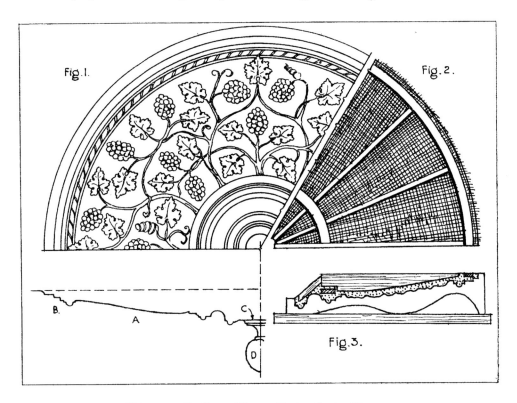

FIG. 107.—Casting a Fibrous Plaster Centre Flower.

might be useful, but wax is superseded by the jelly process, which is fully described elsewhere. Fig. 103 shows the jelly mould, slipper, and cast. Otherwise the two processes are identical. The annexed sketch, Fig. 107, illustrates one method of casting a fibrous "centre flower" in a wax mould, 3 ft. in diameter. A portion of the plan, with section, is shown in No. 1. Take this section to distinguish the various parts of the centre flower. A is the body, B the border, C the centre, and D the seed, or drop. In the old "solid cast work" the border is cast separately in short lengths. In fibrous work the border is cast with the body. It will be seen that the centre C is cast separately. A bed, as shown on the section, is made on the body to fix the centre to. This method saves a considerable quantity of wax when moulding, especially if the centre has a deep projection. It also gives greater freedom for handling the model when moulding, and the mould and cast when casting. The seed D is also moulded separately first, because it is often dispensed with when a metal rose is used with the fittings ; and second, to allow the centre to be moulded in one piece.

No. 2 shows a portion of the wax mould of the body with a portion of the canvas, and plaster and laths in position. The inner and outer rim laths, which are plainly shown, are $1\frac{3}{4}$ in. wide, $\frac{1}{4}$ in. thick, and as long as can be cut out of a deal board. The outside radius should be $\frac{1}{4}$ in. less than the mould rims, to allow a space for the plaster and the canvas to be turned up and over the laths. Cut sufficient rim laths to complete the circles, and extra pieces to overlap the joints. The joints need not butt accurately, any little inequality being made up with plaster and canvas, or, if space permits, covered with overlapping pieces. Large flowers, or those with deep sections, require six, eight, and even ten ribs to strengthen them. The ribs for this size of flower are $\frac{3}{8}$ in. thick, but ribs up to 1 in. are used for large ones. Ribs $\frac{1}{8}$ in. thick are used for smaller and thinner flowers than the above. The outer rim lath for this one is cut to a radius that will give the most depth, to allow the ribs and the " point laths " to overlap.

No. 3 is a section through half of the mould. The canvas should be cut in eight radiating pieces, allowing 2 in. at each side and 4 in. beyond the outer and inner rim laths. Small pieces of canvas are required for the border at H. The border pieces are cut to the general outline. It is not necessary that the pieces should be cut accurately to fit all the curves. If the edges are deep, leave a margin to be turned over ; and if thick, turn over straggling edges, making up any little parts with small pieces of canvas. Galvanised iron wire, bent to the contour of the outer line of the cast, is sometimes used to strengthen thin or tender parts of casts. Cut sufficient laths and canvas, and oil and wash the mould. Gauge the " firsts," and carefully brush into the sunk-in parts, and then the " seconds " as before. Lay the border pieces of canvas first, brush and press into the angles of the outline of the border, and make up any uncovered parts with small pieces. Next lay the canvas for the body one piece at a time to overlap, leaving the rim margins unbrushed. Lay the rim laths in position, and brush them and their beds as before. Turn over and brush the margins. Lay the four rib laths, cover with canvas strips, and brush. Lay canvas and brush the point laths, and make up outer rim and rule off flush. Put plaster and canvas dots on the top edges of the inner rib laths, and rule flush with the outer mould rim. The dots are to prevent the cast from drooping in the centre while drying, and also keep the cast in shape when screwed up. Should the canvas not overlap enough to complete two layers, make up with small pieces and brush. Then brush over the whole surface with " seconds," to bind all the margins together and finish off. Place the wax mould in warm water until it becomes pliable ; take out and ease round the rim and take the cast gently out. Large wax moulds which cannot be put in hot water may be softened by pouring hot water over the back of the cast, or by fomentation with old sacks or canvas.

Undercutting Fibrous Plaster.—It is often desirable to undercut some parts, such as fruit, flowers, and foliage, which have been stopped down on the model to allow a wax mould to draw ; and as fibrous plaster is thin and difficult to cut clean, it is necessary to make provision for this. This is done by first stiffening a portion of " seconds " with dry plaster, and then working it with a small tool round the proposed undercut parts in the mould, and before this is set the mould is filled in as before. If the undercut parts in the model are large, it is best to make plaster pieces at the parts before the mould is made. The small seams caused by the joints at the plaster pieces are easily taken off with a small tool or a fine file. Undercutting by hand is the best way for small parts. The work is more free, and less mechanical in appearance when done by hand.

Fibrous Plaster Cornices.—Mouldings of any considerable length may be made in fibrous plaster. They are generally made in 8 ft. to 18 ft. lengths, or in convenient lengths for two or three casts to make up the length of a room. For example, if a room is 33 ft. by 20 ft., the mould would be made 13 ft. long, out of which would be cast three 11 ft. pieces to make up the full lengths of each side, and two 10 ft. lengths for each end of the room. Short pieces are cast out of the same mould. The mould is made longer than the longest cast required, to allow a bed for the " mitre stops " that are used for forming internal and external mitres, and also for square butt joints on the casts, hence the reason for the above mould being 13 ft. The extra length of mould is regulated by the projection of the cornice. Fibrous plaster cornices are often cast in " reverse moulds." This useful part of plastic " art " should be mastered before attempting the casting of fibrous plasterwork. A quick way of producing fibrous plaster enriched cornices is by the use of jelly moulds. A moulding piece is first made by running a length of moulding, preferably in clay, for new work, on a bench, then fixing the enrichments, keeping both ends jointed. The model is then cased, moulded, and the casts made.

Mitre and Joint Stops.—Mitre stops being required before the cornice cast is made, the method of making them is given first. Mitre stops are made of plaster, and are used as fences to form mitres and joints in cornices, etc. They are laid on the casting mould, and being movable, any desired length of cornice (less than the length of the mould) can be made, and each length with any desired form of mitre or joint at both ends of the cast.

No. 2, in Fig. 108, shows the method of making mitre and square joint stops. It also shows the section of a " reverse " mould for a plain cornice, about $7\frac{1}{2}$ in. by $7\frac{1}{2}$ in., with sections of the laths used for the cornice cast. LHE is a left-hand external mitre stop; LHI is a left-hand internal mitre stop; and S is a square joint or butt stop. Right-hand mitres are, of course, cut to the opposite angles. Mitre stops are made by first covering a sufficient length of the mould with damp paper over the contour of the mouldings. The paper allows the plaster piece to leave the mould freely and prevents chipping. Gauged plaster is then laid on the papered surface to the desired thickness and ruled square with the mould rims. If wood rules are laid flat on the rims to act as fences, no ruling off is required. The plaster (for small mouldings) is made up to the square of the rim lines, so that the mitre stops will act as ruling-off bearings, or points for proving the square of the cast when being filled in. When mitre stops are not made up to the square, boards cut to the square are fixed at the mitre stops as guides for testing the squareness of the casts. This is only necessary where the space between the mould's surface and the square of the rims will only admit of the laths and a sufficient thickness of plaster and canvas, which makes up the cast nearly to the square of the rims, as shown by the sections and the dotted lines in Nos. 3, 4, and 5. Where there is ample space and the laths well within the square, as shown in No. 2, a thickness of from 2 in. to 3 in. will give sufficient strength for the stops and width of bearing for ruling off or testing the square of the cast. After the plaster piece is taken off, the various lengths of the stops are set out and sawn to the required angles. The mitres are best sawn in a mitre box. Each stop should be lettered to save confusion. All measurements for stops and cornices should be taken from the wall line. If the cornice is large, or has acute angles, or is difficult to draw in places, the stops must be made in two or more longitudinal sections.

To Cast Fibrous Plaster Plain Cornices.—Fig. 108 also shows a method of casting plain cornices having various profiles. No. 1 shows a reverse mould (in plaster) on a running board, with the plaster, canvas, and laths in position. This cornice has a ceiling projection of 12 in. and a wall depth of $10\frac{1}{2}$ in. RB is the running board or bench; S is the section of the mould, the dotted part being the plaster or clay; CR is the " ceiling rim "; and WR is the " wall rim " of the mould. These rims, the

" striking-off edges " of the mould, represent the ceiling and wall lines. No laths, canvas, or plaster must protrude beyond the square of these lines. The ceiling and wall lines indicated by the dotted lines in Nos. 2, 3, 4, and 5 are horizontal and perpendicular respectively. FP (No. 1) is the first coat of plaster and canvas. The unbrushed canvas margin lies over the mould rims and on the board, ready to be turned over when the ceiling and wall laths are laid in position. The various laths, before being canvased and brushed, are also shown in position. C is a " ceiling lath "; W a " wall lath "; and B a " body lath." The ceiling and wall laths are about 2 in. by $\frac{1}{4}$ in., and the length of the cast. Larger cornices require thicker and wider laths. The body lath is about 2 in. by $\frac{3}{4}$ in. The extra thickness is to enable the lath to better carry the weight of the cornice until fixed ; two or more ceiling or wall laths may be used to make up the desired thickness of a centre body lath. Larger cornices require two

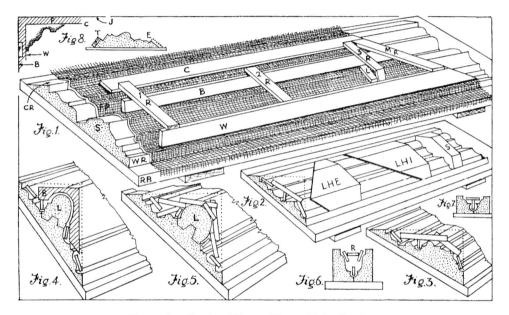

FIG. 108.—Casting Fibrous Plaster Plain Cornices.

or more body laths ; the centre (main) lath should be placed on edge at a prominent square member, as at B. This secures the most strength for the cast, and strengthens the part which is most handled in fixing. R shows the " rib laths." No. 1 overlaps and No. 2 butts against the ceiling and wall laths, forming a lap and butt joint alternately, thus giving greater strength. It sometimes happens that space will not permit of overlapping joints ; butt joints are then compulsory. With rough laths and canvas, well and closely laid and brushed, the joints will not come asunder where there is no great weight or strain. It requires considerable force to pull a well-brushed piece of canvas off a rough lath. No. 3 shows a rib lath in two pieces, a plan adopted when the cornice will not allow a single straight lath. The joint is strengthened by means of a " lap lath " L. Where space is limited, the lap lath is placed against the joint ; but where space permits, a stronger joint is obtained by placing it over the joint. MR, a " mitre lath," is placed to strengthen the mitre. Rib laths vary from 2 ft. to 5 ft. apart, according to the strength requisite to support the moulding. Rib laths take the place of cornice brackets, connect the ceiling and wall laths, and stiffen the whole moulding.

Thin laths, laid flat, are sometimes used to strengthen the splayed edges of mitres. In order to show the position of the mitre laths more clearly, the " mitre stop " is omitted.

Having shellaced the mould and stops, set out on the mould the length of the proposed cast, fix the stops with clay, and grease the whole surface. Cut the necessary quantity of laths and canvas, lay in a convenient place, and keep each kind and size separate, to save time and confusion. Cut two sheets of canvas the length and width of the mould, allowing a margin overlapping the ceiling and wall laths. Measure the length of the canvas with a rod and the width with a string, following the contour of the mouldings. Cut an ample quantity of long and short canvas strips to cover the body and rib laths, and a number of small pieces to cover lap and butt joints. Gauge and lay the " firsts " and " seconds," and lay and brush the first sheet of body canvas as before. Lay each sheet to follow the contour of the mould and leave an equal margin at the mould rims. Press and brush from the centre of the mould and work outwards. Lay the second sheet in a similar way. Lay the ceiling and wall laths in position, keeping them close to the mould rims, to strengthen the outside edges of the cast. Lay them in place for strength and position for screwing through when fixing the cast. Turn over the margins, press into the angles, and brush. Lay the body laths, taking care that their positions give strength. Where practicable, laths should be laid flat and on edge alternately ; it gives resisting force to strains and weights.

When the body laths are canvased and brushed, the rib and mitre laths are laid, canvased, and brushed. Cover all lath joints with extra strips and well brush. Make up the rims of the cast or bearing parts at the ceiling and wall lines, and rule off flush with the mould rims. When the laths can be got close to and nearly flush with the mould rims, the canvas and plaster alone will make up the cast rims. When all is set, remove the stops, ease the cast at the ends, and take it out of the mould and place on a straight board to dry. Should the cast warp slightly, it will come straight in fixing. Warping is usually caused by inferior laths and too rapid or unequal drying. If excessive, or straight from the mould, weight the cast down or screw to a straight board until dry.

No. 3 shows the section of a reverse mould for a plain cornice, 1 ft. by 6 in. deep. The positions and sections of the rib laths are all shown in their positions, as already described.

No. 4 shows the section of a reverse cornice mould, 9 in. by 15 in. deep. Two body laths are required for this size and form of moulding. Brackets are sometimes used in place of rib laths for such curved work as this. Cut brackets to overlap or butt up to the longitudinal laths, as shown by the bracket B. Large brackets are made up in two or more pieces of timber, but are seldom used for general work. Small curves are made up with short laths, as in No. 5. L is a loose piece in the mould, requisite in this section for withdrawing purposes, and is made with a keyed joint, to keep it in position while the cast is being filled in.

No. 5 shows a reverse mould 12 in. by 12 in. This requires a loose piece, as at L. The laths also show. The curve of the cove is made up with short laths, according to the size of cove. This is only given to illustrate the general principle of forming curved ribs where brackets are not obtainable.

No. 6 shows a rib moulding (4 in. by 4½ in.) and laths. R is a rib lath, every 3 ft. to 4 ft. Two longitudinal laths are used for small mouldings, in the form of a T, as No. 7. The top lath supplants the rib laths and is used for fixing through.

No. 8, the section of a cornice, having little thickness at the ceiling and wall faces, is given to illustrate a method of gaining space, to allow thickness for ceiling and wall laths, where the members are otherwise too thin. It may also be resorted to where an increased thickness of laths is required, to give greater strength for large work. B is the brick (or other) wall face ; J the joist line ; P lime plaster ; F a wood fillet for fixing purposes ; C the finished ceiling line ; and W the finished plaster face. Extra thickness is obtained by extending the outer lines of the ceiling and wall members, as shown by the dotted line at E in No. 9, when setting out the reverse mould, or by laying a rule on the rims, as. at T. The extra thickness must not exceed the brick face and joist level, and be fixed on to the same. All sketches of fibrous cornices here given are taken from the finished ceiling and wall faces. In each case there is space for all laths.

To Cast Fibrous Plaster Enriched Cornices : Bedded Enrichment System.—Enriched cornices are best cast in reverse plaster moulds. The method is expeditious, accurate, and clean. Enrichments in cornices may be " bedded," " fixed," and " cast." Each process possesses merit advantageous to special purposes.

Fig. 109 shows the method of casting enriched cornices in fibrous plaster by bedding ; also the method of " moulding " and " casting " fibrous enrichments. No. 1 shows an enriched fibrous plaster cornice about 1 ft. 5 in. in projection by 11 in. deep, with enrichments " bedded." No. 2, an enlarged section of the reverse mould, showing the fibrous enrichments, Nos. 4, 7, 12, and 9, and laths laid in position. The numbers in No. 2 correspond with the respective moulds of the enrichments, Nos. 4, 7, 12, and 9. The dotted lines indicate the back surface of the casts, which is made rough.

After all the enrichments are cast, lay them in the cornice mould, arrange the joints and mitres, and fix the casts with small plaster dots, as No. 2. Cut canvas strips the length of the cornice mould, and as wide as will cover the girth of the plain members between the enrichments, with a margin to lie over the joints and on the enrichments. Two strips are also required to cover the plain member at the ceiling and wall lines, allowing a margin to be turned over the laths. Lay the long strips and brush as before. Lay a second canvas coat in the same way, and turn over and brush the margins at the ceiling and wall lines C and W. Insert three body laths B, B, B, canvas, and brush ; then the two rib laths R, R, and the top lath L as before. (Some men lay the canvas over all the plain and enriched members in one sheet, following on with another sheet. This may be good for large mouldings and enrichments, but it is an unnecessary waste, there being four canvas coats over the enriched members, besides another coat for the body laths.) Lay two long canvas strips over the enrichments and well brush. The two long canvas strips and the laths give ample strength for ordinary sized cornices, such as No. 2. In large cornices, laths are laid in the cavities of the dentils, as at Z, Z, from the inner face angles to the rib lath, each way, at right angles, and connected with the rib laths at intervals. The amount of timber required for fibrous cornices will not nearly equal that required for bracket and lath of solid cornice work of equal girth. Common-sense judgment is necessary for spacing the laths to obtain the greatest possible strength. A lath $1\frac{1}{2}$ in. by $\frac{1}{4}$ in., fixed in proper place and angle, will afford as much strength as one twice the size laid thoughtlessly. Laths laid to connect others, such as rib laths, are canvased and brushed round the laths and the body of the cast only, leaving the spaces between the laths and the cast quite clear. In many cases canvas strips bound round the ends of the laths, and where they touch the cast well brushed over, will be sufficient. In pen drawings, sections of solid plaster mould-ings are shaded by parallel lines. In this and the following diagrams crossed line shading indicates fibrous plaster. Architects use colours to distinguish the different materials of their sections, but this cannot readily be done in a book of this character.

Moulding Fibrous Plaster Enrichments.—Moulds for casting low relief enrichments were formerly made of wax or plaster, gelatine being now used for under-cut work. Wax moulds were made in lengths from 3 ft. to 5 ft. long for small work, and from 5 ft. to 10 ft. in plaster, or even 12 ft. in some cases. There is no reasonable limit to the lengths, as fibrous casts may be got out the full length of the cornice. If need be, moulds are made by casting and putting together as many repeats as will make up the required length. They are fixed on a bench ground according to the length of mould required. For bedded work, the plain members on each side of the enrichment are run on the bench. Joints must be carefully made, so that there will be no trimming on the casts, as the canvas comes close to the surface and edges, and cannot be trimmed so neatly as solid plaster. Fibrous casts are made much thinner than solid plaster casts. If the section at the joints is deep or undercut, when using wax, make a plaster piece, as shown at P, No. 14, Fig. 109, to allow the mould and the cast to withdraw, and form fitting ends to the casts, as described for a jointed mould in Chapter XIII. A long mould is best made with wood sides and ends to strengthen and keep it straight. Ordinary laths or running rules are used, and are let in while the material is soft. The wax, plaster, or gelatine, as the case may be, adheres to the wood fences, thus giving strength. When the moulds are done with, the wood is freed from the mould and kept for future use. These moulds are termed "framed moulds." The sides and ends of the frame should be nailed or wadded together in position.

No. 3 shows the sections through the moulding fences and wax mould of the dentil, on the moulding board M B. G is the ground of the moulding piece. B is the "backing" which carries the dentils D, forming a "lapping part" of the plain members at the top and bottom of the dentil. The lapping parts keep the casts in position while being canvased and brushed, and make a better joint than if made at angles, or at the joints of plain and enriched members. The backing and lapping parts will be further understood by comparing B B, No. 5, which is a sectional view of the cast, with No. 2. The sections of the plaster moulding pieces on all the figures are indicated by a dotted surface, as also applies to the plaster fences F F, No. 3. The section surfaces of the wax moulds are shown black. On No. 3, L L are sections through the frame laths. S is a stay which is placed at intervals to support the mould. The lower frame lath is temporarily fixed to the fence with thin gauged plaster, and then placed in position and secured with clay or plaster dots, as shown at C. The high fence is fixed in a similar way. After this the wax or plaster is poured on until it reaches the level of the low frame, when it is worked up over the side of the high frame, and then the stays put in where required. The wax is worked up by the aid of a gauging trowel. For clay work, use the fingers to draw the wax when near the model, so as not to injure the model. After the wax is set, take the fences off and then the mould, and lay it on a board, as at No. 4, which is a section through the mould, ready for filling in. The section, No 3, is taken through a dentil; the section, No. 4, between the dentils. No. 6 is a section through the moulding piece and mould of the "bed mould" enrichment. This is moulded in a similar way to the dentil, with the exception that plaster fences are not required. The wood laths, or running rules L L, which form the frame, act as fences. No. 7 shows the section through mould ready for filling in. No. 6 is taken through the egg, and No. 7 through the spindle of the bead and the egg and the dart. The dark line in the black surface is the profile of the egg, and the line above is the profile of the sinking between the egg and the dart. No. 8 shows sections through the moulding piece, mould, and frame laths. P is a plaster profile, or "bed," to receive the beads. The backing B and the spindle of the bead just above B are run with the bed. The beads are then fixed over the spindle, the whole thus forming the moulding piece. The backing and lapping parts are also seen at B, which is a sectional view of a cast of the bead. The frame laths L L are laid on the moulding piece and the wax poured on as before. No. 9 is a section through the bead mould and No. 8 through the spindle. No. 11 the section through the moulding piece of the soffit, and the frame laths L L ready for moulding. The undercut enrichment is moulded with gelatine, which is poured on until flush with the top edges of the frame laths. No

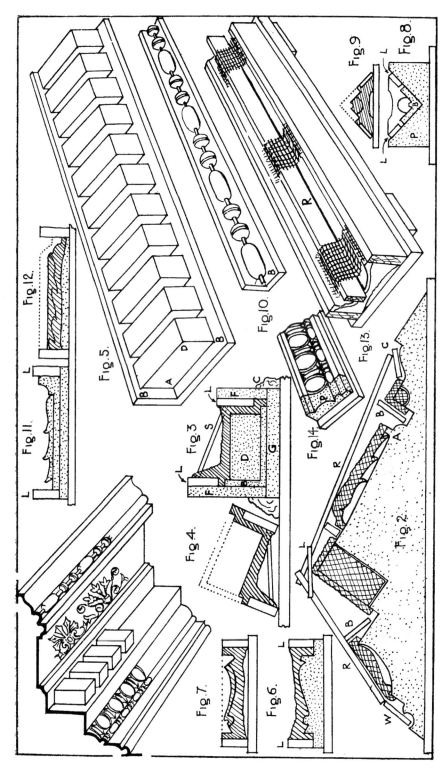

FIG. 109.—Casting Fibrous Plaster Enriched Cornices by the Bedded Enrichment System. Reverse and Framed Wax Moulds for Enrichment.

" case " is required, hence the term " open jelly mould." If the mould is wide, or thin in parts, the jelly is only run until about 1 in. from the frame edges, and the difference made up with plaster, as No. 12. Two ways are shown for forming the bearing and lappit parts of the soffit. The inner side is formed with a plain member, as on Nos. 11 and 2. This is necessary, because the foliage on the soffit extends to the plain member, leaving no margin for a bearing or lapping part. On the outer side the foliage does not extend to the plain member, thus leaving a plain margin on the soffit, which is used as a bearing and lapping part. Provision for this must be made in setting out the reverse run mould, to form a raised part in the width of the soffit in the casting mould, as at A, No. 2. Where practicable, the latter way is the best, as there are no plain mouldings to cast in short lengths, therefore no joints in the plain members, and a better lapping joint is obtained. This will readily be seen by comparing the joint at the cavetto members at each side of the soffit, No. 2. A dentil should be modelled and moulded to repeat the full length of the mould, with a slight draft on both sides, springing from the inner angles and diminishing diagonally from A to D, No. 5. The face and end of the dentil being equal in width, the inward draft is imperceptible, especially in a row of dentils. This allows the mould to leave the moulding piece and the cast to leave the mould, without excessive dragging or fear of chipping. Where there are several moulds required, it is advisable to have a solid moulding piece. This is often compulsory, from the fact that the short casts fixed on the ground come away when the first mould is taken off. A solid model is then taken from this mould. If the enrichment is deep at parts and has but little draft, these parts in the first mould will draw up and form ragged edges. Trim the edges off and smooth with glass paper or with Dutch rush, using paraffin oil as a lubricant. Smith's metal is an excellent material for moulding enrichments for reverse moulds. For permanent moulds it is a good substitute for wax.

Casting fibrous enrichments for bedded work is a simple process. Two sheets of canvas are used, but no laths, unless the work is large, such as a frieze or cove, girthing over 6 in. or 7 in. The backs and edges of the casts need to be rough to give a key when canvased and brushed with the cornice. After the first two or three, casts will take out easily. When the plaster is set, place the moulds (if wax) in warm water to make them pliable. It will be seen that the wax moulds are hollow at the back to economise wax and to be more easily warmed and made pliable. The frames give sufficient strength to a mould, however thin the wax may be. As the casts are thin and have no laths, they are difficult to take out without collapsing. This is avoided, and the cast strengthened by placing a piece of running rule on the cast and then laying strips of canvas about 9 in. or 10 in. apart, and brushing the ends that lie on the cast. These rules are termed " hand rules." They afford a good leverage and give a point of resistance to the end of a file or chisel when prizing the cast up, and a good grasping place to lift the casts out of the mould. No. 13, Fig. 109, is a view of and section through the mould and cast of the bed mould, with the frames at each side. R is the hand rule, with three strips of canvas, ready for the ends to be brushed. Two rules are used for wide casts. When the casts are out, the strips are cut on both sides and the rule freed for the next cast. The brushed strip ends are left on the cast. When the casts are extra thin or difficult to draw, a canvas strip is brushed over the full length of the hand rule. As previously stated, the dotted lines on the moulds indicate the back surfaces of the casts, but no nicety is required for the backs, as they may run below the edges of the frames, as shown at No. 12. This enables the cast to be drawn out more freely. When filling in the dentils, small pieces of canvas are required to fit each dentil, in order that the canvas may be brushed into all the angles and to render the cast light, yet strong.

Casting Fibrous Plaster Enriched Cornices : Fixed Enrichment System.
—Enrichments for this system are cast separately and then fixed on the cornice cast.
The general process is similar to that used for solid work, except that the fibrous casts
are made in long pieces, and fixed on the cast of the cornice with fine nails, and sometimes
with putty and plaster. The enrichments are cast with two coats of canvas for large
work and one coat for small work. Two small laths, each from $\frac{3}{4}$ in. to $1\frac{1}{2}$ in. wide and
from $\frac{1}{8}$ in. to $\frac{3}{8}$ in. thick, are laid along each side of the cast and the canvas margins turned
over and brushed. These laths are " fixing laths " for fixing purposes. When casting
the cornice, corresponding laths are inserted at the beds of enrichments to receive the
fixing nails. The moulding pieces and moulds for the enrichments are formed in
similar lengths and in a similar way to that described for bedded enrichments, with
the exception that no bearing and lapping parts are required. The profile must be
made to fit the bed of the enrichments on the cornice mould, and is done when setting
out the reverse running mould. The casts are fixed with fine sprigs or French nails
of brass, using plaster for the side and end joints, as described for fixing fibrous cornices.
Small thin casts may be fixed with plaster. This was the first system used for forming
fibrous enriched cornices, and is still the most common and the most easy,
resembling the old " solid " method. The completed cornice casts are not so light,
nor the joints between the plain and enriched members so strong, as by the " bedded "
and " cast " systems, but it allows more freedom for seeing and arranging the mitres.

Casting Fibrous Plaster Enriched Cornices : Cast Enrichment System.
—Enrichments by this system are cast with the cornice. The moulds of the enrichments are laid in the cornice mould, and the enriched and plain members cast in one
operation. The moulds are made in long pieces with wax or jelly, and can be used
as " loose pieces."

Fig. 110 shows the cast enrichment system. No. 1 is a section through an enriched
cove cornice. The projection of the modelling is shown by dotted lines : B is a bed-
mould enrichment ; SP a sunk panel. These may be constructed in two ways : first,
as in the present case, the straight styles are cast with the cornice, as at SS, No. 3,
which is a section of the casting mould. The circular styles are cast and then fixed
between the straight styles. For this purpose a moulding piece of the combined
circular styles and patera is made, moulded, and the required number of casts got out.
The plan of the combined styles and patera is shown at No. 4. G is the ground of
the moulding piece. This also illustrates the method of making a moulding piece
for a jelly mould. One end of the ground has splayed angles to form a distinction from
the other. This serves as a guide for placing the case on the moulding piece and the
jelly mould in the case when casting in proper position not to injure the model, a method
adopted when joggles are not used. The second method is the reverse. First run
the cornice casting mould ; the face of the styles must continue across as S to S, No. 3,
to form a bed for the panels. Moulding pieces of the sunk panels are made, moulded,
cast, and fixed on the surface SS. No. 6 shows a plan of styles and panels, as placed
in the cornice mould. SS are the sections. All made-up parts should be fixed with
plaster and secured with screws.

No. 3 is a section of cornice mould, with the jelly moulds of the enrichments in
position. The plaster mould is dotted and the jelly moulds black-lined on sections.
The plaster bed must be a $\frac{1}{4}$ in. larger than the jelly mould to allow for fixing, as shown
by the space between the moulds. The top mould A is also of jelly. The frame rules
are in each case shown in the moulds. Although not here necessary, the mould A is
shown as a " loose piece," as desirable sometimes.

To make jelly mould loose pieces for a plaster reverse mould, run profile P precisely
as for the enriched part (as a ground for making and moulding the enrichment) with

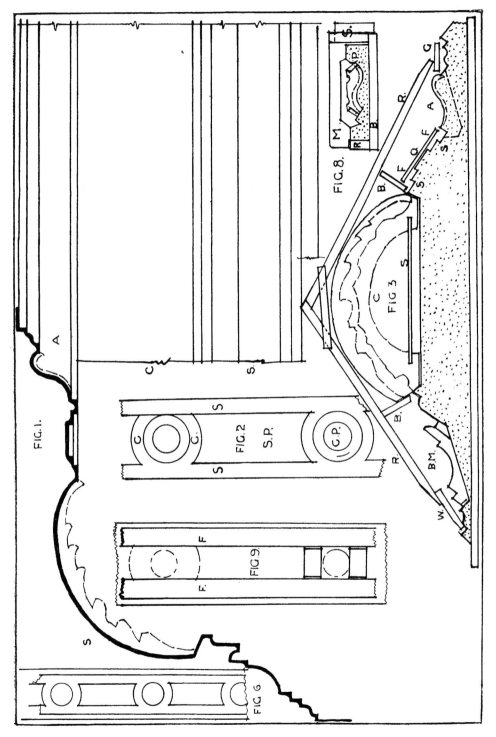

FIG. 110.—Casting Fibrous Plaster Enriched Cornices by the Cast System.   Combined Plaster and Wax Reverse Moulds.

a running mould. It is difficult to get a series of jelly moulds to accurately " bed " in the main mould, therefore a " run plaster case " is used to give uniformity. Run a mould of the section of the bed. When making the jelly mould, leave the back rough to give a key for the case. Shellac and oil the exposed parts of the plaster profile. Lay gauged plaster over the whole surface and form the back with the running mould. B is the board on which the profile P is run. The dark-lined surface is the jelly mould. M is the running mould with a rebated slipper S to work on the side of the running board. The mould with its plaster back is shown in position at A, No. 3. The cove mould C, No. 3, is of jelly. A case for this mould must be used and is indicated by the dotted surface. S is one of the stays placed at intervals to strengthen the mould. Jelly moulds are best made the full length of the cornice cast. Allow for a bed for the enrichment mould when setting out the reverse running mould.

Fill in the mould as described for previous cornices. No. 3 shows the laths for the cornice cast. The fixing laths FF are laid, canvased, and brushed with the cornice cast. No. 9 shows the fixing laths, on plan. The portion of the cast is indicated by the dotted lines. Similar laths are used for the casts. Corresponding laths afford fixing points for the nails or screws. The method is the same as that for " fixed enrichments." A slightly different method is adopted for bosses. First form a series of fixing holes in the cast, each hole being made in the panel to receive a boss by fixing a raised " die " on each panel surface, as shown at D, Nos. 3 and 9. The dies may be cast or cut out of a plaster ground. The diameter of the dies should be about 1 in. less than that of the bearing parts of the bosses to allow a bearing on the panel, as shown by the dotted line at D, No. 9. The double line is the die and the dotted line the boss. When the cast is being filled the fixing laths FF, RR are used for fixing to strengthen the edges of the holes. Canvas is laid over the dies, but not brushed on the raised surface. When the cast is set, cut the unbrushed canvas in three or four places, towards the centre, to form " tags." These are left on the cast and are used for fixing the bosses to the cast. The pateræ are fixed by two or three fine nails or screws. Turn the tags down into the bosses and well brush to give secure fixing and a sound joint. Supplement by brushing tow over the inside joints. When brushed, tow clings to dry fibrous work better than canvas.

Fixing Fibrous Plaster Cornices.—For fixing fibrous work, screws are preferable to nails, and not so apt to jar or chip the work. Brick or stone walls need plugging. Wood fillets are fixed to the plugs to give a fixing ground for the cornice. Fix through the ceiling member of the cornice to the joists. If the longitudinal joists are not in line with the ceiling member, a special fillet must be fixed between the joists for screwing to. If the walls are of lath and plaster, fix to the studs. Fixing grounds must be inserted at the joint where large cornices are made in two or more longitudinal sections. Iron girders or framework to be cased with fibrous plaster must be perforated, drilled, or arranged for plugs or wedges to receive fixing fillets. Concrete work can be constructed with wood plugs, fillets, or concrete fixing blocks in the work. When fixed, joints, mitres, and countersunk screw holes are stopped with plaster gauged with size water. Wet the parts to be stopped and made good with size water, to stop the suction. Only brass screws or nails should be used, to prevent rust and discoloration of surface. Cornices should be fixed on the floating coat. If the walls are previously " set," cut down to the floating coat, allowing a margin about 1 in. wide, and afterwards make good. This makes a better joint than fixing direct on to the finished surface. When it is imperative to fix on a finished surface, the cast rims must be true, strong, and well stopped to prevent the joints opening. When fibrous work has to be fixed up to old plasterwork, the walls (unless lathed) must be plugged at intervals for fixing points. Joints between fibrous and solid work should be stopped with plaster gauged with lime

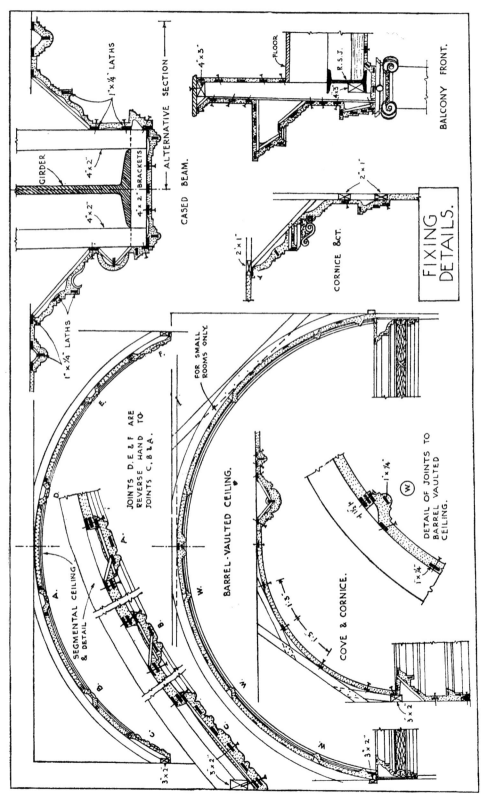

FIG. 111.—Fibrous Plaster Vaulted Ceilings, Cove, Cornice Front, and Balcony Front, etc.

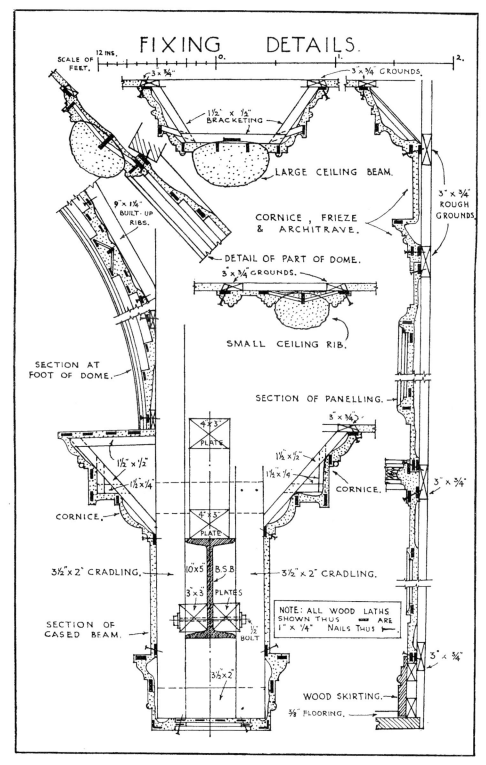

FIXING DETAILS.

SCALE OF FEET.

12 INS.

0.   1.   2.

3 x ¾"

3" x ¾" GROUNDS.

1½" x ½" BRACKETING

LARGE CEILING BEAM.

9" x 1¼" BUILT-UP RIBS.

CORNICE, FRIEZE & ARCHITRAVE.

3" x ¾" ROUGH GROUNDS.

DETAIL OF PART OF DOME.

3" x ¾" GROUNDS.

SMALL CEILING RIB.

SECTION AT FOOT OF DOME.

SECTION OF PANELLING.

3" x ¾"

4" x 3" PLATE

1½" x ½"

1½" x ¼"

1½" x ½"

1½" x ¼"

3" x ¾"

CORNICE.

CORNICE.

4" x 3" PLATE

3½" x 2" CRADLING.

10" x 5" B.S.B

3½" x 2" CRADLING.

3" x 3" PLATES

½" BOLT

NOTE: ALL WOOD LATHS SHOWN THUS ▭ ARE 1" x ¼" NAILS THUS ⊢

SECTION OF CASED BEAM.

3½" x 2"

3" x ¾"

WOOD SKIRTING.

⅜" FLOORING.

FIG. 112.—Fibrous Plaster Panelling, Ceiling Beam, Beam Casing Entablature, and Coffered Dome.

putty water, slowed with size water. Putty water prevents expansion and renders plaster more tenacious. Stop wide or deep joints with plaster and canvas. When the rims of casts have thick laths, fix on to the brick face and joist line. This should be decided before the mould is made, or difficulties may arise when fixing.

Fig. 111 gives sections and details of two fibrous plaster vaulted ceilings, a cove, a beam casing, cornice and balcony front, showing the customary placing of laths and fixings in fibrous plasterwork generally. Two layers of canvas are, of course, used: the first layer laid in the "firstings," afterwards turned over the edges of the second and over the second layer on top of the lath, viz., the first layer should be cut 3 in. to 6 in. larger all round than the cast, and brushed and turned over the edge laths and second layer of canvas.

Fig. 112 illustrates the lath and canvas construction of fibrous plaster wall panelling, a large ceiling beam and a beam casing entablature and part of a coffered dome. The usual placing of the 1 in. by $\frac{1}{4}$ in. laths is indicated with stronger laths at the fixing points. It is better to use two 1 in. by $\frac{1}{4}$ in. laths instead of one 1 in. by $\frac{1}{2}$ in., as in the former case the two laths correct one another in case of warping and twisting, which often occurs.

Measurements and all dimensions for fibrous plasterwork should be taken from the actual work, or from arranged figures. Unless this precaution is taken, it may be necessary to alter, by cutting or making up, to fit the structional work which, most likely, will vary from drawings. The expense of alterations has generally to be borne by the plasterer. When setting out fibrous work for cornices and ceiling or wall panelling, allow the extra thickness required for the lath framing in large casts, also for wood fillets, or wall battens for fixing purposes. Allow about 1 in. for lime plaster, but the thickness for fibrous work will vary from 1 in. to 2 in., or 3 in. for large casts or heavy work.

Fire-resisting Fibrous Plaster.—When plaster, fibre, and wood are used in combination, unless there is a sufficient body of plaster to protect the wood backing and great precautions are taken, fibrous plaster may be overcome by fire as any other woodwork in the construction of buildings. The plaster surface will resist fire. The back requires protection. This may be given by well brushing the wood and canvas with plaster gauged with slag dust, fine engine ashes, tile, brick, terra-cotta dust, or by covering these parts with slag wool in a dry state, or mixed with plaster. Canvas is incombustible if steeped in a strong solution of borax, or a solution of phosphate of ammonia with sal-ammoniac. Wood is partially protected by immersion in either of these solutions.

"Expanded metal" (see Fig. 45, Chapter VIII) may be substituted for wood backing and lathing and, in some cases, wire-netting for canvas. When the Alexandra Palace was destroyed by fire in 1873, it was stated in a newspaper that "the rapid progress of the fire was due to the fibrous plaster ceilings and decorations." This is incorrect. The rapid spread of the fire was entirely due to the constructional woodwork supporting the fibrous plasterwork. The draughts drew the flames to the woodwork and fed the fire. The fire originated by a plumber's "devil" on the roof. Fragments of fibrous plaster were found among the ruins, blackened and scorched on the outer surface. In some instances the wood backing was charred to the plaster surface. When the Oxford Music Hall was burned, in 1868, a small portion of fibrous plaster resisted the fire, but the greater portion was destroyed by inward fire and falling walls. Some fragments found in the debris showed that the plaster had to some extent resisted fire and water. Fibrous plaster may resist fire and stay its progress, but unless the woodwork on which it is fixed is fire-resisting there is little safeguard against fire.

Fibrous plaster decorative sheets have been used as a decorative covering for walls and ceilings, and for wood, stone, and iron surfaces. They can be made to any size. The design having been modelled, is jelly moulded and casts made to form a moulding piece and jointed to suit the design. The thickness of the moulding piece ground must not be more than $\frac{1}{16}$ in. Mould with jelly or plaster, as desired. Jelly is good for most purposes; it is clean, sharp, and pliant for a large flat surface. Fill the mould with extra fine plaster, gauge with best size water, and lay and brush a sheet of extra fine thin canvas. No wood is required. Take out the cast and lay it on a flat surface to dry. It can be rolled up in loose form. The cast can be rendered very tough by dressing with a strong solution of hot glue. The casts may be fixed with strongly gauged putty, plaster, and size water. If the walls are dry the casts can be fixed with a paste composed of white lead thinned down with linseed oil and gauged with fine plaster. Spread the fixing material evenly on the wall and press the cast on to it with flat pads or brushes. Stop the joints the usual way.

Muslin Plaster Casts.—Fine and thin casts for plaques, delicate panels, etc., can be made with one or two sheets of fine open muslin and plaster. The casts are light, strong, as thin as paper, flexible, and may be bent to any curve. They can be fixed with glue, white lead, or plaster, and may be used for a variety of decorative purposes by fixing a series of casts on to a canvas ground and fixing that in one piece.

Plaster and Tow Casts.—Tow, well chopped and gauged with plaster and size water, can be used with advantage for small thin work, also in thin or narrow parts of moulds where canvas would be too thick to turn over. A little tow is excellent, when dipped in gauged plaster, for fixing plantings on fibrous or solid work. Fix the planting on the face of the main cast with " seconds," in which short chopped tow has been mixed. Turn over the cast, unless it is in a position to work at from both sides, and brush with " seconds." This makes a strong, clean joint. When casting for plantings, tow may be used for the whole cast, or for parts, according to the size or nature of work; in either case the tow should be dipped or brushed with plaster, but leave the edges in a loose, dry state, to brush over the joint of the main cast, in fixing. This gives a strong key and unites the pieces. When making circular casts for planting, a combination of canvas and tow will be found useful. Use canvas for the inside parts, and tow for the small parts and outside edges. No wood or wire is required for small work, if tow, saturated with plaster, is used for the edge. Tow is used with plaster for modelling the figure, for theatrical decorations and properties, also for fibrous plasterwork in France. Tow is very strong and tough.

Rapid Plastering.—Plaster slabs were used by Egyptian, Saracenic, and Moorish plasterers. Slab plastering is used for producing ceilings and partitions in plaster or cement, whereby the operation of lathing, pricking up, and floating may be dispensed with. The delay necessary for lime plaster to dry, after each of the above-named operations, is thus avoided, as the foundation or body of the ceiling is made beforehand and requires only to be nailed up, and then set with a thin layer of plaster (or cement) in the ordinary way. The present form of plastic slabbing is the outcome of fibrous plasterworking.

Some slabs consisted of a layer of plaster, two sheets of canvas, and a lath in the sides, in all about $\frac{1}{2}$ in. thick, the sides and ends bevelled to overlap. Slabs can be made to any desired size or form, but are generally made 2 ft. 6 in. wide, and in lengths from 3 ft. to 4 ft., so that the joints will come central with the joists. For special purposes the lengths and widths, whichever way fixed, must joint on the centre of the joists. When dry they can be cut with a saw to fit an angle, or make up small parts. They are generally made from $\frac{1}{2}$ in. to $\frac{5}{8}$ in. thick, according to the class of work and to the distance apart of the joists. For instance, slabs $\frac{1}{2}$ in. thick on joists 12 in. apart will stand the strain of trowelling while being set, and will resist vibration, overhead rolling, or the falling of heavy bodies ; if the joists are 14 in. or 15 in. apart, the slabs should be $\frac{3}{4}$ in. thick. Increased thickness also renders ceilings or partitions more sound-proof. Slabs are made with a rough face to receive a finishing coat when fixed. The other side being smooth, they can be used for temporary building by fixing the smooth surface outward, afterwards stopping the joints with plaster and colouring the whole as required.

Fibrous plaster slabs can be advantageously used for counter ceilings, for pugging or deafening boards, also for covering wood or iron work as a protection from fire. They may be used for warehouses and similar buildings, where time is a desideratum. Plaster being the principal material and the chief bulk of their construction, great care is requisite in its proper gauging and general manipulation, otherwise the slabs will be soft in body and unequal in surface hardness. Plaster that is excessively or unequally gauged becomes soft and hard in patches, and will not stand the test of time like the old-fashioned lime and hair plasterwork, which is improved by repeated gauging and working. It may be thought that the setting coat will give a hard and uniform surface. The setting will certainly cover and (for a time) hide the slab's defects, but the work will never be sound, safe, and satisfactory. No veneer, however strong, can be sound on a weak foundation. Soft or spotty slabs can only bring the plasterer's craft into great disrepute. Slabs can be used during frosty weather, when other building work is suspended.

Fibrous Plaster Slab Moulds.—Slab moulds are usually made on a bench, the top surface of which forms the surface of the mould. They are termed " bench slab moulds," to distinguish them from an independent mould. The top of the bench is generally made of plaster or Portland cement, and sometimes of wood ; iron or zinc sheets may be used, but plaster is cheapest and best for temporary purposes. The bench is made to hold four moulds, each one being 4 ft. by 2 ft. 6 in. The frame of a bench of this size generally has six or eight legs. The bottom long rails are fixed on the inside to give greater leg room for the worker. A centering of rough board T, Fig. 113, is nailed on the frame, the joints $\frac{1}{4}$ in. apart, to allow for any swelling after the plastic surface is laid. On the centering fix the bench rules 3 in. (B.R.) by $\frac{3}{4}$ in., planed on the upper and outer surfaces, to form a permanent bench edge and fence to the plaster surface. Two or more widths may be required for the ends of the bench, to allow for fixing points for the mould rules and the clip screws. After fixing the bench rules firm and level, drive nails into the centering surface, about 4 in. apart, projecting, to form a key for the plastic top. Neat plaster for the finished surface does not wear well. A more durable surface is 1 part of ground lime to 3 parts of plaster, gauged stiffly. Hydraulic lime is better than chalk lime for the purpose ; but nothing equals Portland cement, iron plates, or zinc sheets. Plaster must be seasoned with linseed oil ; litharge oil applied hot makes a better and harder surface. Soft soap —although it stops the suction—does not harden the surface, and the plaster is apt to scale and chip. The soap makes it difficult to repair. Having finished the surface, set out the mould sizes. The sides and ends of the moulds are formed with wood " mould rules," $2\frac{1}{2}$ in. wide and $\frac{1}{2}$ in. thick, planed on all sides and edges, and brushed with liquid shellac. The shellac hardens the surface, prevents the oil or grease from being absorbed, allows the slabs to leave the mould freely, and the rules to be cleansed more easily. A are fixed rules, B are loose mould rules. The cross ones fit into sockets in the long mould rules, keeping the cross ones in place. The cross rules A hold the front rule, locked by means of the three clips, as shown in position. C shows a clip, which turns on a screw and is always ready for use. The bench is about 2 ft. 6 in. high. A platform is sometimes useful on the lower rails for storing laths, etc. Canvas is best kept clean, overhead, within easy reach. Mould rules are sometimes held in position by pegs, but the above method is the quickest and most reliable way of ensuring slabs of equal size and form. Smaller slabs may be cast from the same moulds by laying width rules as required. The maker's name should be on each slab for identification, therefore fix a plaster name-plate on the surface of each mould. The other sketches show the making of slabs, as follows :—

Fibrous Plaster Slab-making.—The materials and methods are the same as for plain panels, with an additional coat of plaster to make up the requisite thickness. The canvas must be coarse and open, the frame laths from 1 in. to $1\frac{1}{2}$ in. wide by $\frac{1}{8}$ in. to $\frac{3}{16}$ in. thick, according to the size of slab. Materials for the body coat vary. One of the first used was " coir," the outside coating of coco-nuts, obtained from matting factories. Waste fibre or short ends are used for slab making. Fibre and sawdust in equal parts give good results. Good slabs are made with sawdust and plaster. Waste cork, bark from tanpits, peat moss, shavings, straw, hay, bracken, reeds, rushes, bamboo and other canes (split and whole), and similar materials have been employed as aggregates. Bark or similar materials should be chopped to free from lumps, and dried before gauging with plaster. Coarse plaster alone makes the slabs heavy and brittle : if gauged with fibre or sawdust,

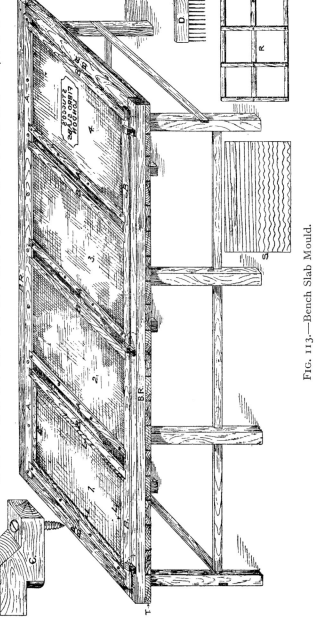

FIG. 113.—Bench Slab Mould.

or both, coarse plaster is less heavy and more tenacious. Oil the moulds with Gallipoli oil (a cheap sweet oil), or grease them with a " tallow pad " by laying $\frac{1}{2}$ lb. of common tallow in a double ply of canvas, about 8 in. or 10 in. square, tied up at the ends with string. Beat hard tallow on a wood block until it will work freely through the canvas. Greasing is more quickly and equally done with a tallow pad than with oil, and the slabs leave the moulds more freely, cleanly, and with less chipping. Moulds in good working order require greasing once or twice per day only, using a solution of soft soap for other casts. Having cut laths and canvas sufficient for a day or more, grease the moulds, and gauge enough plaster to cover the surface of the mould $\frac{1}{8}$ in. thick. This must be stiffly gauged, and quickly. At the same time gauge another quantity of plaster with size water. Scrape out all the plaster and wash the pail after each gauging. Pour the neat plaster into the mould, spread it with a laying trowel, lay a sheet of canvas over it, leaving an equal margin over the rims, and then, with a trowel, press and lay the canvas evenly and close up to all angles and sides of the mould. Charge a large brush (an old stock brush will do) with sized plaster, and brush the whole surface to thoroughly incorporate the surface coat and the canvas. Brush the bed of the laths, lay them in position, as shown at L, No. 1 mould, and then brush the laths and fill up any crevices between the laths and the sides of the mould. While the laths are moist, turn the canvas margins over them and brush thoroughly. Then gauge and lay the body coat flush with the mould rims, and well scratch. The body material usually termed " fibro " consists of coarse plaster, more often than not, gauged with equal parts of fibre or sawdust. The plaster must be stiffly gauged and the aggregate mixed with it until of the consistency of well-tempered coarse stuff. While the canvas is moist, lay the fibro in the centre of the mould, spread with a trowel, rule flush with the mould rims, and before set well scratch the surface with a wire drag, to give a key for the setting coat. One sheet of canvas is sufficient for ordinary work if the plaster is good and properly gauged. Two sheets are used for special work if joists are extra wide apart.

When set, turn the clips, take off the loose front cross rules, insert the blade of a trowel between the slab and the bench, and ease the slabs and lay them on a " slab rack." The novice had better try one mould first, and when he has mastered the gauging, noted the time of setting, and the amount of materials required for one mould, he may fill in two alternate moulds at one time, and while they are setting, fill in the other two. This allows more space and freedom for working, and time for the other slabs to set. Stack the slabs on edge in racks arranged with a $\frac{1}{2}$ in. space between each slab, to allow a free current of air. The racks should be in a drying room, heated by coke fire ; if time or atmosphere permits, the drying can be done by air currents. When dry, store close together on edge, or lay them flat on racks made up of wood fillets about 1 in. by $\frac{1}{2}$ in., until the stack is man high. This prevents buckling. On no account should slabs be laid close together until thoroughly dry, as any contained moisture will render the plaster soft and the slabs weak and flabby. The slab stacks must be in a dry place where there is a strong current of air. R (Fig. 113) shows a slab rack. D is a wire drag formed of a wood stock, 6 in. by 2 in. by $\frac{3}{4}$ in., into which is fixed steel wires of about $\frac{1}{8}$ in. diameter and about $\frac{1}{4}$ in. apart. The wires should be flattened at the points. The drag should be drawn along the surface in zigzag form, at an angle of 70°, to give a wavy key. A series of zigzag indentations will give a stronger key than straight ones. Both forms are shown on the plan of a slab S.

Setting Fibrous Plaster Slabs.—Fibrous slabs are fixed with $1\frac{1}{2}$ in. galvanised nails having good-sized flat heads, the nails being about 6 in. apart. When the slabs are all fixed, the joints are stopped with plaster gauged with size water, leaving the surface rough. For common work they are set with gauged putty and plaster. If required for immediate use or painting, they are usually set with Parian, Express, or other white cement. Owing to the dry and porous nature of most slabs, it is necessary to correct the excessive absorption before commencing the setting, or the stuff will be difficult to trowel off, and liable to peel. The absorption may be stopped by brushing the surface with size water and following on with the gauged putty and plaster as quickly as possible. If setting with white cement, the slab surface should be brushed with a thin solution of the cement intended for the setting coat, and then following on as before. This is best done by one man brushing the surface with the solution and another following him up and laying the skimming coat with a float. After this is all done, one man lays a thin finishing coat with a trowel and his partner follows up and trowels off.

Fire-resisting Slabs.—As just previously stated, plaster has long been recognised for its fire-resisting qualities. To obtain slabs of the requisite strength, it is necessary to use only those aggregates which are themselves fire resistant. Therefore, wire netting is used in place of canvas, and fine slag, brick, tile, or engine ashes in the place of fibre or vegetable aggregates, for gauging purposes. Wire netting should have a mesh varying from $\frac{1}{4}$ in. to 1 in., according to the required strength of the work. Cut the wire to the size of the mould and lay in the centre of the thickness of the slab. Lay the gauged plaster, mixed with an equal part of fine slag or other aggregate, into the mould, until about half full. Then beat down the stuff and lay the wire in position, make up the remaining half of the thickness with the same gauge, beat and rule off flush with the mould rims, and scratch the surface as before. The moulds are the same as those used for fibrous slabs.

Combination Slabs.—Silicate cotton, an important factor in fire-resisting plastic construction, also known as slag wool or mineral wool, is an incombustible material largely used in conjunction with plaster for fire and sound resisting purposes. It is used with wire netting and applied in sheet form for plaster slabs, pugging, and fibrous plaster casing for iron columns, girders, or wood construction. It is a waste substance from iron-smelting furnaces. The wool is made by playing steam on a stream of molten slag. Its power as a non-conductor of heat is due to the fact that it contains a great volume of air. Material containing a high percentage of air is a poor conductor of heat. Unconfined air is subtle and rapid in movement, and, excepting by its own motion, is slow to convey heat and is the greatest barrier to its transmittal. 192 lbs. (or 1 cub. ft.) of raw slag will make 192 lbs. of slag wool (or 8 cub. ft.), therefore wool encases eight times as much air as the slag does. It is an antiseptic, *i.e.*, a substance which resists or arrests putrefaction ; therefore it is an excellent sanitary material and will not harbour vermin, properties which render it useful for many plastic purposes. Fibrous slabs and all kinds of fibrous work are rendered highly fire-resisting by combining silicate cotton and encasing the back surface of the slabs with a layer, 1 in. thick, of silicate cotton, secured by means of wire netting and fastened to the slabs.

Patent " Simplex " Fire and Sound Resisting Partition Blocks.—These blocks are made and largely used in the construction of partition walls and as linings to brickwork. The blocks, half a super yard by 2 in. thick, can be fixed to brick, wood, concrete, iron, or any kind of existing structure, are fire and sound resisting in a high degree, and are secured by means of metal keys or continuous hoop iron which, bedded in the material, do not corrode.

The blocks can be cut with a saw, and any plaster will adhere to them.

In building partitions it is advisable not to exceed 100 superficial feet without introducing quartering with wood or iron. Solid blocks are made for fixing small water cisterns, shelves, cupboards, etc., to. For large areas, or if plastering with lime plaster, bed the joints with Robinson's cement.

Another advantage is the speed with which they can be fixed ; economy of space and the reduction in weight, $4\frac{1}{2}$ in. brick wall weighing five times as much as a similar area of " Simplex " blocks.

External slabs are made in a similar way to the fire-resisting slabs, with Portland cement instead of plaster. They are about 1 in. thick, the lengths and widths being regulated to joint on the wood standards or framing on which they are fixed. Owing to their hardness when set, provision for screw holes must be made while being cast, by means of pegs let into the mould surface. Where lightness is desirable, coke breeze or pumice stone should be used as an aggregate in the proportion of 1 of cement to 3 of aggregate. Pumice concrete weighs about 25 per cent. less than cement concrete. The slabs are set with neat Portland cement, or Portland cement gauged with lime putty. The smooth face may be used externally and the joints stopped with Portland cement, or panelled by fixing cement mouldings over the joints. The foundation for the slabs is thin wire netting, or perforated metal sheets, tow being employed for acute angles. Slag wool in conjunction with cement, held in position by wire netting, is used for backing up parts exposed to excessive heat. The slabs and mouldings are fixed with screws, but for fire-resisting purposes they are arranged for hanging on metal hooks, or for screwing from the back, so that no metal work appears on the outer surface. The inside fastenings are covered with a similar compound. Although it is not advisable to hasten the setting of Portland cement for solid or constructive work, it may be done for this class of work without fear of failure. The quick setting may be obtained by mixing various materials with cement.

" Mack " Patent Fire-resisting Slabs.—These slabs, having embedded strong hollow reeds of the nature of bamboo, are made from specially prepared gypsum, etc. The reeds form sealed air chambers, and with the plaster make a high class, light, non-conducting material of great strength. The air cells formed by the reeds break up the vibrations of sound and prevent the sound passing through the partitions. The non-conducting qualities are proved by the report of the fire test made by the British Fire Prevention Committee with the $2\frac{3}{4}$ in. slab partition ; the temperature on the fire side was over 2,250° F. ; on the opposite side a little over 100° F.

These slabs are extensively used in the construction of fire and sound resisting partitions, ceilings, puggings, and floors, for the lining of walls, insulation of roofs and ironwork, etc. Partition slabs are 2, $2\frac{1}{2}$, $2\frac{3}{4}$, and 4 in. thick, 6 ft. long, and 12 in. high. They are built up without any intermediate supports, no iron rods or metal keys being required. Ceiling slabs are $\frac{1}{2}$, $\frac{5}{8}$, $\frac{3}{4}$, 1, $1\frac{1}{4}$, and $1\frac{1}{2}$ in. thick, and in various sizes to suit the spacing of joists.

Reed Slabs.—The use of reeds or rushes in connection with plaster dates from the earliest period. Reeds have been used up to the present time in the Midlands for the construction of plaster floors. As a substitute for wood laths, they were employed up to the middle of last century. Reeds are light, tough, and pliable, and form an excellent strengthening material for many plastic purposes. Reed slabs are made in similar moulds and ways to those for fibrous slabs. The whole thickness of the slabs is composed of plaster (fine and coarse in equal proportions), with two layers of reeds placed in the centre of the slab's thickness, one layer crossing the other at right angles. The slabs are stacked and dried as in the case of fibrous slabs. Bamboo is another excellent material for strengthening slabs, or for other plastic work.

Grooved slabs are made in a similar way to reed slabs. They are usually composed of neat plaster, and vary in thickness from 1 in. to $1\frac{1}{2}$ in. Although simple, they are patented abroad, the merit claimed being the form of groove, so undercut that the finishing coat, when applied, will have a perfect dovetail at each groove. The grooves are about $\frac{1}{4}$ in. wide by $\frac{1}{8}$ in. deep and $\frac{1}{4}$ in. apart, formed by means of metal fillets, inserted in channels in the surface of the mould and drawn out when the plaster is just set, before it begins to swell. Flexible fillets fixed on the surface would not be so costly as sliding metal ones, and would answer the purpose equally well. Flexible fillets can be made with rubber, leather, or gelatine, treated with bichromate of potash, which renders them insoluble in water. Undercut grooves may also be made by simply drawing an undercut drag or scratcher across the slab surface while the plaster is soft.

Perforated slabs are an American invention. The slabs are constructed with a series of perforations for fixing purposes, each perforation and the whole slab being strengthened by wires. The moulds are of wood or metal, with a series of wood or metal pins or pegs on the surface. The pegs are tapered, fixed about 9 in. apart in rows (to correspond with the ceiling joists), and left projecting flush with the mould rims. Wires are stretched longitudinally from end to end of the mould, and twisted or coiled round the pegs. They are coiled loose, so that they may draw off the pegs, and are placed near the centre of the slab's thickness. The moulds are then filled in with plaster in the usual way.

Pugging or deafening slabs are made in much the same way as fibrous slabs, their width being regulated according to the space between the joists, the length being 3 ft. and the thickness 1 in. For ordinary work they are composed of coarse plaster and fibre, sawdust, or any other similar aggregates, with a sheet of canvas in the centre. Fireproof pugging slabs are composed of coarse plaster gauged with fine slag, brick dust, coke breeze, or fine engine ashes, having a sheet of wire netting in the centre. They are laid on wood fillets, previously nailed on each side of the joists, and bedded or stopped with coarse plaster gauged with size water. For effective work a double layer of slabs is used, the intermediate space being filled in with slag wool, or coarse plaster gauged with sifted breeze or ashes.

Hardening Fibrous Plaster Slabs.—Several materials and methods are used for hardening neat plaster and fibrous plasterwork, but they are too costly, slow, or unsuitable. After many experiments I have found " litharge oil " give the best result. It is made as follows :—

Litharge oil is composed of 1 lb. of litharge (oxide of lead), 1 lb. of paraffin wax, $\frac{3}{4}$ lb. of resin, and 1 gal. of linseed oil. It is best made in an iron pot over a slow fire. The wax is melted in another pot and poured into the oil pot. The litharge and resin, in a powdered state, are then put in, the solution being constantly stirred. Allow to cool before using, and when required, melt and apply hot on work which has been previously dried. The oil is applied with a brush, and the work should be warm to allow the oil to penetrate into the surface and to work freely. One coat is generally sufficient for ordinary purposes. When two coats are applied, allow the first to stand in a warm place for two or three hours. Then apply the second coat hot. This process renders the work so hard that it will resist a nail. It becomes waterproof and is effectively protected against atmospheric changes. If the back of fibrous work is coated with this oil, the work will resist the action of saline acids and damp. It is also useful for indurating work in exposed positions. The work can be painted and gilded soon after it is cool. This solution does not enter into any great chemical combination with the fibrous plaster ; but being of a hardening nature and filling up the pores, it hardens the work and prevents the action of moisture. It may be used with advantage for indurating ordinary plaster for various purposes.

Damp-proof Slabs.—A cheap and ready method of rendering fibrous slabs damp-proof is by brushing the backs once or twice with a solution of coal tar or pitch. Pitch, Stockholm and coal tar are rendered more durable, damp-proof, and not so readily affected by heat, if mixed with fine brick dust or ground lime. The solution should be well worked on the slabs with a hard, stumpy stock brush. The process is effectual for slabs intended for damp or exposed positions.

Fibrous plaster blocks have been used for constructing partitions, ceilings, arches, and domes. The blocks are made in wood moulds, metal or plaster being used to form divisional parts. They are composed chiefly of strong, coarse plaster. Reeds, sawdust, fibre, wood wool, or ashes are occasionally used as aggregates. They are made in various forms and sizes, according to purpose. For partitions they are generally

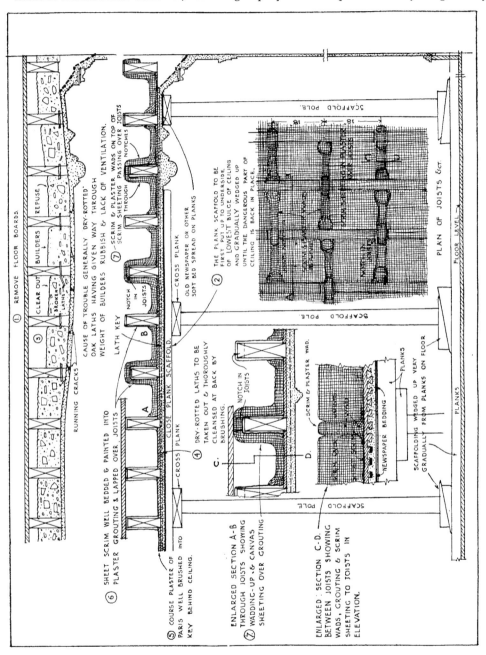

FIG. 114.—Methods of Strapping and Reinforcing Defective Old Plaster Ceilings.

3 ft. long, 1 ft. wide, and 2½ in. thick. Every three blocks of this size measure 2 yards superficial, counting both sides, and each block weighs from 15 lbs. to 25 lbs., according to the size of the perforation, the amount and class of aggregate. They are made with round perforations extending longitudinally from end to end. This is done with rods

covered with brown paper (to allow withdrawal), or rods brushed with a thick solution of clay. The perforations may also be made by tapered rods. They are laid in the mould the reverse way, alternately, to give uniform strength to the block. They are sometimes grooved on all edges to give a key for fixing. They are also made with dowel holes for fixing, the wood or metal dowels being inserted as the building proceeds. When they are fixed between iron or wood joists, the exposed parts of the joists are covered with wire netting as a key for the finishing coat. Domes or arches made in one piece, or in large sections, are generally composed with a skin of fine plaster, backed with coarse plaster and left with a finished face. No originality can be claimed for plaster blocks, the idea being taken from the stalactite ceilings of the Moors.

Strapping Up and Reinforcing Dangerous Old Solid Plaster Ceilings.— Fig. 114 shows in plan, section, and detail some methods of saving dangerous old solid plaster ceilings from falling to destruction. The drawing is self-explanatory in its notes. It occasionally happens that beautiful and valuable old ceilings of historical interest and fame come away and bag down from the wood joists on which they have been worked, and but for the great strength and tenacity of the good old plaster would fall with perhaps disastrous, if not fatal, results. The reason in most cases is that the wood laths on which the ceiling has been worked have rotted and gone to powder for want of ventilation between the joists. It frequently happens that the old builders have swept their accumulated building rubbish into the space between the joists rather than carry it away, and the superincumbent weight and stoppage of air circulation in the course of time causes the mischief.

The remedy is quite simple, but requires most careful handling in the order noted and figured on the diagram. Enlarged sections are shown in the case of single and double joisted floors. The system really comes to supporting the ceiling from below on a well-padded scaffolding, taking up the floor boards overhead, removing all rubbish from between the joists, then gently wedging the bagged ceiling back into its place, removing the dry rotted laths from the back of the solid plaster without injury to the rough key of the plaster, thoroughly brushing, cleansing, damping, scrubbing, and grouting, and reinforcing with strong plaster of Paris and canvas the back of the ceiling, taking the canvas up and over the wood joists. The ceiling then becomes practically a reinforced fibrous plaster ceiling strapped to and over the wood joists of floor above. That is the principle at least.

Where double joists occur, the back of ceiling is cleansed, grouted, and canvased all over, but the canvas cannot be taken over the joists, and has to be supported by wads of canvas steeped in plaster and placed and taken over the joists at about 2 ft. intervals, or as illustrated otherwise in details of Fig. 114.

CHAPTER XVI

" REVERSE " MOULDING

Reverse Moulding: Its Uses and Terms—To Set Out a Reverse Template—To Make a
Reverse Casting Mould for Cornices—Panel Mouldings—Rib Mouldings—Plain
Capitals—Diminished and Fluted Columns and Pilasters—Plain Columns—Hollow
Cores and Column Casts.

Reverse moulding (an English invention) derives its name from the direct formation
of plaster moulds by running the mould itself and at once forming a casting mould
cut from the inner profile of a moulding section, being the reverse of an ordinary running
mould cut from the outer profile of a section. A casting mould made by the " reverse "
method requires no model to mould from. A reverse piece mould for a cornice is
run in plaster in one operation, while an ordinary piece mould is formed from a
model requiring careful manipulation.

Reverse moulding is more expeditious than piece moulding, and a saving is effected
generally, but it is not applicable to work of any degree of good taste or artistic merit,
although largely used for a cheap and rapidly executed commercial class of work. It
is necessary to define the nomenclature adopted, and describe the general process before
the individual parts.

The " ground line " on the sections of the intended moulding represents the bench
line, for setting out the form and position of any loose pieces, and the width of bearings
for the nib and slipper of the template. The " square edges," or " striking off " edges,
forming the rim of the casting mould, are the ceiling and wall lines. A " loose plate "
temporarily screwed to the running mould to form a bed for a " loose piece " is made
where a member being undercut would otherwise prevent a cast from drawing. The
loose piece draws with the cast when removed from the mould, and is then taken off
the cast and replaced in the mould. If a loose piece should fracture, the pieces can be
put in place and surface defects " stopped " with clay or plaster, the seams being
afterwards cleaned off the cast. Large loose pieces are best strengthened with canvas
strips centrally. As there is no swelling in a fibrous cast, the loose piece is easily removed
by tapping. A " core " or bracket of wood, brick, or other rough material is used
in large work to save plaster and prevent swelling. The casting mould is termed " the
mould." The accompanying sketches show how to make a template and moulds
for various purposes. The foundation of reverse moulds is in the setting out of
the template.

To Set Out a Reverse Template.—The annexed sketch (Fig. 115) shows the
method of setting out a reverse template for a cornice. No. 1 is the profile to be
produced. The first consideration is the bench line A. Leave sufficient thickness
between the extreme points of the moulding and the bench line. This body of plaster
constituting the casting mould should not be less than 1 in.; if less, the plaster is apt
to dry and lift from the bench. When forming the bench line, sufficient width at the
ceiling and wall lines is necessary for striking off the mould. Continue the line across

the wall and ceiling lines as a bearing for the nib and slipper of the running mould. Having settled the position and length of the ground line, the plate of the running mould is set out. The space between the dotted line and the inner section of the cornice is the shape of the template and, of course, is precisely the same as the section. A tracing should be taken from the original drawing and transferred to paper (" lining paper " is good enough for the purpose), and the section of the plate and loose piece and its plate set out.

No. 2 shows the section of the mould plate and the loose piece plate C. A is the bench line. The undercutting of the cove which would prevent the cast withdrawing from the casting mould is obviated by making a loose piece as shown, to draw in the direction of the members, *i.e.*, in a line with the longest side of the loose plate. Loose pieces should be made on a flat surface, so that the joint seams may be easily cleaned off. In enriched cornices they should be in an enrichment bed, as any unevenness in the mould is easily made good, and the seam on the cast covered with the enrichment.

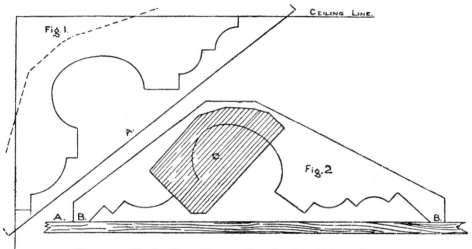

FIG. 115.—To Set Out a Reverse Running Mould for a Cornice.

In the example, one joint is made near the centre of the cove and the other on the line of the fillet. The latter joints at an arris, and unless the loose piece is closely fitted when casting, it will leave a seam requiring skill to clean off. A seam on or near an arris is more difficult to clean off or make good than one on a flat surface. This form of joint, although not so good as the first, is used for special purposes, and is better than on a round member, and a joint on the under part of a member is not so noticeable as one on a vertical member. Loose pieces should be large and strong to bed firmly and steadily, and to stand frequent moving and handling in casting, but must not overweight the cast. Sharp angles in the bed of loose pieces should be cut off, so that the bed may be cleaned out. Avoid a sharp edge which would wear and create dirt in the joint. The loose piece plate should lie well over the stock of the running mould to fix securely.

To Make a Reverse Mould for a Cornice.—Having set out the template and cut the plate for the loose piece, the whole is stoutly " horsed," to resist the force of the plaster when it begins to swell, or set while being run. The stock should be $\frac{3}{4}$ in. to $1\frac{1}{4}$ in. or so in thickness, according to size. The template is greatly increased in strength by using two handles from the slipper to the end of the stock. The fixing point on the stock should extend to the outer member of the profile. Two handles enable one man to push the mould along and another to push and hold the nib of the mould down, so that it will run steady and true and avoid humps. For extra wide mouldings, handles fixed on the top of the slipper, as at 3A, are stronger and better to grip. One handle is sufficient for small work.

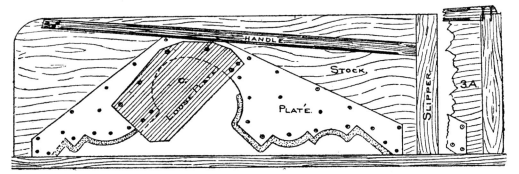

FIG. 116.—Reverse Running Mould for a Cornice Casting Mould.

The method is the example as shown. Fig. 116 shows the loose plate and the loose piece plate screwed on the stock, also the handle and the end of the slipper, the names of the various parts being indicated. The loose plate forms the bed of the loose piece C. The dotted line indicates the continued profile of the main plate, which is the profile of the loose plaster piece. The plaster muffling, an allowance for the

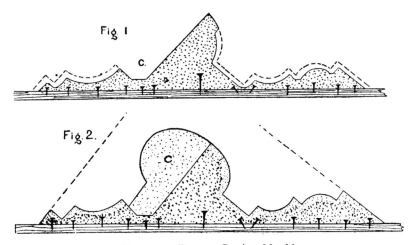

FIG. 117.—Reverse Casting Mould.

No. 1—Section of Mould when run with the Muffled Running Mould.
No. 2—Section of Casting Mould with Loose Piece.

swelling of the main plaster body, is done by adding plaster on the stock, projecting $\frac{1}{4}$ in. below the profile of template, as sketch, dotted on each side of the template plate. In order to make a true and sound joint between the main and loose parts, about $\frac{1}{2}$ in. at each side of the loose piece must be left unmuffled. The moulding is roughed out, the muffling is taken off the template, and the finished surface run off.

Fig. 117, No. 1, is the section of the casting mould when run with the muffled template, leaving a finished surface at the bed of the loose piece C and a finished part at the joints of the loose piece, the dotted lines indicating the thickness of the fine plaster finishing. The bed of the loose piece is then shellaced, oiled, and filled in, the rough surface of the mould being laid with fine plaster, the width being run in one operation. No. 2 shows the section of the complete mould with the loose piece C and the finished surface. The rough core, the thickness of the finished surface, and the joints formed by the unmuffled part of the template are indicated by the darker dotted surface and the lighter dotted surface respectively. By comparing this figure with No. 1 and the section of the running mould, the process will be seen at a glance. With regard to the filling in of the mould, the cast must not extend beyond the dotted lines No. 2, from the rims, viz., the striking-off lines, representing the wall and ceiling surfaces ; any projection beyond these lines would prevent the cast from being fixed squarely. Casts are sometimes fixed to the ceiling joists and wall plugs, and in such cases allowance must be made in setting out the template. The formation of a reverse template for a plain moulding is quite simple, and when the principle of loose piecing is mastered (some mouldings requiring several loose pieces), their use for many purposes will suggest themselves to the thoughtful plasterer.

To Make a Reverse Mould for Sunk Panel Mouldings.—Fig. 118 shows

FIG. 118.—Reverse Moulds for Panel Mouldings.

the method of making a reverse mould for sunk panellings to beams, arches, etc. The section of a sunk panel mould with fixing nails, to prevent the moulding from lifting, is shown at A. One side of the mould is shown with a plaster side piece, if the side or front is to be moulded. The other side shows a board (standing on edge and secured with a rule on the flat) if a plain side is required. E is the section of the template. The section of the template for the moulded side is shown at D. This is sunk and raised to show that the same method of forming the running mould applies to both. If sunk panels are required for an arch, the mould pieces must be run on a saddle. For circular panels on flat surfaces, the mould pieces are run by fixing a radius rod to the running mould, excepting in the case of elliptical curves, where a template is advisable for guidance. The stock in this case representing the profile of the plate of the template, is indicated by irregular lines and the slipper by vertical lines.

To Make a Reverse Mould for Rib Mouldings.—Fig. 119 shows sections of a template I and the mould A for a moulded rib. There are two methods of constructing the mould. By the first, one-half of the mould is run as a fixture and held by fixing nails, and the other as a loose piece, held in position by the side rules J ; at the left side is a fixed rule, and only used if both pieces are movable. J, at the right side, is also a fixed rule, used as a stay for the wedge L, and K is a movable rule placed along the side of the mould. This is better than wedging at intervals between the fixed rule and the plaster, the wedges being apt to fracture the mould. Hot plaster is liable to swell or twist, and pressure at certain parts causes the mould to twist, whereas the movable rule has an equal bearing along the whole length of the cast, and should the half mould get broken the rule will keep it in place. When the mould is filled in, remove the wedges and the side rule, and draw the half mould and cast up to the fixed rule, when the cast is easily removed.

By the second method, both sides of the mould are loose, and held in position by side rules. Another way to hold the pieces together is to use clips as described for slab " bench moulds." If segmental ribs are required and their length does not exceed

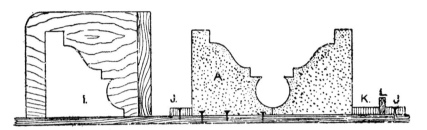

FIG. 119.—Reverse Moulds for Rib Mouldings.

their diameter, the inner half is run first as a fixture, the outer half being run as a movable piece. If a full circle or more than half a circle is required, the mould is made the full length required and cut into sections, to form a piece mould to draw easily from the casts.

To Make a Reverse Mould for a Plain Cap.—The figures in Fig. 120 show sections of the template M and the mould A for a simple moulded cap. When making the mould, run a sufficient length of moulding for the front and sides ; cut to the required lengths and mitres, and place them on the bench. The mould pieces are kept in position as described in the previous example. Moulds for caps to circular, square, or other shaped piers and copings are made in like manner.

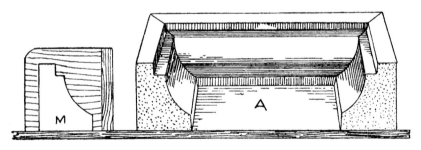

FIG. 120.—Reverse Moulds for Plain Caps.

To Make Reverse Moulds for Diminished Fluted Columns and Pilasters. —Fig. 121 shows two methods of reverse moulding for diminished fluted columns and pilasters ; both are of simple construction and accurate production. No. 1 shows a half section of a mould, the dotted lines indicating the top and centre lines. Two casts are made and screwed together, to form a complete column. The body of the mould A is made first by cutting reverse templates of the necking and of the first fillet of the base, with about 2 in. of the shaft to each. A little more than half the circumference of the necking and base mouldings is run, each being cut to a true half and then fixed on a stout moulding board or bench (similar to T, T in No. 3), so that a man can work on each side. The necking and base moulds are fixed the length of the proposed column apart, lineable with each other and level at the upper or jointing edges. A board is fixed at each side as a fence, the intermediate space being cored with boards, or brickbats and plaster, the surface made up with plaster and ruled with a diminished rule, cut to a contour the reverse of that used for diminishing columns *in situ*. The flutes are formed by setting out in the positions and forms on the ground of the mould, and making a solid one (from which a mould for the other flutes is taken) in the centre of the mould. This flute will allow the half-column casts to draw and is made permanent. The ground should be well keyed, a few nails being driven in and left projecting to give a further key for the plaster with which the flute is formed. Templates

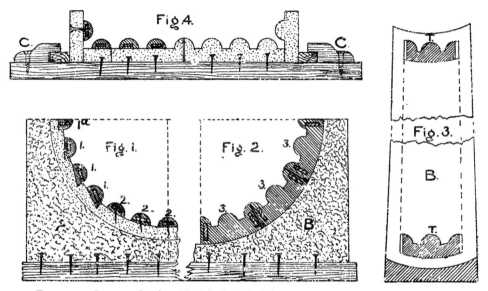

FIG. 121.—Reverse Casting Moulds for Diminished Fluted Columns and Pilasters.

Nos. 1 and 2—Sections of Reverse Moulds for Columns.
No. 3—Plan of Ground for forming Flutes.
No. 4—Section of Reverse Moulds for Pilasters.

are cut to the lower and upper diameter of a flute and temporarily fixed on the body of the mould at the end of the flute lines, then fill in between with plaster and rule with the diminished rule. Remove the templates and form by hand the circular ends of the flute, using the circular end lines on the ground as a guide. A plaster mould is made from this, and the required number of fibrous casts made and fixed on the ground of the mould, with a lath in the centre of each flute cast (as shown) for strength and for fixing through to the mould. Notice that only the centre and two flutes on each side will draw, therefore the other flutes must draw as loose pieces. Two ways of making and fixing them are shown. In one, sinkings are made in the ground to receive the flutes and hold them in position, as at 1 and 1a. The sinking must be cut to a uniform depth, the ground bed being at an angle allowing the movable flute to draw with the cast. A flute is then made on one of the rebated grounds and moulded, the other casts made and being placed in position. Should difficulty occur in cutting the sinkings uniformly, each flute may be formed on its own bed. The half flute, 1a, requires a deeper sinking, to counterpoise the projecting weight. The bed of each flute must be shellaced and oiled before the flute is made. The same principle applies to the other half of the mould. The sinkings allow the undercut flutes to draw with the cast and be taken off and replaced in the mould. Another way is to peg the flutes in position on the body of the mould, at an angle allowing the flutes, nails, or pegs to draw with the cast. For small work the flutes need not have laths, an extra layer of canvas or tow giving ample strength.

No. 2 shows a mould made by the second method. For this a reverse piece mould is made, each piece consisting of a whole flute, two fillets, and two half flutes, as at 3 ; a section of larger diameter is required for the body of the mould B, for the extra thickness of the pieces. This is formed by cutting two templates to fit the upper and lower diameters of the shaft, allowing $1\frac{1}{2}$ in. for the thickness of the pieces, which are fixed the proper width apart, the intermediate space being filled in and ruled off with a straight-edge, as in No. 3. Two templates are cut to the upper and lower sections of the combined flute, fillets, and half flutes, fixed on the ground of the body of the mould (as at T, No. 3), the intermediate space being filled in with plaster and the upper surface ruled off with a diminished floating rule, and the two sides ruled off with a straight-edge. The sides may also be formed by temporarily fixing a fence board on each side of the template (see dotted lines, No. 3). The sides must be straight and the profile formed with a diminished floating rule, to give a true and uniform arris. The model of the flute may be run with a hinged running mould, the ends formed by hand, and the mould and cast produced as before. For large work, laths (inserted as shown) will give strength. The casts are easily removed by the aid of three strips of dry canvas, laid in channels formed in the body,

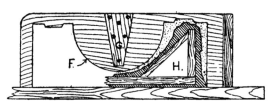

FIG. 122.—Reverse Running Mould, for Reverse Casting Mould for Plain Column.

crosswise (one near each end and one centrally). Cut the strips long enough to lay on the channels under the flutes, and over the sides of body, to afford a grip for withdrawing the cast, and to prevent the flutes from falling off the cast.

No. 3 shows a plan and section of the ground, with the joint lines of the flute and fillet piece set out. T, T are the upper and lower templates in position on the ground, ready for the model of the piece to be filled in at B. This method also applies to the making of single flutes.

No. 4 is a section of a reverse mould for casting pilasters. The flutes may be worked solid as shown on one-half of the section, or cast fibrous and fixed, as on the other half. The sides are held in position with rules and clips C, as described for slab bench moulds.

To Make a Reverse Mould for Plain Columns.—Figs. 122 and 123 show methods of forming reverse moulds for plain columns and hollow moulds and casts. Fig. 122 shows the section of a reverse template for running a mould for a plain column 4 in. diameter to any length. F is the profile of the template, G is a wood cleat, screwed on the stock to strengthen the deep part, and H is the section of a hollow core, used for hollow moulds and casts. Great care must be exercised in cutting the mould plate to ensure true fitting of the joggles (see section, Fig. 123). This is best done by roughing out the profile on a sheet of zinc and cutting it through the centre, the two halves to fit close at the joint when fixed on the stock ; both sides may be placed together in a vice and filed in one operation, so that the two profiles will be exactly alike and ensuring the joggles fitting accurately. This method of cutting and filing the half plates together is useful in making templates for rib mouldings, etc. In making a mould, say, for a column 4 ft. long, run a full 8 ft. length of moulding, cut the piece in two, place one on top of the other, and bind with hoops to keep them together while casting. This mould and the others here illustrated may be called a " run plaster piece mould," the pieces and joggles being run instead of made by hand, as in the case of ordinary plaster piece moulds. The run joggles prevent the mould pieces from moving sideways, but not lengthways. Any displacement of the pieces while casting would cause distorted casts, so the run joggles are interlocked at each end, stopped by cutting off about 2 in. at both ends of the raised joint, oiling the cut parts to prevent cohesion, placing this mould piece on the other, and filling in the sunk joint at the ends with plaster, the sinking being previously keyed and wetted. Intermediate " stop joints " are made by removing a part of the raised joint and cutting a hole through the sunk joint to pour in the plaster to form the " stop " of the joggle.

At one angle of the section a triangular shaped block of wood is shown. In large moulds it is used as a core to save materials and lighten the mould ; one is fixed at each side on the bench before the mould piece is run, after which the mould is made. The dotting of this section indicates the fine and coarse plaster. It does not follow that because there are no loose pieces the template should not be muffled. When the mould is roughed out with a muffled template, it allows the plaster to swell before the fine plaster face is run, and with greater ease and accuracy. Fine plaster for a large mass is an extravagance. Sometimes the cast must be of a given thickness to fit a structural iron column, or the inner surface of a definite profile, which can be done by fixing templates on the ends of the mould for ruling off, or for working straight or curved rules. The section of a quarter of such a template is shown at T, Fig. 123.

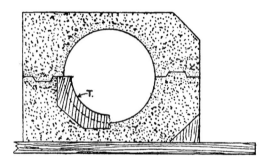

FIG. 123.—Reverse Casting Mould for Plain Columns, showing Run Joggles.

Hollow Cores.—The making of hollow cores is explained by Fig. 122. H shows the section of a hollow fibrous plaster core. This method is more economical for permanent than for temporary purposes, is useful for large moulds that must be moved about, is half the weight of solid work, and is doubly strong. Proceed as follows : The wood frame is made less in diameter than the actual size, to allow for plaster, canvas, and the finishing coat of fine plaster. Lay a coat of " firstings," followed by " seconds " with canvas, on the bed and place the frame in position, allowing plenty of canvas at the ends to overlap the frame. Then brush another strip of canvas over the joint. Before the stuff is set, pass the muffled template to and fro to clear any excess of plaster. The surface should be left rough as a key for the finishing coat of plaster. A little teased tow stuck into the soft fibrous work and left loose on the surface, affords a good key. The finishing coat should be laid and run while the core is green. Gauged stuff brushed on has a better key than if laid with a trowel, especially if following the curves of mouldings. The hatched lines round the frame H, Fig. 122, represent fibrous plaster, and the dotted section the finished surface of fine plaster.

Hollow Column Casts.—If casting hollow cement columns, stand the mould on end and place a tapered wood core upright in the centre, securing it at the bottom by inserting the end into a socket previously made in the wood ground. The core is easily removed after the stuff is set by tapping with a hammer. Pack gauged cement in at the top and ram home with a piece of rule padded at the end with felt, to protect the surface of the mould. The core is easily removed after the stuff is set by tapping with a hammer. If a hollow cast of plaster is required, the mould, if large or heavy, is rolled on the bench while the plaster is setting, or slung with ropes from the roof and made to revolve. If fibrous casts are required, one-half of the mould is filled with a lath at each edge. The joints are ruled flush with the edges of the mould. When two casts are made they are placed together, screwed through the edge laths, and further secured by a long strip of canvas soaked in plaster. The wet canvas is pulled to and fro over the joint and pressed on by a stumpy brush on a lath from each end of the mould, which is then turned over, the other joint being treated in the same way. Another way for white cement or fibrous plasterwork is to place a rough, fibrous plaster core in the mould and fill in the space between the core and the mould. The core must be " green " and rough, so that the surface material will adhere to it. When set, release the mould and the cast as one piece.

CHAPTER XVII

COMPOSITIONS

Gesso—Woods—Walter Crane's Recipe—Ceiling in Gesso—Gesso Duro—How to Begin to Paint Pictures : Method of Making and Manipulating—How to Fasten Linen on Panels —Laying Grounds—Preparing a Fine Ground—Preparing a Ground for Gesso Sottile —To Smooth the Surface of a Panel—Planing Gesso Sottile Surfaces—Smith's Patent Metal.

THE materials used for **Gesso, Papier-mâché, Compo,** and **Carton-pierre** are placed in a group by themselves, being altogether different from the plaster group, in that all require glue (or size) to set and combine them into a hard and durable substance, whereas limes, plasters, and cements need water only to make them set hard.

" Gesso," as we know the term in England, is applied and restricted to painting in relief and thus linking up the art of the painter and sculptor. It is a term frequently misused for stucco, but quite different in every way. In Italy the word gesso is used for plasterwork generally, as " stucco " is in Scotland and " plaster " in England.

Gesso is a very ancient form of material, largely used decoratively by the Egyptians, who doubtless discovered the process. Like most ancient processes, it is very simple. Its remote ancestor was evidently the craft of painting in " slip " clays on vases or other fictile productions, and in this form it still survives on the commonest earthenware, and in those most refined and beautiful works in *pâte-sur-pâte,* whereon M. Solon records the art history of our time—works which shall be valued in the future as we now value a Greek cameo. From the use of clay to that of chalk the transition is easy. Calcined chalk (whiting) was found to be the most perfect ground or surface for displaying the beauty of gold and to receive painted or gilded decoration ; to wit, the wooden statues and pictured panels of the earliest times, as the Egyptian mummy cases and other work, which the dryness of the African climate has preserved to us.

We have it at Pompeii in conjunction with painting and stucco decoration, and in the decoration of the Roman tombs of the Via Latina. We have it, united with painting, in the diapered backgrounds, gilded enrichments, nimbi of saints, and jewelled accessories of kings in early Italian pictures. We find it used by the illuminators of the Middle Ages, under the burnished gold of glorified initial letters.

To render whiting or gesso stable some viscid liquid, such as glue or size, had to be mixed with it. This was found to be a convenient vehicle for modelling low relief by painting, and thus gesso took its place as an accessory decorative art of the painter. The early Byzantine painters used it as a ground for "tempera" painting and for painting diaper and other small patterns in relief, for the gilded portions of pictures.

A visit to the National Gallery will reveal much gesso work by the early painters.

Our museums contain much decorative relief work described as gesso which is not executed by this method, being moulded or pressed work. It is not possible to mould, press, or cast gesso, which is ornament in relief applied to various materials put on warm with a brush. Applied decoration cast from moulds, or squeezed on to a ground by a mould into a doughy substance, which adheres to the groundwork and leaves an impression, is " compo," or composition.

The principal use of gesso is in the formation of a groundwork on to which gold may be applied. Its perfect surface enhances the true beauty of gold. On carved wood several coatings of gesso were applied to soften the sharp arrises and to broaden the hollowings, because sharp or strong shadows are detrimental to the beauty of gold or gilding.

The retable in Westminster Abbey is an illustration of its use as an architectural accessory. During the Renaissance of decorative art it covered the cassoni, or gilded marriage coffers (of which there are some fine examples in the Victoria and Albert Museum, from which Plates CXVIII and CXIX are illustrated), the larger articles of furniture (Plate CXV), and the panels of the wainscoting. Gesso became, in general, the foundation for the more delicate and refined work of that period and lingered till the latter half of the eighteenth century. In modern times, Sir E. Burne-Jones, Mr G. T. Robinson, Mr Walter Crane, Professor Lethaby, and others have given an impetus to the art of gesso working. Mr Robinson at first used plaster instead of whiting, with glue and a little oil to render it fluent. This produced a remarkably hard body, capable of being either laid on with a brush or modelled up with steel modelling tools. When gilt it looked like wrought gold. It adheres so closely to glass, marble, porcelain, or polished wood, that purposed fracture of the base on which it is laid will go through the gesso without chipping it from the surface Whiting is easier to work than plaster. The beginner should use the best gilder's whiting, which is much purer than the ordinary whiting of commerce. The glue should be of the best make, macerated in cold water until it will not swell. The linseed oil should be of the oldest and cleanest kind. The quantities for each vary, according to the nature of the work proposed. It is difficult to give any definite proportions, but a few experiments will readily enable the worker to ascertain the mixture best suited to his purpose.

A very good recipe for gesso is as follows : 12 oz. of best gilder's whiting ; 9 oz. of parchment size ; 3 drops of cold drawn linseed oil.

The size should be put into a basin, perfectly free from grease, and the basin placed in a saucepan of cold water over a stove with slight heat, until the jelly or size is thoroughly melted, which should be accomplished in about thirty minutes. The water must not become of warmer temperature than may be comfortable to the finger. The whiting must be pounded with a pestle in a mortar until very fine, then made warm, the melted size poured into the mortar, mixed with the whiting as poured in, and stirred for about five minutes. The mortar should then be placed into the saucepan of warm water and put on the stove for about ten minutes, after which time three drops of cold drawn linseed oil may be added and quietly stirred for five minutes. The mixture may then be poured off into the basin in which the size has been melted, and allowed to cool for twenty-four hours before it is used. In very cold weather less time will suffice.

When required for use, melt some of the mixture in a basin placed in a saucepan of water, as before described for melting the size.

It is important that the water should not be hot or warmer than may be comfortable to the fingers ; nor must any water get into the basin of size and whiting when being mixed. The gesso mixture should be of the consistency of thick cream. If too thick, add diluted size, melted down as before described ; equal parts of water and size.

This gesso may be applied to any rigid material. If quite free from any trace of grease, the gesso will adhere to the foundation with great strength.

Woods.—Oak, cedar, lime wood, mahogany, and ebony are all suitable woods on which to apply gesso. No wood having a greasy nature, such as teak or pine, will take gesso well.

A wide, flat, hog's hair brush, a No. 2 sable brush, and a No. 2 sable tracer will be found useful for applying the mixture.

When preparing a foundation on which to model, a coat of the mixture should be spread equally with the wide hog's hair brush, by dipping the brush into the mixture and drawing it over the panel (or other foundation) until the brush is empty, and repeating this process until the panel or foundation is equally covered. When the first coat is quite dry and hard, it should be rubbed down with glass paper until the wood looms through, when a second coating may be applied and glass papered as before. The gesso must not be touched with the fingers after being brushed on to the panel. When the second coating of gesso is quite dry and hard and glass papered, a coat of best orange shellac, dissolved in methylated spirit, should be spread and allowed to dry hard. Gesso will take some days to harden, but will dry very hard and tough. The surface of the panel will then be ready for working on the relief modelling. The beauty of the modelling will depend on the peculiar quality of surface which the gesso naturally takes from the flow from a full brush and not touched (until hard). It is best left unaltered and not disturbed by scraping. The modelling must be gradually built up, and be given a coat of shellac on top of every two coats of gesso. In modelling, the brush should be held as vertically as possible to assist the flow of the gesso from the brush on to the background, and into the shape of the design spaces which are to be flooded with the mixture, gradually adding more of the mixture as increased relief is wanted. The best character of work is direct and simple. It might perhaps at first sight be thought that a material such as gesso had no particular restrictions or limitations of use essential to character or style. On the contrary, it has most delightful and charming characteristics peculiar to and arising directly from the nature of the medium itself and from the tool or tools, which an artist may tend to emphasise and develop rather than to hide. In the flowing on and building up of a design, brush and medium will combine in favouring particular forms such as dots, blebs and spots, arrangements of lines and stringy forms, branch, leaf, scroll work, and forms such as naturally flow from a brush full of thick, treacly paste. Success depends partly on the consistency of the medium, which should be neither too thick nor too thin, thin enough to flow, but thick enough not to overflow the outline of the pattern, partly on precision and nicety of touch, and partly on the aptitude of the user to put together such arrangements of line or form as best suits the medium and its proper purpose.

One may even see some resemblance to the nature of gesso in modern cake confectionery, where the artist squeezes pattern work of spirals and curls, waves and lines, dots and blebs of white and tinted sugar upon a sugar ground.

Walter Crane's recipe for the preparation of gesso is as follows : Boil 1 part of powdered resin in 4 parts of linseed oil and 6 parts melted glue, and mix well together, warm. Soak whiting in cold water until quite soft, and add to the above mixture to make it of the consistency of thick cream. Mr Robinson did not use resin, and thinks it is not at all necessary. It may retard absorption of moisture of the material by the ground, but is apt to cause the work to flake off from it. Absorption may be prevented by other means. Gesso is less liable to crack when the resin is omitted.

The mode of applying gesso depends greatly upon requirements and on the foundation upon which it is to be applied. It can be applied to any rigid, non-greasy material. If to wood, which is to remain visible, the surface should be given a thin coat of French polish. If the surface is to be covered with gesso, glue thin canvas or " skrim " over it, for a key, and scrumble with thin glue. If the foundation is fibrous plaster, trace on the design outline, " scratch " the ground thoroughly, and stop any absorption with a thin coat of shellac or two coats of thin glue. The foundation will then be ready to receive the modelling. If the relief is to be high, boss up the higher portions with fine tow (or cotton wool) steeped in gesso. When partially set, paint with a full brush over it, coat by coat, with fluent gesso until the general bulk and form is attained. Use thin glue and water when any absorption begins to appear. The finishing coats and finer work should contain a little more oil for the mixture to dry smooth and even. It may be finished with a modelling tool. To do this, let the work dry, and afterwards soften the surface by applying glue water from a vessel containing the mixture, placed in a saucepan of warm water. The gesso must be kept at one consistency; if it chills it becomes "ropy" and may flake in drying. With a mixture thickened with stiffened glue and more whiting, modelling may be done as with clay or wax. It must not be put on thickly, and the finger and tools must be oiled. When a high degree of finish is required, it may be worked up with graver or small tools, and the surface polished if required with fine pumice stone or Dutch rush. This, however, is not the province of gesso, the beauty of which depends on the natural smoothness of surface due to its fluid application from a brush point. Any other process is an abuse of gesso as a vehicle of art.

Stamps or dies (for other purposes) may be moulded in a mixture of plaster of Paris and flour paste, which, when rolled out thin, will form a ground for gesso. This is the "pastiglia" of the Italians. Its adaptability may be seen in the model of part of the Villa Madama, in the Victoria and Albert Museum.

The whiting may be stained any colour, and by applying relief of one tint on to a groundwork of another, models somewhat resemble cameos. This mixture may be gilded, lacquered, or painted. In the two latter cases more labour and little oil must be used.

There are various patent ready-made materials to be had for working in gesso. These consist of a fine powder, sold in tins, which needs only to be mixed with cold water to turn it into a paste of any consistency, according to the quantity of water used.

Most of these tinned preparations may serve a purpose, but they cannot compare with the genuine medium of Italy for beauty of working and finish.

They appear to have flour and sugar ingredients, and work rather too sticky and pasty; but they dry slowly, and are open to modelling and retouching and variety of treatment in their own particular way.

Gesso duro is hardened or durable plaster. Gesso sottile is gauged with whiting instead of plaster. Gesso grosso is specially prepared plaster.

The following extracts from the MS. of Cennino Cennini (a pupil of Agnoli, himself a pupil of Giotto), written in 1417, and translated by Mrs Merrifield in 1844, will be interesting and invaluable in connection with gesso and tempera painting, dissolving glue, the use of plaster, glue, and linen, and recipes for gesso grosso and gesso sottile :—

How to Begin to Paint Pictures.—In the first place, a panel of the wood of the poplar, lime, or willow tree must be prepared on which to paint the picture. Let it be made quite smooth. If it be defaced with knots, or if it be greasy, you must cut it away as far as the grease extends, for there is no other remedy. The wood must be very dry; and if it be such a piece that you can boil in a cauldron of clean water, after the boiling it will never split. Let us now return to the knots, or any other defect in the smoothness of the panel. Take some glue (colla di spicchi) and about a glassful of clean water; melt and boil two pieces (spicchi) in a pipkin free from grease; then put in a porringer some sawdust and knead it into the glue; fill up the defects or knots with a wooden spatula and let them remain; then scrape them with the point of a knife till they are level with the rest of the panel. Examine if there be any nail or other thing that renders the panel uneven, and knock it into the panel ; then provide some pieces of tinplate, like quattrini (small pieces of money), and cover over the iron with them ; and this is done that the rust of the iron may not rise through the ground. The surface of the panel cannot be too smooth. Boil some glue, made of parchment shavings, till the water be reduced to one-third of what it was at first, and when put on the hands, if one hand stick to the other, it is sufficiently boiled. Strain it two or three times, put half this glue into a pipkin, add a third part water, and boil well together ; then, with a hog's hair pencil, large and soft, pass a coat of the glue over the panel, or foliage, or pyxes (cibori), or columns, or whatever you work upon, that is to be covered with a ground (ingessare), and let it dry ; then take some of your first strong glue (colla forte) and pass twice over your work, letting it dry well between each coat of glue, and it will be glued to perfection. Do you know the effect of the first glue ? A weak water or liquor is absorbed from it by the wood, which operates exactly as if, when fasting, you eat a few comfits and drink a glass of wine, which gives you an appetite for dinner ; so this glue prepares the wood for the glue and grounds to be applied afterwards.

How to Fasten Linen on Panels.—Having thus spread the glue, get some linen cloth, old, fine, and white, and free from grease. Take your best glue, cut or tear this linen into large or small strips, soak these in the glue and spread it with your hands over the surface of the panel, remove the seams and spread it well with the palms of your hands, and leave it to dry for two days. And remember it is best to use glue when the weather is dry and windy. Glue is stronger in the winter. For gilding, the weather should be damp and rainy.

How to Lay Grounds of Gesso Grosso on the Surface of a Picture with a Spatula.—Where the panel is very dry, take the point of a knife like a rasp (mello), rasp it well, and make the surface quite even. Then take some gesso grosso, that is to say, volterrano, purified and sifted like flour. Put a porringerful on the porphyry slab, grind it well with this glue as you would grind colours, collect it, and put it on the surface of the pictures, and with a very smooth and rather large spatula cover the whole surface, and wherever you can use the spatula do so. Then take some of this ground plaster (gesso), warm it, take a soft hog's hair pencil, and give a coat on the cornices and foliage and on the even surfaces with the spatula. Give three or four coats on the other parts of the cornices, but on the other level parts you cannot use too much. Leave it to dry for two or three days. Then take the iron rasp (mesella) and level the surface ; procure some small iron rods, which are called raffiette, such as you will find in the painters', who use several kinds of them. Pick out all the cornices and foliage which are not flat, and with these make every part of the surface of the ground smooth and free from knots.

How to Prepare a Fine Ground (Gesso Sottile) for Pictures.—You must now prepare a plaster for fine grounds, called gesso sottile. This is made from the same plaster as the last, but it must be well washed (purgata) and kept moist in a large tub for at least a month ; stir it up well every day until it almost rots (marcise) and is completely slaked, and it will become as soft as silk. Throw away the water, make it into cakes and let it dry, and this plaster (gesso) is sold by the apothecaries to our painters. It is used for grounds for gilding, for working in relief, and other fine works.

How to Prepare a Ground of Gesso Sottile on a Picture, and How it is to be Tempered.—Having laid on the gesso grosso, rubbed down the surface and polished it well and delicately, put some cakes of the gesso sottile into a pipkin of water, and let them absorb as much as they will. Put a small portion of it at a time on the porphyry slab, and without adding any water to it, grind it to an impalpable powder. Put it then on a piece of linen cloth, strong and white. When you have ground as much of it as you want (for you must consider what quantity you will want, that you may neither have to make two portions of tempered plaster nor to throw away any good plaster), take some of the same glue with which you tempered the gesso grosso. You must make sufficient at one time to temper both kinds of gesso. The gesso sottile requires less tempering than the gesso grosso; the reason for this is that the gesso grosso is the foundation of all your work, and that how much soever you press the gesso grosso, a little water will still remain in it. For this reason, make the same kind of glue for both. Take a new pipkin which is free from grease, and if it be glazed, so much the better. Take a cake of this gesso sottile and scrape it fine with a knife as you would cheese, and put it into the pipkin. Put some of the glue on it and stir the gesso as you would a paste for making fritters, smoothly and evenly, until there are no longer any lumps. Procure a cauldron of water and make it very hot, and put into it the pipkin containing the tempered gesso. Thus the gesso will become warm, but will not boil, for if it should boil it would be spoiled. When it is warm, take your picture and a large and very soft pencil of hog's bristles, dipped in the pipkin, and taking up a proper quantity at a time, neither too much nor too little, spread it evenly over the level surfaces, the cornices, and the foliage. It is true that in doing this the first time you should spread and rub the gesso with your fingers and hand wherever you can, and this will incorporate the gesso grosso with the gesso sottile. When you have done this, begin again and spread it with the brush, without touching it with the hand. Let it rest a little, but not so long as to dry thoroughly; then pass over it a third time with the brush, and let it dry as usual. Then give it a coat on the other side, and in this manner, always keeping the gesso warm, give the panels eight coats. Foliage and relievos require less, but you cannot put too much on cloths. This is on account of the rasping or rubbing down, which is done afterwards.

How to Begin to Smooth the Surface of a Panel on which you have Laid a Ground of Gesso Sottile.—When you have finished laying the ground (which must be done in one day, even if you work at it in the night, in order to complete it in the usual way), let it dry in the shade for two days and nights at least. The drier it is the better. Tie some powdered charcoal in a piece of linen, and sift it over the ground of the picture. Then, with the feather of a hen or goose, spread this black powder equally over the ground, because the panel cannot be made too smooth, and because the iron with which you rub the picture is smooth also. When you remove it, the ground will be as white as milk, and you will then see whether it requires more rubbing with the iron.

How to Plane Surfaces on which Gesso Sottile has been Laid, and of what Use the Planing is.—Take a flat raffietto, about as wide as a finger, and gently rub the surface of the cornice once; then, with a sharp rasp (mella arrotata), which you must hold as freely and lightly as you possibly can, rub over the surface of the panel with a very light hand, brushing away the loose gesso with the feather. And know that this dust is excellent for removing grease from the pages of books (carte de libre). In the same manner rub smooth the cornices and foliage and polish them as if they were ivory. And sometimes, for you may have many kinds of work, you may polish cornices and foliage by rubbing them with a piece of linen, first wetted and then squeezed almost dry.

The bands of old linen evidently serve the purpose of the sand in the Egyptian method, give a tooth for the plaster, help to hold the panel together, and prevent soap or resin from rising through the gesso surface. Apparently, linen was used for the best coffins in Egypt in the same way. Gesso volterrano is (according to Mrs Merrifield) plaster of Paris, obtained from gypsum quarries near Bologna. Vasari gives a long account of this gesso volterrano in his life of Andrea Verrocchio, who used it to make

PLATE CXV

(*a*) and (*b*) DETAIL OF TWO MIRROR FRAMES, DECORATED IN GESSO. (ENGLISH, EIGHTEENTH CENTURY.)

(*c*) TOP OF SIDE TABLE DECORATED IN GESSO. (ENGLISH, EIGHTEENTH CENTURY.)

PLATE CXVI

A RENAISSANCE PICTURE FRAME, DECORATED IN GESSO. (ITALIAN, SIXTEENTH CENTURY.)
(*Victoria and Albert Museum.*)

PLATE CXVII

DECORATED CIRCULAR BOX IN GESSO (ITALIAN). (*Victoria and Albert Museum.*)

PLATE CXVIII

(*a*) and (*b*) DETAIL OF MARRIAGE COFFERS IN GESSO WITH FIGURES, ETC. (BOTH ITALIAN RENAISSANCE.)

PLATE CXIX

(*a*) and (*b*) DETAIL OF MARRIAGE COFFERS. (ITALIAN RENAISSANCE.)

PLATE CXX

(*a*) DOORWAY IN COMPO. CARTON-PIERRE (MODERN) IN
GEORGIAN STYLE.

(*b*) DETAIL IN GLAZED TERRA-COTTA, BY LUCA DELLA ROBBIA.

Plate CXXI

Chimney-piece in Wood Decorated in Compo. Carton-Pierre. (Adam Style, Late Eighteenth Century.)

PLATE CXXII

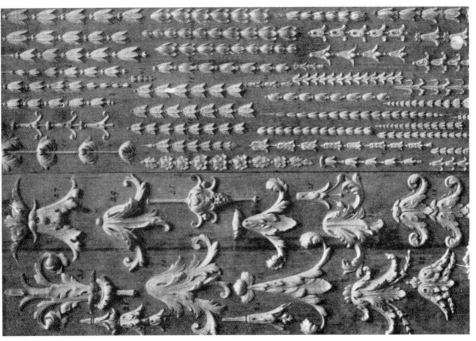

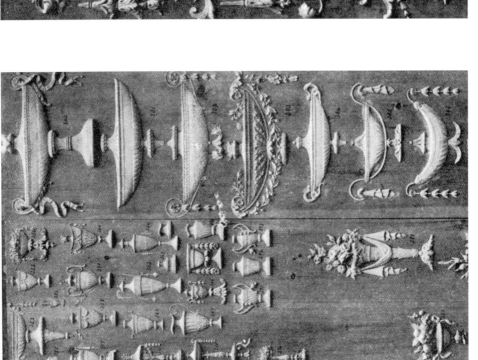

(a) EXAMPLES OF STRIP VASE DECORATION IN CARTON-PIERRE.

(b) EXAMPLES OF PAPIER-MÂCHÉ ENRICHMENTS.

(From the original moulds.   *Vide also* Plates XXX, XXXA.)

casts from dead persons. It will be noted that the gypsum for the final coating of gesso is thoroughly slaked by keeping in water for some weeks.

A very fine example of gesso work exists in the old cathedral church at Coire, or Chur, Switzerland. There is there a box (claimed to be of ninth-century work) entirely covered with gesso, on which a design in low relief has been roughly scrolled. The gesso has been polished, like ivory. At the corners, which are chipped, linen can be seen next to the wood, as Cennino Cennini advises.

Smith's patent metal (an improvement on Spence's composition metal) is used for casts and moulds. Reproductions in this metal give the most delicate lines and forms in figures and foliage. Having a durable nature, unaffected by acids, lime, or damp, it has advantages for moulds for concrete, Portland cement, and white cement castings. It is useful for casting composition enrichments, fibrous plaster enrichments, and for moulds of enrichments in reverse moulds for casting fibrous plaster cornices. Casts of this metal, from moulds with a polished surface, are as polished as the moulds. Deeply undercut metal casts can be produced from gelatine moulds. This metal is dissolved and used as sulphur is used, but iron filings are not required. Piece moulds of this metal are made as with wax.

CHAPTER XVIII

COMPOSITIONS (*Continued*)

Papier-mâché—Manufacture and Uses for Decorations—Stage Properties—Papier-mâché Moulds—Paper Casts Without Moulds—To Make Paste—Permanent Paste—Carton-pierre—Recipes—English and French Carton-pierre—Fibrous Slab or Patent Wood—Pâte Coulante—Paste Composition—Making Sulphur Moulds for Composition—Recipes—London Composition—Sulphur Moulds—Casting and Fixing Composition.

Papier-mâché, as its name proclaims, is of French origin, but the use of the material at the present day is almost extinct. Good examples are to be found in French buildings of the sixteenth century. The grand trophies and heraldic devices in the Hall of the Council of Henri II in the Louvre, as also decorations at St Germain and the Hotel des Fermes, on ceilings and walls, are executed in papier-mâché. In 1730 a church, built entirely of papier-mâché, was erected at Hoop, near Bergen, Norway. The inside and outside are covered with this material, which was made waterproof and nearly fireproof by an application of vitriol water and lime slaked with whey and white of eggs. The decorations of the Pantheon, London, were executed in papier-mâché by Bielefeld. In 1847, E. F. Bielefeld obtained a patent for making moulds for this material, also for making papier-mâché maps in relief. In 1858, White and Parley obtained a patent for improvements in the manufacture of papier-mâché and carton-pierre. The dome of the Palais de Justice of Brussels (weighing 16 tons) is composed of this material.

Papier-mâché Manufacture.—Papier-mâché work usually requires a back and front mould of brass for a cast generally about $\frac{1}{8}$ in. The paper and ingredients are mixed up in a machine, rolled into sheets of the required size, placed into moulds, and subjected to hydraulic or screw pressure. The casts are placed in a drying room to harden, and when dry, trimmed and finished. This substance was used for the decoration of wood cornices; the enrichments are pressed in parts and afterwards joined up by mounters. The moulds are made of brass, copper, type metal, box-wood, or sulphur. Large pieces, such as panels, etc., are backed with wood to strengthen them.

Another process is that of glueing or pasting layers of paper together, and subjecting them to high pressure until all become one.

Another method is to make a composition of paper pulp and resin, placed in moulds, and with layers of strong paper pressed into a homogeneous body.

Papier-mâché Stage Properties.—Modellers and plasterers often find employment in the property rooms of theatres in modelling, moulding, and making grotesque masks, heads of animals (the bodies of which are made of wickerwork), and architectural decorations for solid or built scenes. Papier-mâché properties are produced from plaster piece moulds. Large sheets of brown and blue sugar paper are pasted on both sides, and folded for the paste to absorb. The first part of the paper process is known as a " water coat." Sugar paper is soaked in water, torn in small pieces, and laid over the face of the mould, to prevent the actual paper work from adhering. Brown paper is then torn into pieces about 2 in. sq., and laid over the water coat, followed by coats of sugar paper similarly laid until thick enough for strength. The pieces of paper are laid overlapping, and care taken that each coat of paper is well pressed and rubbed into the crevices with the fingers, and a brush, cloth, or sponge, to work out the air, obtain complete cohesion of the paper layers and a good impress of the mould. After being dried before a fire, the paper cast is taken out of the mould, trimmed up, and painted. A clever man, with colours and a little hair, can give each mask taken from the one mould a completely different appearance. Coloured papers enable any uncovered part of the previous layer to be seen and covered over. Some property men dry the mould and oil or dust the surface with French chalk to prevent adhesion of cast to mould. Others paste one side only of the sugar paper used for the first coat.

Papier-mâché Moulds.—A cast is sometimes required of some part of a building, furniture, or an ornament, which cannot be moulded in plaster, or squeezed in wax or clay. A paper mould may be made as follows : Brush several sheets of sugar paper with clean cold water, and lay sheet on sheet to keep damp. When pliable (not wet) lay small pieces of the paper on the object to be cast, and press and rub them on with the fingers, modelling tools, and a brush. When the object is covered, lay four or five coats of brown paper (previously pasted) as before into every part. When dry, remove all carefully. If possible, make a case (by laying plaster over the back) before removing the paper mould, otherwise a plaster case may be made after removal. When dry, give the mould a coat of linseed oil ; let it stand for twenty-four hours ; then coat it with shellac and cast from it.

To Make Paper Casts Without Moulds.—Paper casts suitable for some purposes may be made without making a mould. To prevent mould and cast from sticking together, oil or dust the mould with French chalk before proceeding as follows : Paste some sugar paper and brown paper on one side, dip the former in water, and roll it in a damp cloth. Fold the brown paper and set it aside, ready for use. Then tear the sugar paper into the required sizes, and lay it piece by piece until the object is covered in, pressing it well into parts with brush and modelling tool ; no ridges or lumps must be on the surface. Then lay a coat of brown paper smoothly and uniformly in thickness. Finish with a coat of sugar paper, leaving the surface smooth and fair. When dry, carefully take it off the model and coat inside with glue. If the model is on the round, as a figure or vase, cut the paper cast vertically up both sides with a sharp knife, to free it from the object. If the model is undercut, cut one side only and ease off by degrees. If removed carefully the cast will spring or bend back to its place. Then glue and paste the joints over with paper. If the pasted papers, when laid aside to absorb, should become fixed or difficult to open, dip them in water to free them.

To Make Paste.—Paste may be made with flour and cold water well worked together, and boiling water poured on and the mass well stirred.

Permanent paste (as used in Italy) is made as follows : Dissolve 1 oz. of alum in 1 qt. of warm water ; when cold, add flour and stir until a thick paste ; then add $\frac{1}{2}$ oz. of resin, 1 oz. of sugar of lead (lead acetate), and boiling water as required to thicken.

Carton-pierre has a paper basis, like papier-mâché. It was first introduced by M. Mizière, a Parisian modeller, and further carried out by M. Hire, also a Parisian modeller, who reduced the paper to a pulp, mixing it with plaster and dissolved glue. This substance was coarse in texture, had to be coated with plaster, and again cleaned up by hand. M. Romagnesi reduced the paper pulp to a fine state, added glue, and mixed whiting as required; he was thus able to take very fine lines from delicate originals.

The decoration of the principal apartments of the Tuileries, some in the Louvre, the Palais-Royal, and the internal decorations of later France and Belgium, are mostly of carton-pierre.

The ingredients used and the proportions vary. Some use more glue than others. Some use plaster to make it set more quickly, and china clay. The English carton-pierre is much stronger than that of the French, who use a larger proportion of whiting.

Metal moulds are sometimes used for stock patterns. Plaster piece moulds are mostly used for carton-pierre, and the dough-like mixture is hand pressed into the mould in the following manner: The moulds are seasoned with linseed oil, or shellaced and oiled as required. The soft carton-pierre, or dough, is rolled on a smooth slate or other solid slab, and is mixed with fine whiting, to which a little plaster is sometimes added to give it the required consistency. No more should be stiffened than can be conveniently used, as it may become too stiff to press easily. Cut a small piece off and roll on the slab to give it a smooth face, and press it into the mould with the point of the forefinger and a small wooden tool. When this piece is firmly and evenly pressed, the ragged joints should be cut clean and square, then wetted with water to make a better joint for the next piece to be laid on. Centre flowers and foliage, etc., are cast without any ground, and in order to strengthen the several parts, thin copper wire is embedded in the weak or thin parts. Very thin wire is also carried across from one weak part to another, as in tying one weak tendril to the main stem, to support it until fixed. The wire is then cut off. When the cast in the mould is all pressed and made flush at the edges and rim, it is allowed to stand in a warm place to get firm. Should there be any hollow places in the back of the cast, they are filled up with dry plaster or fine sawdust to keep the cast from sinking. A board large enough to cover the mould is then placed on the top and drawn backwards and forwards, to level the dry filling. The mould is now turned upside down, care being taken to keep the board close to the rim of the mould. The case of the mould is removed, and then the plaster pieces one by one. The cast is kept on the board, and placed in a warm place until properly set. The seams caused by the joints of the mould are now cleaned off by the use of gouge files or small tools, and afterwards sand-papered. The plaster or sawdust on the back, to keep the hollow parts from sinking until set and cleaned up, is cleared out, and as this material becomes very hard, it is necessary to make small holes in the stems and other places before the cast is set, so as to admit of fine brads, screws, or needle points for the purpose of fixing. When fixed on wood, it is usual to glue it on and drive needle points into the cast to keep it in its place until the glue is set. A thin paste of carton-pierre is also used for fixing it on plaster, further supporting it by the aid of screws or fine brads. Carton-pierre casts can also be made by pressing in jelly moulds.

The following proportions are used by the best London and Paris makers. It will be seen that some use alum. This is to prevent the dough from turning mouldy, or smelling offensively. Some use plaster and whiting in equal proportions for stiffening; others use only whiting. The better the paper, the stronger the carton-pierre. Old ledgers, or paper made from rags, give the best results. The paper used for wrapping oranges makes strong work.

Recipe.—2 lbs. of best glue dissolved in 2 qts. of water, to which is added $\frac{1}{2}$ lb. of flour, and $\frac{1}{2}$ lb. of good paper reduced to a fine pulp by boiling and beating. The paper is weighed dry. This mass is all boiled together for one hour, and allowed to simmer for one hour, after which it is poured out on to a slab and stiffened with sifted whiting. In all cases the whiting should be dried, so as to be more easily ground fine and sifted.

Recipe.—2 lbs. of best town glue, dissolved in 3 pts. of water, $\frac{1}{2}$ lb. of flour, $\frac{1}{4}$ lb. of ground alum, and 1 lb. of paper. Cut or tear the paper into small pieces, and boil for ten or twelve hours. While hot, add the dissolved glue, also hot, then shake in the flour, alum, and $\frac{1}{4}$ lb. of fine sifted whiting. Stir this mass well, pour out on to a bench, and beat it well, adding sifted whiting until of the consistency of dough. Fine plaster and whiting are added as required for use. The paper should be taken out, strained, and beaten with a wooden beater, having one end studded with lath nails, to reduce the paper to a fine pulp; boiled again, and strain off superfluous water, which would weaken the glue.

Recipe (London).—To make a 2 lb. batch: 1 lb. Scotch glue, $\frac{1}{4}$ lb. paper, 5 pts. of water, and 14 oz. of flour. Paper used for packing oranges is employed for the above, torn to shreds, and mixed and boiled with the other materials. A small proportion of chloride of zinc added to the pulp will toughen papier-mâché or carton-pierre.

Recipe (London).—To make 60 lbs. carton-pierre: 14 lbs. china clay, 14 lbs. plaster (white), 2 lbs. best glue, 2 lbs. paper, and 2 lbs. flour; add water and boil.

Plates CXX-CXXII show some architectural features in Georgian and Adam style in carton-pierre or compo.

French Carton-pierre.—$2\frac{1}{4}$ lbs. of glue dissolved in 7 pts. of water, $\frac{3}{4}$ lb. of paper reduced to a pulp. Add the glue hot to the hot pulp, boil the mass together, add best French whiting, and stiffen with plaster for pressing.

French carton-pierre was, during the last generation, greatly employed in London for internal decoration.

Fibrous Slab or Patent Wood.—The name given to an invention patented by E. F. Bielefeld, which consists of rolled slabs of carton-pierre. The dome, 140 ft. diameter, of the Reading Room of the British Museum, designed by S. Smirke, R.A., 1856, is lined internally with this material. The panels, composed of three pieces, are 22 ft. long by 11 ft. 6 in. wide. They were raised in their spherical form to a height of 110 ft., and fixed in one piece to the ironwork.

Pâte coulante (liquid paste) is a cheap form of carton-pierre, used for work not exposed to much wear. It is more quickly and cheaply produced than carton-pierre, being poured into gelatine moulds like plaster, and thus avoiding hand pressing.

Pâte coulante may be made in two ways. One is to mix equal proportions of plaster and ground whiting with as much dissolved glue as will enable the mixture to run freely, adding ground alum as required. Alum hardens plaster and hastens its setting, thus promoting quicker working. The other method is to add fine tissue paper pulp to the plaster, whiting, and glue.

Compo, or Composition.—Attributed to the invention of M. Liardet, a Swiss clergyman; has been used in France for the decoration of buildings, picture frames, and mirror frames since the time of Louis XIV It was introduced into England about 1767 by Robert Adam, who used it for the low relief decoration of ceilings and walls, chimney-pieces, doors, and window shutters. The work designed by the Adam Brothers is remarkable for its delicacy, crispness, and cleanliness of modelling, resembling wood-carving when painted. It would be a libel on the art of wood-carving to say that compo ornament cannot be distinguished from it. The probability is that the moulds were produced from soft wood-carved models (Plates CXXI, CXXII); but the technical qualities, although similar to the public eye, are quite different. It has withstood the test of a century and a half, the material being as hard to-day as when new. Compo was first made in London by Italian workmen, who jealously guarded the secret of its preparation, which was eventually discovered, made, and shown by Mr John Jackson, in the form of balls strung on threads and small ornaments. It was then largely used for the decoration of houses, chimney-pieces, mirror and picture frames, furniture, musical instruments, chandeliers, and other work as a substitute for wood-carving ; in Edinburgh, Glasgow, Dublin, and elsewhere it is now used in ornamental wood mouldings on shop fronts ; the composition seems harder and better preserved than the wood on which it was fixed—good evidence of its durability.

Composition or " paste compo " is still used for mirror and picture frames, ship saloons, and interior woodwork.

Owing to its flexible nature, paste compo is useful for application to circular work. When hard it will not easily chip. It can be painted and gilded. There are various ways and quantities of materials used for making paste compo, each maker having a special recipe ; but all are similar, as follows :—

The following quantities are used by different makers of repute—

Recipe.—3 lbs. of best town glue dissolved in as much water as will just cover it, $1\frac{1}{2}$ lbs. of resin, 3 gills of linseed oil, $\frac{1}{4}$ lb. of Burgundy pitch. The glue is allowed to swell in the water for four or five hours, and then dissolved by means of heat in a water bath. The oil, resin, and pitch are melted in a separate pot (taking care that it does not boil over), and when cooled, is poured into the pot containing the melted glue, all being well stirred together. It is afterwards poured on a slab, or clean smooth bench, on which is formed a ring of well-dried and sifted whiting. It is then well mixed up, kneaded, rolled, and beaten, until it becomes a smooth, tough, elastic kind of dough or oil putty. No more whiting is used than will make a stiff dough. Divide the batch into cakes and put them aside until required. They are softened by steaming when required for pressing.

Recipe.—Best glue, $2\frac{1}{2}$ lbs. ; resin, 2 lbs. ; linseed oil, 1 pt. The ingredients are melted, mixed, and rolled until doughy, as described above.

Recipe.—Good Scotch glue, 3 lbs. ; resin, $\frac{1}{2}$ lb. ; linseed oil, $\frac{1}{2}$ pt. ; boiled oil, $\frac{1}{4}$ pt. ; Burgundy pitch, $\frac{1}{4}$ lb. ; Venice turpentine, $\frac{1}{4}$ lb. The ingredients are mixed as before, the Burgundy pitch and Venice turpentine being mixed with the resin and oil.

It will be seen that the proportions are all similar, being nearly 1 lb. of resin and 1 gill of linseed oil to 1 lb. of glue. When Burgundy pitch is used, the quantity of resin is less, and the quantity of oil is regulated according to the strength of the glue. The best glue only should be used. The whiting should be well dried and ground fine, or it will lie in small, dry patches in the work and spoil it. Gilder's London white is best. When a screw press with swing ball is not at hand, an ordinary copying press may be utilised for small work. Some plasterers use a compo mostly of glue and whiting and a small quantity of resin for gallery fronts, or other places not exposed to wear and tear. This is hand pressed, but is not so strong as the machine-pressed work.

London Composition.—The following quantities will make a 16 lb. batch. This is an old recipe and is mostly used in London shops. Dissolve 16 lbs. of town glue and 5 pts. of water in one pot, and dissolve 9 lbs. of ground resin and $3\frac{1}{2}$ pts. of linseed oil in another pot. When both are dissolved, pour the glue into the resin pot and stir well with a stout stick. Sprinkle in sifted whiting until of the consistency of thin dough, and then turn the mass out on a slab and knead it well, adding whiting as required.

Composition for picture or glass frames is made as follows : Dissolve 7 lbs. of best Scotch glue in $2\frac{1}{2}$ pts. of water, then add 5 gills of linseed oil, $3\frac{1}{2}$ lbs. of resin, and $\frac{1}{4}$ lb. of pitch. Boil the whole together, keep stirring until dissolved, then add as much sifted whiting as will make it into a stiff yet pliable dough. It is then ready for pressing into the mould.

The addition to either of the above recipes of 3 oz. of coarse sugar, dissolved in water to each pound of glue will keep the material more pliable, and assist in combining better with the linseed oil. The glue for fixing is further improved by adding $1\frac{1}{2}$ oz. of sugar and 1 oz. of linseed oil to each pound of glue.

The late G. Baldwin, a London foreman plasterer, made compo and carton-pierre a study, and improved both considerably. He introduced the use of Burgundy pitch and Venice turpentine, which prevent paste compo from shrinking ; the latter toughens it. Compo is kept in condition for use in a " steamer," with a close-fitting lid, the bottom being perforated to admit hot steam. The batches are kept warm and pliable under old blanketing, or flannel, to retain the steam. For a small job, a shop hand can turn an old oil-can or pail into a steamer by fixing a perforated bottom half-way down, the original bottom being knocked out, or well perforated ; or a small pail may be placed inside a larger one, the bottom of the former being well perforated to admit steam. An old pail without a bottom will do for the outer receptacle ; place the pail in boiling water, which must not reach the dough.

Moulds are generally of sulphur, brass, copper, iron, pewter, box wood, or pear wood. Smith's metal is excellent for the purpose. Wood moulds have to be carved in the reverse.

Sulphur moulds are made by dissolving sulphur (sticks) over a slow fire in an iron pot and stirring to prevent burning. When melted, allow it to stand until cool enough to pour. Plaster originals must be soaked in water and treated as for wax moulding. Let the melted sulphur stand until a thin skin has formed on top ; break the skin at the side of the pot and pour out. Take the mould off the original before the sulphur contracts by cooling. To strengthen the mould to resist screw pressure, place steel or iron filings in the back of the mould before it cools. When remelting, the filings will sink to the bottom of the pot and require continual stirring, or they may form a solid lump, or fire the sulphur. Should this happen, remove and cover the pot with an old plaster or cement bag to extinguish the flames. It only requires attention to prevent this. Burnt sulphur does not run freely or take so fine an impression as when pure.

When melted, remove the pot, stir the contents for a few minutes, and allow to cool, as previously described. When the mould is full, ladle some filings from the pot and place in the back of the mould. When the mould is taken off, bed it with Parian cement or plaster into a wooden block or case to ensure a close $\frac{1}{8}$ in. below the level of the block (to protect the mould from screw pressure), and with a 3 in. margin round the mould. If the mould is deep, bind and clamp the block with iron to strengthen it. Cast-iron cases are also used for stock designs.

Sulphur (brimstone) is a yellow, brittle solid, insoluble in water, but soluble in carbon bisulphide, oil of turpentine, and benzole. At its lowest fusing temperature (about 100°) it becomes a semi-liquid of light yellow colour ; this, heated to about 150°, becomes viscid, dark coloured, thick, and too tenacious to be poured ; at a higher temperature it regains its fluidity and dark colour. When boiling it becomes an amber-coloured liquid. Limestone sulphur will mould delicate medallions, plaques, metal panels, etc.

To Cast Composition.—When ready, the mould is smeared with linseed oil, thinned with paraffin oil (sweet oil is a bad ground for paint). A piece of warm, soft compo is rolled smooth to the length and width of the mould and pressed into it by hand, $\frac{1}{4}$ in. above the level of the block, to allow for pressure. A wet board about the size of the block is placed on the compo and the whole put into a powerful screw press, the compo being squeezed into every part of the mould. The pressure unites the wet board and the compo, so that when taken out of the press the compo is removed from the mould adhering to the board with a ground of compo about $\frac{1}{4}$ in. thick. The cast is cut (with a broad, double-handed knife) from the ground, which is then peeled off the board, returned to the steamer, and warmed up again. Mould and board are again free for another cast. It is usual to have three or four boards to each mould ; a cast can then harden a little, when it is more easily cut. Casts harden and shrink before being fixed. Fresh casts are exceedingly pliant and supple and may be bent to any form, concave or convex, with ease. Hard casts may be made pliable by steaming, or by laying on their backs on hot steamed flannel. Casts are fixed with glue and needle points. If casts are soft the backs may be dipped into or brushed with hot water ; by thus softening the glue in the compo, a cementing paste is formed that will adhere to wood ; the former way is the better. Casts require to be jointed like plaster casts ; joints must be as square as possible (with no hollows at the abutments) and may be stopped with soft compo. If cut true and square and the ends are well pressed together, little or no stopping will be required.

CHAPTER XIX

PLASTERERS' MEMORANDA, QUANTITIES, WEIGHTS, AND RECIPES

Quantities of Plastic Materials Required for Various Works—Concrete Quantities—Water Quantities—Weights of Materials—Chemical Names—Measuring Plasterers' Work—Squaring Dimensions—Recipes for Indurating, Fireproofing and Waterproofing, and Polishing Plaster—Cleaning Plaster Figures—Whitewashing—Distempering.

A.—PLASTERERS' MEMORANDA, QUANTITIES, AND WEIGHTS

Weights and Cubic Contents and Quantities of Materials Required per Superficial Yard

Laths.—Length, from 2 ft. 6 in. to 4 ft.
Width, about 1 in.
Thickness—" Single laths," $\frac{1}{8}$ in. to $\frac{3}{16}$ in.
Lath and a half, $\frac{3}{16}$ in. to $\frac{1}{4}$ in.
Double laths, $\frac{1}{4}$ in. to $\frac{3}{8}$ in.
125 laths 4 ft. long = 1 bundle.

A bundle contains from 360 ft. to 500 ft. run, most frequently the former number.
30 bundles of laths = 1 load.
Laths are usually spaced from $\frac{1}{4}$ in. to $\frac{3}{8}$ in. apart, according to their strength and nature of plaster.
A bundle containing 360 ft. run (or 400 ft. nominally), nailed with butt joints, will cover about $4\frac{1}{2}$ superficial yards.
A bundle of 3 ft. laths requires about 660 nails, and one of 4 ft. laths 630 nails, if nailed on to joists 1 ft. from centre to centre.
Lathing nails are from $\frac{3}{4}$ in. to $1\frac{1}{4}$ in. long, according to the thickness of the laths. They are either wrought, cut, or cast iron, and they should be galvanised for white cement work.
About 350 $\frac{3}{4}$-in. cut nails = 1 lb.
1,000 laths and 11 lbs. of nails will cover 70 superficial yards.
A bundle of laths and 500 nails will cover about 5 superficial yards. Sawn laths are generally used in America. They measure about $\frac{1}{4}$ in. thick, $1\frac{1}{4}$ in. wide, and 4 ft. long.

Hair.—A bushel of dry hair weighs from 14 lbs. to 15 lbs. For best work, 1 lb. of hair is allowed to 2 cub. ft. of coarse stuff, and 1 lb. to 3 cub. ft. for common work.
A barrel's bulk is 5 cub. ft.

Plaster.—14 lbs. (London style) = 1 bag.

$$\begin{array}{rcl}
7 \text{ bags} &=& 1 \text{ bushel.} \\
1\tfrac{1}{4} \text{ bushels} &=& 1 \text{ cwt.} \\
2 \text{ cwt.} &=& 1 \text{ sack.} \\
10 \text{ sacks} &=& 1 \text{ ton.}
\end{array}$$

Parian Cement.—Four bushels of cement, gauged with an equal quantity of sand, will cover 10 superficial yards $\frac{1}{2}$ in. thick.

$$\begin{array}{rcl}
1 \text{ sack of Parian} &=& 2 \text{ cwt.} \\
1 \text{ cask of Parian} &=& 2\tfrac{1}{2} \text{ cwt.}
\end{array}$$

Keen's Cement.—A cask contains 4 bushels, and when gauged with sand in the ratio of 1 part of cement to 2 parts of sand, will cover about 15 superficial yards $\frac{1}{2}$ in. thick. One sack of Keen's = 2 cwt.

Martin's Cement.—One cwt., gauged with equal proportions of sand, will cover about 7 superficial yards $\frac{1}{2}$ in. thick.

Robinson's Cement.—One cwt. of cement and 1 of sand will cover 7 superficial yards $\frac{1}{2}$ in. thick. One cwt. of cement and 2 of sand will cover 11 superficial yards $\frac{1}{2}$ in. thick. One cwt. of cement and 3 of sand will cover 15 superficial yards $\frac{1}{2}$ in. thick. One cwt. of neat cement (No. 1) will cover 15 superficial yards $\frac{1}{8}$ in. thick. These proportions are by measure, not weight. One cwt. cement equals about $1\frac{1}{2}$ imperial bushels.

Adamant.—Adamant (No. 2) for floating walls, weighs 155 lbs. per sack, and will cover 7 superficial yards. Adamant (No. 2) for floating laths, weighs 130 lbs. per sack, and will cover 7 superficial yards. Adamant (No. 3) for setting coat, weighs 140 lbs. per sack, and will set 30 superficial yards.

Sirapite.—One ton mixed with an equal portion of sand will cover about 120 superficial yards $\frac{3}{8}$ in. thick; 1 ton of pure sirapite will cover about 300 superficial yards.

Granite Plaster.—$1\frac{3}{4}$ tons of render on " sawn laths " will cover about 100 superficial yards $\frac{1}{2}$ in. thick, and 1 ton of **X** or finish will cover about 300 superficial yards.

Restall's Adamantine Plaster.—For wall work an admixture of 1 part sand to 2 parts adamantine is allowed for a floating coat, which is skimmed with pure adamantine only. No admixture of sand is allowed for ceiling or lathwork.

One bag of pure adamantine (180 lbs.) will cover about 6 superficial yards.

Mastic.—One cwt. of mastic and 1 gal. of oil will cover 5 superficial yards $\frac{1}{4}$ in. thick.

Fibrous Plaster Slabs.—Slabs $\frac{1}{2}$ in. thick weigh when dry $2\frac{1}{4}$ lbs. per superficial foot. Fourteen lbs. of nails will fix 100 superficial yards.

Gelatine.—Two lbs. of gelatine when dissolved will cover about 1 superficial foot $\frac{1}{2}$ in. thick.

Wax.—5 lbs. of moulding wax will cover 1 superficial foot about 1 in. thick.

Silicate of Cotton.—One cwt. will cover 100 superficial feet about 1 in. thick.

Limewhite.—Limewhite once done requires 1 cub. ft. of slaked lime per 100 superficial yards; twice done, $1\frac{2}{3}$ cub. ft. of lime.

Whitewash.—100 yards superficial " once " done requires about 12 lbs. of whiting, ½ lb. of blue-black, and 1¾ gals. of size.

100 yards superficial " twice " done requires 21 lbs. of whiting, ¾ lb. of blue-black, and 2¾ gals. of size.

1 firkin of double size = 48 lbs.

2 dozen whiting = 1 cwt.

Lime.—100 tons of blue lias lime yield 59.37 tons of quicklime ; 1,583 bushels of ground lime, 2,063 bushels of slaked lime.

74 gallons of water are required for slaking 1 ton of quicklime.

1 ton of quicklime	=	30 bushels.
1 ,, ,,	=	27 bushels ground lime.
3 bushels ground lime	=	1 sack.
9 sacks ,,	=	1 ton.
2 yards of lime	=	1 ton.

21 bushels (striked), or 27 cub. ft. of lime or sand = 1 cub. yd.

3 bushels of lias lime	=	1 sack.
9 sacks ,,	=	1 ton.
36 bushels ,,	=	1 load.

One cubic yard of lime, 2 yards of sand, and 3 bushels of hair, will cover 75 superficial yards, if rendered and set on brick, and 70 yards on lath, or 65 yards render, float and set on brick, and 60 yards on lath. One cubic yard of coarse stuff equals 1 cart load.

Lime Plastering Quantities.—Quantities of lime, sand, hair, and water required per superficial yard for various classes of plastering :—

Render only, ⅜ in. thick	Lime (unslaked)	.15 cub. ft.
	Sand	.23 ,,
	Hair	.1 lb.
	Water	1.2 gals.
Render and set, ½ in. thick	Lime	.22 cub. ft.
	Sand	.23 ,,
	Hair	.12 lb.
	Water	1.8 gals.
Render and float, ⅝ in. thick	Lime	.25 cub. ft.
	Sand	.38 ,,
	Hair	.17 lb.
	Water	2.0 gals.
Render, float, and set, ¾ in. thick	Lime	.32 cub. ft.
	Sand	.38 ,,
	Hair	.18 lb.
	Water	2.6 gals.
Setting with putty and plaster, ⅛ in. thick	Lime (unslaked)	.10 cub. ft.
	Plaster	.03 ,,
	Water	1.00 gal.

For rough walls the quantities should be slightly increased. The first coat on lath requires about one-tenth more coarse stuff than rendering.

The following is the method of calculating the above proportions to ascertain the amount of materials required for any given quantity of work to be executed. Multiply the quantities given in the above tables by the number of superficial yards of work required to be done. Example—What quantities of lime (unslaked), sand, hair, and water will be required to render 50 superficial yards and $\frac{3}{8}$ in. thick ?

Process.—Lime

$$
\begin{array}{r}
.15 \\
50 \\
\hline
7.50 = 7\frac{1}{2} \text{ cub. ft.}
\end{array}
$$

Sand - -

$$
\begin{array}{r}
.23 \\
50 \\
\hline
11.50 = 11\frac{1}{2} \quad ,,
\end{array}
$$

Hair - ·

$$
\begin{array}{r}
.1 \\
50 \\
\hline
5.0 = 5 \text{ lbs.}
\end{array}
$$

Water -

$$
\begin{array}{r}
1.2 \\
50 \\
\hline
60.0 = 60 \text{ gals.}
\end{array}
$$

And in a similar manner for other descriptions and quantities of work.

Selenitic.—Three bushels of selenitic = 1 sack. 34 bushels = 1 ton.

Reduction in Bulk of Materials.—The reduction in bulk of dry cement when mixed with water is 10 per cent. of the total ; of sand, 20 per cent. ; and of sand and cement in equal proportions, 19 per cent.

Porosity.—The relative porosity of limes and cements is as follows : Common lime mortar (1 to 2), 100 ; plaster of Paris, 75 ; Roman cement, 25 ; and Portland cement, 10.

TABLE I.—QUANTITY OF MORTAR PRODUCED FROM ONE IMPERIAL BUSHEL OF VARIOUS LIMES AND CEMENT

Description.	Lime or Cement.		Sand, Number of Bushels.	Water, Number of Gallons.	Quantity of Mortar in Cubic Feet.
	Weight in Lbs. per Bushel.	Number of Bushels.			
In lump—					
Stone lime (Plymouth)	70	1	3	12	$3\frac{1}{2}$*
Lias (Keynsham) -	80	1	3	$9\frac{1}{2}$	$3\frac{1}{12}$*
,, (Lyme Regis) -	70	1	2	$8\frac{1}{2}$	$2\frac{3}{4}$†
	70	1	3	$8\frac{1}{2}$	$3\frac{1}{4}$†
Ground—					
Lias (Keynsham) -	63	1	3	$6\frac{1}{2}$	$3\frac{1}{8}$
,, (Lyme Regis)	74	1	2	6	$2\frac{3}{4}$
Roman cement	72	1	...	$6\frac{1}{4}$	$1\frac{1}{8}$
	72	1	1	$6\frac{1}{2}$	$1\frac{3}{4}$

* Six gals. of water are required to slake, and 6 gals. to mix each bushel.
† Two gals. are required to slake each bushel.

Roman Cement.—One cask of Roman cement holds $3\frac{3}{4}$ cub. ft., and the weight is about $3\frac{1}{2}$ cwt. Three bushels of cement = 1 sack. One bushel of cement and 1 of sand will cover $4\frac{1}{2}$ superficial yards $\frac{1}{2}$ in. thick.

Portland Cement.—Two centals (200 lbs.), London trade custom = 1 sack. Two bushels, Midland trade custom = 1 sack. One cask of Portland holds about 4 cub. ft. One cask varies from 375 lbs. to 400 lbs. gross, general London custom, for export.

TABLE II.—SUPERFICIAL YARDS, RENDERED WITH PORTLAND CEMENT GAUGED WITH VARIOUS PROPORTIONS OF SAND, AND IN VARIOUS THICKNESSES

Proportions	Thickness.				
	$\frac{1}{2}$ in.	$\frac{5}{8}$ in.	$\frac{3}{4}$ in.	$\frac{7}{8}$ in.	1 in.
1 bushel of cement, neat	$2\frac{3}{4}$ yds.	$2\frac{3}{8}$ yds.	2 yds.	$1\frac{1}{2}$ yds.	1 yd.
1 ,, ,, and 1 of sand	$4\frac{3}{8}$,,	$3\frac{3}{4}$,,	$3\frac{3}{8}$,,	$2\frac{3}{4}$,,	$2\frac{1}{4}$,,
1 ,, ,, and 2 of sand	$6\frac{3}{8}$,,	$5\frac{1}{2}$,,	$4\frac{3}{4}$,,	4 ,,	$3\frac{1}{4}$,,
1 ,, ,, and 3 of sand	$8\frac{1}{2}$,,	$7\frac{1}{2}$,,	$6\frac{3}{8}$,,	$5\frac{3}{8}$,,	$4\frac{1}{4}$,,

Note.—$\frac{3}{4}$ in. is the usual thickness.

TABLE III.—QUANTITY OF MATERIALS (IN VARIOUS GAUGES) REQUIRED TO MAKE ONE CUBIC YARD OF GAUGED PORTLAND CEMENT AND SAND

1 and 1 { Cement — 12.62 bushels.
Sand — 12.62 ,,
Water — 30 gals.

1 and 2 { Cement — 8.37 bushels.
Sand — 16.74 ,,
Water — 25 gals.

1 and 3 { Cement — 6.37 bushels.
Sand — 19.11 ,,
Water — 23 gals.

One cubic yard of gauged Portland cement and sand will render 70 superficial yards.

Comparative Strength of Portland Cement and Sand, in Various Proportions.—At the end of one year after setting, 1 of Portland cement and 1 of sand is about three-fourths the strength of neat cement; 1 of cement and 2 of sand is about one-half the strength of neat cement; 1 of cement and 3 of sand is about one-third the strength of neat cement; 1 of cement and 4 of sand is about one-fourth the strength of neat cement; 1 of cement and 5 of sand is about one-sixth the strength of neat cement.

Weight of Various Cement Concretes having Various Aggregates in Lbs. per Cubic Foot.—The concrete consists of 1 part of cement to 3 of aggregate. As the weight of different kinds of the same class of aggregates varies, the average weights of the concrete are given :—

TABLE IV —WEIGHTS OF VARIOUS CONCRETES

Pumice stone concrete	70 lbs.
Coke breeze concrete - -	80 ,,
Brick concrete -	120 ,,
Limestone concrete -	130 ,,
Slag concrete -	140 ,,
Gravel concrete -	145 ,,
Granite concrete -	145 ,,

TABLE V.—WEIGHTS OF VARIOUS PLASTIC MATERIALS PER CUBIC FOOT IN LBS.

Ashes -	37 lbs.
Clay, common - - - -	125 ,,
,, modelling - -	120 ,,
Cement, Portland - - -	78 ,,
,, Roman - - -	60 ,,
Chalk - - - -	125 ,,
Gravel - -	112 ,,
Gypsum, natural	140 ,,
Hair, ox, dry - - - - -	11 ,,
Lime, grey chalk, in lump -	44 ,,
Limestone - -	53 ,,
Mortar, old -	90 ,,
,, new -	110 ,,
,, well tempered - - -	115 ,,
Plaster of Paris cast -	80 ,,
Red pine wood	36 ,,
Sand, dry - -	100 ,,
,, wet - -	130 ,,
Shingle - -	95 ,,
Thames ballast - -	110 ,,
Wax - - -	60 ,,

The weight of a superficial yard lath plaster, float and set ceilings of good quality is about 98 lbs. If of inferior quality, it would be about 8 lbs. less.

Rough-casting Quantities.—For 100 yards superficial of rough-casting (two coats on lath) the following quantities are required: 25 cub. ft. of lime, 50 cub. ft. of sand, 16 lbs. of hair, and ¾ yd. of prepared gravel for the dash coat. A quarter tub of lime putty should be mixed with every tub of gravel for the dash. To cover 100 yds. superficial in any of the tints named herewith, the following quantities of ingredients are required : For a blue-black, 5 lbs. of lampblack ; for buff, 5 lbs. of green copperas, to which add 1 lb. of fresh cow-manure, strained and mixed with the liquid dash. A fine terra-cotta colour is made by using 14 lbs. of red metallic oxide mixed with 5 lbs. of green copperas and 4 lbs. of lampblack. The addition of 10 per cent. of alum solution to the liquid dash will give brilliancy and permanency to the colours. Various tints of these colours may be obtained by varying the quantities given.

Concrete Quantities.—One sack of Portland cement (10 sacks to 1 ton), gauged in the ratio of 2 of cement to 5 of aggregate, will fill in 12 ft. run of moulded spandrel steps, 12-in. tread and 7-in. rise, or about 5 cub. ft.

Concrete paving slabs 2 in. thick weigh about 26 superficial lbs., or 9 superficial yards to 1 ton.

Concrete Foundations.—It takes about 1 cub. yd. of brickbats, stone, etc., to form 10 superficial yards of dry foundations 3 in. thick.

Concrete Quantities.—One sack of Portland cement (10 to the ton) gauged with 2½ sacks of aggregate will cover 4½ superficial yards 2 in. thick. One ton of Portland cement, gauged with 2½ parts (in bulk) of aggregate, will cover about 40 superficial yards 2 in. thick. The quantities vary according to the closeness and compactness of the dry foundation. The quantities are also the same for granolithic paving.

Granite Concrete Paving Quantities (Various Thicknesses).—One sack of Portland cement (10 to the ton) and 2 sacks of crushed granite will cover the following surfaces :—

TABLE VI

12½ superficial yards	½ in. thick.
6¾ ,,	,, 1 in. ,,
4½ ,,	,, 1½ in. ,,
3½ ,,	,, 2 in. ,,
2 ,,	,, 2½ in. ,,
2¼ ,,	,, 3 in. ,,

A sack of granite weighs nearly the same as a sack of Portland cement, so that when calculating by weight, the bulk of each can be reckoned about equal.

Weight of Various Aggregates.—The following materials weigh 1 ton, as filled into carts :—

| 21 cub. ft. of river sand. |
| 22 ,, ,, pit sand. |
| 22 ,, ,, Thames ballast. |
| 23 ,, ,, coarse gravel. |
| 24 ,, ,, clean shingle. |

Water and Heat Memoranda.—A medium-sized pail will hold 3 gals. of water. A pint of water weighs about 1 lb., and is equal to about 27 cub. in., or a square box 3 in. long, 3 in. wide, and 3 in. deep.

1 gal. of water equals	272.123 cub. in.
1 ,, ,, (United States)	231.0 ,,
6¼ ,, ,,	1 cub. ft.
1 cub. ft. of water weighs	4 lbs.

Salt water is heavier than fresh, and weighs 64.11 lbs. per cub. ft.

Water freezes at 32° F., and boils at 212° F.

The following table shows the relative heat-conducting power of various materials:—

TABLE VII

Silicate cotton or slag wool	100
Plaster of Paris	125
Sawdust	163
Coke breeze - -	230

Bushel Box.—A box 13 in. × 13 in. and $13\frac{1}{8}$ in. deep will hold 1 bushel of Portland cement. Another size, 12 in. × 12 in. and $15\frac{3}{8}$ in. deep. All inside measurements.

1 bushel contains - - -	2218.192 cub. in.
1 bushel contains (United States)	2150.42 ,,

Timber.—Timber is now largely used by plasterers in the construction of fibrous plaster and for concrete moulds and centering. A brief description of the terms and sizes may prove useful.

Timber is cut into various sizes, and the timber merchants use the terms " planks," " deals," " battens," " boards," " scantling," and " quartering." Planks are pieces of wood 11 in. wide, $2\frac{1}{2}$ in. or 3 in. thick, and may be bought in lengths from 8 ft. to 21 ft. Deals are 9 in. wide, $2\frac{1}{2}$ in. or 3 in. thick, and of the same lengths as planks. Battens are 7 in. wide, $2\frac{1}{2}$ in. thick, and likewise of the same lengths as planks. Boards are of less thickness than planks, deals, or battens, and are distinguished by their thickness as " half-inch board," " three-quarter board," " inch board," and so on ; but they are often spoken of as so many " cuts " as " three-cut," " four-cut," " five-cut," etc., which means that the plank or deal, 3 in. thick, is divided by the number of saw cuts mentioned ; thus, five cuts would divide the plank or deal into six boards, each being $\frac{1}{2}$ in. thick, less the portion cut away as sawdust. Scantling simply means a quantity cut to any desired size for any purpose.

In a London deal standard there are 120 deals. 12 ft. × 9 in. × 3 in. = 1,080 superficial feet = 270 cub. ft.

121 deals = 100.
100 superficial feet of planking = 1 square.
 50 cub. ft. of squared timber ⎫
600 superficial feet of 1 in. planks or deals ⎬ 1 load.
400 ,, ,, $1\frac{1}{2}$ in. ,, ,, ⎭

One square of centering requires 12 boards 12 ft. long and 9 in. wide.

An allowance of one-third to one-half is usually made for centering, etc., on reconverting to use.

Wood for special templates, squares, thin or circular strips, or laths for fibrous plasterwork, is not so liable to crack or warp if steamed or boiled in hot water for three or four hours, and then slowly dried.

Value of Plasterwork.—In 1874 Major Seddon, R.E., made a series of experiments with a view to ascertain the amount of labour and material required for a given number of yards of plaster and cement work. The results are given in the subjoined table. The cost of scaffolding and carriage of materials are not included in the prices.

The prices for labour and materials may be altered to suit local and present rates. These trials are valuable, inasmuch as it is certain that no vested interests were concerned, and that the experiments were made under proper conditions.

TABLE VIII.—ANALYSIS AND COST OF MATERIALS AND LABOUR
FOR PLASTERWORK (SEDDON, 1874)

Materials and Labour Required for 10 Superficial Yards. Description.	Value. s. d.	Render One Coat and Set.		Render, Float, and Set.		Lath, Plaster, and Set.		Lath, Plaster, Float, and Set.		Portland Cement. Render, Float, and Trowel, 1 Cement and 2 of Sand.			
		Quantity.	s. d.	Quantity.	s. d.	Quantity.	s. d.	Quantity.	s. d.	Quantity.	£	s.	d.
Chalk lime, cub. ft.	0 4	5	1 8	6¼	2 1	5½	1 10	6¾	2 2	...		...	
Sand	0 1½	5	0 7½	6¼	0 9¼	5½	0 8¼	6¾	0 10	6		...	
Sand, washed, cub. ft.	0 3	...	...	...	...	...	...	...	...	6	0	1	6
Hair, dry, per lb.	0 3	2½	0 7½	3	0 9	2¾	0 8¼	3¼	0 9¾	15		...	
Water, per gallon	...	20	0 1	25	0 1	22	0 1	27	0 1	15	0	0	1
Lath (lath and half) per bundle	2 0	...	...	...	...	2¼	4 6	2¼	4 6	...		...	
Lath nails, per lb.	0 1½	...	...	...	...	4	0 6	4	0 6	...		...	
Portland cement, per bushel	2 6	...	...	...	...	...	...	...	...	2½	0	6	3
Plasterer, per day	5 6	⅓	1 10	½	2 9	½	2 9	¾	4 1½	1¼	0	6	10½
Labourer, per day	2 9	⅓	0 11	½	1 4½	½	1 4½	¾	2 0¾	1¼	0	3	5¼
Apprentice, per day	1 6	⅓	0 6	½	0 9	½	0 9	¾	1 1½	...		...	
Cost, per 10 yards	...	...	6 3	...	8 6¾	...	13 2	...	16 3½	...	0	18	1¾
Cost, per yard	...	...	0 7½	...	0 10¼	...	1 3¾	...	1 7½	...	0	1	9½

CHEMICAL NAMES OF COMMON SUBSTANCES USED BY PLASTERERS

Common Name.	Chemical Name.	Chemical Formula.
Lime	Oxide of calcium	CaO
Slaked lime	Calcium hydrate	CaH_2O_2
Muriate of lime	Chloride of calcium	$CaCl_2$
Plaster of Paris	Sulphate of lime ; also selenite	$CaSO_4$
Chalk	Carbonate of calcium	$CaCO_3$
Copperas or green vitriol	Sulphate of iron -	$FeSO_4$
Blue vitriol	Sulphate of copper -	$CuSO_4$
White vitriol	Sulphate of zinc	$ZnSO_4$
Oil of vitriol	Sulphuric acid - -	H_2SO_4
Potash -	Oxide of potassium -	K_2O
Red lead	Oxide of lead -	Pb_3O_4
Sugar of lead	Acetate of lead -	$Pb(C_2H_3O_2)_2.3H_2O$
Iron rust	Iron (ferric) oxide	Fe_2O_3
Alum, dry	Sulphates of aluminium and potassium	$K_2SO_4, Al_2(SO_4)_3, 24H_2O$
Common salt	Chloride of sodium -	$NaCl$
Soda	Oxide of sodium	Na_2O
Sand	Oxide of silicon	SiO_2

Plaster and Concrete Colours on Drawings.—Plasterwork on architectural drawings is indicated by a grey colour ; cement work by sepia or Payne's grey ; and concrete by a blue colour.

Measuring Plasterers' Work.—Plasterers' work when entered into the dimension book is generally treated with the following abbreviations : " F.P." stands for fibrous plaster ; " R." for render ; " R.S." for render and set ; " R.F.S." for render, float, and set ; " L.P." for lath and plaster ; " L.P.S." for lath, plaster, and set ; " L.P.F.S." for lath, plaster, float, and set ; " W.S.C.W." for wash, stop (claircolle), and whiten ; " L.W." for lime white ; " L.O." for labour only ; " L.M." for labour and materials ; " P.C." for prime cost ; " dd." for deduct ; " cub." for cubic ; " super." for superficial ; " yds." for yards ; " ft." for feet ; " in." for inches ; a tick or dot also placed after a figure or figures is intended to describe feet, while two dots means inches, thus 3′ 9″ stands for 3 ft. 9 in.

Various forms of plasterwork are measured by the yard and foot superficial, per foot lineal, and per inch girth. *Per yard superficial* includes render and set, trowelled stucco on brick lath, lath and plaster on walls and ceilings, fibrous slabs, and plain face ; render, float, and set in cements for floors, walls, and ceilings, lime whitening, or colouring, washing, stopping and distempering.

Per Foot Superficial.—Cornices (over 6 in. girth), plaster and cement soffits, bands, margins, fascias, panels, dados, pilasters, columns, and large plain coves.

Per Foot Lineal.—Plaster or cement reveals, skirtings, narrow bands, and margins, arrises, beads, quirks, reveals and string-courses, and enrichments.

Per Inch Girth.—Mouldings 9 in. girth and under, and enrichments with circular profiles. Centre flowers, capitals, trusses, etc., are numbered ; the cost of modelling is generally allowed for in the prices, but as the modelling is a distinct and important part of the work, the cost of same should be charged as a separate item, the design and nature of the labour, and the quality, being carefully described, and any speciality always mentioned.

Enrichments are numbered and charged separately according to schedule. Measure ceilings from wall to wall, and take out one projection of cornice. Measure walls from the top of skirting or wood grounds to half-way up the height of cornice for lathwork, and one-third for brickwork. Plasterwork, if circular on plan, is measured one and a half times the girth by the height, and the area added to the plain work. If circular work is described and allowed for in the specifications, the girth is taken single. Panelled work is taken by the round of the panel, as square arris or moulding, and describing the girth of the moulding.

All enrichments to be taken distinct from the cornice, which is to be taken as plain, cornice being girthed in full.

All mitres over four in number to be charged each at the price of a foot run of moulding. Stops charged the same as mitres. Return mitres are charged as two.

Dubbing out with tiles or gauged stuff, in order to get an extra thickness or projection, or if the work is out of upright, is measured by the foot superficial, unless for narrow string-course, when it is taken by the foot run. Internal and external work is always kept separate, and the various kinds of work, materials, and number of coats are always fully described.

Deduct all openings, with the exception of small oblong or circular windows, or ventilators, and columns, where the labour working round them is more than if the space had been done. Additions or joints with old work are measured 1 ft. over the joints, to allow for the labour cutting and making good the joint. Patches are not measured, but charged time and materials.

For small triangular parts and closets, where shelves are in, it is customary to add one-half of the measurement to the measurement, to allow for extra labour of plastering such work.

Cement floors are measured by the superficial yard describing the proportions of sand (or other aggregate) and cement, but small works, such as hearths, cisterns, etc., are taken by the superficial foot.

Squaring Dimensions.—Lineal measure relates to length only. Superficial measure to length and breadth. Cube, or solid measure, to length, breadth, and thickness. If feet are multiplied by feet, the product will be feet. If inches are multiplied into feet, every 12 of the product will be feet. If inches are multiplied into inches, every 12 of the product may be reckoned as an inch, and any number less than 12 as parts of an inch. If parts of an inch are multiplied by feet, every 12 of the product will be 1 in., and any number less than 12 will be parts of an inch. If parts of an inch are multiplied by inches, every 12 of the product is 1 part, and any number less than 12 are seconds.

There are various methods of squaring dimensions. The following are generally used. The primary object in all cases is to find the contained number of square or superficial feet and parts of feet, and having found the number, divide by 9, which gives the number of superficial yards. The dimensions of length and breadth expressed in feet and inches are multiplied together by duodecimals, and the result is the number of " superficial " feet and parts of a foot.

The first method is usually known as cross-multiplication, and will be explained by the following example. Find the contents superficial of a wall 11 ft. 4 in. long and 7 ft. 5 in. high. The process is as follows : Set down the figures with a cross between them, thus—

$$
\begin{array}{cc}
\text{Ft.} & \text{In.} \\
11 & \times 4 \\
7 & 5 \\
\end{array}
$$

Ft.		In.				
11	×	7	=	77	0	
5	×	11	=	4	7	
4	×	7	=	2	4	
5	×	4	=	0	1	8 pts.

Total contents   84   0   8 pts.

The following simple method of calculating for multiplying feet, inches, and parts, and which holds good either in cubic or square measurements, is to remember feet × feet give feet ; feet × inches give inches ; inches × inches give inches ; inches × parts give parts ; parts × parts give thirds, etc.

Example.—11 ft. 4 in. × 7 ft. 5 in. are multiplied thus—

Ft.	In.	Pts.
11	4	
7	5	
4	8	8
79	4	
84	0	8 *Ans.*

Another method may be shown by example :—Find the contents (superficial) of a wall 14 ft. 7 in. long and 9 ft. 2½ in. high.

Process.—Set the figures down thus—

Ft. In.　　Ft. In.

14　7　×　9　2½

Ft. In. Pts.

14　7

9　2　6

―――――

7　3　6

2　5　2

131　3　0

―――――

140　11　8 *Ans.*

A quick way. Find the superficial contents of a ceiling 20 ft. long and 18 ft. wide.

Process.—180 × 2 = 360 superficial feet.

Find the contents (superficial feet) of a margin 21 ft. long and 18 ft. wide.

Process.—As 18 in. equals 1½ ft. ; thus 21 × 1½ = 31½ superficial feet ; or 31 ft. 6 in. superficial.

To find the superficial contents of a cylinder or column. Multiply the diameter by the length, and the product by 355, and divide the last product by 113 ; the quotient is the superficial contents. Another way is to multiply the circumference by the length ; the product is the superficial contents.

Another way still is that the superficial contents are found by multiplying half the diameter by itself, and the product by $3\frac{1}{7}$; or, in other words, multiply the square of the radius by 22, dividing by 7 ; the product is the superficial contents of the whole circle. If it is only half a circle, multiply by 11 instead of 22.

To Measure Triangles.—Triangular pieces of work are measured by taking the length of one of the sides by half of its perpendicular distance from the opposite vertex (point of angle) ; these dimensions, when multiplied together or squared, will give the superficies of the triangle. Other irregular figures are measured in the same way, by dividing them into triangles.

To Measure Irregular Widths.—If a wall or other surface is wider at one end than the other, add the width of both ends together ; half the sum is the mean width, then multiply the mean width by the length.

Cube or solid measure is not much required in ordinary plasterers' work, but as artificial stonework is coming largely into use, and being done by plasterers, the following examples are given :—

The dimensions of length, breadth, and depth, expressed in feet and inches, are all multiplied together by the usual method as employed in superficial, and the result is obtained in cubic feet, 12ths, and 144ths. Thus to find the contents of a pilaster, 11 ft. 3 in. long, 1 ft. 2 in. broad, and 11½ ft. deep.

Process.—First multiply 11 ft. 3 in. by 1 ft. 2 in., which gives superficial feet, 12ths, etc., and multiply that result by 11½ in., which gives cubic feet, 12ths, etc.

Thus—

	Ft.	In.		Ft.	In.		In.
	11	3	×	1	2	×	11½

	Ft.	In.
	11	3
	1	2

1	10	6
11	3	0

| | 13 | 1 | 6 superficial feet. |

Multiplied by   11   6

	6	6	9
12	0	4	6

12   6   11   3 cubic or solid feet.

The 12th of a cube foot must not be confounded with the cubic inch, as it really contains 144 cub. in.

A quick way for the same operation is to find the contents (cubic) of 6 caps, each 1 ft. by 1 ft. 2 in. by 1¾ ft.

Multiply together the length, breadth, and depth of one cap in feet, and the largest fractions of a foot, and multiply by the given number of caps, thus—

$$\frac{1 \times 7 \times 7 \times 6}{6 \times 4} = 12\tfrac{1}{4} \text{ cub. ft.}$$

An old way to find the contents (cubic) of a window head 6 ft. long, 10 in. wide, and 7 in. deep.

Multiply the length by breadth, and the product by the depth. Multiply this product by 12, and divide by 1728. The result is 2 cub. ft. and $\frac{1584}{1728}$.

Thus—

6 ft.

10 in.

—

60

7 in.

—

420

12 in.

—

840

420

—

The inches in a solid foot 1728)5040(2 ft.

3456

—

The inches in a quarter foot 432)1584(3 quarters, 288 in.

—

288

A short way is performed thus—

$$6 \text{ ft.} \times 10 \text{ in.} \times 7 \text{ in.}$$

$$
\begin{array}{cc}
\text{Ft.} & \text{In.} \\
6 & 0 \\
& 10 \\
\hline
5 & 0 \\
& 7 \\
\hline
2 & 11 \\
\end{array}
$$

A method of calculation for showing the contents of a cubic foot in cubic inches is :— Find the contents of a concrete block 12 in. by 12 in. by 12 in. Multiply the length by the breadth, which gives the superficial contents. This multiplied by the depth gives the cubic contents. Thus—

$$
\begin{array}{l}
12 \text{ in.} \\
12 \\
\hline
144 \text{ superficial contents.} \\
12 \\
\hline
1728 \text{ cub. in. or } 1 \text{ cub. ft.}
\end{array}
$$

The diameter of a circle being given, find the circumference. As 7 is to 22, or as 113 to 355, so is the diameter to the circumference.

Example.—Find the circumference of a circular panel moulding, the diameter of which is 12 ft.

Process.—Multiply the diameter by 355, and divide the product by 113. Thus—

$$
\begin{array}{l}
\quad\ 355 \\
\quad\ 12 \\
\hline
113)4260(37 \text{ ft. } \tfrac{79}{113} \text{ of a foot} \\
\quad 339 \\
\hline
\quad 870 \\
\quad 791 \\
\hline
\quad\ 79 \\
\hline
\quad 113 \\
\end{array}
$$

The circumference being given, the diameter is found by dividing the circumference by $3\tfrac{1}{7}$.

Example.—Find the diameter of circular panel moulding, the circumference of which is 11 ft. Thus—

$$\frac{11 \times 7}{112} = 3\tfrac{1}{2} \text{ ft.}$$

Another way is : Multiply the circumference by 113, and divide the product by 355.

To find the area of an ellipse, multiply the long diameter by the short diameter, and by the decimal .7854, and the product will give the area.

To find the cubic contents of a true tapered pyramid, whether round, square, or triangular.   Multiply the area of the base by $\frac{1}{3}$ the height.

To find the cubic contents of a cylinder.   Multiply the square of the radius by the thickness, both in feet and fractions of a foot, and the product by $3\frac{1}{7}$.

Another way is to multiply the square of the diameter by the thickness, both in inches, and divide by 2200, and the product is in cubic feet.

Another way : Multiply the square of the diameter by 7854, and the product by the length.

A cylindrical foot is the solid contents of a cylinder, 1 foot in depth and diameter, and is equal to 1728 cylindrical inches.   Cylindrical inches + 7854 = cubic inches.

To find the superficial contents of a circle.   Multiply the half diameter by itself, and the product by $3\frac{1}{7}$, or in other words, multiply the square of the radius by 22, and divide the product by 7.   This gives the superficial of the whole circle.   If it is only a half circle, multiply by 11 instead of 22.

Example.—Find the contents of a circle, the diameter of which is 12 ft.

Process.—First square the half diameter, or radius.   Thus—

$$
\begin{array}{r}
6 \\
6 \\
\hline
36 \\
22 \\
\hline
72 \\
72 \\
\end{array}
$$

$$7)792(113\tfrac{1}{7}.$$

Another way is to supply the square of the diameter by the decimal .7854 ; or multiply the circumference by the radius, and divide the product by 2.

And yet another way : The diameter being given, multiply the square of the radius by $3\frac{1}{7}$.

Example.—Find the area of a circle panel, the diameter of which is 36 in.   Thus—

$$\frac{3 \times 3 \times 22}{2 \times 2 \times 7} = 7.07 \text{ ft.}$$

B.—RECIPES FOR PLASTERWORK

To Harden Plaster Casts.—Numerous patents have been obtained and many methods used for hardening plaster casts.   The following are some of the most simple and effective methods.   In order to obtain the maximum of hardness, the plaster should be gauged as firm and as quick as is possible.   When plaster is hardened by soaking or coating with a solution, the work should be perfectly dry, and also warm, so that the solution may penetrate more easily.   Where practical, the casts should be immersed in the solution.   The work of hardening and polishing should be done in a clean, dry, and warm room, free from draughts of cold or damp air, or dust.

The addition of about 5 per cent. of good cornflour to plaster renders it hard and tough. This admixture is useful for casting plaques and similar ornaments. Ground rice is used for a similar purpose.

Plaster casts can be made extremely hard and tough by adding pulverised marshmallow root to the plaster, also by gauging the plaster with the water in which marshmallows have been boiled. If the plaster is gauged with 4 per cent. of finely pulverised marsh-mallow, the setting is retarded for about one hour. When dry, it may be filed, sawn, or turned. With 8 per cent. of marsh-mallow the setting is further retarded, but the toughness and hardness are increased. This may be rolled out on glass in thin plates. It may be used as a substitute for carton-pierre, also for the manufacture of enrichment or mouldings that have to stand rough usage, also for frames, brackets, panels, etc. This material will take a good polish. Plaster casts may be rendered hard by soaking in or brushing with a hot solution of strong alum. Plaster casts formed with marsh-mallow, as above, and soaked in a hot solution of alum, renders the casts as hard as stone and as tough as wood, and capable of receiving a polish equal to marble. A sharp blow will cause an indentation rather than shatter it. It forms a good surface for paint or gilt. Plaster casts are rendered hard by soaking in or brushing with a hot solution of stearic acid and soda lye. Plaster casts are hardened by soaking in a hot solution of stearine. The casts by this method may be polished by rubbing with soft rags or cotton wool, also with a soft brush. Plaster casts may be rendered hard and impervious to damp by soaking them in a hot solution of paraffin wax. They may also be rendered hard and tough by soaking in linseed oil for ten hours, then air drying and soaking again for six hours. Warm glue size is also used for a similar purpose, and also by soaking the casts in strong solution of potash alum. Soaking in sulphate of zinc is also useful for this purpose. The immersion should not exceed two hours ; if immersed longer the plaster will become friable. Plaster immersed in a strong solution of borax, gradually heating it, becomes nearly as hard as marble, and may be polished in like manner. Plaster casts immersed in paraffin oil become hard, and assume a fine surface.

Plaster and Portland cement (cast or laid) work may be rendered hard and tough by gauging the material with from 10 to 15 per cent. of minion. Minion is the siftings of ironstone after calcination. Signor Abati, of Naples, found that by combining plaster with the minimum quantity of water, by the application of steam, filled into moulds and submitted to hydraulic pressure, the cast became as hard as marble and as susceptible to polish.

New Mode of Hardening Plaster.—Mr Julhe, in a note presented to the Academie des Sciences, describes some experiments that he has performed with a view to rendering the use of plaster still more general. Of all materials used in building, plaster is the only one which increases in bulk after its application, while mortars and cements, and even wood, undergo shrinkage and cracking through drying. When applied in sufficiently thick coats to resist breakage, it offers, then, a surface that time and atmospheric variations will not change, provided it be protected against water. But it is necessary to give this material two properties that it lacks—hardness and resistance to crushing. This is what Mr Julhe proposes to effect by his process. Six parts of plaster are mixed with one of finely sifted unslaked lime. This mixture is used like ordinary plaster for moulding any object whatever, and, when once dry, the object is soaked in a solution of a sulphate having a base precipitable by lime, and the precipitate of which is insoluble. These form sulphate and oxide of lime, both of them insoluble, which fill the pores of the object and render it hard and tough. Sulphates of zinc and iron are the salts that answer the purpose best. With the first the object remains white, and with the second it gradually assumes the tint of sesqui-oxide of iron (rust).

Polishing Plaster Casts.—Plaster casts can be made to take a high polish. Those which are to be polished by friction with other substances should be made as hard as possible. The plaster should be gauged firm, and used expeditiously. When a soft-gauged plaster is necessary to allow it to be run into closed up moulds, the cast may be partly hardened by dusting the back with dry plaster to absorb the moisture. Gauging with alum water hardens plaster, but causes it to set too quick for manipulation in certain kinds of moulds. This may be overcome by adding size water (which also hardens plaster) to the gauging water. The setting may be regulated to any required degree. Casts intended to be polished should be covered with paper or cloths until dry, and kept in a dry and warm place.

The following are the best known methods for polishing plaster casts :—To 4 lbs. of clean water add 1 oz. of pure curd soap, chipped and dissolved in a glazed pot ; next add 1½ oz. pure white beeswax cut into thin slices. When it is all properly mixed, it is fit for use. The figure must be dried, and suspended by a string. It is then dipped into the liquid varnish, and when taken out, allowed to stand for about three minutes ; stir up the varnish, and then dip the figure again. Cover it up in a dry place, free from all dust, for six or seven days, after which take some soft rag or cotton wool, and gently rub the figure until it has received a brilliant gloss.

Another Way.—Plaster casts soaked in olive oil in which white wax has been dissolved by heat, or casts soaked in dissolved paraffin wax, will, when dry, take a fine polish. The casts should be hot when put into the hot solution. The polishing is done with French chalk and cotton wool. If the polished casts are left in a smoky room, they will acquire the appearance of old ivory. Plaster casts can be made to assume any colour by dissolving in the water for gauging any desired colour in powder.

Another Way.—Soak the casts in a hot solution of white beeswax and glycerine. When dry, polish with French chalk and cotton wool or sable hair brushes.

Another Way.—Take clean skimmed milk, and with a clean soft brush coat the figure until it will absorb no more. Gently blow off all superfluous milk from the face of the object, and lay it in a place perfectly free from dust. When dry, it will have the appearance of polished marble. A great deal depends on the amount of care bestowed on the skimming of the milk. Plaster gauged with milk and water will enable the casts to be polished.

Another Way.—Plaster casts thoroughly dry and brushed with two coats of clear linseed oil, and kept for a while in a smoky room, will take a good polish, and acquire the appearance of old ivory.

Another Way.—Dissolve ½ oz. of soft soap in 1 qt. of water, and then incorporate 1 oz. of white wax. The cast is dipped in or brushed over with this mixture. When dry, it may be polished with soft rag and French chalk. Another way is to give the cast a thin coating of white shellac, then paint over this a good coating of boiled soft soap, and polish when dry with a soft dry rag.

Another Way.—A beautiful varnish for plaster casts may be made by fusing ½ oz. of tin and ½ oz. of bismuth in a crucible. Melt together, then add ½ oz. of mercury. When perfectly combined, take the mixture, allow it to cool, and add the white of an egg. The casts must be dry, and free from stains or dust.

Another Way.—The cast must be perfectly dry, and free from scratches and dust. Give it a coat of linseed oil, and allow it to stand until dry, after which give another coat, and French polish in the ordinary way. If a figure or bust is required to be white, make smooth with white size, and varnish with hard white varnish.

Another Way.—Take 2 parts stearine, 2 parts Venetian soap, and 1 part pearl ash. Grate the stearine and soap, and mix with 30 parts of solution of caustic potash. Boil this for thirty minutes, stirring all the time. Add the pearl ash dissolved in a little clean rain water, and boil for five minutes. Stir until cold, and mix with more lye until it is quite liquid. Before use, it should be allowed to stand for a few days, keeping it properly covered up. Let the figure be clean and well dried. Coat with a soft brush or sponge until the figure will absorb no more. Allow it to stand well covered up, and give another coat. When dry, rub with soft rags or a brush. This will give a beautiful polish. The liquid may be kept for years if properly covered up. Should the surface not have the required degree of gloss, the operation must be repeated. This liquid has the property of hardening the plaster.

Another Way.—Take a clean cast, well dried, and coat with white wax. Place it before a fire until the wax is absorbed. A good polish may then be obtained by friction.

Another Way.—Plaster may be polished with French chalk until it shines like glass. The cast when nearly dry is dusted with the finest French chalk, and gently rubbed with cotton wool. Repeat the dusting and rubbing until a bright polish is obtained, taking care that the chalk does not cake and injure the face of the cast. When perfectly dry, it may be dusted and rubbed again to give a good finish. For deep parts in a cast, where it is difficult to use the wool, use a camel hair brush. French chalk can be used as a help in the final polish in most of the other methods described.

Plaster for Casting Metal.—Plaster mixed and gauged with equal parts of powdered pumice stone makes a heat-resisting mould for casting fusible metals.

To Restore Plaster.—Plaster that has lost its hard and quick-setting properties by dampness or exposure to air may be partly restored and used for gauging coarse stuff by boiling in an iron pot or pail, keeping the plaster continually stirred with a stick or iron rod.

To Waterproof Plasterwork.—A solution for protecting plaster exposed to the weather is composed of 6 parts of linseed oil, boiled with one-sixth of its weight of litharge, and adding 1 part wax. The plaster surface must be clean and dry before the solution is applied. It is laid on hot with a brush. A warm dry day should be selected for using the solution.

Plaster to Set Quick.—Plaster may be made to set rapidly by adding alum. The alum should be previously dissolved in water, and the alum solution added to the pure water when gauging. Alum water also increases the ultimate hardness of plaster. White vitriol, dextrine, chloride of sodium (common salt), sulphate of potassium, or gauging with warm water.

Plaster to Set Slow.—The setting of plaster may be retarded by adding or gauging with size water, ammonia, or stale beer. Sulphate of zinc added to the water has also a marked effect in retarding the setting and increasing the ultimate hardness of plaster.

Modelling Composition.—Mix 200 parts of soapstone powder and 100 parts of the best wheat flour, and stir the mixture carefully into 300 parts of melted white wax, not too hot. This mass can be coloured at pleasure.

American Modelling Wax.—Melt carefully over a moderate fire 2 lbs. of yellow beeswax, add $4\frac{1}{2}$ oz. of Venetian turpentine, 2 oz. of lard, and $2\frac{3}{4}$ lbs. of bole, and mix thoroughly. Then gradually pour the mixture into a vessel with water, and thoroughly knead several times with the hands. The wax should be melted at such a low temperature that no bubbles appear on the melted surface.

American Paste Composition.—Mix together 13 parts of dissolved glue, 14 parts pulverised litharge, 8 parts white lead, 1 part plaster, and 10 parts of very fine sawdust. This composition is extensively used in the manufacture of picture frames, and as a substitute for carton-pierre, etc.

Plaster Imitation of Old Ivory.—Ivory carving may be so closely imitated that only an expert can detect the difference. Ivory carvings, or rather castings, when mounted in metal, wood, or plush frames, have been sold in great numbers and at highly remunerative prices, at exhibitions and art dealers' sales. The process is simple, but requires a considerable amount of skill on the part of the craftsman. The moulds are generally taken from real ivory, carving wood, or art metalwork. Superfine plaster is used. The water is tinted with fine yellow ochre. For the general colour of old ivory, add ½ oz. to each pound of plaster. When the casts are thoroughly dry, they are dipped into spermaceti and suspended until the excess of the spermaceti has run off, and when the cast is nearly dry, but still sticky, fine yellow ochre is sprinkled on. The prominent parts are wiped with fine rags or cotton wool. The success of the work greatly depends on the art displayed in laying and wiping the ochre. The ochre is dusted through a fine muslin bag. Sometimes the grain or spots (as seen in old ivory) is obtained by brushing, stippling, or dabbing with small tool brushes having the hair cut square, short, and wide apart. If the cast is too large to be dipped, it can be brushed over with warm spermaceti quickly and evenly, taking care that the spermaceti does not cake. In both methods the casts should be warm, and the ochre ground to a fine powder. To imitate new ivory, gauge with the tinted water, and when the cast is dry, dip it for fifteen minutes into a solution of spermaceti, white wax, and stearine in equal parts, then polish with cotton wool.

Fictile Ivory (*French Process*).—The cast is made by gauging the plaster in the proportion of 1 lb. of superfine plaster and ½ oz. of the finest yellow ochre. They are thoroughly mixed by passing them through a fine sieve, and then gauged with clean cold water, to which a few drops of the best glue water have been added. The cast is first allowed to dry in the air, then carefully heated in an oven, and when the cast is thoroughly dry, and still warm, it is soaked for a quarter of an hour in a bath containing equal parts of white wax, spermaceti, and stearine, heated a little beyond the melting point. The cast is set on edge to allow the superfluous wax mixture to drain off, and before it is cool the surface is brushed with a soft tool brush to remove any wax that may have settled in the crevices. When the cast is cold, it is finally finished by polishing with cotton wool.

To Take Plaster Casts of Natural Objects.—By this process plaster casts of the most delicate objects of natural history can be reproduced. The material of the mould is modelling wax. As it becomes soft and plastic by the application of heat, though in a cold state it is perfectly rigid, it takes the most minute markings and striations of the original to which it may be applied without injuring it, and the microscopic structure of the surface of the original is carefully reproduced in the cast. The method is briefly this : Cover the object to be cast with a thin powder of steatite or French chalk, which prevents the adhesion of the wax. After the wax has become soft, either from immersion in warm water or from exposure to the direct heat of the fire, apply it to the original, being careful to press it into the little cavities. Then carefully cut off the edges of the wax all round, if the undercutting of the object necessitates the mould being in two or more pieces, and let the wax cool with the object in it until it is sufficiently hard to bear the repetition of the operation on the uncovered portion of the object.' The steatite prevents the one piece of the mould sticking to the other. The original ought to be taken out of the mould before the latter becomes perfectly cold and rigid, as in that case it is very difficult to extract. Then pour in plaster, after having wetted the moulds to prevent bubbles of air lurking in the small interstices ; and if the mould be in two pieces, it is generally convenient to fill them with plaster separately before putting them together. Then dry the plaster casts, either wholly or partially. Paint the casts in water-colours, which must be fainter than those of the original, because the next process adds to their intensity. The delicate shades of colour in the original will be marked in the cast by the different quantity of the same colour, which is taken up by the different textures of the cast. After drying the cast, steep it in hard paraffin. Cool and polish the cast by hand and cotton wool with steatite.

To Paint Cement.—Caustic lime which is not in a state of combination in cement saponifies the oil used in painting. Consequently painting on cement is only practicable when, under the influence of the air, carbonic acid has united with the caustic lime to form carbonate of lime. Various expedients have been resorted to in order to allow the cement to be painted as soon as finished, but the best results have been obtained by the use of casein. Fresh white cheese and fresh slaked fat lime are added to the desired colour. This solution hardens rapidly, and is insoluble in water, a formation of albuminate of lime taking place. The solution, composed of 3 parts of cheese and 1 of slaked lime, is well mixed, and the colour added. Only earth colours, or oxides of iron, should be used. Inorganic colours, aniline, Prussian blue, and white lead should not be used. The caseous lime should be prepared as required for daily use. The mural paintings at the Berlin War Office were done with this solution.

Oil paint on cement is likely to be thrown off by the formation of crystals beneath it ; while, if it remains in place, it usually presents a mottled appearance, owing to the unequal absorption of the oil from the paint by the cement. The common way of remedying both these difficulties has been to wash the cement surface with acids before painting it. This dissolves any crystals that may have formed, and acts upon those spots in the cement which have become slightly carbonated by the action of the atmosphere, so as to restore the absorbent quality, which the formation of a superficial carbonate tends to diminish. Where acid is used, it should be sulphuric acid, made very dilute. Muriatic and acetic acid, which are often employed, leave the cemented surface impregnated with chloride of calcium or acetate of lime, both of which are very deliquescent, and by keeping the surface damp, prevent the proper adhesion of the paint. A better application even than sulphuric acid is, however, to be found in carbonate of ammonia. The crystals of the ammonia carbonate should be exposed to the air until they effloresce partially into a white powder, which is bicarbonate, and more suitable for the purpose than the original carbonate. About ¼ lb. of the ammonia salt should be dissolved in 9 qts. of cold water, and the cement surface washed with the solution. As soon as it is dry, the paint may be applied, and will adhere well and resist the atmosphere. The carbonate of ammonia is best applied when the cement surface is about three weeks old. For prepared surfaces, perhaps older than this or more exposed to the weather, silicate of soda is sometimes useful. This should be prepared by dissolving the syrup silicate of soda of commerce in four times its bulk of water. Three coats should be applied, and after the last the wall must be thoroughly washed to remove any signs of silicate, or it will effloresce and throw off the paint.

Cement Wash.—Cement wash is composed of Portland cement and water. A small percentage of putty lime is added where a lighter shade is required. A solution of sulphate of zinc is sometimes added to give the wash greater permanency. Cement wash is used for colouring cement or stucco façades, walls, etc.

Sanitary Whitewash.—Whitewash is one of the most valuable sanitary articles in the world. Its cheapness and easy method of application bring it within the reach of all. It prevents not only the decay of wood, but conduces greatly to the healthiness of all buildings, whether wood or stone ; outbuildings and fences should be done twice a year. There are various recipes for whitewash, but the following is one of the best. Into a large clean tub put 1 bushel of lime, and slake it with boiling water, covering it up during the process to keep in the steam ; strain the liquor through a fine sieve ; then add 3 lbs. of sulphate of zinc, 1 lb. of alum, and 2 lbs. of common salt, the alum and salt being previously dissolved in hot water. Various colours are obtained as follows : For a cream colour, add 3 lbs. of yellow ochre ; pear or lead colour, add lamp, vine, or ivory black ; fawn colour, add 6 lbs. of American umber, 3 lbs. of Indian red, and 1 lb. of lampblack ; for stone colour, add 8 lbs. of raw umber and 4 lbs. lampblack ; terra-cotta colour, add 4 lbs. Venetian red, 2 lbs. of purple brown, and 2 lbs. of yellow ochre. Limewash with 1 lb. of coarse brown sugar added to each 15 gals. of water will adhere so firmly that splashes on wood or iron will require to be scraped off.

Fire-resisting Whitewash.—Slake freshly burnt lime ; add as much water as will reduce it to the consistency of cream.   To every 10 gals. of this liquid add 2 lbs. of alum, 24 oz. of subcarbonate of potash or commercial potash, 1 lb. of salt, and 1 lb. of plaster.   The above are added separately, and in the order named, being constantly stirred.   The whole is then passed through a fine sieve.   When required for use, it is heated to boiling point, and applied in a hot condition.   If the wash is intended for old walls, the addition of a small quantity of fine sand will tend to preserve and strengthen crumbling walls.

A Cheap Whitewash.—A good whitewash that will not peel or crack is made by adding 1 part salt to 3 parts stone lime.   If used for granaries, sheds, or where there is a difficulty in fixing scaffolding, it may be quickly applied by using a hand fire-engine or a large squirt.

A Brilliant Whitewash.—Take half a bushel of good unslaked lime, and slake it with boiling water, covering it during the process to keep in the steam.   Strain the liquor through a fine sieve, and add to it a peck of clean salt previously dissolved in warm water, 3 lbs. of rice ground to a thin paste, and stirred and boiled hot, $\frac{1}{2}$ lb. of powdered Spanish whiting, and 1 lb. of clean glue, previously dissolved by soaking it, and then melting in a water bath.   Add 5 gals. of hot water to the whole mixture.   Stir it well, and allow it to stand for a few days well covered up to prevent dust getting at it.   The whitewash should be laid on quite hot.   This can be done by heating on a stove as required.   One pint of this liquid will cover a square yard of surface.   This whitewash retains its brilliancy for years.

Mould-proof Whitewash.—Whitewash when used in cellars or dairies is liable to turn mouldy.   This may be prevented by adding 1 oz. of carbolic acid to each gallon of whitewash.

Washable Whitewash.—Herr Reschenschek gives the following quantities to form a washable whitewash, which, it is said, will not lose colour, and the hardness of which will increase by wetting and washing.   Mix 3 parts siliceous rock powdered, 3 parts crushed marble or sandstone, 2 parts porcelain clay, 2 parts warm freshly slaked lime. This will form a wash, which in time will solidify like stone.   Any colour which can safely be used with lime can be added to the ground colour.   The wash is put on thick, allowed to stand for a day to dry, then frequently wetted with water, and it soon becomes waterproof.

To Make Whiting.—Whiting is pure white chalk ground to a fine powder.   It is mixed with water and size for whitening walls and ceilings.   It is made as follows :— Take 6 lbs. of whiting and just cover it with clean cold water, let it stand for six hours, mix it with 1 qt. of best double size, and then leave it in a cold place until it becomes like a jelly.   It is then diluted with water until of a thick creamy consistency.   One lb. of the jelly will cover 6 superficial yards.

Distempering.—Distemper, or destemper, from *tempera*, a term used in fresco painting, is applied to water-colours or pigments ground in water, beer, etc.   Painting scarcely comes within the category of plastering, but distempering (also whitewashing) was a part and parcel of the plasterer's craft in ancient times.   Even at the present time this kind of work is done by plasterers in many parts of the country, therefore a brief description of distempering is here given.

The preparation of ceilings and walls for the finishing in distemper is of vital importance to the ultimate result, inasmuch as if they are not properly prepared they will rarely turn out well at the finish.   The first thing to be done is to stop the suction, for except the finishing colour lays on cool, and without any or very little suction, the work is apt to be more or less rough, and will gather or accumulate more colour in one part than in another, and consequently will look shady. And here the fact may be noted which shows the necessity for the use of a preparation. It will almost invariably be found that one part of a wall or ceiling will have a greater power of absorbing colours than another part. It will be observed, as with a first coat of paint, that some parts are glossy, and others dry dead, that is, the paint has sunk into or been absorbed on the dead parts, while on the glossy part it remains on the surface, owing to the unequal finish of the plasterwork. Of course, in oil painting this is remedied by successive coats of paint. It therefore becomes necessary that some means should be adopted to stop this power of absorption, and for this purpose various preparations are used. The following has been recommended as a suitable preparatory coat, and will be found to answer the purpose very effectually. " Mix about 12 lbs. of the best whiting with water to the consistency of soft paste. Add sufficient parchment or other size to bind the colour fast. Add about 2 oz. of alum, and the same weight of soft soap dissolved in water. Mix well together in a pail, and strain through a coarse cloth or a metal strainer." Of course somewhat similar proportions will answer for any quantity. The colour should now be tried on paper, and dried before a fire or otherwise, in order to test whether sufficient size has been used to " bind " the colour, and to prove that the tint is exactly what is required. The finishing coat can be laid on without disturbing the first one. The alum and soft soap contribute to this effect in a great degree, and help to form a semi-impervious coating upon which the finishing coat will work cool and without suction. Caution must be observed not to have the size too strong, or it will be very liable to chip, especially in rooms where much gas is used.

In order to produce good work, two things are essentially necessary in the mixing of the distemper, namely, clean and well-washed whiting and pure jellied size. The whiting should be put to soak with sufficient soft water to cover it well and penetrate its bulk. When the whiting is sufficiently soaked, the water should be poured off, which will remove any dust or foreign matter from the whiting. It should then be beaten up or stirred until all the lumps are broken, and it becomes a stiff, smooth paste. A good workman will do this carefully with his hand, and will manipulate it until it is quite smooth; but it may be done most effectually with a broad stick or spatula, and then strained through a metal or other strainer. The size should now be added, and the two lightly but effectually mixed together. Care should be taken not to break the jelly of the size any more than can be avoided, and this may be best done by gently stirring the mixture with the hand. If the jellied state is retained intact, the colour will work cool and lay on smooth and level. Then size, whether made of parchment clippings, glue, or any other material, should be dissolved in a sufficient quantity of water to form a weak jelly when cold. In practice it is found that distemper mixed with jellied size will lay on better and make a better job than when the size is used hot. Colour mixed on the former plan works cool and floats nicely, while the latter works dry, and drags and gathers, thus making a rough ceiling or wall, and the difference in the labour required is very much in favour of the jellied size. A little alum added to the distemper has a good effect in hardening and helps it to dry out solid and even. It is customary in some cases to give the ceiling or wall a couple of coats of oil paint previous to the application of the distemper. This stops the suction and gives a richness to the colouring; but if, as frequently happens, the wall gets low in temperature during a continuance of cold weather, when a change takes place the condensation is so great that the water runs down in streams to the top of the skirting, and the colouring matter thereby becomes stained.

With regard to the method of laying on distemper colours, it may be accepted as a fact that the sooner they dry after they are laid on the better. The best plan is to close the windows and doors, and stop the free circulation of the air as much as possible while the distemper colour is being laid on. This prevents it drying too quickly, and enables the workman to lay the colour on more evenly and with less danger of showing any pieces; but the moment that the wall or ceiling is covered, the windows and doors should be thrown wide open, and as much fresh air admitted as possible. This free circulation of air absorbs and carries off the moisture from the walls. The evaporation is quick, and a good job results. If the distemper does not dry quickly, it becomes slightly discoloured and shaded. One great point to be aimed at is, of course, a level and uniform surface when dry, and this desirable result can only be obtained by the colour being laid on of a proper consistency, and with every attention to equality.

When ceilings are badly stained and discoloured from the accidental overflow of cisterns, water-closets, etc., the only effectual method of treating them is to wash them off with clean water, and give two coats of oil paint before the distemper is applied. Other processes are adopted, but as they cannot be depended upon, it is much better, in the first instance, to incur a little extra expense, and paint the discoloured ceiling in oil colours.

The following hints for mixing various colours in distemper, etc., by which at least a theoretical knowledge of the subject can be acquired, which will greatly facilitate progress in mastering the practical details, are given by the author of the " Painter's and Grainer's Handbook."

The best size for distemper colour is made from parchment clippings. These are put into an iron kettle filled with water, and are allowed to stand for twenty-four hours, until the pieces are thoroughly soaked; then boil for five hours, occasionally taking off the scum. When the liquid is sufficiently boiled, take it from the fire, and strain it through a coarse cloth. If the size is to be kept for a length of time, dissolve 3 oz. or 4 oz. of alum in boiling water, and add to every pailful. The size must be boiled again till it becomes very strong. It must then be strained a second time, put into a cool place, and it will keep for several weeks. It is cheaper and safer to buy size ready-made from a maker of good repute.

Pink.—Dissolve in water separately whiting and rose pink. Mix them to the tint required, strain the colour through a strainer, and bind the size.

Lilac.—Take a small quantity of indigo, finely ground in water, and mix it with whiting till it produces a dark grey; then add to the mixture some rose pink. Well mix and strain the colour, and a beautiful lilac will be the result.

Light Grey.—A small quantity of lampblack mixed with whiting composes a grey. A wide range of shades may be obtained from the darkest to the lightest grey.

French Grey.—Take the quantity of whiting required, and soak it in water, then add Prussian blue and lake which have been finely ground in water. The quantity of each of these colours should, of course, be proportioned to the warmth of tint required. This is a handsome and delicate colour for walls. Rose pink may be substituted for the lake; but it does not make so brilliant a colour, neither is it so permanent.

Orange.—This is a mixture of whiting, French yellow or Dutch pink, and orange lead. These ingredients may be proportioned according to taste. This colour cannot be worked except in a size jelly, as the orange lead is a colour which has great density, and will sink to the bottom, separating from the other colours.

Buff.—A good buff may be produced by dissolving separately whiting and yellow ochre in water. A little English Venetian red should be added to give a warm cast. Mix with size, and strain as before directed.

Drab.—(1) Dissolve whiting in water, and grind some burnt umber very fine in water. Mix to the tint required. Raw umber will make a drab of a different shade. (2) Dissolve separately some whiting and yellow ochre in water. Take a quantity of each, and mix them together. Grind a little lampblack very fine, and with it sufficiently stain the colour to make the tint required. (3) Another shade may be obtained by adding a little Venetian red. By diversifying the proportions of these pigments a great variety of colours may be produced. These are all permanent colours, and may be depended upon.

Salmon.—An excellent salmon colour may be made by dissolving whiting in water, and tinging it with the best English Venetian red. A little Venetian red, mixed with lime whitewash and a quantity of alum, will answer very well for common purposes.

Paints and Washes.—The following paints and washes, which are extensively used in America, will be found useful for various purposes :—

Flexible Paint.—Slice $2\frac{1}{2}$ lbs. of good yellow soap and dissolve it in $1\frac{1}{2}$ gals. of boiling water, and grind the solution while hot with $3\frac{1}{2}$ gals. of good oil paint. It is used to paint on canvas.

To Prepare a Zinc Wash for Rooms.—Mix oxide of zinc with ordinary milk of lime, and apply the mixture in the same manner as whitewash. When dry lay on a coat of solution of chloride of zinc. This combines with the oxide, and forms a solid coat with a lustrous surface.

Quickly Drying Oil Paint.—Boil for fifteen minutes in an earthenware pot 1 part of soft curd in 3 parts of water. Pour the mass through a colander, wash it with cold water, and press out the water in a linen cloth. To 1 part of the curd add $\frac{1}{4}$ part of unslaked lime and $\frac{3}{4}$ part of water. The fat slime thus formed is triturated in oil or water with the various pigments. Walls, ceilings, stairs, in short anything of stone, plaster of Paris, or zinc, can be painted with this. If the paint is to be used on wood, add $\frac{1}{16}$ part of linseed oil. Ochre, chrome yellow, Berlin blue, indigo, lead, and zinc are best adapted for colouring substances. The mixture dries so quickly that three coats can be applied in one day. It is entirely without odour, and costs about one-third of ordinary oil paint.

For recipes for Gesso, Carton-pierre, and Compo see Chapters XVII and XVIII.

MISCELLANEOUS INFORMATION

The Plasterers' Company.—The Worshipful Company of Plasterers was incorporated in 1501. King Henry VII by his charter, dated 10th March, incorporated the Worshipful Company of Plasterers under the title of " The Master and Wardens of the Guild or Fraternity of the Blessed Mary of Plasterers." Their grant of arms by Thomas Hawley, Clarencieux, is dated 15th January 1546. A confirmation of their charter of incorporation, dated 11th June 1667, grants them the usual privileges of a guild ; a livery, a master, two wardens, and thirty-two assistants.

Their arms are " *Azure* on a chevron *gules*, between a trowel and two hatchets, handles of the second headed *argent* in chief, and a treble brush in base proper ; a rose gules seeded or, between two fleurs-de-lis of the first." " Let brotherly love continue " is their motto. Their book of ordinances is an interesting volume. In 1686 occurred one of those " 'prentice " riots so famous in the old time, and five of the prisoners proved to be of the Plasterers' Company. In an Act passed in the sixth year of William and Mary, 1694, it is stated that " whereas the Masters and Wardens of the guild or fraternity of the Blessed Mary of Plasterers, London, are, and very anciently have been, a brotherhood or guild, and for confirmation or strengthening of their privileges have obtained several royal grants, whereby the original constitution of the said fraternity or guild ought to be and consist of all persons using the trade of a plasterer in the city of London and liberties thereof." A fine was inflicted on those *practising the art* without being a member of the guild.   A statute was passed in the first year of the reign of James I, 1603, c. 20, which enacted that no plasterer should exercise the art " of a painter in the city of London or suburbs of London."   An apprentice was exempt from the meaning of the Act.   The penalty was £5, but a proviso allowed plasterers to use whiting, blacking, and red ochre mixed with size, without oil.   This was a very important statute ; it cleared up the disagreements existing in 1575 between plasterers and painters, the latter retaining their privileges by becoming incorporated in 1581.

Plasterers do not appear to have restricted themselves to the mystery of pargeters. In 1579 and 1585 two orders were made by the Court of Aldermen for settling matters in dispute between the tilers and bricklayers and the plasterers, as to interfering in each other's trades.   The observance of these orders was enforced by an order of the Privy Council, dated 1st June 1613, and a general writ or precept issued to the same effect on 13th August 1613.

The Plasterers' Hall is situated in Addle Street, Wood Street, Cheapside, London. Unfortunately, it is now used as an office and warehouse.   Malcolm, who wrote in 1803, states that the rooms were much ornamented with work peculiar to their profession, and the best artists belonging to it were doubtlessly employed.

Wages.—Plasterers' wages have shown a good deal of fluctuation.   The standard rate in July 1914 was 11½d. per hour ; in 1925 the rate was 1s. 9½d., and now (1927) stands at the same figure, according to the schedule of the plasterers' union. This figure represents an increase of 87 per cent.   According to authorities on building estimating, an addition of 20 per cent. must be made to the basic figure of 187 per cent. to allow for reduced output and shorter hours.   This figures out at 37.5, making a total percentage of increased cost of labour of 124.   But the shortage of skilled men is such that rates above the standard figure, sometimes reaching as high as over 2s. per hour, are frequently paid.

Hawk Boys.—In London and the South of England plasterers formerly had attendants called " hawk boys," each pair of plasterers having one to wait upon them. The hawk boy's duty was to knock up, gauge, and serve materials, keep tools clean, and warm their food.   The materials were gauged in a banker, placed on the floor or scaffold.   The boy gauged the materials with a " server."   When he had finished a gauge, he shouted " serve," and lifted as much as would fill a plasterer's " hawk."   If the plasterer was on a mid-scaffold, a smart hawk boy could " throw " a serverful of stuff quite 10 ft. high.   Their wages were from 2d. to 2½d. per hour, and a few coppers on pay-day as " tool money."   Hawk boys are now past history, and better so !   As the boys grew up, knowing the names and uses of the tools, a cute boy developed into a so-called plasterer, to the detriment of apprenticeship.

Regarding Plastering Literature.—Some authors when describing plasterwork make palpable mistakes.   It is probable that the writer who first introduced the subject as a part of his work was so engrossed with his own particular branch that he could not give plasterwork due attention, or that, aware of his want of plastic knowledge, he left the subject to some careless underling, who was either incompetent to give reliable information, or in his search for information was imposed upon, and in turn imposed upon his employer.   Other authors or would-be teachers of plasterwork blindly followed, like a flock of silly sheep following a leader.   Only recently the Plasterers' Company offered a series of prizes to plasterers' apprentices for the best description and examples of about a dozen branches of the plasterers' craft, and as many of the branches named were new, the students were referred to a well-known work on Building Construction.   On referring to this work, a few short notes are to be found, which are not only insufficient, but wholly incorrect and misleading.   It would take up too much space to enumerate even one-fifth of the errors, but the following are fair samples.   It is stated that " trowelled stucco is laid in pieces about 4 or 5 ft. square, and the workman, with a float in one hand and a brush in the other, floats the work until it is as smooth as *glass*." Now it only requires a modicum of intelligence or thought to see that it is impossible to get a partly soft or moist surface as smooth as glass with a wood float. Of course the work is scoured with a hand-float, but it is the hard, smooth, and straight edge of the trowel that gives the polish and renders the surface as smooth as glass. Again, laying the work in small pieces is entirely wrong. In fact, it is never done by plasterers in the manner described. If laid in small pieces, it would make a series of joints, which would be unsightly and difficult to make smooth and true. Floating is described as " consisting of fine stuff with the addition of a little hair, and derives its name from being laid on with *floats*." Now a novice knows that floating consists of coarse stuff, and that it is laid on with a laying trowel. It derives its name from the fact that it is a second coat " floated " on the first coat, to form a solid straight surface for the setting coat. Another reason for the name is that the surface is made straight (not smooth) with a floating rule. It is also stated that " common stucco is laid on with a brush like whitewash, smoothed with a straight-edge, and then rubbed with a hand-float, and brought to a hard and glossy surface." I have been in the trade and a seeker of plastic knowledge for over forty years, and I have never seen or heard of laying setting stuff with a brush (instead of a trowel or skimming-float), or of smoothing being done with a straight-edge. This is used, as its name implies, to make the surface straight. As to the glossy surface, it is done with a trowel, not by a float. It is by the contact and friction of two hard surfaces (the consolidated setting stuff and the trowel) that the gloss or polish is obtained.

The term " fine stuff," which is used by some authors for " setting stuff," should be entirely discarded. There are several degrees of fineness in most plastic stuffs, such as coarse, fine, and superfine plaster ; coarse, fine, and superfine Keen's. Even in " coarse stuff " there is often a finer quality used for floating ceilings (especially for panelled ceilings) than what is used for lathed walls, and rendering, first-coating, etc. Therefore, the term, as applied to " setting stuff," is vague and often misleading, especially as there are several degrees of fineness in this stuff, such as coarse, common, and fine, which are used for different kinds of setting and stuccowork. It seems ridiculous, or like gilding gold, to name the finest degree of this stuff as fine fine stuff. Fine stuff is described by some authors in their passing remarks as " slaked lime saturated with water until of the consistency of cream   for some purposes a small quantity of hair is added." Now the veriest tyro will see that this is simply lime putty. No mention of sand is made. Lime putty is described as similar to fine stuff, but always used without hair. Even in lime putty there are two degrees of fineness—the ordinary run lime, used for coarse stuff, and the fine putty used for running mouldings and making setting stuff. Hence the necessity for the general use of the term " setting stuff," and the denomination of the other degrees of fineness, as fine or coarse, as required for the class of work.

Some authors also speak of " coarse gauged stuff," whereas it should be gauged coarse stuff. The stuff may be of different degrees of fineness, but the gauging can only be medium or strong gauged, *i.e.*, using more of the material which has setting powers. The gauge may also be stiff or soft, but not coarse gauge. This then would rather imply that it was carelessly or improperly done. Coarse stuff is a term solely applied to the material used for the first or second coats of lime plastering, or when coreing or roughing out work with coarse plaster. Coarse or rough may be correctly applied to denominate the degree of fineness of any material, such as coarse plaster, etc.

APPENDIX

NOTES ON SOME RECENT DEVELOPMENTS IN AMERICAN PLASTERING

In addition to a widespread use of concrete for all classes of structures, the past few years have witnessed a great development in the use of various forms of plaster and the varieties manufactured. It is felt, therefore, that the following brief and possibly disconnected notes may be of some interest to English plasterers as well as providing concise information for American readers.

For dwelling-houses and commercial and industrial buildings the possibilities of plastering in the U.S.A. are almost boundless, and the next few years will probably see a remarkable upward leap in its application, with cement-stucco exteriors for every class of building—churches, halls, clubs, apartment buildings, and private houses.

An interesting but ephemeral use of stucco is in the preparation of buildings and scenes for filmwork, an application of enormous utility, variety, and extent.

In some cases stucco is used to imitate the appearance and structure of ancient or historical buildings. This practice, possibly permissible as an archæological exercise for study, is bad in principle and unsound as art, with whatever degree of skill the craftsmanship may be carried out.

One of the most striking developments of the art, especially under the clear skies of California, is the advent of brightly coloured stucco—an application of the modern feeling for bright colour which has not yet reached England or the European Continent. For this Mr O. A. Malone, President of the Californian Stucco Products Co., known as " the man who put colour into California," is largely responsible, and to the preparation and use of coloured stucco—the so-called " Jazz Plaster "—he has devoted much labour and experiment. Many of the film stars at Hollywood have their private houses built of brightly coloured stucco, rivalling the hues of Nature herself in that bright and vivid region.

According to Mr Malone, pale blue bungalows, shell pink apartment buildings, and bright yellow mansions decorated with coloured spots may line the streets in the near future. Even the usually drab farmhouse will be coloured in pastel tones, and office buildings will stand in brilliant shades. Moreover, exterior and interior wall surfaces will be rough mottled, spotted, or finished to give the effect of light and shadow, instead of a plain flat expanse. Mr Malone is stated to have worked out a method of piling colours on the plasterer's hawk that, when applied to a wall, gives effects equal to the gorgeous colour combinations of colour artists.

It is debatable whether such methods could be effectively employed with the grey towns and weather of this country, which has never succeeded in the application of bright colour to the exteriors and interiors of buildings.

Reasons of space render it impossible to devote anything approaching adequacy of treatment to the innumerable ramifications of this vast and interesting subject. The following notes and brief specifications may be recorded as typical examples selected from a great store of available information. But the American stucco manufacturers issue in many cases well-prepared and fully-illustrated booklets on the characteristics and methods of use of their stuccoes, and are always ready to send copies and supply information exhaustively to anyone interested.

The collection of this information, of which only a small portion can here be utilised, is due to the interest and enterprise of Mr George Cole, Plasterer, of Alhambra, San Francisco, to whom it is a pleasure to express the warmest gratitude.

I. Standard Plastering Specifications prepared by the Contracting Plasterers' Association of Southern California

Note.—It is assumed that the building to be plastered has been properly constructed and prepared for lathing and plastering : that studding and joists have been spaced 12 in. or 16 in. on centre ; that proper nailing has been given at all corners and angles ; that walls are straight and plumb ; that all grounds are in place which are to serve as a guide for the plasterer, and that grounds are $\frac{7}{8}$ in. thick for three-coat work, $\frac{3}{4}$ in. thick for two-coat work over wood or metal lath, and $\frac{1}{2}$ in. thick where plaster is to be applied to walls of brick, tile, or concrete.

INTERIOR WORK

Wood Lathing.—All wood lathing shall be done with a good sound quality of Oregon pine lath, free from bark, pitch, or pitch pockets or cross grains. Laths shall be thoroughly wet before being applied.

For lime mortar plaster the lath shall be spaced $\frac{3}{8}$ in. apart ; for Hardwall plaster, $\frac{1}{4}$ in. apart.

Laths shall be nailed at every bearing with threepenny fine nails. Perpendicular joints in the lathing shall be broken every eighth lath. No laths shall be set vertical to fill out any corners or other space.

Metal Lath.—Metal lath shall be either galvanised or asphaltum dipped. For ceilings the lath shall weigh not less than 3 lbs. per square yard when tied to steel, or $2\frac{3}{4}$ lbs. if attached to wood with supports spaced not greater than 16 in. on centre.

On walls the lath shall weigh not less than $2\frac{1}{2}$ lbs. per yard when applied to steel, and $2\frac{3}{10}$ lbs. per yard when applied to wood.

Metal lath applied to steel shall be fastened with galvanised wire of not less than No. 18 gauge.

Metal lath applied to wood shall be secured with not less than fourpenny wire nails, driven to at least $\frac{7}{8}$ in. penetration, and bent up to engage at least one strand without breaking.

Keene's Cement.—For the best results, Keene's cement should be used neat, or with as little lime as possible. In many cases the practice has obtained of adding so much lime to Keene's cement in order to achieve economy and easy-working qualities, that the cement has but little more strength than an ordinary lime putty finish.

When lime is used to give extra plasticity, not more than one pail of lime putty should be added to each 100 lbs. of Keene's cement. When not mixed with lime, Keene's cement will have almost the hardness of marble with all its beautiful finish.

HARDWALL PLASTER

Wood Lath : Two-Coat Work.—The first coat mixture shall consist of 2 parts of clean, sharp sand free from loam or silt to 1 part Hardwall plaster. Darby with as little water as possible and rod around angles, base, windows, and doors. The second or finish coat will be found under heading of " Finish Coats on Hardwall Plaster."

Wood Lath : Three-Coat Work.—The first or scratch coat shall consist of a mixture of 2 parts of clean, sharp sand free from loam or silt to 1 part Hardwall plaster put on with sufficient force to ensure a good clinch and scratched with a metal scratcher or broom. Scratch coat shall be thoroughly set before applying second coat.

Brown or second coat to consist of a mixture of 3 parts of clean, sharp sand free from loam or silt to 1 part of Hardwall plaster. This work should be rodded and darbied to a plane slightly back of grounds to allow for finish coat. Use as little water as possible.

Finish coat will be found under heading of " Finish Coats on Hardwall Plaster."

For base coats on plaster board use same directions as specified for wood lath. Metal lath shall be plastered in three coats. Scratch coats to consist of sixteen shovels clean, sharp sand to one sack Hardwall plaster, this coat to be well scored with metal scratcher, to provide ample key for brown coat. Brown coat to be applied after scratch coat has thoroughly set ; mixture to be eighteen shovels clean, sharp sand to one sack Hardwall plaster. Use same precaution as specified for base coat on wood lath.

FINISH COATS ON HARDWALL PLASTER

Sand Finish.—To consist of twelve shovels screened sand to one sack screened Hardwall plaster, screen to be No. 14 or No. 16 mesh. Apply this coat even with grounds, and float to even texture with carpet float.

Smooth, Hard Finish.—To consist of lime putty and plaster of Paris, or screened Hardwall, gauged strong enough to make a hard, durable wall free from chip cracks.

Plastering behind Wainscoting.—Where plaster is applied back of wainscoting, it shall be of two coats and $\frac{3}{8}$ in. thick.

Plaster on Concrete.—Where plaster is applied to concrete, brick, or tile or plaster blocks, the surface shall be thoroughly cleaned and wet before plastering is applied.

EXTERIOR PLASTERING

All exterior surfaces of wood construction to be covered with waterproof felt paper, lapped 2 in. starting at bottom of wall before applying metal lath.

Metal Lath.—Metal lath shall weigh not less than 3 lbs. per square yard, and shall be galvanised or armco iron or other acid-resisting lath. The lath shall be applied with fourpenny nails driven not over 8 in. apart and to at least $\frac{7}{8}$ in. penetration, and bent to engage at least one strand of wire. Vertical laps shall occur at supports, and stapled or nailed not more than 4 in. apart.

Plaster.—The character and quality of sand and lime shall be the same as specified for interior work.

The cement mortar shall be applied in three coats, each coat not less than $\frac{1}{4}$ in. in thickness, the whole finishing not less than $\frac{7}{8}$ in. thick.

The scratch coat shall be composed of 1 part Portland cement, 2 parts sand, and not more than 10 per cent. lime putty or hydrated lime. To this shall be added cattle hair or long fibre of a quality only sufficient to bind the mortar.

This coat shall be applied with sufficient force to thoroughly embed the lath and the surface roughened with steel scratcher to give a bond for the second coat.

When scratch coat is set but before it is thoroughly hardened, the second coat shall be applied. This coat shall be composed of 1 part Portland cement, 2½ parts sand, and not more than 10 per cent. of lime putty or hydrated lime. This coat shall be floated to a true and even plane.

After the second coat has cured for at least two weeks, the finishing coat shall be applied.

The finish coat shall be of a character and colour as desired by the owner.

The second coat shall be sprayed with water occasionally for several days, so as to allow the cement to thoroughly set before drying out.

II. Portland Cement Stucco prepared by the Portland Cement Association (of Chicago, America), available in a Wide Range of Colours, and adapted for a Variety of Textures

CONDENSED SPECIFICATIONS

General

1. **Preparation of Surface.**—All hangers, fasteners, trim or other fixed supports or projections of any kind shall be in place previous to the application of stucco. In masonry backing the surface shall be cleaned thoroughly before stucco is applied and shall be sufficiently rough to provide a good mechanical bond for the first coat.

2. **Flashing.**—Flashing shall be in place previous to the application of stucco in the following locations : at the top and along sides of all openings wherever projecting trim occurs ; across the wall and under coping, cornices, or brick sills with mortar joints, flashing to project beyond upper edge of stucco ; under built-in gutters and around roof openings ; at the intersection of walls and roofs ; and at all other points where flashing would prevent water from getting behind the stucco.

3. **Water Protection.**—All horizontal exposed surfaces, which are of stucco, such as copings, cornices, belt courses, shall be given sufficient fall to prevent water from accumulating on such surfaces. In general, the construction shall protect the surface against excessive concentrated water flow, all horizontal projections being provided with overhanging drips and watertight joints. Stucco wall surfaces shall be stopped 6 in. above grade line.

Materials

4. **Cement.**—Portland cement shall conform to the current standard specifications of the American Society for Testing Materials.

5. **Fine Aggregate.**—Fine aggregate shall consist of clean sand, screenings from crushed stone or pebbles, graded from fine to coarse, passing when dry a No. 4 screen, with not more than 20 per cent. through a No. 50 screen, free from dust or other deleterious materials.

6. **Water.**—Water shall be clean, free from oil, acid, strong alkali, or vegetable matter.

7. **Colouring Materials.**—Only permanent mineral oxides that are fully guaranteed by the manufacturer to be unaffected by lime, cement, or weathering shall be used in colouring.

8. **Hydrated Lime.**—Hydrated lime shall meet the requirements of the standard specifications of the American Society for Testing Materials, and when used shall not exceed one-fifth the volume of the cement.

9. **Reinforcement.**—Reinforcement shall consist either of expanded metal cut from sheets not less than 20 gauge in thickness with openings not less than $\frac{3}{4}$ in. by 2 in. nor greater than $1\frac{1}{2}$ in. by 4 in. in size, the fabric to weigh not less than 1.8 lbs. per square yard, or wire fabric composed of wires not smaller than 18 gauge used with openings not less than $\frac{3}{4}$ in. square or with wires not smaller than 14 gauge used with openings not greater than 2 in. square.

Construction

10. **Proportions.**—Mortar for both scratch and brown coats shall be mixed in the proportions of five (5) sacks of Portland cement, one (1) 50 lb. sack of hydrated lime, and 16 cub. ft. of sand.   The finish coat, if not a prepared Portland cement stucco, shall be of like proportions to those used in the previous coats, with such additions of mineral colouring pigments as necessary, but in quantities not to exceed 6 per cent. of the volume of the cement used.

11. **Mixing.**—Dry mixing of ingredients shall be carried on until the colour is uniform ; wet mixing until the consistency is uniform.   It is positively essential that a definite system be used which shall produce uniform mixes for scratch and brown coats. The quantity of water shall be determined by trial and thereafter used in the proper proportions.

12. **Framing.**—Spacing of studs shall not exceed 16 in.   Studding shall run from foundation to rafters without intervening horizontal members, tied together below second floor joists with 1 in. by 4 in. boards let into the inner faces of the studs.   In open construction without sheathing the spacing of studs shall not exceed 12 in.   The corners of all walls shall be braced diagonally to secure the necessary rigidity of the structure. Bridging of studding with 2 in. by 4 in. braces shall occur at least once in each story height.

13. **Sheathing.**—Sheathing boards shall not be less than 6 in., nor more than 8 in. wide, dressed to a uniform thickness, laid horizontally and fastened securely to each stud.   Over the sheathing shall be laid, horizontally, beginning at the bottom, any standard asphalt saturated roofing felt weighing 15 lbs. per square, the bottom layer lapping the baseboard and each strip lapping the strip below, and all flashing at least 2 in.

14. **Application of Reinforcement.**—Reinforcement shall be placed horizontally, fastened with approved furring devices not more than 8 in. apart over the surface. Vertical laps shall occur at supports, horizontal joints being lapped and tightly laced with 18 gauge annealed wire.   The sheets shall be returned around corners at least 4 in. in sheathed construction and 16 in. in open construction.   Corner beads shall not be used.

15. **Furring.**—All reinforcement shall be furred out from the studs, sheathing, or base $\frac{3}{8}$ in. by any device which will not reduce the effective section of the scratch coat.

16. **Half-Timbering.**—Embedded trim or half-timbering shall be securely nailed directly upon sheathing or studs, and shall have the inside corners of vertical members grooved, into which the mortar of the first coat shall be forced, forming a watertight joint.   All joints on horizontal members shall be flashed.

17. **Masonry Walls.**—Concrete, concrete block, brick, hollow tile, and similar

walls shall be rigid and constructed upon solid footings, all units being set in Portland cement mortar. The surface on which stucco is to be applied shall be clean, free from all dust, dirt, or loose particles, preferably rough and of coarse texture. Wood lintels over wall openings shall not be used. Monolithic concrete walls shall be roughened by hacking, wire brushing, or other effective means. Concrete block, tile, or brick units shall have the joints cut back even with the surface. Clay tile shall be hard burned with dovetail or heavy, ragged scoring. Clay brick walls shall be composed of rough, hard-burned clay brick, and if painted or waterproofed shall be covered with reinforcing fabric before overcoating with stucco.

18. **Wetting the Surface.**—Immediately preceding the application of the stucco, the surface of the wall shall be evenly wetted but not saturated. Water shall not be rapidly absorbed from the plaster, nor remain standing on the surface.

19. **Retempering.**—Retempering by the addition of water shall not be permitted.

20. **Consistency.**—Only sufficient water to produce a workable consistency shall be used.

21. **Application of Stucco Coats on Frame Construction.**—The application shall be carried on continuously in one general direction without allowing the stucco to dry at the edges. If it is impossible to work the full width of the wall at one time the joining shall be at some natural division of the surface, such as a window or door. The scratch coat shall be shoved thoroughly through the metal reinforcement, forming a solid mass against the sheathing paper, thus completely encasing the metal. This coat shall be $\frac{1}{2}$ in. thick fully, covering the face of the reinforcement, and shall have its surface heavily cross-scratched to provide a strong mechanical key or bond. Allow this coat to become thoroughly dry. It shall be wet down but not saturated before applying the second coat. The second, or browning coat, shall be at least $\frac{1}{2}$ in. thick over the face of the first coat, and shall be rodded straight and true in every direction, or left untrue, giving a wavy effect, as the desired finish would suggest. If the finish is to be a float type finish, the second coat shall be brought to a good even surface with wood floats. This coat shall be wet down for at least three days and allowed to become thoroughly dry before the finishing coat is applied. The finish coat shall be applied not less than one week after the application of the second coat, and shall vary in thickness from $\frac{1}{8}$ in. to $\frac{1}{4}$ in., depending upon the texture of the finish coat.

22. **Scratch Coat on Masonry Walls.**—Mortar shall be trowelled on to a thickness of approximately $\frac{1}{2}$ in., heavily cross-scratched and allowed to become thoroughly dry before the browning coat is applied. (From this point on use specification covering "Application of Stucco Coats on Frame Construction." See paragraph 21.)

23. **Freezing.**—Stucco shall not be applied when the temperature is below 32° F., unless protected with canvas and heat sufficient to prevent freezing for a period of at least forty-eight hours after application.

24. **Curing.**—Each coat shall be protected from drying rapidly from effects of intense sunlight or wind until it has sufficiently hardened to permit sprinkling. Each coat shall be kept moist by sprinkling for at least three days following its application.

25. **Back-Plastered Construction.**—In back-plastered construction, the metal lath shall be attached directly to the face of the studs by an approved furring device and the mortar of the first, or scratch coat, applied with sufficient force to push it through the openings of the metal lath forming keys behind. The back-plastering coat shall not be applied until the scratch coat has hardened sufficiently to prevent injuring the keys of the scratch coat. The back-plastered coat shall not be less than $\frac{1}{2}$ in. thick back of reinforcement, composed of the same proportions and materials as the scratch coat, and shall be applied from side to side of the hollow space between studs. The application

of the browning and finish coats on back-plastered construction is identical with other methods as previously given.

26. **Open Construction.**—In open construction a standard 15 lb. asphalt saturated roofing felt shall be applied directly on the outside face of the studs, being fastened by flat-headed roofing nails on 12 in. centres. Vertical laps shall be 12 in. and horizontal laps 6 in. over the lower course. Metal reinforcement shall be applied over the entire surface held in place by approved furring devices, lapping at least 2 in. on all horizontal laps and at least 6 in. on all vertical laps. All horizontal laps between the studding shall have at least one tie with No. 18 annealed wire. All vertical laps shall occur on studding and shall be laced with No. 18 annealed wire. All metal reinforcement shall be returned around corners at least 16 in. Corner beads will not be permitted.

27. **Finish Coat.**—The finish coat shall be of the colour and texture agreed upon by the owner and architect. If prepared Portland cement stucco is used it shall be applied according to the manufacturer's specifications. If a field mix is used for the finish coat it shall be applied in accordance with the practice outlined here. In all cases the architect will furnish samples of texture and colour which shall be inspected by all bidding contractors. A definite decision shall be arrived at as to colour and texture before bids are taken, in order that bidding shall be done intelligently.

COLOURING MATERIALS

Mixing of mineral pigments with the finish coat should be resorted to only when prepared machine-mixed materials are not available in the desired colours. Mineral colours should be used, as mortar, organic or aniline pigments are likely to fade under the action of the lime.

The finer the materials are ground and the better distributed through the mortar, the more their colour is imparted. Another important requirement is high tinting value. Although the unit first cost will be higher, it is advisable to use such as the least amount will be required to obtain a definite tint. Simple tests indicate how well any pigment will unite with the cement. Place quietly a small quantity of the powdered pigment in a glass of water and watch its settlement, or make a thin wash mixture with neat Portland cement; allow it to stand and observe if separation of pigment particles from the cement occurs. Additions of most inert admixtures somewhat reduce the strength of the stucco, but not appreciably unless the amounts are large. Generally, additions of colouring material not greater than 6 per cent. of the cement weight will produce any but the darker tints.

It is impossible to arrive at definite colour formulæ applying to colouring materials, since the variations in the colours of the sands as well as the pigments themselves would make such but approximations. Best results are obtained by experiment. Small panels should be made, using different percentages of pigment with uniform methods of mixing. In obtaining the more delicate shades the use of white Portland cement in the finish coat is convenient.

Polychrome colour effects used with certain textures add variety. There are several ways of producing these in the finish coat. An amount of each of the coloured mortars may be placed separately on the mortar board, and smaller amounts from each pile are laid together on the hawk, the trowel then being used to cut through and apply this vari-coloured mixture to the wall. Or the colours may be blended by combining the coloured mortars on the mortar board and proceeding as usual in applying the mixture to the wall with the hawk and trowel. Thin washes, made of mixtures of colouring pigment, cement, and water in tried proportions, may be brushed on the surface as a stain.　Any polychrome surface may be blended by rubbing with a scrub brush or wadded piece of burlap, which removes most of the stain from the higher points.

A general guide to colouring materials for various tints in stucco is as follows : Reds and pinks—red oxide of iron ; yellows and buffs—yellow oxide of iron ; greens—chromium oxide ; browns—brown oxide of iron ; blues—ultramarine blue ; greys or slate effects—-manganese black, drop black, or Germantown lampblack.

III. Estimating Plastering Costs—An American Table for Plasterers

This table is designed to show the quantities of material and labour required for 100 square yards of lathing and plastering. It was worked out by a plastering contractor for his own use, and although it obviously cannot cover all types of work, it does take up some of those most commonly used and gives the principal items of material and labour that enter into each.

In referring to these figures, it should be remembered that the accomplishment of both material and labour varies from job to job even on the same type of work, and also that there may be a big difference between one job and the next—particularly in labour—due to the kind of finished work required by job specifications.

At best, the table is a guide to be qualified in the light of experience. The single item of labour will probably vary more than anything, and hence no attempt has been made to show a difference in time between similar operations such as scratching in over metal lath and wood lath. But notwithstanding such variations, it is thought these figures will serve as a guide in estimating the average job.

A blank column is included for foreman's time. No figures are shown because they will depend upon the size of the crew and also upon whether the one in charge also uses the trowel.

Lathing and Furring

Material and Labour Required for 100 *Square Yards*

LATHING AND FURRING.					
Material.				Labour.	
Type of Construction.	Steel Channels.	Lath.	Wire or Nails, Lbs.	Lather's Hours.	Foreman, Hours.
Standard wood lath, 1½ in. × 48 in.	...	1,450	10 lbs. nails	8	...
Narrow wood lath, 1 in. × 48 in.	...	1,950	13½ lbs. nails	11	...
Metal lath on wood studs	...	105 sq. yds.	8 lbs. nails or staples	8½	...
Metal lath on steel studs	(1 in.) 500 lbs., or 1,000 lineal ft.	105 sq. yds.	20 lbs. wire	41	...
Plaster board on wood studs	...	900 sq. ft.	7 lbs. nails	7	...
Beam and cornice furring	...	110 sq. yds.	8 lbs. nails or staples	25	...
Beam and cornice furring	(¾ in.) 700 lbs., or 1,750 lineal ft.	110 sq. yds.	40 lbs. wire	100	...
Suspended ceilings	(2 in.) 555 lbs., or 325 lineal ft.; and (¾ in.) 380 lbs., or 980 lineal ft.	105 sq. yds.	108 ¼-in. hanger rods and 20 lbs. wire	38	...

Plastering

Material and Labour Required for 100 *Square Yards*

PLASTERING.							
Material for Base Coat.				Labour for Base and Finish Coats.			
Kind of Base.	Cement Plaster, 100 lb. Sacks.	Wood Fibre, 100 lb. Sacks.	Prepared Plaster, 100 lb. Sacks.	Kind of Work.	Plasterer's Hours.	Plasterer's Labour, Hours.	Foreman, Hours
Wood lath	9 to 11 (sanded 2 to 1)	14 to 17 (no sand)	22 to 24	Scratch on concrete	5½	3	...
Metal lath	17 to 20 (sanded 2 to 1)	22 to 27 (no sand)	45 to 50	Scratch on wood lath	5½	3	...
Plaster board	8 or 9 (sanded 2 to 1)	13 to 16 (no sand)	20 to 22	Scratch on metal lath	5½	3	...
Brick and clay tile	14 to 17 (sanded 3 to 1)	18 to 20 (sanded 1 to 1)	35 to 40	Scratch on plaster board	5½	3	...
Pyrobar tile	10 to 12 (sanded 3 to 1)	14 to 16 (sanded 1 to 1)	25 to 28	Brown on brick or tile	6	3½	...
Concrete	Use bondcrete for base coat over concrete, 14 to 16 sacks per 100 sq. yds.—no sand			Brown on scratch	6	3½	...
Material for Finish Coat.				Lime putty finish	8	3	...
Kind of Finish.	Gauging Plaster, 100 lb. Sacks.	Finish Hydrate, 30 lb. Sacks.					
Gypsum sand float	3½ or 4	...		Gypsum sand float finish	9	3½	...
Lime putty	1	4					
Sand.							
For 2 to 1 mix estimate ¾ cub. yd. of sand to 1,000 lbs. plaster							

IV. Directions for Plastering Furnished by the Nephi Plaster and Manufacturing Co., Utah. Gypsum Quarries at Nephi, Utah. Makers of the Plaster used in the Panama-Pacific International Exposition, San Francisco

Care of Plaster.—Plaster must be stored in a dry, cool place ; circulation of air through the warehouse should be avoided. Plaster should not be placed on the ground or against a damp wall, or in any damp place, when delivered to the building.

Lathing.—Use 1⅝ in. by ⅜ in. white pine or fir lath, free from knots, sap, and bark, to be spaced not less than ⅜ in. apart, and securely nailed with threepenny galvanising lathing nails. Break joints every fifth lath and leave space of ¼ in. between ends of lath. Lath not to be extended through partition walls. If only cedar lath obtainable, they should be spaced ¼ in.

Green lath should be used if obtainable. Where only dry lath are procurable, they must be thoroughly wet with clean water for two to five hours before plaster is applied.

Note.—Wide keys, space left at end of the lath, and laths thoroughly wet and expanded as above stated, will prevent buckling. There is no good reason for cracked or buckled walls. Such a result is usually the result of poor headwork, poor lath, or both.

Sand.—*Quality.*—Use only clean, sharp sand, free from loam or dirt, etc., and as free as possible from mica. Avoid quicksand. Sand should pass through a 10-mesh and remain on a 30-mesh sieve.

Plastering on Wood Lath.—This should be three-coat work, scratch, brown, and finish.

Scratch Coat.—*Quantity.*—For wood lath, the first or scratch coat should be composed of 1 part of " Nephi " fibred Hardwall plaster to not more than $1\frac{1}{2}$ parts (struck cubic measure) of sand, flushed off without tamping or shaking. This is to be applied promptly after lath are thoroughly wet, and with sufficient pressure to fill key, spreading a good coat over the lath.

Browning.—After the scratch coat is thoroughly set, but before it has dried out, the second, or browning coat, may be applied. For this a mixture of 1 part " Nephi " Hardwall plaster to not over 2 parts sand should be used. This should be straightened with rod and darby. It is not necessary to use float.

Grounds to be $\frac{7}{8}$ in. thick, including the lath.

If for labour, or other reasons, the contractor is aware in advance that he is to permit the scratch coat to become thoroughly dried after setting, it should be, at the time of application, roughened by either brooming or scratching, and then dampened before the second or browning coat is applied. We recommend that the browning coat be applied after the scratch coat has set, but before it has dried out. Where cedar lath are used, the browning should be permitted to dry before finish coat is applied, this to prevent staining.

Plastering on Metal Lath.—This should be three-coat work, scratch, brown, and finish. Grounds to be not less than $\frac{3}{4}$ in. On account of the open key, a rich scratch coat is necessary. Use equal parts of " Nephi " Hardwall plaster and clean, sharp sand, struck cubic measure. The same treatment as for wood lath, with reference to dampening of scratch coat, etc., is to be employed before second coat is applied. The second or browning coat is to be composed of one part " Nephi " Hardwall plaster and not more than 2 parts sand. Our recommendation again is to apply browning after scratch coat is thoroughly set, but while it is still damp.

In hot weather the first coat on metal lath may dry out to a considerable extent before setting takes place. Should such a condition arise, the scratch coat should be wet a few hours after it has been put on. Great care should be taken to prevent scratch coat drying before setting ; to avoid this, in certain cases, the setting time may be hastened.

Plastering on Plaster Block, Tile, Brick, or Stone.—This should be two-coat work, brown and finish. Grounds to be sufficient to plumb and straighten walls, but not less than $\frac{5}{8}$ in. Darby and float brown coat if necessary, but use water sparingly in order not to kill set of plaster by overworking after crystallisation or setting has commenced. Surfaces should be dampened before mortar is applied ; this to prevent suction of water from the plaster.

Three parts of sand to 1 of " Nephi " Hardwall plaster may be used, if the plaster will carry such quantity of sand and still maintain a desirable plasticity for easy working. Pure rock gypsum plasters will vary to some extent in sand-carrying capacity, atmospheric conditions, and age of the product modifying somewhat. It may be necessary to use less than 3 parts of sand to secure a desirable plasticity for the sake of conserving labour and getting even grounds, but not more than 3 parts sand should be used in any event.

Plaster Board.—First fill the joints between the boards, after same have been dampened. After the plaster has set, the whole wall should be dampened and browning mortar applied. The plaster board and grounds should be at least $\frac{7}{8}$ in. thick unless otherwise specified by the architect. Quantities of sand in this browning coat to be not more than 2 parts sand, struck cubic measure, to 1 part plaster.

Plastering on Concrete Walls, Ceilings, Beams, and Columns.—This should be two-coat work, brown and finish. Grounds to be sufficient to plumb and straighten the walls, but not less than $\frac{5}{8}$ in.

Brown Coat.—To 1 part " Nephi " unfibred Hardwall, add 1 part sand for brown coat. A rich, highly adhesive mixture is required.

Application.—After pouring Portland cement or cement concrete, in practically all cases a scum of free lime, or cement dust, or an alkali " bloom " appears on the surfaces approximating forms. Part of this will adhere to the forms and part to the concrete surfaces.

This thin film or scum has but little tensile strength and tends to absorb moisture and prevent suction. The following directions are essential to follow, in order to secure a satisfactory result and to assure proper adhesion of plaster to the concrete surfaces.

First.—Put up a staging, take a steel brush, designed for the purpose, and thoroughly brush the ceilings and walls, cutting slightly into the solid concrete, thereby roughening it somewhat, and at the same time removing all soft substances, either of free lime, alkali, or unset or partially set concrete.

Second.—After the walls have been thoroughly brushed, they should be hacked with a hatchet or some suitable instrument designed for that purpose. The hacks or notches should not be further than 2 in. apart. After the ceilings and walls have been thoroughly brushed and hacked, they should be thoroughly washed by hosing, thereby ridding the walls of all loose substances. While the ceilings and walls are yet damp, apply " Nephi " Hardwall plaster to fill out grounds and bring to a straight and even surface, ready to receive the finishing coat.

For white, hard coat, use 1 part " Nephi " finishing plaster to 2 parts of well-seasoned lime putty, mixing with clean water. Apply and trowel to a smooth, hard, even surface.

When wood lath have been used, the finishing coat should not be applied until the browning coat is thoroughly set and dried. Where the browning has been placed on wire lath, brick, clay tile, plaster board, or concrete, the finishing coat may be applied while the browning is still damp.

An excellent sand finish may be obtained by using 1 part " Nephi " unfibred Hardwall plaster to 1 part of fine screened or washed sand, the mixture being floated with a cork or carpet float. This finish is particularly adapted for tinting or where decorated walls are desired.

" Nephi " casting plaster, owing to its whiteness, uniformity in setting, and ultimate strength, is well adapted for ornamental work. For heavy cornice work, rough with a muffled mould, using " Nephi " Hardwall plaster in the same proportions as for scratch coat. If it is necessary to hasten the setting time, add a little lime putty to each batch. The cornice can then be immediately finished by taking off muffle and finishing with equal parts of " Nephi " finishing plaster and lime putty.

For sticking ornaments in or to a cornice, or elsewhere, use " Nephi " casting plaster ; some prefer to mix with glue size. (Do not use any lime putty.) If the cornice is very dry, the surface to receive ornament and back of ornament itself should be well scored and wet, and stuck with pure " Nephi " casting plaster.

V. Oriental Stucco

Manufactured by the United States Gypsum Co., Chicago

Oriental stucco base coat is a prepared base, factory mixed, for Oriental stucco finish, and is ready for use by adding water only. Oriental stucco finish is prepared from a formula based on old stuccoes, and is made in white and nine standard colours. Its ingredients are automatically weighed and machine mixed, thus ensuring right proportions and a thorough uniformity. It is delivered ready for use by the addition of clean water only.

Both mix easily with water, and work easily under the trowel. Oriental stucco finish has maximum covering capacity, and the colour effects obtainable with it are permanent. The setting time is so regulated that the workman can take the necessary time to apply it properly, thus avoiding unsightly shadows and joinings.

SPECIFICATIONS

Oriental stucco base coat and Oriental stucco finish are supplied in paper bags containing 80 lbs.

Oriental stucco base coat is a Portland cement base, water-resisting and plastic, including the correct proportion of sand. Oriental stucco finish is a hydraulic lime base, waterproof and non-staining, and is mixed with mineral colours.

Add clean water only to Oriental stucco base coat and Oriental stucco finish to make them ready for use. Oriental stucco may be applied over metal lath, wire lath, tile, brick, and concrete. It is adaptable for overcoating old cement-stucco walls and masonry surfaces.

The base coat is to be applied in two coats as with Portland cement stucco. The first coat should be scratched and allowed to dry thoroughly ; then followed with a brown coat properly floated. The brown coat must be allowed to dry to permit shrinkage ; then wet down before applying Oriental stucco finish.

The scratch coat should not be less than $\frac{1}{2}$ in. thick, the brown coat $\frac{3}{8}$ in., and Oriental stucco finish $\frac{1}{8}$ in. to $\frac{1}{4}$ in. thick, making the total thickness average $1\frac{1}{8}$ in.

One ton of Oriental stucco base coat $\frac{1}{2}$ in. thick as a scratch coat over metal lath, wire lath, concrete, and brick with flush joints should cover approximately 40 square yards. If joints on brick are raked, about 30 square yards will result. Applied $\frac{3}{8}$ in. thick as a brown coat over the scratch coat, 1 ton should cover 50 square yards.

One ton of Oriental stucco finish will cover 150 to 200 square yards. With a light dash, a greater covering capacity can be obtained.

For best results, Oriental stucco finish should never be applied to a thickness greater than $\frac{1}{8}$ in. to $\frac{1}{4}$ in.

INDEX TO TEXT

INDEX TO PLATES AND ILLUSTRATIONS IN TEXT

N.B.—The Plates are numbered in Roman numerals; the numbers of the text illustrations (ordinary figures) refer to the pages on which they occur and not to their figure numbers